Blantyre
Glasgow Road South

The Real Story

Paul Veverka,

Blantyre Project Publication

By Paul D Veverka

Copyright © 2018 Paul D Veverka

All rights reserved.

ISBN: 1548797359
ISBN-13: 978-1548797355

DEDICATION

This book is dedicated to two remarkable Blantyre men who have inspired me, motivated me, kept me on track and above everything else, become good friends. In no particular order, Alex Rochead & Gordon Cook this book is for you both. For several years, I have thoroughly enjoyed our late night emails, calls, meetings and walks, especially where we went exploring or hunted down some unique old, mysteries.

Alex, your passion for Blantyre is astounding. You have such an ability for rapid record retrieval and such foresight to have taken photos of Blantyre in years gone by. I will always remember us both digging in the Clyde riverbank to find that elusive Blantyre Priory Tunnel and hope to read a book by you one day.

Gordon, I'm proud to say, perhaps unwittingly, you most definitely have become my mentor in recent years. There's no other individual in Blantyre that knows more about this town or who has collected as much memorabilia, as yourself. There is no other person, with exception of my wife in Blantyre, that I respect more. Every conversation with you is my learning experience and I suspect you probably see my pursuit of Blantyre knowledge as 'borderline obsessive!". Let it be known....I'm always in awe of your knowledge, but of your filing system....perhaps less so!

Thank you sincerely. If I live to learn half of what you both know about Blantyre, I'll be happy.

By Paul D Veverka

CONTENTS

	Acknowledgments	i - ii
	Featured Contributions list	iii
	List of Photos & Illustrations	vii -xv
	QR Codes	xvi
	Foreword	xvii
1	**Introduction to Blantyre**	Page 1
	Blantyre Parish	Page 2
	Earliest mention of Blantyre	Page 3
	Origins of the name	Page 4
	No longer a village	Page 5
	Boundary myth	Page 7
	Modern Blantyre	Page 7
2	**Glasgow Road – Birth to Redevelopment**	Page 9
	Early Glasgow Road	Page 9
	Expansion of Glasgow Road	Page 10
	20th Century Glasgow Road	Page 11
	Decline of Glasgow Road	Page 13
	Redevelopment of Glasgow Road	Page 14
	Clydeview Shopping Centre	Page 19
3	**Exploring Boundaries: Burnbank**	Page 21
	Forgotten former farms	Page 21
	Road Splits & bends	Page 22
	Burnbank	Page 24
	Greenfield	Page 25
	Birdsfield Street	Page 27
	Blantyre Lodging House	Page 28
	Official Boundary	Page 29
	Greenfield Bridges	Page 32
4	**Burnbank to Springwell Place**	Page 35
	Greenfield Foundry	Page 35
	Birth of Springwell	Page 46
	Evolution of Springwell	Page 47
	McLelland's Land, Springwell	Page 48

	Welsh's Land, Springwell	Page 52
	McDougall's Land, Springwell	Page 55
	Tram Accident 1904	Page 61
	Springwell Piggery	Page 61
	McLelland boys in bother	Page 63
	Smellie's Buildings, Springwell	Page 64
	Springwell Slaughterhouse	Page 70
	McNair's Land, Springwell	Page 71
	Springwell Social Club	Page 75
	Gambling at Springwell	Page 75
5	**Springwell Place to Auchinraith Rd**	Page 79
	Springwell Place	Page 79
	Semple's Land (Dalzell Place)	Page 80
	Allison Place	Page 85
	Miller's Buildings	Page 92
	Fields at Springwell	Page 98
	Blantyre Golf Course	Page 99
	Springwell Poultry run	Page 104
	Cattle maiming	Page 106
	Auchinraith Railway Junction	Page 107
	Springwell Housing Scheme	Page 109
	Eastern Railway Bridge	Page 124
	Western Railway Bridge	Page 129
	Michikas vrs Lanarkshire Trams	Page 133
	Vandalism at Springwells	Page 134
	Chamber's Buildings	Page 135
	A725 East Kilbride Expressway	Page 140
	Rosendale Place	Page 144
	Auchinraith Fairground	Page 154
	Caldwell Institute	Page 155
6	**Auchinraith Rd to Herbertson St**	Page 163
	Springwell Farm	Page 163
	Henderson's (Kelly's) Buildings	Page 166
	JR Reid Printers	Page 178
	Gavin Watson Printers	Page 181
	Anderson's (Botterills) Buildings	Page 184
	Burleigh Church	Page 189
7	**Herbertson St to Jackson St**	Page 197
	Origins of Herbertson Street	Page 197
	Telephone Exchange	Page 199

	Stonefield Parish Church Manse	Page 201
	Fatality on Glasgow Road	Page 202
	Minister under the influence	Page 202
	Roberts Land	Page 203
	Police Station	Page 206
	Avon Buildings	Page 212
	Blantyre Co-operative Society	Page 218
	Blantyre Co-op Central Premises	Page 226
	Glasgow Road Industrial Estate	Page 235
	Jackson Street Eastern Homes	Page 236
	Origins of Jackson Street	Page 237
8	**Jackson St to Church St**	Page 239
	Jackson Street Western Homes	Page 239
	Sprott's Buildings	Page 240
	Merry's Rows	Page 247
	Alois Schlothauer	Page 254
	Origins of Elm Street	Page 255
	Masonic Hall / Elm Court Flats	Page 256
	Nazarine Church	Page 256
	Elm Street Playpark	Page 259
	Stonefield Parish Church	Page 260
	Rev Thomas Pryde	Page 269
	Rev Duncan Finlayson	Page 270
	St Andrew's Church	Page 271
	Hitler's Pianist	Page 272
	Youth Centre not meant to be	Page 274
9	**Church St to Logan St**	Page 275
	Origins & Evolution of Church St	Page 275
	Abbeygreen Manse	Page 276
	Abbeygreen Building	Page 277
	Abbeygreen Hall & Rooms	Page 279
	Boys will be Boys	Page 285
	The Masonic Buildings	Page 286
	Priory Place & The Priory Bar	Page 294
	St John's Wood & Episcopal Church	Page 300
10	**Logan St to Craig St**	Page 301
	Origins of Logan Street	Page 301
	The Winks Inn	Page 302
	Turner's Buildings (Central Buildings)	Page 304
	Blantyre Post Office	Page 315

	Clydeview Shopping Centre- East	Page 319
11	**Craig St to Victoria St**	Page 325
	Origins of Craig Street	Page 325
	McVaney's Land	Page 326
	Central Garage (Harper's Garage)	Page 328
	Nimmo's Buildings	Page 332
	Bloomfield Cottage	Page 337
	Stonefield Parish Infant School	Page 340
	Stonefield Parish School	Page 342
	Major John Ness, headmaster	Page 349
	James Aitchison, headmaster	Page 352
	Clydeview Shopping Centre - West	Page 353
12	**Victoria St to Priory St**	Page 361
	Origins of Victoria Street	Page 361
	Stonefield Farm (Hastie's) & J.C Forrest	Page 363
	Hastie's Farm (Post World War 2)	Page 371
	Bobby Brown	Page 379
	Annfield Terrace	Page 383
	Blantyre Markets	Page 388
	Victoria House Care Home	Page 390
	Stonefield Burn	Page 391
	1930's Council Homes	Page 392
	Toll Brae	Page 393
13	**Priory St to Stonefield Rd**	Page 395
	Origins of Priory Street	Page 395
	Wooden Office, Yard & Field	Page 399
	Coats Buildings	Page 400
	Coats Tenements	Page 400
	Nicola's Hair & Beauty Salon	Page 400
	Stonefield Tavern (Teddies Pub)	Page 400
	Coats House & Bake-house	Page 409
	Co-op Emporium	Page 411
	Clydesdale Bank	Page 414
	Alarming Break in	Page 416
	Stonefield Ind. Co-op Buildings	Page 417
	Co-op Original Building	Page 420
	Caught Faking Cheques	Page 423
	Clydeview	Page 424
	Gray's Buildings (YMCA)	Page 432
	Broomknowe Cottage	Page 441

	Clydesdale Bank Building	Page 445
	Dervoch Cottage	Page 448
	Electric Street Lights	Page 450
	Minto's Buildings	Page 451
	Broompark Place	Page 453
	Clyde Cottages	Page 460
	Workshops & Yard	Page 464
	Valerio Court	Page 467
14	**Stonefield Rd to Bardykes Rd**	Page 469
	Exploring Stonefield Road	Page 469
	Clive Place	Page 471
	The Old Original Bar	Page 476
	Stonefield Cottage	Page 484
	Westneuk (Stonefield House)	Page 487
	Community Centre	Page 492
	Mayberry Grange	Page 496
	Blantyre Trams	Page 497
	Roselea	Page 504
	Rowan Place	Page 508
	Glasgow Road Villas	Page 510
	Eastern Bungalow	Page 511
	Arnot	Page 512
	Western Bungalow	Page 513
	Brownlea Cottages (Jeanfield)	Page 514
	Korek	Page 515
	Blairhoyle	Page 516
	Clifton	Page 517
	Laurel Cottage	Page 518
	Oakbank	Page 519
	Modern Homes	Page 520
	Campsie View	Page 521
	George Bowie	Page 522
	Daldorch	Page 524
	Dalveen	Page 525
	Dunedin	Page 526
	Orwell (Larchmont)	Page 527
	Dunallan Loop	Page 528
	Modern Flats	Page 530
	Walkers Buildings	Page 531
	Volunteer Arms Pub (Cross Guns)	Page 534
	Causeway Shott (Douglas Place)	Page 538
	Cloudhowe Terrace	Page 540

	Westend Place & The West End Bar	Page 542
15	**Bardykes Rd to Priory Bridge**	Page 557
	Origins of Bardykes	Page 557
	Bardykes Grove	Page 558
	Caldergrove	Page 561
	Bardykes Mill & Mill House	Page 564
	Priory Bridge	Page 567
	Road Alignment	Page 574
	Spittal & Dalton Accidents	Page 575
	Caldergrove Row	Page 577
	Archaeology at Dalton	Page 578
16	**Glasgow Road South Business Directory**	Page 581
	About Blantyre Project	Page 607
	About the Author	Page 609
	And Finally	Page 611

ACKNOWLEDGMENTS

As a future historical reference aid, it is important that 'Blantyre Glasgow Road – The Real Story" is accurate and clearly records factual records, events and dates. As well as my own research, I was offered or sought assistance in making this book as interesting as possible. Many people showed me a great deal of kindness, patience and involvement. In recognition of this, and in no particular order, it is necessary to say a special thanks to the following people and businesses who were instrumental in permitting their information:

1. The staff at Blantyre library, Glasgow Road (for their continued interest, support and permitting presentations, a huge source of data collection.)
2. The staff at Hamilton Reference library (for putting up with me and my constant queries and their diligence in having archives ready for me coming in.)
3. Mr. Jim Brown, High Blantyre (Photographer – for a couple of photos. Please check out his many thousands of photos online at the Flickr Website)
4. Mr. Gordon Cook (fellow history enthusiast & Chairperson of Blantyre Heritage Group for sharing his inspirational Blantyre knowledge & photos. As this book evolved, I knew it would end up being dedicated to you Gordon.)
5. Mr. Alex Rochead for his excellent help each time I got stuck. (Thank you for record retrieval, pointing me in the right directions and all your support. It was a 'no brainer' that this book should jointly be dedicated to you.)
6. Mr. Neil Gordon & his family (dec. The late Community Historian – for the invaluable archives, pointers and inspiration from a time before the internet.)
7. The Hamilton Advertiser (Scottish & Universal Newspaper Group)
8. Mrs. Betty McLean (for kindly providing an original Gilmour's Directory with so many wonderful photos of old Glasgow Road)
9. National Library of Scotland Records, Edinburgh
10. Online Ancestry Databases, Scotlandsplaces, Scotlandspeople (I'm fairly sure your company's stock value has increased dramatically, the amount of credits I spent whilst researching this book!. In seriousness, the book could not have been written without this unprecedented, paid access to old records, perhaps the stumbling block previously for any historian as to why a book of this nature hasn't existed until now.)
11. British Newspaper Archives, paid subscription to old news stories.
12. Burnside Crescent Action Group (1978) documentation for their Springwell story.
13. Gavin Watson Printers website and information from Director, Tom Brown.
14. Historic Environment Scotland Purchased Aerial Photography license for print. Order number : IMSL-IR-100909 for permitting use of 1950's aerial images.
15. St Andrews Parish Church Website for part of the Stonefield Parish Church story.
16. Church elders of St Andrews for kind permission in sharing Church bible photo.
17. My family for providing modern photos of Blantyre.
18. Mr. George Crawford, for his information on Rev. Duncan Finlayson.
19. Mr. Tony Wildsmith, for information on Dr Keir Fisher of Glasgow Road.
20. Mrs. Rosemary Harper, for the photo and history of the Brown Family.
21. Mr. James McGuire, for his foresight in photographing some of Glasgow Road in the late 1970's prior to redevelopment.

22. Mr. Bill Beers and Mr. Jack Owens, for photos of Stonefield Parish School.
23. 'Glasgow and Lanarkshire Illustrated' for Major Ness information and photo.
24. Mr. Scott Allison, for his photo of Hastie's Whisky bottle
25. Mr. James Bridges, for a photo of Mr. McDade's gold watch 1889
26. Mr. Anthony Smith, for use of his Glasgow Road fire photo 1970's.
27. Mrs. Catherine McRury for the photo of YMCA outing in 1945.
28. Mr. Robert Stewart, for his family photo of Stonefield Cottage in 1959 and additionally for the valuable commentary and his knowledge of the Stonefield Road junction area.
29. The Owners and staff of 'The Old Original Bar' for their access and assistance during November 2017.
30. Mr. Jimmy Cornfield & his family (dec. The late Community Historian – for permission to feature his poem.)
31. The ladies of the Women's Guild in High Blantyre Old Parish, for their interesting tales and comments.
32. Lanarkshire Tramways by Ian L Cormack, MA for a perfect insight into trams.
33. Mrs. Jean Richardson for family photos and assistance with Roselea History.
34. Mrs. Margo Clayton for her interesting history on the Bowie family.
35. Mr. John Reid (the printer) for his interesting telephone calls and information relating to his printing business.
36. Mr. Lon McIlwraith for his interesting insight into Hastie's and wonderful pictures of his grandfather, Bob Brown.

To all the countless other individuals who have emailed me daily with stories and photos and taken an interest. To a loyal reader base who buy each Blantyre Project book as it is released.

Finally, to 13,400 wonderful people who freely subscribe to The Blantyre Project Facebook page whose lively discussion and comments each day have enabled much of this history to be pieced together in such a wonderful way.

This deluge of social media comments on each article was essential in piecing together many of the stories in this book and provides an added layer of interesting, community detail from the lives who lived on Glasgow Road, actually those who walked it, who shopped on it, all on a scale never been seen before. I've selected featured contributions to use within the book and thanked them personally for their input.

FEATURED CONTRIBUTIONS

Sincere thanks go to the following people, listed here in alphabetical order for their memories, knowledge and helpful input exclusively from social media, emails, telephone conversations and interviews. Their wonderful commentary has helped bring this book alive in a special manner.

ADDISON, Mrs. Lillias
AITKEN, Mrs. Marianne Stark
ALLAN, Mrs. Liz
ANDERSON, Mr. Daniel
ANDERSON, Mr. Stephen
ANDERSON, Mrs. Joan
ANDERSON, Mrs. Maggie
ANDERSON, Mrs. Nora
ARKWRIGHT, Mr. Steven
BAIRD, Mr. Alan
BALDWIN, Mr. Bruce
BARRETT, Mr. Thomas
BARRY, Mr. Dave
BLACK, Mrs. Andrena
BLACK, Mrs. Margaret
BOYD, Mr. John
BOYLE, Mrs. Mary
BRENNAN, Mrs. Anne
BROWNLIE, Mr. Robert
BROWN, Mr. Jim
BROWN, Mrs. Rae
BRUCE, Mrs. Julie
BURNS, Mrs. Elaine
BURNS, Mrs. Margaret Brown
CALLAGHAN, Mr. Andy
CAMBRIDGE, Mr. James
CAMBRIDGE, Mrs. Mary
CAMPBELL, Mrs. Donna
CANNING, Mr. Jim
CARTWRIGHT, Mrs. Senga
CAULLEY, Mrs. Rena
CLAYTON, Mrs. Margo
COCHRANE, Mr. Jim
COCKBURN, Mrs. Eleanor
COOK, Mr. Gordon
CORNFIELD, Mr. John
COSH, Mr. Fraser
COUSTON, Mr. Ray
CROMBIE, Mrs. Carol

CROSSAR, Mrs. Marie McVey
CROWE, Mr. Stephen
CRAWFORD, Mr. George
DALY, Mr. John
DAVIDSON, Mrs. Catherine
DICKSON, Mr. David
DICKSON, Mr. William
DILLON, Mr. Thomas
DOCHERTY, Mr. Michael
DODD, Mr. Stuart
DOLAN, Mr. Steven
DONNELLY, Mr. Patrick
DONNELLY, Mr. Steven
DOONIN, Mrs. Sharon Morrison
DOWNIE, Mrs. Maureen
DUNCAN, Mrs. Margaret
DUFFY, Mr. Colin
DUNSMUIR, Mr. Gordon
ELDER, Mr. Graham
FARMER, Mrs. Margaret
FAULDS, Mr. James
FISHER, Mr. Drew
FORREST, Mrs. Christine
GAFFNEY, Mrs. Laura
GARDINER, Mrs. Collette Macguire
GILL, Mr. Stevie
GOLDIE, Mrs. Anne Gemmell
GORDON, Mr. Fairlie
GRAHAM, Mr. Bill
GRAHAM, Mrs. Susan
GREEN, Mrs. Arlene
GRIEVE, Mrs. Helen
GROGAN, Mrs. Anne
HAMBLEY, Mr. Henry
HARTLEY, Mrs. Lesley
HARPER, Mrs. Eliza
HARTMAN, Mr. Thomas
HARTMAN. Mrs. Ann

By Paul D Veverka

HERD, Mrs. Ann Marie
HUNTER, Mr. Bill
HUNTER, Mrs. Elaine
IRWIN, Mrs. Bridget
JACK, Mrs. Liz
KANE, Mr. Den
KELLACHAN, Mr. Gerald
KELLY, Mr. Gerry
KIRKBRIDE, Mrs. Mary
KRAWCZYK, Mr. John
KRAWCZYK, Mrs. Valerie
LADDS, Mr. Chris
LE GRANDIER, Mr. Anton
LEE, Mr. Garry
LINDSAY, Mrs. Moyra
LOBBAN, Mr. Bill
LOVE, Mr. Alan
LYNGHAM, Mr. John
LYNCH, Mr. Andy
LYNCH, Mrs. Deborah
MACFARLANE, Mrs. Moira
MACGUIRE, Mrs. Marian
MALLAN, Mr. Kenny
MALLORY, Mrs. Jennifer
MARSHALL, Mrs. Linda
MARTIN, Mrs. Lisa
McALLISTER, Mr. Jim
McCALL, Mr. Stephen
McCALLUM, Mrs. Maureen
McCOURT, Mr. John
McDONAGH, Mr. Michael
McDOUGALL, Mrs. Caroline
McGAULLEY, Mr. John
McGREGOR, Mrs. Elspeth
McGUIGAN, Mr. Matthew
McKEOWN, Mrs. Ann
McILWRAITH, Mr. Lon
McINNES, Mr. Alister
McINTOSH, Mr. David
McLAUGHLIN, Mrs. Maura
McLEAN, Mr. John
McLEAN, Mrs. Betty
McLEOD-WOLOHAN, Mr. Robert
McMILLAN, Mrs. Debbie
McMILLAN. Mrs. Marie
McNAMEE, Mrs. Thea Boreland
McNEIL, Mrs. Michelle

MEECHAN, Mr. Eddie
MIKKELSEN, Mrs. Carolyn
MIKKELSEN, Mr. Serge
MILLIGAN, Mrs. Irene
MORRISON, Mrs. Etta
MORTON, Mrs. Janet
MUIR, Mrs. Nina
MULLEN, Mr. William
MULLINGS, Mrs. Abigail
MUNDAY, Mrs. Helen McGowan
MURPHY, Mrs. Catherine
NEIL, Mr. Matthew
NORTHFIELD, Mr. Len
O'BRIEN, Mr. Peter
O'DONNELLY, Mr. Thomas
PACHECO, Mrs. Moira Mulvaney
PATERSON, Mr. Andy
PATERSON, Mr. Ian
PEMBERTON, Mrs. Linda
PITCAIRN, Mr. Colin
RICHARDSON, Mrs. Jean
QUIINN, Mrs. Anne
ROBERTS, Mrs, Linda Gilmour
ROCHEAD, Mr. Alex
RODWELL, Mrs. Marie
ROONEY, Mr. Phillip
ROUSE, Mr. James
RUSSELL, Mrs. Margaret McLaughlin
SAUNDERS, Mrs. Janet
SEMPLE, Mrs. Irene
SIMMONS, Mrs. Margaret
SINCLAIR, Mrs. Ann
SLATER, Mr. Duncan
SMITH, Mr. Anthony
SMITH, Mr. Martin
SNEDDON, Mrs. Catherine
SPIERS, Mrs. Elaine
STARK, Mrs. Janette
STEVENSON, Mrs. Carol
STEWART, Mr. Robert
STIRLING, Mr. James
STONE, Mr. Jay
SUMMERS, Mrs. Teresa
SWEENEY, Mrs. Karen
TABOR, Mrs. Julie
TAYLOR, Mrs. Helen Lawson
THOMSON, Mr. David

THOMSON, Mrs. Sheena
TIERNEY, Mr. John
TREMBLE, Mr. Stuart
TRUSSLER, Mrs. Evelyn
WALKER, Mr. Gerry
WARD, Mrs. Natalie
WEAVER, Mrs. Elizabeth
WEIR, Mrs. Elizabeth Cushley

By Paul D Veverka

LIST OF PHOTOS & ILLUSTRATIONS

Figure	Description	
1	Welcome to Blantyre sign	Page 1
2	Blantyre Parish Boundaries	Page 2
3	Town Statistics	Page 5
4	Crossbasket Castle Interior	Page 8
5	Sketch Glasgow Road 1850's	Page 10
6	Glasgow Road Tram in 1910	Page 11
7	Glasgow Road 1930's	Page 12
8	Glasgow Road Tenements 1977	Page 15
9	Clydeview Shopping Centre 2015	Page 19
10	Roy's Military Map 1752	Page 21
11	Glasgow Road Burnbank Overlay	Page 22
12	Greenfield Boundary in 1859	Page 23
13	Glasgow Road splits 1859 map	Page 24
14	Populated Greenfield Area in 1898	Page 26
15	Limetree, Burnbank as it is today	Page 27
16	Blantyre Lodging House 1910 map	Page 28
17	Trades Hotel, Burnbank 1940's	Page 28
18	Noel Kegg's Tool Business 2010	Page 31
19	Noel Kegg demolition day 2016	Page 31
20	Greenfield Bridges in 1892	Page 32
21	Site of Greenfield Bridge, Glasgow Rd	Page 33
22	1898 map of Greenfield Foundry	Page 35
23	1882 Notice of Dissolution	Page 37
24	Drawing showing interior of Foundry	Page 39
25	1910 map of Greenfield Foundry	Page 41
26	Photo children playing at Greenfield	Page 42
27	1936 map of Greenfield Engineering Works	Page 44
28	First Buses Depot off Glasgow Road 2017	Page 45
29	1859 Map of Springwell	Page 46
30	1898 Map of Springwell	Page 47
31	1898 Map showing McLelland's Land	Page 48
32	Location Line Drawing of McLelland's Land	Page 49
33	1898 Map showing Welsh's Land	Page 52
34	Location Line Drawing of Welsh's Land	Page 53
35	1910 Map showing McDougall's Land	Page 55
36	Location Line Drawing McDougall's Building	Page 56
37	Photo of Children in 1900's tenement	Page 56
38	Duncan McDougall Death Certificate 1925	Page 60
39	Pigs in Piggery	Page 61
40	1898 Map showing Smellie's Buildings	Page 64
41	Location line drawing Smellie's Buildings	Page 65
42	Traditional Fleshing (butchers) shop	Page 68
43	1910 Map of Springwell Slaughterhouse	Page 70
44	1910 Map of former McNair's Land	Page 72

45	Location Line Drawing showing McNair's Land	Page 72
46	Miners playing 'pitch n toss'	Page 76
47	1910 Map of Springwell Place	Page 79
48	1910 Map of Semple's Land	Page 81
49	Our sketch of Semple's Land, Springwell	Page 82
50	1915 Sale Advert for Semple's Buildings	Page 83
51	1910 Map of Allison's Place, Springwell	Page 85
52	Location Line Drawing of Allison's Place	Page 86
53	Back of Tenement Stairs	Page 87
54	Death Certificate Miss Ann Allison Heriot	Page 88
55	1910 Map showing former Miller's Buildings	Page 92
56	Location Line Drawing Miller's Buildings	Page 93
57	1910 Map showing Blantyre Golf Course	Page 99
58	Blantyre Golf Club opened with success	Page 101
59	Ladies Golf Fashions of the 1910's	Page 103
60	Photo of Springwell Poultry Run c1930	Page 105
61	1898 Map showing Auchinraith Junction	Page 107
62	Photo of Auchinraith Railway Junction 1960's	Page 108
63	Photo of Auchinraith Signal Box 1960's	Page 108
64	Aerial view of Springwell overlaid on map	Page 110
65	Aerial view of Springwell Housing Scheme 1950	Page 112
66	Photo Veronica Greer, Springwell resident 1978	Page 114
67	1978 Photo of Burnside Crescent	Page 115
68	Photo Burnside Crescent Action Group 1990	Page 117
69	Photo Burnside Crescent 1990	Page 118
70	Further Photo Burnside Crescent 1990	Page 119
71	Photo Burnside Crescent Houses in Winter 1990	Page 122
72	1936 Map showing Eastern Railway Bridge 1	Page 124
73	Photo rebuilding Eastern Railway Bridge 1931	Page 125
74	Photo Eastern Railway Bridge work 1931	Page 126
75	Photo Railway Bridge Work at night 1931	Page 126
76	Photo Railway Bridge ready for girders 1931	Page 126
77	Photo Railway Bridge girders arrive by rail 1931	Page 126
78	Photo New girders ready 1931	Page 127
79	Photo Inspecting completed deck 1931	Page 127
80	Photo Completed Eastern Railway Bridge Deck	Page 127
81	Photo Completed renovated Railway Bridge 1931	Page 128
82	Photo Demolition of Eastern Railway Bridge 1980	Page 127
83	Comparison of 1898 and 1910 maps of Bridges	Page 128
84	Location Line drawing of former road bridge	Page 130
85	Photo work begins on Bridge 2 replacement	Page 131
86	Photo work progresses on 1932 Western Bridge	Page 131
87	Photo New Western Bridge 1932 arrives	Page 132
88	Photo Western Bridge from Chalmers Land	Page 132
89	Photo Glasgow Road between the Bridges 1931/32	Page 133
90	1936 Map showing Chamber's Land	Page 135
91	Aerial Photo Chamber's Land 1950	Page 136
92	Location Line Drawing Chamber's Land	Page 138
93	Photo opening 2nd phase EK Expressway in 1978	Page 141

94	Photo East Kilbride Expressway today	Page 142
95	1936 Map showing Rosendale Place	Page 144
96	Photo of Rosendale in 1971	Page 145
97	Aerial View of Rosendale in 1950	Page 149
98	Photo Rosendale Residents in 1968	Page 152
99	Photo Rosendale & Auchinraith Social Club	Page 152
100	Aerial View of Fairground in 1950	Page 154
101	1936 Map showing Caldwell Institute	Page 156
102	Photo James Caldwell MP 1888	Page 157
103	Photo James Caldwell MP 1898	Page 157
104	Photo Caldwell Institute façade 1936	Page 158
105	Photo Alex Crawford and Family 1946	Page 160
106	1859 Map of Springwell Farm House	Page 163
107	Rare Photo Springwell Farm House c1876	Page 165
108	1910 Map showing Henderson's Buildings	Page 167
109	Photo of Henderson's Buildings in 1903	Page 169
110	Photo of James Kelly, Celtic Director	Page 170
111	Photo of James Kelly with Celtic Management	Page 171
112	Alexander Barrie Advert at Henderson's Buildings	Page 173
113	Photo Typical Scottish Fire brigade 1940	Page 174
114	Aerial Photo Henderson's Building in 1950	Page 175
115	1962 Map remaining Henderson's Buildings	Page 176
116	1970's Photo Henderson's Buildings	Page 177
117	Satellite aerial overlaid on 1898 map	Page 178
118	Photo Gavin Watson Printers 2017	Page 182
119	1910 Map showing Anderson's Buildings	Page 184
120	Photo Anderson's Buildings 1903	Page 185
121	Photo Pawn-broking sign	Page 186
122	Location Line drawing Anderson's Buildings	Page 187
123	Photo Botterill's Building in late 1970's	Page 188
124	1910 Map United East Free Church (Burleigh)	Page 189
125	Photo East Free Mission Hall, Herbertson St	Page 190
126	Aerial Photo Burleigh Church & Hall 1950	Page 191
127	Photo of Mosaic saved from Burleigh Church	Page 194
128	Photo of modern Herbertson Street 2017	Page 198
129	Photo Herbertson Street mid 20th Century	Page 198
130	1910 Map Telephone Exchange	Page 199
131	Photo of Typical 1920's Telephone Exchange	Page 200
132	Photo of Stonefield Parish Church Manse 1948	Page 201
133	1936 Map Roberts Land, Herbertson St	Page 203
134	Location Line Drawing Roberts Land	Page 205
135	1910 Map showing former Police Station	Page 206
136	Photo former Police Station in 1900	Page 207
137	Rare Photo old Police Station in 1900	Page 208
138	Photo of Blantyre Police Officers in 1908	Page 210
139	Location Line Drawing former Police Station	Page 211
140	1910 Map showing Avon Buildings	Page 212
141	Photo of Avon Buildings in 1933	Page 213
142	Photo of Avon Buildings in 1978	Page 214

143	Photo of derelict Avon Buildings in 1978	Page 216
144	Avon Buildings Photo 1910	Page 217
145	Photo Blantyre Co-op staff in 1930's	Page 220
146	Photo interior of Co-op Store in 1930's	Page 221
147	Photo of Co-op Tokens and checks	Page 222
148	1936 Map showing Co-op Central Premises	Page 226
149	Photo of Blantyre Co-op Central Premises 1933	Page 227
150	Aerial Photo of Co-op Central Premises 1950	Page 228
151	Photo former Central Premises in 1979	Page 231
152	Photo demolition of Central Premises in 1979	Page 232
153	Photo Central Premises & Avon Buildings 1977	Page 233
154	Photo Central Premises & Avon Buildings 1978	Page 233
155	Photo Central Premises looking west 1978	Page 234
156	Photo Central Premises at Herbertson St 1978	Page 234
157	Photo Glasgow Road Industrial Estate 2017	Page 235
158	Photo Jackson Street Homes (East) in 1950	Page 236
159	1962 Map showing Jackson Street	Page 237
160	1898 Map Jackson Street Western Homes	Page 239
161	1910 Map Sprott's Buildings	Page 240
162	The 1881 Census for Sprott's Buildings	Page 241
163	1950 Aerial Photo of Sprott's Buildings	Page 242
164	1950 Advert for Smiddy Inn	Page 243
165	Photo Kidd's Buildings (formerly Sprotts) 1977	Page 244
166	Photo Derelict Kidd's Building 1978	Page 245
167	1936 Map Merry's Rows short before demolition	Page 247
168	Photo of Merry's Rows in 1913	Page 248
169	Photo Mrs Slater & Katie 1930	Page 253
170	Photo Mary, Sarah, Agnes & Katie Slater 1930	Page 253
171	Photo Ellen, Sarah & Katie Slater at Merry's Rows	Page 253
172	Mrs Slater at 1 Priory Street during 1940's	Page 253
173	Photo German Camp Knockaloe during WW2	Page 254
174	Photo Elm Street in 1950	Page 255
175	Photo Former Masonic Hall now flats 2016	Page 256
176	Photo Nazarine Church Mission Hut 1952	Page 257
177	Photo Nazarene Church Hall in 2016	Page 258
178	Photo Elm Street Playpark in 1978	Page 259
179	Photo Children's Painting at Elm Street 1990	Page 259
180	1962 Map of Stonefield Parish Church	Page 260
181	Aerial Photo Stonefield Parish Church 1950	Page 260
182	Photo Interior Stonefield Parish Church 1930's	Page 262
183	General Booth on motor car tour of 1904	Page 263
184	Photo Booth addresses crowds on tour 1904	Page 264
185	Photo Stonefield Parish Church fire 1979	Page 267
186	Photo Stonefield Parish Church winter 1979	Page 268
187	Photo of Rev Pryde's 1880 bible	Page 269
188	Photo Rev Duncan Finlayson & daughter 1948	Page 270
189	Photo St Andrew's Church being built 1982	Page 271
190	Photo Pianist in the 1950's	Page 272
191	Photo Barrett & Co at 19 Church Street 1970's	Page 275

192	1910 Map showing Abbeygreen Manse	Page 276
193	1962 Map showing Abbeygreen Building	Page 278
194	1898 Map showing Abbeygreen Hall & Rooms	Page 279
195	Photo Rev John Burleigh	Page 279
196	Photo Abbeygreen Hall in 1903	Page 280
197	Photo Abbeygreen Hall, Glasgow Road 1903	Page 281
198	Photo Dr. David Keir Fisher	Page 282
199	Photo Fisher's Surgery Plaque 1920's	Page 282
200	Photo Church Street and Glasgow Road 1937	Page 283
201	Photo Abbeygreen Hall at Masonic Buildings 1979	Page 284
202	1910 Map showing Masonic Hall	Page 286
203	Photo Masonic Halls in 1905 after opening	Page 289
204	Photo Interior of Livingstone Masonic Hall 599	Page 290
205	Aerial Photo of Masonic Buildings in 1950	Page 291
206	Photo of Masonic Buildings in 1970's	Page 292
207	Photo of Masonic Stained Glass Windows	Page 292
208	Photo of Masonic Buildings being demolished	Page 293
209	1910 Map showing Priory Place	Page 294
210	Photo of Priory Place & The Priory Bar 1977	Page 295
211	Photo of the Priory Bar & Glasgow Road 1930's	Page 298
212	Photo of Priory Lounge at Logan Street 1977	Page 299
213	Photo folks inside Priory Lounge 1970's	Page 299
214	Photo of St John's Wood 2016	Page 300
215	Jane Logan Death Certificate in 1866	Page 301
216	1859 Map Showing Winks Cottage	Page 302
217	Location Link drawing showing Winks Inn	Page 303
218	1910 Map showing Turner's Buildings	Page 305
219	Photo of Turner's Buildings in 1903	Page 306
220	William Buchanan Death Certificate 1895	Page 307
221	Photo Browns Ironmongery Store 1920	Page 310
222	Photo Blantyre Scouts at Central Buildings	Page 313
223	Photo Turner's Buildings in 1975 looking east	Page 314
224	Photo Vacant Land on Glasgow Road 1978	Page 314
225	1910 Map showing Stonefield Rd Post Office	Page 316
226	Photo Blantyre Post Office in 1955	Page 317
227	Photo Blantyre Post Office demolished 1997	Page 318
228	2017 Map of Clydeview Shopping Centre East	Page 320
229	Photo Clydeview Shopping Centre East 2017	Page 321
230	Photo Clydeview Shopping Centre East 2009	Page 322
231	1898 Map showing McVaney's Land	Page 326
232	1906 Painting showing McVaney's Land	Page 327
233	Location Line drawing showing McVaney's Land	Page 328
234	Photo Harpers Garage in 1934	Page 329
235	Aerial View of Central Garage 1950	Page 330
236	Photo Central Garage 1978	Page 331
237	1962 Map showing Nimmo's Buildings	Page 332
238	Photo Nimmo's Buildings / Hills Building 1950	Page 335
239	Photo Nimmo's Buildings looking east 1979	Page 336
240	1910 Map showing Bloomfield Cottage	Page 337

241	John Watt Death Certificate 1925	Page 339
242	Aerial Photo Bloomfield Cottage 1950	Page 339
243	1936 Map with Stonefield Parish Infant School	Page 340
244	Photo Stonefield Parish Infant School	Page 341
245	Photo Stonefield Parish Infant 'wee' School 1977	Page 341
246	1910 Map showing Stonefield Parish School	Page 342
247	Photo Stonefield Parish School 1907	Page 343
248	Photo Pupils and teacher in 1896	Page 344
249	Photo pupils and teachers in 1911	Page 346
250	Photo Ness's School in 1946	Page 347
251	Photo Ness's School in 1951	Page 348
252	Photo Major John Ness in 1890's	Page 349
253	Photo Ness Obelisk in Cemetery 2017	Page 352
254	2017 Map Clydeview Shopping Centre West	Page 353
255	Photo Casper's Nightclub interior 1990	Page 357
256	Photo ASDA Entrance in 2017	Page 359
257	Photo Salvation Army in 2016	Page 359
258	Photo Glen Travel in 2015	Page 359
259	Photo Lorraine Harkin Hairstylists in 2009	Page 359
260	Photo Mehran Takeaway in 2010	Page 360
261	Photo Blantyre Library (previously Caspers) 2016	Page 360
262	Photo ASDA Petrol Station 2017	Page 360
263	Photo Victoria Place (Honeymoon) in 1946	Page 362
264	1859 Map Showing Stonefield Farm	Page 363
265	Photo John Clark Forrest	Page 365
266	Illustration of Hastie's Farm break-in	Page 366
267	1898 Map Stonefield Farm (Hastie's)	Page 368
268	Photo Hastie's Farm Whisky Bottle	Page 369
269	Photo Hastie's Farm Entrance 1960's	Page 370
270	Photo Hastie's Farm renovated in 1975	Page 373
271	Photo of Bobby Brown and Boxers 1975	Page 374
272	Photo of Hastie's Farm night out 1970's	Page 375
273	Photo Zeigfields Advert 1986	Page 377
274	Photo Bob Brown with dog at Hasties	Page 379
275	Photo Interior Hasties Pre 1975	Page 381
276	Photo Kathy Brown at Petrol Station 1962	Page 382
277	1910 Map Annfield Terrace	Page 383
278	Annie-Logan Forrest Birth certificate 1866	Page 384
279	Photo Annfield Terrace looking east 1910	Page 384
280	Photo Annfield Terrace in 1936 looking east	Page 386
281	Photo clearance of retaining walls Annfield 1970's	Page 388
282	Photo Contemporary Market in 2013	Page 389
283	Photo Victoria House Care Home 2016	Page 390
284	1898 Map showing Stonefield Burn	Page 391
285	Photo 1930's Council Houses in 2016	Page 392
286	1859 Map showing the Toll Brae	Page 393
287	1936 Map Council Homes on Glasgow Rd	Page 395
288	Photo Slater Family 1 Priory St in 1938	Page 396
289	Photo Winnie Ewing at Priory Street 1967	Page 397

290	Photo Winnie Ewing vowing for votes 1967	Page 398
291	1859 Map showing Wooden Building & field	Page 399
292	1910 map showing Coat's Buildings	Page 400
293	Location Line drawing Coats Tenements Buildings	Page 401
294	1950 Aerial Photo of Coat's Tenements & Tavern	Page 402
295	1898 Map showing Stonefield Tavern	Page 403
296	Photo Stonefield Tavern Exterior 2009	Page 404
297	Photo Stonefield Tavern in 1910	Page 406
298	Photo Barman Davy at Stonefield Tavern 2016	Page 408
299	1910 Map Coats House & Bake-house	Page 409
300	Illustration of Bake-house	Page 410
301	Photo Stonefield Tavern, Coats Buildings 1910	Page 411
302	Photo Construction of Co-op Emporium 1954	Page 412
303	Photo Opening of Co-op Emporium 1954	Page 412
304	Photo Derelict Emporium 1981	Page 414
305	Photo Clydesdale Bank 2015	Page 415
306	1910 Map Stonefield Independent Co-op Buildings	Page 417
307	Photo Co-op Buildings in 2015	Page 418
308	Map Co-operative Building 1962	Page 420
309	Photo F McDade's Gold Watch presented 1889	Page 420
310	Photo Blantyre Co-Op 2 Buildings 1979	Page 421
311	Photo Blantyre Co-Op 2 Buildings 1990's	Page 422
312	1910 Map Clydeview	Page 424
313	Location Line Drawing Clydeview	Page 425
314	Photo Clydeview Fire early 1970's	Page 428
315	Photo Clydeview Building 1981	Page 429
316	Photo Glasgow Road South 1983	Page 430
317	1936 Map showing Grays Buildings	Page 432
318	Illustration Mary Blantyre 1813	Page 433
319	Photo Grays Buildings 1981 facing east	Page 434
320	Death Certificate of Mary Blantyre 1901	Page 435
321	Death Certificate of John Gray 1928	Page 436
322	Photo YMCA outing in 1945	Page 437
323	Photo Derelict YMCA Building 2010	Page 438
324	Photo Apple Bobbing at Halloween 1970's	Page 439
325	1898 Map showing Broomknowe Cottage	Page 441
326	Photo Broomknowe Cottage 1981	Page 442
327	Photo Broomknowe Cottage J. Potts 2015	Page 443
328	Photo Broomknowe Cottage 1979	Page 444
329	Photo Clydesdale Bank 1979	Page 444
330	1936 Map showing Clydesdale Bank	Page 445
331	Photo Clydesdale Bank & Glasgow Rd 1981	Page 446
332	Photo Ladbrokes & Lanarkshire Law 2015	Page 448
333	1898 Map showing Dervoch Cottage	Page 449
334	1910 Map showing Minto's Buildings	Page 451
335	Aerial Photo Minto's Buildings 1950	Page 452
336	Location Line Drawing Minto's Buildings	Page 453
337	1962 Map showing Broompark Place	Page 454
338	Death Certificate of Henry Oliver	Page 455

339	Photo Minto's Buildings & Broompark Place 1903	Page 456
340	Photo Hughes Photography & Patons 1979	Page 458
341	Photo Broompark Place 1979	Page 458
342	1936 Map showing Clyde Cottages	Page 460
343	Photo Clyde Cottages 1979	Page 463
344	Photo Stonefield Road Junction 1979	Page 463
345	1936 Map showing Joiners Workshops & Yard	Page 464
346	Photo Café de Royal in 1920's at Stonefield Rd	Page 467
347	Photo bottom of Stonefield Road in 1920's	Page 468
348	Photo Valerio Court in 2016	Page 468
349	Photo Stonefield Road at Glasgow Road 1915	Page 469
350	1859 Map showing Clive Place	Page 471
351	Photo Clive Place Public House 1890's	Page 472
352	Photo Horse & Carriage at Clive Place 1890's	Page 475
353	1962 Map showing Old Original Bar	Page 476
354	Photo Old Original Bar exterior in 2009	Page 477
355	Photo showing date stone Old Original Bar	Page 478
356	Robert Craig's Death Certificate 1917	Page 478
357	Photo William Francis (Frank) Benham 1921	Page 479
358	Photo Old Original Mob early 1970's	Page 481
359	Photo Exterior Old Original Bar in 2015	Page 482
360	Photo Interior Old Original Bar November 2015	Page 483
361	1859 Map showing Stonefield Cottage	Page 484
362	Photo Robert Stewart at Stonefield Cottage 1959	Page 486
363	Photo Stonefield Cottage in 2015	Page 487
364	Sketch Victorian Concert Hall	Page 488
365	Location Line Drawing of Westneuk	Page 490
366	1910 Map of Stonefield House	Page 491
367	1962 Map Blantyre Community Centre	Page 493
368	Photo Community Centre in 1995	Page 494
369	Photo Yoga Class Community Centre 1978	Page 494
370	Photo Play-scheme Community Centre 1978	Page 495
371	Photo Derelict Community Centre 2001	Page 496
372	Photo Mayberry Grange in 2015	Page 496
373	Photo Blantyre Tram 1903	Page 497
374	Photo Blantyre Trams Opening Day in 1903	Page 498
375	Photo Motherwell Tram Powerhouse 1903	Page 499
376	Photo Lanarkshire Trams ready to be deployed	Page 500
377	Rare Blantyre Tram Postcard from 1907	Page 501
378	Photo lifting Glasgow Road tram cobbles 1930	Page 503
379	1962 Map showing Roselea	Page 504
380	Photo Councilor Richardson during 1940's	Page 505
381	Photo Jock & Jean Richardson early 1970's	Page 506
382	Photo Roselea Garage and Roselea Cottage 2017	Page 508
383	Photo Rowan Place May 2015	Page 508
384	Photo Wheatlandhead Farm fields 1940's	Page 509
385	Photo Eastern Bungalow in 2016	Page 511
386	Photo Glasgow Road Villa "Arnot" 2016	Page 512
387	Photo Glasgow Road Western Bungalow 2016	Page 513

388	Photo Glasgow Road Brownlea Cottages 2016	Page 514
389	Photo Glasgow Road House "Korek" 2016	Page 515
390	Photo Glasgow Road House "Blairhoyle" 2016	Page 516
391	Photo Glasgow Road Villa "Clifton" 2016	Page 517
392	Photo Glasgow Road Villa "Laurel Cottage" 2016	Page 518
393	Photo Glasgow Road Villa "Oakbank" 2016	Page 519
394	Photo Modern Homes 2016	Page 520
395	Photo Glasgow Road Villa "Campsie View" 2016	Page 521
396	Photo George Bowie 1856-1906	Page 522
397	Photo Williamson Watson Bowie 1855-1931	Page 523
398	Photo Glasgow Road Villa "Daldorch" 2016	Page 524
399	Photo Glasgow Road Villa "Dalveen" 2016	Page 525
400	Photo Glasgow Road Villa "Dunedin" 2016	Page 526
401	Photo Glasgow Road Villa "Orwell (Larchmont)	Page 527
402	Photo Crashed bus at Dunallan Loop 1935	Page 529
403	Photo Modern Flats on Glasgow Road	Page 530
404	1936 Map showing Walkers Buildings	Page 531
405	1936 Map showing Volunteer Arms Pub	Page 534
406	Photo Rifle Volunteers 1870's	Page 534
407	Photo Ottoman Troops at Gaza in 1917	Page 537
408	1916 Map showing Causewayshott Place	Page 538
409	1962 Map showing Cloudhowe Terrace	Page 540
410	Photo Cloudhowe Terrace 2016	Page 540
411	Photo Cloudhowe Terrace east end 2016	Page 541
412	1936 Map showing Westend Place	Page 542
413	Photo Westend Place in late 1880's	Page 544
414	Margaret Craig's Death Certificate 1895	Page 545
415	Photo Miners at Westend 1880's	Page 545
416	Photo Robert Henderson 1950	Page 549
417	Photo Aerial View of Westend Place 1953	Page 551
418	Photo MacNeil Gravestone at Barra	Page 552
419	Photo Exterior West End Bar 2016	Page 553
420	Photo Interior West End Bar 2016	Page 554
421	Photo Callaghan Wynd Title Deed map	Page 559
422	Photo Bardykes Grove 2016	Page 560
423	1898 Map Caldergrove Estate	Page 561
424	Photo Caldergrove Hospital WW1	Page 562
425	Photo Caldergrove Servant's Kitchen 1982	Page 563
426	Photo Bardykes Mill ruin 2004	Page 564
427	1859 Map Bardykes Mill & Mill House	Page 565
428	Photo Ruined Bardykes Mill 2004	Page 567
429	1910 Map Priory Bridge	Page 568
430	1817 Sketch Priory Bridge	Page 570
431	Photo Priory Bridge 2007	Page 572
432	Postcard Spittal Bridge and Tramcar 1910's	Page 574
433	Photo Bad Bend at Spittal 1920's	Page 575
434	Photo Spittal Crash 1967	Page 576
435	1896 Map Caldergrove Row	Page 577
436	Photo Archaeology find at Dalton 1930	Page 578

QR CODES

Throughout this book, on occasion, you'll see QR codes, just like this one. These are interactive links that take you straight to websites with more information about the subject and contain multimedia content that you can view on a smartphone or tablet.

To visit the QR links you need a smartphone or tablet with a free app called a "QR reader" that you can download from your device's Android or IOS app store. Just point the device's camera at a QR code and follow your QR readers instructions to scan the code and visit the recommended website.

Of course, this is just a little added bonus to the book. You WON'T need a smartphone to read and enjoy the rest of this large book, the good old fashioned, normal way.

FOREWORD

"It is with tremendous excitement, absolute commitment and utmost motivation that I write these opening words. It is now winter 2016/2017 and I find myself sitting this evening, in a rented flat in Stonehaven, in Aberdeenshire, some 137 miles away from my home in Blantyre facing the prospect of working away from home for 2 years. I'm a commercial manager with a construction company and work has once again taken me from my home town and family. I knew when accepting the works contract, (for my sanity) I would need to find something productive to do each evening when back in from work and this book represents exactly that.

Tackling a complex subject as detailing the history of all the buildings, ownership and businesses on Blantyre's busy Glasgow Road was always going to be difficult and certainly the reason no such book exists…. until now.

With hundreds of photos and so much to tell, I know already that a book on Glasgow Road needs to be split into both South and North sides, not just to make it economically viable to sell commercially, but more importantly to tell that history in detail, in a deserving manner, without assumption, or reliance on just one person's account. It just cannot be done in one book. So, this book, strictly only the SOUTH side of Glasgow Road is just one half of that enormous task, and as such, in time a sequel will be required. In these pages, contributions from hundreds of people are featured, those who lived there, remembered it, touched and felt that history, all combined with a layer of factual presentation and hundreds of original images, maps and illustrations.

Ladies, Gentlemen, Boys and Girls, in a fifth of a MILLION words, I present "Blantyre Glasgow Road South – The Real Story"'

Paul Veverka, January 2017

By Paul D Veverka

CHAPTER 1
INTRODUCTION
BLANTYRE

Writing an entire book about the businesses, properties and people of Glasgow Road, Blantyre was always going to be a monumental task, which ultimately will perhaps appeal mostly to a very niche and specific part of the population. However, with nobody approaching the subject previously in any real historical detail, it is certainly a story worth exploration and recording. This book, a first of its kind, opens below with some words about Blantyre and a brief introduction to its primary thoroughfare, the busy, Glasgow Road.

Every attempt has been made at great time, cost and effort to ensure the research contained in this book is accurate. Whilst records have been relied upon heavily for the oldest part of Glasgow Road history, social history and memories from interviewed contributors account for much of the post WW2 history, as well as a reliance upon personal recall in more modern times. The outcome is a good mix of accurate history, especially around property construction and ownership, but with an abundance of social, interesting history and stories thrown in.

Figure 1 'Welcome to Blantyre' sign pictured in 2012 by Robert Stewart

Blantyre Parish

Blantyre is a civil Parish in South Lanarkshire, Scotland, with a population of 17,505. The Parish is situated in the northwest of the Parliamentary district of Hamilton. From north to south the length of the parish is six and a quarter miles long. It extends for six miles in length, from north to south, and varies greatly in breadth, not averaging more than one mile in the whole; it comprises 4170 acres, of which, excepting 200 acres of moss land and plantations, all is or was once, arable.

It should be noted that when referring to Blantyre Parish, that it does not refer to the town of Blantyre. The former village of Blantyre is actually in Blantyre Parish, which comprises of much land in all directions around Blantyre's populated centre.

Its boundaries consist mainly of rivers, but also in a few places, by roads and fence lines. The Parish is bounded by the River Clyde to the north and northwest forming a boundary with Glasgow, Uddingston and Bothwell. To the west the boundary is parts of the Rotten Calder river forming a boundary with East Kilbride and Cambuslang. The boundary to the east is primarily formed by the Park Burn, but also of field boundaries before the Park Burn rises separating Blantyre from Hamilton. The boundary to the south is the Rotten Burn. It is incorrect to say Parish boundaries are all rivers or water.

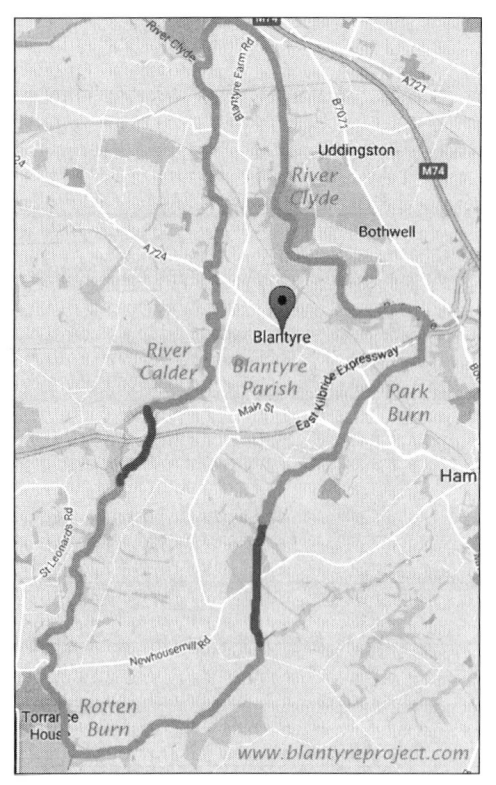

Figure 2 Blantyre Parish Boundaries

Whilst Blantyre Parish predates 1845, it should be noted that from 1845 to 1930, civil parishes formed part of the local government system of Scotland: having parochial boards from 1845 to 1894, and parish councils from 1894 until 1930.

The civil Parish of Blantyre can be dated from the 1700's, after ceasing to be a Barony. Several failed attempted have been made through the ages to make Blantyre a Burgh. However, it would take until 1845, for legislation to be enforced which gave parochial boards power to administer the poor law.

Described in 1846, the parish is in the presbytery of Hamilton and synod of Glasgow and Ayr; that year, the minister's stipend was about £184, with a manse, and a glebe valued at £16 per annum. The parish church at that time was not in good repair. Located in the Kirkton graveyard, it was erected in 1793, and only held about 300 persons. The lands formerly belonged to the Dunbars, of Enterkin, in which family they remained till the Reformation, when they were purchased by Walter Stewart, son of Lord Minto, treasurer of Scotland, upon whom, on the suppression of monastic establishments, the ancient priory of this place was bestowed by James VI, who also created him Lord Blantyre. The scenery is, in many parts, exceedingly beautiful; the parish is generally well wooded, and diversified with gently undulating eminences and fertile dales. The rateable annual value of the parish was £8280.

In the 1859 name book, it was described as, "A Parish in the Middle Ward of Lanarkshire, bounded on the west by Cambuslang and East Kilbride; Glassford on the south; Hamilton, and Bothwell, on the east; and on the extreme north by Old Monkland, This Parish at its widest part is not more than two miles, and about six, from north to south, Nearly the whole has been feued off the Right Honbl. [Honourable] Charles Lord Blantyre, who possesses the patronage, The ruins of "Blantyre Priory" is the principal antiquity in the Parish, "Blantyre" village has the Parish Church, and School, as well as an adventure School in it. "Blantyre Works" employ a great number of the population – Copied from Name Sheets of 11 – 14 of this Parish – R. H"

Civil parishes in Scotland, as units of local government, were abolished by the Local Government (Scotland) Act 1929. By 1975, following the Government Land Act 1973, local councils revised how former Parishes were managed.

The geographical area is sometimes still referred to as Parish, however, for purposes to compare and against previously published statistics.

Earliest Mention of Blantyre

In 1234-1241, the Earl of Lennox granted a charter of the lands of Killheryn (Killearn) to Stephen Dunbar of Blantyre. There was also an inquisition in 1263 to ensure that his son Patrick Dunbar inherited the estate. Patrick (3rd of that name) The Earl of Dunbar is thought to have founded the

Priory late in 1269. Another early written record of the name Blantyre was in 1275 where the Priory was included in a list of Scottish ecclesiastical establishments which were taxed by Pope Clement IV to raise money to finance yet another crusade against the Saracens. This document was known as Bagimond's Roll, named after the Pope's emissary, Baiamund De Vicci, who was sent to collect the hated tax.

The name is also mentioned in early 14th Century charters as being "Blantyr", "Blaentir", "Blauntyre" and "Blanntyre". Over the centuries, it has also been referred to as "Blantir".

Origins of the name, Blantyre

Since the 13th Century, there have been many versions of the name 'Blantyre'. It has been referred in documents as Blantir and Blantyr before the more modern 'Blantyre.' There are several theories as to the origin of the name but the exact is unknown. The Reverend Stevenson, writing in 1790, suggested that it was two Gaelic words meaning 'Warm Retreat'. Another suggestion, from the Reverend Wright, writing in 1885, was that it was Gaelic, meaning 'Field of The Holy Men'.

It would suggest that the old spelling Blantyr is a Gaelic corruption of LLANTYR. Llantyr contains two Welsh words – LLAN meaning 'consecrated' and TYR meaning 'ground/land', the consecrated/church ground being the Blantyre Priory itself. The old sixteenth century communion cups belonging to the Old Parish Church have no letter E in the spelling of BLANTYRE, suggesting the 'e' was added after that time.

There was no real consistency in the spelling until the 18th Century, when maps were forced to use a consistent name.

In 1936, J.A Wilson suggested a Welsh origin from Blaentir meaning a "promontory" as a description of the northern part of the Parish around which the Clyde flows.

Rev. A McKenzie in 1952 had a different suggestion after the early missionary 'Blaan' or 'Blane' who came from Ireland in the 6th Century. One thing is for certain, we are now called "Blantyre" on maps and documents as has been the case for several Centuries. However, no matter where you go in the world, people always seem to encounter others who know about the local dialect being pronounced, "Blantir" or more harshly, "Blantur". As writer of this book, I experienced this myself at a bus stop on the Polish – Czech border in 1989, when a local resident corrected my 'Blantyre' to 'Blantur'!

No longer a village

Did you know Blantyre is officially a "town" and has been for some time. Blantyre being described as only a 'village', is an old, inaccurate notion not many people under 50 years old use and there's good reason for that, for the former village of Blantyre became a town in May 1975.

Fondly but incorrectly referenced, some Blantyre residents of a 'certain age' will I'm sure always refer to Blantyre as a village, as they remember the old days and descriptions or perhaps be simply unaware the change was made. It's a mindset that won't change for some people, and no big deal really, as the term "village" conjures up images of small, quaint, friendly places. When I enquired in 2012 to South Lanarkshire Council Planning, they confirmed to me that Blantyre is a 'town' rather than village. I decided to investigate more just in case. Other historians don't seem to have written much about this before. Some clarification was much needed, especially after I noticed a rogue assumption elsewhere that Blantyre "couldn't be a town, as it didn't have a town hall or mayor", despite those two requirements only applying to classifications in England! (Of course in Scotland, there are no mayors, official post holders known as Convenors, Provosts, or Lord Provosts depending on the local authority).

41	Kirkintilloch	19,020	Town	East Dunbartonshire	55°56'N 4°09'W
42	Peterhead	17,790	Town	Aberdeenshire	57°31'N 1°47'W
43	Blantyre	17,400	Town	South Lanarkshire	55°48'N 4°06'W
44	St Andrews	17,010	Town	Fife	56°20'N 2°48'W

Figure 3 Blantyre is currently the 43rd largest town in Scotland

However, you can see perhaps how the mistake is made. Pathe News referred to Blantyre as a town as early as 1930's, despite it still being officially a village back then. Many other newspaper reports prior to WW2 described Blantyre as a town or village, or simply didn't bother at all about finding out the real classification for their reports. Rightly or wrongly, an elderly generation perpetuated the term 'village', even beyond its "sell by date" in 1975. So, some evidence, as it was actually quite easy to check.

The Scottish Government shared their clarification with Blantyre Project, after enquiry, adding, "A town is usually a place with a lot of houses. Generally, the difference between towns and villages or hamlets is the sort of economy they have. People in towns such as Blantyre usually get money from industry (factories etc.), commerce (shops etc.) and public service (working for the town), not agriculture (growing food), as may have been the case in Blantyre in previous Centuries. The subject can be difficult for people who lived on either side of the 1973 Government Act who may not wish to adopt change or just be unwilling to believe its happened.

Although modern wards consider population, the number of people who live in a place does not in isolation tell us if its a town or a village although it can be a factor in helping to classify designations. For example Bothwell nearby to you has less than half the population of Blantyre but residents there often refer to themselves as a 'conservation village'. For the record, when referring to Blantyre, we use the classification, town, but it would be worth checking with the local authority. We hope this clarifies your enquiry."

Classification of land in Scotland is actually different from the rest of the UK. With exception of crown, Parishes, Burghs, boundaries, councils and subsequent later wards are all treated differently, thanks to Scots Law. South Lanarkshire Council wrote back to me, backed up by Hamilton Reference Library, commenting,

"The Local Government (Scotland) Act 1973 was an Act of Parliament of the UK that altered local government in Scotland on 16 May 1975. That day, the county council was abolished and the area absorbed into the larger Strathclyde region, which itself was divided into new Council Areas in 1996. With it came the declassifications of Parish's within Lanarkshire, and a modern step forward to reclassifying and acknowledging growth in villages and towns. Although towns and new towns existed in Lanarkshire prior to 1975, the recognition that some villages were prospering or growing beyond village classification had to be incorporated, leaving Lanarkshire with 13 towns of "Biggar, Blantyre, Bothwell, Cambuslang, Carluke, East Kilbride, Hamilton, Larkhall, Lanark, Lesmahagow, Rutherglen, Strathaven and Uddingston. The classification of 'town' was assigned to Blantyre due to its size, nature of its economy being industry based, a quantum shift away from agriculture and farming and on the noted basis that it held a regular market and fair, something a village does not."

The evidence was there in black and white and it changed the way I describe Blantyre, always taking care to mention it's a town, rather than darting back and forth between village and town. The term 'village' is dying.

With South Lanarkshire Council, the recognised official authority on the subject confirming Blantyre is a town, the Scottish Government, reference library officials and land registration all confirming the same, with not one small reference left to us being a village except in memory, the case was clear and closed.

Like it or not. Blantyre is now a town.

Blantyre Boundary Myth

A modern myth seems to have manifested in recent years. It is said that you cannot cross the Blantyre Parish Boundary without stepping over water, based on the fact that the Parish Boundaries are the River Clyde to the North, The River Calder to the West, The RottenBurn to the south and the Park Burn to the east.

Sadly, this is not true. Fanciful and would have been a great piece of trivia had it been correct. You can most definitely get out of Blantyre Parish without passing over water.

The myth is properly corrected in the definitive Blantyre book, "Blantyre Explained". Meantime, the accessible boundary areas into Blantyre Parish, without crossing water, can be seen in the darker shaded boundary areas of the aforementioned Blantyre Parish map in Figure 2. The problem is some folk perpetuating the myth, have just simply incorrectly assumed the Parish Boundaries are all rivers, when actually they're not. Some parts of the official boundaries are roads, others are field fence lines.

There are areas on the west of the Parish near Crossbasket and Basket that the boundary is not the River Calder, but actually old roads and fence lines. More significantly the boundary to the east is only partially the Park Burn, but importantly, is comprised of hundreds of feet of field boundaries, to the south before the ParkBurn rises at Park. It disproves the myth entirely, for clearly you can enter Blantyre Parish by land without crossing over streams and rivers. Blantyre is an island? Nice idea, but wrong nonetheless.

Modern Blantyre

Whilst Blantyre's weaving and coal mining heritage has fallen away, the town still thrives on Industry with various Industrial Estates of different sizes providing good employment, primarily for self employed businesses. In recent decades our schools have all been rebuilt providing state of the art education for the pupils of today. Homes continue to be built, with a new development of 195 private houses underway in High Blantyre by Avant Homes.

A plethora of small shops still exists, mostly located around Glasgow Road and Main Street. We're still surrounded by green spaces, thankfully with beautiful woodland to the Calder at the west and open expansive fields to the south. Although somewhat hemmed in by the Clyde to the north, the areas is still pretty and woodland grows again, where once was heavy industries. We live in a beautiful area, with easy access to good transport links that make commuting to Glasgow or within Lanarkshire very easy and affordable. Blantyre has changed vastly over the Centuries but a strong sense of community remains with frequent local events, environmental groups and people generally looking out for each other with a degree of civic pride.

We have a lot to look forward to. Rumours of a planned further renovation of Glasgow Road's Clydeview Shopping Centre are coming to the forefront. New Homes are being built in Victoria Street. The woodland at Greenhall is being regenerated with hopes and discussion underway to improve the woodland trails and reinstate former bridges over the Calder. A new University is being built to the south, although being classed as Hamilton, is still definitely within Blantyre and should benefit our community as such. Our population is steady with no more people leaving, than arriving, as it has been for a few decades. Our wonderful David Livingstone Centre has in July 2017 just been given £6m of funding to renovate the centre into a world class tourist destination, something that can only bolster Blantyre's economy further. Recent renovations to the Vic's Club and the construction of beautiful places to eat out like Carrigans, The Parkville Restaurant on Glasgow Road and Redburn Inn are putting Blantyre back on the map. Crossbasket Castle in High Blantyre, also doing that by being our only 5 star luxury venue, fit for the most amazing weddings and meals.

Figure 4 Venues like renovated Crossbasket Castle, put Blantyre on the map

CHAPTER 2
GLASGOW ROAD
BIRTH TO REDEVELOPMENT

Early Glasgow Road

The main road from Glasgow to Hamilton and beyond to Lanark seems certain to have existed in Medieval times. Its very likely that even in the 13th Century at the time of the founding of Blantyre Priory, our oldest building, that a rough dirt track existed in the location we now know as Glasgow Road today running from northwest to southeast. Travellers on foot or on horse, carts and carriages would have seen nothing more than hedge or tree lines on both sides of the track, with untouched landscape for as far as they could see either side.

By the mid 1700's, Blantyre's population was still only around 500 people, most of them concentrated around the High Blantyre cross area. Small individual hamlets existed, such as Auchinraith, Barnhill and Bardykes to name a few. Low Blantyre and Glasgow Road however at this time was incredibly sparsely populated with just a few individual farms scattered just off the track. From south to north, even in 1750, only farms such as Newhouse, Woodside, Wheatlandhead, Cottshill, Bardykes and the Priory Bridge Mill were accessed from the road which would later become Glasgow Road. Even counting the population of these farms, it is safe to say that as late as 1750, the population along Glasgow Road was still under 50 people.

The construction of Blantyre Mills on the Clyde in 1785 caused a population explosion with an influx of workers coming to Blantyre, mostly weavers, seeking employment. A workers village sprang up and the track leading perpendicular from Glasgow Road down to the village, which would later become known as Station Road was formed.

Tolls were collected on the Glasgow to Hamilton Road at a tollbooth situated at the corner of Glasgow Road and Station Road, taxing passing trade for the privilege of using the road for their business. Around this area the small hamlet of Stonefield started to form.

By the end of the 1850's, Glasgow Road however, was still very rural, indeed some farms like Newhouse had disappeared, replaced by Springwell House and Stonefield Farm. In 1859, from the boundary at Burnbank, all the way northwestwards to the bottom of Stonefield Road, there was still literally nothing but Springwell House, the isolated Winks Inn, Stonefield Farm and a few thatched houses opposite, the aforementioned tollbooth and a few homes opposite and a public house called Clive Place at the bottom of the Stonefield Road track. With the exception of Stonefield Cottage and Westneuk, there was nothing else built either side of the Glasgow Road track until you reached Priory Bridge's Black Mill at Blantyre's Western boundary. An estimate of population in these building would be between 150 – 200 people. However, things were about to take a drastic change with the discovery of coal in the next decade.

Figure 5 Sketch 1850's Glasgow Road

Expansion of Glasgow Road

The arrival of coalmasters who sunk pits in 8 different places in Blantyre brought a huge population surge with workers coming from all over for the plentiful coal mining jobs. To the east of Glasgow Road at the boundary of Burnbank industries like Robertson's of Springwell and the Greenfield Foundry offered plenty of employment, alongside the nearby Greenfield Collieries. Hamlets like Springwells, thrived and grew in such an ideal location. Businesses had excellent infrastructure with railways cutting through Blantyre in many places. Further west tied miners cottages at Craighead Rows and Merry's Rows housed the miners and their necessary services sprang up on either side of Glasgow Road, with property owners choosing to build traditional 2 or 3 storey tenements to rent out, usually with shops on the lower floors.

In the 1870's and 1880's churches, schools, halls and public houses all appeared, with several side streets, some of them significantly large being created as communities all along Glasgow Road expanded out.

By the end of the 1890's, Glasgow Road had become very densely populated, the population of Blantyre tripling in only 3 decades. More new churches were built, many pubs and more homes, including large villas now starting to appear along the north side of the street.

20th Century Glasgow Road

1903 saw the arrival of trams in Blantyre, with lanes laid from Burnbank all the way to Stonefield Road outside the St Joseph's Church, being built around that time. The line was extended westwards later in 1907 to carry on into Halfway. There is no doubt that the trams further assisted the prosperity of businesses in those boom years.

Figure 6 Glasgow Road Tram in 1910

By 1910, most of the properties on Glasgow Road on either side, had started to merge with each other, residents packed into homes, forcing the build of further homes like Mount Pleasant in Springwells and more villas this time on the south side, opposite the Parkville, then the home of the doctor. The exception to all this were homes and businesses on Glasgow Road in Springwells, which still sat in isolation, separated from the hive of activity on the rest of the street, by the railway lines crossing nearby. Further streets off shooting at perpendicular angles all along Glasgow Road were appearing, as were small parks and ground for recreation. By this time homes stretched almost all the way to the Westend, although not really beyond to the west.

The depression and strikes of the 1920's did not affect the expansion of the street to any visible extent, certainly on maps and by the 1930's with the selling of homes to private individuals, Glasgow Road had become an urban collection of private properties of hundreds of people, with population in their many thousands.

In October 1928 Mr. William Marr, at a council meeting took protest to the decision to employ only men from Hamilton and Blantyre to undertake the proposed Glasgow Road widening work and asked that the skills of men outwith these areas were also considered to ensure the job was done as efficiently as possible. In perusal of their intention to curtail the tram service, the Lanarkshire Tramways Company suspended the service of tramcars between Blantyre and Cambuslang, distance of four miles on Friday 10th May 1929. Work began that month. This was to see the removal of tramlines and the construction of a much wider Glasgow Road. Residents were to lose part of their gardens. By September 1929, several public buildings had also lost part of their front grounds and gardens to the widening operations. This included St Joseph's Church and School, David Livingstone Memorial Church and Low Blantyre School. Pictured in the 1930's, is the completed work to Glasgow Road, tramlines removed and this whole scene, must have at the time felt very modern and attractive.

Figure 7 Glasgow Road in 1936 following removal of tramlines

The Decline of Glasgow Road

Businesses came and went and slowly but surely the buildings got older, some not maintained too well. By the 1960s', well before the redevelopment of Glasgow Road got underway, there were 36 shops on Glasgow Road and 13 pubs, a large number you may think, but not as great as it had been 50 years earlier. A large proportion of these shops were dominated by the Blantyre Co-operative Society, which were popular with lots of residents.

The East Kilbride News from Friday, June 28th, 1968, touched upon Glasgow Road looking unchanged for 70 years! Nothing could now be more further from that statement, with the subsequent 1970's redevelopment of Glasgow Road transforming the old character through demolition of the old buildings, into the modern streetscape of today. The article touches upon the "ugly scars" on Blantyre by these old tenements, many of which were boarded up. Remember, this is reported in a 1968 context and although the following strays sometimes from the subject of Glasgow Road, it is worthy of inclusion here in this book as a reminder that Blantyre looked relatively unchanged. "Look clearly at this photograph. It was taken perhaps 60 years ago. Yet today, without the tram, the similarity is striking. It is a photograph of Glasgow Road looking towards Stonefield from a point just east of Herbertson Street. On the right are the Co-op buildings, while across the road that licensed grocers shop on the corner of the building is still a licensed grocers shop today. Well known Hamilton and Blantyre grocer, Andrew Gilmour, who also had a shop in High Blantyre near the Post Office, once owned it. The photograph is one of a collection in a booklet issued by Mr. Gilmour to his customers. Others show scenes from the banks of the Clyde, the old mill, Priory Colliery at the height of production and the old hermit's hut at Calderwood Castle.

One of these booklets has come into the possession of "East Kilbride News" reader Mrs Janet Tennant of 12 John Street, Blantyre (now in my own possession via Betty). Now 73 years of age, Mrs Tennant has lived in Blantyre all her days and remembers many of the old scenes. Turning these pages of history, she recalls, "Gilmours also had a drapers shop where I used to buy trousers at 1/11 a pair." Mrs Tennant's boys were Tom, now living in Bath and George who is a salesman with Robertson of Springwells, the mineral water firm. The Blantyre woman also has 2 daughters Mrs Janet Mackie and Mrs Elizabeth Graham. Mrs Mackie is the wife of Mr. Willie Mackie, the Co-op butcher at High Blantyre and lay pastor of Blantyre Nazarene Church. Mr. Mackie's father, who lived above the shop where his son now works, died about 10 years ago, aged 84. It was after his death that the book of photographs was discovered amongst his possessions and passed to Mrs Tennant. Although firmly steeped in the past, Mrs. Tennant also has an eye for the future and she speaks proudly of her granddaughter, 8-year-old Sandra Graham, who is dancing her way to fame with Mrs. Hislop's School of dancing. Sandra has already gained many medals and cups and she participated in last Saturday's dancing competition at the Community Centre. From her home in John St, Mrs. Tennant looks across at the rear of tenements, which are now an ugly scar on Blantyre's main thoroughfare. She also sees the public park, which one-day if county plans are realized, will stretch right to Glasgow Road. Indeed, at a recent Council meeting, Councilor Frank MacDonagh raised the question of whether the park could not be immediately extended to the road at the site of the former, "Blantyre Gazette" works, now recently demolished.

As for the building where Andrew Gilmour had his shop, only 3 of the 7 shops are still occupied by a butcher, baker and grocer. The pend close is still there and people still live above in the houses. Of the rest of the lower properties, only the former Victoria Cafe survives, as a development fund headquarters for appropriately enough, the Blantyre Victoria Football Club."

By the end of the 1960's, several properties had started to become boarded up and unfit for purpose, forcing some tenants and shopkeepers to move. The tenements were cold, badly insulated if at all and almost all in need of re-wiring and plumbing. Timber rot, rising damp and woodworm were amongst other problems, not to mention many still with unwelcome outside toilets. As the colourful and vibrant 1970's approached and especially seeing the accomplishments in modern new towns like East Kilbride, something had to be done to save Blantyre's retail district. A grand plan was unveiled by the Council but sat shelved for many years due to the perceived disruption it would all cause.

Redevelopment of Glasgow Road

On 3rd May 1977, plans were submitted to Hamilton District Council Ltd by CMS Ltd for the redevelopment of the area that would eventually become ASDA. This included the entrance to Logan Street from Glasgow Road and the lower part of Craig Street, as well as existing infant school and the Central Garage, although it was noted at that time the Stonefield Parish Primary School had been cleared. These plans had been discussed for many years.

The area was certainly large, and at the time of this acquisition, it may not have been known that Asda or a supermarket was going there, but more likely the council thought they could put that large piece of land to better use. The plans also "ringfenced" the existing post office at the time, not to be touched, which is why that vacant piece of land near the end of Logan Street sits outwith Asda's boundaries today. It's also interesting to see that the houses at the bottom of Logan Street had their back gardens halved with the proposal.

When the proposal got underway, local houses and shops were provided with a little pamphlet on the 1970's plans to develop Glasgow Road. It showed the redevelopment of the town centre had been thought about since 1972 and that also the recession of the 70's and lack of council funding was likely to blame for it not happening earlier than the late 70's.

Some of the plans changed, but others like the Clydeview Shopping Centre, extension of the park, sheltered housing in the park and the arrival of Asda, very much happened. The 1977 booklet given to residents is transcribed here fully: "Hamilton District Council- Blantyre – Town Centre Redevelopment"

Background – The inhabitants of Blantyre have been deprived for a number of years of a proper town centre with adequate modern shopping facilities. In addition, the degree of dereliction and decay in the town centre is very severe and of great concern to Hamilton District Council.

Figure 8 Glasgow Road Tenements boarded up in 1977

These problems were emphasized in the redevelopment plans produced by the former Lanark County Council and approved by the Secretary of State in 1973. However, due to the severe restrictions on government spending, money was not forthcoming for the development. Hamilton District Council have since come into being in 1975, treated the problems of Blantyre Town Centre as a top priority and have now enlisted the assistance of the Scottish

Development Agency who will provide the financial backing for the redevelopment process.

The major private developer who will be included in this scheme is Associated Dairies Limited who have now reached an agreement with the District Council and have received full planning permission for the development of the major part of the new shopping centre.

The Scheme – The redevelopment scheme which has been prepared by Hamilton District Council is based on the plans approved by the Secretary of State and is comprised of the following main components:

Shopping Centre – the new shopping centre which will be located to the south side of Glasgow Road between Victoria Street and Logan Street will consist of ASDA superstore together with approximately 20 shop units, public houses, offices, etc. and a large carpark.

Service Industrial Site – An area has been allocated at Herbertson Street at the east end of the Town Centre to accommodate local tradesmen displaced by the redevelopment and the accommodation of other local small trades.

Park Extension – It is proposed to extend Stonefield Park up to Glasgow Road to provide a landscaped frontage to the town centre and additional recreational facilities. In addition, a major landscaping facelift will be given to all derelict and vacant land within the Town Centre.

Sports Centre – A site has been earmarked in the scheme for this much-needed facility on the north side of Glasgow Road, although money for its construction is not immediately available.

Old Persons Housing – Twenty five pensioners houses are planned for a site in the western corner of Stonefield Park.

What Happens now – Acquisition of Land and Property – The first step in carrying out the redevelopment scheme is the acquisition by Hamilton District Council of all land and property necessary for the scheme. It has been decided because of the multiplicity of ownership and the existence of certain legal difficulties to use the Council's powers of Compulsory purchase. Every person with any legal interest in land and property to be required will receive in the near future the compulsory purchase documents, which will include explanations of the procedures and your rights of objection. In the event of the Secretary of State confirming the Compulsory Purchase Orders, entry by the Hamilton District Council will be aimed at causing the least possible disruption to lives and livelihoods of those involved.

Rehousing – Hamilton District Council will rehouse in suitable alternative accommodation all those residents displaced by the redevelopment and wishing a District Council House.

Relocation of Shops – Hamilton District Council will make every effort to afford the opportunity to all shopkeepers displaced by the redevelopment to relocate to the new shopping centre, prior to the removal of the premises.

Relocation of Local Tradesmen – Again the District council will make every effort to ensure that those tradesmen wishing to remain in business have the opportunity of relocating within the Blantyre area. Compensation – Most owners of land and property of land to be acquired will be entitled to compensation, which will be negotiated by the District Valuer but in the event of disagreement, the matter will be settled by the Lands Tribunal.

Start of Construction – It is anticipated that work will be started sometime on the site in 1978 however, some environmental improvement works could start before the end of this year (1977). Further Information –If you require any further information, or clarification on any matter relating to the town centre redevelopment, please do not hesitate to contact the planning department at 123 Cadzow Street, Hamilton, or phone Hamilton 21188 Extension 274. Mr Calvart.

In 1978, it was agreed in March that some money would be put into the 1978/1979 Council budget to at least let the long awaited Blantyre Sports Centre get started. The budget for that year had just £126,000 set aside to get the work started. The latest council estimate for the whole building at that time was £875,000 but that was being reviewed constantly, the cost rising every few months.

The Sports centre had been proposed as early as 1970, the swimming pool as early as 1973 so it was a great relief to many people in Blantyre to finally hear the news that work would get started. Councilor George McInally said, "It has been a long wait but we know the town is definitely getting a centre and a start has been made. There will be a 6,325 square foot sports hall with a swimming pool around 25 yards long x 12.5 yards wide."

In addition, costs permitting, the council hoped to build a small training pool, or children's pool, a sauna suite, a restaurant, a cafe above the pool, a lounge, a small gym, offices as well as the necessary changing rooms.

In 1978, planners changed the location of the Sports Centre from the East end of John Street (where Devlin Grove now is), over to the West side of John Street in its present location. This was done to let the Sports Centre be part of the newly landscaped Stonefield Park and Glasgow Road. The space created on the east side of John Street was earmarked for housing.

During 1978, it was admitted by Architects that plans were somewhat lavish, and a series of cuts were made to save on the escalating costs. Removal of the separate restaurant was implemented by proposing to make the cafe sell a wider variety of food. Plans for the separate lounge were dropped altogether.

In 1978, work was done to install foundations, run in electricity and water services, although Councilors high hopes of the whole Centre being opened in 1979, were not to be met due to budget constraints.

We look back often criticizing the redevelopment of Blantyre in the late 1970's, but it should be noted back then, that with many of the buildings an eyesore, there WAS an appetite for redevelopment and providing something modern for the future. In March 1978, MP and Doctor, Maurice Miller gave a grim warning that objections were now limited to just a few townsfolk, that were currently holding up the whole process.

In a statement, he said he had written to the Secretary of State for Scotland and Asda to find out just what stage the development had reached. The statement concluded that if those few objectors withdrew their objections, Asda could commence work by the end of June that year providing many much needed jobs to Blantyre.

The Scottish Development Agency and Government had given the all clear to the development but the District Council were dealing with 4 objectors to the Glasgow Road redevelopment. The council hoped to come to some sort of agreement with the 4 objectors, so that the process would not be held up further.

The problem these objectors had was due to their compulsory order forced removal from premises on Glasgow Road and finding somewhere new, suitably as busy as before.

When Asda unveiled plans the year before in 1977, they stated in local newspapers, that without objection, they could get their store opened with 200 new jobs in under one year from the date of planning approval, but it took a couple of years due to contest and objection from the Co-Op.

The full story of Glasgow Road's 1970's redevelopment will be told in our separate book, a sequel to this, "Blantyre Glasgow Road North – The Real Story"

> Blantyre Project Social Media:
>
> **Bill Lobban:** "I remember when parts of Craig Street were demolished in 1979 to make way for the supermarket. My wife Mary lived at number 33 with her father and mother Archibald Baillie and Mary Baillie nee Lamond. I was quite excited about it all. Harper's Garage was still there at that time and the infant school being used as an Annexe for Calder Street, with Stonefield Primary School at the corner of Glasgow Road and Victoria Street already gone."

Clydeview Shopping Centre

Clydeview Shopping Centre is a contemporary shopping centre fronting on to Glasgow Road. It is located near Blantyre Asda supermarket and was opened in October 1980, a major part of Glasgow Road's redevelopment. It comprises of 2 storey retail units to the east and west of a central pedestrian precinct leading from Glasgow Road to Asda. Clydeview takes its name from the postoffice building, formerly at 249 Glasgow Road. The centre occupies the land between Logan Street and Victoria Street, at its boundary with Glasgow Road.

Figure 9 Clydeview Shopping Centre , Glasgow Road 2015

The land the centre occupies was subjected to extensive redevelopment during 1977 – 1979. The following properties previously occupied the site, running west from Logan Street to Craig Street was the Post Office, then a long tenement called Central Buildings in which was located the Co-op Chemist. Harpers Garage was situated on the other corner of Craigs Street, followed by a small tenement containing 2 shops with 4 houses above. Adjacent to this was a 3 storey building known as Whifflet Place and final, next to it, Low Blantyre Primary School (Stonefield Primary or Stonefield Parish Primary School) at the corner of Victoria Street.

The purpose built Clydeview Shopping Centre enjoys a frontage to Glasgow Road with extensive free car parking facilities to the rear.

Leases have proven to be expensive, business rates extortionate by comparison to other local towns, resulting in many of the units still being unoccupied in 2017.

However, we end this chapter about renovation and redevelopment, with a note of positivity. Throughout 2017, Asda representatives met with members of Blantyre Community Council, to discuss plans to demolish part of Clydeview Shopping Centre and replace it with a more functional, modern building, hopefully addressing rent and rates. It's an exciting plan and will change the way many people currently perceive the ailing and outdated "shopping centre with no shops."

The Centre is explored more thoroughly later in the book. The scene now set, we take you next to the main feature.

CHAPTER 3
EXPLORING BOUNDARIES
BURNBANK

We begin this definitive, epic journey of historical analysis of Blantyre's Glasgow Road at its most eastern end, at the Parish boundary we recognize at Burnbank. However, just before we immerse ourselves in all things 'Blantyre' lets start a little further eastwards again beyond the boundary of the Park Burn, something worth doing to explore what was happening on the outskirts of Blantyre centuries ago and how it helped shape the roads we know today.

Forgotten Former Farms

Like much of Blantyre and the surrounding villages of the time, this land was initially rural with fields and hedge rows as far as one could see, all in open expanses. Roy's Military Map of 1752 denotes the area as largely being farm fields belonging to two former farms. 'Newhouse' on the Blantyre side and 'Nether' or "Nitherhouse" on the opposing, lower Burnbank side.

Figure 10 East Boundary Crossing Highlighted on Roy's Military Map 1752

Both of those ancient, former farms are no longer there and indeed the names are now lost and forgotten to time. What is apparent from Roy's map and the previous graphic, is that the main road from Glasgow to Hamilton was along what we now know as Glasgow Road with Blantyre at that time being some 14 miles from the centre of the City. You'll notice also that it was one straight road, (as military and main roads often were), going from Blantyre, past 'Newhouse', later to become Springwells and past 'Nitherhous', a name that would later evolve into the more recognizable name of 'Greenfield.'

Road Splits & Bends

When we think of this area in a modern context, a long straight road at this point, certainly does *not* come to mind. Where Blantyre now merges into Burnbank, it's quite evident there's a huge awkward bend in the modern road near the modern Parkburn Industrial Estate.

The bend is easily explained and was not there on Roy's map of 1752. The road originally ran in a straight line directly into the village of Burnbank, but today is in a different more westerly position, branching off from the former straight road now with that awkward sharp turn. The following graphic shows a black dotted line for the former Burnbank road overlaid with modern road map. The split in the large circle, is the boundary. So why did this happen?

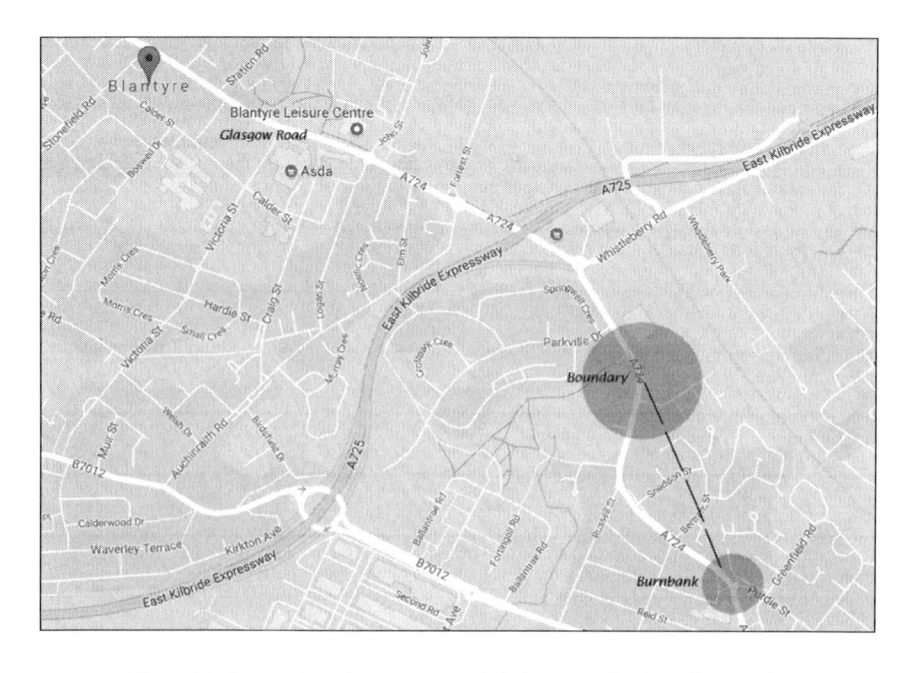

Figure 11 Glasgow Road once ran straight into Burnbank in the 1700's

Well, to answer that, we need to go back to the former farm, 'Nitherhous' which could be found in land tax rolls for Hamilton in the 1600's. There is no reference to this farm by the tax rolls of 1797 and one can only assume it was demolished. Instead later in 1859 maps on that exact land, still slightly outwith Blantyre and within the enclosures formerly denoted on Roy's map, is the farm of 'Greenfield.' i.e. Nitherhous became Greenfield, most likely due to new ownership or a rebuild of the property.

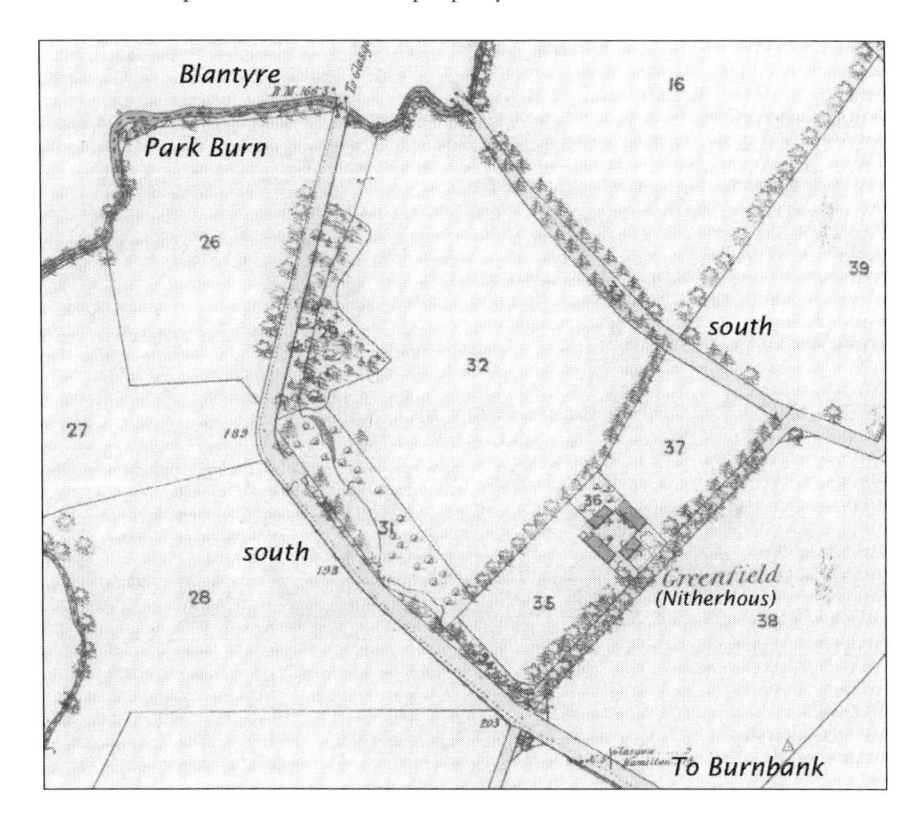

Figure 12 Boundary area at Greenfield in 1859

According to Forrest's map, prior to 1822, the main Glasgow to Hamilton Road split at the Blantyre boundary. No longer just one road, but now with a main southern road leading to Burnbank (as we know it today) and the northern road leading into Greenfield Farm and later into Greenfield Village, a road no longer there. In 1859, the configuration at the Blantyre boundary looked as shown above.

To the north where the roads crossed the Park Burn at the Blantyre boundary, they were bridged with stone & timber bridges, the larger one being the Greenfield Bridge to the south. Benchmarks or Masonry marks on the map indicate this bridge was likely built of stone, perhaps from the nearby former quarry behind Limetree, to the left of the southern road.

On the Blantyre side of the boundary to the north, the split can be seen more easily on the 1859 map. A footway to the north of the road, which even then would be just a rough dirt track, barely large enough for two carts to pass, crossed the split and continued on the southern road to Burnbank. We see the bridge locations at each point, the road crossing over the Park Burn, the dotted line signifying the Parish Boundary. The map suggests some woodland around either bank of the burn.

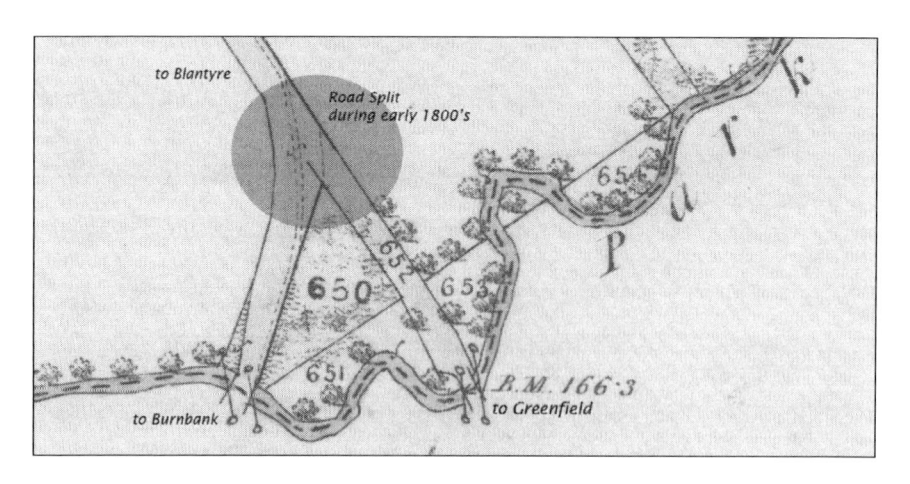

Figure 13 The 1859 maps shows the road split into two

Burnbank

We tend to think nowadays of Burnbank being our most immediate 24mphasiz to Blantyre, the two almost merging. However, it is worth remembering that at one time, a whole other village separated the two, in the form of Greenfield, which evolved from a single farm, to being a whole community. Burnbank, takes its name from the Wellshaw Burn, also known as the Shawburn running through the east of the village, and not the more westerly and distant Park Burn. Wellshaw Burn has been culverted for most of its passage through modern Burnbank. In historic times this stream's confluence with the Clyde lay within the district but now lies in neighbouring Whitehill. The area around the burn was still open country in some regards as late as the 1901 Census which records a Romany family "living in a field near Shawburn, Burnbank."

Burnbank has existed in one form or another since at least the late fifteenth century when a grant of lands was made to Sir John Hamilton of Newton. A further grant of lands to Sir John Hamilton of Zhisselberry (which is later recorded as Whistleberry) also included the lands in and around Burnbank. At this time the extent of the area accepted as Burnbank included the modern districts of Whitehill and Hillhouse and the area around Peacock Cross on the Burnbank Hamilton border. Predominantly rural, with a number of plantations (Whistleberry Plantation and Backmuir Plantation being most prominent) to feed the lace industry in Burnbank and Hamilton which had been sponsored since before 1778 by the then Duchess of Hamilton Elizabeth Campbell, 1st Baroness Hamilton of Hameldon. With the Industrial Revolution, Burnbank lost its rural identity becoming a mining village. Burnbank, like Blantyre, Springwells and Greenfield, was therefore a village in its own right.

The population of Burnbank had grown so great by the 1870's that a committee of citizens decided to apply for the erection of a Burgh of Burnbank. At the same time residents of Burnbank's western 25mphasiz Blantyre re-acted by petitioning for the erection of a Burgh of Blantyre. Both cases came before the Sheriff Court sitting at Glasgow. The Sheriff gave extra time for the petitioners for both causes to familiarize themselves with the arguments of their opponents and to respond in turn. The Provost and Burgesses of the existing Burgh of Hamilton, alarmed at the prospect of one (or possibly both) petitions being successful and thus creating a heavily industrialised, modern and vibrant western rival in turn petitioned the Parliament of the United Kingdom giving rise to the Burgh of Hamilton Act 1878. Blantyre was refused to become a Burgh, but by this Act, Burnbank was absorbed into Hamilton – ending its own burghal aspirations.

Greenfield

Greenfield was a village or hamlet in its own right. The sleepy, rural scene in Figure 3, with just a farm owned by Mr Hamilton in the 1820's and the Potter family in 1859, was short-lived and this whole area would quickly give way to industry with the discovery of coal. As the population expanded in the 1860's and 1870's workers came to find employment in Greenfield Collieries Pits 1 and 2, as well as the newly formed Greenfield Foundry which sat on the boundary itself (explored later) and of course in 1870 with the arrival of Robertson's Aerated Water Factory just over the boundary in Springwells.

During the 1870's and 1880's, many more houses were built. Miners lived in tied cottages at both Old and New Greenfield Rows, the latter built on the banks of the Park Burn. All these miners homes were small and hemmed in by railway lines.

Greenfield quickly became an established village, with its own pubs, school and even its own station opening on 1st April 1878, which would later be rebranded Burnbank Station. The railway branched off the nearby busy, Strathaven junction. Railways featured heavily on the dirty landscape, not just the passenger lines, but several sidings to assist the heavy industries.

Greenfield was incorporated into the burgh of Hamilton in 1878, although as the surrounding population grew, it quickly became known as Burnbank itself. Running through the centre of Greenfield was the old Glasgow to Hamilton Road, branded with a street address, officially known as 'Glasgow Road', as it was in Blantyre in the 1890's, turning sharply at the bend on the left of the above graphic, heading up, towards Blantyre.

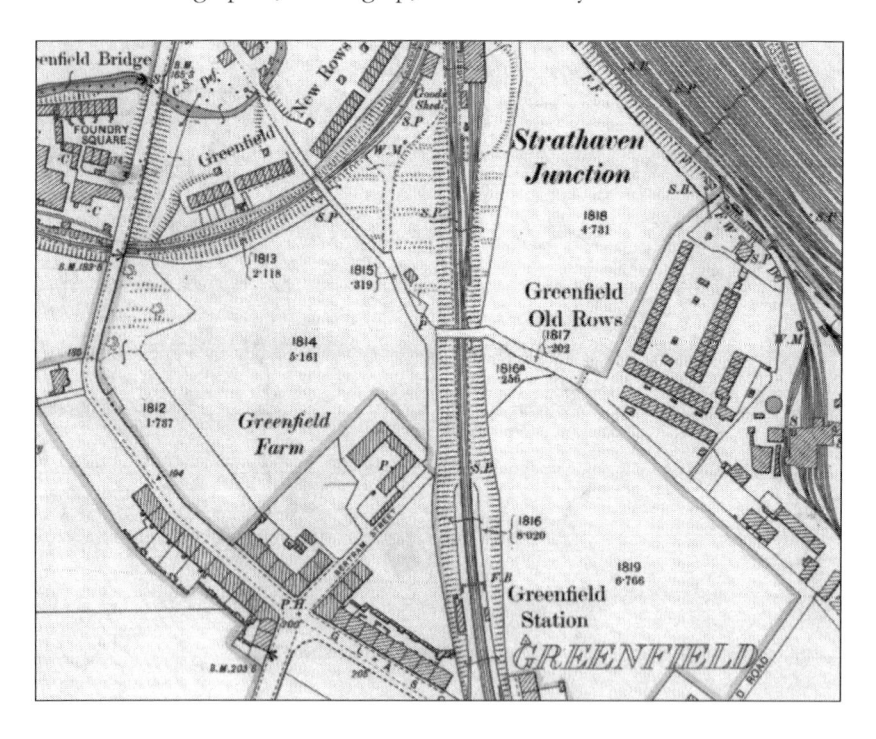

Figure 14 Populated 'Greenfield' at Blantyre's Boundary in 1898

With the demolition of Greenfield Farm between 1898 and 1910 and subsequent closure of the colliery, the name 'Greenfield' would decline more and more throughout the 20th Century, slowly replaced by Burnbank, in time being built upon right up to the Blantyre boundary.

When in 1903 tramlines were laid along Glasgow Road in Blantyre, Greenfield and Burnbank, this only served to further populate the area with good access to homes and businesses for all. It was an affordable means to readily travel in and out of each village. Convenient tram stops were situated all along Glasgow Road, primarily beside major businesses or public buildings. Even by 1903, it was safe to say rural charm here had well and truly gone.

Birdsfield Street

In 1907, a new street was formed in Greenfield/Burnbank, just off Glasgow Road, near the bend before crossing into Blantyre. It was to be a dead end, but constructed wide, the Park Burn at the end of end with earthworks formed to protect against flooding. Birdsfield Street was created and was to officially belong in Hamilton Parish, despite its name connections to the Brick & Tile works and Farm a short distance away in High Blantyre.

The street was adjacent to an old detached house named 'Limetree', built of stone in one and a half storeys with a large, arched doorway, facing out on to Glasgow Road. Limetree is still there today.

Figure 15 Limetree, in Burnbank, as it is today, dating from 1890's

On Birdsfield Street, two small semi detached villas were built that year on the south side. However, it is the large red sandstone building directly opposite them that is of interest and worthy of inclusion in this book. Many people in Blantyre will remember the former Trades Hotel, or as it was also commonly known, the Model Hostel or to give its official title, the Blantyre Lodging House.

The building was so well known, often associated with Blantyre despite sitting on the opposing bank of the official boundary. In a book that explores all of Glasgow Roads' buildings, it would be amiss not to mention it here. After all, it did sit just off Glasgow Road and even had a convenient tram stop. The Lodging House is shown in the highlighted area of this 1910 map below.

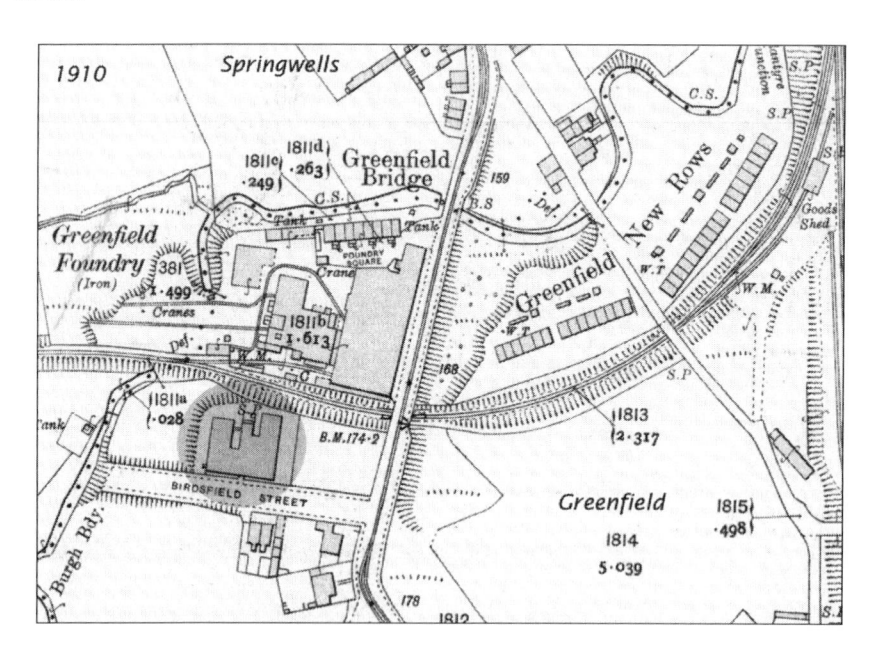

Figure 16 Blantyre Lodging House north side of Birdsfield Street built 1907

Blantyre Lodging House (Model Hostel / Trades Hotel)

Blantyre Lodging House was located at Birdsfield Street in Burnbank. Its identity was often blurry, for whilst it initially carried the name Blantyre Lodging House, it was certainly located over the Parkburn boundary, and into Hamilton Parish, rather than Blantyre. As such, I do still consider this a Hamilton building.

It was built by public subscription with the

Figure 17 Lodging House became Trades Hotel

company Blantyre Lodging House Ltd asking for people to subscribe with shares. Subscription closed on Friday 5th July 1907. Take up was great with directors thinking they may have had to close the subscription before the actual closing date. The prospectus asking for shares had been published slightly earlier on Friday 21st June 1907 and appeared in local newspapers like "The Motherwell Times."

It cost £8,000 with the amount raised from 2000 x £1 cumulative preference shares and a further 6000 x £1 ordinary shares. A 5s deposit could be made payable on application with the balance permitted to be paid up.

James Bell of Motherwell was Architect and one of five directors. The other directors were James Burns, the town clerk of Motherwell, Thomas Chambers a wood merchant of Motherwell, Blantyre's own James Kelly, spirit merchant and justice of the Peace and David Kemp, a painter of Motherwell.

The company was proposed to be formed on 21st June 1907 with the purposes of constructing a model lodge house. It was noted an excellent site had been found already at that time. It was conveniently sited, near public works and with a tram stopping right outside the gate. It was considered the finest location for building such a lodging house.

It opened on Saturday 3rd October 1908 as "Blantyre Lodging House", with all the latest fixtures and fittings. When it first opened there was a handy tram stop just outside at the Glasgow Road, at the entrance to Birdsfield Street. The triple storey building was made of sandstone and was entirely fenced off. When it opened, there was plenty of ground surrounding it offering recreational space foe the residents, or if they wanted to sit out on forms (seats). These seats were placed outside at various intervals for the lodgers. This was considered very important, for it was noted at the time that none of the other model lodging houses in Lanarkshire, or indeed Scotland offered a place for residents to sit outside, smoke and enjoy themselves without actually being on a public street.

The lodgers came in through a big entrance hall, after which it had a large well lit dining hall and a recreation room with kitchen on the ground floor, modern toilets and changing facilities as well as drying rooms were all at the back. A small shop was located within the building, exclusively selling items to residents.

The whole building was advertised as being well ventilated (a must in these hostels) and the big stone staircase led up to dormitories on the first and second floors. These were subdivided into wooden cubicles, which could accommodate 260 guests, each with a bed. Older folk may remember the iron stairway at the back which was the emergency route in case of fire, which in these places was always a hazard, in fact the ceilings were made out of asbestos or some similar fire retardant material.

Throughout the 1940's and 1950's, shares often came up for sale in local newspapers as they passed hands. Local historian and resident, Gordon Cook added, "I'm pretty sure a lot of the shareholders then were Blantyre residents too, the shares came up for sale from time to time. Some men preferred to live there permanently though not out of necessity. When, around 1973 I waited for the Motherwell bus at 5:20 a.m. the men could be heard at the 'model' coughing in increasing numbers as they began to wake up."

In pre WW2 years the hostel, perhaps reflecting it was not in Blantyre, was known as the "Trades Hotel". It was then known as the Model Hostel and home to many homeless people or those down on their luck.

Mr. Hugh McClelland (known as Hughie) was a local character who lived in the Model Lodge in Burnbank, Hamilton, not far from Springwells. He roamed around the Blantyre and Burnbank areas living on handouts from local inhabitants. He was tall, had long unkept hair, wore a ragged coat, and the legs of his trousers were ragged and frayed, all of which gave him a wild appearance.

When drunk, he would rant and rave at the top of his voice. Not knowing he was harmless, strangers would run away from him in terror, but it was claimed Hughie was a well-educated and knowledgeable man who had turned his back on the world and fallen on harder times.

Blantyre Project Social Media:

James Stirling: "I can remember Hughie. He used to walk out in front of the Chieftain bus when it went up Hill Street and when it stopped he would comb his hair by looking in one of the windows."

Betty McLean: "I too remember Hughie. One Friday night I was helping to scrub the floor in the Salvation Army in Forrest St. It was dark and the door opened, in came Hughie saying, 'I'm Jesus the son of God.' We girls screamed. He was a harmless soul but scared us that night."

The building was bought over by Tool Hire company 'Noel Kegg' in early 1975 and they traded there until 2010, for a while also known as Toolstop (the name of Noel's sons company).

In 2010, Toolstop moved to larger location nearer the M74.

Figure 18 Noel Kegg's Business at Burnbank in 2010, pictured by Jim Brown

In August 2014, the building was wrapped in scaffolding, many people speculating that it was to be renovated. However, on Thursday 6th October 2016, the building was completely demolished, as below in our photo that day.

Figure 19 Blantyre Lodging House demolished on 6th October 2016

Official Boundary

Anyway, we digress. Let's get back to Blantyre and the boundary itself. The official Blantyre Parish boundary at this location is the Park Burn, a stream which rises at Blantyre Park, further and higher to the south west. Other tributaries like the Red Burn flow into it further to the west and it flows in a north easterly direction towards the River Clyde, its confluence not far from Bothwell Bridge. The boundary is marked by a heavy dotted line on some of the previous maps in this chapter.

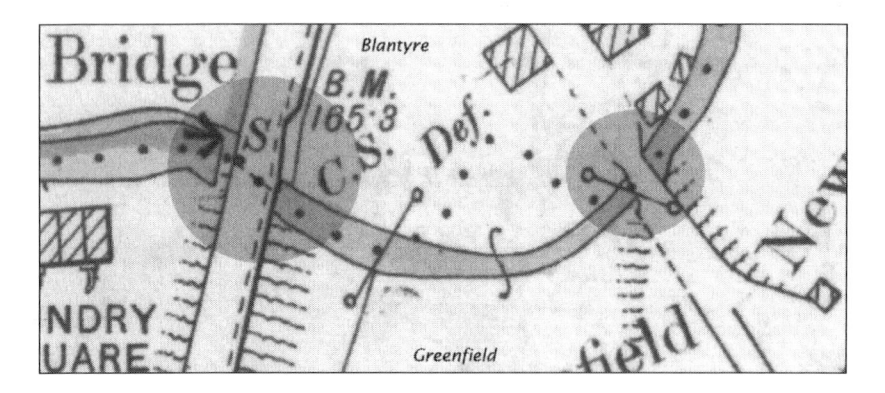

Figure 20 Greenfield Bridge & Greenfield New Row's Bridge in 1892

Greenfield Bridges

The boundary was crossed by going over either of two bridges. Highlighted in the larger circle above was the main Greenfield Bridge, adjacent to the Greenfield Foundry. Known as the Greenfield Bridge it dated from between 1747 and 1822 and allowed people to cross from Hamilton Parish into Blantyre. This bridge was made of stone with a footpath on its eastern side, that road being the Glasgow Road. It likely had improvements made in 1903 when trams started crossing into Blantyre.

Work to improve the bridge appears to have taken place in 1933 when the tramlines in this area were removed, for the 1936 map carriageway looks slightly wider with pavements on either side. Hamilton Town Council agreed on Wednesday 18th January 1933 to ascertain from the Ministry of Transport if a grant would be available for the widening of the road and bridges if it was arranged to proceed with a reconstruction and widening of the thoroughfare from Birdsfield Street, Burnbank to the burgh of Hamilton's boundary at Greenfield Foundry at Blantyre. In the event no grant being available, the Town Council decided to lift the tramway rails and setts and to relay the roadway in the same fashion as had been done slightly earlier in Blantyre.

The approaches had earth embankments with the bridge elevated above the burn. The bridge existed post WW2, but was demolished in the second half of the 20th Century, redundant when the Park Burn was culverted at that location. The bridge would have been exactly where the junction is today into Park Burn Court Industrial Estate. The whole area lies on a low lying plain and it took the creation of the long culvert to finally stop flooding in this region.

To the east, a smaller bridge, perhaps made of timber or stone of a less substantial nature existed. This bridge may have been very old as part of the original Glasgow to Hamilton road before the sharp bend and southern more substantial road was created. In the late 19th Century, this bridge primarily was used by miners accessing the nearby Greenfield Colliery and also by families living at the tied Greenfield New Rows beside the bridge. The smaller bridge is also no longer there, its site now where the first junction is within the modern Park Burn Industrial Estate.

Figure 21 This is how the former location of Greenfield Bridge looks today

Blantyre Project Social Media:

Chris Ladds: "Regarding the old name 'Nitherhous' than became Greenfield Farm. Found in Volume one of late 1600s land tax roles for Hamilton Parish - Netherhouses / Netherhousis / Nitherhouses / etc.... So it will be some sort of subordinate dwelling perhaps a pendicle of a larger nearby farm, or simply lower down given slope. Probably a small cluster of simple farm buildings like an old Scheeling which was replaced by time renamed to Greenfield.

Liz Jack: "We could see the Model Hostel from our house. We would run past it thinking the old men would catch us. Parents told us if we were bad they would come and take us away!"

Blantyre Project Social Media:

Jim McSorley: "When St Joseph's Secondary School closed, we were moved to Greenfield Annex in Burnbank in 1972. I lived in High Blantyre and walked past the Model every day. Once my friend and I went inside as children, into the large entrance hall and saw the poor souls inside. These guys probably served in WW2, something we didn't think about as kids."

Caroline McDougall: "I remember the Model Hostel wee too. The old men used to sit on the wee wall outside smoking. They would also say hello to everybody passing. Occasionally, some of them were drunk, but there never seemed to be any disorder."

Elspeth McGregor: "In the 1950's and 1960's, Limetree Cottage was owned by Miss Dick and her sister, who taught commercial subjects from there."

CHAPTER 4
GLASGOW ROAD SOUTH
BURNBANK TO SPRINGWELL PLACE

Greenfield Foundry

No documented history has previously been compiled about the story of Greenfield Foundry, so following many days work, it is hoped you enjoy this effort. The Greenfield Foundry, later known as 'Greenfield Foundry & Engineering Works' was a former large iron foundry business located to the east of Springwell, Low Blantyre, at the boundary with Burnbank during the late 19th Century and into much of the 20th Century.

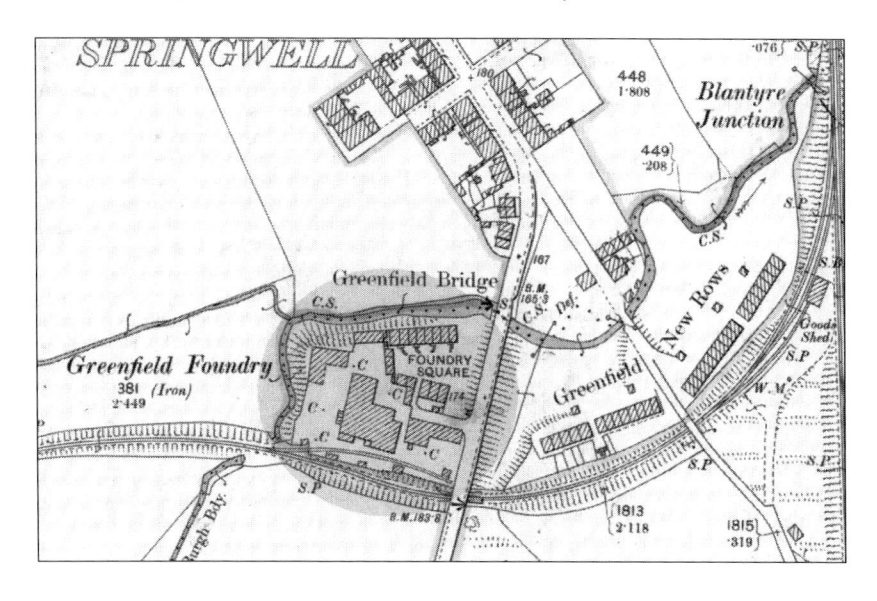

Figure 22 Greenfield Foundry in 1898 at Blantyre's boundary

The foundry was fairly unique as it represented one of the only buildings that spanned two Parishes, parts of the business latterly on either side of the boundary. However, it didn't start off like that, its beginnings focused on the Burnbank side of the Park Burn boundary. It was the arrival of this business in the 1870's, the nearby Robertson's Aerated Mineral Water Factory, and sthe 1880's inking of nearby Greenfield Collieries, that would help grow the detached Blantyre hamlet of Springwell, which prior to that was simply a farm and a couple of small houses.

In 1877, the year of the Blantyre disaster, Taylor & Henderson, ironfounders of Hamilton were the engineers and smiths who ran the business, "Taylor & Henderson Foundry". Buying a plot of unused land, a field around 1 acre in size adjacent to the Parkburn, the partners constructed a moderate sized foundry, where they intended to manufacture items, including rainwater goods, kitchen ranges, stoves, furnace pans, stable fittings, railing bars, balcony panels & general castings. The land was suitable as the railway spur to the south and Parkburn to west and north formed enclosures, protecting somewhat against intruders and theft.

The business first appears up and running in 1878, according to Naismith's Directory. At that time, the manager of the foundry was Mr. James Dunlop of Springwell. The foundry was a private endeavour and it opened with the official name, "The Greenfield Foundry Company" and does not seem to be tied to the collieries, the name taken from the nearby Greenfield Farm, whose former land it had been built on.

It is said that the owners tried to do well by their employees and in 1880 they built the Greenfield Foundry Square, a row of 24 small, terraced homes for their workers to the north end of their site, immediately beside the ParkBurn. The homes were well built, but small, double storey (12 up, 12 down) with only one room and a kitchen in each. Small outdoor washhouses and toilets were located on the west side of the square and formed an enclosed perimeter separating the foundry to the south and west. Steps on the south elevation of the foundry house accessed upper storeys. To the south of the square were the managers and office staff homes with private outdoors toilets at the back. Mr. Lachlan Taylor, one of the business owners who also owned nearby shops and another brass foundry, was fairly "hands on" and lived at 23 Foundry Square, in one of the manager's homes.

Workers entered the foundry from Glasgow Road, the gated entrance to the foundry being straight ahead and the open entrance to foundry square homes leading off to the north. The premises consisted of the offices near the entrance, the main foundry located in the middle of the plot and workshops and pattern rooms at the far west.

However, incoming cash was not managed well. Owing to bad debts, on 21st April 1882, Taylor & Henderson's partnership was dissolved via liquidation. Despite the foundry building on the successes of astonishing construction efforts in nearby Blantyre and Hamilton, Taylor and Henderson went their separate ways.

An offer was made from Andrew Kesson and Duncan Campbell, successful founders in Glasgow already established at Carntyne. Their partnership 'Kesson & Campbell" then bought over the assets of the dissolved company and in 1882, they renamed it simply, "The Greenfield Foundry".

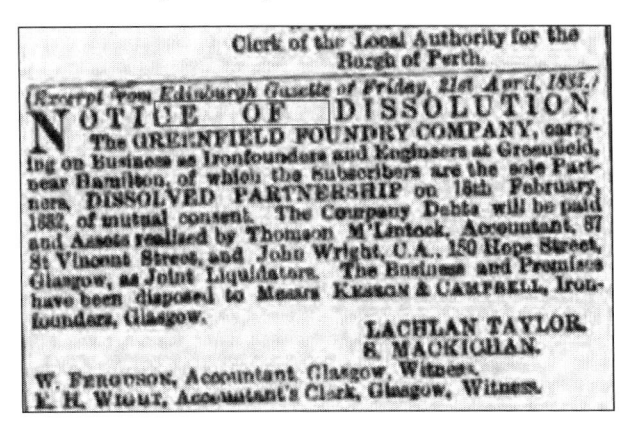

Figure 23 Notice of Dissolution in 1882

Subscriber businessman, Samuel Potts, also funded the venture. The company put out an advert in the newspaper wishing all to know the foundry would be run under "Kesson & Campbell". On 5th July 1882, job adverts appeared in the paper, including asking for office clerks, perhaps to deal with the untangling of orders. The liquidators of Taylor & Henderson pursued debt collection for some time, including £116 owed to them by Messers Merry & Cunningham at Auchinraith Colliery.

To give an idea how much the adjacent area of Greenfield changed in the 10 years previous to this, in 1875, the valuation roll has 12 entries for the area. By 1885, just a decade later, it had 948 entries!

On 28th May 1887, unmarried brothers James Cook (17) and Thomas Cook (20) died in the Udston Colliery Disaster along with their father Richard (50). The men were all miners living at the Foundry Row in Greenfield Foundry and one can only image how Richard's widow must have suffered following that day.

On Sunday 20th May 1888, the manager discovered that thieves have entered the foundry overnight and had attempted to steal money. However, they clearly underestimated that the foundry money was kept in a safe and bolted down by foundry castings. Attempts were made to open it with an iron bar. However, the safe was untouched and the thieves took items of little value instead. In July 1891, Mr Kesson was fined for breaching the Factory Act for employing 3 boys before the regulated starting hour in the morning.

Seeking a quieter life, Mr Kesson was approaching retirement and wanted his share of the business before doing so. On Wednesday 30th March 1892 at 2pm the whole Greenfield Foundry and Foundry Square homes were put up for sale by public auction in Glasgow. The entire property and grounds were for sale and advertised as being in the heart of Lanarkshire's coalfields. The advert stated, "There is ample room for extending the works and a railway siding into them. The foundry having a large trade." The rental of the foundry was £133 per year. The foundry square homes were also up for sale, noted as being in good condition and all presently let out for moderate rents, which could be increased. The rental of the square was £128 12 shillings. The reserve price put on the whole lot was £2,500. The auction came and went, the foundry unsold, perhaps to the relief of the workers in the tied homes.

However, Mr Kesson clearly wanted his share of the business and the foundry remained for sale for a year until a further public auction on 12th April 1893 for the reduced upset price of £1,700. The grounds were noted as being 1 acre, 3 roods.

On Thursday 24th October 1894, Mr Andrew Speed who was employed at the foundry was walking home that evening to his home in Uddingston, after leaving work. He was taking the short cut using the railway line when he died suddenly, after being struck by a locomotive.

Late on the evening of Monday 6th May 1895, a sinister and indecent outrage was committed on the Blantyre on the wife of James Rankin, of Baird's Rows, Stonefield, while she returned homewards from Hamilton. The woman stated that while she was nearing Greenfield Foundry, some men who would not let her pass blocked her path. She was then verbally and physically attacked by a number of men near the gates, and in an endeavour to escape she crossed into the field opposite, running at a pace near the Parkburn where she was caught up on, and in the darkness overtaken, thrown on the ground, her mouth stuffed, her body kicked and beaten, and finally assaulted in the most brutal and shocking manner for any woman. Her assailants then left her where she lay. The woman was found some time afterwards completely exhausted, and was taken in a state of shock to her home. Dr Sinclair declared her injuries to be of most brutal description and confined her to bed. The police lost no time in getting clues together interrogating men in the foundry, and leaving her bed the next morning escorted by police in the most brave action, the woman pointed out the men face to face in their own workplace. Five young men, all-living in Hamilton were apprehended in connection with the outrage and taken to the jail.

Figure 24 Drawing showing interior of the foundry in the 1890's

Greenfield Foundry was not without further crimes and accidents. John Mullen of 4 Low Blantyre Road, Greenfield had the contract with the foundry to go out and cut the surrounding grass parks, keeping the railway verges clear of hay and weeds. On Saturday 25th August 1895, whilst working next to the line, a momentary lapse of concentration was fatal as a locomotive buffer struck his head; the wheels severing his arm clean off. The train did not stop for some time, despite efforts from the driver. Unmarried, the Irish immigrant was taken back to Ireland for burial.

By 1895, the valuation roll shows the 24 foundry square homes still mostly all occupied, but not always by foundry workers. By then, miners and labourers of the nearby Greenfield Colliery were mostly renting them. That year the occupants were 1 George Webster, 2 William Henry, 3 John Buchanan, 4 Empty, 5 William Murray, 6 Robert McNeil, 7 George Hutchison, 8 David Morrison, 9 John Smith, 10 George Lauder, 11 James Hamilton, 12 Thomas Stevens, 13 James Hutchison, 14 James Rodger, 15 Archibald Frew, 16 John Lamont, 17 Neil McNeil, 18 Alexander McDonald, 19 Andrew Haddell, 20 Robert Hunter, 21 John Milligan, 22 Henry Sneddon, 23 Alexander Matthews and 24 Charles Smith.

On 20th May 1896, Andrew Kesson, one of the owners retired. The partnership was dissolved that day, but the Greenfield Foundry carried on with partner Duncan Campbell forming an 39mphasiz new partnership with Robert Bayne Jardine Binnie, along with subscriber Samuel Potts. For a short time, they continued however as "Kesson & Campbell", the name well known.

By 1898, no less than five large cranes adorned the yards outside. A loading platform and siding had also been constructed near the North British

Railway spur to the south of the site.

One can only presume at the difficult and hot working conditions inside the foundry. It would have been a dangerous place, especially in those times before proper health and safety. Scalding hot steam, fumes, and chemicals, sharp metal and faulty equipment would have contributed towards many minor accidents. A notable fatality occurred in 1898 when on Wednesday 21st September; 28-year-old James Farrell lost his life. He had been on duty to attend to the furnace and around 11am, a box of molten metal was sent up to him. Everybody left for lunch and noticed James wasn't there. Upon searching he was found overcome by fumes, his body slumped over and into the carriage, his lifeless head completely submerged in the liquefied metal. Doctors Forbes and Lees arrived but their efforts to revive were not needed.

Later in 1900, in an effort to rebrand the foundry, the venture partners removed the name Kesson with permission from "Kesson & Campbell" and made their partnership more permanent renaming the business, "Campbell, Binnie & Co." The owners added to the former name of Greenfield Foundry and it became "Greenfield Foundry & Engineering Works."

Campbell, Binnie & Co were makers of the Globe Patent Double-Acting SteamPump, allegedly the best pump in the market for Distilleries, Brewers, Chemical Works, Contractors, &c. Makers of Lockwoods Patent Oscillating Furnace Bars, and General Ironfounders, Engineers, Millwrights, Machine-Makers and Smiths.

On Thursday 9th March 1900, an explosion at the foundry severely injured five workers. A barrel containing 8 gallons of naphtha burst and exploded covering the men in the flammable liquid. The injured were John Pollock (41) of 2 Foundry Square, Malcolm Jack (27) of Foundry Square, James Neil (57) watchman of Semple's Buildings, Springwell, William Crowr (23) clerk of Brandon Street, Hamilton and John Stalker (21) clerk of Greenfield Old Rows.

On Monday 2nd September 1901, a cycling accident happened at Greenfield Foundry, whereby a young man named James Robertson (16), residing with parents M'Alpine's Buildings, Stonefield, Blantyre, received injuries of a serious nature. Robertson was proceeding towards Hamilton when he ran into another cyclist coming riding in the opposite direction. Both men were thrown heavily to the ground. When picked up Robertson was found to be unconscious, and was carried into the office of the foundry where a doctor attended him. He was then taken home. Dr Wilson, Blantyre, then attended him and ordered his removal to the Royal Infirmary. The other young man was able to proceed home.

On Saturday 10th September 1904, a sad accident is reported to have occurred about half-past one o'clock on the railway bridge near Greenfield Foundry. It seems that three boys, two of them brothers named Dunn, aged ten and seven years respectively, residing in Johnstone Street, Hamilton, and another boy called Brownlie, had gone Cambuslang with a vanman bringing milk from that place to Hamilton. On the way back the vanman stopped at his father's house at Springwell, and placing feeding bag on his horse's head went inside, leaving the boys in the van. It supposed that the horse must have tramped on the feeding bag and drew off its blinders and bolted. It ran along the footpath until opposite the foundry, where the van capsized down the embankment. Brownlie had jumped off, but the Dunns were both thrown underneath. A passing motorcar to Blantyre conveyed the younger boy to his home, where, on examination by Dr Walker, it was found life was extinct. The elder brother was unhurt.

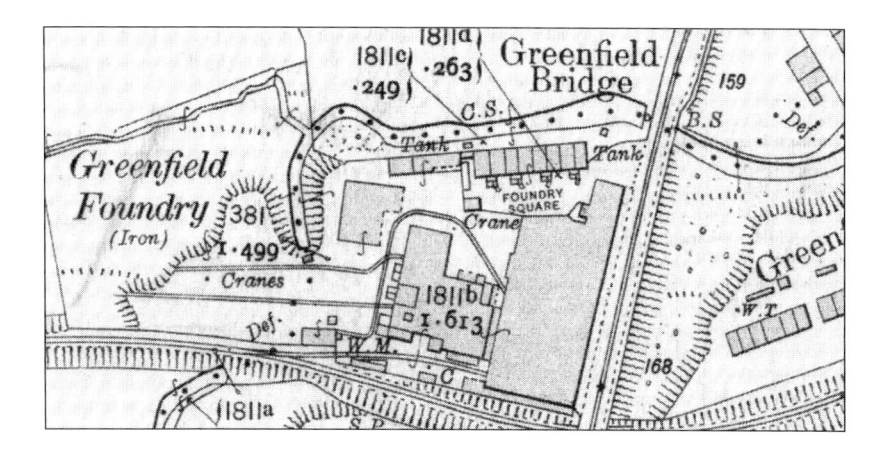

Figure 25 Greenfield Foundry 1910 map showing expansion

The business thrived in the first part of the new Century. Planned expansions came to fruition when between 1900 – 1910 part of the Park Burn was culverted and landscaped over to the west, offering a materials laydown area for the foundry and further space to operate cranes. Beyond to the west and north were still all fields at the time, but it meant Greenfield Foundry was now operating in both Hamilton and Blantyre Parishes.

Around that same time a weighing machine was added beside the railway. However, the greatest change was the demolition of the office managers house in the foundry square and of the offices themselves, creating space for a large foundry workshop right along Glasgow Road, accommodating new offices within. It meant the previous foundry entrance was redundant and another was created opening up Glasgow Road directly into Foundry Square immediately beside Greenfield Bridge, gated off at the southwest to separate the business from residential.

The arrival of trams in 1903 brought easier commutes for those workers who lived outwith the foundry. The nearest tram stop was just outside the nearby Birdsfield Street to the south. In 1900, Mr Muir Robertson, jun., partner of 'Messrs William Robertson & Son, civil and mining engineers, Glasgow, said his firm were engineers for many of the collieries in this district, and for the Greenfield and Udston estates. The Greenfield estate was one of the largest growing mining estates in the district, and was in process of development. He considered that the proposed tramway would be a very great service to the Greenfield, Springwell and Burnbank districts, and among other things, would quicken the development of the Greenfield estate.

Fields surrounding the foundry still kept their rural charm as this postcard from 1908 shows. You can see the square ground cleared behind the foundry in readiness to build Blantyre Lodging House, later that year.

Figure 26 Children in the Hay in 1908. Greenfield Foundry to the left, Burnbank to right

On 21st April 1911, the North British Railway submitted plans for a railway siding alteration and some tracks were laid within the foundry itself, meaning little disruption for any loading operations to their line.

In 1912, Campbell, Binnie and Co had to pay a worker £275 in damages after a court case proved that the worker had been crushed due to their machinery and negligence of maintenance of the equipment. The worker was left lame for much of his life.

Fire broke out in the foundry joinery shop on 20th January 1914 and the fire services were called. Arriving promptly, water was fetched from the Park Burn nearby and the fire quickly put out before it spread to the pattern shop adjacent. Damage was negligible.

During WW1 in 1915, the Foundry continued operating and worker R.H.Reid patented a device for washing coal that could separate materials of different sizes. War affected the foundry just as much as it did other businesses. Men left their employment to head off to fight and employee numbers reduced during that time.

On Saturday 2nd March 1916, workers stopped at lunchtime to hold a little service, where guest of honour was William Webster of the 6th Scottish Rifles. William was presented with a beautiful gold watch with a suitable inscription of his bravery on the battlefield. William who was a sergeant had won the DCM medal and was home on leave and had been an engineer at the foundry, before the war. It was his third visit home from the trenches after being injured 3 times by bullets. The Rechabites raised the money for the watch. He left to go back to the front the following Saturday.

His co-workers John Crookson, Ernest Rogerson and Gilbert Stodart, all privates were not so lucky and did not return from war. During the war years the employees and owners of the foundry subscribed heavily to donation to Blantyre Ambulance, Blantyre Hospital and Blantyre Jubilee Nurses as well as major hospitals in Glasgow. In April 1918, co-workers awarded John Black a gold watch after his return from France and service in the Scottish Rifles.

On 12th August 1924, the partnership of Campbell, Binnie & Co was dissolved due to the retirement of Mr Binnie. Mr William Reid was to take his place, the business re-emerging that day as "Campbell, Binnie, Reid & Co".

In 1924 and 1925, the new business partners decided to expand the business further. They demolished the remaining old homes in foundry square, which had become damp (presumably from consistent flooding at the nearby ParkBurn) and culverted the Park Burn to the north. They then bridged over Blantyre's boundary into a field opposite on the Blantyre side and created another workshop and stores, almost doubling the size of the original foundry. Again, this meant the entrance moving, south this time.

By the mid 1920's Greenfield Foundry & Engineering Works was once of the largest buildings in the area and employer of a couple of hundred people, stretching right up to homes in Springwell.

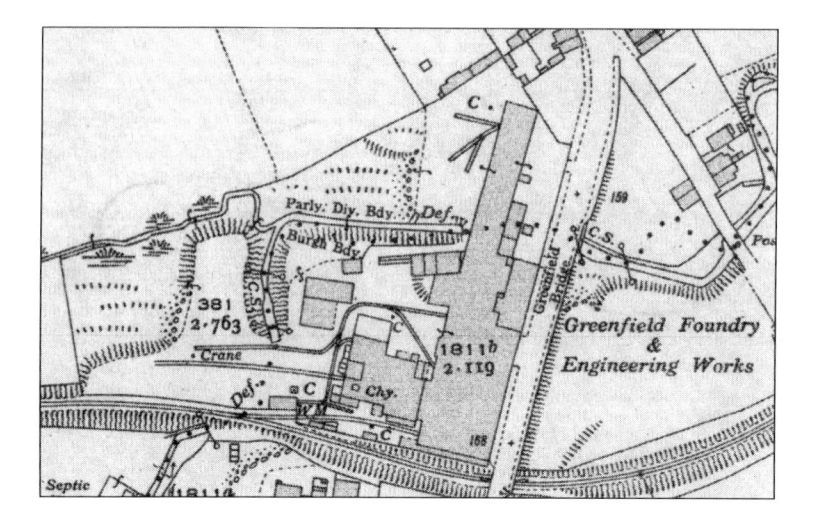

Figure 27 Greenfield Foundry & Engineering Works 1936 Map

Fire destroyed most of the old foundry records in 1927. About midnight on 31st August, fire broke out in the office premises of Messrs Campbell, Binnie, Reid. & Co. The office adjoined the main works, and consisted of a two-storey building with a loft above, where plans and records were stored. It seems that the fire originated in the loft, which was completely destroyed. Damage by water and smoke was also done to the drawing office and the counting house on the ground floor. The damage was estimated at several thousands of pounds. The fire though did not interfere with the work in the foundry.

In 1933, following the removal of the old tram lines on Glasgow Road outside the foundry, the road was widened making it more substantial, just as had been done in Blantyre a few years earlier.

Towards the end of WW2 in May 1945, Campbell, Binnie, Reid & Co was fined £20 for not maintaining safe temperatures for their workers. Their business was wound up in the mid 1950's and bought over by Charles Ireland, who primarily ran a scrap merchants business from the site. It was then heavily fenced off and guarded, with a report that a 2nd World War ammunition was found out in the yard. Charles Ireland's business did evolve and was successful, becoming a limited company in the form of Ireland Alloys on 2nd September 1964. They remained at that site until the mid 1970's before moving to custom built premises on Whistleberry Road.

On Wednesday 21st November 1973, a Mr Hannaway attempted to open the safe with an oxy acetylene torch after losing the key. Not realizing there safe contained dynamite, he succeeded only in blowing both his legs off! The explosion was heard throughout Low Blantyre.

With Ireland Alloys having cleared many of the old buildings, the open space was ideal for vehicle storage. First Buses Depot now is situated on the site of the former Greenfield Foundry. The large depot at Springwells houses many buses with familiar white and purple livery.

Figure 28 First Buses today, in 2017 on former site of the Foundry

Blantyre Project Social Media:

Serge Mikklesen: "I remember all the smells, iron, sulphur, burning as you walked past that metalworks. The never ending stream of men pouring out at the end of shifts, mostly turning right, heading home to Burnbank. Workmen all looked the same, but you could always tell the odd manager or two coming out with a briefcase or a tie on. Reading your article and seeing how far back in history this works went, it must have employed thousands of men."

Carol Stevenson "The back yard used to flood often. In times of heavy rainfall, you could hear the water gushing below the ground in various large culverts. The Parkburn was notorious for it, never properly resolved until recent years. Dips and hollows sometimes appeared in the embankments and roads after heavy rainfall which would need filled in. It took until the creation of the little Industrial Estate opposite Ireland's before water problems were sorted."

"Read More about **Greenfield Foundry** online. Scan our handy QR Code for more narrative and photos at Blantyre's History Archives. See Information at the start of this book for more information on using this added feature."

The Birth of 'Springwell'

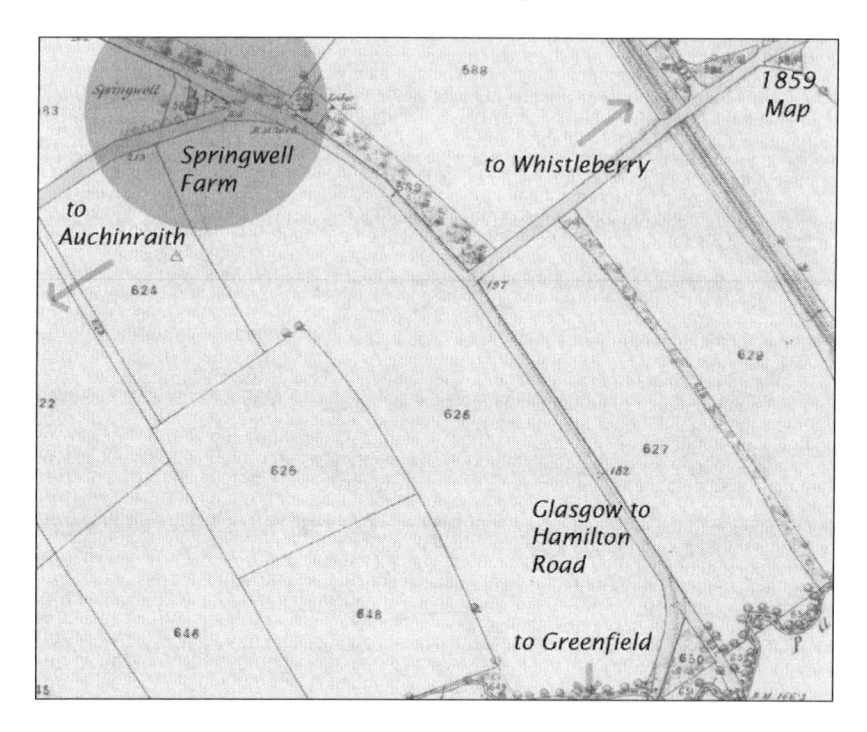

Figure 29 Springwell Map of 1859 shows only 1 farm and empty fields

The Springwell area of Blantyre took its name from a moderately sized but prominent, former farmhouse that once stood detached and isolated on the Glasgow to Hamilton Road. The farm was situated at its junction with the track that would later become Auchinraith Road. Springwell Farm was built in the mid 1700's but was demolished in 1876 meaning photos are rare and sketches even more so.

The name was 'Springwell' and not 'Springwells' which only appears in more modern times with an 's' at the end, named after the 3 wells at the junction. This farmhouse at the fork in the road, (a building explored later in the book) was the birth of Springwell as a small hamlet and very much the early beating heart of this area's history.

The 1859 map in the above illustration shows the expansive fields of Springwell Farm, fields that would later be acquired for building upon, especially around either side of the Glasgow to Hamilton Road. To the west was Blantyre, still largely undeveloped, to the south east, the rural charms of Greenfield farm. This chapter deals with the land to the south of the main road and the hamlet of Springwell, which was about to expand hugely.

Evolution of 'Springwell'

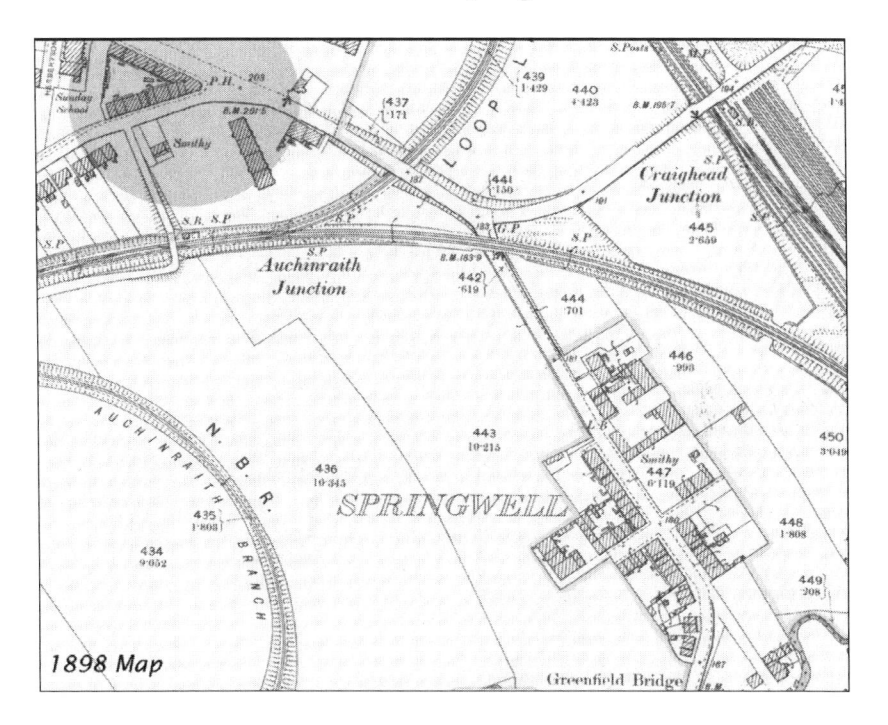

Figure 30 Springwell map 1898, 40 years after previous illustration

The above illustration on this page shows by comparison to the previous image, just how much Springwell changed and grew in only 4 decades. The 1898 map primarily shows expansion of the railways with the Auchinraith railway junction and Craighead junction noticeably crossing over the former Springwell Farm fields. The Auchinraith rail junction forced a realignment of Whistleberry Road junction at the Glasgow to Hamilton Road. The farm is gone at the top left but in its place is a plethora of new businesses and homes, the start of massive development of this main road into Blantyre.

However, meantime our journey continues with the exploration of the south side of the new hamlet of Springwell which had grown in population by many hundreds of people in that short space of time.

Blantyre Project Social Media:

James Faulds: "Springwell was a great place to be brought up. We all had a great time as a family and my older sister still lives there with her family, the Cambridges in Springwell Crescent. Not many of the original old families left."

Now you may think that Springwell as a hamlet "sprung" up initially around Robertson's of Springwell, the large aerated water business but this was not the case. Robertson's Aerated Water Business was founded in 1890 but Springwell formed properly with the first few homes appearing much earlier around 1877/1878.

It was almost certainly the nearby Greenfield Foundry being constructed in 1877 that brought mass employment to the area, as well of course as the Greenfield Colliery, sunk in the 1860's. The 1875 valuation roll still has the fields of Springwell empty with exception of the aforementioned farmhouse.

The first settlers to build modest homes in what would become Springwell hamlet were mostly miners, craftsmen, carters and foundrymen. It was those men with the foresight to buy inexpensive land from the farm of Springwell in the late 1870's and 1880's that did well. The way to prosper was to build your own homes with whatever you could afford, then sell them on, or even better rent them out. Quite often those entrepreneurial miners and foundrymen left their employment a little later due to their successes, to become employers of others. It was a good life plan to follow and that's exactly what people did.

McLelland's Land, Springwell

Using the 1898 map below for reference, our very first building on Glasgow Road within Blantyre Parish is the former "McLelland's Land."

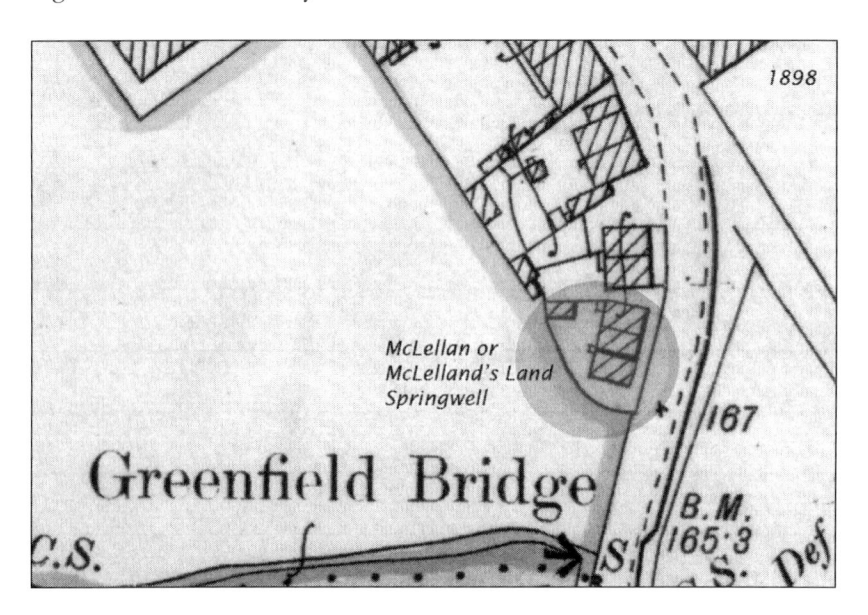

Figure 31 Former McLelland's Land, the start of Glasgow Road, Blantyre

McLellan or McLelland's Land (depending on various census information) was a small, former plot of land about a third of an acre on the south east of Springwell, near the old fork in the road. The name Land or Laun, as in old Scots dialect really refers to the buildings themselves, which at this location were stone or brick built and single storey.

McLelland's property opened out directly on to the Glasgow to Hamilton Road and comprised of 3 small houses, each with 2 rooms and at least 1 window in each room and a nearby workshop to the south. The property was terraced, the nearest to the Parkburn being the workshop. This left another 2 homes in the block, attached on the north side, the middle one being the largest and the farthest divided into 2 homes.

Throughout this book, reference will be made to properties that are no longer here and given the age of some of them, sometimes there are no photos. To provide an idea of how such buildings looked, this publication contains the exclusively unique idea of providing 'location line drawings' overlaying the former buildings shape and profile in a ghost image, into a modern context. It is hoped this gives the reader an interesting idea of size, locations, shape and context.

Figure 32 Location Line Drawing showing former McLelland's Land

You'll notice the property boundary in the above image looks to be sitting out in the road. The overlaid location is correct, but remember when first built, the modern 1930 road widening hadn't happened yet. A washhouse and outdoor toilet was located to the rear of the property, which was fenced off separating the land from neighbours. Behind to the left, were empty fields.

This was one of the earliest properties in Springwell and the edge of Blantyre.

McLelland's Land was built between 1881 and 1885 but surprisingly not by a McLelland. The property was constructed by Mr. John Welsh, a miner who arrived in Blantyre within that timeframe. However, he was the owner for only a short time before selling the entire property, perhaps as early as 1886. It was new owner William McLelland, a miner known well to John that bought the houses, for the purposes of renting them out. We'll be coming back to John Welsh a little later in this chapter.

In the 1885 valuation roll, John Welsh was living at the first house nearest the boundary, which had a rateable value of £3 per annum. In the other 2 houses John MacSwan, a moulder was renting for £6 and in the last house Mr. William McLelland, a miner renting for the reduced rent of £3. Perhaps William and John were friends, for shortly after, William bought the entire 3 houses from John and became the new owner for at least the next 20 years. The suggestion of this is strong, for in the 1891 census, a Welsh family member was visiting William that day.

It seems that the workshop was formed in 1891, something denoted on a later valuation roll, part of the homes converted to suit. This was done to suit William McLelland's own purposes for the workshop was initially used by William for his own new business as a carter. (a person who conveys goods by cart). William had given up the mining profession and was self employed. He may have been letting part of the workshop out to a joiner also by this time. William had family nearby across the road at Burnside near the Parkburn, and therefore was living close to his brother.

His property would have benefited from water being run into the district in 1891, the valuation roll of 1895 noting that improvement to the area. McLelland's land sat in an elevated position high above the Parkburn and was distant and high enough to not be affected by its frequent flooding. In 1895, the occupants were William Mclelland, Robert Ewen who was an engine dealer and John Kenney, a miner renting for £5 per year.

By 1901, William was conducting his business from the workshop but had outgrown living in these small homes, deciding to rent his own house out as well. In 1905, John Penman was living in the largest house paying £8, 8 shillings rent, David Spence a miner paying £6 and Samuel Marshall, a labourer also paying £6.

By 1915, William was no longer the owner, the property being in the possession of William Alston Dykes solicitors held in trust via Alexander Peter or Rosebank Avenue, Blantyre. William McLelland had died in 1906. A little later, in 1915, during those trying times, Alexander Forrest, a joiner was renting the workshop for £2 per annum where he would do so for some time until the mid 1920's without any rent increases. Catherine Donnelly a widow was renting the first house her rent going up from £8, 12 shillings to £9, 12 shillings between 1915 and 1920. In a period of stability for tenants, John Cowan a miner was renting the second house, his rent increasing from £6 to £7, 13 shillings in those same 5 years. In the last house was Malcolm Penman a bricklayer who saw the largest rent increase in that period from £5,17 shillings to £7, 13 shillings.

By 1915, properties along the Glasgow to Hamilton Road had been given postal addresses with proper numbering, rather than known by building names. McLelland's Land was officially 1, 3 and 5 Glasgow Road, the southern side properties all being odd numbers. Some tenants had changed again by 1925. Still held in trust, the homes were rented by Richard Lyle, a miner for £12, and William Williamson an Engineer for £8, 10 shillings. Only aforementioned John Cowan occupied his house for more than 10 years. He was to die between 1925 and 1930 and his widow, Janet Cowan is noted in the 1930 valuation roll living there as head of the house. Her neighbours that year were Alexander Bowes a General Dealer with a rent of £12 and William Emslie, a fitter, perhaps working nearby at Greenfield Foundry.

By the time McLelland's Land was demolished sometime following an "unfit for purpose" demolition order in 1933, they had existed for half a Century had seen around 15 families living at that location. Given that the tram lanes outside the property were lifted in 1930 and the road widened shortly after, it seems likely that McLelland's land was purposely demolished to accommodate modernization. Today, there is a large billboard where the property once was, situated in a small grassy triangular plot and no trace of any building at all.

Blantyre Project Social Media:

Patrick Donnelly: "There were McLellands across the road from this too."

"Read More about **McLelland's Land** online. Scan our handy QR Code for more narrative and photos at Blantyre's History Archives. Further information, photos and commentary from readers are added from time to time."

Welsh's Land, Springwell

The immediate neighbor to McLelland's Land to the north, still on the same south side of Glasgow Road was Welsh's Land or Laun. A building with a similar story to McLelland's, given that it was built by somebody else, but became known differently for the long term owner's surname.

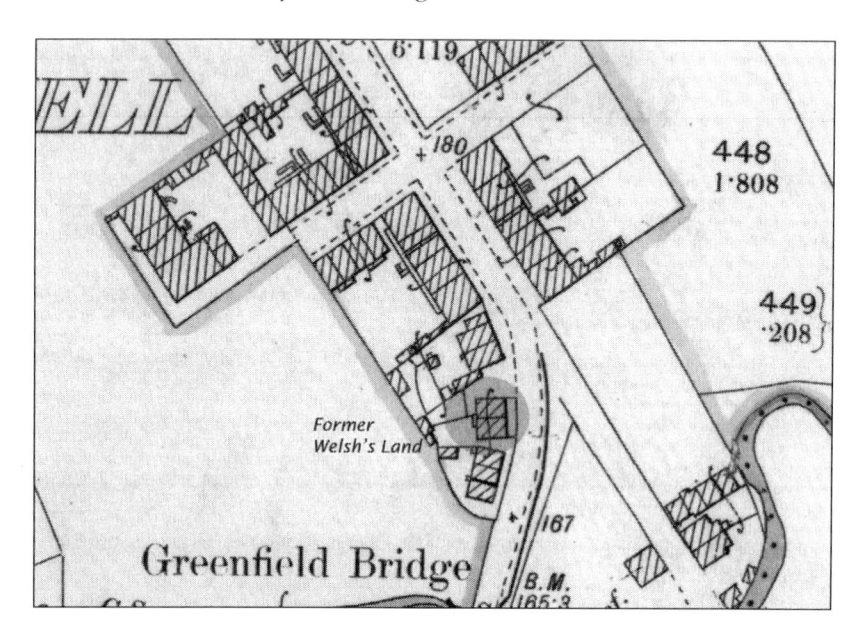

Figure 33 Welsh's Land or Laun highlighted on the 1898 Springwell map

The property was simply 2 houses, of equal, modest size, built of stone or brick in one storey. It is quite likely they mirrored each other in terms of layout. Built between 1881 and 1885 by Mr. William Semple, a stonemason, the houses were slightly larger than McLelland's buildings to the south and opened out on to Glasgow Road.

Born in 1838, William Semple came to Blantyre in 1881 with his wife, Christina. As a stonemason by trade and employer of others, he would have been well known and would certainly have been involved in the construction of tenements along Glasgow Road. Building these 2 small homes was a business venture, and in 1885, they were rented out to miners Henry Thomney and Andrew Frame for £4 per annum.

However, in November 1894, whilst working for Warnocks & Horsburgh, wrights and builders in Rutherglen, William Semple was injured and on 28th November took them to court suing them for £500. (around £60,000 in todays money). In early 1895, William collected all his assets and his injury monies and would go on to build other properties in Springwells. To do this, he had to sell his two properties in this article, which he sold on to Mr. John Welsh, a coalminer. Whilst Semple owned the buildings for only 14 years or so, John Welsh and his family would be the long term and only other owners of this property right up until the 1930's.

The buildings therefore became known primarily as Welsh's land from 1895 and that year Alex McLaren a brakesman was living in the southern house and John Welsh and his family occupying his new purchase in the northern house.

Figure 34 Location Line Drawing showing former Welsh's Land

The houses were deeper than nearby McLelland's and would have occupied the space in between where today two large billboards are erected. Outside wash-house and toilets were located in the far corner of the land, which initially had a dividing fence in the back garden. The house would have made an excellent vantage point for watching people coming and going, to and from Blantyre as well of course as being a suitable location for miners.

By 1903 as trams ran past for the first time, John Welsh had moved out to 15 Victoria Street, left his profession as a miner and had become a coalman. Born in England in 1868, he married a lady named Marion McClelland in Hamilton in 1888. John Welsh should not be confused with a teacher or inspector of the poor of Blantyre, all three with the same name.

In 1905, his acquaintance, (we previously eluded their friendship) William McLelland was living in John's former home, the other house rented by James Stoddart, a miner. Perhaps William McLelland wanted to be near his own property for in any case, the dividing fence was brought down and by 1910, the back gardens of Welsh's Land and next door McLellands, were all open, with some of the old outbuildings removed. William had moved out again by 1915 and Welsh's Land once again was rented out to miners, this time to Duncan McCorkindale and Robert Moore, each for £10, 3 shillings.

Welsh's houses each only had 2 rooms, each with a window, likely front and back. By this era the southern property had address 7 Glasgow Road and the adjoining house, further north was 9 Glasgow Road.

On Saturday 7th August, Mr. Moore renting at 9 Glasgow Road was charged with beating up a 13 year old boy over a matter about their dogs fighting in the street. It was thought the man had been egging on the dogs to fight and the boy simply tried to remove his own pet from the situation.

In 1920, Duncan McCorkindale was still renting the same house, the other house at number 9 rented by James Coffey, a miner and both paying rent to John Welsh.

> Blantyre Project Social Media:
>
> **Ann Boyd** "I had no idea this place existed. I drive by the spot every day to and from work but now I can point out to my colleagues what used to be there."
>
> **Simon Stevens:** "I think the Welsh family were highly connected to the McLelland's. The families didn't just have properties on the south, but also at the north side of Glasgow Road, near the Parkburn. I can't recall when this was, but I connect these names with this area from my childhood in WW2 years."

In 1925, John Welsh was 57 years old and would pass away shortly after in Victoria Street in 1928. That year George Wilson, a miner and Duncan McCorkindale both renting for the princely sum of £12, 12 shillings. Following his death his widow and wife, Marion Welsh continued to let the property out but only a short time.

By the time of the 1936 map, Welsh's Land is gone, likely demolished at the same time as the adjacent McLelland's land to make way for the early 1930's road widening improvements to Glasgow Road. The building was declared unfit for purpose in 1933 and was subjected to demolition orders.

Today, nothing remains of Welsh's Land, the name and building forgotten and confined to the realms of history, but hopefully brought to some life again by this book.

McDougall's Land (Springwell Cottages)

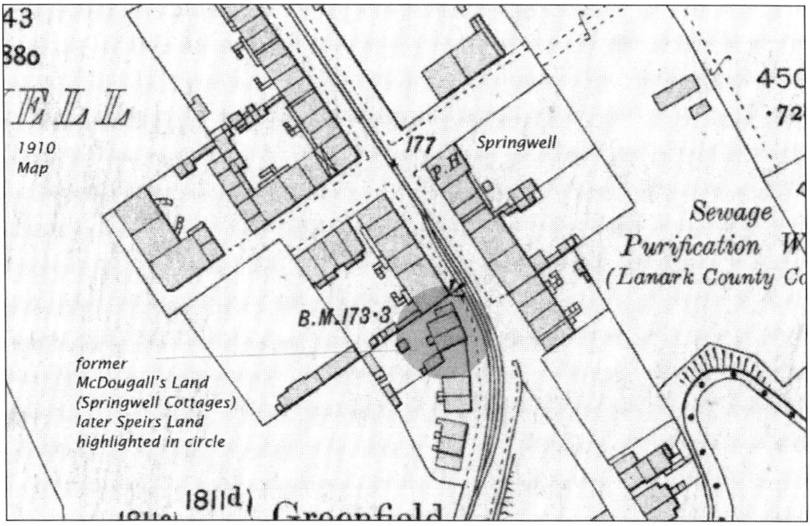

Figure 35 McDougall's / Speirs Land highlighted, Springwells 1910

With exception of Springwell Farm, one of the oldest properties to ever exist in the hamlet was "McDougall's Land" or to give it its original official name, "Springwell Cottages". During the lifetime of this former building, like others nearby it would change hands a few times, be used as personal home for the owner and was also later used primarily to rent out to miners and their families as a means to supplement income.

McDougall's Land was a 2-storey former tenement divided in half, forming 4 houses, 2 up and 2 down. It was of average size for a tenement and each house comprised of 2 rooms, each having 1 window. It opened out on to Glasgow Road and was situated at the former fork in the road, right at the bend.

The stone built property was constructed in 1876 by Mr. Duncan McDougall, a miner of Greenfield Colliery, who arrived in Blantyre that year following a spell living at Hamilton. He was one of the first people to approach the Farm of Springwell to buy land from them and it should be noted when he did, no other properties with exception of the farm existed in Springwell. He was a "Springwell Pioneer" so to speak.

The fact a miner could afford land and to build this property suggests he had savings and that likely he managed to secure an inexpensive deal for his plot. It paved the way for McLellands and Welsh's plots.

Duncan McDougall was born in Tollcross in 1837 the son of Duncan McDougall and Jeanie Hastie. He was 39 years old when he came to Blantyre with his wife and 5 children. In 1881, the family all lived together in one of the homes, but it was crowded whilst he let out the other three.

Figure 36 Location Line Drawing of McDougall's Land in context, Springwell

Life would have been fairly cramped with so many people inside the modest property, especially with so many young children. It would have been a busy household, no doubt the kids having the freedom to explore all the fields of Springwell and Burnbrae Farms behind to the south.

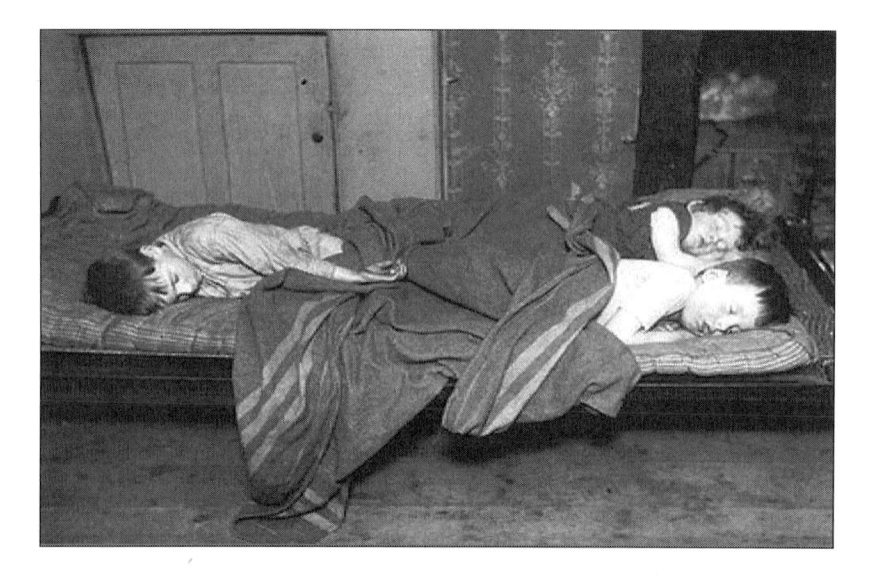

Figure 37 Children had to bunk up several to a bed inside tenements

In 1885, just 9 years after construction, the McDougall family and relatives occupied all 4 of the homes, spreading themselves out more comfortably. In the first house to the south was George Speirs, (Duncan's brother in law who was also a miner.) In the adjacent home was Duncan (44) and his wife Mary Speirs (44) and some of their children. In the third home son George McDougall (24) and in the fourth home was another son John McDougall (22). The men all worked as miners. The proximity of McDougall's Land to other properties to the north, on one occasion included it as part of Springwell Place in census information. This may have been an error, for McDougall's Land was certainly separate.

Living beside your family, each in separate homes, within the one building, perhaps felt a comfortable existence for the McDougall's, by comparison to many of the miners who lived nearby at Greenfield Rows in spaces a third of the size.

By the 1891 census, Duncan (54) was there with Mary (53) and sons James (18), Alexander (16 born in Blantyre), Hugh (13) and daughter Jane (11). With grown up children George (30), John (28), Catherine (26), Robert (26) and Margaret (21) all having moved out by then, in all it is known that Duncan McDougall had 9 children!

In 1892, Duncan sold all his homes to brother in law George Speirs, who was still one of his tenants. It's unknown why he did this, perhaps to raise fast capital for another venture or daughters weddings. It had been McDougall's land for a lengthy 16 years, the best part of a generation. Even after the sale of the 4 homes, occupancy didn't change much with George Speirs, Duncan McDougall and George McDougall all continuing to live in their same homes. However, by 1895 John Ritchie, a miner was renting the 4th house instead of John McDougall whom by then had moved out.

George Speirs rented to Duncan McDougall for £7 a year from 1892 for as long as he owned the property, never changing his brother in laws rent, a condition perhaps part of the deed of sale.

Around 1892, George took the opportunity to expand the property by building a small workshop on the side, adjacent to the north. Opening out on to Glasgow Road, the single-story workshop was modest and rented out to Alexander Lennox, a shoemaker, where he would conduct his cobbler's business for a few years. The workshop was small, may not have had windows and was possibly made of tin cladding or timber. Alex Lennox would have been kept busy making boots and shoes for the miners and their families for Springwell was a busy place in the 1890's. His starting rent was £3 per annum, which never rose throughout the life of this workshop.

Mr. George Speirs was a miner, an incomer to the area. Born in 1840 to parents George Speirs Senior and Margaret Miller, George, like Duncan was also born in Tollcross and worked in Hamilton before coming to Blantyre around 1880/1881.

Initially working for Dixon's Collieries, George and family first lived at Hall Street, the tied cottages to the colliery further west at Stonefield. Grief and tension in that community would still have been high, just 3 or 4 years after so many miner's in those local streets lost their lives in the Blantyre Pit Disaster.

He married twice in his lifetime. His first wife Elizabeth Strachan died young in Blantyre in 1879, aged 39 at 19 Hall Street. George was left as a single father of 4 young children with daughters Annie (12) and Margaret (8) and Janet (6) and son Thomas (10). However, he married just 3 years later in 1882 to Christina Aitken and for a fresh, new start he took up lodgings that year at McDougall's Land, buying it all from Duncan in 1892, 10 years later.

In 1905 George Speirs and family occupied the first house, Duncan McDougall in the second (previous owner now a tenant), vanman James McLelland was in the third home. (We'll come back to James McLelland a little later for his story is an interesting one.). James Pollock a carter occupied the 4th home for £4 per year. The previous shoemakers' workshop, was now a fruiterer by the name of John McKinnan renting for £3 per year.

George had also taken time to expand his interests by building a stable in the back garden, also being rented for a further £3 by the fruiterer for maintaining the horse for his delivery cart. An outbuilding joining on to the house on the south side had also been converted into a small narrow, one storey home. Likely not well built with inadequate warmth, it was rented by Patrick McDade a labourer in 1905, but had been demolished a short time later by 1915, most likely due to being unfit for purpose.

With the McDougall's Building in the hands of owner George Speirs, it became known for a short time at the end of the 19th Century and first decade of the 20th Century as "Speirs Land", (which should not be confused with a building of the same name around this era in High Blantyre). The fashion for naming a building after the owner was on its way out when, at the turn of the Century, the Glasgow to Hamilton Road became known simply as 'Glasgow Road' and buildings along it were given proper postal addresses, each house numbered with the odd numbers on the south. In 1915 George Speirs therefore lived at 11 Glasgow Road, Duncan McDougall at 13 Glasgow Road, James McLelland a craneman also at 13 perhaps looking after elderly George. The workshop then an ice cream shop was 15 Glasgow Road and the 4th house 17 Glasgow Road occupied by John Hamilton, lorryman at £4 per year.

By 1915 the workshop was empty and would be demolished by 1920. This may not be surprising. By the First World War, Blantyre, Greenfield and Burnbank had expanded enormously, offering tremendous business opportunity. That's where profit and trade lay. Springwell was becoming a hamlet, detached and trapped between those popular areas. George may have lost the workshop due to economic progression elsewhere and the same was for his stables, as it was abandoned too. Things were about to change even more the following year.

On 28th November 1916, Mr. George Speirs died, aged 76. His son Thomas Speirs moved from nearby McNair's Land into 17 Glasgow Road at one of his father's homes and was there when the death was registered. In 1920 with Thomas Speirs inheriting the 4 houses, John Tenant was renting 11 Glasgow Road, Duncan McDougall as always at number 13 Glasgow Road, James McLelland now at 15 Glasgow Road (15 became a house after the workshop was demolished.) However this caused some problems, for earlier the building next up the road had been given number 17 beyond the number 15 Glasgow Road workshop. When it was demolished, it meant there were two number 17s. One at McDougalls Buildings and the other in the block further, up not yet explored here.

Thomas was not as lenient on rent as his father had been and in 1920 Duncan McDougall's rent increased from £7 to £8,11. James McLelland's was raised from £4 to £4,18 shillings. Thomas also fenced off the large open plan space to the rear after demolishing the small separate house. The former stable was turned into a piggery, considered far more lucrative a business.

Blantyre Project Social Media:

Margaret Brown Burns: "I used to go to McDougall's shop for my 'chippit' fruit. What a good thing to read all this!"

Sheena Thomson: "I can remember McDougall's delivery van coming round the houses to us in Morven Avenue during the 1960's."

Steven Donnelly: "How amazing it must have been to see trams going by the windows from this little house. Families there probably felt closer to Greenfield and Burnbank than they did to Blantyre. How fantastic to see articles bringing these old, lost properties back to life by means of maps and sketches. Telling the story of Glasgow Road has been long overdue in Blantyre."

By 1925, the occupation hadn't changed much although Thomas had moved into 11 Glasgow Road. Thomas was a miner and only owned McDougall's Buildings for 60mphasi. 10 years. On 18th December 1918, his cousin David Ferguson died at that house, aged 33.

On 21st December 1925 Duncan McDougall died aged 88. His death certificate lists 'senility' and it would trigger a different path for the property. Upon his death and their inheritance, Robert and James McDougall, Duncan's sons who had grown up in the building, bought all 4 homes from Thomas Speirs in early 1926. It was an end to 34 years of Speirs ownership. If there was any doubt to that, in 1930 James McDougall occupied 11 Glasgow Road, his brother Robert at 13 Glasgow Road and all change at 15 with Irvine Fleming a miner renting for £5,4 shillings and a single lady, Barbara Paterson at number 17.

The property had come full circle and was once again truly "McDougall's Land."

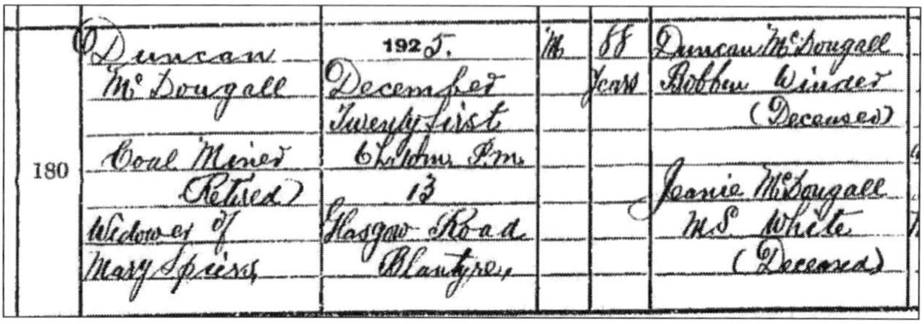
180
Duncan McDougall
Coal Miner (Retired)
Widower of Mary Speirs
1925. December Twenty first 6h 10m P.m. 13 Glasgow Road Blantyre
M
88 Years
Duncan McDougall Bobbin Winder (Deceased)
Jeanie McDougall MS White (Deceased)

Figure 38 Duncan McDougall Death Certificate in December 1925

The 1930's saw many changes. The road outside widened, the Greenfield Foundry expanded so much at the south it practically touched the boundary fences of McDougall's property and of course neighbouring properties McLelland's and Welsh's Buildings were demolished, the land cleared. The piggery was sold off to a man named McCallum.

McDougall's Building was home to many other people throughout the 20th Century and existed well beyond WW2. Robert McDougall would operate a Fruit and Veg business, growing some of his produce at the back during the mid 20th Century. His burgundy delivery van was a regular sight right up until his property was completely demolished in the 1960's.

Today, there are billboards and grass on the land it once occupied. It was an old part of Springwell that had gone forever.

Tram Accident 1904

DID YOU KNOW?

On Thursday 29th September 1904, an alarming collision of two tramway cars took place outside McDougall's Buildings. There was only a single line at the place and owing to the heavy fog the drivers did not observe each other until a collision was inevitable. The impact was heavy, the passengers were knocked about – and considerably. Mr Tennant, a butcher noted shortly in this book, was the person most seriously injured. He was coming down on the outside stair and was thrown down the steps, out to the ground. Both cars were badly damaged. John sued for £2,000 in damages in 1905.

Springwell Piggery

The Springwell Piggery was formed in 1916, when Thomas Speirs, the new owner of McLelland's Buildings cleared the yard at the back and fenced off the large open plan space. He sold the former stables that year, which was of no use to the Speirs family and the buyer was a Mr. William McCallum Junior of 64 Auchinraith Road. It is unknown how the Speirs family took the news when they learned of the plans for land outside their home.

Figure 39 Blantyre Pig Breeding became less popular through the 20th Century

By 1925, William McCallum had sold the piggery business and land to Robert McDougall, the son of the former owner of McDougall's Buildings. The land initially owned by his father, now returned to the family. This allowed Robert to give up his mining profession and he became a pig breeder, moving away from nearby 29 Glasgow Road back into the family home at McDougall's Buildings the year after. Pig rearing may not seem the best job, but by comparison to the working conditions in the mines, so far underground, it may have been much more tolerable. There may have been chickens kept in the same area.

It will take a person of a certain age to remember this piggery, for it was removed around 1955. It was relatively tucked away off the Glasgow Road at Springwell, behind buildings and should not be confused with the piggeries accessed from Craighead or John Street.

Piglets were weaned and removed from the sows at between two and five weeks old and placed in sheds or nursery barns. Farmed for their slaughter weight, for the purposes of providing meat, piggeries became less common in Scotland rural areas during the latter part of the 20th Century.

Contaminants from animal wastes sometimes could enter the environment through pathways such as through leakage of poorly constructed manure lagoons or during major precipitation events. Regulations became stricter and pig farming became less of a small business pastime, with individuals becoming more unable to compete with larger, intensive pig farming operations.

Blantyre Project Social Media:

Ann McKeown: "Hubby says he thinks it closed in 1955. He says the guy who owned used to go round Springwell houses and leave tins. People put in their food scraps and someone came round evenings and fed the pigs with them the collected scraps."

Anne Brennan: "There was a tenement building across from Miller's Fireplace shop. I lived there from being born in 1960 until 1964. No piggery there by then."

Steven Arkwright: "By god it smelled awful during the summer. You could smell it all over Blantyre in the 1950's."

Teresa Summers: "I'm sure they kept birds too, chickens, geese or turkeys and the like. I can't remember for certain though."

McLelland boys in bother

Let's backtrack a little to Mr. James McLelland. James if you recall was renting a house at McLelland's Buildings and also happened to be the son of William McLelland, the owner of neighbouring McLelland's Land explored earlier. When William McLelland (miner and carter) died in 1906, James unfortunately went "off the rails" somewhat and lets just say, he was in the newspaper often, for not the best reasons.

On Wednesday 20th February 1907, James found himself standing in Glasgow Sheriff Court, turned out in his best suit. The accusation against him was serious for stealing £108 (about £15,000 in today's money), along with a gold watch, 2 gold rings, 2 silver albert chains and a purse from his mother, who was a widow, living at Springwell. An agent for James, stated to the court that the accused's father had been a carter and died 6 months earlier, leaving considerable property and over £300 in money. (nearly £50,000 today). The family were distrustful of banks and the sum of money was kept at home at McLelland's Buildings, in their home within an 8 day clock in the front room.

About 3 weeks before the court date, the brother of James had appeared in court charged with taking £100 from the pot without permission. The problem was since the death of the father, the widowed mother had been drinking heavily and the pot of cash was depleting. A curator of the money had been appointed in courts at an earlier date, the intention being on resolving through legal process who was entitled to what. However, James and his brother, worried by this situation took it upon themselves at different times to help themselves to a share, before any legal authority instructed them. Looking at this situation, it must have been very difficult for them to see such a large sum of cash being kept at home and not to touch it.

One evening, James had got very much the worse for wear with his mother in a drinking session and it is then whilst under influence that he abstracted the money and the articles. He then fled to Edinburgh, but was later caught, the money returned with exception of £16 spent. James pleaded guilty telling the court he thought he had only taken his legal third share, leaving two thirds to be split between his brother and mother. The matter in court actually proved quite complex, for in truth, there was a high likelihood that a third of the money did belong to James, or indeed soon would. The judge explained this to him and asked if he wished to change the plea to not guilty. James did and was sentenced on the diminished plea.

However, even as early as July 1900, James's brother John McClelland had broken into a house in Burnbank and stolen items, being jailed for 40 days. It is not unnoticed that this was long before the father's death.

Smellie's Buildings, Springwell

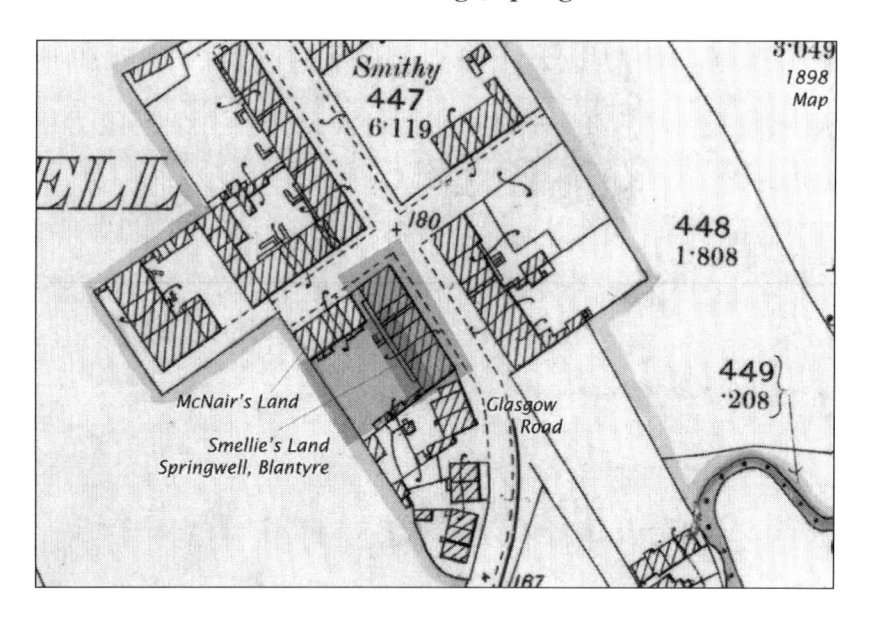

Figure 40 Smellie's Buildings (Pronounced Smiley's), Springwell

Moving again northwestwards, further into Springwell, we next arrive at the former Smellie's Land or Smellie's Buildings (pronounced 'smiley'), a surname well known throughout Lanarkshire.

Smellie's Buildings at Springwell should not be confused with his buildings at Craig Street, Stonefield, which also was Smellie's Land. These pages are about his Springwell properties on Glasgow Road, sometimes incorporated in census information as part of nearby Springwell Place.

The subjects consisted of a block of four, two storey stone tenements, with frontage directly on to Glasgow Road, commissioned by owner Alexander Smellie, a nearby flesher (butcher). The buildings were to be Alexanders's retirement present to himself.

Alexander Smellie was born on 1st January 1852 in Carluke and married his wife Ellen (Helen Finlayson) in Larkhall in 1875. The couple set up their home there initially, with Alexander working as a butcher. In 1877 their daughter Mary was born, then a son John in 1881, both born in Larkhall. By 1885, the family had moved to Springwell, Blantyre renting a house at Allison Place (a tenement block) and working from a corner shop of at the property.

A daughter, Jeannie would follow in 1892, born in Blantyre.

By 1895, Alexander Smellie was working 3 different shops in Allison Place at numbers 12,13 and 41 (not the numbers of Glasgow Road, but the numbers within Allison Buildings). Working with them was his wife's sister Kate. Alexander had already by that time bought houses in the newly formed Craig Street and was renting them out, further to the west in Blantyre, choosing to live at 43 Craig Street. He would later move to a larger home at 55 Craig Street by 1925.

In 1896, Alexander retired from being a butcher, not due to age as he was only 43, but having acquired so many homes in Craig Street and presumably from savings, he was able to step away from working that lifestyle and became a factor of homes. Expanding his property empire was key to this succeeding and having bought an empty square acre of Springwell land, directly beside his previous rented shops, he set about building his own tenements and shops.

In 1896, he constructed 4 terraced, two-storey stone tenements of varying sizes, on the south side of Glasgow Road, between McDougall's Land and the entrance to Springwell Place, slightly stepped due to the fall of the land.

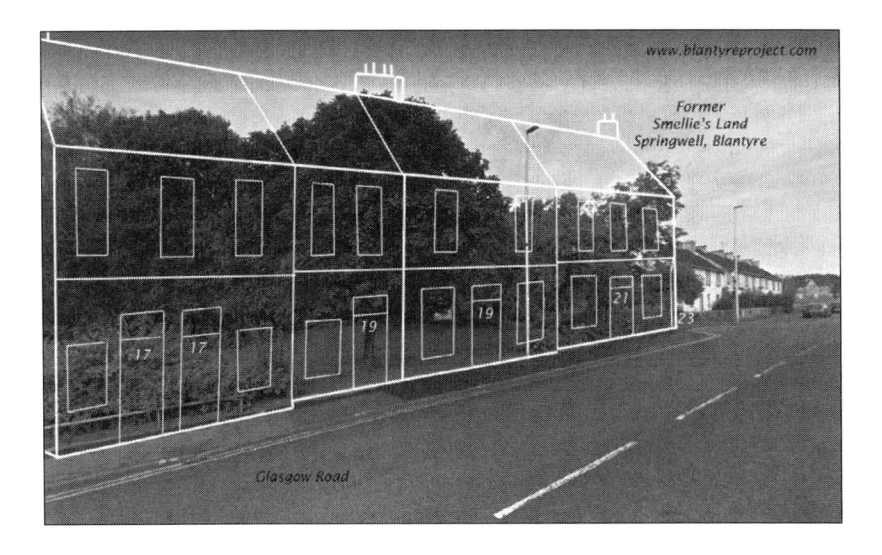

Figure 41 Location line drawing former Smellie's Buildings, Springwell

With no photos of Smellie's Buildings forthcoming, we once again show how the tenement looked with a location line drawing, putting size, location and scale into modern context. This was quite a latter addition for Springwell, with many homes, shops and tenements around it by its time of construction. All together the buildings comprised of 13 homes and 2 shops, both at the western side at the corner with Springwell Place, (a former side street leading off Glasgow Road.)

The corner shop was let to John Tennant, a butcher, who was likely filling the vacancy created from Alexander's sales departure in the area. Next door was James Allan, a relatively short lived tailor shop.

The back of the property was an open square yard with outside toilets. The upper homes were accessed by one single flight of steps at the rear with a long upper terrace leading to the doors. However, by 1908 an additional flight of stone steps had been built, with more private entrances created, possibly due to the homes being further subdivided to maximize rental capacity.

By 1905 Alexander had bought a similar good sized square plot of land at the south of Smellie's Buildings and had constructed a hayloft, stables and a slaughterhouse. Of note then also, was his acquisition of the adjacent, existing 8 one-storey houses going by the name of McNair's Buildings which ran north to south along the east side of Springwell Place. From 1905, the name 'McNairs' was gone, these homes incorporated into Smellie's Land.

In 1905 the tenants renting Smellie's Buildings (including McNairs) were mostly miners, carters or enginemen and their families. They were as follows; Mrs. Margaret Nelson, Samuel Liddell, Marion Davidson, Thomas Speirs (later to own McDougall's Land), John Brenigan, Joseph Irvine, Agnes James, Boyd Thomson, William McGill, John Gray, Thomas Jamieson, Robert King, Hugh Wood, John Law, David Allan, George Hutch, Robert Nelson, Robert Lawson, Charles Neilson John Tennant and Alexander McGregor. You'll notice 21 tenants, but only 18 houses, so some of these people may have been living in split or smaller rooms.

Rents ranged between £4, 9 and £5, 13 shillings per annum, with exception of tenant John Brenigan living in a double property paying £8, 11.

Around this time Smellie's Buildings on the Glasgow Road were given postal addresses, namely homes 17 and 19 in the east, then 21 (shop) and 23 (corner shop) moving west.

Blantyre Project Social Media:

Betty McLean who lives in Canada commented, "William McGill, one of the tenants in 1905, was my great, grandfather."

Valerie Krawczyk of Church Street, Low Blantyre added, "I believe that Alexander Smellie was my great, grandfather!"

Alister McInnes commented, "I was born there at 22 Glasgow Road.'

Tragedies at number 19

DID YOU KNOW?

At 19 Glasgow Road the Swain family were renting in 1916. Tragedy struck the family when little Eddie, the 1 year old son of James and Margaret died on 27th April. Following the infants death, the family moved out and new tenant was Gavin McLelland. However, fate was not finished with 19 Glasgow Road.

In August 1918, it was reported that Private Gavin McLelland of the Scottish Rifles, who was the fourth son of Hugh and Grace McLelland of Hamilton, had died. Gavin had left 19 Glasgow Road to head off to war, which during his time away was vacant. However, injured in a fight against the Germans, he died from his wounds. Another Blantyre solider taken by war.

In 1914, McNair's Buildings went on fire, with everything gutted inside. The story is told later when we properly explore this, but the properties were rebuilt.

By 1915, whilst war raged in Europe, John Tennant was still renting the butcher shop at 23 Glasgow Road, for £12 a year. He was doing well for he had bought the hayloft, stables and former slaughterhouse from Alexander Smellie. John Tennant, who you may remember earlier in the book receiving compensation for being injured in a tram accident in 1904 had also moved out to Burnbrae Cottage in High Blantyre Road. John Tennant would operate his butchers business from 23 Glasgow Road from around 1896 until the early 1920's. In 1920 he was paying £16 a year rent. By 1925, David Berry was the shopkeeper, signifying an end to Tennant's butchery business between 1920 and 1925. John passed away in 1947.

Fleshing or butchery was and still is, a traditional line of work. In the industrialized world, slaughterhouses used butchers to slaughter the animals, performing one or a few of the steps repeatedly as specialists on a semiautomated disassembly line. The steps include stunning (rendering the animal incapacitated), exsanguination (severing the carotid or brachial arteries to facilitate blood removal), skinning (removing the hide or pelt) or scalding and dehairing (pork), evisceration (removing the viscera) and splitting (dividing the carcass in half longitudinally).

These practices would have been done at the back of the property in

John's slaughterhouse, situated some distance from homes. It may be he utilized the neighbouring piggery to obtain much of his meat and poultry.

Figure 42 Fleshers were a vital part of community private food shops all over the UK

After the carcasses were chilled (unless "hot-boned"), John would have had to select carcasses, sides, or quarters from which primal cuts can be produced with the minimum of wastage; separating the primal cuts from the carcass; trimming primal cuts and preparing them for secondary butchery or sale; and storing cut meats. Secondary butchery involves boning and trimming primal cuts in preparation for sale. Historically, primary and secondary butchery were performed in the same establishment, but the advent of methods of preservation and low cost transportation largely separated them. It would have been a messy job, not for the faint hearted, but one necessary to keep the growing Springwell population happy.

Next shopkeeper was David Berry but it is unknown what he sold. He was at 23 Glasgow Road from the early 1920's for only a couple of years.

In 1915, the neighbouring shop at 21 Glasgow Road had changed occupants, being run by Mrs. Margaret Reid, a shopkeeper with James Allan, the tailor, no longer there. This was a short term arrangement, for by 1920, Mrs. Jeanie Lawson, a grocer was the shopkeeper, also renting for £16 a year. (This lady was not Alexander's daughter Jeanie but a wife of a former tenant.)

By 1930, Jeanie Lawson and her sister, Margaret had moved into the larger corner shop where they would continue their grocery business right up until WW2 at that location. Beyond that time, Lawson's grocery shop was also run as a bakery, owned by relative Meg Lawson who may have acquired the whole building after Smellie. By the 1930's, 21 Glasgow Road then became another house for rent, meaning there were 6 homes at 17 Glasgow Road, 8 homes at 19 Glasgow Road and 5 homes at 21 Glasgow Road, as well as the 8 homes at former McNair's land.

Alexander Smellie lost his wife in 1921. He seemed to have done well building good quality homes. Smellie's Buildings existed right into the 1970's and many of the families who lived there doing so through several decades and generations. It's noticed that many of the tenant surnames in the 1930's were the same in 1905.

Today, the site of Smellie's land is nothing more than a little grassy area, with some trees becoming more established, where once the yard was. There is no reminder of the tenement on the site at all.

With his quality homes built in Craig Street, even up until his death on 18th February 1935 in Larkhall, aged 83, Alexander Smellie would have undoubtedly been respected, well known with a good name in Blantyre.

Blantyre Project Social Media:

Alister McInnes: "I lived in these buildings, my grandmother nearby at number 33 Glasgow Road. At the back was a square courtyard leading to back entrances to the houses. Nearby was a shop called "Maggies" at the time a general store. I always looked forward to getting "Blue Riband" biscuits in there. After the building was demolished, many of the residents were relocated to 'the electric houses' in High Blantyre."

Garry Lee: "Directly across from these buildings was an old tenement across the road (McCaffries) where I got my first 'carry-oot' when I was just 15 years old. That building is still there, but the angle its sitting at, makes me think it will soon be demolished."

Anne Brennan: "My family lived at number 19, flat d I think in a single end. We stayed there until 1964 until we got a brand new council house in Camelon Crescent. I still remember the old place in this tenement vividly. It was amazing how much furniture could fit into one room. Davy Sneddon, our new neighbor at Camelon Crescent helped us with the Glasgow Road flitting on the back of his coal lorry, no less! Thank you for all this information, all the memories came flooding back!"

By Paul D Veverka

Springwell Slaughterhouse

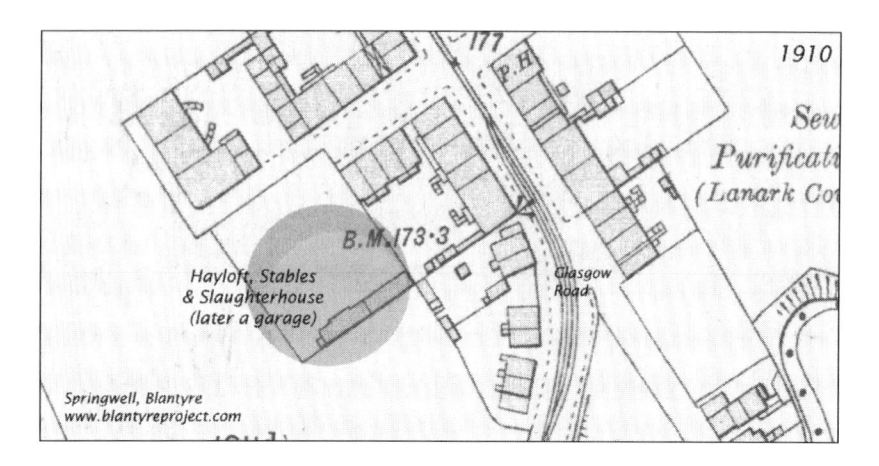

Figure 43 Springwell Slaughterhouse, Hayloft & Stables

Around 1898, Mr. Alexander Smellie bought a 1 acre plot of land to the south of his buildings. Upon it he built a hayloft, stables and a slaughterhouse, as shown in our highlighted map. Entrance to the properties would likely have been off Springwell Place, the road leading from Glasgow Road, just as it is today.

The hayloft and stables were rented out to assist the grocers who were renting his shop. Horses would have been kept to run the delivery carts and the square plot of land would have been an effective paddock. The fields to the south were still part of nearby Burnbrae farms, although by this time, not Springwell Farm which had gone by the late 19th Century. Hay would have been plentiful to buy to maintain the horses, perhaps acquired from these fields as our earlier picture of the field behind Greenfield Foundry showed.

The former slaughterhouse may have been wooden or brick built, a chimney on the map indicating it was the southern property in the paddock. It was initially let out to Joseph Scott, a flesher who may have been helping Alexander previously when he ran his business from Allison Place. It would have been the ideal location to acquire pigs from the neighbouring piggery at McDougall's Land.

The rental arrangement did not get off to a good start, nor did the slaughterhouse. On Wednesday 12th April 1899, Joseph Scott was charged at Hamilton Sheriff Court for supplying diseased meat. Sheriff Davidson took no time in charging Mr Scott following the report from the Sanitary Inspector of the County. It was said that Joseph had a diseased carcass in his slaughterhouse, prepared for sale and intended for food. The Prosecutor learned that Joseph had bought the animal in Glasgow but transporting it back to Blantyre, it had died en route. It had been emaciated, thin and picked up disease quickly following death or from when it was alive. The carcass tested for tuberculosis which would have killed anybody who ate it. The judge was appalled and making an example of Joseph, convicted him and fined him £25 (around £3,000 in today's money.)

This shocking news may have travelled fast in the thriving and busy hamlet of Springwell for Joseph Scott was not conducting business there for much longer, either through termination of his rental agreement, by choice, or being forced out due to lack of business!

Shortly after, when Alexander retired he clearly had no use for a hayloft or slaughterhouse anymore, selling the land and all on to John Tennant, also a butcher, one of his tenants who ran the corner shop on Smellie's Land. By 1915, John had converted the slaughterhouse into a garage, indicating that he may have had an early mechanized delivery vehicle by that time or needed a workshop. As such, the slaughterhouse appears to disappear just before 1915.

Throughout the 20th Century, the property was heavily fenced off with large gates and for the most part of the area, it was left vacant. During the 1960's it was a refuse tip. Today, at least one of those old buildings has been rebuilt in the same location and other larger pitched roof buildings now adjoin them. Use of the land appears to have changed in 2017, where some sort of scrapyard or place where many old dilapidated vehicles are now being stored.

McNair's Land, Springwell

Within the square acre of Smellie's Land was another block of miner's homes, although much more modest, initially known as 'McNair's Land'. These were brick built small, one storey homes, running north to south along Springwell Place, directly behind Smellie's Buildings and opposing Allison Place.

Constructed in 1879 by Mr. James McNair, a builder of Cambuslang, his purpose seems to have been to sell them once built, for by 1881, they were in the hands of a Hamilton lady, Mrs Hannah Craigen. Hannah was a factor of homes and lived at 120 Almada Street at Almada Cottage. She was the bondholder in possession. This was to be a long term investment for her, renting out to 8 families. Or should we say 7 families initially, as up until 1905, one of the homes appears to always have been empty, perhaps used for a different purpose or store?

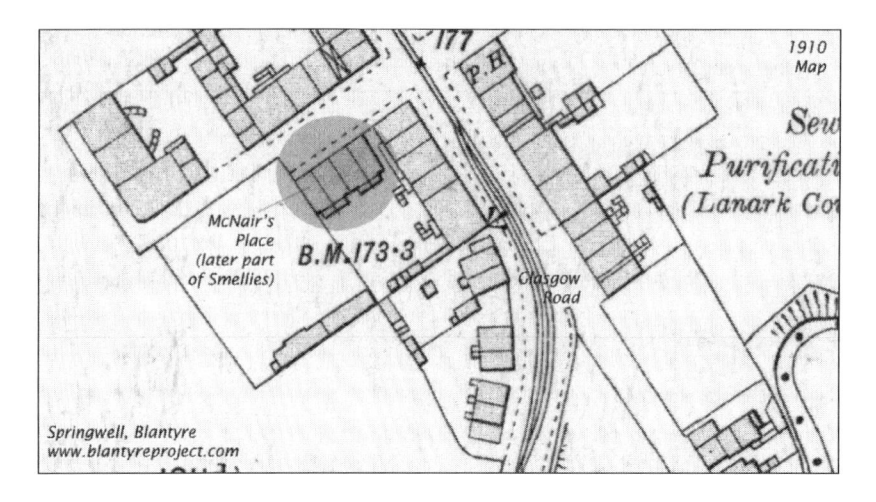

Figure 44 Former McNair's Land (8 single storey homes) on 1910 map

The houses were all of the same size, 2 homes to each block. There were only 2 rooms to each home, only 1 of which had a window. Toilets were out to the rear but adjoining the back of the building. Let to miner's and labourer for similar rents, the homes were often classed as Part of Springwell Place, the dead end street between McNairs and opposing Allison Place. Despite Mrs Hannah's ownership, the buildings remained known as "McNair's Land" until subsequent owners got hold of them.

Figure 45 Location Line Drawing showing former McNair's Land in modern context

In 1885, Hannah was renting out to miners Robert Lawson, Andrew Finlayson, Tom Barr, Dan Richardson, William Carmichael, William Watson

McGill and John Breingan. Rent was £3 and 12 shillings for most of the properties, only 3 being more expensive at £3, 16 shillings per annum.

Ten years later in 1895, rent had increased considerably up to £4, 16 shillings. Tenants that year were Robert Lawson, Peter Devlin, Alexander Russell, Walter Neilson, George Leick, William McGill Watson and John Breingan.

Due to sitting back off that main road the houses didn't originally have Glasgow Road postal addresses, but were numbered 1-8 McNairs Land until around 1905 when due to the purchase of the houses by Alexander Smellie, they were incorporated into Smellie's Land, becoming part of Smellie's Buildings and eventually all of McNair's were allocated as being part of 19 Glasgow Road by 1920.

The name "McNair's Land" vanished very quickly following 1905. Tenants in 1905 were familiar in Robert Lawson, William McGill Watson and John Breingan. Alexander let out the empty property and that year all 8 homes were occupied, the others being Joseph Irvine, Boyd Thomson, Thomas Spiers, Mrs Agnes Jones (w) and John Gray.

On Saturday 30th May 1914, McNair's Buildings caught fire. During the same week elsewhere, suffragists continued to battle for women's vote, the first airmail was delivered over the Channel, war was fierce in Europe and Ireland declared home rule. The alarm was raised about one o'clock in the morning and all the tenants were woken up and required to leave immediately with their families. So rapidly did the fire spread through the building due to timber rafters and wooden internal walls, that none of the occupants had time to go back to retrieve their belongings, clothing or furniture. It was a sad sight as concerned neighbours awoke in nearby Smellie's Building and Allison Place to offer their assistance to the stricken miner's families. Considerable excitement occurred when it looked at a time that the fire may spread to nearby Smellie's 2 storey Buildings, which thankfully did not happen.

When the Lanarkshire County Fire Brigade arrived from Bellshill, it was seen that nothing could be done, the homes and contents all lost. Damage was estimated at around £600. The firemen confining the flames to McNair's Buildings only determined the fire had started by a fallen paraffin lamp, filled with fuel. The tenants burned out were John Briengan, James Reid, Samuel Copland, John McGill, Robert Agnew, Edward Liddle, Charles McGoughan and James Flannigan. Of course all their families were too, with 8 whole families losing their homes and possessions.

You can only imagine the misery in them picking through the ruins as sunlight arose the next day.

The building was only partially insured, but owner, Alexander Smellie ensured the whole lot was rebuilt. However, it is clear from the valuation roll the next year in 1915, that some families never returned. Following the death of Smellie in 1935, the Lawson family who had been living in Springwell since around 1881, acquired the properties, which were adjacent to their grocery shop.

Despite the demolition of many other houses nearby, McNair's Land lasted quite some time throughout the 20th Century right into the early 1970's, ironically possibly due to it being rebuilt.

Unable to find any further remarkable or noteworthy stories for this small block, we'll move on.

Blantyre Project Social Media:

Davy Thomson: "Beyond McNairs Land at the end of Springwell Place there used to be a metal working business called 'Gillans'. It was a busy place in the 1980's. Workers would come out at lunchtime and play footie in the spare ground next to it."

Debbie McMillan: "It's all changed doon that way now. Nothin's the same in oor wee toon anymair."

Moyra Lindsay: "As of October 2017, the former Gillan's place behind the locked gates at the end of this wee cul de sac is currently up for rent."

Serge Mikklesen: "I've seen lorries going in and out of there from time to time. The land is still privately owned and although looks cleared, business owners are using it for storage. The area opposite this will change dramatically in 2018 as Dunn's Food & Drink have submitted plans for extending their premises where the old Robertson's factory used to be. Opposite side of the road I know to this article, but thought I'd mention it."

"Read More about **McNair's Land, Springwells** online. Scan our handy QR Code for more narrative and photos at Blantyre's History Archives. Further information, photos and commentary from readers are added from time to time."

Springwell Social Club – Rejected

DID YOU KNOW?

In May 1929, license was refused for a proposed club in Springwell. The Sheriff saw through the real plan behind the club, which incredibly was proposed for a space no larger than about 6 foot by 5! The report in the Motherwell Times on 31st May 1929 reported,

"Sheriff Mercer has refused the application of Springwells Social and Recreation Club, Blantyre, for certificate of registration under the Licensing Acts in respect of premises at Blantyre, the ground that the premises, if registered, would be used mainly as a drinking club. Objection to the application was taken by the Chief Constable of Lanarkshire. In his interlocutor, Sheriff Mercer explained that an accountant, examined for the applicants, calculated on an estimated attendance of 400, the gross annual drawings for food at £430, from mineral waters at £93, and from tobacco £291.

He accepted the estimate of the objectors of gross drawings at £1139. "I consider." Says the Sheriff, "an estimated membership of greatly exaggerated, and it would, in my opinion, be highly undesirable to attempt to house a registered club membership of anything like that number in apartment 28 feet square."

Gambling at Springwell

Elderly man, Thomas Dunsmuir Hartman lives in Chicago, but is formerly from Logan Street, Blantyre. Around 2007, he wrote a short social history article making it available online about his recollections in Blantyre during the 2nd quarter of the 20th Century. This valuable account gave an insight into life in Pre WW2 Springwell. He writes,

"Part of Springwell's history in those days was Gambling. Every Friday it was not uncommon to see some of the miners wives go up to the entrance of the mines to collect the wages that the miners had made that week. This was before they went and drank and gambled what they had made.

This was indeed a very common occurrence for the miner to go to the pubs directly from the pithead, if she (the miner's wife) was not fast enough to waylay him on his way home invariably he finished up at the pub and most times drank most or gambled what he had made. One can feel the frustration of this life they led and much more so for the women with their children. To the men this was an every day occurrence and the pubs were their only way of blowing off steam.

The Gambling was big! We called it Tossing or Heads and Tails, played with two copper pennies of the realm. You tossed them a good distance in the air and allowed them to fall without touching anyone in the huge crowds which attended these Tossing Schools. Springwell was well known around Lanarkshire for its Sunday after church Tossing School. This was planned in great detail, from the lookout for the police who were stationed at various intersections or highpoints to see any police in the near vicinity and give warning of a raid.

Figure 46 Miners Playing 'Pitch n Toss' for money in the early 20th Century

There was one person in charge of the gambling school and he was called the Baber. It was his job to collect all the bets and to pay out if the lad tossing the coins tossed two tails. Two heads you are a winner, a head and tail you toss again, until you turn up two of a kind. If you say that you have 10-30 men all gambling and most of them big strong miners I think you have to consider this to be a rather large crowd and such a crowd which easily could get out of control especially if they are on the losing side of the toss. So this Baber had to have his own henchmen and he himself was one very capable person to handle a situation when it arrived , and it did! Constantly.

You always found that he was without a doubt the local punch drunk bully and if you did not believe it to be the case he was willing to take you on to prove it to the crowd attending the tossing, and they did come along to try their luck at gaining this position, as it had quite a large financial pay out to the Baber.

If anyone tossed three heads in a row he was a winner and the Baber always got a cut of the winnings. This could go on all day and each time someone tossed three heads in a row he was pocketing a fair amount of money so much so, I can recall as a boy watching the Baber walk away with all of the money. At this particular tossing, he had pocketed so much money that he could compete in the game and finished up the big winner. Who is going to argue with the local toughie.

I have to mention the raids with the police. This was great fun for us kids to watch about 30 men being chased by, at the most at anytime say four police, this was considered a big raid, I think they called in reinforcements from the surrounding police stations. I can only remember two policemen at the Blantyre station. I can never remember seeing anyone caught, just a lot of puffing and grunting going on. I don't think the police ever really wanted to catch anyone. Just a lot of show on their part. Talk about the Keystone cops, they had nothing on this lot!"

Blantyre Project Social Media:

John Cornfield: "My father, Jimmy Cornfield told me about the tossing schools in Springwell. My grandpa Paddy Cox apparently tossed 4 heads in a row and the Baber wouldn't pay out. So my grandpa being a small, quiet man left and told his wife who then told their eldest son Thomas Topsy Cox, the complete opposite of his father and later became a heavyweight boxing champ. He went back to Springwells and told the Baber a wrong had been done. The Baber wasn't having it and brought his own heavy into it, a man Fulston, in his 40's. Despite being in his 20's a fight broke out and Fulston was knocked out. Thomas Cox took the money owned from the baber and the family ate well that night!"

Ann Sinclair: "My father was brought up at 22 Croftpark Crescent, one of 13 children. He often talked about the tossin at Springwell. He also told us about a family Crombie Coat that would go into pawn shop on the Monday and always be retrieved on the Friday, ahead of the dancing at weekends."

By Paul D Veverka

CHAPTER 5
GLASGOW ROAD SOUTH
SPRINGWELL PLACE TO AUCHINRAITH RD

Springwell Place

Springwell Place was a former dead end street on the south side of Glasgow Road. It is first referenced in 1878 and last appearing around the mid to late 1920's.

Although the entrance is still there today, there are no homes or businesses at the address and as such the name has fallen out of use.

This should not be confused with Springwell Terrace which was directly opposite on the north side of Glasgow Road.

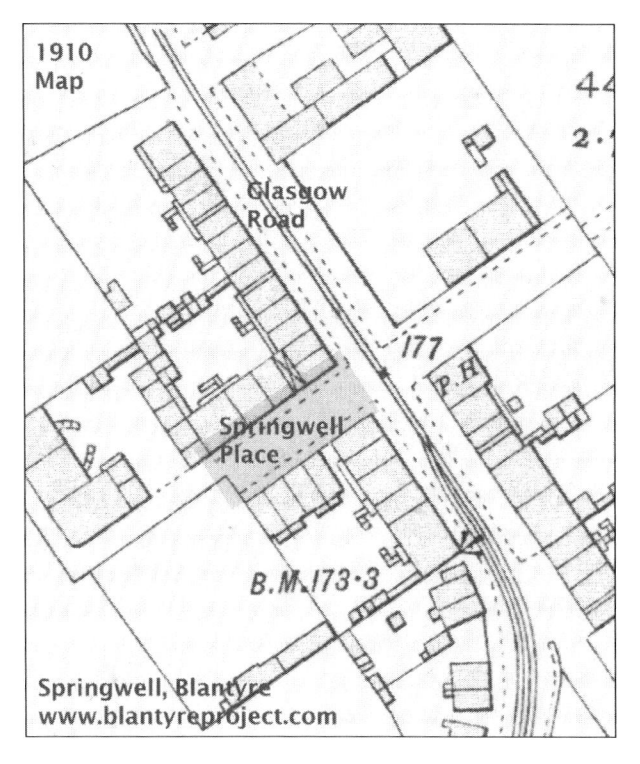

Figure 47 Former Blantyre Street, Springwell Place

Former properties on either side of the road included McNair's Land and Allison Place. Springwell Place was also the only entrance into the former slaughterhouse and Semple's Land, located to the south at the back of Allison Place. A footpath now connects this former Street with High Blantyre's Strathyre Rd.

By Paul D Veverka

Semple's Land (Dalzell Place), Springwell

Born in 1838 in Strathaven, William Semple came to Blantyre in 1881 with his wife, Christina. As a stonemason by trade and employer of others, you may recall from earlier in the book, around that time he built and sold Welsh's Land to John Welsh. You'll see from this chapter that later on in the early 20th Century, the Semple family of masons were an important family for Blantyre's development, responsible for building many homes and shops and almost certainly the primary constructors of Auchinraith Road's houses.

In 1881, William was 43 years old and was living at 37 Allison Place with his wife Christina (42) from Fort William along with daughters Agnes (19) and Gavin (8). Very much a tenant of others at this time, the Semple's fortunes would change with the growing construction boom in Blantyre and Hamilton and work opportunities look to have been plentiful.

Between 1881 and 1885, William along with a neighboring joiner Andrew Frame had together bought a plot of land around 1 acre to the south of Allison Place at the south end of Springwell Place. Upon it, they initially built 2 small one storey homes for themselves and a workshop. For a short time, William was working on a contract in Kilwinning, Ayrshire, moving his family temporarily around 1885, letting his own house out to miner Henry Thomney for a year or so.

However William and his family were back in Blantyre in 1887, occupying the house he had initially built for himself. This is confirmed by their Blantyre presence in the 1891 census behind Allison Place again. William (53), Christina (53), daughters Janet (26), Elizabeth (22) and sons William (20) who was an apprentice Blacksmith and other son Gavin, an apprentice Stonemason helping his father.

In November 1894, whilst working for Warnocks & Horsburgh, wrights and builders in Rutherglen, William Semple was injured and on 28th November sued them for £500. (around £60,000 in todays money). The case must have seemed pretty watertight, for in January 1895 just as it was about to go to court, the company suddenly settled with William for £267, 8 shilling 6d. (almost £40,000 in todays money!)

With new found wealth and perhaps a diminished ability to work due to his injuries, this would go a long way towards securing further personal investments. So, later that year in 1895, William embarked on his next venture. His plan was to build many more homes outright on land already owned and rent out to miners and their families.

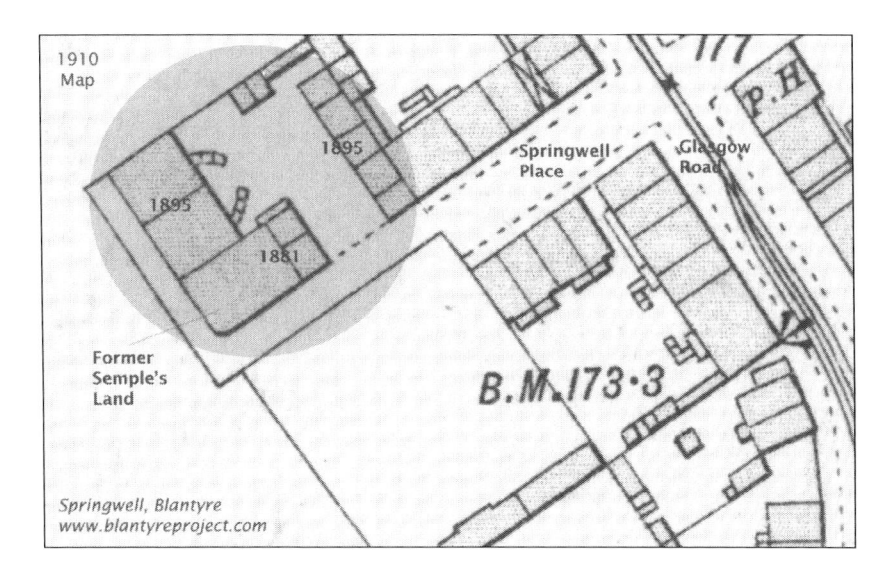

Figure 48 Former Semple's Land on Springwell 1910 Map

In 1895, William after buying out Andrew Frame, built a further 17 homes, all around the perimeter of his square acre. Two large stone tenement blocks were constructed, each with capacity to rent out to 6 families. A further 5 single storey houses were built from brick or stone too, and when finished, along with his former 2 single storey homes, the enclosure had a courtyard type appearance. This was Semple's Land and part of Springwell Place.

William moved into the largest, which at £10 rated value was one of the largest in Springwell of the 19th Century.

The next 2 largest homes were occupied by his former business partner Andrew Frame and James Divine, both masons. They were renting from William for £8, 10 shilling per annum. The other 16 houses were let to miners, carters and in one instance, a widow each for £5, 10 shillings.

Other tenants in 1895 included miners and labourers, John Gray, William Nichol, Hugh Grant, Thomas Gray, Joseph Gray, Thomas McCall, William McEwan, James Clelland, Thomas Gray, Henry Steven, James Downie, Matthew Sorbie, James Forbes, Mrs Marion Davidson, Edward Briggs, William Waddell and Andrew Gibson.

With a guaranteed income coming steadily in, between 1895 and 1901, William could afford to upgrade his home and he is noticeably absent from Blantyre in 1901, choosing to move away to 2 Oxford Street, Shettleston, Glasgow.

However, in 1905, he still owned all 19 of the houses letting the double storey homes out for £6,10 shillings and the single storey houses, offering slightly more space for a family, at the lucrative, decent rent of £8, 10 shillings.

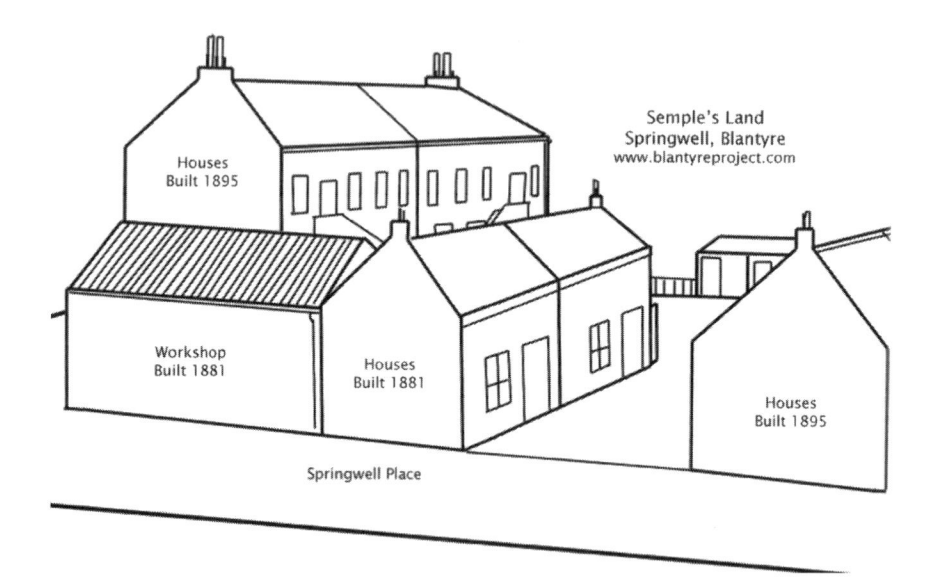

Figure 49 Our Sketch of former Semple's Land, Springwell

Much more of a presence and more well known were his sons William Semple Junior and Gavin Semple both masons. The successful brothers by 1905 had acquired many of the former Springwell Farm fields, especially those along nearby Auchinraith Road and had started to construct homes. Indeed, it is safe to say that William and Gavin Semple were the constructors of Auchinraith Road houses. Not just houses at the top, but major properties like Melbourne Place and Radnor Place as well as the opposing Bute Terrace. Gavin Semple, b1873 was especially prominent in house ownership.

Tragedy struck the family when in 1907, William Semple Senior died at his home in Shettleson, aged 68. Brothers William Junior and Gavin inherited their father's property at Semple's Land and set about splitting some of the homes, as was commonplace in that era, in order to maximize rental capacity. Their 18 homes ended up being 26 miners homes, which would have seen inadequacies in space manifest. William and Gavin lived in their respective new villas one of which was 'Dunedin' on Glasgow Road.

By 1915, the Semple brothers, too old for war, had built further homes on Auchinraith Road along with partner William Ritchie, a joiner of High Blantyre. They owned shops there too, a smithy and had moved their attention to building several of the large villas on Glasgow Road beyond Parkville.

In July 1915, something prompted the Semple Brothers to sell the land and property at Springwell. Perhaps due to the buildings becoming hard to maintain, or subsiding (as some buildings to the north were) or perhaps due to consolidating their property empire to new, better built homes, they put Semple's Land up for sale.

The houses still hadn't sold by October, so the price was dropped to just £625 (around £60,000 in todays money), which even at that time was inexpensive for 26 homes and the land itself. The advert states £173 rental capacity, meaning any purchase should have in theory been in profit just after 3.5 years. If there was nothing wrong with these buildings, on the face of it, it appears a bargain.

New Owners

Two local men formed a partnership to buy the land and houses later that year. Mr Charles A Easson of 58 Auchinraith Road and Mr Thomas H Bell of 52 Glasgow Road. Each man owned their own homes at those addresses but had no other property. It is unknown how much they paid for the private purchase.

The name Semple's Land was gone by the end of 1915. By 1920, the partners renamed their land and homes 'Dalzell or Dalziel Place', which continued to be part of Springwell Place. Most tenants continued to live there even with a hike in rents by the new owners.

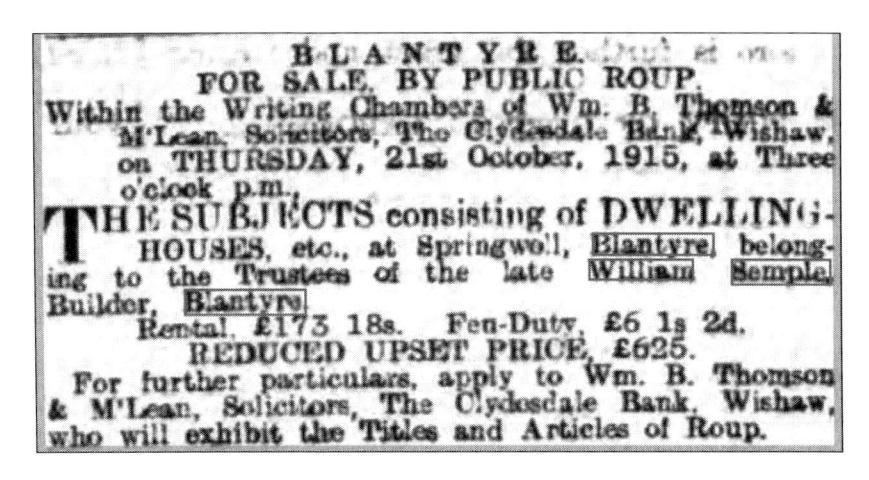

Figure 50 Sale Advert for Semple's Buildings in 1915

At the Sheriff Court, on Friday 1st June 1917, Abraham Swain, Semple's Buildings, Springwell, was charged at the instance of D. W. Hiddleston, solicitor, acting for Blantyre School Board, with failing to comply with attendance orders issued in respect of his two children, Mary and Martha. He admitted the offence of keeping them out of school, and was fined £2, together with £1 3d of expenses, or twenty days' imprisonment.

Also in 1917, authorities reported that a large increase in the number of people paying rates in Springwell had been reported in that previous year, indicating at that time the whole area was becoming very populated.

Easson & Bell continued to rent out the 26 houses right up until 1927, no doubt making a good return on their investment. Near the General Strike ending in 1926, the sanitary department were trying their best to force landlords to introduce running water, sinks, toilets etc. improving their premises, but many were reluctant to spend the money, so a lot of properties were just left to decay year after year. Add to this they may have been badly built in the first place and it paints a horrible picture. By the end of 1927, because of its sub-standard condition, Dalzell or Dalziel Place had been completely decanted. However, the owners then, without any legal permission from the Council, let the properties out again at the beginning of 1928. There were 13 one-apartment houses and 6 two-apartment houses and 9 of these were re-let to what must have been fairly desperate people. Eventually, the Council obviously got wind of this and started legal proceedings against them.

First, they traced the "reputed owner" and fined him £5 (or 30 days' imprisonment) and then they went after the tenants. Seven of the tenants removed themselves after being threatened by the Sheriff, who then ordered the other two to quit within 14 days. After the fortnight passed, there was still one defiant tenant refusing to budge and he was summarily convicted and fined £3 (or 15 days' imprisonment), it was after all this that the buildings were finally of no use to anybody.

Dalzell Place was entirely demolished in 1929, the land cleared entirely. Some of the buildings had only lasted 32 years. Residents of Dalzell Place made good use of brand new Blantyre council houses moving to the Crescents and to Welsh Drive. The square acre formerly Semple's Land would be acquired by the council a decade later in preparation for their new expansive Springwell Housing Estate.

The grassland occupying that space now is still owned by the council today.

Allison Place, Springwell

One of the largest and oldest properties in Springwell on Glasgow Road was the well known and heavily populated former 'Allison Place.' Constructed in 1878 by Robert Lindsay for John Heriot of Wishaw, his daughter Ann Heriot, (a teacher) would be the long term owner, from the moment they were built.

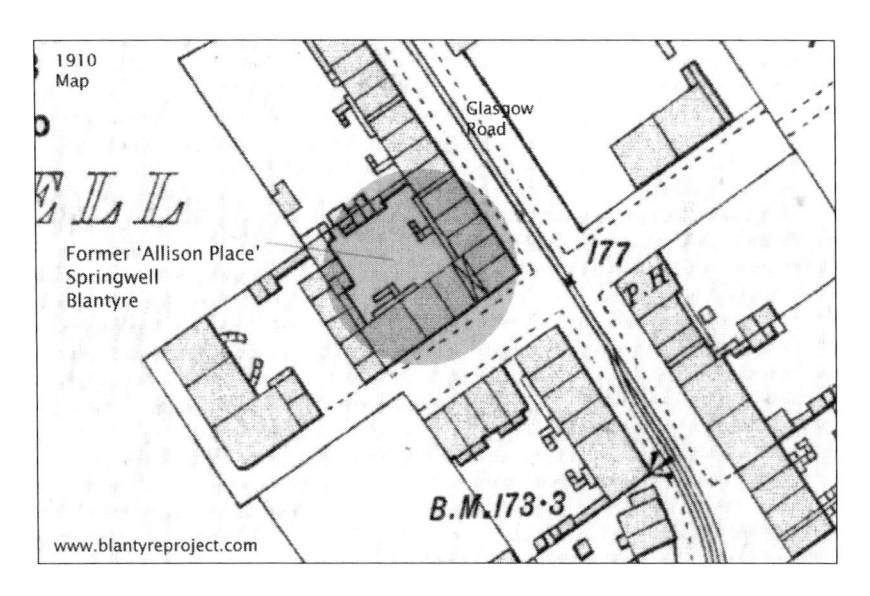

Figure 51 Former Allison Place, Springwell on our 1910 map

Allison Place takes its name from Ann Heriot's middle name, her mother's maiden name of Allison. (Correct with two 'l's). The property consisted of 6 large tenement buildings configured in an L shape, with frontage on Glasgow Road and Springwell Place. It was directly opposite where the modern Dunn's Food Offices are today.

The buildings were all two storey, built of stone, timber and slate. A wider, pend close led from Springwell Place into the back courtyard, and a narrower pedestrian close from Glasgow Road into the courtyard further to the west. Steps to upper levels were located at the read, out of sight from the main road.

When constructed there were initially 35 homes located in these tenements, people densely packed in, primarily miners and their families.

The number of houses increased in the first decade or so and before Glasgow Road postal addresses, they were labeled 1-41 Allison Place.

Sewers outside Allison Place

On 26th August 1879, notice was given under the Public Health Act by authorities, that a sewer should be laid between Allison Place heading towards Springwell Cottages at the Burnbank boundary. The proposal was most descriptive. The Glasgow Road, then a turnpike road owned by the Cambuslang and Muirkirk Road Trust had a ditch running along the side of it, in front of new properties. The laying down of a sewer was determined to be the only way the foulness and offensive smells could be removed, as it was known that wastewater, raw sewage and other 'matters' were constantly thrown into the ditch as it was at the time. The motion was passed and Springwell got its first sewer, the sewage works being located tnear the Parkburn to the rear of the yards of the north side of Glasgow Road. It would take until 1893 for the sewer to be extended from Allison Place into Blantyre up to Herbertson Street.

As well as homes, two popular shops were located at the western end. In 1885, five of the 35 homes were still empty to be let, but the other 30 all occupied. Ann also owned a blacksmiths or smithy in the rear yard but it fell out of use rapidly and was even unused by 1885, quite probably due to a large, established blacksmiths across the road on the north side, directly opposite. One of the shops was occupied by John Miller, a grocer and the other by Alexander Smellie, a butcher.

Both these individuals would later have aspirations of their own property ownership at neighbouring buildings.

Figure 52 Location Line drawing former Allison's Place, Springwell

Quarrel on the Stairwell

During one dark evening in late October 1893, four persons (three men and a little girl) were quarreling over an unknown matter at a wedding reception in an upper house at Allison Place. They took the argument outside to the back stair landing of the tenement.

Suddenly, the handrail they were all leaning against broke and all of them ended up 14 feet down on the ground in the back yard. The men allegedly continued to fight in the fall! All the men were little worse for wear, but the girl whose surname was Lees was rather seriously hurt. It turns out 2 guests went outside to fight and the other 2 people came out to try to stop them.

Figure 53 Tenement Back Stairs

Owner Miss Ann Allison Heriot was born in 1833 and was therefore middle aged by the time she took ownership of Allison's Place. The daughter of John Heriot, a baker and Christina Allison, she did not live in Blantyre ever, but clearly fancied the business of factoring out these homes. She lived first in Dennistoun, but later moved to 12 Albert Drive, Crosshill, Glasgow. She would be single all her long life.

By 1895, as the Century drew to a close, her smithy in the backyard was still empty as was the adjacent stable. John Miller and Alexander Smellie still occupied the shops on the ground floor. However, Ann had split some of the homes and there were now 41 houses, only 1 of which was empty. Conditions must have been difficult with whole families squashed into those small homes.

Tenants renting from Ann Heriot for rents between £3, 12 and £7, 4 shillings in 1895 included miners John Gray, John Lockhart, Daniel Murdoch, Peter Morton, John Murdoch, John Stewart (engineer), Francis O Brien (pensioner), miners William Rooney, Robert Fleming, William Colvin, Joseph Irving, John Cobrough, Edward Bradley, a Mrs Jones, Mark Stewart, Joseph

Robb, James King, James Crawford, Peter Gowan, Hugh McPhail, Margaret Neilson, Patrick Callaghan, Walter Neilson, James Davidson, Alexander Livingstone (joiner), Charles Russell, George Rennick, Mrs John Galbraith, John Wilson, David Cameron, Mrs Elizabeth Neilson, Mrs McLachlan, James Lawson, and John Miller (grocer).

In September 1900, whilst local newspaper told of a rumoured tram system coming to Blantyre shortly, the butchers shop was let to others and Mr John Lees, a confectioner moved in to form a sweet shop. This was due to Alexander Smellie constructing his own neighbouring buildings.

By 1905, residents of the 41 homes of Allison Place would have been quite used to the trundle of the new trams cars going past their windows on Glasgow Road. Ann Heriot's abandoned smithy was now being used as a lumber room, perhaps a store for firewood. The stable was still unused. John Miller continued his grocery business in one shop and the aforementioned John Lees running the other shop as a confectionery business. Five of the homes were empty that year.

Sharing Ownership

In 1907, Miss Heriot was 74 years old. Becoming eldery she sold a share of her property at Allison Place to Mr. Daniel Paterson, of nearby 1 George Street, Burnbank. They are both noted as co owners in 1915. This may have been getting too much for Ann to manage by then 37 homes (some joined together again) and she likely did it not just for a cash sale, but for some assistance in maintaining the aging buildings. Daniel Paterson may have been more hands on and known to tenants, for there are references in this era to 'Paterson's Buildings in Springwell', despite the name Allison Place still existing. Mr Paterson also bought some farm fields further to the west.

The smithy, now lumber room and stable were still used in 1915 but the shops had both changed hands. John Miller (grocer) had moved out and Robert McDougall Grocers had moved in. At the end the sweet shop was gone by 1912, and instead was shopkeeper John Crop (business unknown).

Around this time Allison Place was also allocated Glasgow Road postal address. From east to west, numbers 25, 27, 29, 31 and 33 were assigned and it is around then we see the old numbering of 1-41 Allison Place disappear for good. Many of the families living there even in those war years had the same surnames as previous decades, indicating they may have been homes for generations in the same families, rather than transient miners and labourers.

Rents increased steadily every 5 years or so.

Lost Dog

DID YOU KNOW?

In April 1918, during World War 1, Robert McDougall, the grocer who lived at 27 Glasgow Road found a collie dog. As was the custom at the time, he advertised it in the paper for collection by any owner, else he would sell it in 3 days time.

By 1920 McDougall's Grocery was at 27/29 Glasgow Road within Allison Place and shopkeeper/publican John Bell (business unknown) at 31 Glasgow Road. Thirty seven homes were occupied with rent going to both partners.

However, just one month after the valuation roll was conducted, Miss Ann Heriot died at her home in Glasgow on 23rd May 1920. She was 87 years old and had no children or husband. At her death, a nephew from London signed the death certificate.

Figure 54 Miss Ann Allison Heriot Death Certificate in 1920

Daniel Paterson would inherit the other half of the Allison's Place later that year and then between 1921 and 1924, put the whole lot up for sale. Allison's Land was purchased by John Stevenson , a grocer of 67 Clark Street, Paisley, permitting Robert McDougall to continue operating his grocery business from there. Despite being a remote owner, John Stevenson also kept a few homes on the east side of Stonefield Road, near the Anderson Church.

Meantime at 33 Allison Place….

During researching this property, a few stories arose in connection with one of the addresses, i.e. at 33 Allison Place. In May 1923, behind an action which had been brought in Hamilton Sheriff Court was the remarkable story of an alleged treasure of gold and precious stones buried in a churchyard near Edinburgh. The Sheriff made avizandum in the case. The pursuer in the action was Mrs Ona Novasitis, a Lithuanian widow who lived at 33 Allison

Place, Springwell and she sought to recover the sum of £93 from Blades Stephanskis, a miner residing at 51 Auchinraith Road, Blantyre. The pursuer averred that in 1921, and in the beginning of 1922, the defender informed her that he had a treasure, consisting of gold and precious stones, buried in Rosewell, near Edinburgh.

On the strength of defender's reiterated statements she gave him the loan of £13 to enable him to uncover the treasure, being promised that the money would be repaid to her. She later parted with a further two sums, on the same pretexts, obtained the loan of £20 but never saw the treasure, for she was told by the man it is stated, that the nights were too light dig up the treasure then, and that he would wait until the winter came before doing so splitting it with her. Then she learned that the man was not the owner of any treasure, and that the statements made to her regarding it were false and fraudulent. Requests for repayment of the money were made repeatedly to the defender, but he declined or delayed. The money had to be repaid back.

Another story at this address occurred in 1927. On being sentenced in Hamilton J.P. Court on Saturday 22nd January 1927, for theft, William Allen (14), a local Blantyre boy living at 33 Allison Place, Springwells, refused to walk from the dock and, shrieked, "Oh, daddy, help!". He was lifted by an officer and carried, still shouting, to the cells below. The Fiscal described him as "a boy who was training boys, younger than himself to become criminals."

A nine-year-old boy had told the police that he was a member of a gang, which Allen was self proclaimed leader. This younger boy said that his parents had thrashed him because of his association with Allen, and that Allen had treated him brutally when he refused to steal for him. The youngster said he was more afraid of Allen than he was of his parents. He now did what he was told by Allen, and recently, when a lorry with beer bottles was seen standing in Glasgow Road, he on Allen's orders, along with other boys, stole some of the bottles. The liquor was taken to the picture-house on Glasgow Road, where Allen and another boy drank some of it. Allen was charged that Saturday, when pleaded guilty, and admitted four previous convictions. The Justices ordered the boy to be detained in Parkhead Reformatory until he attained the age of 19.

Blantyre Project Social Media:

William Dickson: "I have memories of Caserta's Café and Dougie Frasers shop directly across the road from these buildings. Alongside nearby Robertson's Ginger Factory, this was a great place to be. Happy days for many people."

Before we move off 33 Allison Place, yet another story in the paper that happened just a week earlier than the previous paragraphs. On Friday 12th January 1927, Joseph Malcolmson, a carter of Dalzell Place and his friend Robert McGinn of 33 Allison Place, both carters were up in court for breaking into a signal box at Craighead Colliery and stealing an axe, some matches and a regulations book. Malcolmson also admitted breaking into Castle Park Football ground in Forrest Street and was sentenced to 30 days in prison. McGinn was fined £1.

Blantyre Project Social Media:

Mary Cambridge: "I lived in Springwells for 68 years and in all that time, I never once thought of leaving it. I have a lot of great memories, great neighbours who were so friendly and my grandchildren still like to come and play here."

Senga Cartwright: "How wonderful that this old history is being brought back to life, to the best of my knowledge for the first time. There cannot be many people alive, (if any) that would remember Allison Place."

Patrick Donnelly: "The tenements couldn't have been built very well for them to be demolished so quickly. Perhaps the Council just simply urgently wanted the land to build modern homes."

"Read More about **Allison Place** online. Scan our handy QR Code for more narrative and photos at Blantyre's History Archives. Further information, photos and commentary from readers are added from time to time."

In 1928, the whole of Allison Place, including the outbuildings were demolished, the county council acquiring the land from John Stevenson. Allison Place had lasted exactly 50 years.

In 1933, the Council built 3 large terraced blocks of 2 storey homes on this and neighbouring ground with frontage on to Glasgow Road, directly across from Robertson's Aerated Water Factory. The new homes were given addresses 25 – 41 Glasgow Road and still exist, in good repair today.

Miller's Buildings, Springwell

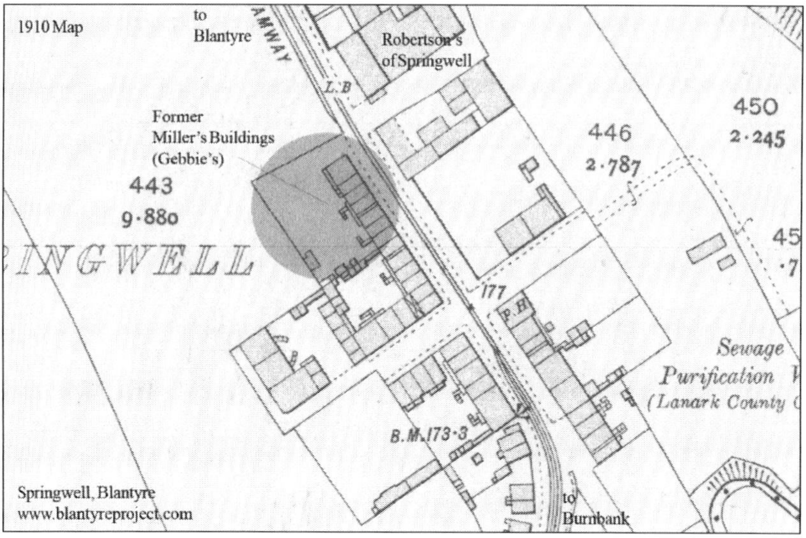

Figure 55 Former Miller's Buildings, Springwell, Blantyre on 1910 map

You may be forgiven for thinking that Miller's Buildings along Glasgow Road was where David Miller's modern fireplace shop was. That would be wrong, for whilst Davy did indeed have a fireplace shop on the north side of the road, it was actually located in McCaffrie's Building in the 1990's and post Millennium. Miller's Buildings was actually on the opposite side of the road, on the south side and was older. Far older and once owned by a relative of Davy. The name is correct with "Miller" and not "Millar". Before we explore that, however, we must go back to the building origins and constructor Francis Gebbie, not forgetting his hired builder, Blantyre's William Roberts, a joiner.

Born in Strathaven in 1830, Mr. Francis Gebbie was the son of a well known Victorian writer. In 1855, at the age of 25, he went to the bar and passed his exams, becoming a lawyer. He rose through the ranks in Glasgow, where he lived and took part in many legal cases and in September 1873 received the promotion to Sheriff Substitute of Mid Lothian. He was transferred on 4th February 1881 to the same role in Dumbarton.

Just prior to that, with the creation of Springwell Place in Blantyre and his office attending to the legal work for the sales of the emerging buildings in this district, Mr Gebbie's interest was peaked when he saw potential in buying a plot of inexpensive land adjacent to the south of the Hamilton to Glasgow Road. Neighbouring Allison Place had already been built and Mr Gebbie intended to let homes of similar construction out to more miners families.

So, in 1879 he approached Blantyre joiner William Roberts, of Stanley Place, Stonefield and together they built what would initially be known as "Gebbie's Buildings", sometimes referred to as an extension of part of Springwell Place. William, a native of Lanark was 28 years old and on the cusp of being married, already had a good reputation of being a Blantyre housebuilder. We'll explore more about William in other parts of this book, for he would later build many homes.

A rectangular plot was secured to build three, double storey stone tenements, internally framed in wood with slated roofs. The buildings were tenement in style with stone steps accessing the upper levels at the rear beside a large open yard. Length was approximately 115 feet with frontage all on Glasgow Road. A pedestrian close was located in the middle tenement offering easy access from front to back.

Figure 56 Location line drawing showing former Miller's Land, Springwell

The 10 houses and shop were quickly sought after by miners and their families, with Robert Longmuir, a grocer taking the shop at the far western end.

Tragic start

Tragedy struck the property pretty fast. It was reported from Blantyre that on 5th January 1881 a girl aged four years, named Martha Burt, daughter of

William Burt, miner, Gebbie's Buildings, Springwell, Blantyre had died through injuries by burning. Her mother was apparently keeping a neighbour's shop, and the girl accompanied her and was playing about when her clothes accidentally caught fire. The flames were instantly put out by means of wrapping a bed-mat, but not until the poor little thing was severely burned about the face, body, and legs. Taken to hospital, she died a short time later. The Burt family moved away, absent from the next valuation roll.

By 1885, only one 1 house remained empty. That year, Mr Gebbie's tenants were aforementioned Mr. Longmuir, Constantine Kelly, Mrs Thomas Cairney, Mrs Donald Ferns, Charles McCallum, John Reid, Edward Burns, Mrs Sim.

Ten years later Francis Gebbie had split many of the homes, making them smaller and had squeezed in 16 families, each paying rent from £5, 9 shillings and up to £8. At the shop was John English, a dairyman. An outdoor dairy building had been built at the back by 1895. John was paying £12, 10 shillings in rent and may have been there since the late 1880's.

New Owners

In 1902, whilst living at Helensburgh, Francis Gebbie retired and put his Blantyre property up for sale. Gebbie's Buildings had existed for 23 years by the time he sold to David Miller, a fellow solicitor and colleague of New Cross, Hamilton. From 1902, the property was known as 'Miller's Buildings' and the change in ownership arrived at the same time as tramlanes outside the front windows.

A sidenote, Mr Francis Gebbie died on 4th April 1908 at his home in Helensburgh. His successes in life, inheritance and hard work had seen him accumulate a fortune. He was 78 years old and had not survived a major operation. He was well respected, well known and his loss was felt by many people. His will left £32,071, a considerable sum, which in today's money would be around £4m!!

Now, you may be wondering why we haven't called the buildings Gebbie's Buildings. The answer is simple, they existed for longer as Miller's Buildings, around 29 further years.

Nothing changed too much when David Miller took over. In 1905, rents were only modestly raised in all 16 homes between £6 and £9 per annum, the dairy now occupied by Samuel Moore.

Tram Disturbance

In 1905, William Sharpe of Millar's Buildings, was fined in 7s 8d or three days for breach of the peace on a tramcar. He had two old tickets in his possession and refused to pay his fare when challenged, and created a disturbance. He explained that he had bought his ticket in Wishaw to take him to Hamilton, but had come off at Motherwell and was resuming his journey on a different car.

By this time, the back of the properties offered views out over farm fields, and the Auchinraith junction of the N.B Railway and Auchinraith Pit Bing would have been clearly visible.

David Miller would not own the buildings for long, passing away in 1907 at his home in Hamilton. He was 57 years old, although his wife Janet Miller inherited the property and would continue to let the houses out to miners families. The buildings continued as "Miller's Buildings".

By 1915, all 16 houses were let out. Glasgow Road postal addresses were allocated and Miller's Buildings became officially 35 – 49 Glasgow Road. The shop at the end became a larger home, occupied by miner Hugh Logan. Rents varied between £8, 4 shillings and £11, 15 shillings.

Events of 1917

In 1917, Mr Logan was one of 40 people injured in a spectacular train collision in Ratho Station, Edinburgh. Although he survived, 11 other people died.

"We broke Into this house. We are the Brass Button Gang and you will find a dead man in this room.—T.B.B.G." This mysterious and cryptic message was found scrawled on a piece of paper attached to the door handle of a room in a house at Craighead Estate. Blantyre, in March 1917. T.B.B.G stood for the Brass Button Gang. This lawless and apparently bloodthirsty and formidable gang of supposed ruffians turned out to be four boys all residing at Miller's Buildings, Springwell. Their ages ranging from 8 to 14—a very harmless looking quartette. The Court was not a little amused when the terrible message, signed T.B.B.G." was read to the Fiscal, and they beheld the miscreants in these four boys, whom their fathers declared had been soundly thrashed for their misdeeds. The Fiscal stated that they had done a good deal of mischief in house, besides taken away a number of articles. As the accused were all at Court for the first time in their lives. Sheriff Shennan continued the case against them till 28th March, and meantime advised the parents to put their heads together and make suitable reparation to the occupant of the house which the boys had partly dismantled.

By 1920 again all 16 homes were let out, although the larger former shop which had become a home 10 years earlier, was now home to James Semple, a miner. In 1925, the shop house was split and Mr. B Fisher operated his business from there working as a cooper. (somebody who made utensils and barrels, usually out of wood). The other part was empty. Rent of this shop in 1925 was a lofty £28 per annum. With the shop split, there were actually 17 homes at Miller's Buildings going forward.

Helped Soldiers to Desert

In 1926, a Blantyre couple at Miller's Buildings found themselves in trouble with the law. The story goes that on Wednesday 3rd November 1926, Mr William Crichton, a pit sinker and his wife Mary Barr, residing at 41 Glasgow Road, were up in court, charged with having aided three soldiers of the Cameronians from Hamilton Barracks to desert! William Crichton was also charged with having attempted to persuade a fourth soldier to desert.

Later rounded up and appearing in the same courtroom, two of the three soldiers who deserted said that one Sunday night on 19th September 1926, they purposely went over the wall at Hamilton Barracks, and proceeded with haste Blantyre. However, it was late and they needed somewhere to rest and decided to hide in the back of a random property at 41 Glasgow Road, Blantyre.

Knowing they were in huge trouble, they camped out in the cold, but were soon discovered by surprised tenant, William Crichton, who did not know them and proceeded to tell William they simply needed clothes.

It was a cold evening, so William took them into his house, gave them something to eat, and put them up for the night. Early next morning he provided them with civilian clothes. Having put these on, they left their uniforms behind, and walked via Edinburgh all the way to England. The gravity of their escape soon dawned upon them and the realization that being away longer would only make it worse for them when caught. One soldier gave himself up to the police in Newcastle, and the other at Penrith. The third soldier, who had come up with the idea about the desertion was not heard of again! However, this is not the most remarkable part of the story.

A fourth soldier was at Hamilton Showground on October 16th, when he was approached by a man who said he knew how to help soldiers desert from the regiment, and that if the soldier had 12 shillings, he would obtain civilian clothes for him. The mystery man wrote the name and address of William

Crichton on a slip and told the Soldier to call to that house in Blantyre, but careful, the person whose name he gave was a known Communist and was not a fan of the army. In court it was stated that William Crichton was not the man at the fair, so either William had an accomplice, or he was being set up!

Back at the barracks that evening, the 4th solider, knowing of the 3 missing soliders and having no desire to leave the barracks himself, promptly gave the name and address and the piece of paper to his corporal.

Police were dispatched to William Crichton's home, made a search and there, they found two military tunics, which were identified as belonging to two of the deserting soldiers theirs. Mr. Crichton in the witness-box, denied the charges made against him forming a story that, going out his work 5.30am one morning, he found the two tunics hanging on his stairwell railing. He took them into the house and told his wife to hang them up. His wife stood by the story.

William admitted that he had the tunics a month before the police called, and considered the tunics were thrown away by others, and never thought reporting his find to the police or the military. Asked if he had fed the deserting soldiers one night, he replied in court saying, "I'm a miner. I can hardly feed myself, let alone the British Army!"

Ultimately though, the Crichton's story did not stack up to the admitted testimonies of the soldiers retrieved from desertion. The fate the soldiers received is unknown. However, Sheriff Shennan found both Mr and Mrs Crichton guilty of the charges brought against them. The Sheriff regarded these unusual offences as very serious, and sent William Crichton to prison for three months with hard labour. Mrs Crichton was fined £3, with the option of fifteen days' imprisonment.

End of Miller's Buildings

An empty property in 1925 was a warning of what was to come. As huge slum clearances took place throughout Blantyre, Miller's Buildings in 1930 were laying empty. All 17 homes vacant, with the exception of Mr Joseph Middleton, who may have been squatting. Many of the former residents were rehoused in the new modern homes at Victoria Street, although with the closure of the pit at Auchinraith in 1930, several other families disappeared from Blantyre altogether.

Miller's Buildings look to have been demolished around 1931. As noted previously, the council then acquired the land and built the current terraced block of council homes in 1933 , numbered 25-41 Glasgow Road.

It wasn't the end of the Miller's business dealings in Springwell. A descendent of David and Janet Miller, another David Miller would return to Springwell in the late 20th Century, setting up "Miller's Fireplace" shop on the north side of Glasgow Road, a story for another time.

> Blantyre Project Social Media:
>
> **Thea Borland McNamee:** "My aunt stayed in the council houses, 41a Glasgow Road, my brother across the landing in 41c and Frank Cummiskey stayed in 41b back in the 1970's, 80's and 90's."
>
> **Den Kane**: "I came into this world in 41 Glasgow Road."
>
> **David Dickson:** "My dad stays in number 25, for nearly 47 years now."
>
> **Senga Cartwright:** "You can see the council put some thought into ensuring the new council homes looked similar in size and location to the buildings there previously. Unusual consideration for them!"
>
> **James Faulds:** "Springwell was the 'Capital' of Blantyre. Never a door locked, kids running around having fun, mothers looking after others kids as well as their own. Sure there was always a couple of neighbours we would torment as kids to get a rise out of them, but it was never anything bad. Taking ginger bottles back to Dougie Fraser's shop across the road, the 'gless cheque' just to get the 5p deposit back for sweets. Good times."

Fields at Springwell

To the west of Miller's Buildings and behind them were open 4 large fields. Prior to 1937, no building was ever built on these fields to the south of Glasgow Road which were hemmed in between Auchinraith Road, Glasgow Road and the Auchinraith Pit further south. In each valuation roll they are named as fields and grassparks in Springwell.

The land in 1875 belonged to Mrs Janet Jackson of Old Place, High Blantyre. Janet was the last owner of Springwell Farm, before it was demolished in 1876. She still owned the fields in 1895 via Trustees of her late mother Mrs Margaret Herbertson. By 1905 after the death of Janet, Dr Grant of Blantyre held them in trust until a buyer could be found. The grassparks were let out that year to James Duncan, a dairyman of Springwell who most likely kept cows in the fields. Mineral rights were let out to Merry & Cunninhgam Coalmasters and it is safe to say with proximity to their pit, these fields must have been mined far below.

New owners for the fields came along in 1913 where 3 widows bought the 4 fields. The ladies were Margaret Paterson of Hamilton, Janet McGregor of Strathaven and Annie NcKenzie of Blantyre Terrace, Edinburgh. The ladies knew each other well and equally shared the purchase. They would go on to own these fields for many years until selling them to the council around 1936 or 1937 for the purposes of building the Springwell Housing Scheme.

Blantyre Golf Course

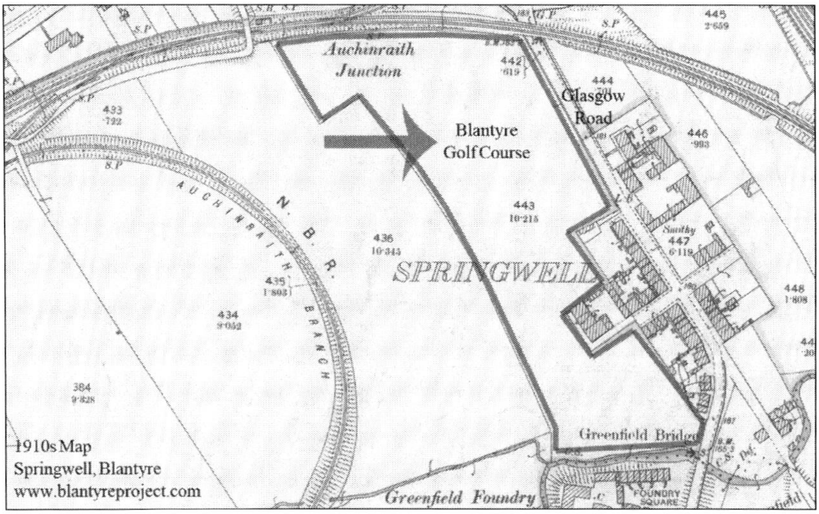

Figure 57 Former Blantyre Golf Course at Springwell 1910's

Some things have been incorrectly written by others about Blantyre's former Golf Club. Contrary to reports, it was not laid out on Merry & Cunningham's mining land, and the course was certainly not abandoned for housing. That cleared up, let's look at some detailed facts.

Blantyre Golf Club was a short lived golf club of the 1910's, a casualty itself of World War One. It was laid out on the northern fields and grassparks at Springwell, on land equally belonging to three ladies I.e. Margaret Paterson, Janet McGregor and Annie McKenzie.

According to "Hughes Sporting Life Magazine" of the era, Mrs. Paterson and her 2 business partners, all widows were keen on "the Advancement of Women". This may have been a reference to the suffragette movement so prevailing at the time, but is also likely associated with the inclusion of women into everyday life and perhaps sports. Why? Well Blantyre Golf Club was to cater for women too and even had preferential rates for them.

Let's be clear though, the club was not owned by the 3 ladies, merely laid out on their land, presumably rented from them. As such, given their interest in including women, perhaps it may have been a stipulation of any rental agreement, that women should be permitted to take part.

A 9 hole golf course was laid out in a northwest to southeast direction in 1913 and enhanced in 1914, which surely would have been a talking point in the community. Given the timings of each annual AGM, it appears the course opened in April 1913. It was entered from Auchinraith Road, by going over the railway and down on to the field. The whole field sloped slightly from the railway towards the Parkburn and the course was considered part of Springwell.

Following enhancements to the course, the first meeting of the Blantyre Golf Club was held in the Masonic Hall, Stonefield, in April 1914, Rev C Scrimgeour Turnbull, President, in the chair. It is a fair suggestion to say that as President, Rev Turnbull likely had a hand in the creation of the club being President for that first year. There was an attendance of about 100, a good indicator that the club had been welcomed and thriving. Meeting business required to appoint a committee and the following officers were elected; Hon president, John Menzies; hon. Vice-presidents, Miss J W Forrest, Woodhouse, Dr William Grant, J.P., Dr J C Wilson and Rev C S Scrimgeour Turnbull, M.A; president, Mr A W Hendry; vice-president, Thomas McCluskey; captain, D S Hardey; vice-captain, J M Thomson; secretary and treasurer, W McGruther; the following were appointed to the committee – Captain Brown, Charles McAra, William Brown, Charles W Easton, J Freeman and Miss G McCallum.

Subscriptions

Subscriptions were set as follows; Gentlemen £1/1s, ladies with 50% discounts at 10 shillings 6d. Juniors(members (under 18) were 10 shillings/6d; Family tickets £1/11s/6d which would certainly represent good value if 2 or more people in the same family wished to participate. During the first meeting, the following inter-club matches were arranged for that coming season; Bellshill, Kirkhill, Larkhall and Motherwell. Although there was no initial clubhouse, members clubs could be obtained from the Masonic Lodge in Glasgow Road. A Pavilion is noted in the 1915 Valuation roll later. Payments were accepted at the Commercial Bank, Blantyre or directly to the treasurer Mr. William McGruther.

Competition Matches & Prize-giving

A report that appeared in the Hamilton Advertiser on Saturday 2nd May

1914 covered the opening day for that second season, a week earlier stating, "The Blantyre Golf Club had their official (annual) opening on Saturday last, (25th April 1914) when an exhibition match was played by T Walker, professional to the Hamilton Club, and Mr. R B Stewart, Kirkhill, which brought about 150 members and friends to witness the game. The professional was in especially good form, and his drives were watched with the keenest interest, although at times he was exceedingly unlucky with some of his tee shots. It was readily seen that Mr. Stewart was an unequal opponent, and the professional ran out an easy winner by 5&4, the scores being Walker 69, and Stewart, 77. After the game the members were refreshed with a cup of tea and cakes, purveyed by Mr McLair and which was greatly enjoyed. Thereafter the members engaged in various competitions, results as follows; Mixed foursome – first, Miss Isa H Tulloch and Peter F A Grant; second, Miss Jessie Orr and Robert Paton; third, Miss Mary Devenney and Robert S F Harris. Stroke Competition (gentlemen) – first, T Haldane; second, Jas Rennie; third, Jas Heggison. Clock Golf – ladies, Miss Weir and Miss Jackson (tie); gentlemen, A M Muir.

At the end of the exhibition match Mr David Harley thanked guests Walker and Stewart for coming to Blantyre, and he said the game had given satisfaction to the large company that had witnessed it. The club is in a prosperous condition, and from appearance it is quite apparent that a successful season is in front of them." Competition matches were seasonal taking place when weather was finer, each July.

Result of the July 1914 monthly medal; First class – John Barry (11), 73; John Sharp (7), 75; John Cunningham (11), 77; Second class – Clydesdale Medal – David Harper (24), 85; Forrest Spoon – Miss Grace D McCallum (24), 98; Miss E Thorburn (24), 106.

Figure 58 Blantyre Golf Club opened with success

The presentation for the seasons prizes was held in the Masonic Hall on Wednesday 28th October 1914. A whist Drive was also held with proceeds going to the War Relief Fund. Mr. John Menzies, president, presented the prizes to the following; Forrest Spoon (1914) – Miss Isa H Tuloch; President's Prize – Miss Meg Dunlop; Kirkton Challenge Medal – 1st Class (1913), David L Harley; Clydesdale Medal – 2nd class (1913), Peter F A Grant; President's Prize – first, Duncan Harper; second (tie), J B Taylor and Thomas Duncan; Captain's Prize – first, Thomas P Black; second, John Cunningham; Special War Relief Medals, given by the captain and John Roberts, Priory Bar, respectively – first class, William Chambers; second class, Thomas P Black.

Impact of War

However, the timing couldn't have been worse. World War One had started and many of the subscribed males were enlisted, although perhaps at that early time, nobody would have any idea of the scale of the horrors that were about to unfold in Europe.

On Tuesday 13th April 1915, the Annual General Meeting of Blantyre Golf Club was held in the Masonic hall, Stonefield. There was good attendance of members with Mr. A Hendry as president, offering chairperson. The minutes were read from the last meeting and finances presented which showed the club to be in good solid standing. It was reported that the club at that time was still in a very satisfactory condition, perhaps through the payment of fees, prior to men being enlisted.

The following officers were elected; president, Thomas McCluskey; vice-president, C McAra; captain, D L Harley; vice-captain, John Sharp; secretary and treasurer, William Mc Gruther; William Brown and James Heggison were appointed secretary and treasurer pro tem on account of Mr Mc Gruther being on active service.

Honorary membership for the year was conferred on all members serving with H.M forces. The "Roll of Honour" which had been drawn up and printed was showing that 29 members were on active service with more to follow. No formal opening of the course would take place this year, and the committee had decided no fixtures list would be issued for the season. The course, which had been greatly improved on the previous year, was now open for casual play.

On 6th January 1917, the Hamilton Advertiser recorded that the Golf Club had raised a total of £9 and 9s, which was to be set aside for its members serving in the Great World War I. The amount was to be reserved for them coming back, for "comforts". More telling was a concert held to raise club funds in September 1917 at the Co-operative Hall, tickets costing 1s.

Clearly the club had started to struggle in 1917, perhaps even earlier in

1916. By 1918, as war loomed into its 4th year and the atrocities of the frontlines became more known to all, running a golf club for recreation and sport may have seemed like a pastime best left for happier times. The impact of war on the UK economy may also have meant subscriptions were a luxury that seemed frivolous in such times. Some of the women members went on to raise funds for the war and especially may not have wanted to pay subscriptions for recreation, or indeed keep up with the expensive fashionable clothes industry that arose around the sport in those years.

The Hamilton Advertiser newspaper, records the proposal to close the club.

From their archives relating to 24th January 1918, "A special general meeting of Blantyre Golf Club was held in the Lesser Co-operative Hall on Thursday evening. The captain, Mr. John Sharp, owner of Chamber's Buildings nearby presided. Owing to the present conditions (assumed war and/or lack of members) there was only a small attendance of the members.

The Chairman, in the course of his remarks, pointed out that it was becoming increasingly difficult to keep the club going, and that in the opinion of the committee the club was in a better position for being wound up than it had ever been.

Figure 59 Ladies Golf Fashions of 1910's

After the secretary had read the statement of affairs, it was moved and seconded that the club be wound up voluntarily. The attention of members is directed to the advertisement re members' clubs, etc." With no known clubhouse ever built, presumably members clubs were permitted to be taken home or still stored at the Masonic Lodge as had been the case in previous years.

Finally, on Saturday 18th May 1918 it was announced that the club had gone into liquidation. It had lasted just over 5 years in the most trying of times. All claims against the club were to be lodged within seven days from this date with the secretary, William Brown, 176 Glasgow Road, Blantyre.

It is said that the late historian Jimmy Cornfield once had the enamel "No trespassing sign", but this is wrong. Jimmy never had it, he only a photo of it. The sign is held by another local gent.

It wasn't the end of Blantyre Golf though. In November 1921 it was told that local golf enthusiasts had an option on "a most excellent and well adapted stretch of ground within easy distance of the heart of the town." It was suggested after a meeting in the Parish Chambers that Blantyre could have "one of the finest golf courses for miles around," while one of the men actually said, "Gleneagles would not be in it!" The following month though, word came from the legal firm of Castiglione & Scott of Edinburgh that the land had been sold, and the golfers were left right back where they had started. Where was the land? It was Greenhall Farm. Later in January 1934. "The Committee recently appointed to make enquiries regarding the proposed new 18-hole golf course for Blantyre have now decided to proceed with the scheme. They have an assured membership of 160 ladies and gentlemen, and it is expected that the total will increase to 300. It is hoped that the course will be open for play next June." However, it didn't go ahead. No course was ever laid out again until the small pitch n putt course at Greenhall in the 1960's.

The former golfing field adjacent to Glasgow Road at Springwell would however, go on to have another immediate use which is explored next.

Springwell Poultry Run

The Springwell Poultry run was a relatively short lived poultry farming operation of the late 1920's and 1930's situated in open fields of Springwell, which prior to the poultry run, had been Blantyre Golf Course.

Several poultry farms sprang up in Blantyre during the 1920's and 1930's, offering an alternative to using land for agricultural purposes. One of the first poultry farms in Blantyre, truly on a large scale was created between 1920 and 1925 and was run by Mr. George Kay from his ground at Woodened, at the end of John Street. Perhaps prompted by his success, others quickly followed and by 1930, as well as Mr. Kay's, poultry runs also existed at Park, High Blantyre run by the Craig family and at Station Road run by the Forrest family. Not forgetting the subject of this article, a poultry farm at Springwell, situated adjacent to Glasgow Road.

Memories of Blantyre Golf Course were long forgotten as the expansive fields in the shadow of Auchinraith Pit Bing were given over to Mr William Tait who rented the field for his own poultry farm for the sum of £10 per annum. The land was owned by the same 3 widows (Paterson/ McGregor/ McKenzie) who had 17 years earlier permitted a golf course to be set out on their fields. Truly this was "Birdsfield" although that name is much older!

Figure 60 Springwell Poultry Farm around 1930, Auchinraith Bing at back

Sometime between 1926 and 1930, Mr Tait's Poultry Farm was up and running with several hundred birds roaming freely around the fields (pictured), being farmed and bred for their eggs and meat. Families who had flocks of this size sold eggs as their primary income source, and chicken meat was a delicacy being reserved for special occasions and holidays only. The average chicken would lay between 80-150 eggs per year. The chicken diet was basically whatever they could forage with occasional handouts of grain, scraps and waste kitchen products. A hen destined for the pot would be fattened up with extra grains and buttermilk if available.

Housing was non-specific, either in the barn with the other animals or separate scattered small outhouses as was the case at Springwell, offering small respite against inclement weather. They certainly didn't have purpose built large coops like we see today, and this led to a high mortality rate of around 40%. Chickens also didn't do well over the winter months due to a lack of vitamin D which is provided during the summer months through sunlight.

Vitamin D was discovered in the early 1920s and led to a small revolution in poultry keeping. Hens could now survive through the winter months with Vitamin D supplements and go on to produce healthier chicks in the spring. The venture was carried out on a grand scale to make it viable as a business enterprise. Adjacent fields around the bing to the south were let out by the widows to Mr. Craig of Bellsfield for his cattle.

William Tait was a poultry keeper who lived at 5 Jackson Street, Low Blantyre and came to Blantyre between 1925 and 1930. The days of his poultry farm were numbered when in 1937, the Council had acquired the land for the large Springwell Housing Scheme. It is unknown if he removed the poultry farm prior to that year. As such, the maximum time the poultry farm could have existed at this location was 12 years and was most likely shorter.

Blantyre Project Social Media:

Sheena Thomson: "My granddad, Tom Gilmour had a chicken run just off Whistleberry Road in the 1950's and early 1960's. He lived at 86 Glasgow Road."

John Cornfield: "Free range chickens and eggs before it became trendy or cared about."

Senga Carthwright: "I've heard this talked about, but never believed!"

Cattle Maiming at Springwell Fields

DID YOU KNOW?

In July 1923, Blantyre police had to investigate what they termed as one of the worst cases of cattle maiming which had ever come under their notice.

On 7th July 1923, a young 15 months' old heifer, belonging to Mrs. Anderson, a dairy keeper, was found about 7 o'clock that Saturday morning lying in a field in the Springwell district in a dying condition with its right hind leg cut clean off. Clearly distressed, the animal died shortly afterwards. The heifer had been stunned and attempts made to cut its throat. That part, the right hind leg containing the femur bone was disjointed with skill and precision that could only point to one conclusion, that the party who carried out the brutal work had some experience of the fleshing/butchery trade and took it from the live animal for consumption of the meat!

Auchinraith Railway Junction

In 1863 the Caledonian Railway opened a loop line branching off their main Glasgow to Hamilton line, sweeping up into Blantyre and heading northwards, under Glasgow Road, over fields at Springwell and onwards through developing Blantyre, up to a new High Blantyre Station.

On 1st May 1882, a spur was added leading from this loop to the main line at Craighead, forming what was to become known as the Auchinraith Junction. The junction sat above the field formerly the golf course and poultry run.

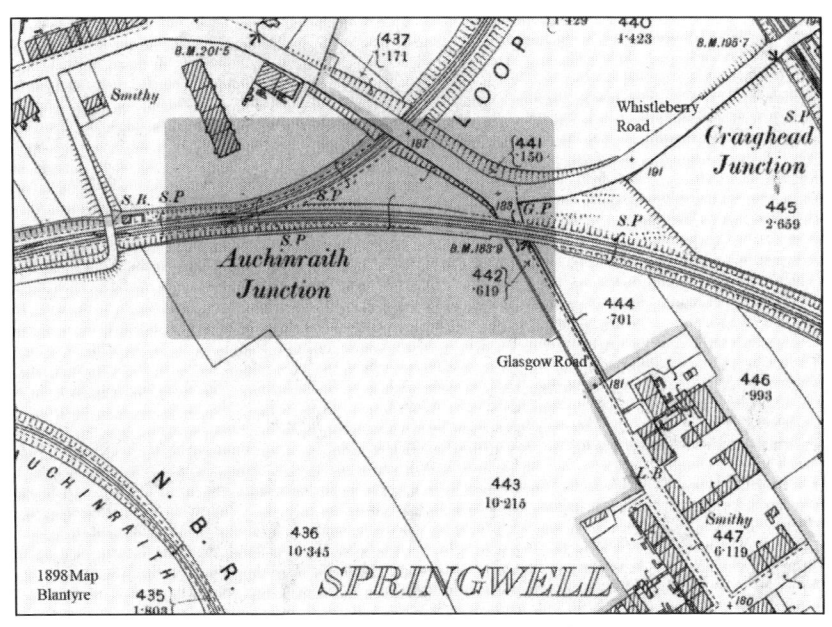

Figure 61 1898 Map showing Auchinraith Railway Junction

A sweeping semi circular branch was added nearby to the North British Railway giving access to Birdsfield Siding and to allow Auchinraith Pits connection to the main NBR Hamilton branch at Blantyre Junction to the north of Springwell. The colliery was already served by the Hamilton and Strathaven Railway line from Auchinraith.

A small path crossed the railway at Auchinraith junction , adjacent to a signal box. The signal box fell out of use in 1925 although was used again during war years and existed right up until the 1960's.

The line ceased operating on 1st June 1960 and the line quickly became weed ridden and unused, serving only on occasion as the odd freight service.

In the following photos from the early 1960's, the Auchinraith Junction is shown, unused and with the houses of Springwell Housing Scheme on the right at numbers 45 and 47 Springwells Crescent.

Figure 62 Former Auchinraith Railway Junction in the 1960's

The gardens and houses to the left of the railway line are no longer there, demolished along the bottom of Auchinraith Road to make way for the East Kilbride Expressway in the early 1980's.

Figure 63 The Auchinraith Signal box ceased operating in 1925.

The exact location of Auchinraith Junction today is now at the top of the slip road coming from Lidl supermarket back on to the A725 heading to EK.

> Blantyre Project Social Media:
>
> **Henry Hambley:** "Great pictures. I lived in Auchinraith Terrace from mid 1950's until 1963. I remember the old signal box at Auchinraith. I remember there used to be one train per day hauling empty coal wagons up to Dixon's pit and returning with full wagons later in the day. It was possible to see this from one or two of the classrooms of Auchinraith Primary school."
>
> **Moyra Lindsay:** "The railway ran behind our house in Radnor Place. We left there in 1952. Coop coal dept. was in the yard at Auchinraith Road just beside the line."
>
> **Andy Callaghan:** "The line ran between Rosendale, where we lived, and Springwell. I fell off the stair to the signal box when I was 5 and broke my arm."
>
> **Bill Graham:** "My Aunt, Jean McDade worked that box as a signalperson during WW2."

Springwells Housing Scheme

On Friday 22nd February 1935, a report appeared in the local Motherwell Times, telling of a drive to tidy up Lanarkshire's towns. The Lanarkshire Slum Drive was initiated which saw Lanarkshire's biggest demolition of residential dilapidated homes involving condemned properties. It was approved by the County Council's Committee. The districts covered were Strathaven, Shotts, Carluke, Douglas, Newarthill, Blantyre and Forth. Displaced families were to be rehoused in new schemes in the eight areas. Many of the properties demolished were several hundred years old. The programme at the time cost nearly £10,000. It is around then we first see the name "Springwells" with an "s" at the end.

For Blantyre, this meant clearance of several old properties in Springwell along Glasgow Road and additionally the clearance of some of the homes at Dixon's Rows further West. Combined with slum clearance of many homes at Merry's Rows and so soon after clearance of Blantyre Works Village homes, Blantyre's housing was in crisis, with hundreds of families either already or proposed to be displaced.

By 1936, the County Council had acquired the 4 huge fields of former Springwell Farm, which previously had been Blantyre Golf Course then subsequently, a poultry run. The fields were bordered by Auchinraith Road, Glasgow Road, Auchinraith Pit and some older homes at the south east of Springwell and were ideal for construction being relatively flat and well drained. With housing shortages manifesting all over Blantyre, and illegal 'squatting' becoming commonplace the plan was to build nearly 400 modern homes at a quick pace, whilst demolishing Blantyre's slums.

The nearby Auchinraith Pit had closed in 1931 and the NBR line leading to it, unused, was dismantled by 1936 and cleared by 1937. County Architects and planners had however to make the housing proposal fit within the site and within the boundary of the existing Caledonian Railway to the northwest.

Figure 64 Springwell Housing Estate built in 1937 - 1939

Five primary streets would be created, accessed from both Auchinraith Road and Glasgow Road. Burnside Crescent, Parkville Drive, Springwell Crescent, Croftpark Crescent and Auchinraith Terrace, the street of which would follow the curve of the former dismantled railway. Plentiful green, open spaces were planned, including the siting of playparks. With 3, 4 and 5 apartments available, this was to be a modern, affordable scheme that Blantyre could be proud of in a modern age.

On Tuesday 26th October 1937, whilst constructing the homes, 22 year old slater, John Blue of Mossend received head and back injuries when he slipped from a roof. He ended up in the Royal Infirmary Hospital.

In January 1939, Mr John Flynn, labourer of 6 Springwell Crescent was charged under the coinage act of possessing a mould which could make half crown pieces. He was remanded in custody for a week.

On Thursday 15th March 1940, a 17-year-old pithead worker was killed when he accidentally fell down the shaft to the pit bottom, three quarters of a mile down, at Bardykes Colliery, Blantyre. He was George Logan, of the Springwell Housing Scheme. The boy's father, William Logan, who was a contractor for the colliery, was in the colliery office at the time, and when informed of the tragedy, he collapsed and had to receive treatment in the ambulance room.

The Brown Tragedy

A terrible, heartbreaking tragedy was felt in Spring 1947 by Blantyre people, Mr and Mrs Matthew Brown. The couple, of 17 Springwell Crescent sadly lost their son Norman Brown, a Navy officer who had been discharged only 3 months earlier. Norman was only nineteen years old. The couple buried their son in High Blantyre Cemetery. Consumed in their grief, it was a week that would change their lives. Not just one day upon returning from the funeral, their other elder son, twenty one year old Alexander Brown also died at the family home. Alexander was formerly a miner, but had not enjoyed good health for almost two years. He had been confined to hospital for some time, but was discharged some months earlier, and had been under medical care at home for some months.

Springwell Crescent Fire

A bricklayer, Frank Dunsmuir (27), was the hero of a fire which broke out in the early hours in the morning of Wednesday 28th December 1949 in his father's home at 29 Springwell Crescent Blantyre. The house, which still exists today is a four-apartment upstairs dwelling, that time in the county council housing scheme. The occupier was Mr. Hugh Dunsmuir, a 61-year-old retired miner, and also living there was his wife, his son, Frank; a married daughter, Mrs. Mary Penman; and two grandchildren, 11 year-old May Lloyd and 15-year old John Fullarton.

All of the occupants of the house were sleeping in adjoining bedrooms when the raging fire, which almost gutted the entire house, broke out in the living-room, and they had to escape in their night attire. Frank Dunsmuir was awakened by the smell of smoke. When he got out of bed and went to the door of the living room he was met by a burst of smoke and flames. He immediately raised the alarm.

By this time the flames had secured such a strong hold on the house that the occupants had to move quickly to reach safety. Frank, with some difficulty, managed to get to his father, who has been in ill-health for some time taking him downstairs, then returned to the bedroom occupied by his mother. Shielding his mother from the flames with his own body, he made haste towards the door and she was removed to safety outside.

Despite the fact that the house and stairwell by this time was well alight, he went upstairs again to get his married sister , Mrs Penman, to safety, but when he entered the bedroom occupied by her he was almost overcome by smoke and could not hear anything when he called for her.

The room was filled with smoke, so much the walls inside could not be seen. He put his arm through a glass window to make an outlet for some of the smoke, his arm immediately bleeding being badly cut.

As onlookers poured out into the street and called the fire brigade, Frank heard from below that his sister was already safe, and had been rescued from another room. With the smoke clearing enough from the room temporarily, he saw his way back to the stairwell and made his way outside to safety, burned and bleeding.

The fire brigade managed to prevent the flames from spreading to the other three houses in the block. The six people who had been living in the burned-out house were left with only their night attire but neighbours and the community of Springwells came to their assistance that night, providing them with food and shelter.

Figure 65 Aerial view of Springwell Housing Scheme 1950

Photo shows an aerial image of Springwell in 1950. Glasgow Road is to the left, Greenfield Foundry & Engineering works at the back.

Springwell Rates Shocker

A Rates shocker came through the letterboxes of Springwell's residents in April 1978. Families from 43 to 81 Auchinraith Terrace found their rates had risen substantially for the coming year of 1978/1979, despite them having fought and won a rates reduction the year before.

The resident had their rates lowered previously due to recognition that the new East Kilbride Expressway being built was right outside their windows. It had been understood that the rates reduction of £1.10 per fortnight (about £8 in todays money) was to be in force permanently, but residents soon found out it was only to be during the construction of the road works.

Mrs Lilliene Walsh, Secretary of the Springwells Tenants Association angry at the decision took the matter up with Councilors, explaining that their situation of facing out on to the progressing road works had not changed. Today, nearly 40 years on, the problem of seeing the expressway isn't anywhere near as apparent as before from those house due to the trees which have grown to quite a size screening much of the road, but there are still gaps, especially at bridges.

Now clearly, with so many families living there for 80 years, the stories are numerous and would take up a book in itself. Of course much of Springwells Housing Scheme is situated away from Glasgow Road, so we won't go into huge detail for this housing scheme. However as the scheme is so large and with such proximity to Glasgow Road to ignore, there is an important point worth exploring about Springwells Housing Scheme.

Springwells – Lack of Budget

With such huge sums of money spent initially on Springwells Housing Scheme in the late 1930's and the apparent happiness of families in their new homes, a problem soon arose in post WW2 years when the council stopped providing any decent maintenance budgets and concentrated on providing public buildings elsewhere in Blantyre. They left Springwells budget each year lacking any meaningful contribution.

From the early 1960's onwards, Springwells started to become even more neglected by the council. The lack of private housing left council rented tenants constantly waiting for the council workers to conduct repairs and improvements and the situation eventually became intolerable. By the 1970's, Springwell Housing Scheme had started to become run down, appearing neglected in many places and worryingly for residents, homes soon started to be boarded up and people started to move away. Combined with an overwhelming, widespread vandalism problem in the 1970's all over Blantyre, Springwells eventually gained the suggestion of being a notoriously rough neighbourhood.

One family living in fear

Bullet holes, smashed windows, broken bottles, terrified women. Young Blantyre soldier Jim Greer must have seen it all during his service in Ulster. However, when he returned home at the end of January 1978, he saw it all again! He returned home to find his mother living in terror in what was yet another vandal attack on their home in Springwells.

His mother, Veronica Greer (pictured) said, "I'm in a state of near collapse. I need to get out of this area and Jim has enough to worry about dealing with events in Ulster. "

Mrs. Greer lived with her 13 year old daughter in Auchinraith Terrace at the time. She told police, "after Jim left last year, windows were smashed and somebody even shot out a window with a bullet! Bricks, bottles, dog and even human dirt has been thrown at our house."

MRS GREER, ready to welcome her son home to a house virtually under seige.

Figure 66 Veronica Greer 1978

Her application to move in Blantyre was turned down on account of her having a home already. The last straw came when she awoke one morning to see her door window smashed out. So, she walked up to the Police Station to report it and on her return found that even during that short visit, vandals had returned and smashed her back windows. Vandalism was a huge problem all over Blantyre in 1978. Some public buildings including churches were broken down and residents blamed a perceived glue sniffing youth culture.

Perhaps the Greer family had been targeted as there were no men in the house at the time.

Springwells – Years of Neglect

However, the neglect of Springwells was not caused by people. It was caused by the council. The people of Springwells were, (as they are today) decent, hard working people, from good, kind families, and a strong sense of community, perhaps more so than anywhere in Blantyre. They looked out for each other.

Instead of rolling over and letting the council walk over them or continue ignoring them with no annual proper budgets, the people of Springwell came out fighting in protest, joined forces with each other in order to turn their situation back round to something positive.

Throughout the 1970's and 1980's tenants groups campaigned for modernization, which was always put off by authorities. Council cuts by Government were blamed and Springwells suffered by becoming hard to let. Tenants complained of lack of repairs to houses, poor roads, street lighting problems, inadequate refuse collections, vandalism never cleaned up etc.

During the 1980's an increasing number of empty houses started to appear. The Housing Department called these 'voids.' In 1990 half of the 110 homes in Burnside Crescent were 'voids' boarded up, although this situation was never as bad anywhere else in Springwells Housing Scheme. The empty houses encouraged vandalism. Houses covered in graffiti, regularly broken into and often set on fire.

Figure 67 Burnside Crescent 1978 – some homes boarded up

Springwells – Ending the downwardly spiral

In 1990, Hamilton District Council decided to sell the entire street of Burnside Crescent to a private developer, a most unusual step which saw them dispose of a problematic area for them. Hamilton District Council officials and councilors took this decision with, they claimed, the full support of the tenants of Springwell. In fact, they claimed that the idea of selling Burnside Crescent (named after its proximity to the Parkburn), came from the tenants themselves. Tenants welcomed the decision to sell. They were living in conditions which were intolerable and dangerous. However, residents then had to fight hard to be rehoused. They were kept in the dark , told wrong information, excluded from discussions and generally treated most shabbily. Eventually, at the start of 1991, they were re-houses. The experiences they went though left many people bitter and determined that no other tenants should ever be treated in that manner.

This remarkable story deserves to be told in detail and it is that aspect in 1990 that is researched here with input and fact gathered from the residents themselves who campaigned. Focus is primarily on how Burnside Crescent, Springwells was rescued from that spiral.

Blantyre Project Social Media:

Mary Kirkbride: "I lived in 13 Springwell Crescent from 1947 until 1973, married and now live in Middlesborough. I can still remember all my neighbours names. We had some great times when we were young."

Catherine Sneddon: "We had many a good time in Springwell playing kick the can and hide and seek. I still remember the boys playing football on the big green."

Davy Thomson: "Springwells had the 'big shoap' which sold everything. I can remember Bridie working in it for many years. Next door was the 'chippy' which would sell wee pokes of chips in the 1970's for 10p. My sister worked in it and we would get the leftovers when it closed. On 5th November each year we'd build the biggest bonfires imaginable in the middle of Croftpark. Some of the older boys would always find a 'spare' telegraph pole which was used as the centre piece of the fire. They never failed to get one every year!"

Moira Mulvaney Pacheco: "My Uncle lived in Springwell and raised Budgies and other kinds of birds in his big hut in the garden and never had any trouble. A lot of good school friends came from Springwell and it was a smashing place to be brought up. Happy families, all looking out for each other. Very happy memories reading all this."

Figure 68 Burnside Action Group in 1990

Tenants fight to be heard

By 1990 Burnside Crescent was perhaps the most poorly maintained street in Blantyre. It was said that if you were offered a house in Burnside Crescent and you could afford to wait for a second offer, then you waited. Some tenants had been in Burnside for many years and would have liked to have stayed. But the houses! People became scared of living in a street where half the homes were empty, where gangs of youths gathered, where police were slow to respond, where the Council refused to carry our necessary repairs.

With Blantyre being declared a Special Initiative area in the mid 1980's, Strathclyde Regional Council clearly stated that they wished to tackle the problems in Blantyre and in particular Sptingwell. The plan was to tackle these along with other agencies, the District Council, the Health Board, as well as the various departments of the Region, such as Social work, Community Education, Police, Roads etc. For the next few years tenants had a succession of professionals from various departments and agencies working in the area to address problems. Some of this was even fruitful. A Block of houses was converted to provide a much needed Pre-5 centre for example. Other work was likely well intentioned. However, it was modernization that tenants wanted.

Blantyre Safe Neighbourhood Project also had good intentions. They busied themselves in surveys, meetings and produced a report concluding it was the standard of housing that was the main problem. The Blantyre Special Initiative formed a Springwell Sub Group made up of residents and officials from Social work, Housing and Police. This group was chaired by District Councilor, Mr. McKillop and Regional Councilor, Mrs Brogan, supported by Coordinator Miss Fiona Robertson.

Figure 69 Burnside Crescent in 1990, half homes boarded up

After a short time, local people however decided to meet separately and formed the Springwell Community Group. Later on this evolved into the Burnside Crescent Action Group, which struggled to get meetings, with authorities preferring to meet the residents group representing all of the Scheme, rather than one street's group.

Then in April 1989, a report appeared in the local newspapers under the headline "Housing Blitz". The District Council had decided to call in a Housing Consultancy , Scotia House, to draw up plans to give Whitehill, Hillhouse and Springwell a facelift. The initial response though was anger as tenants had not been consulted at all. The options were looked at by residents and a new professional arrived in Brian McAleenan, the Project Officer of Springwell Partnership Project. Ten different options were looked at ranging from bringing in Private developers to complete demolition. The idea was that residents would discuss then vote for their preference and take that to the council. The preferred option was to sell Burnside Crescent to a developer after rehousing the remaining tenants. The money paid by the developer would be put back into improving Springwells as a whole and the council got the bonus of being able to claim back the VAT. Springwell rejoiced and envisaged fitted kitchens, new bedroom suites and landscaped gardens. However, unknown to residents, the council still planned to modernize Burnside Crescent and plans to sell to developers were far from being achieved.

Figure 70 Burnside Crescent in 1990, many homes unoccupied

The problem however, was that some residents in Burnside wanted to remain in the area, not be rehoused, and certainly didn't want to buy their own home from a developer. Some tenants refused to go along with the majority plan.

The Council's Decision

By August 1989, as was to be expected, the resident's plan was controversial. Within the Labour Party, opposition to selling off Council houses was strong. Selling to private developers, a first for the area was causing political divides.

In September 1989, Mr McAleenan presented a report to the District Council outlining further detail about how any sell off proposal would work and encouraged the Council to investigate costings for the sale.

On 22nd March 1990, the Policy and Resources Committee finally met to agree whether to sell or not. Many local residents attended the meeting, punching the air and shouting in joy as the Council took the decision to sell off Burnside Crescent for £1m to a Private Developer. Burnside residents, for the best part were pleased on the basis that they thought it meant immediate rehousing. Little did they know the council hadn't even thought of this yet!

Burnside Blight worsens

Even with the 1990 decision made, conditions in Burnside Crescent immediately got worse. Gangs of up to 50 youths congregated there every night, one block of houses became known locally as "the lounge", a favourite gathering point. Vandalism progressed beyond stone throwing and graffiti and on several occasions, cars and debris blocked either end of the street and were set on fire. Taxi drivers refused to enter the street and for the remaining tenants, particularly those with children, were incredibly terrifying. Police were slow and at times non existent. A security firm employed in the area were completely ineffective, admitting this and pulled out.

It was sad to see stigma of the area spreading over Blantyre with others not understanding the situation, wrongly thinking it must have been on tenants making.

Campaigning for Rehousing

No timetable was set in 1990 and residents had no idea when they would be rehoused. Feelings quickly turned to anger at the inaction and lack of communication. Rumours were rife. What would happen to those who refused to leave? Where would they be settled? What if you owned rent? What if the sell off to developers fell through? Nothing seemed to be happening and in Springtime 1990, residents became desperate for answers.

On 23rd May 1990 residents organized an impromptu sit-in in the Pre-5 centre situated on the other side of the Scheme. It was well attended, the offices on the first floor occupied and staff denied access. Eventually, later that afternoon authorities agreed to take a delegation of tenants to the Town Hall. Instead, all the sit in protesters went. Despite this, the result was still no firm assurances on being rehoused but it had made people take notice. The event also attracted huge attention from the press, following deliberate leaks.

The protesters met in meetings throughout May and June that year, the events taking place 3 times a week, forming the Burnside Crescent Action Group. (BCAG). The group organized placards and banners and repeatedly told Councilors, "its not vandalism we have, its terrorism!". An response in June was to install new security firm, "Allander Security" who opted to try recruiting local people. Also in June, MP George Robertson dropped by the Pre-5 Centre and although sympathized when he saw the street, he said it was outwith his hands.

The Council promised they would discuss it quickly and said they would meet with tenants on 22nd June. Meantime, Burnside residents asked their neighbours in other streets to join in their campaign.

The councils promised meeting took place in Springwells Neighbourhood Hall on Friday 22nd June 1990 at 2pm. It was very well attended and the meeting opened in perhaps not the best way with authorities commenting on the nature of the campaigns becoming darker and of troublemaking attitude. However Councillor Malcolm Waugh kept things on track and intimated the plan was certainly to get residents rehoused before the street was sold and work on regenerating the homes started. This was a major step forward and what many tenants wanted to hear. A timetable was presented regarding the developers work, but frustratingly did not have the tenants rehousing on it.

Negotiations and the deal

Now, you may be thinking already, why on earth did the council take so long to rehouse residents. Well, truth be told, like most council related matters, it was to do with money. Unknown to residents at that time, in the background the councils negotiations were not going well with developers. The resale value of each house in Burnside Crescent had dropped from £4,000 to only £1,000 per house! The price the developers were willing to pay had fallen from £1m, to just £400,000 for the whole street. It hugely affected the proposal and the amount available to regenerate Springwells and threatened also to undermine the whole proposal. It was clear the Developers were using the press coverage and urgency of the situation to their advantage.

The "cat was out the bag" on 26th June when one of the tenants attended a meeting in the council's public gallery and heard for himself how the value had dropped. Additionally, it was heard that rehousing may actually take another 6 months. Just one day later when this news was relayed to the BCAG, the angry group decided to properly organize themselves electing committee members and once again staged another sit in, this time in the Housing office on 12th July. An indication of the mistrust of the authorities at that stage was demonstrated by tape recorders being hidden in the room and at future meetings, in case things were reneged upon further.

By the end of July 1990, there were 24 developers lined up and a selection process primarily based around price was continuing. Meantime Allander Security had brought some of the vandalism under control. Part of a problem the tenants group had at this stage was that they became more interested in the money that would go to Springwells as a whole, for this is where they hoped to be rehoused. The developer of course more interested in Burnside Crescent, poles apart from the residents hopes and promises.

Figure 71 Burnside Crescent houses in winter 1990

> Blantyre Project Social Media:
>
> **James Cambridge:** "I was born and raised in Springwell and had great neighbours. I bought my first house there too. Lots of family still live there but it's different these days. Everyone once knew everyone but its very impersonal now, perhaps like everywhere, neighbours keeping themselves to themselves."
>
> **Natalie Ward:** "I grew up in Springwell and loved it. I wouldn't change a thing. Sadly on one point though, the area seems to again be at the bottom of the Council's list in terms of getting anything fixed or done. I hope this is addressed going forward."
>
> **Elizabeth Cushley Weir:** "I loved Burnside Crescent and remember the street games. Mums & dads joined in and stand 'blethering' at neighbours gates."

In August, the situation was alleviated slightly when it was announced by the council that tenants being rehoused would receive a financial payment for being rehoused. This was unexpected and ranged from £300 for people living in houses under a year to £1,500 for being in homes more than 5 years. As residents were being rehoused anyway, the news was considered as a bonus. The news was also welcomed when it was further announced on 22nd August that those owning rents would have their rent debt deducted from the financial payment, again those in debt, seeing this as win-win. Council repair bills for them leaving would be scrapped, for no new council tenants would be moving into these council homes. The financial good news continued when the council agreed to pick up all home moving costs.

The bad news however, issued at the same time as these sweeteners, was that re-housing would take until February 1991 due to plans by the developer. More bad news followed when it was suggested that temporary housing may be the answer in the short term.

The meeting held on 11th September to discuss all this latest news was relatively calm, residents more or less glad that their finances were being considered. Residents more or less accepted they would be spending one more Xmas at Burnside Crescent. At the end of November the council's rent department made a mistake or epic proportions, sending rent demands to all the residents, contrary to the promises made to them by Councilors. The matter was quickly deflated though and appeased.

Finally, on 29th November 1990, Bellway Homes was announced as being the preferred developer. The Christmas period out the way, tenants finally started to get rehoused, many suspicious that the delay in rehousing had entirely been due to awaiting the council to sign the dotted line with Bellway.

By mid February 1991, most of the Burnside Crescent tenants had been rehoused, in homes they found very acceptable and with payments made to them relatively smoothly. The Council had found 50 homes all over Blantyre. It left a mixture of emotions with many people convinced they would have been happy being modernized in Burnside Crescent. The whole process had left nerves shattered, stressed people to the hilt, seen health suffer and of course had seen people live through terror in their own streets for several years. 110 homes were bought by Bellway, which undertook work quickly after, selling them off as private housing no doubt for a handsome profit.

It was difficult for many former Springwell residents to read the Hamilton Advertiser report in February 1991, where Councilor Tom McCabe so openly and blatantly and in true Council propaganda style, had commented how smooth the whole process had been!

Glasgow Road Eastern Railway Bridge

Ok, lets get back to the task at hand and back to examination of Glasgow Road. Crossing over Glasgow Road at its junction with Whistleberry Road once was a railway bridge, leading from Auchinraith Junction to the busy Craighead Railway Junction, part of the Caledonian Railway.

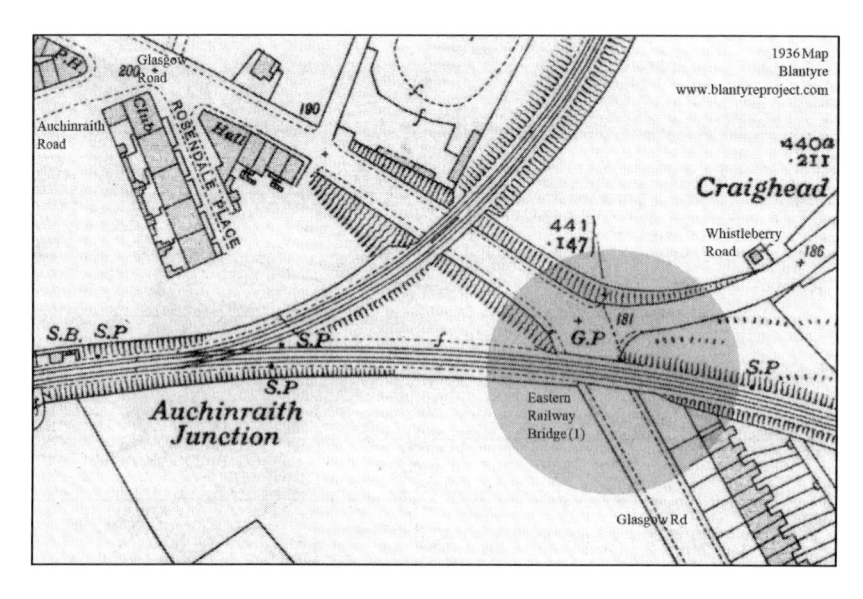

Figure 72 Glasgow Road Eastern Railway Bridge 1936 map

Constructed in 1882, the iron railway bridge traversed over Glasgow Road and could accommodate two passing trains.

Figure 73 Rebuilding Glasgow Road Eastern Railway Bridge 1931

Pictured in 1931, is the arrival of William Arroll Contractors to remove the old 1882 railway bridges all over Blantyre. They started at this southern most bridge, labeled as "Bridge 1" commencing work in September 1931. Pulley cranes were brought to site to remove the old girders, constructing the new bridge in two halves.

A high resolution copy of this photo, when zoomed in is very revealing. Workmen had set up a welfare compound on Glasgow Road, as pictured in the foreground, below the poultry run fields. The compound included a cabin as protection against elements for the workers, jackets seen hanging up on the outside of it. Glasgow Road all along the tramlines was cobbled, although this would change when the lanes were removed shortly after. The road below this bridge was maintained as open, but trams had stopped running, several months earlier. A sign placed in the middle of the bridge in these different days of health and safety, warned tram passengers on upper decks to "Please sit down and mind your heads!"

The remarkable series of photos over the next couple of pages show the different stages of the work, from removing the girders, to placing the new bridge beams into position and a completion inspection. This necessary work also prepared for the widening of Glasgow Road later that decade and it is clear authorities had no idea how rapidly this line would decline afterwards.

By Paul D Veverka

Figure 74 Eastern Railway Bridge 1931

Figure 75 Work at Night September 1931

Figure 76 Ready for new girders 1931

Figure 77 New Girders arrive by rail

Figure 78 New Girders ready 1931

Figure 79 Inspecting completed deck

Figure 80 Completion of Eastern Railway Bridge deck 1931

By the end of 1931, the bridge work had been completed at this location and contractors moved westwards on to the next bridge. Although the line ceased use in 1960, it would take another 2 decades for the dismantled railway and bridge to be entirely removed. Today, no bridge exists at this location, now a small roundabout at the entrance to Lidl, Farmfoods and B&M stores.

Figure 81 The Completed renovated Eastern Railway bridge in Winter 1931

Figure 82 Contractors demolishing the Eastern Railway Bridge in 1980

Lowering Eastern & Western Railway Bridges

When the Lanarkshire Tramways introduced double decker covered trams in 1924, the height clearance at Eastern and adjacent Western Railway Bridges crossing over Glasgow Road at Springwells, had to be considered. This was dealt with by lowering the Glasgow Road by 3 inches at this location. It was not the first time adjustment to height clearance was required at this location as the next article demonstrates.

Glasgow Road Western Railway Bridge

Figure 83 Comparison 1898 and 1910 Maps Western Bridge

Another earlier bridge existed near to Bridge 1, at a more westerly position on Glasgow Road. It was situated where today the pedestrian road crossing is adjacent to Lidl Superstore. The line dates from February 1863, but the bridge actually started out as a tunnel under Glasgow road. The railway leading up from the main Glasgow to Hamilton Line had to cross Glasgow Road and did so by means of a small tunnel, but large enough for 2 trains to pass. It then progressed westwards to Auchinraith Junction then up to High Blantyre Station.

In 1903 upon the arrival of trams in Blantyre, trams could not climb the steep incline up over the railway tunnel, so work had to be done to this structure, and indeed the surrounding railway spur. This involved realigning Glasgow Road, changing its levels significantly at this location by reducing it around 3 or 4 foot and building a new raised embankment to the east of

Chalmers's Land and new western railway bridge. Trains could then go over Glasgow Road, similar to the Eastern Bridge nearby whilst trams and traffic ran under the bridges along Glasgow Road. Comparison of the 1898 and 1910 maps of Blantyre show this to good effect. It is for this reason as demonstrated below, that there is currently an unusual profile and unusual steepness to Glasgow Road at that location today.

The subsequent Western Railway Bridge was known as "Bridge 2", the Western Railway Bridge or sometimes as Whistleberry Railway Bridge. To the immediate west was Chamber's (Chalmers) Land on the south of Glasgow Road and from the mid 1920's onwards, the entrance to the former greyhound racing track on the north side. To its east was the other rail bridge.

Figure 84 In 1898, the road was 4 foot higher and trains ran under a road bridge

After William Arroll Contractors finished replacing the girders on the Eastern Bridge 1 in 1931, they moved attention to Bridge 2 to its west. Work commenced in January 1932 and by March it was well progressed.

Blantyre Project Social Media:

Jay Stone: "I remember the railway bridge across from my Granny's house. We were sent for messages and would need to go under it. Very exciting as there were no paths. You had to watch for cars, then run fast! If you got back safely from the errand (usually with Woodbine for my Uncle, we would be rewarded with a penny or two for sweets. Talk about child safety!"

John McCourt: "I climbed the bridge ladders when I lived in Rosendale"

Figure 85 Work begins in 1932 to replace Railway Bridge 2

Figure 86 Western Railway Bridge 2 replacement progresses 1932

Figure 87 New Western Bridge 2 arrives ready to be placed 1932

The bridge replacement progress photos were taken on 6th March 1932. This and the other bridge were a notable landmark on Glasgow's Road for any early traffic. The railway line ceased to operate in 1960 and quickly fell into disrepair, being dismantled shortly after. Whilst the line was removed, the bridge remained right into the late 1970's before being entirely removed.

The adjacent railway embankment provided a good vantage point on the North side of Glasgow Road for spectators to watch the nearby Speedway. The modern photo was taken from spare ground at nearby Chalmers Land, courtesy G. Cook.

Figure 88 West Bridge 2 in the 1970's

Osadorous Michikas vrs Lanarkshire Trams

DID YOU KNOW?

An action in which Osadorous Michikas, vanman, 102 Main Street, Bellshill sued the Lanarkshire Tramways Company for £500 damages for personal injuries was heard on Thursday 1st February 1917.

Figure 89 Glasgow Road between the Bridges in Winter 1931/1932

It was stated by the Mr. Michikas that on April 5th 1916, he was driving his employer's horse and lorry along the road from Blantyre to Burnbank and he suggested that when he was nearing Whistleberry railway bridge, one of the company's' tramcars was driven into the rear end of his lorry on Glasgow Road, with the result that the lorry was swung round, and his right leg was crushed between the lorry and the sleeper fence on the left side of the road. For the defence, it was stated that the horse panicked and swerved round on the pavement, with the result that the rear end of the lorry was swung round and thrown against the tramcar. Both sides of the story was heard and the hearing was adjourned.

The case resumed on the Friday and the jury were absent for 55 minutes before they came back with the verdict that Mr. Michikas was being truthful and that he should be compensated. Mr. Michikas was awarded £175 in damages, a sum today worth £14,000. However, the tramways company was unwilling to accept the verdict and wished to fight further.

In the Second Division of the Court of Session on Tuesday 26th June 1917, before the Lord Justice Clerk and Salvesen, Guthrie, the Division disposed an application by the Lanarkshire Tramways Company for a new trial stating that it should be refused. The Division refused the motion for a new trial, advised the tramways to drop any talk of further action and re-applied the February verdict in favour of Mr. Michikas, with expenses to him.

> Blantyre Project Social Media:
>
> **James Faulds:** "I remember crossing the railway where the old bridge used to be when we wanted to play fitba at Rosendale Park. Adults used to have a gambling tossing school at the Rosendale side, handy as they could watch for police coming from every direction. Police came often and I remember watching people grab their money to regroup later."

Vandalism at Springwells

In August 1978, vandals turned towards the new leisure area in Springwells on what had previously been an eyesore of wasteground. A £90,000 scheme was underway to turn the ground into a play area, with landscaped grassed areas. However, shrubs had been attacked and up-rooted, as quickly as they had been planted and the project was not due to be finished until the end of that year.

The expensive ash play-park to the south of the Springwell Housing Scheme had been churned up even before it was finished with motorcycles and cars driving upon it and the brand new goalposts were ruined, by somebody actually stealing the crossbar!

By far the worst damage though was 90 young trees uprooted and left for dead, representing half of the total planted at the taxpayers cost. Hamilton District Council commented at the time that the trees had been taken 10 years to grow in a nursery before being planted in Blantyre, and had died in a month of being out the ground. In the end, those 90 trees were NOT replaced, hence today the play area looks fairly open, rather than having the intended wooded perimeter.

Vandalism thankfully decreased gradually following the renovation of Glasgow Road and the improvement of local housing estates alongside the building of several community halls and further small parks.

Chambers' Buildings

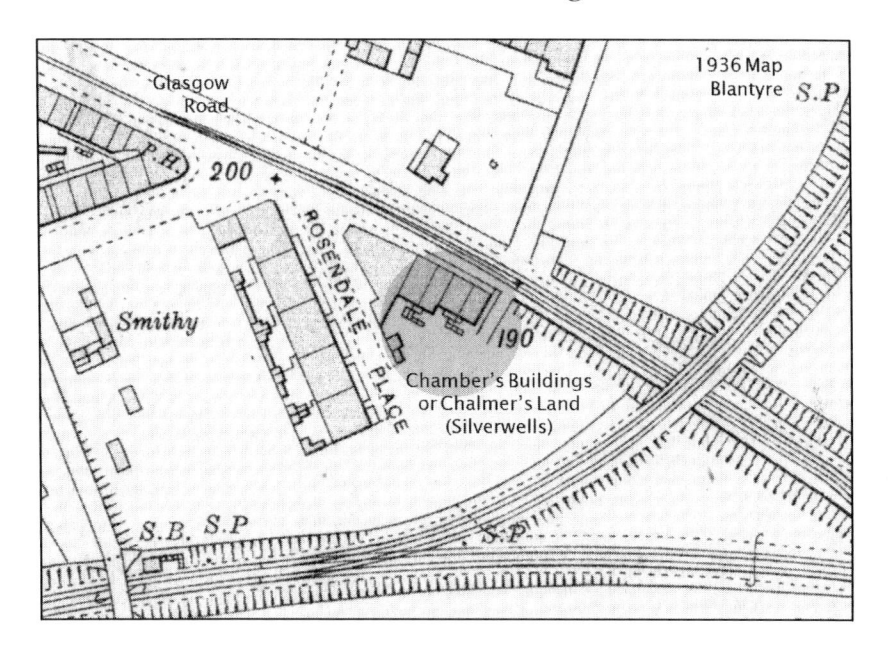

Figure 90 Chambers Buildings on Glasgow Road (1936 map)

Chamber's Buildings was a former double tenement situated on the south side of Glasgow Road, adjacent to the Western Railway Bridge and directly opposite the entrance to the Greyhound Racing track. Unusually for Glasgow Road these tenements were all homes with no shops. The property was initially known as "Silverwells" or Chalmers Buildings, an early adaptation of the surname 'Chambers.' It is unknown how the name Silverwells came about.

Formerly a miner, Mr William Chalmers is noted in 1879 Naismith's Directory as a joiner and builder. He was one of the final tenants who lived at Springwell (Farm) House prior to it being demolished. He may have been related to the Chalmers wood merchants of Motherwell (one of whom would be responsible for the construction of the Model Hostel in later years).

Around 1879, William purchased a small plot on empty farm fields approximately 100 yards in front of Springwell House from owner Janet Jackson of Old Place. The area would surely have felt home for him and the land may have been inexpensive due to its proximity to the "Loop Line" on the nearby Caledonian Railway.

During 1879 and 1880, William Chalmers set about to construct two adjoining tenements, the western one slightly larger in area. The tenements were stone built with slated roofs and opened out directly on to Glasgow

Road, which in those times was still relatively unpopulated. Chamber's Buildings was a relatively early Glasgow Road property. Access to the upper floors was to the rear, the entrance to which was located on the eastern side of the property. The tenements were two storey, but appeared taller due to the addition of attic rooms with dormer windows, which provided the effect of 3 storeys in each building. Initially there were 17 homes squashed into those 2 blocks. The surname of Chalmers around this time was interchangeable with Chambers and the name of "Silverwells" on "Chalmer's Land" was founded.

In 1881, when the houses were completed, William immediately put them all up for sale, which must have been his intention all along for a quick cash profit in such times of booming population in Blantyre. He may have however, continued to operate a small haulage business from the rear outbuildings. Chalmer's Land is noted within Enumeration District 6 in the 1881 Blantyre Street Index.

The buyer was Mr. David Gardiner Dunn (b1831), a Cambuslang coalmaster and he would be the new owner for some time. David lived at 11 Knowe Terrace, Pollockshields, Glasgow.

He was assisted by factor Alexander Peters, a joiner from nearby Springwell. Alexander Peters born in Blantyre in 1854 was an established tradesman, but employed rather than self employed and moved to Silverwells between 1881 and 1885.

Figure 91 Chambers Buildings on Glasgow Road in 1950

In 1891, Alexander Peters was 37 years of age, married to an Islay woman named Annie, a year older. With them were daughters Annie aged 9, Margaret 1 month and sons John 11 and Colin aged 2.

When Alexander Peters moved to Silverwells, 2 of the homes became 1 and Alexander, factor of the houses lived in the larger house, renting in 1895 for £8 per annum. The other 16 homes at Silverwells had rents from £4, 16 shillings and were let out mostly to miners, all payable to owner David Dunn. It is noted that in 1895, Chalmers Land was part of a district with both water and drainage, something that wasn't available in some other parts of Springwell.

Local man drowns

DID YOU KNOW ?

On Saturday 15th August 1903, Mr William Cochrane of Chalmer's Buildings went missing. On Wednesday the following week, the body of the thirty three year old was found in the River Clyde between Caldervale and the River Clyde. It was unknown what happened to him.

New owner

By 1905, the houses had been divided further and 18 homes existed, a number that would remain for the rest of the life of the property.

The name 'Silverwells' vanished between 1891 and 1895, perhaps due to the fact that Silverwells was in name more well known in Bothwell and Hamilton.

The homes in 1895 were let out to widows and miners with rent ranging from £4, 16 shillings up to £8, 5 shillings. One of the homes still belonging to David Dunn was empty that year. At the back was ground belonging to James Stein and John Colvert. By 1896 adjacent Rosendale had been built. By 1900, the adjoining Caldwell building had been built, explored later.

In 1909, David Gardiner Dunn died, aged 78. The property passed to John Grant Sharp of 172 Buchanan Street, as his trustee. In every subsequent census and valuation roll throughout the 20th Century, this building would thereafter always be referred to as "Chamber's Buildings" although the name "Chalmers" was still used verbally from time to time, even with residents.

By 1915, Chamber's Buildings were still occupied by miners and their families, rents from between £5, 13 shillings and £9. The postal addresses of 51-59 Glasgow Road (odd numbers only) were allocated to the 18 houses. More specifically, 14 houses were at address 51 Glasgow Road, and the other 4 homes were individually, 53, 55, 57 and 59 Glasgow Road, the latter addresses being larger.

In 1915, the tenants at number 51 were Robert Buchanan, Richard Wright, Thomas Cook, Jackson Stevenson, Patrick Connor, John Hutchison, Alexander Cook, James McFaulds, John McGuire, William Hendry, John Cook, James McCrory, Michael Stephen and Edward Lawrie. At 53, 55, 57 and 59 were John Beggs, Samuel Dawson, David Buchanan and Thomas Shaw, all miners. It is safe to say the Cook family were well represented at this property.

Figure 92 Location Line Drawing putting Chamber's Buildings in context

Around 1920, John Grant Sharp who owned Chamber's Buildings also owned ground at the back, which was set out as a Quoiting Green by miner John Robertson.

In 1924, John Grant Sharp, who was also Captain of the nearby Blantyre Golf Club died in Cathcart, aged 71. The property passed to Margaret Sharp, acting as executor of John and trustee of David Dunn.

In 1925, she was renting out to many miners families and also ground being used by Archibald Menzies, a blacksmith who lived at nearby Auchinraith Road. In 1930 all 18 homes were still being rented out by Margaret Sharp. The valuation roll that year incorrectly notes James Kelly's properties further west as being Chamber's Buildings too, when in fact the name Chambers only related to these 2 tenements.

Worth noting, Mr. Kelly, local publican did not own Chambers Buildings.

Chambers Building – Deaf man dies on the ice

Tragedy befell a Blantyre man on 21st December Christmas 1927. Along with two others, John (or James as some reports confirmed) Cook (20) of Chalmer's or Chamber's Land, Blantyre set out for stroll, and eventually reached Bothwell Bridge, where a pond beside the river was frozen.

Cook, who was a deaf man, but impetuous youth, suddenly left his companions and slid across the ice. Richard Wright, his friend noticed that certain parts of the ice seemed rather thin, and he called the attention of Cook by signing him using signals he would understand trying to make him aware of the danger. Cook laughed and waved his hand. Suddenly a crack was heard, and the John Cook disappeared, straight under the River Clyde ice!

Richard attempted to cross the ice, but got himself into difficulty in the thin ice, and it was only with a struggle that he reached the riverbank again. The other companion ran for aid, while Richard got to the opposite side and obtained a large branch, which he held over the hole where Cook had disappeared, but all efforts were absolutely in vain. No hands came back up to grab that branch.

It was fifteen hours later, with the aid of Glasgow expert, that the body was recovered by means of grappling-irons. John Cook was popular and well known in Blantyre, where he resided with his mother. His father and sister at the time were in America, and only a few weeks before his death, John had his photograph taken professionally, to send to them for Christmas along with other presents.

The funeral of John Cook (20) took place on Christmas Eve 1927 with crowds of sympathetic spectators lining the streets. Amongst the spectators was Richard Wright, the man who made a gallant rescue attempt. It would not be the last time the River Clyde ice claimed young Blantyre lives.

"Read More about **Chamber's Buildings** online. Scan our handy QR Code for more narrative and photos at Blantyre's History Archives.

Further information, photos and commentary from readers are added from time to time. Learn about QR codes at the beginning of this book."

The end of Chambers Buildings

David Allan & Sons Billposting Ltd leased the gable of number 51 to advertise, something they did at many Glasgow Road properties. Post WW2 years, they erected an enormous billboard directly across from the building on the north of Glasgow Road. During the 1950's public lavatories were built directly across the road from Chamber's Buildings, near the entrance to the greyhound track. The grassy embankment between Chamber's Buildings and the railway line was never built upon.

The area significantly changed at the end of the 1950's and early 1960's. Just before the nearby railway line ceased to operate and was dismantled in 1960, Chamber's Buildings was demolished in 1959. They had lasted 80 years and were likely in need of modernization by comparison to several new housing estates in Blantyre. Proximity to the nearby former Auchinraith Pit and previous underground workings may also have been a factor. Some Chamber's Buildings residents are known to have moved to Wheatlands and to High Blantyre to new homes that had recently been built.

A725 East Kilbride Expressway

The important infrastructure roadway link in the area is designated the A725, which bypasses Blantyre after crossing over Glasgow Road and takes traffic from the Raith Interchange to East Kilbride. It feeds Blantyre at various slip roads. The section from Whirlies Roundabout to Raith Interchange resulted from the need to provide higher quality routes from Hamilton to East Kilbride and replace the inadequate A776 Stoneymeadow Road from High Blantyre and the B7012 via Bothwell Bridge. It was eventually included within the recommendations of the Greater Glasgow Transportation Study as a proposed dual carriageway link to the M74.

Five Centuries separate two Bridges at the end of Blantyre, spanning over the Clyde at Bothwell. One is an ancient bridge, designated an ancient monument and steeped in history. The other is the road bridge built over the water when the final section of £12.2m East Kilbride A725 Expressway was built in 1983. The expressway, so vital to commuters today, was constructed in 3 phases.

The first stage of the Expressway was built between Crossbasket and the Whirlies roundabout at East Kilbride. You would drive out of High Blantyre on to a fast road. Built in 1966 and 1967, it cost over £600,000 at the time, a lofty sum by comparison to the original budget of £382,000. This section of the Expressway was then and still is named officially as Hamilton Road, with the EK Expressway the official name of the future road that was to be built from High Blantyre to Raith. In January 1967, stories were filtering to the press about escalating costs due to unforeseen ground conditions and behind 2 months late. Councilors spun stories about how the straight, modern road would negate the need of Stoneymeadow Road traffic, returning the Stoneymeadow Road back to having a more rural feel. Mr John Adamson, the county roads engineer released progress updates to the press, staying in January 1967, "Road conditions have been worse than we anticipated" but he would not reveal the escalated cost sum and it was not known until completion. During construction, instances of accidents on Stoneymeadow Road were as frequent as ever and the public in general looked forward to a more modern and direct route to East Kilbride, which avoided the traffic hazard of General's Bridge. This section eventually opened in April 1967. There is a wide tunnel under the Expressway at High Blantyre. The tunnel permits water coming off the upper Southern slopes of Blantyre to safely travel under the expressway heading back into the Calder on the northern side of the road. Contractor was James, Anderson & King. Designer was Lanark County Council.

Figure 93 The Second phase of EK Expressway opened in October 1978

2) The second phase was Crossbasket to Auchinraith. This involved removing the pit Bings on Auchinraith Road and at Priestfield, which was done in 1975. It extended the A725 from the present eastbound sliproad at Stoneymeadow Road adjacent to the General's Bridge, and connected to the roundabout at Auchinraith.

It opened in October 1978 its cost spiraling hugely due to unexpected land acquisitions. Further construction difficulties saw the road being re-profiled once the project was underway, and costs ended up being £5.2m. The slip roads at High Blantyre at Douglas Street were added in 1994 and 1995. Contractor was Murdoch MacKenzie Ltd. Designer was Strathclyde Regional Council.

Figure 94 East Kilbride Expressway crossing over A724 Glasgow Road today

3) During 1983, the final section was constructed from Auchinraith down to the roundabout at Raith, which was particularly expensive due to having to overcome the Bothwell Bridge itself. The expressway crosses over Blantyre's Glasgow Road next to the Lidl Supermarket at the site of the former Caldwell Hall and Rosendale Place.

Great care had to be taken around the old Bothwell Bridge protecting it fully as parts of it dated to the 15th century. The Bothwell Bridge was built between 1400 and 1486. According to the expressway architects, evidence of that original bridge is still located within the core of the existing Bothwell Bridge. During the Expressway construction, the contractors were able to dispel a myth that somehow a 5th arch would be under the road approaches.

This was not the case and the bridge was confirmed as only having 4 arches. Of course today, the portcullis tower is no longer there either and the bridge was reconstructed in the 1820's. The Expressway saw a Blantyre wish for better infrastructure be fulfilled that was first mooted a generation before. It was finally completed and opened fully on December 15th 1983 although of course the other sections had been opened for some time before this. The final cost of the whole expressway was around £18million, which by today's standards would have cost £52m.

Councilor Malcolm Waugh of Strathclyde Regional Council upon opening the completed road announced, he had also been personally waiting for that day to happen, which would finally see an end to congestion in Blantyre's Glasgow Road and Main Street. It was also a historic day for William McAlonan who was one of the design team responsible for producing the huge and massively complex Whirlies Roundabout at East Kilbride. Contractor was Murdoch MacKenzie Ltd. Designer was Strathclyde Regional Council. Today, tall trees line the expressway, both sides actually quite green, something which should look even more impressive in a generations time.

> Blantyre Project Social Media:
>
> **Stevie Gill:** "I used to play on the stretch of new motorway on bikes, before it officially opened. What a racetrack that was!"
>
> Speaking of the underpass under the Auchinraith Roundabout shown in the earlier photo, many Blantyre residents wanted to speak out with their story.
>
> **Ray Couston:** "I was chased through this underpass by 'neds' when I was about 14 for simply walking past them at the entrance to the Industrial Estate and keeping my head down. I escaped up the steps into Timbertown. I always later avoided this underpass, even now I still prefer to walk along the mucky path at the side of the road in the daylight. Mentally scarred for life!"
>
> **Donna Campbell:** "This was our playground in the 1970's. Sad to say, but I knew there was a 'glue sniffing brigade' near that underpass."
>
> **William Mullen:** "I got in a fight near that underpass in 1979. The polis came and tried to lift me saying I'd been seen with an axe, no less! However, it was ma stookie they saw, a plastercast on my arm. Walked away a free man."
>
> **Marie Rodwell:** "I lived near the Industrial Estate for 26 years and knew this underpass well. Not one time in all those years did I even want to use it. You just never knew what would be lurking down those dimly lit tunnels out of sight of passing cars and people."

Rosendale Place

Rosendale Place was a former large 3-storey tenement, situated just off Glasgow Road at the corner of Auchinraith Road, commanding an elevated vantage point above and to the rear of Chamber's Buildings and Caldwell Buildings. In the 20th Century, across was road was The Horse Shoe Pub (Kelly's Bar or Kelly's Corner Pub).

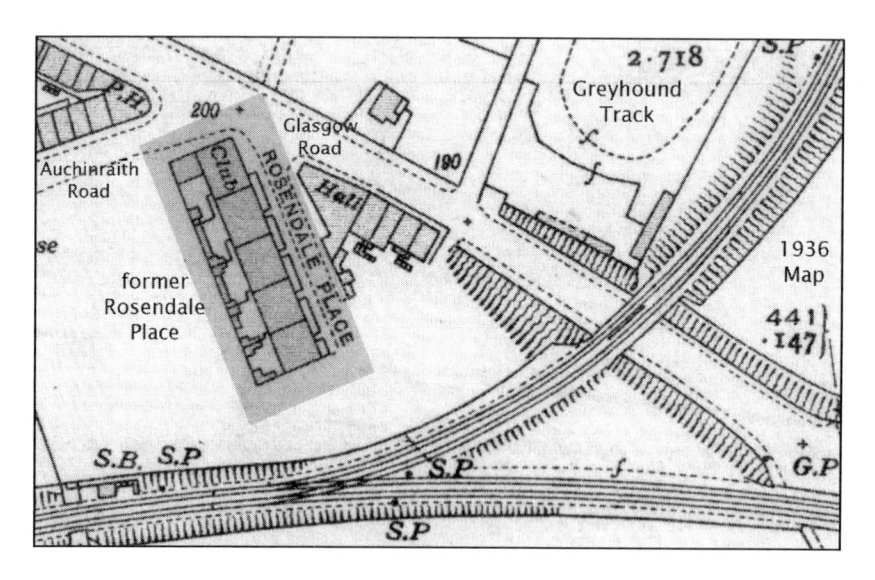

Figure 95 Rosendale Tenements beside Glasgow Road on 1936 map

The building was known as 'Rosendale Place when first constructed, although after 1905, this was the name of the street in front of the tenements. The property was also known simply as "Rosendale" and from time to time, although not in any census or valuation roll, "Rosendale Terrace." They would have addresses 1,2,3,4,5,6,7 and 8 Rosendale and never have Glasgow Road addresses.

In 1896, constructor Mr. Adam Kirk bought a portion of land directly behind Chamber's Buildings from nearby Chamber's Land owner, Mr. David Gardiner Dunn. David would sell off the rest of the land he owned in that area a few years later to the constructor of the Caldwell Buildings.

Born in 1853, Adam Kirk was a joiner and not a native of Blantyre. He lived in at 78 North Street, Whiteinch in Renfrew. His construction would surely have been a talking point, for his building was not in a similar style to the rest of the tenements appearing in Glasgow Road due to its use of red sandstone, rather than granite and darker stone. Construction started in 1897 and on the 1898 map, 4 of the 5 tenements were already built, but with no entrance road formed yet. By 1905, the full 5 terraced tenements including shops at the western end had been completed. Outdoor toilets were built at the rear of the properties, for each tenement, although in later years some relief from this situation was provided when a couple of the toilets were relocated into the dark closes. Speaking of the closes, the entrances were on the north side of the building, entered from the street for the lower floor only. Access to the upper two levels was to the rear via steep stone steps, so common at the time everywhere else. Rosendale was to have the appearance of being a bold, well built property and offered miners families an excellent place to stay close to Auchinraith and Craighead Pits.

Figure 96 Rosendale, Springwell Blantyre in 1971. Glasgow Rd foreground

The imposing height of the three storeys, scale and different design must have made an impressive sight to any traveller coming into Blantyre from the East. However, that would have been short lived for by 1900, Caldwell Buildings obscured most of Rosendale from Glasgow Road. Rosendale was to serve as excellent accommodation for many, many families over the decades. The access road, to be named Rosendale Place was to the front of the tenement extending diagonally behind the Caldwell Halls away from Glasgow Road. It was not entered from Auchinraith Road as others may have reported.

Dispelling incorrect facts & myths

It is previously written incorrectly by 'ainother that Rosendale was "built in the early 1880's and erected by David Dale of the Workers' Village and named after his wife Rose." This delightful comment would have been such a romantic piece of history, if it were true. Sadly the account of the construction date and of how it was named is entirely wrong. We take the bold step of correcting it here so it doesn't get perpetuated further. Inaccurate historical accounts require correction, itself a huge motivator for this book. (Sidenote: David Dale died in 1806, some 90 years before the buildings were actually constructed! Additionally, David only married once to his sweetheart Anne Campbell. History records nothing of a 'Rose' existing in his family).

Rosendale was built in 1896 due to the requirement for proper accommodation following the arrival of the coalmining era in Blantyre. It is said, the name 'Rosendale' was decided in a local competition held in the newspaper press, with both winner and how it was called to be, now lost, never recorded. One theory is that it was given such a flowery, beautiful name due to the immediate proximity to the drab Craighead miner's rows across the road and hemmed in on the other side by busy railway lines, bridges, signal posts and junctions. The back of the building looked out on spare ground occupied by a blacksmith, Alexander Menzies. Even at its time of construction, Rosendale was squashed in amongst pollution and industry. What better way to celebrate the name of a new building, than a "dale of roses." This could also have been a reference to Craighead's gardens not too far off from this location. Or as is more likely, it could simply have been a name owner, Adam Kirk liked.

In 1901, newspapers told of an outbreak of smallpox at Rosendale, affecting one man in his 30s. The report comments on Rosendale being one of the most fashionable buildings in Blantyre.

Early Ownership, Shops and Tenants

Adam Kirk rented out every house to local families. Rosendale was divided into 5 tenements. In number 1 were 11 houses, 1 of which was empty in 1905. In number 2, 11 houses, 3 of which were empty. In number 3, 9 houses, 1 of which was empty. In number 4, 10 houses with 2 empty and in number 5, 7 houses. In all there were 47 homes with handy access to the tram network.

In 1905, Mr. Kirk also owned the shops at number 6,7 and 8. Mrs. Agnes Murdoch was renting the large shops at number 6 and 7. At 8 Rosendale was Antonio Tracendo's ice cream parlour. Antonio lived in a house nearby. It is known that Mr. Richard Pickering was also a shopkeeper around this time.

Families living at Rosendale in 1905 included but not limited to Baird, Bryan, Coletta, Colthart, Crawford, Cumming, Davidson, Dent, Dickson, Dixon, Duddy, Dunlop, Elliot, Francenda, Graham, Hanna, Hewlett, Inglis, Kirkpatrick, Law, MacDonald, Mackinlay, Montgomery, More, Murdoch,

Nicol, Niven, Park, Paterson, Paul, Penrose, Polland, Pritchard, Reid, Scoullar, Semple, Sneddon, Spence, Stewart, Thomson, Tinning, Tinto, Watters and Young. When you consider each of these families had large families of their own, you can begin to imagine the hundreds of people who would have lived at Rosendale.

In 1908, Adam Kirk died young aged only 55 at Renfrew. The properties passed to his trustee Thomas Black & Son, of Cambuslang who would continue to lease the homes out to miner's families. During World War One, all the homes were occupied, but the shops, which had been split into 5 separate shops, were all laying empty, perhaps a casualty of the war years.

In 1912, Mr. Alexander McDermott of Rosendale was walking his Pomeranian Dog when it was run over an killed by a tram. He attempted to sue the Lanarkshire Tram Company and the case ended up in the small claims court. However, the verdict was, if Mr. McDermott was going to be in the habit of keeping an expensive dog, he would have to in future make sure it was kept out of harms way. Alexander left with no compensation.

In May 1912, Mr. Samuel McDermott of 3 Rosendale was in the habit of betting as a bookmaker illegally hanging around the corner of Auchinraith Road and Glasgow Road junction. However, during mid May, following anonymous tipoffs by letter, three police officers hid behind the shops and awaited for the illegal activity to begin, pouncing out at the right moment and giving chase to Samuel down Rosendale Place. Samuel ran home and locked himself in the house, refusing entry to the officers, who eventually broke the door down, taking him away to the Police Station. He was later fined.

The ground behind Rosendale was a favourite for bookies. Taking bets on the open air sports ground across the Glasgow Road, and later taking bets on greyhound racing. News stories tell of people being charged for bookmaking illegally even into the 1930's.

Auchinraith Social & Recreation Club

In 1919, the Auchinraith Social & Recreation Club was formed. A working mans club, especially frequented by miners. The club rented the 5 shops from Thomas Black & Son and knocked them through into the one large premises, the club being attached and on the western end of Rosendale in a part of the building that was one storey with a pitched slate roof. It had address 6 Rosendale. The club, essentially a small hall was situated at the corner of Auchinraith Road and Glasgow Road and was the first building encountered at the foot of Auchinraith Road. Small events and classes were frequent and included Scottish Country Dancing classes, which later moved to the Co-op

Halls. Later that Century the club would give up their lease and obtain their own premises further south along Auchinraith Road, nearer to Auchinraith Primary School.

Latter ownership and tenants

In 1916 Mrs. Agnes Downie of 5 Rosendale was going through legal proceedings for custody of her child away from David Greenhorn, a miner from Burnbank.

War did not escape Rosendale. On 8th December 1917, Lance Corporal Thomas McLean of the Scottish Rifles, died in France.

Ownership was unchanged until 1922 when Mrs. Annie Davidson, or Carlton Miller of London acquired Rosendale from Thomas Black & Son, the trustees of Adam Kirk. She was widow of William Imrie who ran the Blantyre Arms Public House. Houses were rented out for around £6 per annum and she continued to lease out the space for the club. At that time, number 5 was leased out Robert MacManus and Alan Robertson. This was still the same arrangement in 1930.

In June 1928, James Murray, a miner aged 26, of 12 Sunnyside Terrace, Coatbridge was awarded a parchment for heroism in life saving. On the 1st June 1928, he saved 8 year old Archibald Hutton of 49 Baird's Rows, and John Hogg (8) of 3 Rosendale Place who both fell into the water at the junction of the Calder and the Clyde, whilst trying to catch minnows.

Rosendale Quads

A rather rare event was talked about for some time after when it became known that a Blantyre woman had given birth to her 4 children, all on the same day. On 9am on Sunday 6th May 1928, the young Blantyre woman, Mrs Flora McLean, wife of miner, who both resided at Rosendale Place gave birth to quadruplets, to four sons in Bellshill Maternity Hospital. Unfortunately though, this story does not end happily. All four were still-born. Mrs McLean was reported by Dr. H. J. Thomson, of Uddingston, who was present, and later advised press who were keen on the story, that the heartbroken mother, was progressing favourably under the circumstances.

An alarming smash took place on Saturday 16th February 1935 at the junction of Auchinraith Road and Glasgow Road, when a large motor lorry, belonging to Ian Fair, Glasgow, and loaded with bricks, and a light motor van owned and driven Mr J. Baird, baker. New Stevenston. Came into collision.

Both vehicles were travelling towards Hamilton when they collided, the van having come out of Auchinraith Road. They crashed into the telegraph pole. The pole and overhead wires were broken. William Stokes, residing at Rosendale Place, was standing at the pole when the wires fell on him, but escaped injury.

On 2nd December 1938, Miss Alice Sharpe, aged 12, daughter of Mr. Matthew Sharpe, Rosendale was killed by a heavy motor lorry. The lorry, which was proceeding towards Glasgow on the Glasgow Road, had to be jacked up to release the girl. She died while being conveyed by ambulance to the Royal Infirmary, Glasgow.

WW2 didn't start well for one Rosendale resident. Pleading guilty to committing a breach of the peace, Patrick Ward, labourer of 4 Rosendale stated at Hamilton J.P. Court on Saturday 2nd September 1939, that he got into an argument with another man about Hitler. "This other man said Hitler was a good man, and I disagreed with him. I used two or three words, and the police lifted me." Imposing a fine of 10s on Ward, the presiding Justice said— "You can't use obscene language in the street, even when talking about Hitler!"

Figure 97 Aerial View of Rosendale in 1950. Caldwell Institute opposite

1950's onwards

At the Queens Coronation day in June 1953, a huge street party took place out the front of the building, in front of opposing Baird's Rows on the opposite side of Glasgow Road, some of Rosendale tenants attending.

By Paul D Veverka

Rosendale families who latterly lived there in the 1940's – 1970's include Barkey, Beaton, Callaghan, Flannigan, Kelly, McCourt, McCue, McIntosh, Rouse, Slaven, Tonner, Walker and Watson.

Some former residents of the 1950's -1960's remember as children local rivalries between Rosendale children and Springwells, which could often end up in fisticuffs, a shame that this happened as Rosendale was a Springwells building too.

Rosendale (A Magic Place when we were young)

There's a wonderful poem about Rosendale written in 2004 by former resident, Brian Cummiskey. It was Brian's first poem with the late James Cornfield adding some old Scots.

Ah' remember the tenement called Rosendale,
In Blantir took fae whence ah' hail,
An ancient place, a bit o' a dive,
But somehow magical, when yur only five.

Ah' remember ma pals an' thur cheeky wee faces,
Thur wee short troosers held up wae braces,
Playin' outside was always a must;
Kickin' a baw in the stoor an' the dust.

Ah' remember the outside toilet wae dread,
Is it any wunner we peed the bed?
Tae go doon there made me awfy unhappy,
Thir wur times ah' wished, ah' still wore a nappy.

Ah' remember the close wae hardly a light,
The ghosts oan the stairs that gave ye a fright,
An gaun tae bed when the time wis just right,
Tae wait fur the Daleks, that came in the night.

Ah' remember ma da' wae his jet-black hair,
Young an ' handsome an' fu o' flair,
A Blantir Dandy some wid say,
But a gentleman always, come what may.

Ah' remember ma mother, a young Snow White,
Always there tae make things right,
Tender, lovin' an fu o' care,
Wae a heart fu' o' love, for us tae share.

> The family remembers those childhood days,
> In auld Rosendale in oor different ways,
> An' as we remember, happy or sad,
> We'll always be grateful, tae oor mum and dad.

Brian wrote the poem for his father's 70th birthday noting that the ghost on the stair was allegedly seen by his father and remembering the Daleks of Dr Who kid's TV programme, where a lifesize replica of one adorned the Co-op windows nearby.

Blantyre Project Social Media:

Gerry Walker: "I was born there in 1960 before moving to Craigton Pl a few years later. Outdoor toilets and a big sink as a bath. Plenty off room out the back to play though."

David McIntosh: "I was born in no. 3 Rosendale Place in 1942. I remember the Queens Coronation party in 1953, it was held out in the street in front of the building. I'm sure everyone who lived in the building was there."

Susan Walker Graham: "I remember going round the back of the pub on the corner and removing the beer bottle lids that used to have cork on the inside. We would make badges with them!"

Gerry Kelly: "After moving, we ended up in the Electric houses."

In post WW2 years, the building was acquired by the District Council, and similar to other buildings in Springwell, little was spent to maintain it. With Chambers Buildings demolished in 1959 and Caldwell Buildings in the mid 1960's, by the end of the 60's Rosendale was sitting alone on that ground, its frontage now on Glasgow Road. It had fallen into disrepair and was in need of modernization.

Resident's Complain and pursue re-housing

In February 1968, residents of Rosendale Building went to the County Buildings in Hamilton to complain about the state of the housing block and the delay in getting them re-housed. Mothers of young children complained that the chimneys were ready to fall, there were no toilets in many apartments, rain was leaking into the rooms and a tarpaulin protected part of the roof. The building was probably badly damaged during the January hurricane of the earlier month. Quite a number of buildings were damaged that night around Blantyre.

Figure 98 Residents of Rosendale march to the Council in 1968

The complaints were upheld and people slowly but surely started to be rehoused from late 1968. Many residents left for the new housing built at Burnbrae and High Blantyre. By the mid 1970's, Rosendale was scheduled for demolition. It was demolished by 1976, before the opposite building at Kelly's corner, an early casualty of Glasgow Road redevelopment. Like Chamber's Buildings, it had existed for 80 years.

Figure 99 Rosendale & abandoned Auchinraith Club in the late 1950's

It has been said that Rosendale was once where Gavin Watson Printers (formerly JR Reid Printers) now is. That is incorrect, as Rosendale was exactly where the A725 carriageway is now and partially on what is now woodland between the A725 and the Low Blantyre slipway. Nearby to its former location, a modern street to a small industrial area, named Rosendale Way is a nod to the buildings existence.

Blantyre Project Social Media:

Ann Marie Herd "We moved out of No 2 Rosendale on 9th August 1968 up to Burnbrae Road with the Sloan's, Phairs, Kellys, McCools and Darcy families. We thought we had won the pools. What a brilliant time we had."

John Lynaghan: "I remember the shows behind Rosendale."

Colin Duffy: 'Mum mum and her family were all born there in number 2."

Ann Hartman: "I remember as a wee girl in the very late 1950's or early 1960's hanging out ma Auntie's window waving a flag because Royalty was passing through Blantyre. We all had a great view of the car passing by."

Thomas Barrett: "My dad and Aunt Mary worked in the Auchinraith Club at the side of Rosendale. I remember climbing into the building at one end and trying to get out the other side. It was a mission to do that as a 9 year old."

James Faulds: "Rosendale was my playing ground. Up the park playing fitba all day and evening long. I delivered papers there and knew almost everybody in the building. It was a great area to grow up around. I remember the Wilkie family living nearby."

Marie McMillan: "My friend Karen and I often played out the back of these houses. I must have been a 'bad lassie' for one time we got a tin out the bins and filled it with puddle water. We then got our other friend Margaret Rouse to drink it, making her think it was juice. Next thing we knew Margaret was taken to hospital and later recovered, but we got a leathering off of parents."

Andy Callaghan: "We lived at 2 different flats. First at number 2, then into number 1. My dad was a miner working at Cardowan pit. All the miners gathered at the corner of Auchinraith Road to get picked up by the bus. I'd walk down with my dad to wave him goodbye. All the men would be chewing tobacco, smoking, spitting and swearing and laughing. I though my dad was odd as he didn't spit or swear. I wanted to spit and swear and wear a bunnet like these men. We left Rosendale in 1954 when I was 6. I loved that place."

Archie Peat: "A lad named Harry (Smith?) was seriously injured when he climbed up a drainpipe at Rosendale and it came away. Wonder what became of him?"

Auchinraith Fairground (The Shows)

Small travelling fairs are known to have visited Low Blantyre since the 1890's. Initially, simple games and booths for boxing matches, the fair arrived at Springwells on an annual basis, but was displaced from the ground in the mid 1920's, with the creation of the greyhound track.

A spare plot was utilized across the Glasgow Road on the south side, behind the Rosendale tenement and with the arrival of mechanized rides, quickly became an established, welcomed attraction for local children.

Figure 100 Travelling Fair visits Blantyre in 1950 behind Rosendale

The location was ideal, on vacant ground near the Smithy at Auchinraith Road. In the shadow of the signal box, a small pedestrian crossing over the railway led Springwells families straight down into the fair. Centrally located, this site was ideal for families coming from all directions.

The fairground, often called "the shows" was set up in Blantyre each Springtime. Travelling families like Laurences, Dan Taylor's and Irvin's are all known to have brought fairs to Blantyre in the 20th Century. Children took delight in going on rides such as "The Whip", "The Steam Yachts" and "Carousel" as well as playing a variety of fun games on several stalls. It was inexpensive and affordable to most working families. A real treat.

The fair visited this location right up until the late 1970's. Today the exact site is the carriageway of the A725 East Kilbride Expressway.

> Blantyre Project Social Media:
>
> **John Daly** "The shows were also later temporarily at the big field in front of Wilkie's Farm at Bardykes. This was 'all the Christmasses' come at once for the Westend Bar across the road!"
>
> **Jim Brown:** "The fair also had a 'What the Butler saw!'"
>
> **Rae Brown**: "I was gutted when I lost my money down some wooden stairs one time at this fair."
>
> **Janette Stark**: "I remember going there. I stayed nearby in Parkville Drive."
>
> **Robert McLeod-Wolohan:** "I remember this well when I lived at Burnside Crescent. I then afterwards took my own kids to this fair until it stopped abruptly."

Caldwell Institute

The Caldwell Institute was a former 3 storey large building, triangular on plan which formerly sat at the corner of Auchinraith Road and Glasgow Road junction. It had frontage on to Glasgow Road and although the very last building in Springwell, was at times described as being at the start of Stonefield, a hamlet within Blantyre.

Constructed of stone with slate roof it comprised of a large hall with upper rooms, 2 or 3 shops and a large house flat. Sometimes known as the Caldwell Halls, this description is a little inaccurate as the Hall was only one part of the building. It had official name as the Caldwell Institute.

In 1899, Mr James Caldwell, MP for Mid Lanark, as owner funded the construction of his Institute. William Adam & Son (Joiners of High Blantyre with their own sawmill) was appointed as the contractor and by summer 1900, the three storeys of the Caldwell Institute was built, adjoining against Chamber's Buildings. Residents of nearby Rosendale may not have been too happy at having such a large building built so soon outside their relatively new homes.

The building was of unusual design, constructed to fit within the corner piece of land. It was taller than adjacent tenements and had space inlaid on the corner for a clock. It is unknown if the clock was ever fitted. Entrances were off Glasgow Road and Auchinraith Road.

William Adam & Son fell out with Mr. Caldwell towards the end of the build over the matter of £60 worth of additional work. The matter could not be resolved between them and ended up in court, where on 21st February 1901, Sheriff Davidson at Hamilton Sheriff Court heard the case. Mr Caldwell maintained that the contract signed incorporated these changes and the action was dismissed with William Adam and Son liable for costs. It was not the first time William Adam took a client to court at the end of a build!

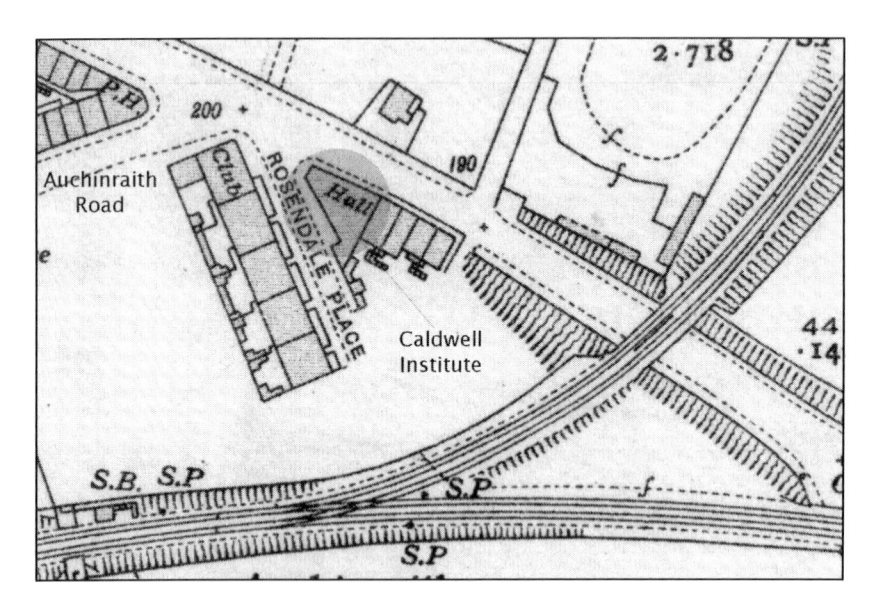

Figure 101 Caldwell Institute shown on the 1936 map

James Caldwell, MP

James Caldwell was a Scottish politician born in 1839. He was certainly no young man by the time he built his Institute in 1899. He was both a lawyer and a wealthy calico merchant of Glasgow and never lived in Blantyre.

He was a new Liberal Unionist MP. His maiden speech emphasized that fair rents fixed by the 1881 Irish Land Act of 1881 had to be paid. He tried to set an agenda on Highland land reform for the Liberal Unionist party and was passionate about this subject. He was first elected for Glasgow St Rollox (UK Parliament constituency) in 1886 as a Liberal Unionist.

In 1890 James went over to the Gladstonians Liberals and stood for them in Glasgow Tradeston in 1892. He was narrowly defeated due to the presence of a Labour candidate. He served as an MP for two constituencies.

James re-entered Parliament as a Liberal MP for Mid Lanarkshire at a by-election in 1894. He campaigned often in Blantyre during that time. The previous Liberal MP, John McCulloch stood down and James triumphed over a Peter MacLiver by 119 votes. He held the seat until he stood down before the January 1910 election.

In 1904 James sat on a Committee considering copyright issues and spoke up for the general public's interest in hearing music ; "copyright is not such an absolute right of property as is claimed but is a "liberty" or privilege , conferred by Parliament with the view of encouraging music in the general community". i.e. he didn't mind about it.

Figure 102 James Caldwell in 1888

The rest of the committee were more minded to side with the music publishers and that it was highly illegal and advised it was downright devoid of morals to copy or take the work of others without crediting them. He was advised by his colleagues that it was the work of a low man of no ability or self worth that did such a thing.

James however felt that the spread of music piracy (at that time distributing printed sheet music freely) was due to the enormous gap between the prices

Figure 103 James Caldwell MP in 1898

charged to the public and the cost of production, but on this instance was certainly on the losing side of the eventual copyright legislation passed. From 1906 to 1910 James was a Deputy Speaker. James died in 1925 aged 86.

Caldwell Institute – Early Years

Figure 104 Rare old image of former Caldwell Institute Building 1936

On 8th October 1900 Mr. Caldwell was canvassing in nearby Cambuslang and it was noted in the newspaper at that time that the Caldwell Institute existed by then. The Institute was more of a public meeting place, a community hall. Many political meeting took place right from the start, some of which may have suited Caldwell's career path. There are stories of 1,000 people packed into the hall to hear speakers during the 1910's. The Hall was located on the first floor, with upper rooms above on the upper storey. It was in these halls that the Stonefield Parish Church held their Sunday school and youth fellowship meetings. The halls were also used for badminton and hired out for social occasions, such as dances. St Joseph's Brass Band often providing the music for some functions. It is known that Blantyre Vics used the hall from time to time.

In 1905, James Caldwell was living at 12 Grosvenor Terrace in Glasgow, one of the most wealthiest addresses in the city. The hall had a rent value of £40 per annum. Mr William Taylor was renting the only house in the building, for £8, 10 shilling his job being the caretaker. Mr. John Sneddon of Springfield Cottage, Glasgow Road was the factor of the homes.

On the ground floor were 2 shops. A small shop was empty that year, but in the large shop was Pasquela Lombardi, confectioners paying a whopping rent of £30 per annum. With rents set depending on square area, this is a good indication that Lombardi's shop occupied much of the whole of the ground floor. Up until 1910 the Holiness mission was using one of the rooms in this building to meet, prior to them building a hut to form the Nazarene Church in Jackson Street.

By 1915 postal address for Glasgow Road had been allocated. The hall was 61/63 Glasgow Road. The Caretakers home also 61/63. The small shop at 65 Glasgow Road was empty as was the large shop at 67 Glasgow Road. Lombardi's look to have moved around 1911. The caretaker had changed and was now John Smith paying rent to the Right Honourable James Caldwell, by then living in London.

One has to wonder what was going on with empty shops around this area in 1915. Whilst the easy answer is that WW1 was taking place, it is not unnoticed that the shops were empty in both Caldwell Institute and the 5 shops nearby in Rosendale. Caldwell Institute would have a long history of those ground floor shops being empty, even well beyond WW1. It is possible the high rates put off prospective shopkeepers or were so high that businesses could not be maintained there.

By 1920 John Smith was still caretaker and the shops were faring a little better. The small shop was subdivided and on one side was Matthew Miller, a boot repairman renting for £9 per annum, who would later move westwards along Glasgow Road. On the other side of the small shop was Thomas McGurk, a confectioner at number 65 Glasgow Road. The large shop at 67 Glasgow Road, again empty.

Change of ownership and use

In 1925 James Caldwell died and his Institute was inherited by his daughter Miss Elizabeth Caldwell, noted as owner in the 1925 valuation roll. It is noted that year that the entire building lay empty, with exception of Mrs. Smith, the widow of the former caretaker. Nobody occupied the shops and they were given over to the storage of Coffins, perhaps for the nearby undertaker who worked at Henderson's Buildings just across Auchinraith Road.

It is around this time that we see the nickname for the property come into play. "The Coffin Hall" was well known as being the Institute building, perhaps also due to the fact the hall was shaped liked a coffin, a narrow western end, broadening out then narrowing again at the east.

Miss Caldwell's ownership would be short. In 1926, with no real connection to Blantyre, she sold the Institute building over to the Central Trustees of the Church of Scotland. The hall, house and shops were now owned by Stonefield Parish Church and their own caretaker was appointed in the form of Mr. Samuel McClements. In 1930, Samuel and his family were the only occupants of the entire building.

From the late 1920's the name Caldwell Institute gradually vanished, replaced by the more common official name as the Stonefield Parish Church Hall, or for the more morbid of Blantyre residents, by the nickname, "Coffin Hall". This name would exist for the remainder of the property's life. Around the same time, the tram stop outside the building became redundant as trams stopped running, replaced by buses along Glasgow Road.

In 1936 the Crawford family moved from the Dales in High Blantyre Main Street into the Stonefield Parish Church Hall building. By 1936, the shops had gone and the lower ground floor knocked through into what would become the Crawford's home. Part of the floor however, was used in 1939 to store mattresses, with no indication any longer of coffin storage.

Figure 105 Alex Crawford and family at Stonefield Parish Church Halls 1946

Mr. Alex Crawford was the Beadle at Stonefield Parish Church from 1936 to 1948 and his position meant tenancy in the Stonefield Parish Church Hall. He supported ministers Rev. James Gibb and Rev. Duncan Finlayson in that time. Their address was 61 Glasgow Road.

George Crawford, (the son of Alex) was born in 1930 was a former resident of Stonefield Parish Church Halls and is one of the boys pictured on the previous photo. Recalling his time at the property, he commented, "Our home was at ground floor level and consisted of a large room with sink, bed, furniture and a small attached bedroom. The rooms were approached from a corridor which gave access to a toilet, clothes washing room complete with an open boiler, a glory hole for small storage and access to a sitting room which had a Chalen piano. Today I regularly play a Yamaha Clavinova. From the sitting room there was access to a bath room. The principle room was across the internal landing from which stairs led (downwards) to a main door and the Shaw hall (left) with kitchen and to the large meeting room (right) Stairs also led (upwards) leading to on the right, a medium sized room, on the left, a toilet room with sink."

He continued, "The principal hall was adjacent. It had a balcony approached from another stairway. The top storey had a toilet room and meeting room. I do remember from the bathroom, the sound of the anti aircraft guns stationed at the Whinns during WW2 and gathering shrapnel and synthetic cords from the streets in the mornings. Each week for one halfpenny we collected Soor dook supplied by Mr Craig from a large vessel situated on a cairt (cart) drawn by a horse. He came from Bellsfield Farm situated off the main street in High Blantyre. Rubbish collection was also made weekly by a horse drawn cart."

During the 1950's it is known that a model railway was laid out in the upper rooms of the building, providing a nice attraction for paying visitors. The whole building was demolished in 1965, some 6 years after the adjacent Chamber's Building. Today, the exact site of the Caldwell Hall is the southern concrete abutment on the modern A725 Expressway Bridge over Glasgow Road.

Blantyre Project Social Media:

Betty McLean: "I remember this well. Very close to where I lived. Kelly's Bar was directly across the road from this hall."

Mary Kirkbride: "My dad always used called this building ' The Coffin Hall. Definitely a nickname for the building used commonly by Blantyre people."

By Paul D Veverka

CHAPTER 6
GLASGOW ROAD SOUTH
AUCHINRAITH RD TO HERBERTSON ST

Auchinraith Road at the junction of Glasgow Road moving westward into Blantyre marks the start of the hamlet of Stonefield, often used to describe much of Low Blantyre. However, before we leave Springwell behind to the east and venture into a much more densely populated area., there is one property that sat on the boundary we still need to look at.

Springwell Farm

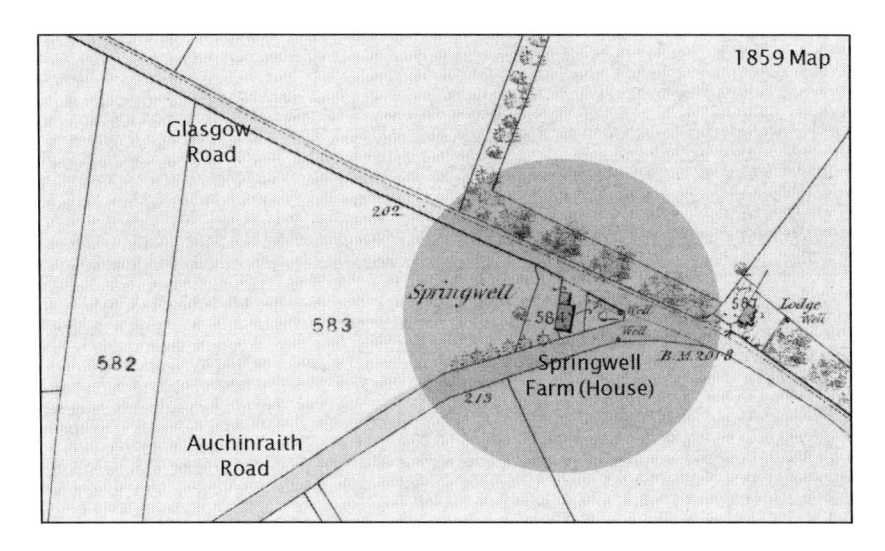

Figure 106 Springwell Farm House on 1859 Map

Springwell Farm is almost certainly the isolated former farmhouse called "Newhouse" marked on Roy's Military Map of 1747. We can therefore say the building was constructed prior to this date, most likely from it's description sometime between 1700 –1747. The name 'Newhouse' appears to have vanished at this location by 1800, (perhaps due to the emergence of a 'Newhouse' Farm at Sydes Brae to the north. The house at Low Blantyre then replaced by the more descriptive, "Springwell". There are indications from census and valuation rolls that Springwell (Farm) house may not have been a working farm by owners, but instead letting out the expansive fields to other farms for use to other farmers, such as nearby Birdsfield.

Valuation rolls and census information as always provide the best detail for ownership. In 1855 Mrs. Margaret Herbertson of Spittal, Cambuslang was the owner of the farm at Springwell, letting out to William Gardner for £60/year. The large rent perhaps indicative of the size of the surrounding fields and farming opportunities. Mrs Herberston may have been the widow of the owner prior to this date. The Herbertson name would later be used for a new street decades later which once formed their western farm boundary. Mrs Herbertson that year also owned a house and grassparks in Springwell which she let out for £4, 10 shillings. She also owned Auchentibber Quarry, letting out for £20/year to Alexander Aitkenhead, a builder. Additionally, she owned 3 homes, one of which had a garden at Auchinraith, most likely along Main Street. Of course these properties were linked by the track stretching north east to south west, which would eventually become Auchinraith Road.

In the 1859 name book, Springwell is described as, "A dwellinghouse in an angle formed by the Parish Road joining the Hamilton & Glasgow T. P. [Turn Pike] Road. There is a small Lodge house on the opposite side of the T. P. [Turn Pike] Road, belonging to the Lands of Craighead. It bears no proper name. The Lodge is the property of Miss Brown" It had changed tenants too with J Craig of Birdsfield working it, Robert Reid occupying it. The description ties in exactly with the time of the previous illustration.

The Herbertson family may have been related to the Jackson family of Spittal and Bardykes. In 1863 Margaret Herbertson died at Spittal and the property appears to have passed to Janet Jackson her daughter through inheritance. In 1865 Mrs Janet Jackson (nee Herbertson), of Spittal, Cambuslang owned Springwell Farm letting it out to James Scott of Auchinraith. She also owned a house, stable and garden in Springwell, as well as a house and loomshop in Auchinraith, including the aforementioned quarry in Auchentibber.

By 1875, Springwell Farm was still isolated, detached and surrounded by fields, although the decade after would see expansive building projects around it. Janet Jackson had moved to Old Place in High Blantyre (in modern day Janefield Place). She was letting Springwell out to farmer Alex Craig of Birdsfield and the house, stable and yard was noted as being in the now forgotten location of "Backside". John Russell of Burnbrae now rented the quarry in Auchintibber and the homes she had in Auchinraith, all occupied. It is likely the fields she owned stretched east of the house all to the south side of Glasgow to Hamilton Road, as far east as the Parkburn.

Between 1875 and 1876, Janet Jackson appears to have sold Springwell Farm, for there is no mention of it after this date and indeed by 1877, it had been demolished and new homes and shops had been built by Mr. William Henderson on the site.

Janet was still alive in 1885 living at Old Place, and although she did not have the farm and fields at Springwell any longer, it is likely she did well through these transactions, with portions of the farm fields sold to many different individuals for development in what would become the hamlet of Springwell. She rented out the mineral rights of Springwell to Merry & Cunningham Coalmasters, giving her a yearly income for the mine workings far below ground she once owned.

This rare, previously unpublished photo taken in the 1870s, prior to 1877 was a Blantyre mystery until now, but this book now suggests it is the former Springwell Farm House shortly before demolition with Auchinraith Road in the foreground, the junction of Glasgow Road just out the picture to the right.

Figure 107 Previously unpublished photo, "Springwell Farm House" c 1876

This former building was the beginning of Springwell, its initial beating heart. Its inclusion in this book is worthwhile and indeed a first, for no other Blantyre historian appears to have written about it yet. In a modern context, it would have been where now the eastern side of Gavin Watson Printers is located.

By Paul D Veverka

Stonefield

The hamlet of Stonefield took its name from Stonefield Farm, further to the west, but their fields stretched eastwards towards Springwell, the boundary being where modern Auchinraith Road is.

During 1846, Samuel Lewis published his topographical dictionary of Scotland. This included some extensive and accurate descriptions of Blantyre's hamlets, which included insights into population and employment. For 1846, in years immediately preceding coal being mined, this provides a wonderful account of how life was in Blantyre before that remarkable explosion growth. It stated, "Stonefield, a village, in the parish of Blantyre, Middle ward of the county of Lanark, 1¼ mile (NE by E) from the village of Blantyre; containing 174 inhabitants. It lies in the north-eastern part of the parish, and on the west bank of the Clyde, which here separates the parish from that of Bothwell. The population of the village is chiefly employed in the manufactures of the district, and a few in common handicraft trades." However all this was about to change with the arrival of many more people in the mid to late 19th Century.

Henderson's Buildings

On the site of former Springwell Farm, throughout the late 19th Century and much of the 20th Century were tenement buildings known firstly as Henderson's Buildings and latterly post WW2 as Kelly's Buildings.

In 1876, the year before the Blantyre Pit Disaster, Mr. William Henderson, a builder of 4 Firpark Terrace, Dennistoun, Glasgow bought the triangular plot of land where the farmhouse had sat only a year or two earlier. He may have been the person who demolished the house to make way for his tenements. Constructed in 1876 and likely into 1877 due to their size, the property was 2 storey, built in tenement style with slated roofs. Set out in a V shape on plan the tenements had frontage on Glasgow Road of around 100 foot and of similar size heading around the corner, going southwards up Auchinraith Road, directly across from later Rosendale building.

Shops on the Glasgow Road ground floor had homes above them. There were no shops on the Auchinraith Road side, only homes. An enclosed yard at the rear was accessed from Auchinraith Road and via 3 pedestrian pend closes, 2 on which were on Glasgow Road.

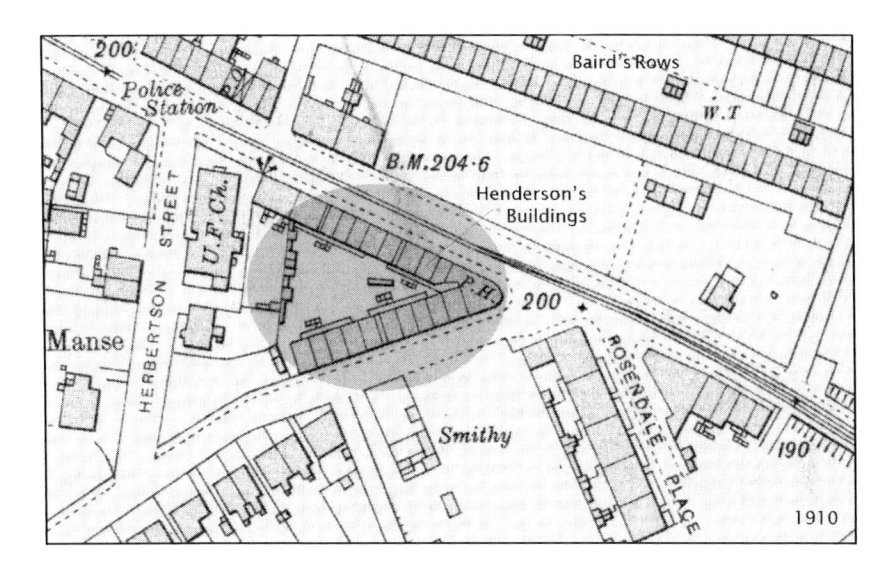

Figure 108 Henderson's Buildings on 1910 Blantyre map

The tenements were located between Herbertson Street and Auchinraith Road, on the southern side of Glasgow Road. The late 1870's and early 1880's was a time of huge expansion of Glasgow Road. Around William Henderson's Buildings other properties and miner's rows were springing up fast on land previously open fields, never been built previously upon. It must have seemed everybody was constructing homes and shops and no doubt would have been hugely exciting for Blantyre residents, then still only numbering around 3,000 people seeing their town expand so rapidly. Blantyre's population was to triple in the next 2 decades and Glasgow Road was a large contributing factor.

In all, William Henderson (b1835) constructed 36 houses within this buildings, including an initial 7 shops, a spirit shop on the corner of Auchinraith Road and a large house being used as a meeting house or hall. He let them out to tradespeople, miners, labourers and their families. Home occupancy was good, and the shops appeared to be in good locations. It is known that between 120 -200 people lived at Henderson's buildings at any one time. Factoring or maintaining the houses, including chasing up rents was managed by James Deans, a joiner (b1850 in Overton), who lived in one of Henderson's homes.

Early Owners and Tenants

The newly established Blantyre Co-operative Society opened the first shop in Henderson's Buildings in August or September 1883, managed by a Mr. John Crow. It expanded nearby as the Co-op prospered till they had occupancy of this area, in which eventually there was an Office, a Hall,

Central Grocery, dept., a Dressmaking and Millinery dept., a Gent's Outfitters, a Fleshing dept., Ante-Rooms and a Boardroom. The Co-op later opened their own central premises nearby and further westwards on the opposite side of Herbertson Street at its junction with Glasgow Road. (explored later). The homes on Auchinraith Road side of Henderson's Buildings faced out to open fields until Rosendale was built. They also looked out upon Archibald Menzie's Blacksmiths at the foot of Auchinraith Road.

In 1885, William Henderson was renting out the hall to William Reid, the spirit shop on the corner was Harvey's Public House, a predecessor to the more remembered 'Horseshoe Bar'. William Harvey was leasing the licensed premises for £99 per year, although his business was fairly short lived and wound up around 1888. (Mr Harvey is not in the 1891 census). In 1885, 2 of the shops were empty, another occupied by Alex McWilliam a flesher and another by William Peters a shoemaker.

In 1888, William Henderson died in Dennistoun, aged only 53, prompting sale of Henderson's Buildings. Mr John Meek was the new owner, buying all shops and homes and continuing to let the same tenants live there. The name "Henderson's Buildings" was retained, already established and Mr. Meek continued to use the services of James Deans as factor. However the shops nd spirit shop ended up with new leases.

In 1895, 34 houses were being rented out between £6, 5 shillings and £7, 10 shillings per year. The Meeting hall was looked after by Mr. William Muir.

The public house on the corner was rented from around 1888 by Mr James Kelly, a well known businessman with connections to the newly established Glasgow Celtic Football Club. James would prove to be an important figure in the history of this building as you will see shortly.

The shops in 1895, now 8 in number saw 2 empty, others occupied by William Young, William Caldwell a tailor, Mrs Robert Kilgour, Malcolm Reid, Robert Docherty, Thomas Lamond & Co watchmakers. All shops were rented out between £8 and £9 per annum. William Caldwell lived in the building and may have been a relation of James Caldwell, given that Caldwell's buildings were built shortly after across the Auchinraith Road. One can imagine Mr Caldwell holding political meetings at the small Henderson's hall in the late 1890's, but needing a requirement for larger premises.

The success of Mr. James Kelly saw him buy out Mr. Meek sometime before 1905, for by then, James Kelly not only owned the pub, but owned all houses and shops at Henderson's Buildings. James was a wealthy, clever man and this latest business endeavour would not have been entered into lightly.

This remarkable photo from 1903, shows clearly the stepped frontage of Henderson's Buildings at Glasgow Road. A time before nearby co-op buildings, a time before trams. Whilst researching this book, it was found that these shops (which feature external indications of their trade) were occupied by John Arbuckle confectioner, John Mathieson jeweler, Torrance Love hairdresser. Can you match up the businesses with their shopfronts?

Figure 109 Henderson's Buildings, East end Glasgow Road in 1903

In 1903 the Henderson Building hall is known, for a short time to have been used to screen the first of silent movies, at a time prior to proper picture houses being built in Blantyre.

In 1905 James Kelly, wine and spirit merchant had 9 shops in Henderson's Buildings as well as his spirit shop, by then renamed "The Horseshoe Bar" at other times known simply as "Kelly's Bar". This may have been a reference to the Blacksmith in the field opposite Auchinraith Road. The pub was located at the corner of Auchinraith Road and Glasgow Road directly across from the Caldwell Institute. As well as the aforementioned shops, there was also Henry Stevens Confectionery shop, Walter Getty a saddler and Mrs Elizabeth Kilpatrick's shop. All shops on Glasgow Road, none on Auchinraith Road. Alex McWilliam flesher had by then moved to McAlpines Building to the west and north side of the Road. Incidentally at that same time James Kelly also owned the pub at McAlpine's Building.

James Kelly, Blantyre businessman

James was somewhat of a character and as well as being Justice of the Peace, was more known for playing as an initial member of Celtic Football club, then going on to be the President of the entire Club. Residing at Thornhill, Blantyre James also had several local business interests in Blantyre amongst them owning Blantyre Engineering Company and owner of several pubs.

James (or Jimmy to most people) Kelly was an all round athlete in his early life noting prizes for his 100 yards sprint. Born in 1865, he had started out in a working career as a joiner in Renton, Glasgow.

Figure 110 James Kelly of Thornhill, Blantyre

He joined Celtic from the famous Renton World Champions team and a glowing football career continued. He was chosen to captain Celtic in its infancy and was even at his death had never been surpassed as a centre half in the Celtic club. He was capped for Scotland 16 times. Eventually he worked his way to become a director of Celtic and also chairman. He did much work for the community in

Blantyre and was especially interested in education, serving on the old School Board.

Exclusively shared here by great grand-daughter Nora Anderson is a picture taken around 1910 with James Kelly on the far left along with other management figures of Celtic Football Club.

Figure 111 James Kelly in 1910 with members of Celtic Management

His business interests included wine and spirits, which saw him move to Blantyre to his residence "Thornhill". He was an elected member of the County Council and Justice of the Peace. He was just as well known in Motherwell as he was in Blantyre. When he died at the age of 66 at Thornhill, Blantyre at 11pm on Saturday, 20th February 1932, the businessman of Blantyre, and of Motherwell, grocer wine and spirit merchant, a director of Blantyre Engineering Co., Ltd., and Prestwick Picture House, Ltd., director of the Celtic Football Club, and at one time a member of the Lanarkshire County Council, left an estate to the value of £35,786. (about £2.2million in 2017 money.) His funeral took place on Tuesday 23rd February 1932 at St Patrick's Cemetery, New Stevenston, but only after Requiem Mass was held at St Joseph's Church on Blantyre's Glasgow Road at 10.30am that morning.

There was representation from people from all over Scotland and as many as 30 cars took place in the funeral procession. His widow, Margaret later that year applied for the licenses of his pubs, by means of inheritance including that of the Black Bull pub in Motherwell. He also had 10 sons & daughters.

> Blantyre Project Social Media:
>
> **Moira MacFarlane:** "I love this history of Henderson's Buildings. My grandparents lived at 81 Glasgow Road. Grandpa's name was John Park and lived there with his 4 children, Sadie, Katie (my mum), David and Nessie. After my grandparent died, my parents took over 81, where we were brought up. I was one of 7 children! We have great memories of Henderson's Buildings. "

Robert Kelly was born in Blantyre in 1902, one of 10 children of James Kelly. Robert was educated at St Aloysius and St Josephs, Dumfries and became a stockbroker by profession. Like his father, he became a director of Glasgow Celtic FC and was chairman of the club between 1947 and 1971. He was appointed to Celtic Board in 1932 following the death of his father.

Remainder of the Kelly years

In 1915 during WW1, James was leasing out a total of 38 houses and 8 shops. By then, homes had been given postal addresses and in Henderson's Buildings the properties (all homes) facing on to Auchinraith Road were evenly numbered from 2 -22 Auchinraith Road. (4 houses at 2,4,6,8 then 10 houses at number 10, then 6 houses at 12,14,16,18, 20 and 22). The public house was 69/71/73 Glasgow Road, then heading west was a small terraced house occupied by Mrs Grew. At 77 Glasgow Road was a house and shop occupied by Alexander McLuckie, a miner.

At 79 Glasgow Road was Mrs Elizabeth White (w) a shop which would later become the undertakers. At 81 Glasgow Road were 7 houses. 83 Glasgow Road was William McInally's hairdressers. Walter Getty the saddler had a shop at 85 Glasgow Road, 87 was empty, 89 Glasgow Road was a house and shop for Malcolm Ritchie a confectioner, 91 was Alexander Barrie's shop (Alex was fitter, see his advert below). Number 93 Glasgow Road was 6 houses and finally number 95 was Blantyre Co-op. So, we can conclude that Henderson's Buildings occupied 69 -95 Glasgow Road.

Kelly's Horseshoe Pub proved popular with miners nearby, the entrance through a tall, narrow, arched doorway on the Auchinraith Road side.

In 1920, some of the businesses had changed. Alex Barrie had moved out of 91 Glasgow Road and Joseph Dunn occupied it. At 83 and 89 Glasgow Road McInally's Hairdressers and Malcolm Ritchie confectioners continued. At 87 Glasgow Road an Andrew McSkimming occupied the premises. Alex Peters of Rosebank Avenue was by then the factor of the homes, acting for James Kelly.

ALEXANDER BARRIE,

Cycle Agent and Repairer,

STONEFIELD,

BLANTYRE.

Figure 112 Alexander Barrie Advert from c 1915

By 1920, the Co-operative had moved out of 95 Glasgow Road, and this larger shop was subdivided between Matthew and Joseph Miller, shoemakers, Matthew still there in 1925. Joseph Dunn was at 91 Glasgow Road. That year, the shops still had a large confectionery occupancy with Malcolm Ritchie still trading at 89 Glasgow Road. Andrew McSkimming at 87, Joseph Barclay a contractor at 85 and Samuel Douglas had taken over McInally's hairdressers at 83 Glasgow Road. Elizabeth White still at 79, Alexander McLuckie still at 77 and of course Kelly's Pub at the corner occupying 69-73.

By 1930, 20 houses were occupied on the Auchinraith Road side again with no shops there. Alex Peters still the factor. The public house still in James Kelly's ownership too although being run then by James Kelly Jnr, son of James. Shops were 79 John Clarke Undertakers and joiner. Perhaps this is whom constructed the alleged coffins stored at the nearby Caldwell Institute? Shop 83 was empty, 85 was John Harrison confectioner, 87 Duncan Cochrane a grocer, Malcolm Ritchie confectionery still at 89 and James Brown at number 91.

Families who lived at Henderson's Buildings in 1930 on the Auchinraith Road side included surnames; Carr, Morgan, McSkimming, Russell, Steven, Park, McCoul, Muir, Crookson, Henderson (Postman), Houston, Brown, Finning, Binning, McGuirk, Lusk, Bryson, Conquer, Bradley and Morton. On the Glasgow Road side, tenants surnames included; Downie, Stevenson, Clarke, Smith, Beggs, Park, Tenant, Wood, Pearson, Cochrane, Ritchie, Brown, Bell, Louden, Paterson, Jones and Elliot. If you can imagine all these were families, some very sizeable, it may give you a good indication of just how many people lived there!

In 1932, James Kelly died, the properties passing to his widow, Margaret then to his son. One can't help but wonder if the elderly lady had any real interest in running so many businesses and properties and it is little wonder that the Kelly family later in the 1950's sold to Glasgow Publican, Eddie McCrudden, a successful businessman with many public houses under his ownership. The public house name of Horseshoe Bar, or Kelly's Bar, or Kelly's Corner was maintained through the rest of its days.

Henderson's Buildings on fire

At nine o'clock on the night of 31st January, 1940 fire broke out in a large two storey building in Glasgow Road owned by Mr James Kelly Jnr, wine and spirit merchant.

The building which had 120 tenants was still known as Henderson's buildings. The ground floor of the building contained 12 shops at that time and the wine and spirit business owned by James Kelly was at the corner of the building at the junction of the two roads (Kelly's Horse Shoe Bar).

Figure 113 Typical Firebrigade 1940

The outbreak originated in the home of a Mrs Elliot in the centre of the building and the fire travelled at great speed towards the eastern end of the tenement engulfing it in flames. Three fire engines attacked the fire from different angles and they brought the fire under control at 11.30 p.m but continued to pour water on to the burning building until well after midnight. The western homes and pub were saved.

The fire took place on one of the coldest nights for years and the bitter conditions caused a great deal of hardship, not only for the people who had lost their homes, but also to the people whose homes had been damaged by the vast amounts of water needed to bring the fire under control. Access to the upper properties was only by stone stairwell in the rear yard which may have made things more difficult.

During the blaze great anxiety was caused by the knowledge that three invalids, confined to their homes by ill health were in the blazing building but they were carried to safety by neighbours. John Tennent whose home was terribly damaged by water lost all of his furniture. John was the secretary of Blantyre and District Ornithological Society and he remembered at the height of the blaze that he had £23 in a drawer in his home. Much to his relief he found the money quite secure when he managed to gain admission to his home. The money had been the proceeds from a recent show and was to be handed over to the Red Cross.

Seven families were left homeless. Mrs. Mary Elliot, widow; John Woods, wife and family; William Davis, wife and family; Alexander Henderson, wife and family; James Loudon, wife and family; John Clark funeral undertaker, and Stewart Raeburn, wife and family. Many of the families in the building lost everything they possessed due to either fire or water/smoke damage, some sadly not insured.

This news report from the Hamilton Advertiser is made all the more bizarre by suggesting it happened on 28th February 1940, when compared to other newspapers who suggest the fire took place on 31st January 1940, a full month earlier. However, it did take place on 31st January 1940 and in was definitely Henderson's Buildings, not Anderson's Building which was adjacent to the west.

The unsafe, damaged portion Henderson's Buildings was demolished, directly across from Gilmour's Buildings. It is confirmed here that 85-95 Glasgow Road was demolished shortly after the fire. It left the whole building substantially reduced in size and with the public house so prominent in what was left, the building appears to have adopted a more prominent name of 'Kelly's Buildings' following WW2. This 1950 aerial photo demonstrates well the gap left on Glasgow Road.

Figure 114 Henderson's Buildings in 1950. Mind the gap!

Speaking of years prior to WW2, Thomas Hartman recalls, "There was a barbers shop for men. Very few of us boys went to the barbers; it was sit doon in the chair, bowl on your heed and all that stuck out from the bowl was chopped off! There was also a watch repair shop next to this and he had a huge clock hanging outside his shop, which a lot of people used as their own time piece. It was large enough that one could see it a block away, if you were sitting on a bus passing the shop, you could see the people just by habit take a glance at the clock. It was much used in those days."

Latter, Post WW2 years

The late 1950's saw some changes to the building with the drastic removal of all the homes along Auchinraith Road belonging to Henderson's Buildings. It is unknown why these were demolished, but proximity to the former Auchinraith Pit may have been to blame, perhaps subsiding. They likely needed extensive modernization and with homes being built in Blantyre in the 1957's some residents appear to have moved to Coatshill. This 1962 map shows who extensively Henderson's Buildings were reduced.

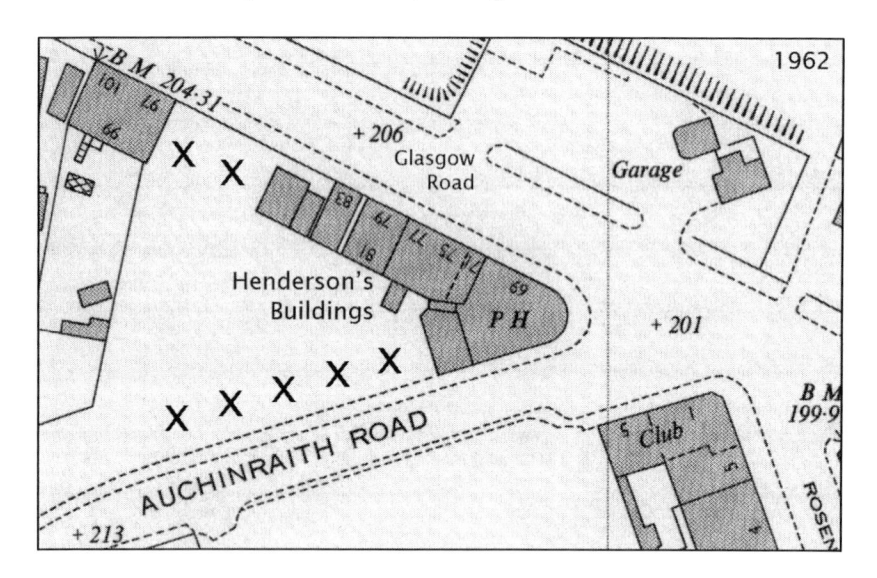

Figure 115 Henderson's Buildings remaining in 1962

During the 1960's Henderson Building was directly opposite O'Neil's Garage on the north side of Glasgow Road. By then Baird's Rows had gone so residents had a view over cleared fields to the side of Grant's Building.

Families who lived there in the 1960's and 70's included the McGuire's (who lived above the public house) and McAlisters. Shops may be better remembered. Heading west away from Kelly's Bar was McVeys Bookmakers, Archie McKays, and a lawyers office.

Finally, in 1977 bought by the County Council as part of a compulsory purchase order for the clearance of Glasgow Road, Henderson's Buildings were boarded up, scheduled for demolition in 1978 but due to planning delays did not happen until 1979.

The land ultimately was just outside the way-leave needed for the new A725 expressway in 1981 and ultimately during the 1980's was sold on to JR Reid's Printers for their relocated business. Today, it is the site of Gavin Watson Printers.

Figure 116 Henderson's Building looking east in late 1970's

Blantyre Project Social Media:

Fairlie Gordon: "My dad served his time at Blantyre Engineering, the factory belonging to Kelly."

"Read More about **Henderson's Buildings** online. Scan our handy QR Code for more narrative and photos at Blantyre's History Archives.

Further information, photos and commentary from readers are added from time to time. Learn about QR codes at the beginning of this book."

JR Reid Printers

J.R.Reid Printers was a former printing business based on Glasgow Road. Starting as an apprentice Compositor (typesetter) with the Hamilton Advertiser in 1964, John Reid registered the Business Name 'J.R.Reid Printers' in May 1969, after earlier in 1965 spending £25 on his first hand-printing machine. His first commercial job on the hand press was 250 business cards for Grant & MacDonald Painters, Stonefield Road, who were charged 15 shillings (75p in today's money).

After qualifying as a Compositor in 1970, John Reid left the 'Advertiser' and tried his hand at selling sewing machines while still running his small print business from his parent's home at 317 Glasgow Road, but decided he was better at printing than selling! In 1972, after being contracted to produce regular sale catalogues for Shirlaw Allan Auctioneers, J. R. Reid Printers rented the old Templetons' Grocers shop at 108 Glasgow Road, near Forrest Street and changed it into a small print factory.

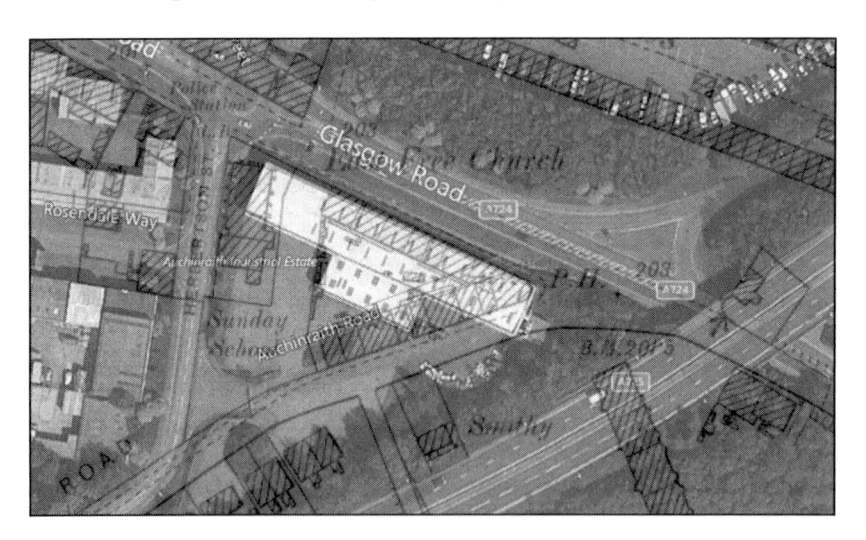

Figure 117 Satellite Aerial overlaid on 1898 Map at former Reid Printers

In November 1972, while still running the printing business, John Reid along with a Mr G. Moon and Miss Jean Nicol of Shirlaw Allan formed 'Blantyre Publishing Company Ltd' to produce a free local newspaper called the 'Blantyre Advertiser'. The newspaper was published fortnightly and was distributed door-to-door throughout Blantyre by Geoff Krawczyk of Pate's Newsagents. Blantyre Publishing Co. Ltd., while using the same premises, was a separate business to J. R. Reid Printers. The 1970's decline of Glasgow Road properties and businesses had an adverse effect on advertising revenues, causing the paper to only be published at Christmas, when the remaining businesses were prepared to advertise. Eventually even the annual publication became unprofitable and the Blantyre Advertiser ceased publication. While the Blantyre Advertiser was in decline in the late 70's, J.R.Reid Printers kept growing each year. In addition to general commercial printing and the Shirlaw Allan auctioneers' catalogues, Reid's started to specialise in theatre ticket printing. They were the sole printers of all concert tickets for the Apollo theatre in Glasgow and business was growing.

J.R.Reid Printers were then advised by their accountant to become a 'Limited Company', but rather than go through all the start-up costs of creating a new Limited Company, it was decided to simply change the name of the now dormant 'Blantyre Publishing Company Ltd' to J. R. Reid Printers LIMITED, the two other directors of Blantyre Publishing Co. Ltd. having previously resigned. This happened in February 1979 and Reid's then traded as limited Company No. SC51794 (until January 2015 when the Company, now under new ownership, was dissolved.)

In 1976 Reid's moved from the 450 sq. ft. Templeton's shop at 108, across the road into the then empty 3000 sq. ft. Central Co-op Grocery building at 109 Glasgow Road underneath the beautiful 'Co Hall' and next to Glen Travel. Then in 1979 John Reid, his staff and their 'mascot' one-eyed Alsatian, Ricky, were forced out of the Co-op Building due to pending re-development which caused the beautiful sandstone Co-op building and Hall to be demolished. J. R. Reid Printers then moved round the corner into new premises at Rosendale Way (where the industrial clothing company now is) and remained there until 1989 when they moved to their own 23,000 sq. ft. custom built building at the corner of Auchinraith Road and Glasgow Road.

The new large building with good frontage on Glasgow Road, is located on the former site of Botterill's Building, Springwell Farm House, Henderson's Buildings and the former Burleigh Church. The custom building is brick built with a red rolltop corrugated roof and is highly visible from Glasgow Road and previously from the expressway. It sits on the bottom of the former Auchinraith Road.

A little earlier in the 1980's, the very end of Auchinraith Road junction with Glasgow Road was blocked off and Auchinraith Road traffic (mostly from East Kilbride) was forced to go down Herbertson Street, past Rosendale Way, on to Glasgow Road. This meant that very northern part of Auchinraith Road was not open to traffic and ran through the current carpark of the printers. It is still visible today in the carpark, untouched due to several services, primarily an old mains gas supply running through it. The location was used as a very large roundabout during the construction of the lower end of the East Kilbride expressway.

In 1990 the Company bought Exacta Print Ltd on West Regent Street, Glasgow and in 1992, J.R.Reid acquired the assets of McClure, McDonald & Co. of Maryhill, including their four-colour press. Acquiring this press along with the McClure press operator enabled Reid's to start producing full four-colour process printing from one press in Blantyre. McClure's produced social and gift stationery for Waverley Stationery Ltd. of Blairgowrie, but later, due to payment issues, J.R.Reid also took over Waverley Stationery Ltd along with their UK wide sales team and various Stationery Brands. The Company name changed slightly over the years but the Company Number always remained the same. With operations in Blantyre, Wishaw, Glasgow and Blairgowrie the name changed to J.R.Reid Printing Group Ltd in 1995; J.R.Reid Print & Media Group Ltd in 2000; and then in 2007, after John Reid left the Company, the name was changed to Reid Printers Ltd.

J.R.Reid Printers Ltd was solely owned by John Reid from its foundation until 2002 when 50% of the shareholding was purchased by Mr I.J.Johnstone who had just sold a chain of pharmacy shops and in 2006/7 I.J.Johnstone 'acquired' the rest of the shareholding of J.R.Reid Print & Media Group Ltd, with John Reid retaining Wishaw Printing Company and Exacta Print Ltd, Glasgow, which is now run by John's son, Innes Reid. John Reid resigned as a Director of the Company he founded 37 years earlier, on 9 March 2007, but is still a Director of Exacta Print Ltd.

In 2007, I.J.Johnstone through his Group Company, GT4 Group Ltd (SC226642) took over Gavin Watson Ltd label printers and Ian Johnstone was appointed a Director of Gavin Watson Ltd on 30 March 2007. The Company operates from the old Reid factory and still employs some ex-Reid staff. The main product of the Company is now labels. Many people utilised Reid's for their printing services over the years and they were a good employer of local people in their time in Blantyre, fondly remembered.

Blantyre Project Social Media:

Jennifer Mallory: "I started working at Reid' in November 1989 and spent 16.5 wonderful years there. We all worked hard and John Reid was great to work for. Everybody respected him and his dedication to the business. I left there in 2006 on good terms and still keep in touch with some people today."

Stuart Dodd: "I started working in Reid's in 1988 and still at the same building today. John was a fair and honest man to work for."

Carol Crombie: "My dad was good friends with John and sometimes looked after Ricky the Alsatian. He was blind in one eye and fierce (Ricky that is!)

Gavin Watson Printers

Having moved to Blantyre in post Millennium years, Gavin Watson Printers is based in the former JR Reid's Printing building on Glasgow Road opposite the slipway on to East Kilbride Expressway. They have address 79-109 Glasgow Road and telephone 01698 826000. The entrance from Auchinraith Road leads into a modest sized car park. The business name is well known and recognised in Blantyre but the company has roots from much further back and away from the town. Gavin Watson Printers were founded over 150 years ago in 1863, halfway through Queen Victoria's reign, when Bismarck ruled Prussia and Napoleon the Third was Emperor of France. The business remained in the Watson family until after the Second World War and was believed to be the first company in Scotland to purchase a lithography printing press which was used to initially immerse itself in the printing of ornate share certificates. Over the years, the company has gained an enviable reputation in wet glue label market for its customer service.

After considerable investment and hard work from all their staff they have gained a formidable reputation for being one of the best wet glue label and commercial printers in the UK. From their purpose built factory they currently produce in excess of 1.3 billion wet glue applied labels annually for clients such as Highland Spring Group, Nestle UK, AG Barr Plc, Diageo, Innocent, Britvic and Baxter's Food Group to name but a few. With direct access to the main motorway networks, they can produce export labels throughout Europe.

Gavin Watson Printers also offer services for security printed products, themselves being part of the GT4 Group, as well as foil & embossing, labeling, flexographic printing, packaging and more regular printing and scanning. The best way to get an idea of the scale of what Gavin Watson does is to look in your kitchen cupboard. If there is anything from Marks & Spencer, Sainsbury, Tesco – or perhaps Harrods – the likelihood is that the label first emanated from the family-owned print shop in Possil or later from Blantyre. In 2002, managing Director Drew Samuel spent over £1.5m on state of the art machinery, investing in the equipment to secure the future of the company. At the time he was overseeing the printing of 20 million labels per week, that's over a billion a year!

Food and drink labeling for major multiples and producers all over the UK accounts for nearly 85% of Gavin Watson's production. It provided a pre-tax profit of (pounds) 150,000 on turnover of just under (pounds) 4m in the financial year to January 2001. Speaking in 2002, Samuel said, "The remainder of production at the 65-employee firm is in security printing – cheques, pass books, giros, and so on, all with specialist security features such as UV threads in the passbooks. That is a smaller part of the business now, but we can say that we have been in security printing for 140 years," said Samuel. "The original Gavin Watson's business in Ingram Street in Glasgow printed those lovely, ornate Victorian share certificates on the first litho press in Scotland – which was made of stone."

The firm was bought by the Bissett family after the war and inherited by Johnny Bissett's daughter and Samuel's wife, Mary, who became chairwoman. Samuel joined as managing director in 1990 at the suggestion of management consultants, leaving behind his successful architectural practice. In 2009, JR Reid's was merged with Gavin Watson Printers, the signage at Glasgow Road changing that year. In 2015, GT4 Group, owner of Glasgow-based labels and packaging printer Gavin Watson and creative agency GT4, acquired fellow Scottish commercial printer Creative Colour Bureau (CCB) in an all-share deal. CCB directors Angus MacDonald and Mark Coll joined the board of GT4 Group, as they planned to consolidate CCB into the larger Gavin Watson site in Blantyre, 10 miles away from their Glasgow premises.

GT4 Group chairman Ian Johnstone said in 2015 that the deal was not expected to result in any redundancies at either printer, which collectively employed around 80 staff and turned over more than £10m. He added, "It made sense to have the two businesses but one lot of fixed costs."

Figure 118 Gavin Watson Printers as it appears today (2017)

Johnstone founded GT4 together with chief executive Tom Brown in 2003 before acquiring Gavin Watson around 2007. CCB was the group's first acquisition since then, although Johnstone said the firm had invested around £3m between 2010-2015, "mostly in the labels business". Quoted in 2015 he continued, "We do a lot of labels for whisky clients and they don't just need labels, they need boxes, cartons, booklets, neck collars, swing tickets – there's a whole load of value-added marketing material that goes along with it and that's something CCB can give us. It became apparent that we were printing different things but on similar equipment and aside from the whisky industry there's very little crossover in our clients." He added that the all-share deal had suited all parties, adding: "If we had wanted to buy for cash they would probably have been less enthusiastic as they wanted to be part of this packaging group we are creating."

Tom Brown, added in 2015, "The relocation of CCB to Gavin Watson's site would take around eight weeks and that the company would then look to invest in some additional finishing and wide-format print equipment. We're looking to invest in some more specialist finishing equipment for things like lamination and spot UV, which a lot of companies just put out. Our philosophy is to deliver to clients on time in full, so we need to have control over production." He added that while CCB had roll-to-roll wide-format devices, it didn't have any flatbed printers and that that was probably an area the company would look to invest in, with the combined spend on that and finishing expected to come to around £500,000. Brown added that both companies were looking to replace an older litho press – in Gavin Watson's case a six-colour Heidelberg CD 74 – and that GT4 would look for a single press to replace both devices, probably towards the end of the year "once we've made sure the specification fits what both companies need". Following the merger to a single site, the company went from a 24/5 to a 24/7 operation. Since their arrival in Blantyre, Gavin Watson Printers have been avid sponsors of several community events, often leading their charitable support to local community newspaper Blantyre Telegraph as well as undertaking printing, often donated for free to Blantyre Community Committee Gala events, Blantyre Oscars and printing for the town's festive events, something greatly appreciated by all organisations.

Blantyre Project Social Media:

Janet Morton: "Just going back to JR Reids for a moment…my first job was in Shirlaw Allan's Auctioneers in Hamilton. In about 1973, John Reid got the contract to print the sales catalogues. A big break for him, the nice chap he was."

Patrick Donnelly: "Did you know, Gavin Watson Printers have an electric charging point for vehicles installed in their carpark in 2017. I think this may actually be the very first one in Blantyre, which given the current surge towards electric vehicles and recent announcement of diesel scrapage, may be looked upon by future historians in Blantyre as something of interest."

Anderson's Buildings

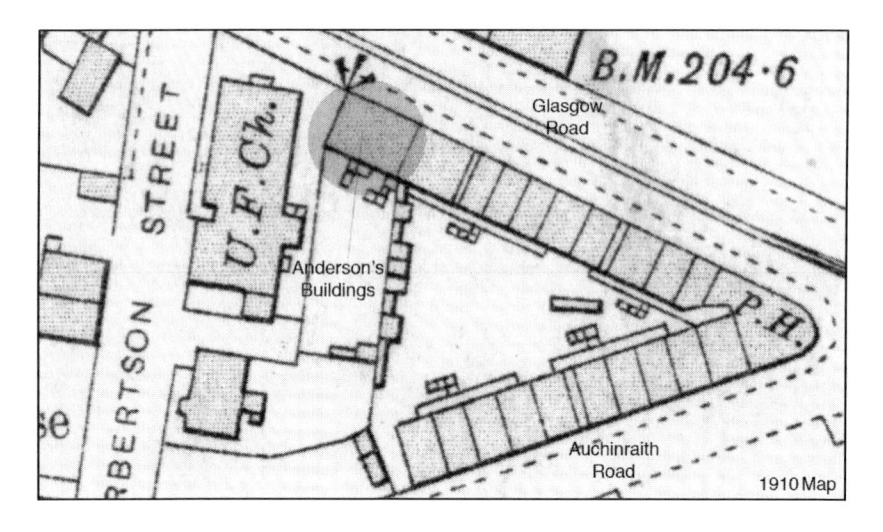

Figure 119 Anderson's Buildings next to Burleigh Church in 1910 map

Situated between Henderson's Building and the United Free Church (Burleigh Church) was the former Anderson's Buildings. The 2 storey tenements were constructed between 1902 and 1904 by Thomas Anderson, a bicycle maker.

The property was directly across Glasgow Road from Grant's Building and made of stone, consisted of 2 shops on the ground level, opening out on to Glasgow Road pavement and 2 houses above. They were directly attached to Henderson's Buildings but slightly lower and of different appearance. There were 5 narrow windows on the upper storey facing out on to Glasgow Road, with chimneys at either end and the middle of the building. The garden at the back consisted of a long, narrow plot of land. Access to the upper floors were on stone steps at the rear yard, entered from nearby Herbertson Street behind the church.

Constructor, Thomas Anderson was a Cycle Agent who made bicycles in those boom times when trams had just started running and lack of motor vehicles. Born in 1865 in Old Monkland, he was an incomer to Blantyre around 1900, noted in the census of 1901 living at Stonefield with older brothers John and Matthew. Clearly his parents were religious people, naming their sons after saints. With them were cousins, the Richardson and Robertson families.

In 1905 first occupants in the 2 houses were Denis McKay a spirit salesman and Matthew Anderson, the brother of Thomas. Matthew was a pitheadman who moved specifically from Springwell to these buildings once constructed, renting from his younger brother. In the shop nearest Henderson's Buildings was Mrs. Ann Robertson, a greengrocer and cousin of Thomas. She rented for £10 per annum.

In the other ground floor shop, next to the church wall was Thomas Anderson himself, conducting his business as a cycle agent. On the outside of his shop was a metal bicycle wheel, which could be seen at a distance by customers, as pictured here in 1903.

Around 1910 postal addresses were allocated to Anderson's Buildings, and from that time onwards the buildings was only known, certainly in census and valuation rolls by the addresses 97, 99 and 101 Glasgow Road .

Tenants and Change of Ownership

In 1915, Thomas was renting out the 2 upper houses, both with address 99 Glasgow Road to William Cunningham a miner and continuing to rent to his brother Matthew. At 101 Glasgow Road the end shop near Burleigh Church was no longer run as a bicycle shop, but instead was occupied by John Marshall, a merchant (possible printer) who lived at the house behind the Burleigh Church Hall on Herbertson Street. John's rent was £18, 10 shillings that year. Whilst researching this era, we found a long lost Blantyre pub, which was situated in Anderson's Buildings at 97 Glasgow Road. Robertson's greengrocers was now Robertson's spirit dealership, immediately adjacent to Henderson's Buildings. The spirit shop was formed between 1905 and 1915 but was short lived and gone by 1920.

Figure 120 Andersons

By the end of the First World War, ownership was to change and Matthew R Anderson, a pitheadman who lived at 99 Glasgow Road in the upper floor was the new owner, buying or inheriting the property from his brother, Thomas. The other house in 1920 still occupied by William Cunningham. The spirit shop was then John Marshall & Son a grocers shop. The other shop was also John Marshall & Son, likely a printers.

The Marshalls therefore rented all shops in that building, but again only for a short time with shops to change occupancy frequently.

1925 saw Matthew Anderson, still owner at 99 Glasgow Road but in the other house was James Botterill, a boot repairman. The name Botterill is interesting given the Botterills ended up owning and running shops here later in the Century. The ground floor shops of Anderson's Buildings in 1925 were occupied entirely by Hill Brothers Ltd, pawnbrokers, renting the larger premises for £28 and the smaller shop for £22. Again, though only for a short time, vacating Anderson's Buildings in 1927.

1930 had Matthew Anderson living away from Blantyre at 134 Dredis Street, Airdrie. His former home occupied by Frank Lyon, a stocktaker. James Botteril occupied the other house. At 97 Glasgow Road the shop was by then James McTavish's Butchers. The larger shop at 101 at the opposite end was split, one half empty, the other half occupied by Charles McElhone, a pawnbroker and competitor of the previous tenants Hill Brothers. Matthew died in 1932 in Airdrie, (75) with tenant James Botterill buying his building.

Figure 121 Pawn-broking sign, leaving customers in no doubt what's inside

You may think the economic depression of the 1920's gave rise to pawn shops in Blantyre, but they existed far before that, and indeed can be traced back to the 1870's. Families like the Fegans, McLindens, Hills all were involved in the pawnbroking industry in Blantyre, some of them like the Fegans even earlier in nearby towns.

Charles McElhone married into the pawnbroking business. He lived at 114 Glasgow Road on the north side of the street with his wife Anne Fegan, the daughter of more established and well known Hugh Fegan pawnbroker. The McElhones ran their own pawn broking business from 120 and 122 Glasgow Road until Anne passed away in 1927, after which Charles moved to Anderson's Buildings. He ran the shop until his death in 1947.

In January 1940, a terrible fire gutted some of the adjacent homes at Henderson's Buildings which must have made Anderson's tenants very concerned. At the back of Anderson's Buildings around this time a small greenhouse was built and 2 outbuildings which may have served as stores for the shops.

Anderson's Buildings existed beyond WW2 with popular shops on the lower part like Botterill's shop, subdivided into Annie Botterill's fishshop and Nancy Botterill's business. Houses remained on the upper level into the late 1970's when the whole building was demolished. Finally, to put all this into context, here is our overlay of Anderson's Building where it would be located today at the western end of Gavin Watson Printers.

Figure 122 Location Line Drawing putting Anderson's into context

Blantyre Project Social Media:

Ray Couston: "There was a Botterills at Coatshill and on Farm Road. We called it Botterils well into it being owned by Spar. Similarly, at Botteril's /Spar on Stonefield Road. We called it Landmark, despite it not being that for about 28 years! I know people who just simply won't change the name, still calling it Landmark to this day. Us Blantyre People are creatures of habit!"

Ian Paterson: "I could cash my giro in the Coatshill Botterill's shop."

Figure 123 Botterills Building (Andersons Building) in late 1970's

Blantyre Project Social Media:

Lillias Addison: "I remember buying baby wool out of that shop."

Michael Docherty: "I got my fingers trapped in a mousetrap in the shop!"

Linda Gilmour Roberts: "My Gran Gilmour was a friend of old Mr Botterill as we lived across the road in the early 1960's. Gran visited them often. Nancy Botterill used to let me choose hair ribbons from the shop, which was a special treat for a 3 year old!"

Liz Allan: "My mum worked for Nancy to help with her mum who lived upstairs. This was around the time Nancy was going out with Yaqcub Ali."

Gerry Walker: "There used to be a rush in our house in the early 1960's on Saturday mornings to run up to Botterills, for comics that came out. It would take 2 of us to carry them back. (Victor, Hornet, Judy, Bunty, Jackie, Twinkle, Dandy and the Beano!) Our house was always very quiet on a Saturday afternoon."

Sheena Thomson: "I know this building well. My Gran and Grandpa Gilmour stayed in Gilmour Place across the road in the 1950's. When I married I stayed in the same flat from 1970."

Burleigh Church

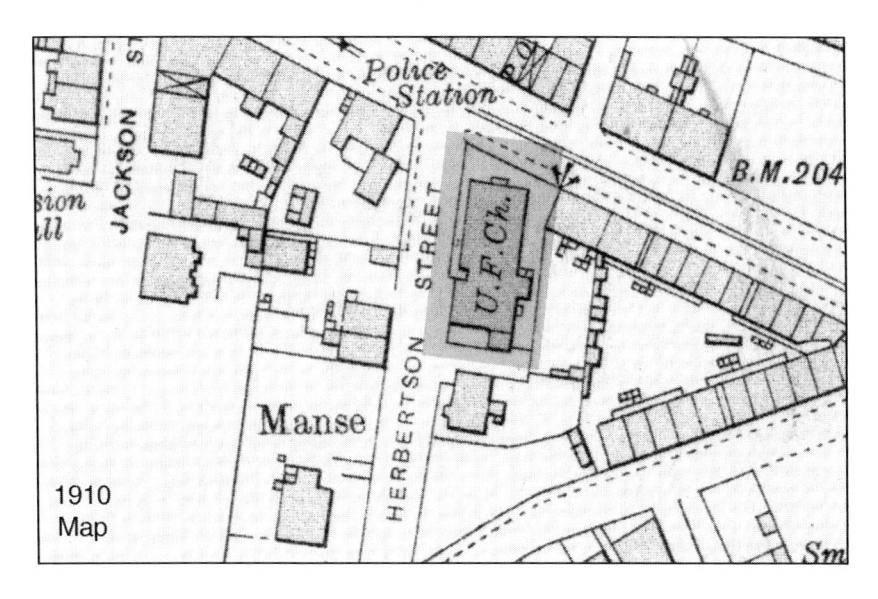

Figure 124 United East Free Church (Burleigh) on 1910 Map

The Burleigh Church was a former church also known as the East Free Church or East United Free Church at Herbertson Street corner of Glasgow Road, Low Blantyre. Before the church was built, the congregation met in a mission hall, which evolved over the years. The story is exclusively revealed by this book.

The Beginnings: The church had its roots back in 1876, at a time when Stonefield and Springwell was in its infancy. At that time in need of further religious outlets, a small mission was set up. Requiring a venue for worship, during its first years, church members rented Dall's Shop in Gilmour's Building on the north side of Glasgow Road for £25 per annum, before moving temporarily in 1877 into a larger shop in Henderson's Buildings for 7 months.

Next, in early 1878, the mission moved temporarily again to the Masonic Hall above the Livingstonian Bar on the corner of nearby Forrest Street and Glasgow Road. (Which would later become the Blantyre Electric Picture Company). It is safe to say the group were choosing locations carefully centered around this area.

Mission Hall: Whilst the mission was at the Masonic Hall, work began on creating a more permanent mission hall nearby at the corner of Herbertson Street and Glasgow Road, Low Blantyre, directly across the Glasgow Road from Gilmour's Building. Construction took place at a similar time to the construction of Henderson's Buildings to the east. A small plot of land was secured at the corner of Glasgow Road and Herbertson Street and by May 1878, a new mission hall had been built, as pictured in this widely distributed photo just over a decade later. Architect was William Gardner Rowan.

Figure 125 East Free Mission Hall, Herbertson Street c1890

The hall was a significant building, made of stone and slate, with large windows at the east and west in the shape of a cross. This was a tradition in church and chapel building where windows were carefully positioned to welcome and see out the light of the day. Four more windows on the north side let in plenty of light. It was heated by coal with fireplaces at each gable. A wooden picket fence was erected around the perimeter and a small tended garden. The entrance was from Herbertson Street where the door faced out upon. Across Herbertson Street was the former Blantyre Police Station, the entrance to which can be seen on the right of the photo. Beyond were fields all the way to Birdsfield at High Blantyre.

The first recognized minister, rather than preachers was Rev. John Burleigh who commenced there in September 1889.

Requirement for a Church

The Church: The small mission flourished and a short time after John Burleigh arrived, the Free Church assembly raised the status of the mission to full church. Plans were drawn up for a permanent church, which was to be built on the ground already bought to the north, encapsulated by the boundary of Glasgow Road and Herbertson Street and immediately nearby to the mission hall. The new church was to be named the 'East Free Church' and would seat over 500 people. The existing mission building next to it would not be redundant but instead would function as a hall only and used as a Sunday school. During 1890 and 1891, a significant budget of £1,620 was raised, which is around a quarter of a million pounds in today's money.

Figure 126 Burleigh Church in front of old mission hall in 1950

The first foundation stone for this permanent church was laid on 12th March 1892 and the church was finally opened on Saturday, 3rd December 1892. It is unknown if it met budget requirements. The new church was a prominent feature and had later allocated address, 103 Glasgow Road, situated on the south side, directly across Glasgow Road from Gilmour's Building. The hall, part of Herbertson Street. In 1895 the church was managed by the Free Church Mission, through Robert Beveridge, treasurer who lived in Hamilton. In 1900 the Church became 'The Blantyre East United Free Church' or EUFC managed by the Trustees of the Evangelical Union Church through John Bryan, a shoemaker in Burnbank. Behind the mission hall in Herbertson Street was only ever one other building on that side of the street. In the early 20th Century it was Blantyre's first telephone exchange.

The early 1900's saw the church have its up and downs with regards to debt on the church buildings and problems with underground workings.

Mr. James Gilmour was the session clerk at the Burleigh.

Rev John Burleigh lived at the Burleigh Manse house, more commonly referred to as Abbeygreen, which was further west at 2 Church Street, which we'll explore later in this book. During his time as minister, he married many, many couples in his church.

By Paul D Veverka

Pre WW1 Years

On Thursday 8th February 1900 Mr. George Kelly and Miss Maggie Robertson on the occasion of their approaching marriage were made the recipients of gifts from their fellow members of the choir of the East Free Church. News reports of the time commented, "The company met in the hall adjoining the church. After tea, the Rev. Burleigh spoke in flattering terms of the respect that Mr Kelly and Miss Robertson were held and in the name of the choir, presented them with a walking stick and reading lamp respectively. Mr Kelly then gave a speech of thanks. During the evening, songs were sung by Messrs T Eadie, J Robertson and Andrew Robertson, bottler of the Springwell Factory. Miss Taggart showed excellent elocutionary power in her rendering of 'Oor Folks'. Games were entered into with great zest and altogether a very enjoyable evening was spent."

On Thursday 26th March 1900 a service of song entitled "General Gordon" was given in the Blantyre East Free Church, by the juvenile choir, under the leadership of Mr. Andrew Robertson. Rev John Burleigh presided. The piece was also illustrated with limelight views. The entertainment on the whole was much appreciated with proceeds in the aid of the African war, for local soldiers families. A nice sum of money was handed over after meeting expenses.

In 1909, the Church roll call was as follows: Minister was still Rev. John Burleigh; Choirmaster, Jas. Robertson; Session Clerk, Jas. Robertson; Clerk of Deacon's Court, Daniel McDade; Church Officer, James Wright; Sunday School Supt., James Murdoch.   Agencies: — Sunday Morning Guild — President, Rev. John Burleigh; Minister's Bible Class; and Guild of Help.

Post WW1 Years

On Friday 2nd October 1914, Rev Burleigh gleefully told the congregation that the church was at last debt free. It was welcome relief and heartening news, given that all news at the time was war related. That same day, the church celebrated 25 years of Rev Burleigh being minister.

In 1915, the church was owned by Trustees of the Stonefield East United Free Church per George Baird, 10 Hospital Road, High Blantyre, a situation that would continue until 1929.

In November 1918 when the armistice and end of WW1 was sounded, the 3 united free churches in Blantyre including East Free came together for a joint service at the larger Livingstone Memorial Church, with ministers from all churches attending and large crowds descending upon the building. What a sight that must have been in Blantyre as the Church Bells rang out in victory and in the name of future peace.

There was great sadness in the congregation when Rev. John Burleigh died on 28th October 1922 and some relief from that grief when Rev. Alexander Ross took over.

Like the Anderson Church at Stonefield Road, The East Free Church joined to form part of the new Church of Scotland in 1929, dropping the terms "free" and was thereafter known as 'Blantyre East Church of Scotland' According to the valuation roll of 1930, the congregation of the "Blantyre East Church of Scotland" owned the church and indeed the nearby mission hall.

Smashed Windows

DID YOU KNOW? During the first week of September 1931, egged on by a companion a Blantyre boy smashed several ornate windows of the church but was later caught out and put on probation.

As you would expect from most churches and halls, several community organisations took place in and around the building. Scouts, Brownies, Sunday school, Women's guild are to name a few.

Around 1945, the "Blantyre East Church of Scotland" was again renamed this time to "Burleigh Memorial Church of Scotland" in honour of the man who had served as the first minister for 33 years.

During the mid 1950's, the pastor was Rev. J. M Barker. Mrs. Roberts became the church organist, a member of the well known family living across Herbertson Street. The Roberts family were regulars at the church, some of the men being elders in their time.

According to former elders, due to dwindling numbers, the first union and readjustment in the town was in 1965 when the Burleigh Memorial Church was united with Stonefield Parish Church to become 'Stonefield Burleigh Memorial Parish Church'. It was decided that the Burleigh would be used as the halls of the new congregation and that the larger, Stonefield building to the west would become the church for Sunday worship. The Burleigh Church Hall was well used for family functions, brownies and guides, wedding celebrations, youth fellowship classes as well as other entertaining and educational pursuits like country dancing, music and singing classes.

As with other churches in Blantyre throughout the 1970's, mysterious fires set their fate most likely caused by widespread vandalism that decade. In 1973, the mission hall at Herbertson Street burned down and was unsalvageable. A year later in January 1974, the Burleigh Church burned down also.

Figure 127 Two Mosaics from Burleigh taken to Hamilton in 1974

The beautiful ornate mosaics salvaged from Cochrane's Chapel, Calderglen that had been in the church in 1925 were thankfully salvaged, cleaned up and then gifted to Hamilton Town Hall, where they still are today above the entrance staircase.

I was astounded by the scale of them! The two mosaics have been lovingly restored and are so colourful with the utmost fine craftsmanship visible in the detail. Vibrant colours jump out and they are each well over 2.5m tall by 1.2m wide. It looks like the original wood backing was lifted out with them. Amazed, I took several photos but felt very sad on two counts. 1. Why are the mosaics in Hamilton now and not still somewhere in Blantyre? 2. Why was there no plaque or story beside them?

To any passers by they are just two random mosaics, when in fact they have wonderful history attached to them from another town. The history is lost in Hamilton and I feel irrelevant there. In that location they serve only as nice decorations on the library wall.

Following the fire, the stained glass windows of the church were allegedly saved also and moved to Ayrshire. The ruined buildings were then demolished a few years before other Glasgow Road tenements. The site of the Burleigh Church is now the western part and offices of modern Gavin Watson Printers.

Rev John Burleigh

Rev. John Burleigh was born in Lesmahagow at a scenic area named Abbeygreen. He was the minister in the late 19th Century and early 20th Century of the Burleigh Church. He was the first minister who commenced at the church on 24th September 1889. John married Marion Braid, the daughter of Andrew Braid a grocer, and he lived with his wife and her father at his home at Coatshill Cottage in 1891. In 1892, Marion had passed away and this coincided with the building of the Church. His daughter married a Mr Fyfe, also in the clergy a minister of Bellshill. John lived with his wife and family at Abbeygreen Manse, at 2 and 4 Church Street, the manse house of the Burleigh Church. He was a 50 year old widower in 1901, remarried Janet Hunter in 1906 in Edinburgh and had 3 daughters. He died on 28th October 1922.

Wedding of Miss Burleigh

Before we leave the Burleigh Church, there's a wonderful description of a 1920's wedding that took place there. None other than Rev Burleigh's daughters wedding! Sadly, Rev John Burleigh had not lived to see it.

Miss Jean Murdoch Burleigh's marriage was held in The East U.F. Church, Blantyre. On Wednesday, April 14th 1926 Rev. Jas. Stanley Fyfe, Duns East U.F. Church, and Miss Jean Murdoch Burleigh, elder daughter of the late Rev. John Burleigh. Much public interest was taken in the event, and at the hour of the wedding, 11.30am, the congregation almost filled the church while many assembled outside to witness the coming and going of the bridal party and guests.

For the occasion, the church had been decorated with roses, tulips and ferns, and made a charming setting for the bride who wore a gown of cream crepe de chine, with lace overdress, and veil with orange blossoms. She carried a sheaf of lilies, and was given away by her mother. The bridesmaids were Miss Elizabeth Burleigh, sister of the bride; and Miss Margaret Fyfe, sister of the bridegroom. Their dresses respectively were of peach and powder blue crepe de chine, and each wore a string of pearls, a gift from the bridegroom, and carried bouquets of lilies, roses and sweet peas. The best man was Mr John Broadfoot, and ceremony was performed by Rev. W. A. Ross. Ushers were Messrs Wm. Hunter and Shannon.

As the bridal party entered the church, Mr John Danskin, junior, played the Wedding March by Wagner. The congregation sang the 2nd paraphrase, and the hymn 'The Voice that breathed o'er Eden,' and at the conclusion the doxology, 'The Lord bless thee and keep thee,' was sung. As the wedding party retired from the church the organist played Mendelssohn's Wedding March. After the ceremony, the reception was held at Abbeygreen at the corner of Church Street, Blantyre and later in the day, Rev and new Mrs Fyfe left for their honeymoon, the bride travelling in a wine coloured two piece suit, with hat and scarf.

> Blantyre Project Social Media:
>
> **Joan Anderson:** "James Gilmour, the session clerk at Burleigh was my grandfather."
>
> **Valerie Krawczyk:** "I attended the Burleigh Memorial Church when I was young. I remember the Daffodil Teas and many social evenings. I also remember the Rev. Barker and his paintings of 'Peenie Paperlegs' who was a bird, which he used in his sermons and addresses."

CHAPTER 7
GLASGOW ROAD SOUTH
HERBERTSON ST TO JACKSON ST

Origins of Herbertson Street

Researching the origins of Herbertson Street proved more difficult than first thought. Nobody has previously written how Herbertson Street acquired its name when postal addresses were allocated around 1910 and the name wasn't in any valuation rolls of that time. Some research in the earlier 19th Century was called for and all became clear when it was found that Mrs Janet Jackson (nee Herbertson) was the last owner of Springwell Farm House prior to it being demolished in 1876. Indeed her family had owned the farm for a few decades before that. The name Jackson and Herbertson are absolutely linked to that same person, related to the Jacksons of Spittal and Bardykes.

Janet's mother in law Mrs Margaret Herbertson was born in Blantyre in 1793, although lived most of her life over the boundary at Spittal Farm. In 1851, she was a widow at the young age of 58 and living with her daughter Janet and her husband Andrew Jackson and their family of young children at Spittal. Along with them are 4 servants. Margaret owned Springwell Farm House, which following her death in 1863 would be inherited by daughter Janet, who would later live at Old Place, High Blantyre.

Herbertson and indeed nearby Jackson Street are both therefore named after the last owners of Springwell Farm, whose former field boundaries became the two small streets leading south off Glasgow to Hamilton Road.

Odd numbered postal address were located on the east side and even on the west. The street runs obliquely from Glasgow Road to Auchinraith Rd.

Herbertson Street has always been a small street and although side streets branching off Glasgow Road are fully explained in another Blantyre Project book, since there were only a few buildings, its worth touching upon them here too.

Figure 128 Herbertson Street as it appears today looking to Glasgow Rd

The following rare photo taken in the mid 20th Century shows how Herbertson Street once looked, a stark reminder of just how much our town has changed. Looking down the street, the Burleigh Church Hall can be seen on the right, the tenements of Glasgow Road north in the distance.

Figure 129 Herbertson Street looking north in mid 20th Century, Burleigh on the right

Telephone Exchange

With the exception of the Mission Hall, there was only ever one other building on the east side of Herbertson Street prior to the 1980's. The telephone exchange may be remembered by some of our older generation being there before 1958, but the building didn't start out like that. It initially was a large, detached house.

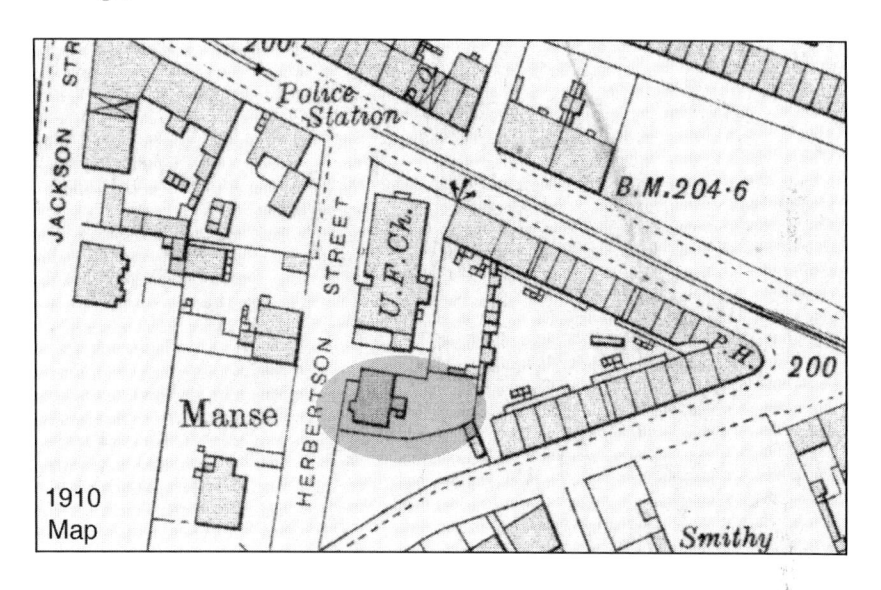

Figure 130 Telephone Exchange started out as a detached house

Between 1898 and 1905, Mr. John Marshall, a printer constructed a detached house behind the mission hall at Herbertson Street. It opened out on to Herbertson Street, the main door facing west. Built of stone in one and a half storeys, it had 2 large dormer windows on the roof and a large bay window on the ground floor.

By 1905, for an unknown reason John was living in Johannesburg, Africa and his house was being occupied by Thomas Moore, an agent. A small workshop had been built adjacent to the house, which lay empty.

According to the valuation roll of 1915, John Marshall's house had been acquired by the bank, owned by the Hamilton & District Economic Building Society and it is noted a liquidator had been appointed, presumably due to payments not being kept up. John had returned back to Blantyre and together with his son continued to operate under new name John Marshall and Son at nearby Anderson's Buildings at 97 and 101 Glasgow Road until 1925.

So what became of the house and the workshop? Well in 1915 the bank was letting the house at 3 Herbertson Street out to the Postmaster General for the Telephone Service with George Carruthers as caretaker. The small workshop at 1 Herbertson Street was now a small house occupied by William McLellan a miner for £5,13 shillings per year.

Figure 131 Telephone Exchange during the 1920's often run by women

The Telephone Exchange was almost directly across from the entrance doors of the Co-op hall, located on the site which now is the car park at Gavin Watson Printers.

The exchange was manned by only one or two women, who must have been privy to every telephone conversation, which took place in those early years.

By 1920, Elizabeth Jamieson (a widow) lived at the large house and likely was one of the operators. In the small house was Christopher Bell McKie, who was a postmaster linesman, operator of the Telegraph. The Telegraph Plant was located within the small house at 1 Herbertson Street. In later years Nancy Donohoe (nee Clark) worked there, a lady with a lovely speaking (and singing) voice.

In 1958, a new exchange was built in Forrest Street, adjacent to Blantyre Victoria's Castle Park Football Club and the premises continued as a house until demolition in the 1970's. Forrest Street equipment was upgraded for the modern era in 1968 and 1969.

Stonefield Parish Church Manse

Stonefield Parish Church Manse was a sizeable house built between 1898 and 1905 located at the top, western side of Herbertson Street near the corner of Auchinraith Road. It was first occupied by Rev Thomas Pryde and had address 34 Auchinraith Road. Thomas died in 1925 at Cardowan.

Figure 132 Jean Findlayson & Family in 1948 outside their manse house

In 1905, the manse had a rateable value of £30. The former stone built manse was a moderate detached sized home, a storey and a half. The door was accessed up a couple of steps and was positioned centrally below a small decorative arch window. Either side on the ground floor were large windows, above them exposed timber rafters along the soffit line. On the upper floor, to the left was a large dormer window and to the right another window, set into a pitched upturned V shape, finished with decorative trefoil timber design. To the north of the manse was land belonging to the Roberts family.

The manse position across Herbertson Street from the UFC Burleigh Church may have confused some people, even more so as the Burleigh Church Manse was further along Glasgow Road at the corner of Church Street. The Stonefield Parish Church manse looked out at the back into a field, then beyond to Merry's Rows. Around the manse was a sizeable garden.

In 1944, Rev Duncan Finlayson came to Blantyre and occupied the manse. It is no longer there today, demolished in 1978 when Duncan left Blantyre and following the fire which consumed the Stonefield Parish Church.

> Blantyre Project Social Media:
>
> Still on the subject of Herbertson Street,
>
> **Peter O Brien:** "I worked in the telephone exchange when it transferred to Forrest Street. During 1968 and 1969, we upgraded the equipment converting the equipment extensively. Also working with me was Jimmy McKinley and Peter Cairney."
>
> **Christine Forrest:** "My Great Aunt Mary Smith (nee Forrest) lived in Herbertson Street in the 1950's to the 1970's. Her first husband Robert Haeburn died in the First World War and she later re-married John Smith. My Great Grandfather lived with her until he passed away in his 90's in 1955 at Herbertson Street. His name was Jock Forrest. My Aunt passed away in the 1970's, long life in the family, she was well into her 90's too. I have lovely memories of visiting her on her ground floor home during the late 1960's."

Fatality on Glasgow Road

Friday 31st January 1936 was a sad day for Blantyre. A four-year-old girl was killed that evening in a road accident on the Glasgow Road, Blantyre. She was little Reta Black, who resided with her grandparents Mr and Mrs John Black at 7 Forrest Street, Blantyre. The girl ran into the street near her home and was instantly killed by a motor bus belonging to the S.M.T. Company.

The accident had happened near the East End, not far from the Herbertson Street junction. The bus was travelling towards Hamilton. It had stopped only 50 yards earlier to let passengers off and at the time of the accident was going at a comparatively slow pace.

Minister Under the Influence

On the 17th June 1939, shortly before the outbreak of WW2, a motor car accident happened on Glasgow Road, Blantyre. Two cars collided, resulting in injuries of three men. When the police were called, it was found that, Lanarkshire minister, John Black Allan of Rutherglen was under the influence of drink! He was charged at Hamilton Sheriff Court on Thursday 22nd June with driving a motor car when under the influence of drink. Allan pleaded guilty, and was fined £15 or sixty days' imprisonment. Sheriff Norman Walker also ordered Allan be suspended from holding a driving licence for 12 months.

Roberts Land

On the western side of Herbertson Street, aside from the manse and Co-op buildings (explored shortly), the only other buildings were at Roberts Land. Contrary to what you may have read by others, there were no tenements located in Herbertson Street near its junction with Auchinraith Road.

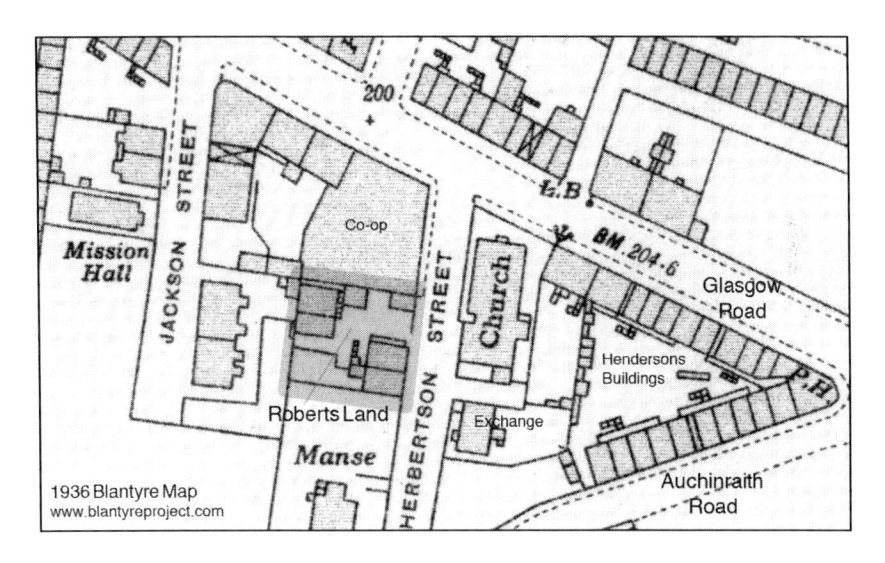

Figure 133 Roberts Land, Herbertson Street on 1936 map

The Roberts family moved to the Stonefield area sometime between 1875 and 1879 although came to Blantyre in the 1860's. William Roberts is a spirit dealer, together with John Roberts at Glasgow Road in 1879's Naismith's Directory. We'll explore John Roberts later in the book. There are other Roberts men related to this line in Blantyre then, such as David Roberts, a joiner at Miller's Land, Springwell in 1885 and who would later build homes at 7 and 9 Jackson Street. However, this article and the Herbertson Street land ownership is specifically related to William Roberts and Thomas Roberts line.

William and his brother Thomas Roberts first lived at nearby Avon Buildings on Glasgow Road at the corner of what would become Jackson Street, when arriving in Blantyre. They're noted as renting homes there in 1885 and may have been the constructors. Both men were to be joiners, William changing profession from spirit dealer, leaving that to another brother John, and deciding to exploit the requirement for house construction.

By 1891, William (born in Shotts in 1850) had established his own joinery business in Blantyre. He is noted in the census as being an employer, living at Stanley Place, just off Forrest Street along with wife Agnes, young sons David and James and daughters Janet, Marion and little Agnes.

Between 1892 and 1894, William Roberts and brother Thomas bought a modest sized square plot of land on the south side of Glasgow Road on the west side of Herbertson Street. It was directly opposite their rented homes. They constructed a double storey workshop, no doubt very secure being directly backed on to the Glasgow Road Police Station. Forming a small courtyard, were also 4 other double storey homes, 2 on the lower floor and 2 above. Their business was not a drop by place for people to buy wood, but instead a workshop used exclusively by the brothers and their employees for the purposes of constructing components for building homes for others.

The first occupants in 1895 were Thomas and William, each taking a lower house on the ground floor. Above them, accessed by stone steps at the rear the other 2 homes were let to Robert Naismith a blacksmith and Elizabeth Lauder a music teacher. A small shop was also built to sell some of their woodwork related items at the front facing out on to Herbertson Street but this was short lived and gone by 1905. This configuration of tenants existed until 1905 when James Robertson a tailor moved into the home formerly occupied by Elizabeth.

The business flourished and the Roberts Brothers were involved in the construction of many homes and buildings in Blantyre. The family were well known as were their extended family involved in other local businesses.

Around the outbreak of World War One, Thomas Roberts retired and moved to Dunoon. By 1915, William Roberts was left in charge of their business keeping an eye on Thomas's share. The workshop had a rented value of £10 per year. Houses in Herbertson Street now had addresses and William Roberts was still in the same house at number 4. Renting at number 2 was Alex Paterson with John Barr and James Sommerville occupying the others for rents of up to £18 per year. The little former shop was now a small street side workhut for family member Jessie Roberts, who had a little dressmaking business behind the police station.

Post WW2 Years

In 1920 William Roberts died in Blantyre, aged 70. Sons James and William Junior formed a company following their inheritance and "J&W Roberts (Joiners)" commenced trading. This was overseen by their Uncle David Roberts who had an interest. David Roberts moved into the house previously occupied by Thomas, and Mrs Agnes Roberts, the widowed wife of William continued to live at the other ground floor home. Upstairs were John Barr and Robert Hamilton, a clerk.

By 1925, the properties had slightly amended addresses due to the earlier arrival of the Co-op near the corner of Herbertson Street at Glasgow Road. Roberts Land still had 4 homes and a workshop, although it would appear by this time the workshop was in a diminished capacity and not operating as a fully fledged sawmill. That year, Janet Roberts, the daughter of William Senior was in the family home, with John Smith a motor driver in the other ground floor house. Upstairs, David Roberts a teacher and John Erskine, another teacher occupied the upper houses for rents up to £24/year. All these properties owned by J&W Roberts.

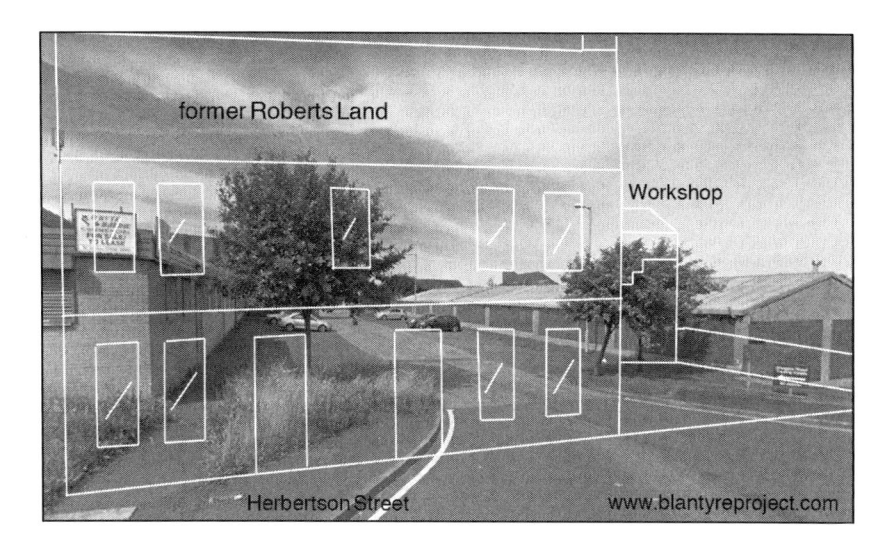

Figure 134 Location Line Drawing of how Roberts Land may have looked

1930 saw changes to the Herberston Street even numbered postal addresses again, due to the expansion and subdividing of shops within the nearby Co-op buildings to the north. The houses were allocated 10 and 12 Herbertson Street on the ground floor and 14 Herbertson Street was the upper floor. John Smith lived at number 10, James Roberts at number 12 and David Roberts and John Erskine above at 14 Herbertson Street. The Workshop at 8 Herbertson Street now also had machinery on the outside. James and William (Bill) Roberts were still the joinery owners (J&W Roberts).

Around WW2, a gap opened up in the wall at the back of the courtyard offering easy access from Roberts Land to family owned houses in Jackson Street. The Roberts family continued to live at Herbertson St, at Jackson Street and Craig Street into the 3rd quarter of the 20th Century. Roberts Land was entirely cleared in 1979 following the council's extensive compulsory purchase order, to make way for building the current small trading estate in which some of Blantyre's Glasgow Road traders were to be accommodated.

Police Station

Our Herbertson Street diversion over, lets get back to Glasgow Road. Prior to the existence of the current Police Station at Calder Street, Blantyre had an earlier police station at Stonefield.

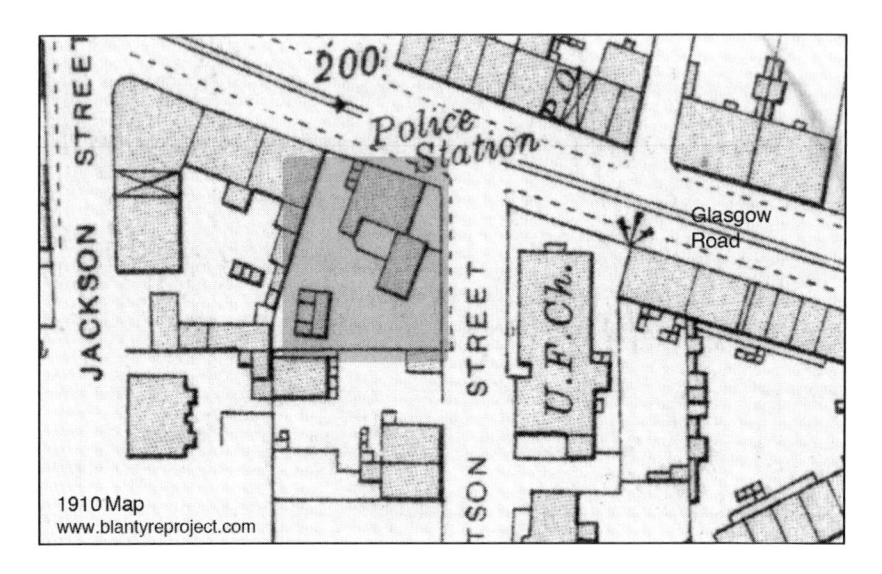

Figure 135 Former Police Station on Blantyre 1910 map

During the mid 1870's with population expanding rapidly, a growing requirement for keeping order and permanent police presence was needed for the expanding mining town. A police building was needed.

In 1875, the 'Commissioners of Police Supply' acquired a plot of land on the main Hamilton to Glasgow Road, near the corner of a track, which would eventually become Herbertson Street. The Police station was one of the earliest buildings in Stonefield, Low Blantyre centrally located between growing areas of Springwell and an expanding Stonefield. Built of stone, of s storey solid construction with a slate roof, it opened out on to the Hamilton to Glasgow Road. A wall was built around the perimeter and the main access in to the back courtyard was through a large stone framed gate approximately 12 foot high (presumably to accommodate slimline police carts or wagons of the era). This entrance was at the corner of what would become Herbertson Street and Glasgow Road.

At the rear of the building were two buildings, one co-joined with the station by a tall wall which almost certainly was the jail (the older term 'gaol' frittered out a few decades earlier.) Another smaller building looks to have been a wagon house or stores.

Certainly there are newspaper stories of police officers responding to incidents in Blantyre as early as 1875, a constable of that year being Mr William Oliver. It is highly likely though that police officers lived in Blantyre prior to this, although were employed out of Hamilton or Glasgow.

Even upon its construction, police officers could never have anticipated just how rapidly Blantyre was to grow that coming decade and incorporating just 3 houses for constables would have seemed adequate.

Walking along this side of the emerging Glasgow Road between 1875 and 1880 must have been an astonishing sight! To see open fields and hedgerows suddenly becomes rows of shop and houses would have been an exciting prospect for incoming miners seeking employment and housing.

Figure 136 Former Police Station in 1900

The station was situated beside the Avon Buildings immediately adjacent to the west as pictured, although the station itself was detached. In 1880, the mission hall was built directly across from the station at Herbertson Street and just over a decade later, Roberts Land was built to the rear of the station. With Blantyre so populated in the 1880's, there are several stories which highlight the fact that 3 or 4 officers, simply weren't enough.

Murderous Assault on Police

Blantyre is no stranger to a party, or a rammy for that matter, but in the early hours of Sunday 16th September 1883, an evening party at a Stonefield residence escalated into argument and quarrel resulting in some disgraceful scenes. Whilst on duty, Blantyre police Sergeant Stewart and Constable

McLeod heard the commotion going on outside the party house and decided to intervene, arresting the two combatants. However, the other people at the party were having none of this and clearly taking sides, struck the Sergeant on the back of the head with a brick. When McLeod dropped his prisoner and came to assist, the police officers were pelted in a fury of stones by some ten people. During the pelting, the Sergeant was struck down and stabbed through the left ear, on the left arm and below the chin, with what could be described as a pocket knife. The police, fearing for their lives, and admitting being outnumbered, left the scene and their prisoners jeered in freedom.

In such days before telephones or police radio, the only way to get back up, was to return to the station, where if you were lucky, other officers would be on duty or could be recalled.

Figure 137 Previously unseen photo of Blantyre Police Station c1900 at Glasgow Road

At the Blantyre Police Station, the bedraggled officers stumbled in to the shock of their colleagues. Thankfully, luck was on their side and two other officers were unusually on duty that weekend. Constable Morton and a young Constable Bruce from High Blantyre were both in plain clothes, but at least were on hand. The four officers proceeded back to the scene of the disturbance and quickly pinpointed one of the people they had tried to apprehend. Incredibly, as they approached the house, directly opposite Mr Scott's shop, Irishman John Kane was violently smashing in his mother's door with a pick axe and was clearly overcome by drink.

When the police officers tried to apprehend him, John Kane smashed the sharp end of the pick on to Officer Morton's skull, in two sharp and quick blows. Kane closed in as Morton fell to the ground clutching his bloodied head. As Kane moved in again, he had to be beaten off by Constable Bruce, a man half his age, and armed with only a small wooden police baton. Upon seeing her "boy" being beaten by officers, Kane's elderly mother lifted the pick axe and made swinging motions towards the officers. The pick was quickly disarmed by the other officers and Mrs Kane restrained, only making John Kane more angry. With Kane's mother is custody, Kane did the cowardly thing, and ran away.

The police officers saw quickly that officer Morton was insensible and delirious and decided to head back to the Station on Glasgow Road with the apprehended lady pensioner. Morton needed medical attention as quickly as possible. On the way there, Morton became unconscious and had to be helped back. This task was made more difficult as by now the house party and spilled out into the street and seeing Mrs Kane being led away, the small crowd decided to pelt the police officers with stones. Back at the Station, Dr Cooper asked for Morton to be transferred to the Royal Infirmary in Glasgow where that evening, upon halfway there, he regained consciousness. The cut to his head was an ugly one and a lot of blood was lost. In an ironic twist of fate, reporters later found out that Morton had only been at the Police Station that evening in his plain clothes, to hand in his notice and leave the police! It was also found out that John Kane, some 2 years earlier had been sentenced to 3 months under the Crime Prevention Act for wielding a pick at another person. Sergeant Stewart was confined to bed and apparently better the next day.

Speaking of which, as Sunday daytime arrived, a huge force from the neighbouring village came and promptly apprehended Patrick Kane, John's brother who had instigated the stone throwing. Mrs Kane was released without charge due to her age. Police Commander McHardy stationed at Coatbridge arrived in Blantyre later in the day to take charge, citing that an example of force should be made and attacks on the police would not be tolerated. The report ends with John Kane still missing, but with the entire surrounding police force looking for him.

Blantyre Riots 1887

DID YOU KNOW ?

On 7th and 8th February 1887, miners in Blantyre rioted in the streets smashing shops and property. At one point, the Police Station was attacked with so much damage done that the local police constables had to release the 2 prisoners in the cells. Many civilians and reinforcement police were hurt in this lively and troublesome commotion.

In 1886 Charles Wilson was in charge of the whole station which then had a rateable value of £45. By 1895 the Police Station and the 3 houses were owned by the County Council. Police officers stationed there were George Taylor, William Lochart and David MacAulay all renting for £5, 4 shillings.

In 1899, Mr. John Braid was a Police constable there, his wife Mary Braid died young on 26th May 1899 at 34 years old at the Police Station. By 1905 Robert Munn was constable, David Richardson the Sub inspector and John Miller another constable paying rent between £12 and £13 per annum.

The Police Station was then allocated the address 105 Glasgow Road, although the address as police premises was short lived, for in 1909, the Glasgow Road Police station was abandoned. Unfit for purpose in those Edwardian Times, with inadequate jail cells, police transferred to a new, larger custom built Police Station at Calder Street (corner Victoria Street.) The new police station being almost ready on 22nd March 1909.

Figure 138 Blantyre Police Force amongst other officers in 1908

In this exclusive unpublished photo from 1908, Blantyre Police officers are pictured with other Lanarkshire officers, although the location is not thought to be Blantyre.

The old Low Blantyre Police Station was bought by the Blantyre Co-operative Society following lengthy negotiations and then entirely demolished in summer 1915, during WW1. They bought the land to build their Central Premises. We end this article putting the station into a modern context.

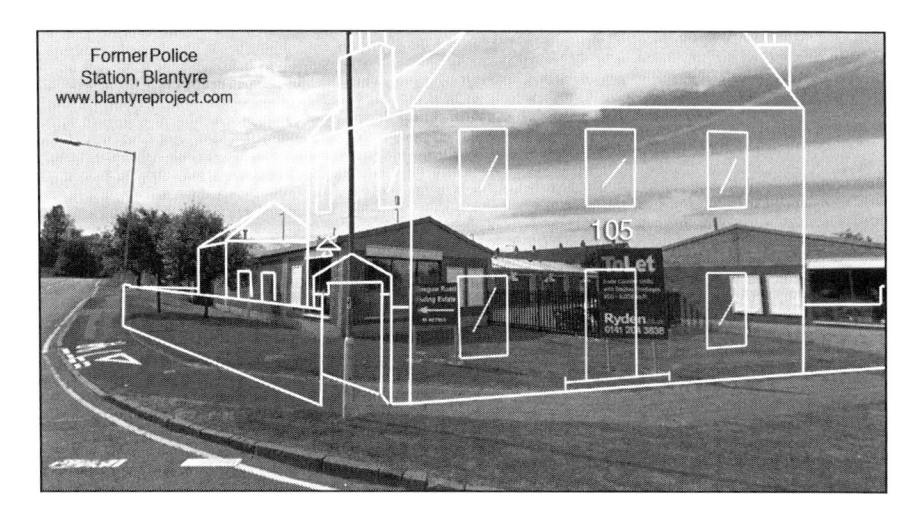

Figure 139 Location Line Drawing putting Police Station in modern context

Blantyre Project Social Media:

Bill Hunter: "Even in the 1960's there were no personal radios for Blantyre Police officers. There was a red light outside the Blantyre Police Station and one outside the High Blantyre Police Office. Should the office man require a constable, he would switch on the appropriate red light to alert the beat man.

The Beat Officer would then call at the relevant station to obtain the message. Or if he was lucky, on Glasgow Road near the telephone exchange, he would ask the telephone lady to call up the station and pass on the message. If you came across a live incident, procedure was to handcuff the accused person to a nearby lamppost and continue on your beat. You then had to call into the Police Station whilst on your beat, to ensure a vehicle was dispatched to retrieve said person. It was 1970 before personal radio's came on to the scene for Blantyre police."

Patrick Donnelly: "I'd be willing to bet, like me, not many people were aware of police stations in Blantyre before the current one at Calder Street was built. Its just something I've never thought about. Driving by this spot many times, I will take pleasure in pointing that location out to my children and work colleagues. "

Avon Buildings

Between 1876 and 1878, two business partners jumped on the construction bandwagon and embarked on a venture to build their own tenements on Glasgow Road. At a time when nearby Henderson's Buildings were being built, a plot of land further west was secured, between two tracks that would eventually become Jackson Street and Herbertson Street.

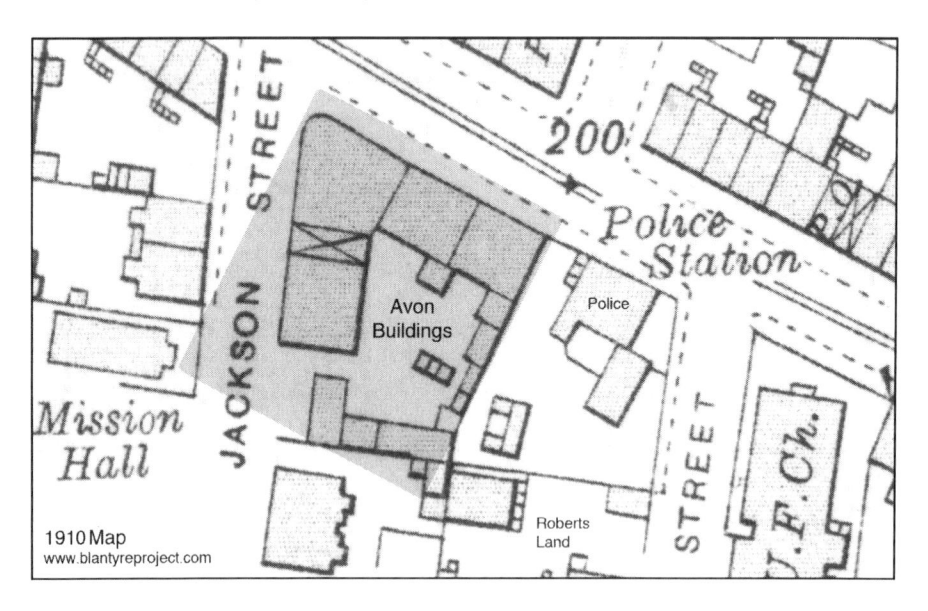

Figure 140 Former Avon Buildings in 1910, which later became part of Co-op

Mr. John Crow of 5 Afton Crescent, Paisley Rd, Glasgow and James Davidson, a grocer were the owners from afar. Seeing that William Roberts, (a joiner who would go on to build nearby Roberts Land) was once of the first tenants, it may be likely that he was their builder. The name 'Avon' may have simply been a reference to the beautiful woodland river stretching from Drumclog to Larkhall, a scenic beauty spot in those Victorian times.

Blantyre Project Social Media:

Anthony Smith: "In the 1950's when I was a young boy I went to these buildings with my mother. The Co-op had 'pick your own shopping' by then. As you entered, there was a fixed stack of 'cubbys' with numbered doors containing wire baskets. You took out the basket, putting your shopping bag in and then did your shopping, actually being allowed to handle the goods! At the checkout, simply a singular tillpoint, you paid for goods and a staff member would give you your shopping bag back. If no baskets were available, you had to wait for one."

Built of stone with slate roof, the property was L shaped on plan, partly on Glasgow Road and partly on the track which would become Jackson Street.

The building was unusual in that the corner had a rounded roof, curved, rather than more traditional angular on most other Glasgow Road tenements. It was 2 storey and initially consisted of 4 upper homes and 4 lower ground floor shops, all with early addresses 1 – 6 Avon Buildings. Four tall prominent chimneys faced out on to Glasgow Road.

Figure 141 Avon Buildings, Glasgow Rd in 1933

The Avon Buildings were located at the corner of the junction of Glasgow Road and Jackson Street and adjacent to the Police Station. In 1879, Mr. Charles Clark was a carter living at these premises. Also at that time, J&G Hogg operated a short lived medical practice named 'The Stonefield Medical Hall."

In 1885, the premises were entirely let out, the owners choosing not to live there. Shops were occupied by (from east to west), Walter Getty saddlers, the middle 2 shops occupied by Blantyre Co-operative Society and the last shop at the corner was Andrew Graham's Dairy.

One of the owners, Mr. Crow was associated with the Co-operative Society and was already managing the first Co-op Shop which opened in 1883 nearby at Henderson's Buildings.

During the remainder of the 1880's, the flourishing Blantyre Co-operative Society were quickly establishing a presence in this area of Stonefield and it was quite apparent they sought out commercial opportunity at every turn.

Figure 142 former Avon Buildings before demolition at Jackson Street in 1978

By 1895, Blantyre Co-operative Society Ltd completely owned Avon Buildings, their secretary John Hamilton of Auchinraith managing the premises. It was likely bought in the late 1880's. The Co-operative expanded the outbuildings at the back, building a store and stables, closing off the open courtyard by a high wall at the back of the building on Jackson Street. This forced the only entrance into the rear through a large pend close on Jackson Street, something which secured the co-op acquisition significantly. The stables kept working horses, kept for their deliveries when pulling cairts (carts) around Blantyre.

Speaking of this back courtyard, elderly man Thomas Hartman recalls this area as a child in the 1930's commenting, "You went through between the buildings into a cobble stoned square. From there it was possible to enter each and every store for the delivery of goods. The public was not allowed to use this entrance, especially with all the horses mingling around. I can still hear the clip-clop of hoofs on the cobble stones and the shout of "Whooh Nelly!" and of course the habitual smell of dung in the air. I remember this was a closed in type square (courtyard) where all sounds and smells being accentuated by the surrounding buildings. It was hustle and bustle of a certain kind. I know about this, for there was I, standing outside the entrance with my pall and shovel, waiting for the , you know what."

In 1895 William Batters, the Blantyre plumber lived in one of the homes. The other 3 homes were occupied by the Dunlop, Clark and Fleming families. Tenants rented for around £8 or £9 per year. The 4 shops were still there.

Getty Saddlers still at the same location, the Co-op running the 2 central shops but having now moved into the larger corner shop at Jackson Street, Graham's dairy vacated by then.

By 1905, the Co-op had turned the Jackson Street side of the building, south of the pend close into their Committee Rooms and offices with registered address 1 Jackson Street. At the rear, a coach house was built which would later become a garage to house delivery vehicles. The rest of the building was to change use dramatically as houses and shops were subdivided to maximize rental and retail opportunities. This appears to be common practice throughout Blantyre in the 1900s-1920's before fashion for larger homes became more desirable. In 1905, instead of 4 shops and 4 homes, there were now 6 shops, 2 workshops at the rear courtyard, the stables, coach house and 10 homes, all contained inside the original building and yard imprint. The businesses were now all owned by the Blantyre Co-operative Society having evicted all private shopkeepers. Those running the shops were now employees.

Prior to WW1 Avon Buildings Co-op shops included a boot shop, repair workshop and butchers shop with back stores. Proper departments were forming too with shops for Hardware, Dairy, Drapery and Grocery. Tenants were mostly employees with jobs such as vanman, flesher and bootmaker.

Need for Expansion

Avon Buildings were initially allocated odd numbered postal addresses of 107-125 Glasgow Road and 1-3 Herbertson Street. With such a flurry of commercial activity here, the Co-op along with other shops in Low and High Blantyre had established themselves as a major factor in Blantyre retail business. Private rented shops like Getty's saddlers shop were forced to move to other nearby properties.

By 1910, new larger premises were needed and planned. The perfect opportunity arose for the Co-op in 1909 when the old Police Station next door to the east was abandoned, presenting opportunity for buildings and land, right next door to their own building. However, the County Council, owners of the old police station buildings and land, likely knew this for discussions were protracted and lengthy, most like through the Co-op not willing to pay the asking price.

However, a deal was done and by 1915, not too long after the First World War had started, the Co-op owned the old Police station, note in the valuation roll that year as being "empty". The police station was demolished by Blantyre Co-operative Society Ltd between April and October 1915, the land entirely cleared at the corner of Herbertson Street by the start of November 1915, paving the way for their new, large Central Premises.

We leave the name Avon Buildings behind in 1915, for following WW1, the premises despite existing until 1979 were later known as part of the Co-operative Buildings, an extension if you like of their Central Premises. The name "Avon" confined to history. In 1915, Avon Buildings had 7 shops and 9 houses.

Once their Central Premises were built, the whole building including Avon Buildings were later given new modern addresses 111 – 127 Glasgow Road, with numbers 107 and 109 disappearing when outbuildings at the back were cleared.

Before moving on, this remarkable picture was taken between 1900 and 1910 and looks west with Jackson Street leading off to the left in the background. Pictured in some clarity are Avon Buildings showing the whole block occupied by the Blantyre Co-operative Society.

Figure 143 Former Avon Buildings in 1978 prior to demolition in 1979

Figure 144 Avon Buildings around 1910 looking west

We pick up the rest of this buildings history when exploring the Co-operative Central Premises next. Today the site is the western part of the Glasgow Road Industrial Estate.

Blantyre Project Social Media:

Elizabeth Weaver: "The staff were always so smartly turned out at the Co-Op. One of our uncles John Scott, worked in the Grocery department at the Co-op in High Blantyre for many years. They had to wear freshly laundered white aprons at all times. Most men back then only had a couple of shirts for work wear but our Granny Scott had to launder and starch the 7 white collars demanded by the co-bosses. Collars had to be fresh every day and they needed 2 for a Saturday! (presumably as staff would get so hot from being so busy that day). The window displays were also immaculate as can be seen in photos in this book."

Moira Mulvaney Pacheco: "When I left school, I worked in the hardware department and drapers in the Co in High Blantyre. The hardware shop had a big fire at the back of the shop to keep it warm."

Maggie Anderson: "The manager of that hardware department was Violet Robertson, I'm sure around that time, 1959 or 1960."

By Paul D Veverka

Blantyre Co-operative Society Ltd

The Co-operative Society has long played a vital part in Blantyre's commerce since the 1880's. It was such a monumental part of everyday life in in this town that it's worth touching upon their history further. Although the Co-op, as an enterprise has roots as far back as 1844, Blantyre's first co-operative was opened on 7th September 1883 at 142 Station Road. It provided reasonable prices for all sorts of commodities including clothes, fire fuel and food. It introduced huge competition into Blantyre at a time when population was expanding rapidly. As miners and their families flocked to Blantyre, they found choice in either becoming a co-op member and the loyalty payments that brought, or sticking to what they knew at all the other local shops. For many people it was a rigid choice and one they stuck to for a long time. Incentives and loyalty dividends were a big attraction.

In late 1883, they also opened a shop at Henderson's Building to the east side of Glasgow Road, rented from William Henderson and occupied it until around 1920. They also rented two central shops at nearby Avon Buildings, a property they would eventually own completely. It all expanded as the Co-op prospered until they had occupancy of much of the building, in which eventually there were the Office, a Hall, Central Grocery, dept., a Dressmaking and Millinery dept., a Gent's Outfitters, a Fleshing dept., Ante-Rooms and a Boardroom. Silent films were shown in the Henderson's Building hall from 1903.

The Co-op or 'Co-operative Wholesale Society' (to give it its full name) had a slow start and Mr. George Pate audited the first balance sheet on January 3rd, 1884. Profits were surprisingly good but larger memberships were needed. During his subsequent years from 1885 to 1891 he served as secretary to the society and took more than a keen interest in the early stages and in particular how he could attract the growing population.

In 1891, Glasgow Road was going through a transformation. New sandstone buildings were being constructed in quality tenements with shops on the ground floor. The Society expanded, building their first dedicated, independently owned premises on Glasgow Road not far from the top of Station Road. Later this new premises became known as Co-op Two, as slowly and surely the smaller premises at Station Road was relegated and was saved from fire in 1931. Part of the Co-op 2 building is still there today, a long 3 storey building above the current funeral parlour. . With the expansion more goods and services were sold and separate departments like clothing or shoes, took off with people employed to act as traveling salespeople, amongst them John Duncan, grandfather of the writer, who sold boots.

On Wednesday 1st March 1900, the annual soiree and concert under the auspices of Blantyre Co-operative Society was held in the Masonic Hall, Stonefield. Mr. Thomas Gray, president, occupied the chair. There was a large attendance. Mr. Daniel H Gerard was present and delivered an address. The programme of the concert was sustained by Miss. Clara A Butler, Miss Alice Golding, Master William C McPhie, Mr. R.C McGill and Mr. Robert Steven, the accompanist. The Children's Gala Day was instituted in 1900. Penny Savings Banking commenced in 1901 and an early form of hire purchase was available.

Years of Prosperity

The large Co-op buildings flourished and membership grew rapidly. By 1903 High Blantyre Main Street had a major co-op building to rival those of Low Blantyre. The High Blantyre Building dates to 1903 as confirmed by the 1903 date stamped on to the cast iron rainwater collection boxes, salvaged in the 1990's and now used as planters at the nearby Priestfield Hall.

Around them grew a supporting network of smaller outlets. Individual Co-op owned Bakeries, grocers, chemists and a funeral parlour were amongst services offered. Some of these outlets were located in Broompark Road, in Dixons Rows, Auchinraith and scattered all along Glasgow Road.

Further expansion came again in 1909 when the co-op entered negotiations to acquire the site of the old Police Station at the corner of Herbertson Street and Glasgow Road. They eventually acquired the police site next to the Avon Buildings and in 1915 demolished the old police building to make way for their new Central premises. A little earlier in 1914 plans were drawn up for a new Co-op building.

At a meeting on 13th July 1916, the Co-operative considered plans of installing a new cinematograph within their new proposed hall. The Cinematograph would run for about 14 years before the 'talkies' put it out of the game (the Co-op couldn't get silent films any more to fit the machine).

One of the managers in the 1920's was Mr. George Muir. Longest serving Co-op manager appears to be Thomas Carrigan who managed Glasgow Road Co-op society for 33 years retiring in June 1927.

During 1929, discussions commenced about the possibility of amalgamation with Stonefield Independent Co-op. A news report in November 1929 tells, "Co-operators in the Blantyre district are waiting for the next move in the deadlock which has taken place in connection with the proposed amalgamation between Blantyre Cooperative Society and Stonefield

Independent Co-operative Society, also in Blantyre. A recent meeting of the members of the former society ended in an uproar, and two directors of the S.C.W.S., who were on the platform, were forced to leave the meeting. The attitude taken up by the committee of the Blantyre Society in their matter of the proposed amalgamation has raised some resentment, and interesting developments are expected shortly."

Figure 145 Co-op Staff at Number 1 Branch in the 1930's

By 1930, the Co-op ownership was expansive. That year, the Society owned 2 houses in Auchinraith Road. A property named Ayton Cottage at number 31 and neighbouring number 33. They also owned a coal yard, garage and petrol tank next to a house at 126 Auchinraith Road in 1930.

Glasgow Road was a street where the Co-operative owned many properties. Amongst them in 1930, on Glasgow Road a drapery shop at number 105, a butchers shop at 107, a grocers shop at 109, a house at number 113, a dairy shop at number 115, a fish shop at 117, a shop at 119, a hardware shop at 121, a boot shop at number 123, a fruit shop at 125 and a bread shop at 127. Not to be confused with Stonefield Independent Co-op further west.

Their property ownership was also apparent at High Blantyre with the 3 storey tenements at Main Street. These still exist today and have addresses 309 to 319 Main Street, the co-op logo carved into the upper stonework. At those address there were several shops located on the lower floor. The Co-op Grocery at number 309, the bread shops at 313, butchers at 315 and a dairy shop at 317. Numbers 311 and 319 were houses according to the 1930 valuation roll. Directly across the road at 254 on the lower floor was their drapery shop, which is now Kathy's. The same address also had a store, now Snips. The Co also owned 252, which was a house.

Figure 146 inside Typical 1930's Co-op Store

Also in 1930, the Co-op owned a tailors shop and workroom at 111 Glasgow Road as well as the Blantyre Co-operative Society Bakery at Auchinraith and stables. They also owned a workshop for boot repairs at 3 Jackson Street that same year.

The Co-op also owned shops in the lower floor of former properties 102 and 104 Broompark Road. This was at Broompark Road near Larkfield Bing, in approximately the location of the current Blantyre Carrigans Restaurant. They also owned 2 houses at number 3 at the former Jackson Street and another house at number 5. The Co-op were also leasing a shop at 88 and 90 Station Road, renting from Charles McIntyre. At Stonefield Road, the society occupied a shop at number 23 on the eastern side and a butchers shop with machinery at number 29.

Nearby, at the junction of Calder Street, at number 33 Stonefield Road, they owned a licensed store, which they leased out to David Gibson & Sons. At Herbertson Street, the Co-Op owned and occupied the Hall and Rooms at number 6, (which was let out at £100 rent a year) the lesser hall, office and boardroom at number 4 and a shop, millinery, petrol pump and tank also at number 4. Their gents department store was at number 2 Herbertson Street. They also owned part of the land at Basket and Auchentibber at this time and had former interests at Calderwood glen. You'll probably gather where we're heading with this. The Co-op was everywhere in Blantyre!

Co-op Tokens & Checks

Figure 147 Co-op tokens used in lieu of money (colour)

Various Co-ops may have introduced their own tokens at different times for their own purposes. For instance, you might find some Societies produced bread tokens while others distributed tokens for milk or coal.

Initially, these checks were integral to the payment of the dividend, the checks being your evidence or receipts of purchases, but latterly in the 1950's and 60's, they were used as cash, having the same monetary value as the coins in circulation at the time. Gordon Cook local historian comments on this as follows, "I would suggest when the carbon copy slips were first issued, giving a copy to the customer while retaining a copy for the Co-op Office in Herbertson Street. After this one would pay with a mixture of cash and checks, and likewise change could be given in the same manner, i.e. 3d cash and a 1d check."

Gordon continued, "You might notice from the photograph that these checks were issued and then re-issued at a later date to replace those that became too worn, got lost, or were stolen (which happened often).

The first time these checks appeared in Blantyre was Thursday 14th January 1897, and they were made of celluloid. They were introduced for the benefit of the butcher, who was seemingly being hindered by having to write a check slip for every customer. The butcher's van (horse and cart) was commissioned in Blantyre around July 1892, so he had been writing out lines for 5 years before he got the new celluloid checks. The Independent Co-op in Blantyre also issued their own checks, same as the original Co-op's but for the name Independent added.

The other tokens are fairly self explanatory, if a child was sent with a token for a pint of milk, he certainly wouldn't be tempted to spend it in the sweet shop, and of course the mother couldn't put it in the gas meter, so milk was assured at the end of the week It was about 1930 before Blantyre caught up with other Societies and began selling milk in bottles. Coal was historically brought from Cambuslang to Blantyre in the early 1800s, but the Co-op in Blantyre didn't enter into this side of business until the winter of 1909.

So having first served a young lad named Alexander McCluskey in late August 1883, after almost 90 years of trading and about 75 years of handling checks, it all came to an end on Tuesday 25th July 1972, when the Society was officially wound up."

Mergers, crimes & other events

At the end of February 1931, negotiations between 4 large Co-operative societies in the area completely failed on coming to a decision to merge each into one large society. Hamilton Central, Burnbank, Stonefield and Blantyre were involved with 3 parties unable to agree to the demands of one particular party. Deadlock was reached and a decision to continue as normal was reached.

Stonefield Independent Co-operative Society merged with Blantyre Co-operative Society on 29th April 1932.

A year later on 31st August 1933, fifteen year old Joseph McCudden of School Lane, Blantyre walked into the Main Street branch of the Co-op, produced a revolver and held up the shop and its customers. During a frightening couple of minutes, the general manager Robert Marshall Robb was assaulted, but not shot. Overpowered on his way out, Joseph was apprehended quickly with nothing stolen and no doubt a hefty sentence following. Indeed, there are many small stories of thefts throughout the decades from these shops, which must have seemed attractive and plentiful targets for people when times were hard.

On 31st December 1935, two men were charged after a raid by detectives on their houses at High Blantyre, which led to an appearance at Hamilton J.P. Court. The two men had decided to stock up for their festive holiday a little earlier than planned, and in a manner most illegal. Mr. David Cunningham, labourer, 10 Cemetery Road, High Blantyre, and Alexander Campbell Anderson, labourer, 8 Cemetery Road, High Blantyre, a 223mphasiz, both of whom were charged with having, between 6 p.m. on December 2 and 5 a.m. on December 3, while acting in concert, broken into the shop of the Blantyre Co-Operative Society at 102-104 Broompark Road, High Blantyre, and stolen three hams, 20 lb. of cheese, three tins of pressed beef, two bottles of sauce, bottle of sweets, and tokens to the value of £83 10s. At the request of the Fiscal, the accused, without being asked to plead, were remanded in custody pending further inquiries.

In the 1952 Statistical Account of Blantyre it is commented "The Blantyre Co-operative society has a very large membership, has commodious premises in Station Road, Glasgow Road, Auchinraith Road (corrected to Herbertson Street) and Main Street.

The staff had to be impeccably turned out. The male assistants had to wear starched collars on their shirts (removable collars) – a clean one every day and two on a Saturday, presumably because they were so busy on a Saturday and the collars got dirtier. All work aprons had to be immaculate at all times and shop assistants' hands had to be scrubbed frequently. There was sawdust on the floor prior to the Co-op becoming self-service, which also was swept and replaced at frequent intervals. Counters adorned the shops all around the walls and there was usually a partially filled butter barrel in the middle of the shop in High Blantyre. In the Main Street premises, also were huge cheeses with a large cheese-wire cutter. The staff members were so accomplished at judging weight that they'd cut it, weigh it, and rarely had to take a bit off or add to it.

DID YOU KNOW

A few other interesting facts about our local Co-op shops. The late local historian, Jimmy Cornfield as a boy of 14 found work at his local Low Blantyre Co-op store as a messenger boy. Like others of his age the job led to a higher position with a trade to be learned. In Jimmy's case apprentice cobbler, before leaving for his time in the army.

During the 1930's, Mr. George Hunter worked for the Co-op as a delivery driver still with horse and cart, but by 1940's and 1950's he had an electric float.

In 1953, the Women's guild celebrated their 50th Anniversary of receiving bulk buy discounts, with a party. The newspaper reported, "Fifty years old and still going strong" – and that was obviously so at the Jubilee Party at Blantyre Central Co-operative women's guild. Cutting the cake were Mrs T. McDonagh the president, Mr Gordon Clark who handed over the cake on behalf of the management, Mrs Sarah Peat a founder member and Mrs M. Mundell vice president. "

The Society was finally integrated into the S.CW.S Retail Group in 1972 and "lost" its named identity then. In 1978 the Co-op tried unsuccessfully to be the new superstore in Blantyre, losing out to ASDA. Today, the brand of Co-op still exists in the town to a small extent, but nowhere near the extent and vital lifeline it was in previous Centuries.

Blantyre Project Social Media:

Davy Thomson: "My Uncle Alex Paterson was manager for the Co-op. He had a flat above John's Superstore in Auchinraith Road, which came with the job. He was also President of the Blantyre Miner's Bowling Club in the late 1960's, or early 1970's."

Mary Kirkbride: "I remember going to the Co-op for butter and cheese. It was amazing how they knew how much to slice. It was then wrapped in paper after being patted down with paddles. Happy memories."

John McGaulley: "My Aunt Mary McGaulley worked in this shop in the 1950's."

Fairlie Gordon: "The Co was a main employer of people in Blantyre for many years. I spent a lot of time in their yard at Auchinraith Road being a milkboy on Wilkie Clarkin's van with Jock Wallace and full time vanboys, Stewart and Peter Reid and Steven Flynn. Some of the other drivers were Rab Shearer, Davie Campbell, John Harliburton, and Jim O'Brien who did the purvies for a while."

Gary Doonin: "My mothers address was 124/126 Auchinraith Road and the Co yard was next door. I remember the yard stored all the vans and milk floats. You could get ginger, cakes and even a cobblers. It was a massive place, looked after by Mr. Stewart, whose wife stayed upstairs in a house overlooking the yard above the shop. They were a very nice couple."

Elizabeth Weaver: "The Co was a busy place in the 1950's. Everybody in Blantyre did their shopping there and there would be long queues at the counters and at the cash desk where you had to give your co-op number. Sawdust on the floor, changed throughout the day if anything was spilled on it. Children would entertain themselves by poking the sawdust around until being told to stop! In those days lots of babies were still carried in their mother's shawls and young children had to wait patiently beside. It was a point often for staff to make an educated guess at quantities as they cut cheese or meat but was usually very accurate, being a daily task. Later on, when prams became the norm, there were rows of prams outside the Co-op. Everyone spoke to babies as they passed, some still in their prams whilst mothers shopped! There was constant activity, everybody knew everybody and a feeling of safety in doing that. Modern parents would be absolutely horrified at the thought of doing that now. Imagine!"

Blantyre Co-operative Society Central Premises

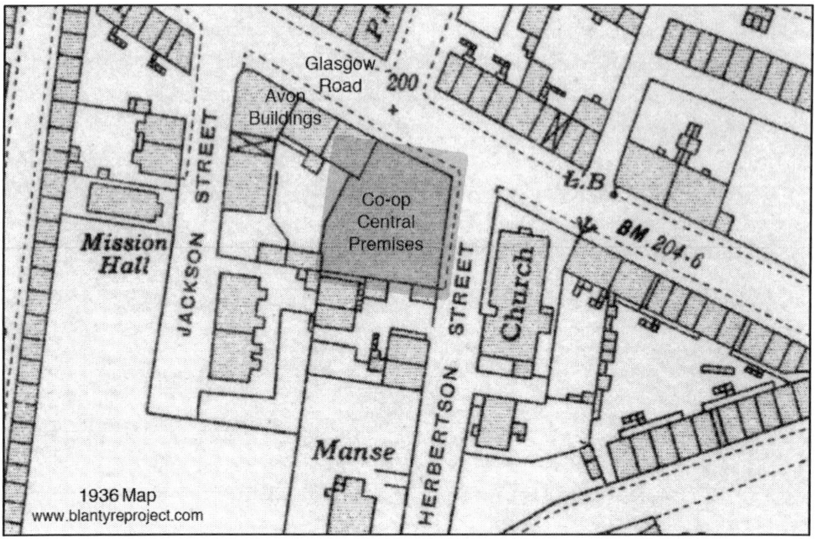

Figure 148 Former Co-op Central Premises on 1936 Map

Blantyre Co-operative Society's Central premises was a former large L shaped, impressive building in Low Blantyre, which contained several Co-op shops, their Head Office and large community hall at the western side of the junction of Glasgow Road and Herbertson Street (opposite Forrest Street.)

Construction had commenced at the start of WW1. Located on the former old police station site, the 'Memorial Stone' of their new Hall, shops and offices was laid on the afternoon of Saturday 6th November 1915 and construction lasted throughout 1916 and into 1917.

Mr R. Lyon, president of the society, performed the ceremony in the presence of the committee, representatives of the Educational Committee and Women's Guild, three of the local contractors engaged on the buildings, Mr Lochhead (architect), and Mr Dow (measurer). Mr Andrew Wright, the builder, on behalf of the architect and himself, presented Mr Lyon with the sliver trowel, suitably inscribed, with which the ceremony was performed. The company afterwards adjourned to the Board Room, where Mr Lochhead presented Mr Lyon with a handsome gold bracelet for Mrs Lyon, associating Mr Wright and Mr Dow with himself in the presentation.

The new buildings, which had been designed by Messrs Cullen, Lochhead and Brown, of Hamilton, were estimated to cost around £10,000, and when they were completed, formed a prominent architectural feature of the town.

The new premises were formally opened by a series of soirees, concerts, and cinema entertainments, which took place on Monday, Tuesday, Wednesday, and Thursday , 12th, -15th February 1917 and again on the same nights the following week. The soirees were given free to members. Mr Thos. Gray, president, occupied the chair during evenings, and was supported on the platform by the local clergy and doctors. A splendid tea was provided, thereafter a fine musical programme was submitted, the following very talented artistes contributing :— Miss G. Amory (soprano) and Mr J. L. Hilton, (tenor), with Mr Jas. Buchanan as accompanist. Addresses were given by a number of co-operators from Glasgow. During intervals in the programme a cinema display was given by the Society's own cinematograph. Altogether, the opening ceremonies proved very successful and were thoroughly enjoyed by the large audiences each evening. Handsome samples of cigarettes and soap, kindly presented by the S.C.W.S., were also distributed during the evening.

Figure 149 Central premises photographed in 1933, Glasgow Road on right

The new premises, which were signed with "Blantyre Co-operative Central Premises" incorporated architectural additions in an early art-deco style and included a large upper hall with good access. The façade made the building much more prominent from other nearby two-storey tenements and shops. Amongst the first uses of the halls, were Burns recitals, concerts, speeches, women's guild and meetings by Blantyre Golf Club. The General manager was Mr. George Muir. The new Central Premises accommodated their own dedicated shops and offices, without having to rent and should not be confused with Stonefield Independent Co-op further westwards.

It is here we pick up the story of adjacent Avon buildings, also owned by the Co-op. Together, from 1917, the whole building became known only as owned by the Co-op. A formidable line of shops was suddenly apparent, and although not quite the longest frontage of shops in Blantyre, certainly was one of the largest. A great place to do your shopping.

Figure 150 Aerial photo of Central Premises & Avon Buildings in 1950

Of course, there wasn't much to celebrate in those first few years. Britain was at war with Germany. On 3rd March 1917, The Co-operative Women's Guild (Blantyre Branch) entertained seventy wounded soldiers from Gateside and Caldergrove Hospitals. The entertainment took place in the Society's new Hall, at Herbertson Street. Mrs Lamond, Guild president, in a few words, welcomed the boys as they sat down to tea. A splendid programme was then submitted, in which the following took part :— Misses Scoular, Mrs Hunter; Mr Smythe, elocutionist, Larkhall; Misses Scoular, Meikle, and Houston (who delighted the audience with their delightful dancing); Miss Porter, pianist; and Mr Higgison, violinist. The guests were then given a cinema entertainment, followed with whist, hat-trimming, and nail-driving competitions, with prizes. A second tea was provided, and the boys each received a box of fifty cigarettes and the nurses boxes of chocolates. On the call of the sergeant, the men gave three ringing cheers to the Guild members who had provided them with such an enjoyable afternoon. Great credit is reflected on the members of the Guild Committee who organised the entertainment. Through the kindness of Mr Moller, general manager of the Lanarkshire Tramways Co., a special tramcar conveyed the soldiers to and from the hospitals.

The Co-op's registered office changed from 1 Jackson Street to 4 Herbertson Street upon the building of central premises which had addresses 105-125, which incorporated Avon Buildings).

In 1920, the Co-op shops in the whole Central Premises (also known as Co-op number 1) block were as follows: The lesser hall at 8 Herbertson Street, Office and board rooms above 4 Herbertson Street which had a dressmakers on the ground floor (although this became a shoe shop in post WW2 years). At the corner at 105 Glasgow Road was the drapery department, at 107 Glasgow Road the fleshers, 109 was the grocery department. Next continuing to head west on Glasgow Road was a tailor's shop and workroom, at 115 was the dairy, 117 was the fish-shop, 121 was hardware, 123 boot shop, 125 fruit corner shop, with 127 bread shop on the opposite corner at Jackson Street.

The large entrance to the offices and halls located on Herbertson Street across from the Burleigh Church led upstairs. Members could collect their dividend from the upper offices, spending their loyalty bonuses. Dances were held often in the upper halls on Wednesdays, Fridays and Saturdays but license did not go beyond midnight. Functions and community groups of all types were often held on the other evenings.

'Rammy' outside the Hall

The halls were no stranger to trouble. A significant rammy occurred outside the hall on the evening of Saturday 30th January 1926. Seven young men from Burnbank had come over to Blantyre to attend a dance in the Blantyre Co-operative Hall. Whilst in there, growing concern and rumour was whispered amongst the males at the dance that there "was to be trouble outside" afterwards. The hall keeper concerned, closed the doors quickly that evening after the dance ended and things "kicked off outside". After the dance the Burnbank men had went outside and a crowd had assembled around them. It is unknown what they had done within the dancehall to enrage so many males from Blantyre. Being pursued, the Burnbank men tried to board a tramcar back to Hamilton, but were surrounded and had to defend themselves, being pursued by a small crowd of men from Blantyre.

What was described then as "regular battle" started on Glasgow Road both on board and off the tram. The car was held up and the driver prevented from moving forward. Blantyre Police arrived and promptly arrested 2 men from Blantyre. When the 2 Blantyre men were arrested, the Blantyre crowd turned on Police with a threatening attitude and started throwing stones at them. During the arrests, the 7 men from Burnbank ran off towards Springwells, but were later apprehended further up the road by police. At Hamilton J.P. Court on Monday 1st February 1926 the seven young men from Burnbank and two from Blantyre were charged with committing a breach of the peace by conducting themselves in a disorderly manner and using obscene language.

The Justices found the charge against one of the men not proven, but all the others were convicted, each being fined £2 each or £1 depending on their involvement.

By Paul D Veverka

Central Premises remembered

In 1930, the Co-Op owned and occupied the Hall and Rooms at number 6, (which was let out at £100 rent a year) the lesser hall, office and boardroom at number 4 and a shop, millinery, petrol pump and tank also at number 4 Herbertson Street. Their gent's department store was at number 2 Herbertson Street. The Glasgow Road premises remained unchanged in use for several decades. During the 1960's onwards 125 Glasgow Road became an electrical shop at the corner of Jackson Street as technology evolved and electrical goods became popular. The Co also owned 127 used as their bread shop.

Many entertainers performed in Blantyre at the Co-op Halls. Robert Wilson the Scottish tenor played at the hall, to the delight of a Blantyre crowd.

On Wednesday 22nd October 1930, the 188th quarterly general meeting of the Blantyre Co-operative Society was held, which ranked as one of the largest and most uproarious ever held the Society's history. The origin was the fact that the committee had dismissed seven of the grocery salesmen in the Central premises one just a fortnight before and the other six the previous Friday. It was fully expected that such a phenomenal dismissal of the servants would create more than ordinary interest. Hence a meeting numbering from 600 to 800 was held. When the time came for general business, the chairman was bombarded with questions relating to the dismissals, and motions and counter-motions were made all at once and pandemonium prevailed until the chairman, Mr. Matthew M'Phail brought the meeting to an end. There was a motion put at the meeting to abide by the committee's decision, and another that the matter be remitted back to the committee with a view to the reinstatement of the dismissed servants. The former motion received scanty support, but for reconsideration a perfect sea of hands responded, and so the whole matter had to be reconsidered by the committee.

In 1949, the Co-op hugely extended their halls and premises at the back, primarily used for stores and further offices. During the late 1950's the grocery department became self service and like many shops in the UK, this caused quite a stir at the thought of actually being able to be trusted to touch the goods before they were paid for!

Following the winding up of Blantyre Co-operative Society in 1972, the property shops were privately let out to local businesses.

"Wheels" was a former cycle shop in the 1970's at 6 Herbertson Street, near the corner of Glasgow Road. Owned by Martin Johnson, it was a cycle repair shop on the lower ground floor. The shop branched out into selling motorcycles in a short lived run up to Christmas 1978.

Figure 151 Former Central Premises private shops in 1979

107 and 109 Glasgow Road became JR Reid Printers, who traded from this location before being moved in 1979 to the same location in the new Auchinraith Trading Estate. They would later move again to custom premises nearby in the late 1980's. 111 Glasgow Road was Glen Travel, 113 the 'Lucky House' Chinese Takeaway and 115 Glasgow Road became Jimmy Pollock's Service Centre (for vacuum repairs) shown on James McGuire's photo above.

> Blantyre Project Social Media:
>
> **Gary Doonin:** "The Co Hall in the early 1970's at Herbertson Street was a place used for playdays for local kids during Summer holidays. It was used a base for Whitehill Accies Football Boys Club between 1976 and 1978 for meetings and the boys would train in the large hall."
>
> **Betty McLean**: "The Co-op Delivery van came round with goods. Normally, my mother would bake cakes, but sometimes, for a wee treat I was sent to the van for 2 cakes. Dick Stewart was one of the drivers. Willie Mackie worked in the butchers co-op shop in High Blantyre Main Street. You had to be careful queuing as the carcasses hung just inside the door! Shopping in those days took a lot of time, going from one place to another. Men usually did leave the shopping to the women. I remember when my father needed new shoes, my mother would head off to the Co-op and it would be several trips later back and forth until she got the size right. Can you imagine that happening today!?"
>
> **Moira Mulvaney Pachecho:** "Different colour tokens for different values"

Following final approval when the council acquired the building by compulsory purchase order in the 1970's, it was demolished by summer 1979. Today, the former Co-op Central premises is the site of the small modern Glasgow Road Industrial Estate at Herbertson Street.

Figure 152 Former Central Premises being demolished in 1979

Some Blantyre history enthusiasts have got this above photo wrong. We'll take the opportunity to correct it. It's not a photo of Blantyre Gaol, the Police Station or Roberts Building being demolished. Taken in 1979, this is the Central Premises and its large hall being pulled down following a disastrous fire. The fire prevented further trading and collapsed the dome earlier in 1978. The excavator sits on the edge of Roberts Land, which was out the picture to the left. The relocated telephone exchange at Forrest Street behind.

Blantyre Project Social Media:

Peter O Brien: "I worked as a vanboy. The driver was Davie Downie. The run started at Auchinraith Road at the Buggy Buildings, on to Hawthorn Place then down to Glasgow Road and finishing at the west end. We must have been super fit to do that all the time and still head off to football practice!"

Elizabeth Weaver: "We used to keep the co-op token checks in a wee china bowl on the sideboard. We were allowed to play with them for pretend shops, but they had to be counted and put back in the bowl, strictly afterwards!"

Figure 153 Central Premises and Avon Buildings in 1977

Figure 154 Central Premises and Avon Buildings 1978

These last few photos were taken in 1978 and 1979, but in the days of poor quality scans are rather blurry. Previously unseen and unpublished, they're still worth inclusion in this book, a reminder of days gone by.

Figure 155 Central Premises looking west along Glasgow Road 1978

Figure 156 Central Premises at Herbertson Street in 1978

Glasgow Road Industrial Estate

Glasgow Road Industrial Estate is the official name for the small industrial units although it has been known locally as Auchinraith Industrial Estate, sometimes known as Auchinraith Trading Estate. It was constructed at the corner of Herbertson Street and Glasgow Road in 1980 by the Council as a means to re-accommodate many traders who were entitled to relocation following the earlier compulsory purchase orders and redevelopment of Glasgow Road.

Located on the site of the former police Station, Central Premises and Avon Buildings, the estate still exists today and is entered from Herbertson Street, via a new street called 'Rosendale Way', a nod to the nearby former building of that name.

The estate consists of 2 blocks facing on to Glasgow Road with parking and yard areas to the rear, where customer entrances are located. One block is large and L shaped, the other block on Glasgow Road is subdivided into 2 smaller buildings. The blocks should not be confused with the larger Scot Industrial Products Ltd building further up Herbertson Street, accessed from the same entrance. It is built of brown and beige bricks with corrugated roofs.

Figure 157 Glasgow Road Industrial Estate in 2016

One of the first tenants was JR Reid Printers in 1980, who relocated to the front of these buildings from their premises demolished on the same spot a year earlier.

Also following demolition of Anderson (Botterils) Building to the east, Botterils also continued trading from this new estate. Braidwood Builders were also initially major occupiers of these premises at the rear.

During the mid 1990's, Motorsport Racing based themselves there, involved in repairing and upgrading of high performance vehicles. Other businesses were MB Upholstery, Dream Kitchens later Palazzo and also Malin Service Centre. Thistle Sporting Goods was also in this industrial estate. They made bags, kilt rolls, pennants etc. and also sponsored Blantyre Vics football club for a while Not forgetting Eurotiles, Morses, TLS Van Hire and Nylon Machining Services.

Modern businesses that occupy the trading estate today include KD Designs, Top to Tail Dog Grooming, Scot Industrial Products at the rear, UPVC Window & Door Company, Horizon Lighting Ltd, Banlaw Systems (Europe) Ltd, Floor Store, RSD Glass works, Parkhill and Orr & Sons.

The letting agent is Ryden and Whyte & Barrie and in recent years, more of these units have punched out the bricks on the front façade to form large plate glass windows on the Glasgow Road frontage. This certainly offers far better advertising. A few of the units currently remain empty in 2017, the most recent business being the arrival of Horizon Lighting, which has a bright lights display in their shop windows during evenings.

Jackson Street Eastern Homes

With exception of the corner of the Avon Buildings, the only other buildings on the eastern side of Jackson Street was a double storey semi-detached tenement.

Between 1906 and 1909, Mr William Roberts, the joiner of Robert land, acquired land to the rear of his property. His new plot was in Jackson Street and he constructed a single detached tenement which had address 5 and 7 Jackson Street.

Figure 158 Former Homes at Jackson St

These were very well built homes, significantly taller than other 2 storey buildings. Less common for tenements, they were built of brick and had bay windows at the front and stairs accessing the upper houses at the rear. In all there were 9 initial homes in the block the first tenants being James Roberts a joiner, Thomas Taylor a plumber, William Smith an enginekeeper, Laurence Craig a barman, Archibald Muir a clerk, Robert Swinton a dentist, Joseph Jardine a pitworker and James Smith enginekeeper. One house was empty in 1915. Robert Swinton's home was larger and he paid £4 a year more in rent, indicating he may have run his dental practice from there.

William Roberts was forward thinking in understanding what his tenants wanted and was one of the pioneering builders in Blantyre to ensure washing spaces, toilets and baths were inside the building in the houses themselves, not in closes, or shared or outside. These homes would have been desirable and naturally higher rents of £13 per year at the time reflected this.

During World War 1, William sold his building in Jackson Street to family member, David Roberts, a teacher who lived at 12 Herbertson Street. Rents were raised up to £21 per annum perhaps telling that in the space of 5 years almost all tenants renting as aforementioned had changed.

By 1936 a further tenement had been built to the south, again owned by David Roberts. With the Co-op renumbering their building, these 2 tenements became known as 7 and 9 Herbertson Street. Owner David may have moved to Bothwell sometime after this.

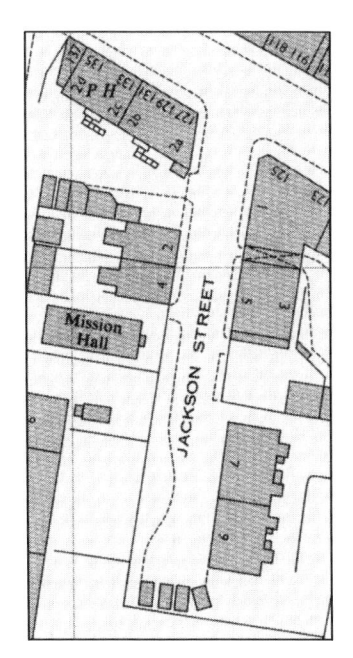

Figure 159 Jackson St in 1962

During the 1960's access was made at the rear gardens into adjacent Roberts Land at the back. A large high stone wall separated the properties and the adjacent Co-op. Around the same time, 4 small garages were built at the end of Jackson Street.

It is incorrectly written by others that Jackson Place or Jackson Terrace was in this street, but those properties were located off Stonefield Road, owned by Dixon's Pits and nowhere near this location.

Families continued to live in Jackson Street homes until they were acquired by the council's compulsory purchase order in 1977.

They were demolished in 1978, a year or so earlier than the demolition of nearby Co-op Central Premises.

By Paul D Veverka

Origins of Jackson Street

Jackson Street was a small dead end street of the 20th Century that developed from a field boundary of the former Springwell Farm. Branching off to the South of Glasgow Road it was suggested to the writer that the street may have taken its name from former Councilor Jackson of Bardykes, who did so much to improve the streets of Blantyre in the early 20th Century. This seems plausible but it is far more likely given the association with nearby Herbertson Street that the name Jackson was honouring the last family to own this land at Springwell Farm.

Aside from the Co-op buildings, there were a few homes on the east and western side. There was also a mission hall at the south western side, but this being too far off course for our Glasgow Road book, we'll leave that to be explored in another book at a later date.

Jackson Street disappeared from maps and from postal addresses in 1980 when the Glasgow Road Industrial Estate was built over it.

Blantyre Project Social Media:

Moira Lees "When I got married, we bought a flat in Jackson Street. This was in 1974 and we got number 7 Jackson Street for £1,800. It was a fabulous big flat and very handy for all the nearby shops."

CHAPTER 8
GLASGOW ROAD SOUTH
JACKSON ST TO CHURCH ST

Jackson Street Western Homes

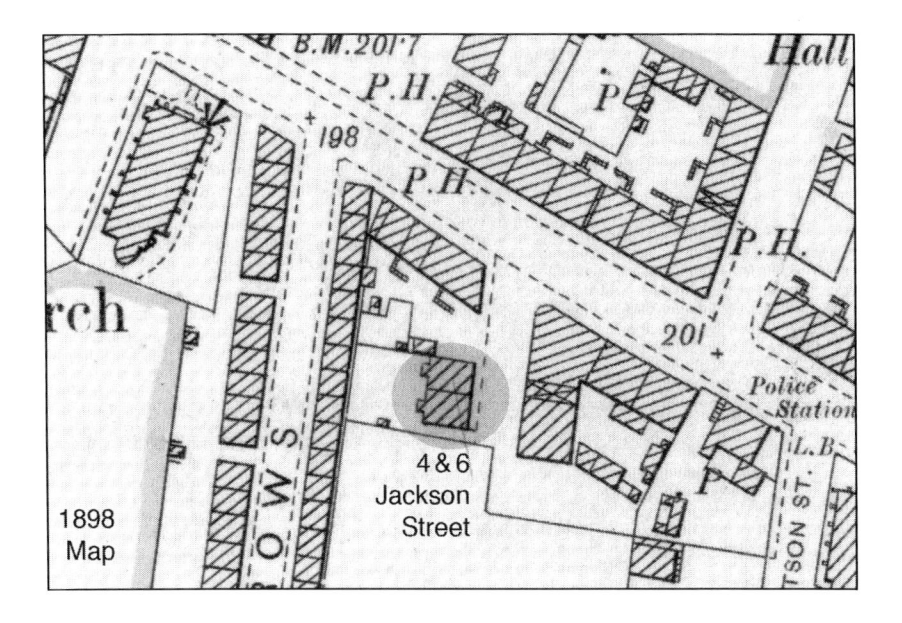

Figure 160 Jackson Street Western Tenement Homes on 1898 Map

On the west side of Jackson Street near the corner of Glasgow Road were semi detached 2 storey tenements with addresses 4 and 6 Jackson Street. These were constructed around 1890 by William Sprott family (sometimes referred to as Sprat.) 4 Jackson Street had the name 'Balgonie Cottage'.

During the early 20th Century they were owned by 2 spinsters, part of the Sprott and Gray families. Margaret Gray was a teacher and in 1915 was renting each house out to ladies by name of Agnes Sprott and Margaret Gray, each for £11 per annum and most likely her family members. The Sprott family owned earlier homes and shops on Glasgow Road nearby and adjacent to these houses. The brick built tenements were demolished around 1977.

By Paul D Veverka

Sprott's Buildings

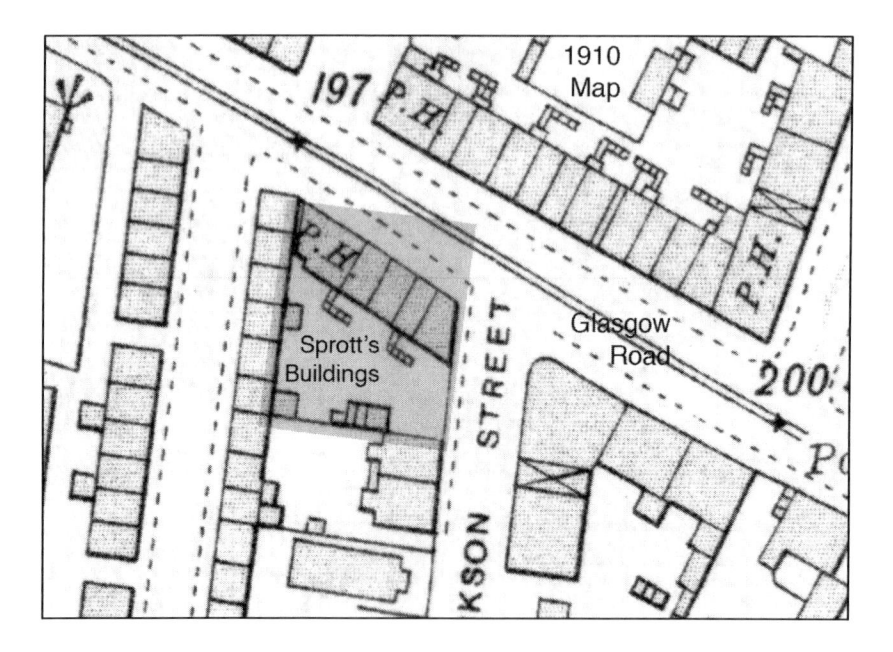

Figure 161 Former Sprott's Buildings on Glasgow Road in 1910

Sprott's Buildings were former double storey stone tenements with frontage on at 127-137 Glasgow Road. Smaller than nearby Avon and Henderson's Buildings they date from the same approximate era.

In the 1870's, George Sprott (b1822) who had previously been a miner changed profession and became a shoemaker, taking opportunity to be involved in the growing expansion of Blantyre's Glasgow Road. In 1879, nearing retirement he constructed these tenements on a plot of unused land, previously fields. Initially 2 shops and 3 houses, they would be hemmed in between a track to become Jackson Street to the east and the newly built Merry's Rows (tied miners cottages) to the west. The prior construction of the rows meant Mr Sprott had to build his property with an oblique angle at one end to make it fit the plot of land.

The name is "Sprott", and not "Sproat", a written incorrect term never used in any documentation, census or valuation (but may have been the local dialect.)

The shops were on the lower floor, the homes on the upper, accessed by stone steps at the rear, entered from Jackson Street. This was to be a home for the large family of George Spott, an investment for their future.

Upon construction in 1879, the intention was to create a public house / spirit shop at the west side. However, when son, Robert Sprott applied for a license that year, he was initially turned down, on the basis of suitability of the premises. The following year, with the building complete, his license was approved. Robert Sprott (b1855) moved from Springwell and would run Sprott's Public House at one end of the building and also a shoe shop at the other end, assisted by his brother George Sprott Junior.

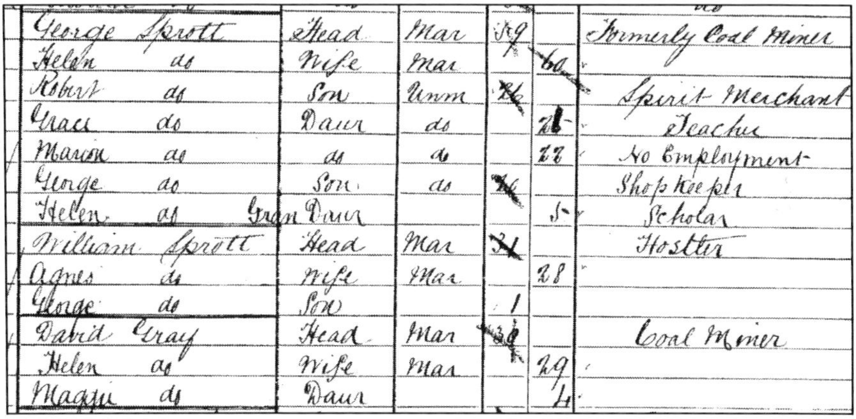

George Sprott	Head	Mar	59		Formerly Coal Miner
Helen do	Wife	Mar		60	
Robert do	Son	Unm	X		Spirit Merchant
Grace do	Daur	do		26	Teacher
Marion do	do	do		22	No Employment
George do	Son	do	X		Shop keeper
Helen do	Gran Daur			5	Scholar
William Sprott	Head	Mar	X		Hostler
Agnes do	Wife	Mar		28	
George do	Son		1		
David Gray	Head	Mar	30		Coal Miner
Helen do	Wife	Mar		29	
Maggie do	Daur			4	

Figure 162 The 1881 Census showing Sprott Buildings occupancy

In 1881 George Sprott is living in one of the houses with wife Helen, and grown up sons Robert and George Junior. With them are daughters Grace and Marion and Helen, who would later live in Jackson Street nearby. His eldest son William Sprott (b1850) lived in an adjacent house with wife Agnes and their son. William is noted as being a "Hostler" or sometimes called "Ostler", a person who keeps horses for others, usually at an inn or public house. In the other house was David Gray a miner and his family.

In 1890, George Sprott Senior died, aged 68, two years after his wife did. Eldest son William Sprott was the main inheritor of the estate, the new owner of Sprott's Buildings and he set about to construct further homes for the family on his land, heading up into Jackson Street. By 1895 he had split the homes and shops up further and there were now 4 upper homes and 5 lower shops (including Sprott's Pub). Homes were occupied by Helen Sprott, William Sprott, David Gray and Walter Neilson, a miner.

Shops in 1895 from west to east were as follows; Sprott & Company shoemakers, Alexander Christie's Clothes shop, Neilsons dressmakers, George Sprott Junior Grocery and Sprott's Public House at the end. It is noted that the public house then sold 'William Younger & Co Family Pale Ale' which cost 2 shilling for each 12 pints.

Figure 163 Sprott's Building in 1950 Licensed Aerial Photo

Change of Ownership, tenants and businesses

In 1900 William Sprott died young aged 50. The full estate was sold on away from family, the new owner being Mr. William Imrie & Son who lived outwith Blantyre. Mr Imrie bought the land, shops, upper homes on Glasgow Road and the homes on Jackson Street adjacent. The buildings and Jackson Street homes are pictured here in 1950, rear overlooking a mission hall.

William Irvine who bought the property was born in Fife in 1847. He married Mary Ann Smith and his profession is noted in census information as wine and spirit dealer. In the 1901 census, he lived with family in Govan despite owning these Blantyre properties and looks also to have owned the Blantyre Arms Public House, elsewhere in Stonefield run by Mr Bremner.

The Sprott family would largely move away with exception of Mrs Sprott, then a widow. Another family member a different William Sprott would perish in 1930 in the Auchinraith Pit disaster.

In 1905 homes were occupied by Mrs Agnes Sprott (w) who died in 1916, Hugh Cumberford a miner, James Cathcart a miner and James Graham, all renting from William Imrie & Son. The shops changed somewhat. That year from west to east were Blantyre Co-operative Society's bread shop, Alexander Christie Clothes shop, Jemima Walker dressmakers, John Machie's Confectionery shop then the Public House.

The Smiddy Inn

The Smiddy transformed from Sprott's Public House and became the

Smiddy Inn in 1900 although of course had been a public house since 1880. The name was given by William Imrie for an unknown reason, for there were no blacksmiths anywhere near this location prior to this or at that time. It may simply have been a "working mans" name he liked, hoping to attract the nearby clientele of miners at adjacent Merry's Rows. (later Elm Street)

The Smiddy Inn was run by William Imrie Junior, who did not live in the buildings, but simply worked there. The public house had address 135 and 137 Glasgow Road and was popular with miners for its wide variety of ales. At the time the Smiddy Inn took up much of the western part of Sprott's Buildings and had a distinctive small single storey store on the western side, which may once have been used for offsales, and would later to become a 'snug'. After his death in 1922, the Smiddy Inn would pass to his widow, then later to another owner Mrs. N Wilson.

It was a real working mans pub. Sawdust on the floor, pipes and had a darts team.

In latter years supporters buses for the football left from this location in Blantyre, right outside the pub. Following acquisition of the Smiddy Inn by Vincey McGuire in the mid 20th Century, it would be renamed "The Smiddy Bar", a name which existed up until its demolition in 1979.

Figure 164 Smiddy Inn Advert from 1950

Change to Imrie's then Kidd's Building

Of course change in ownership of the building, eventually meant that the name 'Sprott' was forgotten perhaps in just one generation, for this building became known for 30 years as Imrie's Buildings and was being referred as such by WW1.

In 1915, 127 Glasgow Road corner shop at Jackson Street was now Samuel Gilmour's Dairy Shop, which would exist there until 1936. Next door at 129 Glasgow Road was George Valerio's Confectionery shop with Alexander Christie Clothes shop now moved out. The Co-op's rented shop had moved further along the building to 131. Next door at 133 Glasgow Road was Isa Botteril's boot shop, then at 135/137 Glasgow Road, The Smiddy Inn. Homes on the upper level had address separated into a,b,c and d.

In 1920, the same configuration existed except at 129 now occupied by John Clark and the Co-op had left 131 which became James Smith's restaurant, perhaps a family member of Mrs Imrie's.

On 12th January 1922 William Imrie died aged 75 in Glasgow and his wife inherited his estate. Mary Ann Imrie (nee Smith) lived in Mount Florida in Glasgow and her son William Imrie Junior would continue to operate the pub on her behalf. During 1925, at 131 James Smith's Restaurant was now Hugh Kidd's Restaurant, a man in his early 30s.

Figure165 Sprott's Building by then known as Kidd's Building in 1977

In 1930 Mrs Imrie was renting all the homes out. Shops were leased by Samuel Gilmour at 127, Hugh Kidd's restaurant at 129 and 131, James Botteril bootmaker at 133 and William Imrie Junior's Smiddy Inn at 135/137. The boot shop also had machinery being leased.

Mary Ann Imrie died in 1930 and the building was bought over by prominent business owner, Mr. Hugh (Hughie) Kidd. From 1931 onwards the building was to be known as Kidd's Building and the name Imrie's Buildings would, like Sprotts, be forgotten to time.

Rest of the 20th Century

Figure 166 Last photo derelict Kidd's Building in 1978

When Samuel Gilmour died in 1936, his dairy at 127 Glasgow Road became Willie Weirs bookmakers. William Weirs (a bookmaking commission agent who had 2 telephone lines in his corner office with Blantyre telephone number 470 prior to WW2. This shop would latterly merge with neighbouring 129 Glasgow Road to become Mecca Bookmakers during the 1970's.

Hugh Kidd's Restaurant which had existed from the mid 1920's would evolve at 131 Glasgow Road into Hugh Kidd's fish and chip shop, remembered by many people as being one of Blantyre's best "chippies." In the 1970's it would become it its final years, 'The White Elephant", a second hand goods outlet which sold toys and household items.

In post WW2 years, 133 Glasgow Road became an extension of the Smiddy Bar at 135 and 137.

Hugh Kidd passed away in 1964 aged 70 in East Kilbride. The whole building was sadly a casualty of the Glasgow Road compulsory purchase order and redevelopment and was entirely cleared in 1979. Sprotts Building by name existed for 20 years, then as Imrie's Building for 30 years followed by Kidd's Building for another 34 years and lastly , by others for its final last 15 years.

The former property if it had survived would have been located on grass in front of flats (home to the Masonic Lodge in 1980) on the south of Glasgow Road at the eastern corner of Elm Street.

Blantyre Project Social Media:

Anthony Smith: "My father used to take us to the 'Dookit Cinema'. If it was still closed, he would go across to the Smiddy for a pint. I had to go and get him when the pictures opened. I was too young to go into the pub, so I just opened the door and shouted!"

Jim McAllister: "My friends older brother took me to a Celtic game on the Smiddy Bus and hid me under the seat so we didn't have to pay the 6 pence fare. That was 1971 Celtic v Ayr semifinals at Hampden. It was a cheap day all round for when we got there, we jumped the fence and never paid to get in!"

Thea Borland McNamee: "I remember this well. It was my wee da's local pub. Granny used to stand at the corner of Elm Street waiting on me coming off the works bus on a Friday to take her in for a 'hauf'. One night, dad didn't come home from work so mum marched up to the Smiddy Bar, and actually plopped his dinner on a plate down for him in the bar! He was never late again. I used to clean the bar when Phil Dolan owned it and he would tell me to keep any money I found on the floor. It was my way of getting tips. I enjoyed a good few nights in there too. Vincey's mum, auld Maggie MacGuire ran it before him."

John Cornfield: "The Celtic bus that ran from the Smiddy was the best supporters bus in the area by far. There were cases of beer and wine in the luggage compartments, and I mean cases! All for a short 30 minute trip into the east end of Glasgow to Parkhead. Happy times."

Alan Baird: "I only ever had a look in once, as I was too young, but if I remember right, it had a parrot in a cage too."

William Mullen: "It was always chaos on that supporters bus!"

Thomas Barrett: "You always got a song on that bus. I remember travelling on it during 1966 and 1967. Great season!"

John Daly: "I remember the Smiddy Bus to Parkhead games too. I swear it was so old even then that the suspension (if that's the right term in those days), was broken and it leant to one side badly even when driving straight. I remember on the upper deck as it was crossing Dalmarnock Bridge, if you looked down through the window, you could just see the Clyde!"

Carolyn Mikkelsen: "Hugh Kidd was my pappy and lived in the flat over the pub. My mum and dad took over the chippie and turned it into a hardware shop. I remember selling them bait for fishing! My mum, Jean Kidd (nee Morrison) now lives in Moffat and is 92. She's as sharp as a tack!"

Betty McLean: "I remember getting a poke of chips ay Kidd's. Walking home on a clear night. Fond memories."

Merry's Rows

Merry's Rows or Raws were built in 1876 to 1878 by coalmasters, Messrs Merry & Cunningham to house the workers of their nearby Auchinraith Colliery at Auchinraith Road. A local dialect of that time had them pronounced sounding similar to Murray's Raws but the name is always written as 'Merry's'. In 1875 or so, around the same time their newly sunk Auchinraith Pit went into production, Merry & Cunningham (Coalmasters) obtained a long narrow field, formerly on the farm of Stonefield. The field is marked number '582' on the 1859 map. Homes were built over 2 years. This was done to expand their existing row of tied homes built nearby slightly earlier in 1874 known as Auchinraith Row.

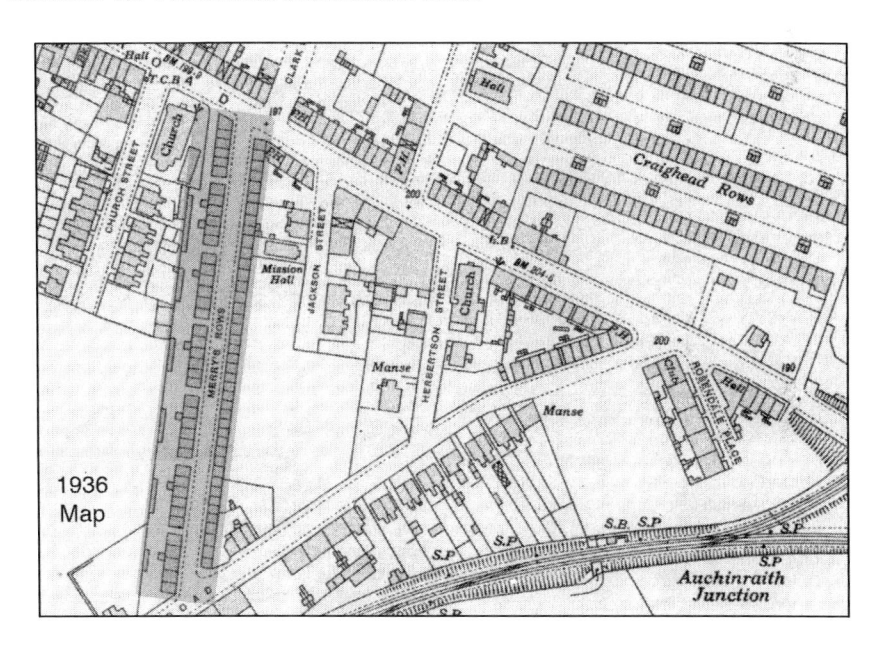

Figure 167 Merry's Rows on 1936 Map (demolished in 1937)

Merry's Rows were 89 houses numbered oddly from 1 to 89 on the west and evenly from 2 to 88 on the east, the upper numbers being near the Auchinraith Road end of the street During the first decade or so they were known as '1-89 Auchinraith' and it would take until the turn of the 20th Century for the name "Merry's Rows" to be more officially used in valuation rolls and census information. There were 50 single apartments, 46 double apartments, 3 three apartments and 1 four apartment house.

The homes were brick built much like other miners rows of the time. The brick was rendered and whitewashed. Homes were all single storey, small and terraced. Every two homes shared a chimneystack. Each home had a front door opening out on to a small pavement at what is now modern day Elm Street, one window at the front, and one at the rear. The windows had wooden shutters on them. Roofs were pitched and slated with grey Scottish slates. Internal walls were not lathed and strapped, but were plastered on top of the brick. There was no damp course and floors were wooden and ventilated underneath.

Living Conditions

Homes on the Eastern side were one continuous block of terraced properties stretching from Glasgow Road to the junction of Auchinraith Road. These homes were one roomed with the bedroom doubling as living area that had 2 beds recessed in the corners.

Figure 168 Merry's Rows photographed in 1913 from Melbourne Place

On the opposite western side of the road the houses, in 7 terraced blocks were larger, two roomed homes. These had one bed in the bedroom and 2 recessed beds in a separate living area. The homes had no hot water and no inside toilet. A coal fire heated the house and oven. The oven was located at the side of the fire and there was no control of the oven temperature; to complete the set-up, was gas lighting and a two-ring gas burner. On that western side, there is evidence that certainly initially, only 6 of the western blocks were lived in, for houses numbered 1 to 13, immediately beside Glasgow Road, do not appear in census records, yet the buildings are shown on old maps, perhaps having another use by the colliery. Coal cellars were located on the west side meaning residents on the east had to cross the street to get to them.

Toilets were six separate outdoor conveniences, situated on the western side of the rows, shared by all residents and upgraded somewhat in the 20th Century. Two water taps provided water in the street in standpipes, serving the whole community. The standpipes were located midway along the road. Adjacent streets were later Church Street, Jackson Street, Glasgow Road and Auchinraith Road.

Pre WW1 Years

There was no time to fetch water, when in March 1889, 2 year old Esther Jane Degnan's nightdress caught alight, quickly burning the girl to death at her home at Merry's Rows.

The homes may not have been built to the best standard and even when sewers were laid in 1892 nearby, the consequences of such improvements would backfire. A report appears in the Glasgow Evening Post on 25th August 1892 stating, "This morning, at half-past four, the back wall of three houses belonging to Merry & Cunningham (Limited), occupied by their miners, fell outwards. On examination it was found that other three were in a dangerous condition, so that six families had to remove their furniture. Fortunately, the roof remained intact, and beyond the alarm injury or damage occurred. The houses, are of the usual type single-roomed brick houses, standing in a continuous block of forty without a break, the back walls being hollow fourteen inches thick. Mineral workings directly account for the occurrence, aggravated meanwhile by the laying of a sewer two feet below the foundation of the wall. For some time past the ground in the vicinity has been showing signs of subsidence."

By 1910, outside toilets had been upgraded and appeared at more frequent intervals including outdoor washhouses. Each family was allocated a washday. The washhouse had a large tub with a opening under it where you would light a fire to heat the water for washing of clothes, the children were next, followed by the men coming home from the pit. The house rent was deducted from the miner's pay and 10% of the remaining was issued in the form of store credit, which could only be used in the Auchinraith Colliery store or shop, a clear sign that old fashioned "truck token systems" was still being abused and used by colliery owners.

Evidence presented to Royal Commission on 25th March 1914 by a visiting housing officer commented, "We visited these two rows of miners' houses on

24th March 1913. They are situated near to the Glasgow Road, in the Parish of Blantyre, and are owned by Merry & Cunningham, coalmasters. They consist of 46 single- and 50 double-apartment houses. They are built with brick, and were erected between thirty and forty years ago, and are a very poor type of house, low ceilinged and mostly damp. The rent per week, including rates, is 2s. 4d. and 2s. 11d. for single and double houses respectively. Within the last five years this property has been included in a special scavenging district, and consequently the sanitation of the place has been very much improved. The water is supplied by means of standpipes at intervals along the front of the row. There are no sculleries or sinks about the place, and all the dirty water is emptied into an open gutter. There is a washhouse to every six tenants, and a flush closet to every three tenants. Bins are in vogue, with a daily collection of refuse. No coal-cellars or drying-greens. A man is kept for tidying up the place."

Education & Tenancy

Children likely attended the nearby Auchinraith School, which was still relatively new. The families living in the houses at that time, according to the 1915 census were: Patrick Skelton at number 13, Robert Graham number 14, John McGauchie at 15, Robert Regan at 16, George Wyndham at 17, William Blair at 18, William Hughes at 19, William MacConnell at 20, John Campbell at 21, Patrick Taggart at 22, William Robson at 23, Robert Duncan at 24, Patrick Donnelly at 25, John Syme at 26, William Gardner at 27, James Kennedy at 28, Hugh Dunsmuir at 29, James Cook at 30, Robert MacConnel at 31, John Bell at 32, John MacGeoghegan at 33, 34 was empty, Thomas Carrol at 35, Peter Ford at 36, William Allardyce at 37, Robert Milligan at 38, John Elder at 39, Robert Black at 40, John Walsh at 41, George MacGregor at 42, James Doyle at 43, Richard Docherty at 44, Frank Wilson at 45, 46 was empty, David Simth at 47, Andrew Burns at 48, Frank Croft at 49, Charles McIvor at 50, David Langmuir at 51, Donald Glen at 52, Andrew Connor at 53, Alexander Martin at 54, William McCall at 55, Patrick Donnelly at 56, Robert Elliston at 57, Hugh Tonner at 58, William J Tennyson at 59, William Lindsay at 60, James Allan at 61, Charles Duddy at 62, Hugh Gallagher at 63, Frank MacInally at 64, Andrew Dyer at 65, James McCormack at 66, John Duddy at 67, Thomas Buchanan at 68, Frank Skelton at 69, Edward Bradley at 70, Thomas Brown at 71, William Anderson at 72, Robert Orr at 73, David Orr at 74, James Connor at 75, James Stevenson at 76, Thomas Regan at 77, James Speirs at 78, Alexander Schlothauer (a German who later renamed the family Slater) at 79, Edward Cummerford at 80, Alexander Dunsmuir at 81, James Orr at 82, William Kennedy at 83, James Hunter at 84, Alfred Harris at 85, Duncan Goodwin at 86, John Pate at 87, Hugh Paterson at 88 and finally John Phillips at number 89.

DID YOU KNOW?

In October 1916, Police arrested David Orr of 74 Merry's Rows who was seen leaving McCaffries pub in Springwell in prohibited hours. Upon arrest, David spoke most unpatriotically of the current war in Europe, adding to his charge.

In March 1917, Mr McWilliam offered his field to Blantyre Parish Council for 12 allotment plots behind Merry's Rows.

The 1930's

Duncan Slater, whose family lived later at number 79, added, "The four households used the one toilet, it was located around the back, accessed by the space between the blocks, Nell said that our toilet was the most popular toilet as Mr./Mrs.Carabine, who lived at #81, had eight children." The Slater family would later move to 1 Priory Street in 1937.

While the above is a 1930's description of Merry's rows, it was typical of the working miners family home in most of Britain even before the First World War. During the war, men who joined the military, traveled and saw how the other half of the population lived; this led to a lot of unrest; the communist party tried to unite the workers, but if any of the men attended a meeting they were sometimes fired and evicted from their tied miners house.

In 1930, Mr. Andrew Kalinsky of 20 Merry's Rows was one of 6 men killed in the Auchinraith Pit Disaster. Other men in the rows were injured.

According to the 1930 Valuation Roll, Merry & Cunninghame at that time still owned the odd numbered houses 13 to 89 inclusive and the even numbered houses from 14 to 88. Following the closure of the Auchinraith Pit in 1931, many families left, but others took up work at Craighead pit and the homes were adopted by the coalmasters there, meaning those particular mining families could stay on. Other homes were taken up by squatters, as the 1930s saw a large housing deficit in Blantyre.

It was said that heading north up Merry's Rows you could be "saintly" and go left to the church, or be a "sinner" and go right to the corner Smiddy Inn, although not on the same day! On the western corner of Glasgow Road and Merry's Raws, beside the bus stop was an open air toilet, very handy for the public houses nearby.

It is no wonder those pubs flourished with so many miners living nearby at Merry's Rows.

> Blantyre Project Social Media:
>
> **Duncan Slater:** "In October 1937, we moved from Merry's Rows into #1 Priory Street. This was a move to luxury, no more running out in the cold to the toilet, no more sharing it with three other families, hot water at the turn of a tap, it was heaven, we could have a bath every night and with only six people in a two bedroom house, we were in heaven."
>
> **Betty McLean:** "So many familiar surnames in this article. Duncan was in my class at school."

"Read More about Merry's Rows online. Scan our handy QR Code for more narrative and photos at Blantyre's History Archives.

Further information, photos and commentary from readers are added from time to time. Learn about QR codes at the beginning of this book."

Sometime after the Auchinraith Pit closed in 1931, the homes and land were bought by the County Council.

Whilst the houses are still all shown on the 1936 map, by then many of them were empty, unfit for purpose and families were promised to be rehoused. In January 1937, the remaining residents of Merry's Rows were told they would have to move out that summer, with the old miners homes scheduled to be knocked down. Some of the last families included the Carabines, Crofts, Duncans, Longmuirs, Patterson and aforementioned Slaters.

Many of the families living at Merry's Rows moved in summer and autumn 1937 to new homes built not far off at Calder Street and Priory Street.

It is thought Merry's Rows were subsequently demolished in winter 1937 to pave way for modern homes and a new street layout. Following demolition of Merry's Rows, Elm Street was formed, joining Auchinraith Road to Glasgow Road at an angle running northwest to southeast, with wider pavements and modern homes on either side.

The next page features the Slater family outside their home at Merry's Rows in 1930, courtesy of Duncan Slater.

Blantyre Glasgow Road South – The Real Story

Figure 169 Mrs Slater and Kate at 64 Merrys

Figure 170 Mary, Sarah, Agnes & Kate

Figure 171 Ellen, Sarah & Katie Slater 1930

Figure 172 Mrs Slater at 1 Priory Street

Alois Schlothauer (Slater)

The Slater's story at Merry's Rows is an interesting one. Alois Schlothauer was born in 1866 in Germany, the son of German parents. He eventually married in Scotland and moved to Merry's Rows in Blantyre in 1902, after obtaining a job at Merry & Cunningham's Pit.

In 1914, when war approached, Alois did not believe he would have to go back to Germany. After all, he had a growing family in Blantyre and at 48 considered himself too old to fight. That year, his wife gave him money frequently in order that he could become a British Citizen, but each time the money was spent on drink. A law was passed asking all foreigners in the UK to register and report to police.

In the May of 1915, Alois duly reported to the local police station, with his personal belongings, on the same day his oldest son, John reported for military service and became a dispatch rider in the "Army Air corps". However, Alois, being of German birth was detained, transported and interned in Camp Knockaloe on the Isle of Man (off the coast of England). The camp was built to hold 5,000 men but by 1917 it held over 20,000 people.

Figure 173 German Camp Knockaloe on Isle of Man during WW2

No letters or communications were allowed between him, and the family back in Blantyre. At the end of hostilities in 1918, he, along with 80% others interned, was deported back to Germany not to return. It was a brutal and severe ripping of a man away from his family and absolutely all family contact ended with Alois, on the day he reported to the police three years earlier.

In 1918, his 2 sons in Blantyre went to Court and changed their surname officially to Slater, something many people did to hide the origin of their name. This was likely primarily for employment opportunities. In 1918, war was still rampant and more men were needed. A ballot at various collieries was conducted, relieving miners of their mining duties and asking them to report for service.

In 1918 Alois' son, John and his half German neighbor William Siegel also from Merry's Rows both found themselves in court for failing to turn up when requested for the next round of their military duty. Each were fined £2 and handed back over to the military. You can imagine what they felt about War and perhaps especially what had just recently happened to their absent father. With thanks to Duncan Slater for this interesting insight into his grandpa's life.

Origins of Elm Street

Following the Lanarkshire Slum clearance drive of the 1930's, and the clearing of Merry's Rows, in 1950 town planners announced a new Street was to be formed where once the miners homes had been.

These were to be modern, spacious double storey homes with gardens, indoor toilets and more than one bedroom.

Elm Street was the name chosen, complimenting nearby new Hawthorn Place leading off and nearby Beech Place just off Auchinraith Road. These names were likely chosen just to reflect nature, greenery and outdoors, a world away from mines, coal and coalmasters and even had a long narrow play park nearby.

Figure 174 Elm Street in 1950

Elm Street still exists today, broad and wide connecting Auchinraith Road to Glasgow Road but due to social housing problems, Hawthorn Place and Beech Place were demolished, the land sold off by the council to make way for private housing nearer the Millennium now named Nordic Crescent.

Masonic Hall / Elm Court Flats

When the Masonic Buildings further west along Glasgow Road were demolished in the late 1970's, the lodge built a new brick building at the bottom of Elm Street, where Sprott's / Kidd's Building had been. The '599 Club' was short lived before moving out in 1988 to High Blantyre. It became "Cobbler's Pub" until a murder in 1992 and in 1993, sold off as modern flats.

Figure 175 Former Masonic Hall, now modern flats. Pictured 2016

Nazarene Church

The Church of the Nazarene is an evangelical Christian denomination that emerged from the 19th-century Holiness movement in North America around 1907. The Holiness work in Blantyre began in March 1907, the following year the American movement commenced.

It was originally called the 'Blantyre Holiness Mission' but changed name in 1910 to become the 'Blantyre Pentecostal Church.' When they initially formed they met in each others houses, those meetings known as "cottage" or "kitchen meetings". However by 1909, just 2 years later they worshipped in the Caldwell Hall at the junction of Glasgow Road and the previous location of Auchinraith Road junction. The hall was shared with Stonefield Parish Church.

In need of a separate identity and to avoid confusion and conflicting service times, in 1910, opportunity arose to buy land and a large Nissan wooden hut was built. The hut was erected further west in Jackson Street and their inaugural service was held on 10th March 1910 conducted by Rev. George Sharpe, the first minister of the church. George was also doing work for the mission at Parkhead. In those early years anybody involved with the church had to abstain from smoking and drinking. The hut faced on to Jackson Street, the rear facing on to the miners homes of Merry's Rows.

Figure 176 Nazarene Church Mission Hut in 1952

Their religious work became a part of the Pentecostal Church of Scotland uniting with the Pentecostal Church of the Nazarene in 1915, with other venue added at Perth, Uddingston and Paisley. In Blantyre the church became known after World War One as "The Nazarene Church", those early names confined to history.

The first resident pastor was Rev. George Dempsie, appointed on 31st August 1910. Since 1907, a total of 24 ministers had served as pastors, the best known of whom was the much respected Rev. William Mackie, who served from 1967 until 1987. Rev. Mackie was a butcher in the Central C0-op on Glasgow Road and sometimes at High Blantyre. A large vacant field was adjacent to the mission hut or "Mission Hall" as it was shown on maps of the era. This field was still vacant right up until the 1950s. In 1924, the Pastor was Pastor McLaglan. By 1931, Pastor Wilkie. In December 1947, Pastor Leslie Roberts was in charge.

When Elm Street houses were still being constructed in 1952, Mr. Bill Clayden, a member of the congregation asked the council to lay a small path to the rear of the church, so people could access it from the new street. With the council agreeing to the request, it was decided by the congregation, they would reverse the layout of the church entirely, amending the insides to suit. This was done with much enthusiasm and almost single handedly by Bill.

After many years of meeting in the old Nazarene Church (hut) it eventually burned down in 1980. A new church, on Elm Street was built on the opposite side and officially opened by Mrs. Janet Mackie. It was dedicated on Sunday 24th October 1982. For nearly 100 years the witness was maintained in Blantyre; a ministry that concluded on Sunday 24th September 2006. The Church was officially closed in its centenary year 2007 when the building on

Elm Street was sold to St Andrew's Church of Scotland whose church is adjacent to it, and named, by the Church of Scotland, "Nazarene Hall".

Figure 177 Nazarene Church Hall in 2016 (Built 1982)

The name lives on – and the work of making Christ known in that community continues. The Nazarene Hall is used every day of the week, for youth and children's work, for Sunday School and community groups.

> Blantyre Project Social Media:
>
> **Patrick Donnelly:** "Going back to the Masonic Lodge / Elm Court flats for a moment. After the lodge moved out in 1989 , Cobblers Bar and Restaurant opened there. It only lasted until 1992, when on 9th October that year, a man was shot in the head in the club and died. The murderers whilst the party continued, took the body back to Elm Court houses nearby, beheading the 34 year old man, removing his limbs and putting him into a sewer in nearby John Street. It made big news, when in January 1993, the body was found in a Bothwell sewage works. The killers were tracked down but only jailed for 5 years for dismembering the body, the murder actually not proven by any jury, although all knew that one of them did it. It was the end of Cobblers and when the building became flats, it was blessed by local ministers, as some tenants knew exactly what had taken place."
>
> **Thea Borland McNamee:** "My brother Dougie bought one of the Elm Court flats. I was always 'creeped' out a little by them and didn't like the fact the toilet had no window!"

Elm Street Playpark

Elm Street, Blantyre 1978
Courtesy: An Historical Dictionary by Neil Gordon

Figure 178 Elm Street Playpark on left in 1978

This view of Elm Street looks north towards Glasgow Road and was captured on camera in 1978 by the late Neil Gordon, just prior to the extensive redevelopment.

To the right is Kidd's Buildings, in front are the tenements on the north side of Glasgow Road and to the left is the former Stonefield Parish Church. In the foreground on the left is the Elm Street Playpark so popular with Blantyre children, although by the time of this picture, the play equipment has mostly gone. Rosie Law once painted a beautiful painting on the wall in the park, which remained there for a long time.

Figure 179 The beautiful children's painting on the park wall in 1990

> Blantyre Project Social Media:
>
> **Catherine Murphy:** "We used to play in the swing park on Elm Street most days coming home from school then up Elm Street and crossed the railway at Auchinraith, by the prefabs to get to our home at Parkville Drive."

By Paul D Veverka

Stonefield Parish Church

The Stonefield Parish Church was located on Glasgow Road at the western corner of Church Street during the late 19th Century and through most of the 20th.

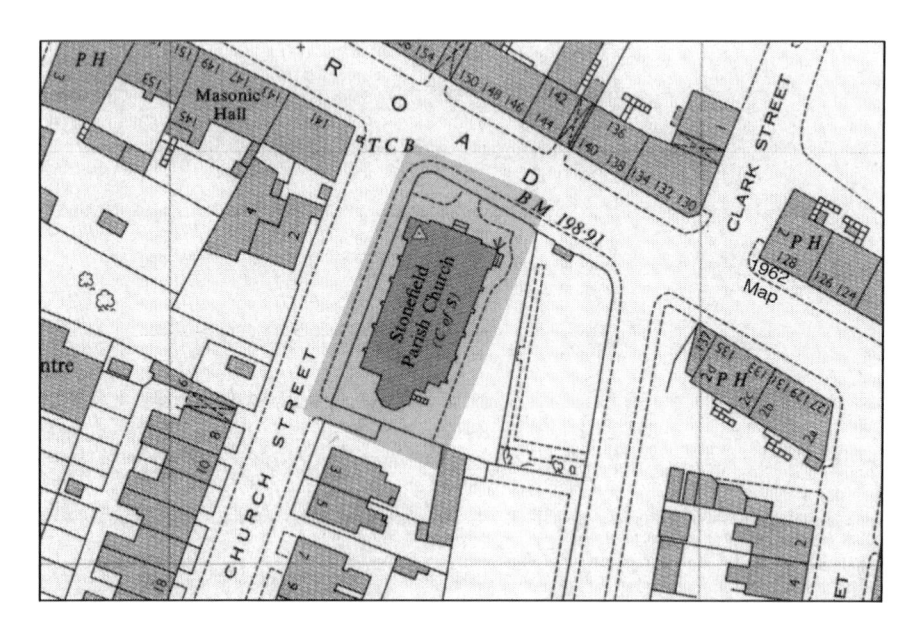

Figure 180 Former Stonefield Parish Church on 1962 map

It was originally noted as being a "Chapel of Ease" later to become known as Stonefield Parish. This "Chapel of Ease" came about as the Old Parish Church built at High Blantyre in 1863, was still subject to overcrowding. Some residents from Low Blantyre had far to walk and so it made sense that another church should be built, which would remain under Blantyre Parish Church. The Provost of Hamilton, John Clark Forrest, a prominent landowner in the town, donated the site for the Church in 1876 although it was not formerly bought until 1878. Like the shops and homes to the east, it was yet another building constructed in the late 1870's.

On 23rd April 1876, a Blantyre Session House record, recorded by Rev Stewart Wright of High Blantyre commented on the greatly increased population of Blantyre and how it now needed a new church. Rev Wright read out the following proposed letter, which was to be distributed throughout the Parish. "Every one acquainted with Blantyre is aware of the thorough change that has passed over the parish. A little time ago it was a retired, thinly populated agricultural district, but now it has become the important centre of a vast mining population. In 1871, the inhabitants numbered about 3500; a census lately taken shows them to have increased to 8000, and we may safely predict, from the evidence everywhere around us, that in five years more the eight thousand will have doubled."

Figure 181 Stonefield Parish Church 1950

Rev Stewart continued, "In these circumstances the minister and the kirk-session feel that there is the most urgent call upon them to be up and doing, so as to provide church accommodation for this vast multitude. Within the bounds of the parish there are at present but two churches, Established and Free, both of which cannot accommodate more than 1300 people. The United Presbyterians have a church on the coannes? Which can hold 400 more, and the Roman Catholics are about to erect a chapel for their adherents, perhaps numbering about 700; so there is thus a large and increasing population for whom it is incumbent upon the Church of Scotland to provide, without unnecessary delay, religious ordinances. Therefore, the minister and kirk-session send forth this appeal to all who love our Zion, and are concerned for the religious instruction of our people, to grant them sympathy and help, that they may, to some extent, meet those spirited demands of their parish.

A site has been promised on the Glasgow and Hamilton Road, in the very centre of the district of Stonefield that is being so quickly populated. The proposed church is to accommodate 900 sitters, and will cost between £4000 and £5000. Grants in aid are expected from the Home Mission, the Baird Trust, and the Ferguson Request; but others, too, must be willing and ready to contribute as God has given them power, if we are soon to see erected here for His service, and to His glory, a "holy and a beautiful house." Your name, as a contributor, will be gladly received by Stewart Wright, minister of Blantyre; or Mr. L. W. Adamson, Rosebank, Blantyre, treasurer. The manse at Blantyre."

The action was made to print this letter and to progress with the new Church to be paid for from funds in the Session accounts and refunded by subscriptions, i.e. it was to ultimately be paid for by the people of Blantyre.

A letter by Rev Stewart Wright appeared in the Glasgow Herald on Friday 1st March 1878, stating, "SIR- Will you kindly insert in your journal the enclosed circular, which I recently issued, and in which I plead for subscriptions to defray the expenses of a new church that is now in course of erection in my parish. The population has so vastly increased that there is urgent need for this new church. The mass of the people are poor, being miners and their families, who consequently cannot afford to give much. The people of Scotland have nobly responded to the appeal, which I issued in behalf of the many families who were rendered destitute by the recent terrible colliery explosion. I feel assured that I shall not now plead in vain for sympathy and help to meet the spiritual wants of those who are still with us."

Building the Church

By 1878 subscription monies had been received to start the build. The Foundation stone was laid by Rev Stewart Wright and John Clark Forrest overseeing a small ceremony in May 1878. Mr. A. J. Smith of Glasgow, architect, drew up the plans for the church, which was 80 feet long and 47 feet wide, and the spire rose up to 100 feet from a large square pedestal feature. Built by William Adam Builders & Joiners of Main Street, High Blantyre, the church was designed in the Norman Gothic style and included an apse behind the pulpit to accommodate a choir and an organ, and all the side windows were of elaborate design with gablets (separate pitched roofs) over them.

It was officially opened on Tuesday 29th June 1880 and including the galleries, could seat 900 people. It is unknown if the £5,000 budget was adhered to. The Church was entered from Glasgow Road via ornate large gates between stone pillars, the entrance on a walled perimeter. Rev. Thomas Pryde was ordained to be the pastorate of the church and was first to do so, when it opened.

Figure 182 Interior of Stonefield Parish Church

A note in the Kirk Session book on 7th August 1880, records the opening event as described by the Rev Stewart Wright of High Blantyre Old Parish.

Noting the opening date and the aforementioned ordainment, it was stated that Rev Wright himself conducted the ceremony and services along with Rev Scott, minister of Bargeddie who spoke from the bible Matthew IX v 37. Rev Wright offered prayers.

After the service the ladies of the Parish presented Rev. Pryde with a pulpit gown, hymnbook and bands. Rev. Pryde said his thanks for the gift and the young minister then shook hands with the leaving congregation. A note was also entered about the glorious church being constructed in such a populous place. It did remain under the Blantyre Parish Church control until 1890 when it was raised to a "Quoad Sacra" Parish with its own Kirk Session and Stonefield Parish Church was then regarded in its own right.

In 1902 the bell from Blantyre mill, which used to summon David Livingstone to work, was presented to Stonefield Church as a coronation gift. It continued to be used as the church bell until it was given in 1922 to Low Blantyre (Stonefield Parish) School. After the 1970's, it was returned back to the David Livingstone Centre, where it now is hung from the gable of Shuttle Row.

General Booth's Visit to the Church

Figure 183 General Booth, stopped at the Church on his 1904 motor car tour

1904 saw General Booth travel through Scotland is his much celebrated motorcar tour, a cavalcade of early cars travelling from Land's End to Aberdeen. William Booth, the evangelist preacher, remembered for being the founder of the Salvation Army was on a grand adventure. This was at a time when motor travel was still in its infancy and Booth covered 1,224 miles in 29 days, speaking at 75 indoor, 36 outdoor, and 53 overflow meetings. During September, he stopped at Stonefield Parish Church to speak about the new car contraption and an audience of 1,500 people packed into the church (that could accommodate 900). Outside 3,000 people had assembled in the open air, quite a considerable percentage of Blantyre's population, given the event had been advertised in advance. Dr Grant presided and afterwards the General was treated to tea.

Figure 184 Booth addresses crowds elsewhere on his tour 1904

Church Life & Ministers

In 1909 the minister Rev. Thomas Pryde was also in charge of the Sunday school. At the same time the session clerk was Donald McLean. Secretary of the Sunday school was a Miss Gray. Choirmaster was William Steven. Harmounium player was Miss Steven.

Treasurer of bible class was Miss Steven. Secretary was Miss J.W Steven.

The Church also had a Senior Women's Guild. During 1909, the President was Miss Shaw. Miss Gray was President of the Junior Guild. Positions of authority within the Recreation and Rambling Club included President, Rev. Mr. Pryde, Treasurer M. McArthur and Secretary George Gray. Rev. Thomas Pryde retired in 1919.

On Thursday evening 21st February 1918, the Junior Choir of Stonefield Parish Church rendered the kinderspiel entitled "Don Quixote" in the Co-operative Hall, Stonefield, Rev. Thomas Pryde, M.A.. presided, and notwithstanding the inclemency of the weather there was a large turnout. The children rendered their several pieces with pleasing effect, and great credit was due to the conductor, Mr. Malcolm Young, for the excellent manner in which he had the young ones trained. By then the Church had address 139 Glasgow Road.

During the 1920's, Rev. W.H. McDiarmid was minister, but left to go to a church in Forfar in June 1929.

During 1921 and 1922, this church faced a serious crisis and the building and congregation was the subject of discussion at the monthly meetings of Hamilton Presbytery. The fabric of the Church had been wrecked by underground workings and this forced the congregation to worship in temporary buildings built alongside the church some time earlier, which quickly became not watertight. A proposed restoration scheme of the old church was discussed at a cost of £4,000 held up extensively as the contractors asked for guarantees that they would be paid.

The Scotsman on Wednesday 28th September 1921 revealed some things about problems at the Stonefield Parish Church – "The serious position in which the congregation of Stonefield Parish Church, Blantyre, now find themselves was the subject of discussion yesterday at the monthly meeting of Hamilton Presbytery. The fabric of the church was wrecked by underground workings; and for some time back the congregation have been worshipping in temporary accommodation, which in turn is now declared to be not wind and watertight. A proposed restoration scheme of the old church at a cost of about £4000 has met with frequent delays on the part of the Baird Trust and the Home Mission Committee, who ask for guarantees of security for the future. The reply to this is that to ask for secure foundations in a mining area like Blantyre is equivalent to asking for the moon.

A remit has once more been made to the Committee already appointed by the Presbytery to consider the whole matter, with power to take expert opinion if thought desirable, also to estimate what financial assistance ought to be given by the Presbytery, and report.".

The church steeple was completely demolished in 1921 to make it safer and garden fetes were still being held in Summer 1922 to raise more money for completing the building repairs.

In 1927, the pulpit of the old Village Chapel / School was transferred to Stonefield Parish Church for use there, a pulpit that David Livingstone himself would have cast eyes upon a century earlier.

Jubilee Celebrations were held in summer 1930 and Rev. E. Sherwood Gunson M.A minister of New Monkland Parish Church during the afternoon service of Sunday 22nd June 1930, dedicated a handsome fumed Oak communion table and chairs, which were a gift of Mr. and Mrs Andrew Wright or Burtonlea, Blantyre. These were in memory of the late Rev. Thomas Pryde. The church that year had a ratable value of £109.

Post WW2 Years

During the 1940's the minister was Rev. Duncan Finlayson. M.A who lived in the Stonefield Church Manse in Herbertson Street. In the mid 1950's it was Rev. R. H. Porter.

The church was well attended by local GPs, businessmen and shopkeepers and had strong links with the Cooperative Society. It did not have halls next to it as every other church did but instead used halls a short walk away at the Caldwell Institute. The exception to this was the temporary hall erected in the 1920's whilst repairs were conducted.

The Church ran two Sunday Schools: a morning one for the congregation's children and an afternoon one mainly for miner's children. Sunday classes were at 12 midday and 6.30pm.

Residents were surprised in December 1946, when many thinking the church congregation was in decline, witnessed the church filled to capacity and more when 1,000 people packed into the building. The occasion was a post war midnight service on that Christmas Eve, a celebration of peace and thankfulness.

Stonefield Church could boast of having 'the finest organ in Lanarkshire'. On the evening of Friday 20th May 1949 at 7.30pm, a service of thanksgiving and dedication took place at Stonefield Parish Church, on Glasgow Road. The occasion was also to acknowledge a most beautiful gift of a 3 manual pipe organ to the church was given from Hamilton Town Hall. With the Second World War ended, an inscription was thought appropriate to be inlaid into the organ itself, which read: "To the Glory of God. In thanksgiving for his safe keeping in time of stress, and as a memorial of those who, for us, laid down their lives 1914-1918 and 1939-1945." The organ was made by Messrs. H Hilsdon Ltd of Glasgow. There were 3 manuals, 27 stops and 15 couplers making a total of 42 stops. It was a remarkable piece of equipment being all-electric. Andrew Wright & Sons Ltd undertook the builders work, T&W Roberts did the joinery, Robert White undertook the electrical work and Charles Messer & Son did the plasterwork. It is unknown what became of the organ.

The organ attracted some of the finest organists. The most famous was 'Hitler's pianist' (explored next). Mr. Hambock became organist of Stonefield Church from 1968-1970.

By the 1960's the last of the coalmines on which Blantyre's prosperity and expansion relied upon, had closed down. This inevitably resulted in a high level of unemployment, which had a 'ripple effect' on many other businesses in the community. Church membership at Stonefield Parish Church never exceeded 600 at its height. This was maintained throughout the sixties, but by the mid-seventies was beginning to show rapid decline.

In 1965, Stonefield Parish Church was united with the Burleigh Memorial Church to become 'Stonefield Burleigh Memorial Parish Church'.

Figure 185 Stonefield Parish Church on fire 1979

In 1976, the Rev James Gregory became the Minister first of the linked charges then of the united congregation. A second union took place in 1978 when the Anderson Church joined the union. At that time the church was renamed St Andrew's Parish Church (Stonefield Burleigh Memorial Anderson Parish Church would have been quite a mouthful!).

On 3rd September 1979, Stonefield Parish Church suffered the fate of many other Blantyre church buildings and was accidentally set on fire. The roof was being restored at the time when a workman left his blowtorch on while he went for his lunch. The building was just 9 months away from its centenary! At first it was thought that repair would be possible with a new roof, but soon it was discovered that the whole remaining church would need to be demolished as a result of weaknesses in the wall and from the land disturbance caused by mining (the reason why the spire had been removed years earlier). The previous photo was taken from Elm Street looking at the back of the church on that very day, the sky thick with black acrid smoke.

In truth, the whole incident was highly suspicious to many people, given the timing and clearance of all other buildings around it.

Figure 186 Stonefield Parish Church in 1979 a year before demolition

Despite losing their church building, the congregation remained resilient. During the next 3 years they travelled further west and met in the Livingstone Memorial Church each Sunday afternoon, boosting the congregation there.

However, the Stonefield Parish Church was a boarded up ruin in Winter 1979 and was demolished in 1980, the land cleared completely to make way for the brand new St Andrew's Church. Stonefield Parish Church has fond memories for many people in Blantyre, especially all those happy couples who married or had children christened there.

Source: Blantyre Project with minor content added with kind permission from St Andrews Church.

> Blantyre Project Social Media:
>
> **Betty McLean:** "To think in those days the churches were full of people. This was a lovely church!"
>
> **Archie Peat:** "Something strange was happening in Blantyre in the late 1970's. It seems several churches were lost in a short period of a few years, and often by fire too!"
>
> **Marian Maguire:** "My husband John was one of the firemen that sad day."

Rev Thomas Pryde

Rev. Thomas Pryde, MA – Thomas was ordained on Tuesday 29th June 1880 as the first pastorate in the Stonefield Parish Church on Glasgow Road. Before Rev. Pryde was ordained by Rev. Mr. Scott of Bargeddie, Rev. Stewart Wright conducted a consecration service, although the church was not formally opened until the following Sunday, the 4th of July. The dinner was enjoyed after the service was held in the old Masonic Hall above the Livingstonian pub.

The ladies of the Parish presented a large bible to Thomas along with gown, cassock and hood. The leather bound bible complete with inscription is still with St Andrews Parish Church today. Thomas retired in 1919 and died in 1925. A communion table and chairs was dedicated in his memory in June 1930, to coincide with the church's Jubilee year. A year after retiring, Thomas had handed back the bible in May 1920 to the Stonefield Parish Church. Knowing a detailed book about Glasgow Road was at last being written, the church has kindly shared this image of that very same bible.

Figure 187 The 1880 Bible as the Church today

Rev Donald Finlayson

Rev. Duncan Finlayson (b1917 – d2012.) Duncan was a former minister of Stonefield Parish Church from 1944. Born in Elgin in 1917 at the end of the First World War, he was raised in Marybank and Strathpeffer.

Duncan was the youngest in a family of three. His father was the factor in a local estate. Educated at Marybank Primary School then at Dingwall Academy, Duncan upon leaving school went directly on to Glasgow University where he gained his MA degree in English and Philosophy, choosing to continue with this Divinity training. He was proud to be awarded runner up in the University's Boxing Championship, which may have occasioned his rather distinctive Finlayson nose! It was at this time in the early 1940's, whilst war raged in Europe, that he spotted Jean in the University Choir and vowed he would marry her, something he did in 1943. Immediately after their marriage they went to Ayr when Duncan became Assistant minister, but it was Blantyre that called in 1944, when Duncan was offered his first charge as minister outright at Stonefield Parish Church on Glasgow Road.

The Church provided a beautiful stone manse at Herbertson Street nearby and it was an ideal setting for the couple to start their family, their first 2 children born there. He also had a cat called "Boots". (pictured at his home in 1948 with his daughter)

His time at Blantyre was relatively short when a move to Glasgow called in the very early 1950's to Church HQ as Associate Secretary to the Foreign Mission Committee. He was then appointed Warden at the Peace Institute, which in 1953 brought him into close association with the Iona Community before another move this time to St Ninians

Figure 188 Duncan, his daughter and cat in 1948

in Musselborough. In 1963 Duncan, Jean and their 4 children (Pat, Duncan, Edward & Iona) moved to St Rules Parish Church in Monifieth, staying there for 6 years.

Duncan had a great desire to tinker and fix things. He had a Mark 2/ 3.4 Jaguar car, which would roar out the manse but he lost it in a fire. For local children, he once tried to make a pedal car buggie but the wheels never quite worked, so he fashioned it into a boat, which never quite worked too, settling for overturning it to become a planter. In 1969 he was appointed first male Principal of St Colm's College in Edinburgh (now closed). In 1978, he and Jean moved to Morvern overlooking the Island of Mull., before finally retiring back to Appin and Stathpeffer. He had come full circle back to the place of his birth.

Duncan and Jean celebrated their diamond-wedding anniversary in 1993 in Tulloch Castle. Jean's failing health prompted the move to be closer to children and Jean died in 2005. Duncan soldiered on his own health failing prompting a move to be close to Iona, his daughter. He passed away at Myrtle Cottage in 2012, aged 95. He was much loved and is said to have had a fun sense of humour, a glint in his eye and liked to exaggerate or fantasize in a playful manner with others.

St Andrew's Church

Figure 189 St Andrews Church being built 1982

On 21st March 1982, the Rev. John Handley, Moderator of Hamilton Presbytery, opened the new and current St Andrew's Church on the same site of the former Stonefield Parish Church. Also in attendance were the Very Reverend professor Robin Barbour, former Moderator of the General Assembly and the architect, Mr. R. Robertson. It was built at a cost of £187,000.

The main sanctuary has seating for 180, but a sliding partition connecting with the hall provides seating for 400 if necessary.

With decline in numbers as part of the modern church's challenge, St Andrew's embarked on a philosophy of mission. The church became a 'mission partner' with St Ninian's Centre in Crieff and a program of mission development began. The laity was challenged to become part of the vision building and the church was structured to develop mission. A Tea Room was established which has become a welcome community resource that continues to this day. A 'Mustard Seed Prayer Group' was formed and healing services were introduced. In 1992, Rev James Gregory retired. Congregation continue to attend this church each Sunday.

Hitler's Pianist

The organist at Glasgow Road's Stonefield Parish Church from 1968 – 1970, was none other than Hitler's pianist! It seemed an unlikely tale but I have learned to give an ear to the extremes of improbability, on the outside chance that it might just be true. A little research demonstrated though, that truth was behind this story. Walter Hambrock was indeed a concert pianist from Vienna, who had married Helen Weir, a lecturer from Airdrie, and had taken the organist's job as the bread-and-butter base for his music publishing business which he ran from Scotland.

His arrival in Scotland by the modest Woods of Strichen, Aberdeenshire was just a minor part of his highly colourful story – he had perhaps been more used to the Vienna Woods, within whose picturesque setting he had grown up in the early part of the 20th century. By the age of 10 he had mastered the preparatory music for the National Academy in Vienna and was playing the piano for the silent films at his local cinema. Studying music in Vienna, he would relax with a book by the tombstones of Beethoven and Schubert and counted among his companions a student called Horst Wessel, who composed the official song of the Nazi Party before dying in a street brawl in 1930.

Moving to Berlin, Walter was heard by Goering and Goebbels, who recommended him to Hitler. Thereafter he played frequently for the Fuhrer, who gave him a signed copy of Mein Kampf. He could tell you about a performance of The Merry Widow where he saw Hitler sitting with the composer, Franz Lehar. It was at the beginning of 1940 that his world fell apart. On his way home from a performance in Holland, a Gestapo hand fell on his shoulder. "What's the meaning of this?" he asked. "You'll find out in Berlin," he was told. Instead of returning to Vienna he was confronted by Martin Bormann, Hitler's deputy, pointing a gun and spluttering: "You played for the Fuhrer and then you played for a Jew!"

He was taken to Dachau and then to the dreaded Flossenburg concentration camp where he witnessed mass atrocities. His wife gained a divorce on the basis that he wouldn't be back. And when he survived the horror and returned to their flat, he was met by another man – wearing his clothes!!

Playing in the ballrooms of Vienna, he also started a music publishing business but, after his second marriage failed, he was at a low ebb when suddenly a Scots lady came into his life. Just as Walter was enjoying the Berlin Olympics of 1936, Helen Weir from Airdrie was rounding off her university career by teaching in Germany. She too was at the Olympics. But it was 26 years later before they met at a friend's house, by which time she was lecturing at the College of Commerce in Pitt Street, Glasgow.

Figure 190 Walter was an accomplished pianist all his life

When Walter came to Scotland to propose, Helen withdrew to her room to think about it. He sat down at the piano and began to play Beethoven's Moonlight Sonata, said to have worked wonders in many a romance. The door opened and Helen came with her answer. Beethoven had won the day! They were married in Airdrie in 1962, went to live in Vienna but returned to Helen's Scotland to live at Strichen, where Walter would run his Austro-Scotia Music Company. So that was how he landed in Strichen, with the perquisite of a splendid house which had been left to the kirk by Jeannie King, a cousin of Mackenzie King, the Canadian Prime Minister. But that going salary as kirk organist was just £48 per annum.

Five years later they were back in Lanarkshire, living in Newmains, where Walter's pupils included talented pianist Tommy McIntyre as well as Neil

Reid, who gained fame as a singer when he won Opportunity Knocks. Walter landed the job of being the organist for the beautiful organ at Stonefield Parish Church. He engaged in this employment every weekend during 1968 – 1970. So much talent, so much courage. But always an obstacle in Walter's life. Misfortune dogged him to his last day in 1979. Having lived to see Stonefield Parish Church burned down that year, final misfortune fell upon him when a snowstorm caused a postponement of his burial at Clarkston Cemetery, Airdrie.

Youth Centre not meant to be

In 1978, a new civic Centre was planned for the corner of Elm Street and Glasgow Road. The plans had been approved by the council and the site was chosen out as part of the Glasgow Road redevelopment plans. The complex project which was to include a community hall and play equipment did not reach the drawing stages, despite the noted need due to the closure of public buildings like the Masonic Hall and the Church Hall.

The council felt some pressure to replace public meeting areas with a new building and budgets were set aside. The final decision was to be put to the Scottish Office.

However, fate intervened, and in a twist of fate, when the Stonefield Parish Church burned down, plans for the new civic Centre were abandoned, when the Church needed to be rebuilt on the intended community Centre spot. Other regional community Centre's were instead later proposed.

CHAPTER 9
GLASGOW ROAD SOUTH
CHURCH ST TO LOGAN ST

Origins & Evolution of Church Street

Like all the southern side streets leading off Glasgow Road, Church Street had its humble beginnings as a field boundary between two fields, in particular at this location, on the former farm of Stonefield. The boundary became a track in the 19th Century and the track would towards the turn of the 20th Century, be renamed Church Street, after the Stonefield Parish Church.

Like Jackson Street further to the east, Church Street was to be a dead-end street, a cul-de-sac if you like, just as it is today. During the 19th Century the street ran only the length of the church. However, by 1910, decent quality stone homes, mostly semidetached had been built on either side of the street, most of which still exist today. These homes were initially owned by Rev John Burleigh and the Batters family. In 1912, a motor house and store was built on the far south western side, the constructor being William Adam of High Blantyre.

In 1970, Mr. Robert Barrett started a car sills repair business at Craig Street but had to move in 1973 when plans of redevelopment began to unfold. He moved to this former motor house at 19 Church Street taking over from the Baxter's Bluebird Buses. R.G Barrett & Co (AutoSills) manufactured car body sills.

Figure 191 Barrett & Co in Church St 1970's

The history of Church Street is explored in other Blantyre Project books. Whilst the distance from Church Street to Logan Street may seem relatively short, a lot has happened in this section of Glasgow Road and we begin by looking at the early beginnings of these properties.

Abbeygreen Manse

Abbeygreen was the former Manse house for the nearby Burleigh Church (East United Free Church) and had address 4 Church Street adjoining to Abbeygreen Building at 2 Church Street.

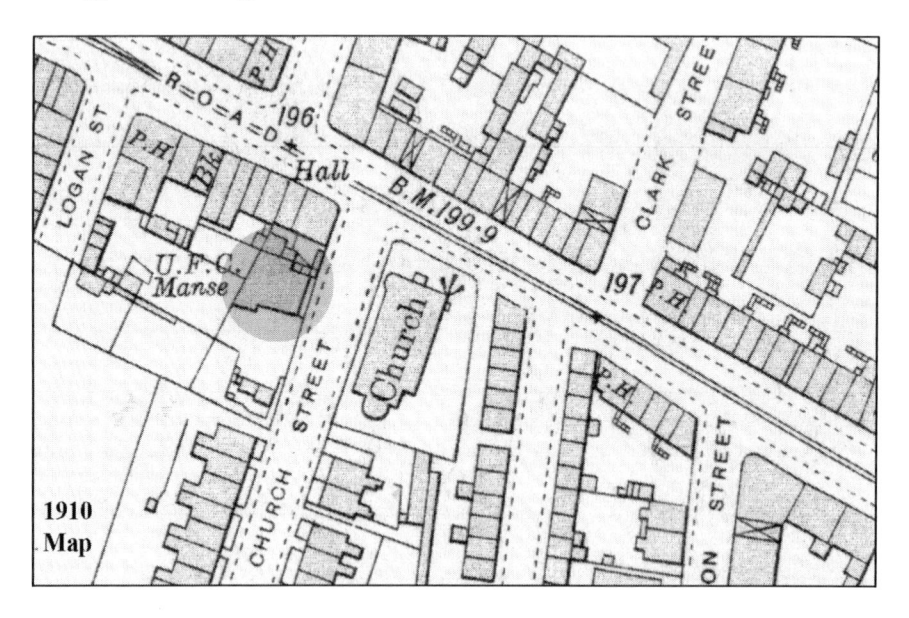

Figure 192 Former Abbeygreen (Burleigh) Manse on 1910 map

Located on the eastern side of Church Street near the Glasgow Road junction, the first mention in documentation appears to be in 1901, where the Rev John Burleigh, then a 50-year-old widower was living with 28-year-old Grace Cameron, a domestic servant hailing from Stonehouse. John's previous wife Marion Braid, 6 years his junior, died on 7th July 1892 at a young age and consequently, he had moved out of his previous home at Coatshill Cottage where he had lived since 1889 with his wife and father in law Andrew Braid (b1912- d1897), a retired grocer.

Abbeygreen Manse house is described as having 5 rooms each with one window or more. In 1905, the manse was owned and occupied by the Rev John Burleigh. According to the valuation roll that year, the buildings were split into two and was called Abbeygreen Manse and Abbeygreen Building, which was let out to Mrs. Grace Lennox (who is not the same Grace noted as a servant girl earlier. This Grace was older and had lived at Abbey Green Building since 1901 when she is noted as being 66 years old).

By 1911, John Burleigh was 60 years old and still single, but living with 35 year old servant Grace Hunter. John would pass away in 1922, leaving the house to a Janet Burleigh, possibly a sister. The adjacent building at 2 Church Street was also owned by Mrs Janet Burleigh. The rateable value of the manse did not change for several decades.

By 1930, Janet still owned adjacent 4 Church Street, often referred to by just the name "Abbeygreen". However, she was not living there at that time. She also owned consulting rooms, which was the hall at 141 Glasgow Road. Abbeygreen is still shown on the 1936 map, although by that time it was not noted as being the manse. It appears that following John Burleigh's death in 1922, the East United Free Church operated from a temporary manse at 306 Glasgow Road, which was simply a house. By 1930, that arrangement did not exist anymore and it appears the new minister at the church moved into the old Stonefield Parish Church Manse in Herbertson Street, as Stonefield Parish Church by 1930 had built a brand new, sizeable manse at 34 Auchinraith Road.

Abbeygreen for a time fell into dereliction but was later home to the Braidwood family of builders. During the mid 1970's it fell under compulsory purchase order and the last owner before it's demolition was a lady, who is now elderly and lives in Hamilton. Many people remember the large, beautiful garden at this former house.

Abbeygreen Building

Abbeygreen Building was a former large, tall building of several homes, which were located at 2 Church Street. The name first appears in the 1901 census and the construction was likely around that time, the previous homes on that site showing a different configuration on the 1898 map. Abbeygreen Building is not to be confused by the former adjacent Abbeygreen Manse. It is likely given ownership by Rev John Burleigh, that he was the constructor and person who created the name Abbeygreen. Strong evidence for this is the fact that Rev Burleigh was born at Abbeygreen in Lesmahagow. i.e. he named his new plot of land, after his birthplace.

The entrance to the houses was crammed into a small space adjacent to the manse at the Hall at the corner of Glasgow Road, and faced out on to Church Street looking across to the imposing height of the Stonefield Parish Church. There are no steps shown on the maps indicating the homes located in Abbeygreen Building were likely all on the one storey.

In 1905, according to the valuation roll, Abbeygreen Building was 6 small homes, a shop and a workshop. Five of the six homes were occupied that year. Renting from John were Mrs Grace Lennox, Mr William Garwood

(Captain of the Salvation Army), Mrs Mary Taggart, Mr Thomas Westwood (miner), and Mr Alexander McCaig (miner). Mr Robert Hunter was renting the shop and running it as a laundry service. Mrs Nellie Lennox rented the workshop working from it as a dressmaker. Overall Rev John Burleigh was receiving an annual rent that year from his tenants of £72 (£8,000 today).

By 1915, John Burleigh owned the adjacent halls at 141 Glasgow Road on the corner of Church Street (explored next), his manse and also 7 homes, indicating that in that previous decade he had split one of the homes further into two although his rental income remained roughly the same. His tenants in 1915 were Dr James H Naismith, Thomas Steel (labourer), David Russell (miner), Priscilla McIlwraith, George Gray (Clerk), Alexander McCaig (Insurance agent) and David McCaig (miner). There was no evidence of any shop or workshop by 1915.

Following John's death in 1922, Mrs Janet Burleigh inherited the properties. According to the 1925 census, the halls at 141 Glasgow Road were by then shops. The 7 houses were let to Mary Ann Heggison, Mary White, John Campbell and the previous occupants named McCaig, McIlwraith and Russell an arrangement that hadn't changed by 1930.

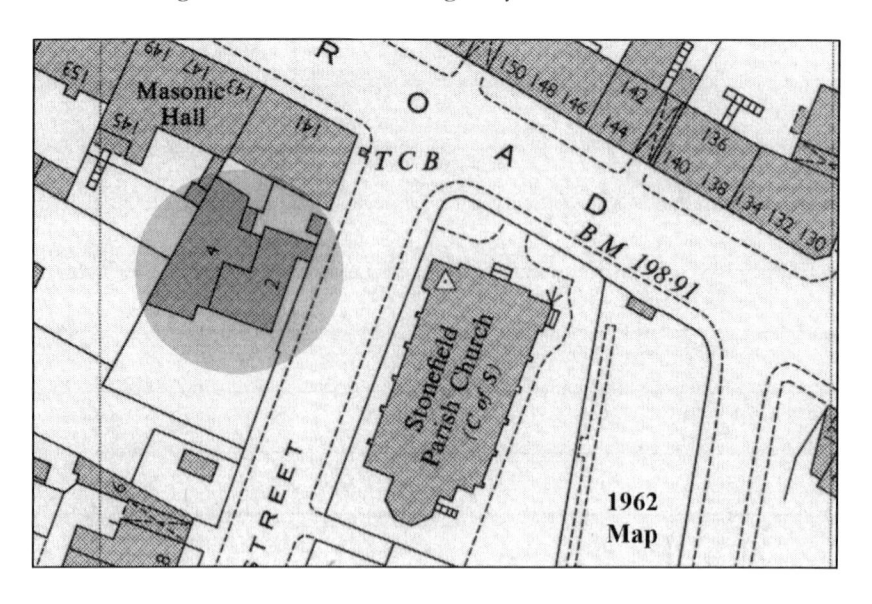

Figure 193 Former Abbeygreen Building shown in front of Abbeygreen Manse in 1962

The site of the old Abbeygreen Building is now a vacant piece of land, which is partially fenced off and in recent years has started to sprout woodland. The adjacent former manse and halls are also no longer there, also vacant land.

Abbeygreen Hall & Consulting Rooms

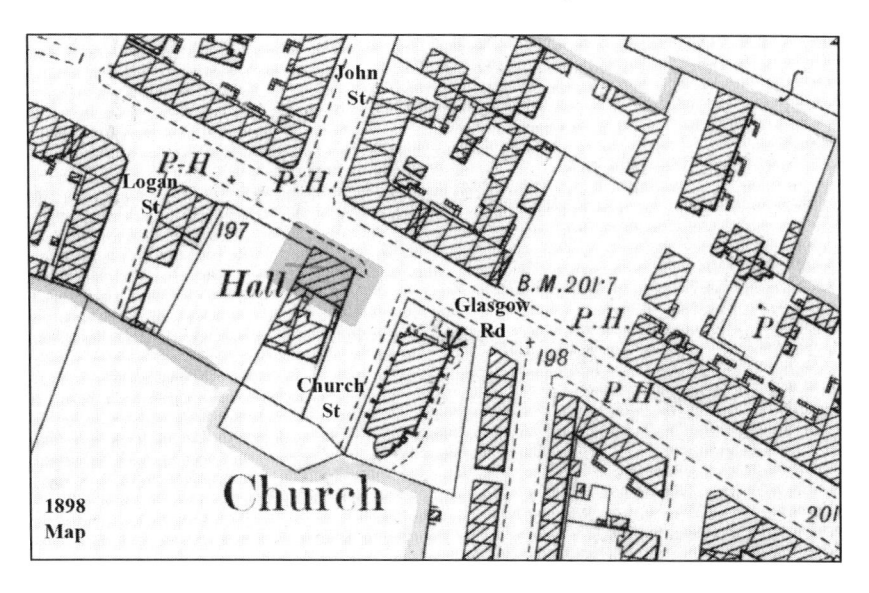

Figure 194 Former Abbeygreen Hall & Consulting Rooms on 1898 Map

At the western corner of Church Street and Glasgow Road, exactly on the junction was the former Abbeygreen Hall & Consulting Rooms. This 2 storey stone tenement building, adjacent to Abbeygreen may have once had the name 'Bothwellview" on account of it facing northwards and perhaps being able to see over the Clyde Braes at one point. It was situated directly across from John Street, so this is entirely possible.

In 1891, the Rev John Burleigh was living at Coatshill Cottage further west. A year later when his wife died, he acquired this rectangular plot of land and constructed Halls for use by the community and should not be confused or called the Burleigh Church Hall, which existed at Herbertson Street.

The Abbeygreen hall & its rooms were entered from Glasgow Road, the building having only 1 door facing out on to the pavement. There were no windows or doors on the gables. John was minister at the nearby Burleigh Church and was well respected and known to many, pictured here from the St Andrews Church website.

Figure 195 Rev John Burleigh

During 1895, it is noted that a shop existed in the ground floor of the building, presumably the hall and rooms being on the upper floor. That year both hall and shop were empty. The hall would certainly have been accessible for many when trams started running up and down Glasgow Road in front of it in 1903.

Figure 196 Abbeygreen Hall on right (looking back East) in 1903

Incredibly, we can date this photo rather accurately. Trams ran from October 1903 and where the billboard is on waste ground, the Masonic Hall construction had started in May 1904, so this creates a 6 months window for when this picture was taken. The long northerly shadows suggesting winter. The postcard very likely taken to celebrate the start of the tram service. The Stonefield Parish Church is behind the hall, although the picture makes it look like it had a steeple (which it didn't!)

By 1905, the hall was again marked 'empty' on the valuation roll, although not to say it wasn't being used often. The shop was occupied by Robert Hunter, a laundryman. Shortly after both hall and shop were given the official address 141 Glasgow Road. The laundry was short lived for by 1915 during war years, beside the hall, within this building was Dr. James H Naismith's surgery. It was the start of a peppered history associated with the wellbeing of Blantyre's population.

Sometime around the end of WW1, Rev John Burleigh moved the requirement for the halls to the vacant and unused Blantyre Works School room and Hall in the Village. The former hall at 141 Glasgow Road and Dr Naismith's surgery were divided and became 2 homes, occupied by Andrew Gillespie and Mrs Ann Jane Higgison, renting for £12 and £7 per annum. It is unknown why the hall moved, but it may simply have been to create the rental opportunity of £19 per annum, whereas before was next to nothing.

Figure 197 Abbeygreen Hall on right, Glasgow Road in 1903

John Burleigh died in 1922 and his estate was inherited by his widow, Janet. It is perhaps telling of the character of Janet Burleigh and her reported caring and assistance to local individuals on the fact that by 1925, the homes were no longer being rented, but instead the rooms were being used by Percival M Hancock, a chemist subletting to William Greenlie Chemists. This was to be the start of a prolonged period where the building would be used for medicine and looking after the health of Stonefield's residents.

Dr. David Keir Fisher

In 1925, the chemist was taken over by the arrival of Dr. David Keir Fisher who would operate a doctor's surgery there for 5 years until leaving Blantyre in 1930. David lived at "The Cairns" at Station Road and rented his surgery space and consulting rooms from Janet Burleigh. He may have left Blantyre due to possibly feeling redundant upon the building of the Health Institute in Victoria Street.

Born on 22nd March 1894, his parents could not afford to fund his medical

Figure 198 Dr David Keir Fisher

training, so Fisher worked as a dental technician for 5 years to save enough to become a medical student in 1913. The next year he joined the 4th Royal Scots Fusiliers, serving in Gallipoli & Egypt, and transferring to a field ambulance unit after recovering from wounds. After the war he returned to studies in both medicine and dentistry, qualifying in both disciplines in 1923. He then worked in general practice in Blantyre, returning to Glasgow in 1930 to work as an anesthetist based at the Dental Hospital.

Appointed a consultant (primarily at the Dental Hospital, but also at the Royal Infirmary) on the inception of the NHS in 1948, he retired from GRI in 1959 and the Dental Hospital in 1961. Fisher was a dental anesthetist in the traditional style, but hypnotherapy was a major clinical interest and he founded the Scottish branch of the British Society of Medical and Dental Hypnosis.

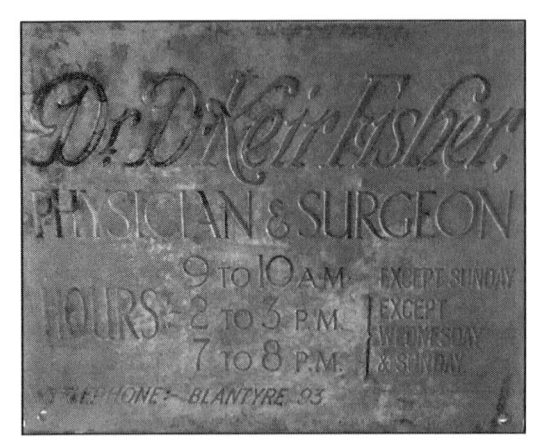

Figure 199 Plaque from former Fisher's Surgery

Predeceased by his wife, he had a daughter and twin sons. He maintained strong links with the church and remained active into retirement, travelling to the Upper Nile in his 90th year, and contributing considerably to the discussion of a clinical meeting only two weeks before his death in Dec 1985.

During researching this book, a Blantyre resident, Mr. Taylor showed this plaque from Dr. Fisher's former surgery. It reveals further information, such that his telephone number was Blantyre 93.

Using the plaque, we know his 1923-1930 surgery was open 9am – 10am except Sundays, 2pm to 3pm and 7pm to 8pm except Wednesdays and Sundays. The plaque probably came off the front of the building outside his surgery when the property was demolished in 1979.

1930's onwards

After Dr. Fisher moved away, the ground floor had a spell as a millinery shop, selling women's clothes. In 1937 Janet Burleigh had moved away and passed away that year too, at Cathcart, Glasgow. That same year, the following photo was taken showing a post tram era, renovated road surface and Church Street leading off to the left.

One of the only Telephone Boxes in Blantyre at the time was located at the corner, perhaps due to its proximity to the nearby Telephone Exchange.

The photo shows a huge crack rippling up the side of the Abbeygreen Hall, caused by subsidence, which was so prevalent in this area. Indeed the nearby Church Steeple had been removed the previous decade and in the following decade a nearby tenement in Logan Street collapsed. In this photo, the crack looks repaired.

Figure 200 Church Street and Abbeygreen hall on left looking west 1937

The new building owners in post WW2 years appears to be the Masonic, buying the building attached to their own and continuing to let out the shop. In the 1950's and 1960's it was occupied by a Dr. Hutchison's surgery and latterly before its demolition in 1979, it had been 2 homes.

Figure 201 Abbeygreen Hall before demolition 1979. Billboard at Church St

David Allen & Sons Billposting Ltd

This is perhaps a good time to talk about advertising billboards, something that was commonplace throughout the 20th Century on the many gables along Glasgow Road. David Allen & Sons Billposting Ltd were a national advertising business known to exist in 1916 and was part of the larger David Allen company formed in 1857. Their Head Office for Scotland was at 21 and 23 Cathcart Street, Greenock and they made their money by leasing wooden hoardings from building owners and charging customers to advertise on them. In some cases, the business attempted to buy the hoarding outright, to ensure they didn't have to rent it themselves. This was commonplace, but created a mixture of leased and owned hoardings. They did this throughout Scotland in the first half of the 20th Century, and Blantyre was no exception. The company leased gable walls of buildings, (mostly on Glasgow Road) to advertise.

In 1930, according to the valuation roll, amongst the places leased was the gable of 57 Glasgow Road (Chambers Land). They also owned and advertised on the hoarding next to the Central Garage at 163 Glasgow Road. They also owned hoarding and a sign on the gable of 225 Glasgow Road belonging to

Margaret Nelson and their own hoarding at 289 Glasgow Road. They also leased hoarding on the side gable of 254 Glasgow Road (now Good Taste Takeaway), which faced on to Station Road in 1930, but was later obscured when the Broadway Cinema was built.

They also leased the hoarding on the gable of 244 Glasgow Road (now Stacks Café), on the north side, facing into the park. They leased a board at Craighead near the racing track. They owned the hoarding at 2 John Street, near the Castle Vaults. Also, they owned a billboard hoarding at 14 Merry's Rows on the western side of the street at Low Blantyre. At number 5 and 6 Stonefield Road, they leased hoarding for advertising from Hamilton Investment & building society. At High Blantyre, they owned a hoarding near Lint Butts at Main Street, directly across from Cemetery Road. They also owned and advertised on Whistleberry Bridge.

Blantyre Project Social Media:

Valerie Krawczyk: "Where the small wood is now at Church Street used to be the beautiful garden at Abbeygreen. It was very well kept at all times."

Betty McLean: "The Salvation Army Officers lived at Church Street. The second house on the right, near the top. It was likely rented as the Officers changed frequently."

Boys will be Boys

All along Glasgow Road by the 1890's, were telegraph and telephone poles. You may have noticed on old postcards and photos, these poles which were situated very often along the pavements on both sides and had whit electrical insulators at the top. These were small, white caps or surrounds to protect the insulator from rain and of course to assist the efficient delivery of the electricity and signals. The caps were made of a substance almost like porcelain and were extremely fragile.

In the late 19th Century, a craze that boys chose as a pastime, was the deliberate vandalism of these electrical insulators, by throwing stones up towards them to shatter them. Can you imagine clusters of boys trying this activity at night or day, whilst one boy acted as a lookout? The opportunity to conduct this 'fun sport' would have been frequent. By February 1900 though, numerous complaints had been made about this wanton destruction and it reached a climax when on examination, it was found that between Springwells and Spittal, upwards of 60 insulators had been broken. Police action "sentenced" boys to receive five stripes or lashings with the birch rod cane.

The Masonic Buildings

In 1904, Livingstone Masonic Lodge 599 abandoned their small hall at the north east corner of Forrest Street and Glasgow Road junction after 27 years and looked to the future in building a new hall fitting for the 20th Century. Their old hall later became a pub called "The Livingstonian."

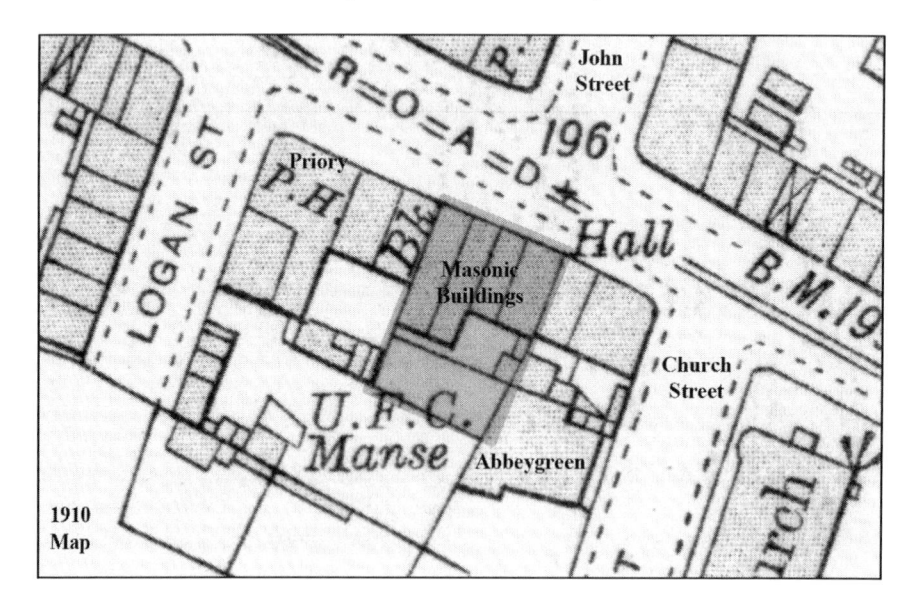

Figure 202 Masonic Buildings, Glasgow Road on 1910 Map

Their search took them to the opposite south side of Glasgow Road, further along in a more central location and a prime plot of land was found situated on vacant ground. Following a false recollection by an old timer online, others have incorrectly copied and published that the building 'was constructed in 3 stages', but that's certainly wrong. It was built all at once, in one stage, situated firmly between 2 existing buildings, i.e. Burleigh's Hall and rooms at Church Street corner and the opposing building at Logan Street corner owned by the late James McHutchison, (which later housed the Priory Bar.)

During researching this book, it was discovered that John Roberts, an adjacent spirit merchant renting the public house at the corner of Logan Street, bought the corner property from the Trustees of James McHutchison in 1904. He then extended his owned Bar by building 2 shops and 2 houses eastwards up against the new Masonic Hall. John Roberts and the Masonic built their new buildings at the same time in 1904, filling up the gap between 2 older, existing buildings, completing the block, directly across from John Street.

The design being selected and all the trades lined up, work began early in 1904. It is possible the nearby Roberts family of joiners were involved in the timber work for this construction, their relative being John Roberts, perhaps assisted by William Adam, also a joiner and prominent member of the lodge.

By Saturday 21st May 1904, the foundation stone of the new Masonic Hall was ceremonially placed in position.

The hall was of impressive design. Whilst some of the building consisted of more traditional 2 storey tenements with shops on the lower floor, the hall was located on the upper floor and had a pitched, impressive frontage, similar to classic Greek designs. Constructed of stone with slate roof the building had 4 windows above the shops on the east and 3 large, tall stained glass windows above 2 further shops to the east. A flagpole was erected above the pitched roof. The building would have address 143 – 149 Glasgow Road although later Livingstone Masonic Lodge 599 would acquire the Robert's extension and eventually would own 143-155 Glasgow Road.

A year after trams opened, the placing of the first foundation in 1904 was by far the largest ever Masonic occasion in Blantyre. Amid great pomp and ceremony Bro Colonel R. King Stewart, Provincial Grand Master of the Middle Ward laid the stone in the traditional manner. The public and visitors assembled at Low Blantyre Public School, Glasgow Road, almost every town in the area was represented, Coatbridge, Holytown, Carluke Larkhall, 3 Lodges from Hamilton, the Major Ness Lodge from Burnbank, there were Lodges from Glasgow, Bathgate, Strathaven and others.

There were between 300 and 400 assembled in marching formation, and encouraged along by the Cameronian Pipe Band, the Blantyre Silver Band, and the Palace Colliery Band, they made their way to the old Masonic Hall at Forrest Street where a meeting had been going on, the office bearers from this meeting then joined the procession and they went their way up Herbertson Street, right into Auchinraith Road, up to High Blantyre Main Street and down Broompark Road into Stonefield, where they halted at the bottom, at a point known as Priory Place not far from their new hall. This was to allow the Provincial Grand Lodge Brethren to take the point in the march and lead them the rest of the way to the New Hall in Glasgow Road. With these members all wearing full regalia and the stirring music of the bands. The thousands of spectators were not disappointed and it was great spectacle.

On arrival at the new premises on Glasgow Road, the dignitaries took to the platform erected for the day's proceedings. Already on the platform was the Stonefield Musical Association led by Brother W. Steven, and when silence was called for, the choir led in singing "God Save the King." R.W.M.

Nimmo then called on Bro. King Stewart to lay the foundation stone. For this endeavour he was presented with a silver trowel by Bro. W. Kerr, and a mallet by Bro. William Adam.

What followed was a very intricate Masonic ritual, but before the stone was finally lowered into place, a sort of time capsule was put in place. A jar or "bottle" as it was called containing newspapers of the day and other documents was meant to be sealed in the cavity behind the stone bar but by some strange omission the usual coins of the realm had been neglected. Major Ness, a prominent Blantyre figure, teacher and member of the Lodge came to the rescue and immediately offered a commemorative set of coins presented to him during the Jubilee of Queen Victoria in 1897, a great sacrifice as the coins were of value and could not be replaced. It is not known if the jar containing them was ever recovered when the old hall was demolished.

The rest of the day witnessed many speeches, anthems, prayers and Masonic ceremony. Because of all the symbolism connected with craft, this was a much more important day in the calendar of Lodge Livingstone 599 than the day when they entered their new premises for their first meeting almost a year after building began.

Costing about £2,400, the P.G.M. Colonel King Stewart consecrated the new hall on Friday 3rd February 1905. He was assisted that day by Brothers W. T. Hay, Master-Depute and Colonel Peter Spence, Substitute-Master, as well as other office-bearers of the Provincial Grand Lodge.

One of the prominent features of this new chamber was a window portrait of Dr. David Livingstone, who's virtuous life was extolled by Colonel King Stewart at the laying of the foundation stone. That day the Colonel had said, "I don't know if Dr Livingstone was a Mason, but this I do know, he followed out in his life what every Mason ought to do. His life was a noble example for us to follow, and we ought all to endeavour act up to his principal of doing good to our fellow men."

Early Shops and Masonic Life

In 1905 the hall was managed by Robert Proudfoot who lived in the Gate Cottage on Station Road near the Blantyre Village Works. The first ever shop the largest in this building at 143 Glasgow Road was occupied by James Miller a bootmaker, of no relation to the Millar family who would own shops further west in later times. Then, to the west was the large wooden door, an entrance to the upper hall and rooms. The 2 shops at 147 and 149 Glasgow Road under the hall were James Greenhorn butchers and Gorden G Grieg Printers & Stationers, renting for £18 per annum.

Figure 203 Masonic Buildings upon Construction in 1905

This incredible photo from 1905 shows these opening businesses. On the right is James Houston grocers within John Roberts' Building. In 1909 the following people held these positions. R.W.M., Bro. John B. Stewart; I.P.M. Bro. Thomas Watson; D.M., Bro, Alex. Reid; S.W., Bro. James Morris; J.W. Bro. John Donaldson; Secy., Bro. John Beecroft, 7 Auchinraith Colliery, High Blantyre; Treas., Bro. Donald Macleay, P.M. All Lodge meetings were held in Freemasons' Hall. Regular meetings on 4th Thursday of each month at 7:30 p.m. Monthly meetings of the Hall Committee were held on 3rd Monday of each month at 7:30 p.m.

This hall was also used by the women's guild throughout the 1910s and 1920s. Mrs Lamond was the patron of the guild, the hall being used for the meetings and parties. The hall had address 145 Glasgow Road.

Livingstone Masonic Lodge 599 was renting out to entirely different shops during WW1. By 1915, James Miller had moved away, perhaps unable to compete with the nearby Co-op boot shop. Instead, at 143 was William Baxter & Son a fruiterer. At 145 the hall was being managed by Daniel J Sprott of 4 Jackson Street. 147 Glasgow Road with its gas lamp outside was no longer James Greenhorn butchers, but was still a butchers. In 1915, it was run by Gilbert Harper who would operate his business until moving in 1922. (he would later establish Harper's Garage in 1934 slightly to the west, the same year as his death.) 149 still had the same use as a printers, but was by then run by Hugh Graham, who passed away in 1937.

By 1920, with the competition of public transport, William Baxter's family would go on to run a bus company from their home at Church Street. Moving into 143 Glasgow Road was John Bowie, Fruiterer, renting for £23 per annum. John was a distant relative of the writer of this book. This address would go on to have a long tradition of being a family fruit and vegetable shop and florist.

Between 1921 and 1925, perhaps wishing to downsize, John Roberts sold his 2 shops and 2 houses above on Glasgow Road to the Masonic Lodge. The lodge would continue to rent out the shops and now owned addresses 143 to 155 Glasgow Road. In 1925, the Masonic properties were John Bowie fruiterer at 143, the hall at 145, Archibald Whittle butchers at 147 and Hugh Graham Printers at 149 under the hall. At 151 was the Commercial Bank with 2 homes above at 153 and James Mathieson Jewelers at the end at 155, next to Roberts Priory Bar. James lived above the shop.

Figure 204 Interior of the Masonic Halls. Windows at Glasgow Road

On Saturday 5th February 1927, the Masonic Lodge celebrated their Jubilee (50 years) anniversary. Thomas Richardson RWM presided. The Provisional Grand Lodge of Lanarkshire was received. Bro Sir Robert King Stewart, the PRWGM, complimented the office bearers and brethren of Lodge Livingstone on their great success since their conception. 250 people attended and long service medals were given to T. Geddes and Alex Livingstone, member of the Lodge for 40 years. Z. Nimmo, A Russell and Alex Reid were also given long service medals.

In 1930, shops had changed slightly again with Mrs. Marion Young's fruit shop at 143 and Matthew Lennox a watchmaker at 155. Archibald Whittle was still at the butchers under the hall, now occupying both shops, one of which contained butchery machinery. 151 Glasgow Road was the Commercial Bank of Scotland.

Figure 205 Licensed photo of Masonic Buildings 143 – 155 Glasgow Road in 1950

> Blantyre Project Social Media:
>
> **Lillias Addison:** "Davidson the butcher was my Uncle, John Davidson"
>
> **Margo Clayton:** "Mrs. Marion Young was a Bowie too"
>
> **Jim Donnelly:** "We used to have our rock band rehearsals in the hall during the late 1970's."
>
> **Thea Borland McNamee**: "I used to go into Bowie's for my lozenges. They were oblong in shape and had little sayings on them, similar to love hearts."
>
> **Serge Mikkelson:** "This block always felt like a mini shopping centre. As well as some popular shops, people used its decorative, distinctive features as a quick glance to see how far along Glasgow Road you were. Well, at least I did!"

In post WW2 years, the correct order of the shops is noted as Bowie's at 143 Glasgow Road, who would come back to occupy the fruit shop. During the 1970's people may remember the shop as Tandem Shoe Shop. The hall remained at 145 Glasgow Road and the butchers at 147 and 149 would become James Aitkenhead butchers then during the 1960's, taken over by Davidson's Butchers, a family who lived at Broompark Road in High Blantyre. The Commercial Bank at 151 became the Scottish Clydesdale Bank, which would later move further west along Glasgow Road.

Figure 206 Masonic Buildings during the 1970's. Pictured from John Street

The Masonic halls were subjected to compulsory purchase in 1977 and scheduled for demolition the following year, delayed slightly by politics.

Figure 207 The Windows

Before the demolition the beautiful stained glass mosaic windows, which featured Livingstone and Major Ness were carefully removed and at great expense to the lodge were renovated to restore their beautiful colours.

Each window features opaque glass of many colours. Red, browns, yellow, greens and blues. Amongst the masonic icons were images of Major Ness and Dr David Livingstone. Some are long and tall and have more than a hint of early art-deco about them. They were then moved to the new Lodge at the bottom of Elm Street, a modern brick building far less impressive than the former Hall. Their time there from 1977 was to be short lived until the hall was sold in 1988 to make it into a restaurant and bar named "Cobblers" (later flats after 1993). The windows were again carefully removed and followed the lodge to their next premises at the Masonic Hall at High Blantyre, alongside Lodge Kilwinning 557.

The windows, create by James Benson, stained glass maker are currently in storage in the basement of the hall. Speaking of the windows, Bill Andrew, a member of this lodge added, "They were always considered one of the most beautiful temples in the area if not Scotland because of this. The Glasgow Road building had a special aura when you walked and you truly felt the history in the building (at least I did) and a big part of this was the windows."

Figure 208 Masonic Halls being demolished in 1978

Pictured in late 1978 is the demolition of the Masonic Halls commencing with the Priory Bar at the far eastern end, directly across from the former Post Office. It was a final, brutal end to these iconic buildings. Demolition had been scheduled earlier than this, but was delayed by final planning objections, ironed out in Autumn 1978.

Today, on this ground between Church Street and Logan Street is a small patch of woodland, which has been rather fast growing in the last couple of decades. The land is currently vacant.

By Paul D Veverka

Priory Place and The Priory Bar

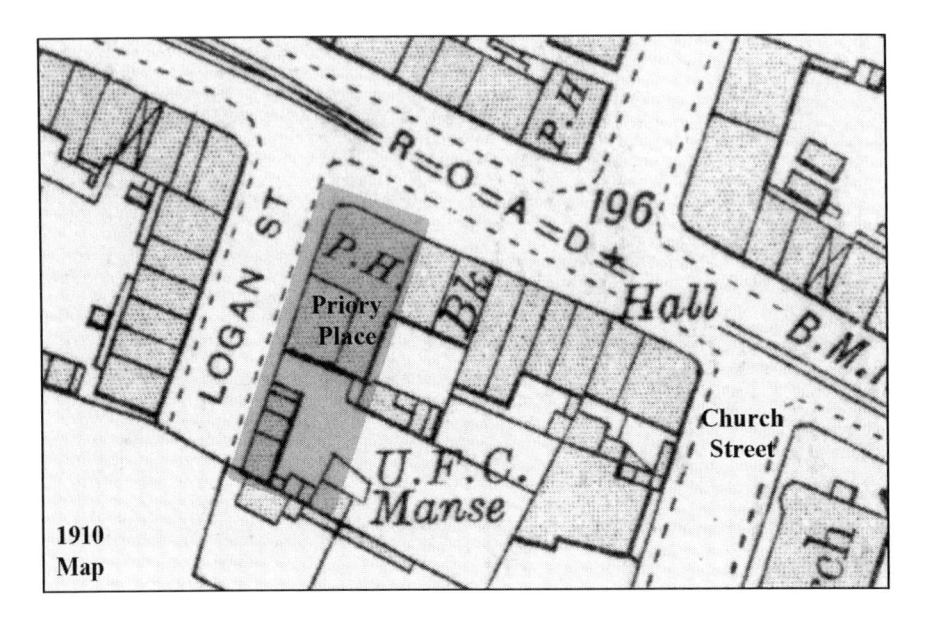

Figure 209 Priory Place on 1910 map at corner of Logan Street

Priory Place was a former 19th and 20th Century building situated at the eastern corner of Glasgow Road and Logan Street junction. It comprised primarily of a popular public house (named the Priory Bar) but also had upper homes and shops.

Naming the Building

Constructed by joiner James Walker around 1889 into 1890, the 2 storey stone corner tenement had frontage on both Glasgow Road and the dead end street that would later open up and become Logan Street. Mining was at the forefront of Blantyre Industry by this time and the name 'Priory' being attached to this building likely signified a nod to the Priory ruin or recent colliery, both with strong connections to Blantyre. Or simply, it may have been just a popular, liked name. Constructed on behalf of owner James McHutchison, the building was to predominantly house a bar, shops and houses. His public house was to be "The Priory Bar" a constant and consistent name which would exist until the demolition of the buildings, regardless of their ownership.

James constructed the Public House facing out on to Glasgow Road which had 5 upper windows on that side and 4 large plate glass windows. At the side and immediately adjacent was a house, separated into 4 small homes. The whole block was to be named "Priory Place" and would become well known in Blantyre.

Figure 210 Priory Bar at Priory Place, corner of Logan Street 1977

James McHutchison

Remote owner, Mr. James McHutchison was a merchant of Bothwell Parish. Born in Clarkson in 1842, he was a licensed grocer. During the 1890's, he lived at Cookshill Place, Bothwell with his wife Bessie, a Bothwell woman, who was 10 years his junior. A successful man, employer of others, his home had 6 windows in it, suggesting a modest size by comparison to the neighbours. It is not thought he had children. Perhaps seeing this a rental investment, his ownership of Priory Place was however, incredibly short lived.

James died in 1891, aged only 49 and as a public house owner, it may be easy to make a connection as to what he died from.

Priory Place passed in 1891 to the Trustees of James McHutchison, to be held in trust. This looks to have prompted a change in occupation of the buildings. In 1895, Mr. George Robertson was occupying a small house at the Logan Street side of Priory Place as well as a stable for £11/year. George was a fruiterer and ran his small, rented shop on the lower floor, not far from the Logan Street entrance. Above the pub lived John Roberts, the son of William Roberts who ran the 'Volunteer Arms' pub further along Glasgow Road.

John Roberts took over as occupier of the pub in 1891 renting the public house for £55 / year from the Trustees of James McHutchison. During this time, Priory Place was separated from more easterly Abbeygreen Hall & Rooms by a large space of vacant land.

John Roberts

Mr. John Roberts was born in Paisley in 3rd December 1849 and had rather an interesting life worth sharing here.

He was baptized on 30th December 1849 at Middle Church, in Paisley. In the early 1860's his family moved to Blantyre. He was the 3rd child to father William, a police officer and mother Mary. John had 5 brothers and sisters. He was a middle child and grew up to become a plumber with a Bothwell company. When he was only 16 (about 1865) he joined the Blantyre Rifle Volunteers. He was allegedly one of the best shots and represented the Battalion on more than one occasion at Wimbledon (the biggest event in the calendar). He was also at the famous 1881 'Wet Review' that Major Ness was so proud to be a part of in Edinburgh before the Queen. In 1871, the census records them as living at "number 6" in Blantyre, and although doesn't say where, it is known that they were at newly built Causewayshot westwards on Glasgow Road by 1881. In 1885, John Roberts lived at the Avon Buildings, an area of Glasgow Road that many of the Roberts family would not stray far from.

Working as a Plumber and living at Walker's Buildings in 1891, John changed profession that year to become a spirit merchant at Glasgow Road. His brother William, had by then started his own building company nearby.

John went on to become a member of the old School Board, and may be featured in some old Blantyre photos of curlers and the bowlers as he was keen on both. In his latter part of life from 1905, he had been the outright owner of the corner buildings at Logan Street and proprietor of the Priory, before he died aged 83 in 1932 in a nursing home in Glasgow.

The Priory Bar and Shops of Priory Place

In September 1899, John Roberts successfully appealed against the County Council raising his rates from £55 to £120, managing to agree upon £100/year. The Priory Bar was clearly successful, for by 1904, John Roberts had the funds sufficient to buy Priory Place from the Trustees of James McHutchison. Perhaps motivated by the Masonic Lodge building their impressive building to the east, John set about to construct an extension to Priory Place on Glasgow Road, building out fro the pub eastwards. This was done at the same time as the Masonic Buildings were constructed and by 1905, there were no gaps in buildings between Church Street to Logan Street. The 1905 valuation roll shows just 1 home occupied by John Roberts, which he had extended above the pub with attic rooms. Owner and occupier of the Priory Bar, his new extension was to be let out to James Houston grocers and in 1905, the other shop he had built was still empty, as were the two homes above them, perhaps still to be finished.

John Roberts was well known and much respected. In 1914 he sponsored the Blantyre Silver Band on several outings, the band using a field nearby to practice. During the 1910's, as treasurer of the Blantyre, Cambuslang & Rutherglen Ploughing Society, John let this organisaiton use his building for their annual meetings. James Pettigrew of Malcolmwood Farm presided.

By the start of WW1, Priory Place extension had address 151, 153 and 155 Glasgow Road. John Robert's Priory Bar had address 157 Glasgow Road and 1 Logan Street. John's home above was 3 Logan Street. He was letting out 151 to the Bank managed by William McGruther, 153 as 2 upper flats and 155 to James Mathieson. These properties (the extension) would be bought completely from John, by the Livingstone Masonic Lodge 599 in 1922, explored earlier in the book.

The bar looks to have struggled for suitable staff during war years with several advertisements asking for qualified assistance. Its central location on Glasgow Road made it easily accessible and successful, often frequented by miners and likely more frowned upon by some of the adjacent Masons who were accustomed to non drinking and self prohibition.

The Priory Bar located entirely on the ground floor was of modest size by comparison to other larger bars in Blantyre. The private rooms at the back used for meetings and later small parties, meant the bar was located in the front room only. A horseshoe shaped public bar, with plenty of space for bar staff to work meant initially little space for punters to stand, although the layout of this changed during the 20th Century. The private room had a window that slid on a small metal rail, allowing people in the room to be passed drinks directly from the bar or indeed to directly order more. In time a lounge bar, separated from the main bar could be entered from Logan Street. Located beside this in George Robertson's former grocery shop was later in the mid to late 20th Century, a bookmakers. Prior to that, direct off-sales were offered from time to time as licenses changed.

Like butchers shops and other pubs, sawdust was put on the floor to assist cleaning and soak up any spillages, although truth be told, it is said this was purely to do with the uncouth habit of men spitting tobacco and spitting in general. The sawdust was cheap and readily available and changed often.

Figure 211 The Priory Bar in the 1930's. Glasgow Road looking east

Shortly before this photo was taken, John Roberts passed away in 1932. He would miss the extension and building of council homes nearby at Logan Street, something which would only bolster the fortunes of the Bar.

Upon his death, William Black was the next manager of Priory Place for widow Helen Roberts, but only for a short time. In March 1935, upon returning home from Motherwell one evening, William was found dead in his chair at Priory Place, aged 57. He had suffered a brain hemorrhage.

Blantyre Project Social Media:

Maggie O'Brien: "I was in the Priory Bar the very last day it was open. Mary was behind the bar. It was a sad day."

Robert McLeod-Wolohan: "This was my local pub, although I frequented most pubs in Blantyre! I was in their darts and dominoes team and I loved having a pie and a pint in there. However, it didn't beat the Castle Vaults, which if I remember over the road was the only pub you could get drunk in, using tic. "

Anthony Smith: "Priory Bar 1967. This was the first pub I ever had a drink in. McEwans Screwtops at 2/ 3d a bottle. I remember when lager and lime became popular too. The barkeeper asked you to take your pint and would add lime, asking you to taste it, adding lime again and again until he got it just right for you. Happy days!"

John Murray of Rutherglen bought the pub in 1935. Brewers such as Youngers, Tenants and later Scottish & Newcastle were later involved with the Pub and the building remained in private ownership. From 1966 until 1972 Jimmy and Mina McInally managed the Priory Bar, then Mina herself for 2 further years when Jimmy died in 1972.

Figure 212 The Priory Bar at Corner of Logan Street late 1970's

During the 1970's Davie & Jean Tallis ran the pub, before passing that mantle over to relatives.

In 1974, Ben and Mary Meechan (a relation to the Tallis family) were the last landlords until Priory Place was bought by compulsory purchase order in 1977, then was demolished in late 1978, ahead of the nearby adjacent Masonic Buildings.

The Priory Bar was popular and appreciated by many for the great evenings had in there with friends and family, singing songs until late, its sports team, including darts and bowls.

Figure 213 Priory Lounge during 1970s

The Priory Bar still is fondly remembered by many.

St John's Wood & Episcopal Church

During the 1930's, situated between Logan Street moving east was a small wooded area, which ran through to Church Street. The wood ran alongside the drill hall, what we know now as "Terminal One" Youth building. The name "St John's Wood" was common to the 1930's and 1940's era and was less used post WW2, and unknown why St John's name was chosen.

In the corner of the 2 acre woodland on the Logan Street side between Priory place and the Drill Hall was a small green wooden hut with some seats and a stove that various clubs from around Blantyre used as a meeting hall. In the 1920's this small wooden hut was officially the Episcopal Church. However, it changed use by 1930 used more by local community groups. The iron railings surrounding this plot were removed for WW2 efforts.

In later decades, it was used as the Racing Pigeon hall adjacent to Priory Place, which was next to the Priory Bar Lounge i.e. beyond large green doors where the beer was delivered. Next to the small hall, the local Doocot. Owners would spend a lot of time looking at the sky to see the birds coming home and then try to get them to land to get the ring off their leg, putting it into their time clock. There are still people with old pigeon lofts in their back gardens at Logan Street although this little hut is long gone.

Figure 214 Location of former St John's Wood, pictured in 2016

This land is currently vacant although a 'for sale' sign has been erected 2017. It's in a prime, central spot for development and we predict confidently that it will be put to use again. If not and with trees already sprouting again, perhaps alternatively, it will see a return of the name, "St John's Wood".

CHAPTER 10
GLASGOW ROAD SOUTH
LOGAN ST TO CRAIG ST

Origins of Logan Street

Logan Street started off simply as a Auchinraith field boundary during the 19th Century, likely land belonging to the Craig family. By the 1870's a small dead end street was formed when Priory Place was constructed at the eastern junction to Glasgow Road and the opposing 'Turner's Buildings' to the West.

An eminent man of the 19th Century in Blantyre had been Colonel John Clark Forrest, and by the 1890's a street, 'Forrest Street' had already been named in his honour. Just after the turn of the 20th Century, around a decade after his death, further streets leading off Glasgow Road were also given proper postal addresses in connection with this man. To the north John Street and Clark Street. To the south, Logan Street, named after John's wife.

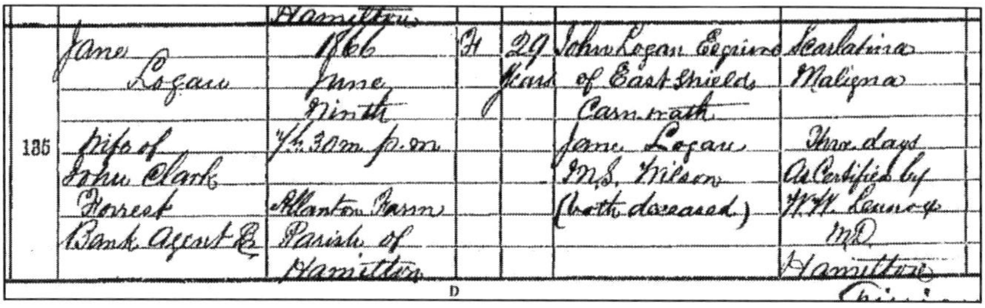

Figure 215 Jane Forrest (nee Logan) death in 1866 at only 29 years old

On 9th June 1866, at just 29 years old, Jane Forrest (nee Logan) had died from scarlet fever at her home in Hamilton, John by her bedside. Despite being only 34 years old, John was inconsolable and chose to devote the rest of his life to work and career, never remarrying again. A military man at heart, he rose through the ranks to become the Captain of 16th Lanarkshire Rifle Battalion. He passed away in 1893 and is buried in High Blantyre kirkyard. Council homes were built in Logan Street in 1933 and the large former drill hall, became Elizabeth Scott Centre, now Terminal One Youth Centre.

Winks Inn

In the 18th Century, if you walked along the Glasgow to Hamilton Road near where the junction of Logan Street is today, you would be walking along a countryside, narrow muddy road, with stone dykes or hedgerows on the south side, rough footpath across the road on the north, with endless fields, part of the farm of Stonefield beyond on either side.

Even until the 19th Century, this was a particularly desolate part of Blantyre in those rural, sleepy days. The traveller would very much feel he or she was leaving Blantyre and heading out into countryside.

During the 1800's, considered literally in the middle of nowhere, on the very outskirts of Glasgow Road and at a time before any tenements, was a small property called "The Winks Inn." Of unknown construction date, it may have been as old as the late 1700's. This was located exactly where the eastern part of Clydeview Shopping Centre is today, approximately at 'Kaos Skate Shop'. At that time there was no indication of any street leading off Glasgow Road adjacent to it. Behind the inn, only a long narrow field leading from the Glasgow Road southwards joining far off at Auchinraith Road.

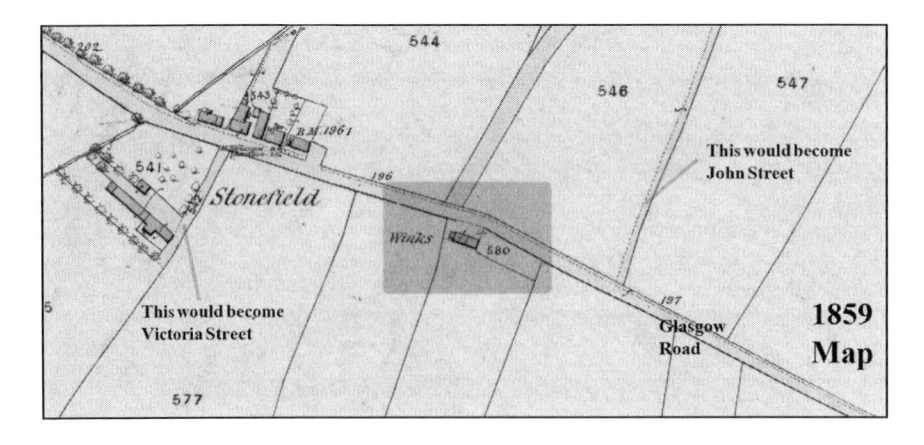

Figure 216 Winks Inn shown on the 1859 Map of a very rural Blantyre

The Winks Inn would have been popular with coaches and travelers and had an area to the eastern side, perhaps a paddock to accommodate the horses? On the 1859 map, an adjoining building may have been a stable. A small building attached to the west may have been a store or outside lavatory.

By this time, the Inn was a home, rather than business, keeping the name Winks, and renamed to Winks Cottage, often referred to in the village as simply "Winks". Early information is few and far between. Thankfully, an accurate 1859 description exists of Winks Cottage in the Valuation Roll, as follows, "A thatched cottage, formerly an Inn, but now occupied by Cotters. (Sidenote: A cotter was "a peasant farmer. It was occupied by Mr. J Craig who also owned Birdsfield) considered by the Proprietor, W. Forest Esqr. The best authority for this name. It is on the lands of Stonefield." It is most likely that Mr. W Forest was a relation of John Clark Forrest (2 r's) who may have inherited these lands either side of Glasgow Road and who was also responsible for providing land for the Stonefield Church further east.

Figure 217 Location Line drawing showing how Inn may have looked in modern context

This mock up photo shows how the thatched cottage may have looked against the modern backdrop and in context of the Clydeview Shopping Centre, the location being correctly assessed.

Today, there's no evidence of Winks Cottage, but it must have existed only a short time after the description, as by 1877, land had been sold by this Forrest family in order to build further tenements along this stretch of road.

Blantyre Project Social Media:

Evelyn Trussler "Can you imagine how many people have walked at this location near the old RBOS at Clydeview and never realized that an inn used to be there. It's all going to change again soon. Planning dept at South Lanarkshire Council have received ambitious plans to demolish this part of the centre and turn it into new retail units. It will be a 4th complete rebuild of this area. From an early Inn, to modern state of the art retail units."

By Paul D Veverka

Turner's Buildings (Central Buildings)

One of the most populated buildings ever on Glasgow Road was the former Turner's Buildings, or as they were also known, Central Buildings.

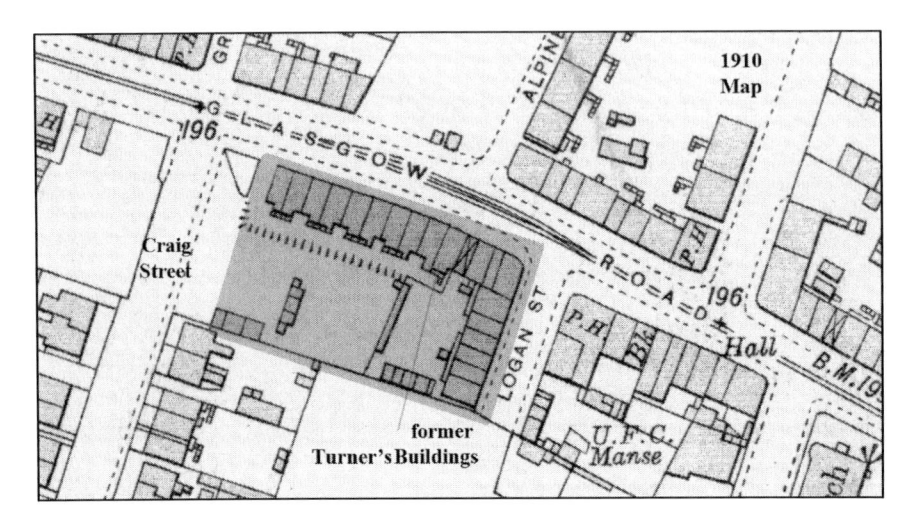

Figure 218 Former Turner's Buildings (Central Buildings) on 1910 Map

Before we explore this, lets clear up something. Central Buildings was not 'located between Craig Street and Victoria Street'. That wasn't the case, it was further east between Logan Street and Craig Street. Neither was Hill's Pawn Building located in it. The name Central Buildings and Turner's Buildings are actually interchangeable for the same former properties and should not be confused either with the Central Premises (Co-op) previously explored.

Turner's Buildings were constructed between 1877 and 1878 by Architect, Mr. George Turner, who did not live in Blantyre. Named after him, it is referred as so in the 1879 Naismith's Business Directory.

The properties were L shaped on plan leading from Logan Street where the buildings were taller at 3 storeys, around the western corner of Logan Street junction with Glasgow Road, then after a pend close, became 2 storey with frontage on Glasgow Road to just over three quarters of the way towards Craig Street. The land at the corner of Craig Street was never built upon until the later Clydeview Shopping Centre. Built partly of brick, part stone with slated roofs and tall chimneys there were initially 28 homes although in later decades these would be split into 44 homes. The land was low lying and was built up on a small embankment to enable the frontage opening out on to the street. Confirmed also by the raised kerblines at the corner of Logan Street.

The houses located on all floors were mostly let out to miners and their families and unlike other nearby tenements, some of the houses were also located on the lower floors. When first built there were 3 shops, 2 of which were Alexander McGill Ironmongers on the corner and further west, James Hill Tailors & Clothiers.

Sad Child Fatality

DID YOU KNOW? On Thursday 25th June 1885, a child of four years of age named Elizabeth Livingston was knocked down outside the building by a runaway horse. She never regained consciousness and died that evening.

The 1880's and 1890's

By 1885, Mr. George Turner was bankrupt. It is unknown what caused this given the rental capability of his premises. Keith Patrick solicitors acted as creditors whilst John Mitchell of Stonefield Road acted as temporary factor of the homes. There is a strong possibility that money may have been an issue for George even whilst the buildings were being constructed, perhaps downsizing from 3 storeys to most of the homes being 2 storeys. As will be seen later, some of these homes were not built to a good standard which would later have disastrous consequences. That year, the 2 shops were Richard Livingstone a wine merchant, JG Birken & Co of Bridgeton and Mrs Marion Potters drapers. As you'll see shops changed often in these buildings!

In 1887, twenty three year old single man, William Denniston of Turner's Buildings was killed in the Udston Colliery disaster. Also that year, as 500 miners rioted through Blantyre, two of the prisoners eventually taken to the nearby police station were 50 year old James McGuire and 18 year old John Gilhooly, both of Turner's buildings. With so many people living at these properties, news stories are plenty.

Between 1887 and 1895, William Buchanan, a spirit merchant of Melville Drive, Motherwell bought Turner's Buildings. Born in 1842, William was the owner of the Black Bull Inn at Merry Street, Motherwell as well as other homes there. This was to be a grand investment with William preferring to continue living at Motherwell. It is around this time we first see the name "Central Buildings" appearing for these properties, likely a name chosen by William to leave behind the old "Turners Building" legacy. However, with residents of many generations living there, the name Turner's Buildings and Central Buildings would both be used right throughout the 19th and 20th Centuries, referring to the same properties.

Figure 219 Turner's Buildings 3 storey and 2 storey on right in 1903

In 1895, Central Buildings in the time before postal addresses were numbered from 1-24. Houses 9,10,17 and 18 were split into two, totaling 28 homes. The shop at the corner was empty that year and in the 2 storey section at Glasgow Road was James Gibson Musician's shop and William Baxter fruiterer.

James Gibson Musician

Born on 8th June 1868, James McRae Gibson was originally from Dunoon and was the son of Alexander Cameron Gibson. He had a natural flair for music, and by 1881, at the age of 12 following a family move to Blantyre, he started playing as organist for High Blantyre Old Parish Church.

On 22nd April 1889, when he was 21, he married his sweetheart Jeannie McNaught at Kirkton High Blantyre. Jeannie was a Blantyre woman, born at Smithycroft, High Blantyre on 20th October 1865. James ran his music business from 2 Central Buildings. He is noted in the 1895 census as being a musician and is said at one time to have led an orchestra. He was not the only family member to be involved with music, for nearby that year at 9 Central Buildings was another James Gibson Jnr, noted as being a music teacher. The relationship was father and son.

James Senior was also an organist for High Blantyre Old Parish Church for 7 years, the church being exactly adjacent to Smithycroft, the home of his wife before they married. It is quite probably this is how they met. He was a pianoforte tuner and also a member of Blantyre Kilwinning Masonic Lodge. In 1891, they appear in the census at Adam's Land, High Blantyre, which was not far from Smithycroft and adjacent to the old Parish Church Halls. With them was 1 year old, first daughter, Agnes.

Before 1900, they family left for Hawick, then later in 1912 moved to Dunville, Canada, taking a ship from Scotland to Seattle. His family moved with him. During his lifetime he had 11 children (3 daughters and 8 sons). He died at home in Canada on 15th November 1937, aged 69. His wife, Jeannie died on 16 March 1947 in Dunville, Canada.

Grisly end of William Buchanan

William Buchanan's ownership of Turner's Buildings was to be short lived when on 8th September 1895, he was violently murdered in the most brutal manner, aged just 53. Let's take another 'pit stop' to tell that grisly story.

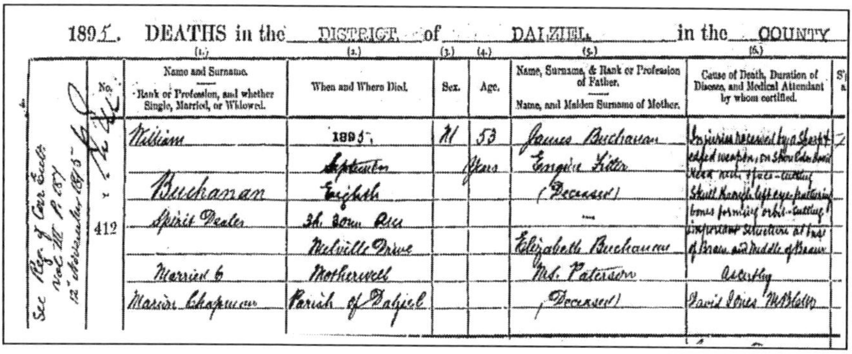

Figure 220 William Buchanan's Death Certificate 1895

That evening, William Buchanan had been out with friends discussing the results of the days yacht races. He left the company late in the evening to walk the short 50 yard distance back to his home in Melville Drive, Motherwell. On the dark path at the back of his house, William was surprised to see his nephew, 18 year old Mr. William McQueen of Glasgow standing there with a revolver in one hand and a knife in the other! The nephew proceeded to shoot William who fell to the ground heavily. There, lying injured he was sat upon by the nephew, who took out the knife and drive it through William's right eye socket into a depth of 4 inches, almost to the back of his head. William died instantly from lacerations to his brain.

His son, witnessing the incident had run for help and came back with police and some of the friends who had been in William's company earlier.

The group was confronted by McQueen, brandishing the revolver at them saying "Don't come any closer or I'll blow your brains out!". Behind him, William lay dead on his back, in a huge pool of blood, with further cuts to his face. McQueen made off quickly, turning back occasionally to let off a volley of shots, which missed the party bouncing off the road.

A young man by name of MacFarlane took it upon himself to give chase to McQueen and later bravely pointed to police where he had gone. McQueen was arrested that night, openly admitting the murder. The revolver was taken in as evidence but the knife was missing and would not turn up for a few weeks until some boys found it on an embankment some distance away.

In court in November 1895, McQueen was charged with murder and given a life imprisonment, but pleaded insanity. He insisted God had told him to do it. It later transpired a family feud have been bubbling away in the background, the details of which were over money and not disclosed.

Turner's Building Young Girl's Sad career

In late February 1900, at Hamilton Sheriff Court, Elizabeth McCann, a 12-year old Blantyre girl stood in the dock awaiting to be charged. She was the daughter of William McCann, a miner who resided at Turner's Buildings.

She was charged with 3 different acts of theft from shops in Blantyre. The offences were committed between 24th January and 22nd February 1900 and the articles stolen were all items associated with keeping warm and dry in that winter. Five boys' jackets, six pairs of boots and one pair of shoes, all of which were promptly taken to be pawned.

The theft is telling of a cold winter but there is more to the story for she was not intending to keep them for herself. Instead the court heard how the girl had been encouraged by her mother to steal the items from the shops and also told where to take them to afterwards, for the purpose of pawning them. The girl was told to bring her mother the proceeds of the thefts. In answer to the Sheriff, little Elizabeth was told she got 2d from her mother on each occasion she took money home after each pawning, and she would happily spend the full 2d on sweets and ice cream.

It was suggested by the court that a usual stance for this type of incident would be for the girl to be sent to a Reformatory School, but the court noted there was no such Catholic Institution of its kind in Scotland for girls at the time and instead asked for a period of 3 months to monitor her behaviour in future. It sounds that Elizabeth had got off lightly.

20th Century Shops, Tenants & Ownership

In 1905, Turner's Buildings was called 'Central Buildings' in the Valuation roll. Owned by the Trustees of the late William Buchanan, the property was being managed by John Hastie an ironmonger and the 28 houses were now divided into 44 houses, including those at Logan Street corner.

Postal addresses had been allocated and there were now 5 shops. At the corner of Logan Street at 159 Glasgow Road on the ground floor of the 3 storey building, and directly across from the Priory Bar had been until 1903, Torrance Grocery, run by Mr John M. Torrance. However by 1905, it was occupied by Hugh Whyte. That year, in the 2 storey at 161 Glasgow Road was Marion Rae's Dairy, 163 Glasgow Road was Marion Greenhorn's Butchers. Further along at 167 was William Baxter's Fruit shop and at 169 was John Bryson's Drapers.

Turners Buildings / Central Buildings were allocated 159 – 187 Glasgow Road, all odd numbers. 20 houses at 165, 8 homes at 171-185 with 10 upper homes at 187 divided into a,b,c and so on. By 1915 the Buchanan estate had passed to William's widow, Mrs. Marion Clifton Buchanan (nee Chapman). Still living in Motherwell, she owned these 44 homes including 4,6,8,10,12 and 14 Logan Street, the 3 storey tenements. Shops had changed again. 159 was James Bryce Ironmongery, 161 Samuel Park's Dairy, 163 was James Powell (jnr) Butchers. 167 and 169 was combined as Charles Easton Drapers.

Mrs. Buchanan still the owner in 1920, with same shops as 1915, with exception of Samuel Brown an ironmonger moving into 159 Glasgow Road at the corner and at 167-169, John Davidson Drapers.

Brown's Ironmongery Store

Samuel Alexander Brown was born in 1878 in Glasgow, Scotland. In post WW1 years he ran an ironmongery shop at the corner of Logan Street for a short time. He was still running the shop until the time of his death in March 1921, aged only 43. The address on his death record was 49 Aitken Street, Glasgow. This was his home address indicating he may not have lived in Blantyre, despite renting the shop from around 1918.

After his death, Samuel's widow, Elsie Blair Meek (who was originally from Forfar), took over the running of the shop but she was soft on the local families who would send barefoot children along to obtain goods without the means to pay for the items. The business later 'went under' by 1923.

Three of the surviving children of Samuel and Elsie were admitted to

Quarriers Orphanage at Bridge-of Weir in 1923. The only child to escape the orphanage was Elizabeth Agnes Alexander Brown (1918 – 1997) who was only two years old at the time of their father's death. A fifth child, known as 'baby Sam' died as an infant.

Figure 221 Brown's Ironmongery Store in 1920 corner of Logan Street

The man at the centre of this previously unseen photo is Samuel Alexander Brown. The lady on the left is likely be his wife. We do not know the identity of the lady on the right, but she is most likely a shop worker. The name of Logan Street can be seen on the photo. In the window reflection, across Glasgow Road is McAlpine's building. The former name of the shop, 'Torrance Grocery' can be seen faintly on the Logan Street upper side.

Change in Ownership

In 1921, Marion Buchanan died, aged 78 and Turner's Buildings were inherited by her daughter Miss Marion Chapman Buchanan, a single lady. All 44 homes were let out. The 5 shops in 1925 were James McGeachie Ironmongery at 159, Charles & Marion McCabe at 161, James Powell Butchers still at 163, James Maxwell & Son Chocolate Manufacturers at 167 and John Davidson Drapers still at 169. However, life was not kind to Miss Buchanan and she died in 1925 in Wishaw, aged 48 after suffering pneumonia whilst recovering from an ear operation.

On Saturday 23rd January 1926, a disastrous midnight fire took hold of these buildings.

The 2 storey tenement premises occupied by Mr. William McManus, provision merchant, 183 Glasgow Road, Blantyre was discovered to be on fire about midnight. The converted shop was on fire and difficulty was experienced by the tenants in the houses above the shop in making for the street, owing to the dense smoke. The fire brigade was summoned to find the shop a raging furnace and for a time the houses above were in danger.

Alter a long fight the firemen were able to get the outbreak under control and about two o'clock on the Sunday the flames were fully extinguished. The shop was completely gutted, and the damage was estimated at £600. Insurance covered the rebuild and renovation of the damaged shop and homes.

Blantyre Men in Trouble

John Stirling (18) and James McGrorty (20) were charged with having between 18th and 20th February 1927 breaking into a magazine store at Gartshore Pit 11 and stole 2 boxes of explosives and detonators along with breaking into a shop and stealing Players cigarettes and one and box of chocolates. They pled guilty.

Turner's Buildings were bought in 1925 by James Little of 175 Stonefield Road, a prominent businessman, joiner and property owner in Blantyre. (James would in 1932 go on to buy Crossbasket House in High Blantyre). In 1930 William Henderson Ironmonger was renting 159 corner shop, Marion McCabe a spinster at 161, James Powell Butchers still at 163, Mrs Little drapers at 167 and John Davidson's drapers at 169. James created 2 more shops. 183 burned down in 1926 and 185 had been converted and was that year consulting rooms for Dr Adam Stewart's surgery. Dr Stewart had telephone number Blantyre 109 and lived at the new homes at 51 Small Crescent. However, all was not well with Turner's Buildings. The 3 storey building at the corner of Logan Street was now in a deplorable condition and some families had moved out, feeling ill or in danger.

The Wartime Collapse

About one o'clock on the final Sunday afternoon in August 1940, considerable excitement prevailed among tenants of Central Buildings. Word soon spread that a large portion of the three-story property situated at Logan Street had suddenly collapsed and many tons of bricks, mortar and some wood crashed down into the back court. For some time this property had been condemned and the tenants had been compelled to leave it, but three families comprising of nineteen persons had been "squatting" in the property.

The property or at least a large portion of it was simply a shell, for the greater part all the internal woodwork and supports had been removed and it had for a long been expected that sooner or later there would be a collapse.

Mr. Robert Limerick an Oncostman employed in a local colliery with his wife and five children who had been squatting in a two room and kitchen house on the top flat, supplied the local news reporter with an account of their experiences. Mr Limerick said he had gone to his work at ten o'clock that morning and did not arrive home till about six o'clock at night. His wife, however, said that she and the children were having dinner when the terrific crash of falling masonry was heard and every moment she expected that the roof would fall in on them. On going to the outside landing she nearly collapsed with fright when she saw that her house at some height was separated only six feet from the huge gap made in the property, and her children were in hysterics.

The house the Limerick family were residing in beggared description and it was inconceivable to think that human beings could live under such deplorable conditions, with no water or sanitary accommodation available. In 1939, Mr. Allan Chapman, M.P. for Rutherglen division, paid a visit to the Limerick's home and said it was a tragedy that people were compelled to live in such a place. As if living in wartime wasn't difficult enough, the collapse threatened their very home. A huge block of bricks and mortar, weighing at least half a ton, was brought down by Mr. Limerick by tying two clothes stretchers together and after a few minutes he managed to get it dislodged from its threatening position.

The other two families, who live at the second flat, were in no danger when the collapse took place and were removed from the gap in the property. The 3 storey block along Logan Street with address 2,4,6,8,10 and 12 Logan Street and also part of Glasgow Road, namely the corner 159-165 Glasgow Road was then demolished entirely.

Latter Years

The space occupied by the collapsed part was bought over by the Post Office who would construct their new building on the corner site in 1953.

The Little family would sell the remaining part of Turner's Buildings with addresses 167-187 Glasgow Road to others in post WW2 years. Families living there during the 1960's included the Dunsmuirs, Mackies and Mains.

Figure 222 Blantyre Scouts march past Turner's (Central) Buildings in the 1950's

Shops would change again too. 167 became a sweet shop, then later the Co-op Chemist. Next door at 169 John Davidson's Butchers became Janette Robertson's Ladies Hair stylist with telephone Blantyre 152.

At the end of the block at 185 Glasgow Road, not far from the corner of Craig Street, the doctors surgery changed hands several times including in the 1960's , premises for Doctor Gordon.

Figure 223 Turner's Buildings on right looking East in 1975

Bought by compulsory purchase order, the remaining businesses and tenants were asked to leave in 1977, the buildings boarded up for a short time afterwards. The properties were then demolished later that year to make way for the Clydeview Shopping Centre and modernization.

Figure 224 Vacant land showing raised embankment Turners Building stood on 1978

> **Blantyre Project Social Media:**
>
> **Patrick Donnelly:** "When James Little bought Crossbasket in the early 1930's, he no longer wanted Turner's Buildings. They were sold very inexpensively (rumoured to have been given outright) to Jane Little, a spinster and family member. She certainly owned the buildings even prior to 1935."
>
> **Rena Caulley:** "I lived in Central Buildings. I was born in 1941 and just love Blantyre and all its history."

"Read More about **Turner's Buildings** online. Scan our handy QR Code for more narrative and photos at Blantyre's History Archives.

Further information, photos and commentary from readers are added from time to time."

Blantyre Post Office

From as early as the 1850's, Blantyre had in those times 2 posts offices. The Low Blantyre post office located in the gatehouse at Blantyre Village Works had adjacent gates that could close off the village to the outside area. The other post office located also in a populated area in High Blantyre at Main Street, on a site where the Apollo pub would later be located.

By the 1890's, the post offices had changed location. The Low Blantyre Post office had moved to large new tenement premises at their main Post Office at 7 Stonefield Road. This important building was located at the bottom of Stonefield Road for just over 3 decades located between Benham's shop and Valerios café. Blantyre postmistresses were Miss Isabella Stewart and her assistant Marian Kilgour. In WW1, on the window was the famous poster of Lord Kitchener pointing for "More men – God save the King".

The Village post office, still retained was used as a sub post office. In High Blantyre, the post office moved across the road to the tenement which formerly stood where now is the car park entrance to Kirkton Park.

For the convenience of the residents in the Stonefield district of Blantyre a further sub post office was opened in early February 1900 in Gilmour Place under the charge of Mrs. Arbuckle, stationer. This was much welcomed at the time and was noted as being a great convenience to the inhabitants of the area. Mr Sam Douglas actually cut people's hair from within the post office. It was often called the "wee post office". Mr Eddie Dobson lived above the wee post office.

By 1910, the Village sub post office had moved from the Gatehouse to a new tenement, further north at Ulva Place, where it existed for many decades.

That year, High Blantyre's sub post office was on Main Street directly across from Lint Butt's on the lower level of a tenement. It was adjacent to the bank, situated on Main Street, at the corner of Cemetery Road. A Mrs Darling worked in this post office around WW2. In the 1960's, it became Jim Hobson's butchers shop. It was located next to Brown's shop (which previously had been the bank.) The High Blantyre Post office would later move back near McLean's Shop, then in 2016, move to Family Shopper where it is at present.

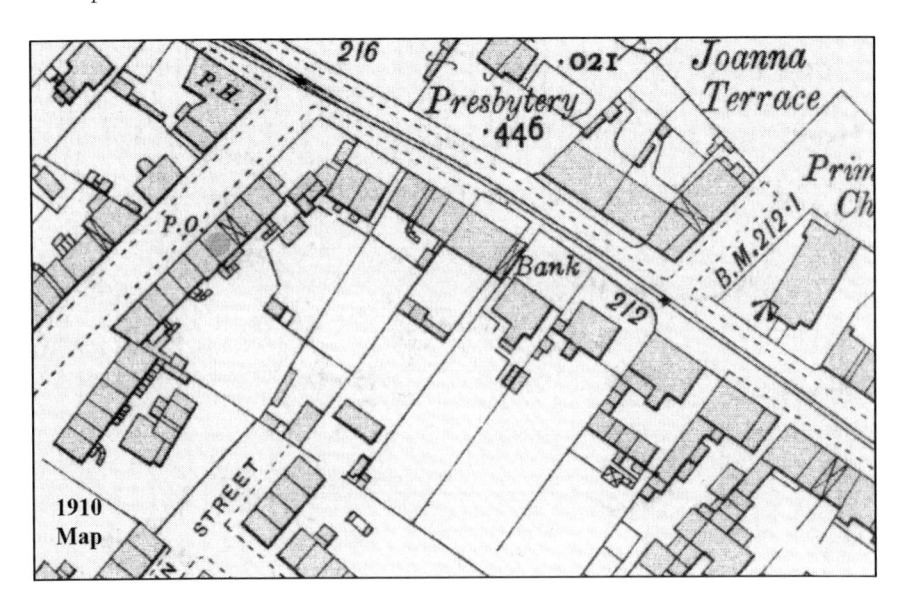

Figure 225 Former Post Office on Stonefield Road on 1910 Map

During the mid 1920's, the main Post Office at Stonefield Road closed and the post office moved to a rented building named, "Clydeview" at 249 Glasgow Road immediately adjacent to the YMCA. This was to be Blantyre's main post office until 1953. This old place of business was apparently very cramped and unsuitable for the type of work being carried out by the postal authorities, conditions that they had suffered for years.

Low Blantyre post office on Glasgow Road started construction in 1953. It was located on the vacant ground where the collapse had taken place of Turner's Buildings 13 years earlier, exactly at the western corner of Logan Street.

Figure 226 The new completed post office in 1955 beside Turner's Buildings

The dating stone on the new Post office showed the commission date of 1953, along with of course the Royal Mail insignia, quite iconic for the postal service set into a stone at the top of the building. The new Post Office was opened without any ceremony whatsoever on Monday morning 25th October 1954, when business was conducted 'as usual' at 9 a.m. Built of stone blocks, single storey the new public building had a solid construction look, one which certainly was unique in Blantyre and almost art deco in places, bordering on municipal. The gable of adjacent 2 storey Turner's Buildings was reinforced.

Soon afterwards in early November 1954, the Blantyre Gazette recorded that there was a call for a pillar-box and a stamp machine to be placed at the site of old premises (next to the Y.M.C.A. further along Glasgow Road on the same side). In the new building, which was welcomed warmly in Blantyre, customers would go in one door and out the other and were impressed by the speed in which the counter staff could stamp things from stamp pads to pension books and postal orders. A phone box was located in the inside of the building. The Post office also catered for Car Tax, Family Allowance, Postage, Premium Bonds and Savings Accounts. A popular feature to this building was the ability to pick up a parcel from the office, rather than having to go to Cambuslang. A lady named Betty was the cleaner for many years.

The post office had address 165 Glasgow Road. When the council bought the surrounding land in 1977 in advance of Asda, this little site where the post office was located, was "ringfenced" off and left out of the sale, the requirement for the postal building continuing. As such, once Asda was built a few years later the post office, appropriately named "Clydeview" after the old premises was maintained and indeed provided the name for the new shopping centre. The PO moved to temporary premises at Clydeview during the mid 1990's. After demolition in 1997, rubble was left, landscaped over to create a grassy area near the Asda Petrol station, which today, is vacant.

Figure 227 Demolition of unused Blantyre Post Office in 1997

After the building was demolished, several Blantyre people were interested in acquiring the masonry date stone to protect and ensure it didn't get put in a skip. Amongst them was Blantyre man, the late Jimmy Cornfield. Jimmy had struck a deal with the foreman of the wrecking crew, and when he returned with the cash he was told the deal was off, the worker saying his boss has told him it wasn't for sale and that someone else had taken it. The location of the stone is unknown, but perhaps another local person beat Jimmy to the 'prize'.

The Post Office then moved further along Clydeview Shopping for a short time. Afterwards the post office relocated west along Glasgow Road to the rear of the Londis supermarket, on the same southern side of the road. Difficult to park there, it feels perhaps a little inconvenient but remains an important, popular resource for the people of Blantyre.

Blantyre Project Social Media:

Henry Hambley: "Lovely, functional building!"

Elaine Hunter: "I remember it well. I used to go up there with my Nana when I was a wee girl. I'd play with the fountain pens and blotting paper in the booths, whilst she was at the counter."

Bruce Baldwin: "I worked as postman there. Great memories! Lots of fun with the front counter staff. It was a great place to work with guys like Bill McGlynn, Alex Young and Malky Muir back in the 1960's."

Maureen McCallum: "My dad was Bill McGlynn. He worked in the sorting office at the back. I worked there a few times when it was busy at Christmas."

John Krawczyk: "Remember it well! When I was a student from time to time I worked there as a postman."

Eddie Meechan: "I used to run in one door as a child, and out the other!"

Carol Crombie: "I played in it too! I loved skidding around the shiny floor and loved the style of it inside, playing in the booths and phone box."

Anne Grogan: "I wished we'd preserved some of these old Blantyre buildings. Saddens me when I visit my old home town."

Clydeview Shopping Centre – East

Clydeview Shopping Centre is a contemporary small shopping centre fronting on to Glasgow Road, currently with partially occupied businesses.

It is located near Blantyre Asda supermarket and was opened in October 1980. It comprises of 2 storey retail units to the east and west of a central pedestrian precinct leading from Glasgow Road to Asda. The retail units have large display frontages with matching doors protected by roller shutters. Sizes range from 1212 sq ft/112.6 sq m to 3780 sq ft/ 351.2 sq m over 2 floors.

'Clydeview' takes its name from the post-office building, formerly at 249 Glasgow Road which relocated to a more modern premises in 1953. The centre occupies the land between Logan Street and Victoria Street, at its boundary with Glasgow Road. The shopping centre is built in two blocks, an eastern and western side. This article is about the east side, formerly on land that was Turner's Buildings and Craig Street. Craig Street prior to 1979 ran down to Glasgow Road near to where the central hard landscaping now is. The land the eastern shopping centre occupies was subjected to extensive redevelopment during 1977 – 1979. When the shopping centre first opened, brick planters decorated the area, as well as young trees. However, some planters were removed, replaced with more robust paving in 1990.

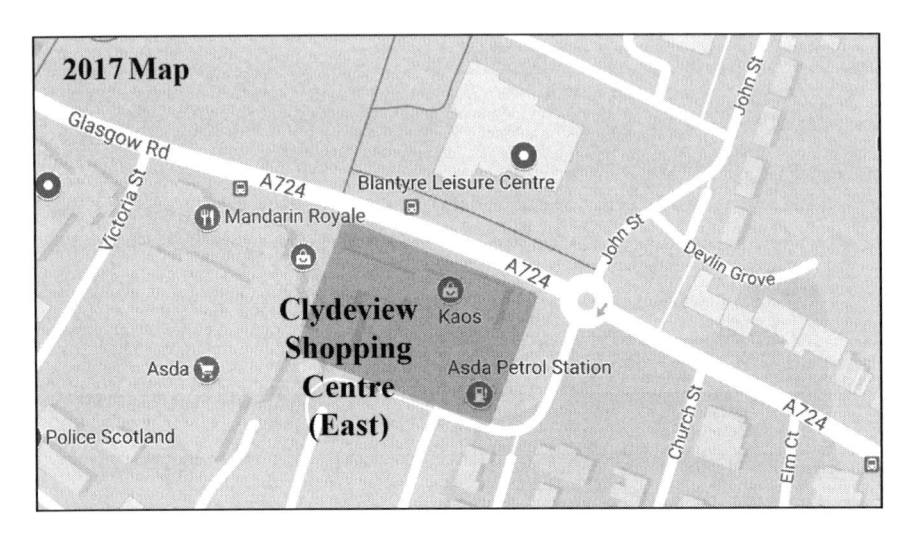

Figure 228 Clydeview Shopping Centre (East) in 2017

The purpose built Clydeview Shopping Centre enjoys a frontage to Glasgow Road with extensive free car parking facilities to the rear and today, the centre is anchored by ASDA nearby who also own and rent out the units.

Over the years, there has been at least 53 shops and businesses on the eastern side including Malcolm Campbell grocers, Just Video, Video Express, Global Video, RS McColl, Supersweet, B2B Hair Styling, Greggs, Betfred, Marie Curie, Munro the Butcher, Quids In Poundshop, Hawkhead Carpets, Jem Carpets, MDC Motor Shop, Farmfoods, Capital Frozen food, Craft at Home, Rapture Clothes, John Fernan Ladies hairdressers, Theresa Mulholland Hairdressers, Weaver Wines, ATR Curry House, Tandoori Nights Indian Takeaway, Mr Kebab Takeaway, Happy Place Chinese Takeaway, Iceberg Frozen Food, Awans Takeaway, Kenny's Tattoo Parlour, Cartys Solicitors, The Curry House, Country Feeds Pet Shop (Gibbs of Galston), Clydesdale Electricals then very briefly The Post Office, Lorraine & Sabrina's Hairdressers, Gillian Baker Family Law, Gostelaw Family Law, Blantyre Criminal Lawyers, Little Bo Beep Wool Shop, Kaos Skateshop, Rinaldi's Chip Shop, Luciano's Fish and Chip Shop, Stepek Electricals, Royal Bank of Scotland, The Abbey National, Sue Rider Charity Shop, Cantors Furniture shop, Mr Saver, Ace Clothing, 'Land of Leather' Italian Furniture Leather shop, Masons Furniture Shop, and Capital Options (Car & Life Insurances).

Sadly, some of the units have been unoccupied for many years and as of 2017, still are. The centre has been a huge talking point in Blantyre in recent years with many people angry at the possibilities wasted, caused by high rent and rates, non-competition terms and conditions and poor maintenance. In Springtime 2017, following a petition started by local lady Amanda Dawson, Blantyre Community Council added the item for discussion on their monthly agenda, inviting Asda representatives to come along and explain potential solutions to getting the units occupied. As of September 2017, there is a strong possibility that these eastern units will be demolished entirely to pave the way for modernized, rebuilt units for traders. Such a radical development for the town makes this worthy of inclusion in this book. Some businesses, like the Royal Bank of Scotland have already left, closing their doors for good, others have been given notice.

Figure 229 Clydeview Shopping Centre (East Block) in 2017

Addresses were all Clydeview Shopping Centre and none were given numbers along Glasgow Rd. Let's now look at a few of the former, more well-known businesses at this location.

Abbey National

Abbey National plc was a UK-based bank and former building society, which latterly traded under the Abbey brand and Santander name. Along with RBOS, it was one of two banks to occupy the Clydeview Shopping Centre in 1981, in the retail units adjoining the Asda shop at Glasgow Road.

The Abbey was in a unit where the façade changed direction, where now Baker Criminal lawyers are based, facing out on to Glasgow Road. When it opened, adjacent shops included Rinaldi's Chipshop (later Luciano's) and Rapture's Clothing Shop (which had a hairdresser above). It had an ATM outside the façade, which is remembered as being one of the first in Blantyre.

Ex-Boxer, Jim Watt officially opened the Abbey National to the public, signing autographs and handing out signed photos. The entrance was on the left and the frontage was all window glass. The Abbey National had white signage with red writing. It had postcode G72 0QD and is remembered for having a good savings programme for children and adults alike with customers receiving a small pay-in book, first manually written into, then during the mid 1980's, typed into with each incoming or outgoing transaction.

The children's savings had "Mickey Mouse" pay-in books. In 1989, with branches at Hamilton also being rebranded, the Blantyre branch closed down for good, causing much frustration and forcing many people to change their bank in Blantyre to either the Royal Bank of Scotland or further up Glasgow Road to the Clydesdale Bank.

Figure 230 Clydeview Shopping Centre (East Block) in 2009. Busier times!

Royal Bank of Scotland

The Royal Bank of Scotland, (under that name) has been in Blantyre since the 1960's at Glasgow Road. First located on the ground floor of a 2-storey tenement on the opposite North side of the road at 166 Glasgow Road it was adjacent to a pub. Rita Clark started working there in 1972 and added that when the pub put their fire on, smoke would come through the walls into the bank, as the tenements were so old. New premises were needed badly.

During the construction of Clydeview Shopping Centre and with the subsequent demolition of the Glasgow Road tenements, bank staff worked temporarily from a portacabin at 188a Glasgow Road. The bank opened in 1981 at Clydeview Shopping Centre. Rita would later move back to Blantyre branch in February 1996 when she became manager. A long-standing employee was Caroline Lee who worked at the Blantyre branch at Clydeview Shopping Centre from 1981 until 1996. A former manager was Stephen Morley, one of many staff who worked there over the years.

To huge disappointment, the Royal Bank of Scotland closed down at Clydeview Shopping Centre on Tuesday 20th June 2017 and planning permission was granted for the ATM being removed shortly after.

Munro Butchers

Munro Butchers was a former butchers chain shop at Clydeview Shopping Centre in the 1980's, which is now occupied by Marie Curie. In August 1995, Property group Asda Property Holdings linked up with Dewhurst managing directors Roger Reeson and Eugene Lines.

Asda Property purchased the freehold premises occupied by Dewhurst, the largest chain of its type in Britain, and leased them back to the new MBO company, Dewhurst Butchers, which by then had bought over the Alex Munro chain of butchers. (In Scotland Dewhurst traded as Alex Munro). However, Munro Butchers in Blantyre was solely a 1980's business and closed down in the late 1980's rumoured to have been due to competition being imposed from Asda. There were also shops in Rutherglen, Motherwell, Cambuslang and Hamilton at the time. Jimmy Scott worked in the popular shop and former employees remember the multitude of different characters coming in for their meat.

Country Feeds (Gibbs of Galston)

Gibbs of Galston was a large pet shop and pet store formerly located in the Clydeview Shopping Centre in the late 1980's. It was officially called, "Country Feeds" located in one of the larger units, near the corner carpet shop and faced out on to Glasgow Road. It was one of the earlier businesses to open at the shopping centre and had operated for some time before closing temporarily in the late 1980's. It re-opened again in the early 1990's with Mrs Mack from "Take the High Road" being a rather unsuccessful opening attraction. However, it closed for good around 2002. Today, that particular retail unit has been closed for years. People have become accustomed seeing closed shutters.

Blantyre Project Social Media:

Anne Gemmell Goldie: "My first Saturday job was in Malcolm Campbell's Grocers. ASDA staff used to come in and take a note of all our prices for the fruit and vegetables. We had a right laugh at them!"

Deborah Lynch: "I worked in the Post Office in 1996 not long after it left their building. We relocated to the east side of Clydeview before moving to the west. The old PO was demolished in 1997."

Allan Love: "Ace Clothing burned down. We got loads of smoke damaged Farrah and Waffle trousers! Half of Blantyre had Harrington jackets that week. The whole town smelt like Bonfire night and you could hear washing machines running in every home!!"

John Tierney: "How can I remember Mason's Furniture Shop and the Video Shop in Clydeview, but not able to remember my wife's birthday?!"

Kenny Mallan: "The MacKinnon family ran Raptures Clothing shop in the late 1980's / Early 1990's."

Thomas O'Donnelly: "Clydesdale Electrical. The arch enemy of Stepek further up the road."

Elaine Speirs: "I remember taking my full piggybank to the portacabin bank when I was just 4. I howled when they broke it, but was pleased they gave me a new one!"

Lesley Hartley: "I had a wee Saturday job in the butchers when I was about 13 or 14. It was 1987 or 1988. I got paid in cash and butcher meat1"

Ray Couston: "I can't wait to see the back of the Clydeview Shopping Centre. What an eyesore these vacant buildings have been!"

CHAPTER 11
GLASGOW ROAD SOUTH
CRAIG ST TO VICTORIA ST

Origins of Craig Street

Craig Street leading between Glasgow Road and Auchinraith Road, started off simply as a field boundary. At some point during the 1870's, a track was formed along the edge of this field and upon expanding nearby population, became a small road, initially called, "The Slag Road."

Perhaps due to the proximity to the Auchinraith Pit, the name may have been given from the pit ash used to form the rough road surface, an effort made to prevent the track being muddy. It was a quick route to get from Stonefield up to Auchinraith, most notably for miners who chose to settle on Glasgow Road. Poorly drained, the northern corner was hardly built upon.

By 1898, nothing at all existed either side of the Slag Road, not even at the corners of a busy Glasgow Road, with exception of the Congregational Church midway up the Slag road, where it is today. At that time, the church sat isolated beside this track completely surrounded by empty fields. At the top of the Slag Road, at the junction with Auchinraith, near to Auchinraith Pit Rows, the road ran under the raised railway track.

The most radical change this road ever saw was in the short period from 1898 to 1910 which saw quality, well built homes built on either side from Glasgow Road up to the church, then up the eastern side towards the brand new Auchinraith School. These houses would have had a lovely, rural view across open fields before any of the Crescents were built. Such construction deserved the renaming of the road, for who would want to live on a road named after 'dirty, auld shale deposits'? The name 'Craig Street' was chosen after prominent former land owner, Mr. James Craig of Birdsfield, sponsor of the church, owner of the farm fields and constructor of some of the homes.

With other property owners including the Smellie family, Craig Street had arrived and would have been a desirable place to live in the 1910's by comparison to some of the nearby more populated and older, miners homes.

McVaney's Land

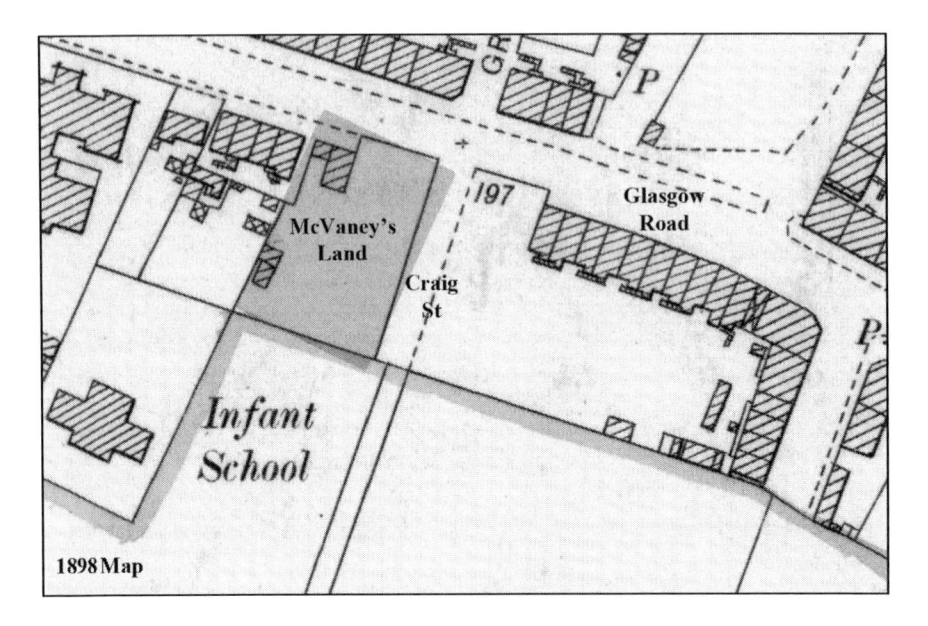

Figure 231 McVaney's Land shown on 1898 Map

Born in 1840 in Ireland, William McVaney (McVenny in some census) and his wife Agnes Gilmour moved to Blantyre during the 1880's. In 1891, they lived at Greenside Street (then named Green St) on the north side of Glasgow Road, not far from the traffic lights are now at Clydeview Shopping Centre.

Sometime between 1892 and 1894, directly across from his rented home, William bought a fairly decent sized plot of land at the western corner of the Slag Road, (later Craig Street). The rectangular plot looked out upon fields to the south and was located quite near the Stonefield Infant School. Upon his land, he built a small house and adjacent shop all on one storey, with a byre to the back. William McVaney was a dairyman and whilst he utilized the byre, his little shop was in 1895 leased out to Miss Marion Russell, a dressmaker.

The house and shop was likely built in stone or brick, for one cannot imagine in the 1890's building a wooden structure amongst so many other 'modern' stone tenements. Needless to say, the little house was unusual, out of place and dwarfed by other more prominent buildings all along Glasgow Road. The house had a pitched roof, the shop to the west being smaller, possibly both known as 'Park Place'. Wooden fences surrounded it.

However, this was to be short lived premises and does not appear to have been previously explored by Blantyre historians until now.

On 13th September 1896, William McVaney died aged 56 due to sudden heart problems. Dr. Grant confirmed his passing and his death certificate was duly signed by a loyal friend by name of McKerrell in Henderson's Buildings.

His widow Agnes McVaney is not in the Blantyre 1901 census, perhaps telling that she moved away. In 1905 she still however, owned the little house but that year it was empty as was the shop and byre. The couple never had any children, so it's possible the area had too many sad memories for her and she moved away from Blantyre. There's a possibility though that with good frontage on Glasgow Road, Miss Russell's dressmaker shop may have existed right up until 1905. Between 1905 and 1910, the byre at the back was demolished and by 1915, the shop and house had been demolished too, the land vacant and a prime spot on a thriving, bustling busy Glasgow Road.

I own a wonderful painting of McVaneys in 1905, which was drawn by modern local artist Harry Rankine, showing all the charm of that era.

Figure 232 former McVaney's House & Shop in 1906 looking east

Following WW1, the land would be purchased and would later become the site of the Central Garage, then in more modern times, the Western side of Clydeview Shopping Centre. It is difficult to imagine how much this has all changed. In the following drawing, we've highlighted how the building would have looked in a modern context to give you an idea of where it was exactly.

Figure 233 Location Line Drawing McVaney's Land (small house and shop) gone by 1915

Central Garage (Harper's Garage)

The Central Garage was a former vehicle garage in the 20th Century once situated on a fairly large plot of land at the western corner of Craig Street and junction of Glasgow Road. The approximate location today is where the central traffic lights and hardstanding is at Clydeview Shopping Centre.

The garage would also be known as Harper's Garage, but Harper was not the original owner and indeed there were 2 owners before him.

Sometime between 1921 and 1924, Mr. Thomas Johnstone bought former McVaney's Land, which at that time was entirely clear. Seeing opportunity in the growing popularity of mechanized vehicles Johnstone constructed a repair shop and petrol tank. Thomas Johnstone was a motorbus proprietor and mechanic and his repair shop is noted in the 1925 Valuation roll. The repair shop had a front entrance out to Glasgow Road, and was long stretching its length on Craig Street, with a pitched roof.

My Johnstone's ownership came to an abrupt end, when in March 1927, Mr. William Mullen sued Thomas Johnstone for personal injuries he sustained in a vehicle accident, asking for nearly £1,000. In court, he settled for £350, but had to put up his repair shop up for sale in order to make the injuries payment. It is unclear if this bankrupted Johnstone.

In 1927, The Blue Line Motor Spirit Company Ltd bought out Mr. Johnstone and opened the premises naming it "The Central Garage", a name first appearing in the 1930's valuation roll. Managing their garage and petrol pump, renting it from Blue Line was Mr. Gilbert Harper, a motor hirer since 1919, and who had previously been a flesher at the Masonic Buildings. This was the primary Garage in Blantyre, the most well known for repairs throughout the 20th Century. In the 1930 valuation roll, it is noted being at 163 Glasgow Road but we suggest this may have been an error in the roll and that the garage was actually at 189/191 Glasgow Road. At that time Mr. Robert Patterson was a driver at the garage.

Gilbert Harper had in 1899 fought in the Boar War. He moved to 4 Craig Street in 1922 which was situated 2 houses up from the garage on Craig Street on the same side. He may have previously used small garages and a former coachhouse at the back of his home prior to renting the Central Garage in 1927 for £35 per annum. His business looks to have flourished for in 1930 he had moved home to a larger house 'Forestlea' at 16 Craig Street.

Figure 234 Harper's Garage traded as G Harper Ltd. Photo N. Gordon

When Gilbert died in November 1934, Barbara Harper took full control of the Central Garage and that year concluded the purchase of the premises from former Blue Line Motor Spirit Company Ltd. Trading under the name G Harper Ltd, family members are pictured with their renamed "Harper's Garage". Following Gilbert's death, the garage and G Harper Ltd was managed by James Ramage, a motor hirer until he started his own business in the 1940's. The Harper family extended the building to the west in the 1940's.

In the 1960's, Brian McLaughlin who owned a local undertakers/lorry business and a mechanics business in Glasgow Road (Felix Mclaughlins) purchased Harper's garage and gave it back its original name of "The Central Garage". As well as repairs and motor sales, Brian also leased out Limousine cars for funerals and weddings and continued to be successful and used frequently by Blantyre residents. It was still often referred to as "Harpers."

This prompted a major rebuilt of the garage to accommodate more vehicles. The extensive renovations saw older parts of the building removed at Craig Street and rebuilt with larger more rectangular frontage on to the more busy and prominent, Glasgow Road.

During the 1960's and 1970's, cars appeared in the showroom windows. Vehicles such as Austin / Morris 1000's, Minis and later Cortina made an appearance and often tempted locals. A common service was repairing punctures and as well as providing petrol, the garage sold pink and blue paraffin.

Figure 235 Aerial View of Central Garage during 1950

When petrol rationing started in the 1970's, staff were very generous to Blantyre people, letting them fill up perhaps more so than other garages. It created many loyal customers. Across the road was Hart's Building which housed the Cosy Corner Public House and Peter Valerio's ice cream parlour.

Further up from the Garage was 'Watts' the dentists and later Oreste's Chip Shop.

Figure 236 Central Garage in 1978 prior to demolition in 1979. Photo J McGuire

The garage was next managed by Willie Richardson, his wife Peggy and her sister Isa MacMillan. These 'Richardsons' were of no relation to the family who later ran the garage of that name further west. One September weekend the garage was robbed, the same day as a garage at High Blantyre, and despite being only a few hundreds yards away, and to frustration of staff and owners, the police took hours to get to the scene.

Many people worked there as mechanics, clerks, attendants over the years including Kenneth Crombie. Marion Aitchison worked in the garage up until it closed. The site of course changed forever when it was demolished in 1979, to pave the way for Blantyre's development and the subsequent building of Clydeview Shopping Centre and Asda.

Blantyre Project Social Media:

Eliza Harper: "Thank you for this detailed history. I read online with annoyance in 2016 (on another Blantyre website) that 'Gilbert was the original owner.' This is not the case. Gilbert was neither the original owner and in fact never even owned the Central Garage at any time, only renting. It was after his death in 1934 that the family through his estate, bought the garage after closing their existing little garage in the 1930s nearby at 16 Craig Street. The Central Garage was a much more prominent business location and good investment."

Nimmo's Buildings

Moving west of the Central Garage we come next to a former 2 storey stone tenement named 'Nimmo's Buildings.' During the late 19th Century and throughout the 20th, this building changed hands several times and was also known as "Whifflet Place" then for a short time "Hills Pawn Building." However, during its lifetime for the longest period and in census information it was referred to as 'Nimmo's' and that being relevant to the original constructor, is the primary name in this article.

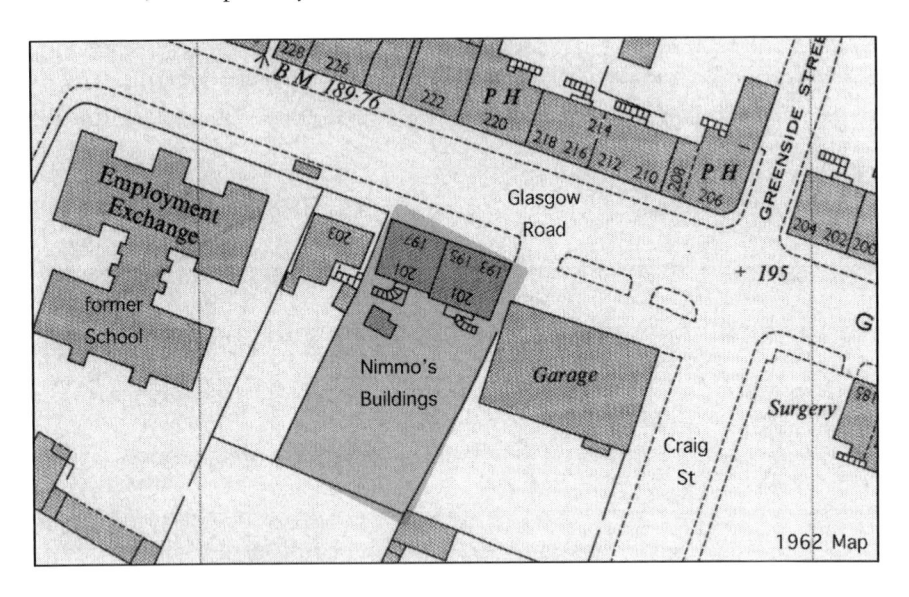

Figure 237 Nimmo's Buildings in 1962 next to Central Garage

The original owner and constructor of these buildings was Mr. John Nimmo, a former miner of Greenfield Colliery near Burnbank. In 1874, John clearly fancied a change in profession and is noted thereafter as being a grocer. The 1875 valuation roll confirms John Nimmo as owner and importantly notes that the tenants had been there "for less than a year." His tenements were built at the same time as the nearby Stonefield Parish School was being built and when he first let his 6 houses out to miners families, they must have thought themselves very fortunate for their children to be so close to the school.

The buildings were constructed in 2 small blocks with frontage on Glasgow Road. The ground floor with shops, the upper floors, homes, a configuration common for many tenements on the expanding street. Access to the upper floors were via stone steps to the rear, accessed from a small lane neat to the eastern gable. At the rear were also a couple of glass houses suggesting the early tenants may have grown some food there or attempted some gardening.

John Nimmo opened a grocer in one of the lower 2 shops and in the other initially was Robert Watson Bakers. However, all was not well financially and John, being a miner likely staking all his savings on the venture was soon in financial difficulties. In May 1885, John Nimmo was declared bankrupt and his property was seized by "Hamilton Savings Investment Building Society Bondholders" acquiring the building as collateral. The circumstance prompted retirement for John Nimmo, but he would continue ironically, renting a house in the property he actually built right up until his death in 1903.

In 1895 the building society still owned the property which was now 4 homes and 3 shops. In Nimmo's grocers, John's son Zachariah Nimmo a former coalman was renting the shop. Zachariah went from being a coal miner to grocer and later to barman. He was well known in Blantyre and highly connected with the nearby Livingstone Masonic Lodge 599 reaching the heights of Vice President near his death in 1936, aged 80. In the second shop was William Morrison a stationer. In the third shop James Bryce an ironmonger. Amongst the tenants in the upper homes in 1895 were Andrew Arbuckle, John Nimmo, Alexander Forrest and Daniel Cairney, a barman.

Change in Ownership and tenancy

Between 1899 and 1900, David Kerr a restaurateur bought Nimmo's buildings. Converting the ground floor grocers on the eastern side into a restaurant, he acquired a beer license and opened a Public House serving food which was called "The Ale House". The pub had a rent value of £40 per annum. With 3 shops, David a member of the Masonic Lodge lived with his family in one of the 6 homes.

David Kerr was living at Nimmo's Buildings in the 1901 census. Born in 1861, the 40 year old was an Ale Merchant and married to Margaret Fleming (39) and with them Mary Ann Breen, a 15 year old servant girl. Following John Nimmo's death, David looks to have named the building "Whifflet Place" perhaps to rid of the Nimmo's legacy and to give the place his own stamp. Whilst researching this book, the only connection found to Whifflet, (a place in Coatbridge) was that it was the birthplace of his wife Margaret. However, with such short ownership, David's renaming would not 'stick' and the properties continued to be referred to as 'Nimmo's' for some decades after.

In 1905, along with his restaurant pub, William Wright shoemaker had moved into the premises formerly occupied by William Morrison stationers.

In the other shop was Robert Sherkis ironmonger. By 1905 the greenhouses at the back of the building had been demolished. In 1905 the Edinburgh brewery who supplied ale to David Kerr was dissolved. Being a merchant for this brewery clearly impacted David's business and he is missing from Blantyre in the following years, the buildings look to have been bought off him that same year.

The next owner was Mr. Hugh Mair, a spirit merchant of Woodside Avenue, Hamilton. Hugh looks to have taken ownership of "The Ale House" licensed restaurant in 1905 or so which was to have address 193/195 Glasgow Road. In 1915 the adjacent shop had been converted to "rooms" which were empty. Further west on the ground floor at 199 Glasgow Road, a former shop was now a house. Upstairs above at 201 Glasgow Road was another 4 homes. Amongst the tenants were William Sullivan a barman of the opposing Central Bar across the street and Mr James Kelly, another barman. By 1915 Nimmo's Buildings had address 193-201 Glasgow Road, where 201 were all the upper homes.

Military Medal Awarded

A military medal was gained in October 1917, the recipient being Private Peter Dorrington, of the A. and S.H., whose wife and family resided at 201 Glasgow Road, Blantyre in an upper house at Nimmo's Land. He was a stretcher-bearer, and it was for a particular act of gallantry in bringing in wounded that he was awarded the honour. Private Dorrington was an old campaigner, having been through the Boer War in 1899. At the outbreak of WW1, the old martial spirit in him revived, and he immediately re-joined the colours for the services. During WW1, he had seen a lot of active service but was severely wounded at the Battle of Loos. Prior to joining up he worked as a miner in Craighead Colliery.

Further Owners & Change in use

In 1920 Mairs "Ale House" was the only commercial premise with all other premises being 7 homes. Hugh Mair died that year, aged 47 at his home in Hamilton and Nimmo's Buildings were inherited by his widow, who continued to run the public house until around 1922. The Ale house had existed from 1899 until 1922 before being used for another purpose.

Around 1922, Hill Brothers (Pawnbrokers) Ltd of Glasgow bought Nimmo's Buildings. The Ale House was converted into their large Pawn Shop which had a rated value of £20 per annum. In 1925, both adjacent ground floor properties at 197 and 199 were empty. Hill Brothers were already in Blantyre at Anderson Buildings further east, but they closed that premises in

1927 and focused their efforts in Blantyre at Nimmo's Buildings. During the 1920's Nimmo's Buildings consisted of 7 houses and the pawn shop and it is in that decade that the name "Hill's Pawn" building came into local use. These were boom times for the pawnbroking business, a decade of depression, miners strikes, unemployment and all the misery of life's situations that would drive some Blantyre people to part with treasured possessions for a fraction of what they were really worth.

Figure 238 Two storey tenement – Nimmo's Buildings / Hill's Building in 1950

In 1927, the Central Garage opened up adjacent to Nimmo's Building. By 1930, Hill Brothers still owned Nimmo's Buildings their pawn shop rated at £45 a year, more than double what it had been just 5 years earlier. 197 is not noted as being used in 1930, 199 Glasgow Road by then a house with 3 homes above them all at 201 Glasgow Road.

Hill's Pawnbrokers was relatively short lived at just over a decade, before others acquired the building in the late 1930's. New owners restored and re-opened the public house as "The Ale House" prior to 1936. All the building at the back were cleared by 1936. The pub, supplied by Bernard's Brewers of Edinburgh would remain at this location until the late 1950's before closing down for good and becoming Whyte's Plumbers. They had moved from the north side of the road beside the Gazette offices to this larger shop at 195 Glasgow Road. During the late 1960's this became Oreste's Chip shop, fondly remembered by many people as being one of the best in Blantyre and recognizable by a large blue door.

At 199 Glasgow Road, the shop in post WW2 years became Haddow's dental surgery. When Haddow's moved directly across the road, Alex Watt dentists moved into Nimmo's building at the former Haddow's surgery. Watts remained there into the 1970's. Haddows and Watts surgeries had a feeling of similarity about them, with the waiting room seats looking the same.

Figure 239 Nimmo's Buildings end gable pictured looking east in 1979 before demolition

Demolition was again the all too familiar story of Glasgow Road redevelopment and Nimmo's Building was gone by 1979, paving the way for the construction of Clydeview Shopping Centre. Today, the corner 'Salvation Army' charity shop of the western side of Clydeview Shopping Centre stands on the site of former Nimmo's Buildings.

> Blantyre Project Social Media:
>
> **Nina Muir:** "In the last picture there, I remember old men sitting on the benches, wearing hats, smoking their pipes, watching the world go by. Their wives on the other hand were at home cleaning, cooking or scuttling up the road to get the messages."
>
> **Arlene McWilliam Green:** "I would sit on the wall opposite and watch the older ones going into Rascalz nightclub, wishing I could go in, yet I was only 14. We sat on that wall having blow dried our hair in the sports centre, wearing our blue eye-liner and wishing we were all older. The only thing salvaging the moment was amazing Lightbody's chips, the best in Blantyre! Move on another year or two and we managed to 'blag' out way in the sports centre bar and eventually into Rascalz."

Bloomfield Cottage

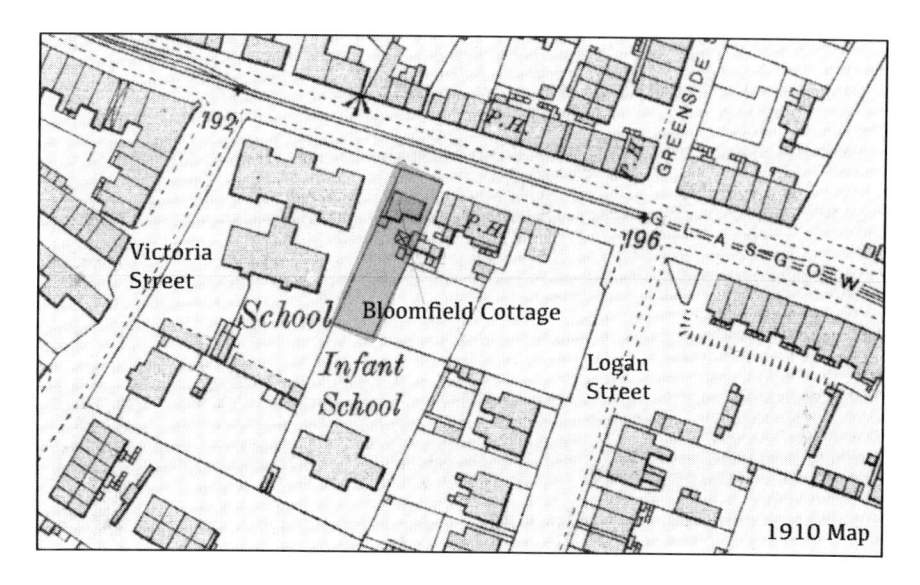

Figure 240 Bloomfield Cottage on Glasgow Road Map 1910

'Bloomfield Cottage' was a former detached home on Glasgow Road sandwiched in a long narrow strip of land between Nimmo's Land to the east and the Stonefield Parish School to the west.

It dates from 1874 with construction ongoing into 1875, built at the exact same time as nearby Nimmo's buildings and the school. This confirms that with the exception of McVaney's Land, all buildings built between Logan Street and Victoria Street were constructed at the same time.

The original constructor and owner was Mr. Hugh Dickson. Born in 1838 in Nitshill, Renfrewshire Hugh came to Blantyre in the mid 1870's and was employed as an enginekeeper for William Baird Collieries. Buying land off John Clark Forrest, he constructed a detached house which had frontage on to Glasgow Road. The fact he called it a cottage is perhaps misleading, for this was way grander than any 'cottage'. Built of stone, it was 2 storey's high, but with attic rooms and a different appearance from more traditional tenements, it gave the appearance of having 3 storeys, taller than nearby Nimmo's Buildings.

A lane led down the eastern gable accessing the rear yard, which was long and had a wall at the end separating it from the later infant school. Bloomfield Cottage was as deep as it was wide and upper levels were accessed by L shaped free standing stairs at the rear. At least one glasshouse was at the rear.

It is unknown why the name 'Bloomfield' was chosen by Mr. Dickson. The name connects to Northern Ireland and also Lancashire and seems very typically un-Scottish for a man who was born and lived in Scotland. Another possible connection was during the 1870's, the Bloomfield Gold Mines in America were making people rich and causing headlines around the world. Perhaps Hugh just liked the name and wanted his own building to prosper?

Hugh Dickson and his family were the initial tenants, confirmed living there in his newly built house in the 1875 valuation roll. Rent was feuded from JC Forrest for £8 per annum.

The 1881 census has 41 year old Hugh still at Bloomfield Cottage with wife Bethia, who hailed from Carluke. With them was son, William. At some point between 1882 and 1884 Hugh moved out of Bloomfield Cottage and into the small miner's tied cottages at 66 Craighead Rows on the north side of Glasgow Road near Forrest Street. Now, whilst this downgrading may seem bizarre, it perhaps made huge financial sense, for still owning Bloomfield Cottage in 1885, he now had rental income by letting it out, which he did to Mrs. William Scott (a grocer).

For unknown reason between 1886 and 1890, the Dickson family had enough of Blantyre and moved away, leaving behind the miners rows and selling off Bloomfield Cottage. Perhaps disgruntled by mining life, disillusioned by the Blantyre riots and 1880's hardships or finding opportunity elsewhere, the Dicksons packed up and didn't return to the town.

Change in Ownership

Bloomfield Cottage, with its distinctive 2 large pitched roof dormers facing on to Glasgow Road was next bought by Mr. John Watt, a shoemaker whom in 1885 had been renting a house nearby at Henderson's Buildings.

Born in 1840 in Lanark, Hugh Watt was the son of John Watt Snr shoemaker and Margaret Morrison. Hugh (junior) was skilled at shoemaking and had been working in Blantyre during the 1880's, clearly doing well enough to be able to buy Bloomfield. The 1870's to 1890's were prosperous times for many tradespeople in Blantyre owing to the population boom ad opportunities brought to the forefront for many.

Certainly, by 1891 John Watt was living at Bloomfield, then aged 51 with wife Margaret Nish, born in Dunbartonshire and 4 years younger. John was neither employed nor self employed, a good indicator that others were running his shoe business for him. The house had a rated value between £10 and £12 per annum. By the First World War, Bloomfield Cottage had official postal address 203 Glasgow Road, but the house name was also kept. John had retired by 1915. In 1918, Lilley Tait, his domestic servant living at Bloomfield got married.

Between 1921 and 1924 John Watt moved from Bloomfield Cottage to 'Avonbank' in Station Road, where he died in 1925, aged 85, outliving his wife. Dr Cowan Wilson confirmed the death and Marion Forrest, a guardian signed the death certificate.

Figure 241 John Watt, owner of Bloomfield - Death Certificate in 1925

Peter Morton, a miner bought Bloomfield Cottage between 1921 -1924. The house continued to have a rated value of £12 per annum. Family member John Morton was janitor of the adjacent school. Bought over by William & Arabella B Stewart in the early 1930's. Later lived in by the Ward and Goodlet families, during the 1950's, it was still there on the 1962 map and was demolished in the late 1960's. Being a private house, unusually for Glasgow Road with no shops, this former property often is overlooked and forgotten.

Figure 242 Bloomfield Cottage (tall, with darker roof in middle) in 1950

Bloomfield was exactly where Glen Travel's shop was at Clydeview Shopping Centre. Glen Travel moved further west opposite the junction of Station Road in November 2017.

By Paul D Veverka

Stonefield Parish Infant School

'Stonefield Parish Infant School' being a bit of mouthful, the toddlers school in Low Blantyre was nicknamed by locals as "The Wee School." It is incorrectly written in publications by others that the infant school was immediately behind Stonefield Parish School, but this wasn't the case. The former infant school was actually situated more to the west, behind Nimmo's Buildings and Bloomfield Cottage. It was located just off Victoria Street not far from the Stonefield Parish School, on central ground.

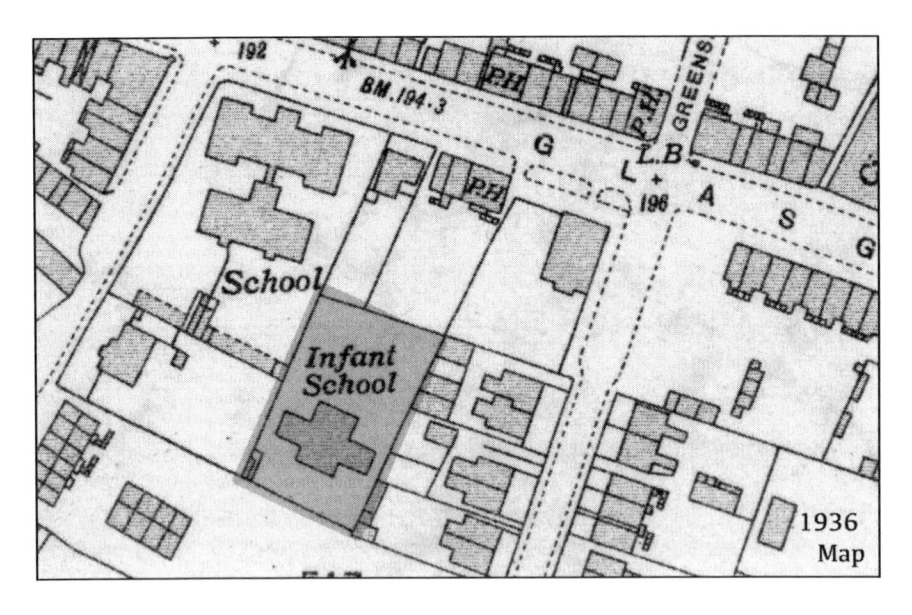

Figure 243 Stonefield Parish Infant School on 1936 map

The infant School was to have a different look and feel about it by comparison to the adjacent School for primary age pupils due to the use of a different Architect to set different style. Built of stone blocks with slated roof, it was designed to provide a remedy to an overcrowding infant department in the Stonefield Parish School, the idea was approved by the local Parochial Board on 12th October 1891.

The building was in the style of Scottish Renaissance, designed by Architect Alex Cullen of Motherwell, who would later design Auchinraith School. Stonemasons James Aitkenhead & Son were the builders, (whose father had previously built Stonefield Parish School adjacent some 16 years earlier). This was a busy time for Aitkenhead Builders who were also building High Blantyre Church Halls.

The school had two large classrooms heated by coal fires accommodating

200 infants and additional space for 100 more if needed. A vacant site on spare ground was chosen and £1,800 budget assigned to the project.

The official opening of the infant school took place at 2pm on 10th April 1893. The main building had a small annex adjacent to it, which was used as a dining room. The annex had a white roof and was later used by Calder Street Secondary School as a technical drawing and metalwork classroom.

Figure 244 The front of former Stonefield Infant School

Figure 245 Infant 'wee' School boarded up in 1977

From as early as 1960, the whole of the infant school was used as an Annex for Calder Street Secondary School, then later Blantyre High for Metalwork, woodwork and technical drawing classes. It still served that function in May 1977, but at that time the county council had acquired the building and land in advance of demolition to make way for the Asda shopping centre. The fate of the school sealed, it was demolished in late 1977 as part of the extensive Glasgow Road area redevelopment. This prompted the building of a new block at Blantyre High in 1978 for the aforementioned technical classes. Not a Glasgow Road building, let's move on.

Stonefield Parish School

Monday 25th October 1875 was a monumental day for Blantyre. In previous years the Village school at Blantyre Works had been filled to capacity and throughout 1875, no less than two new schools were being built. The first being Stonefield Parish School (affectionately known as Ness' School) located on the later nightclub Casper's nightclub site, where the current Blantyre library now stands. The second was the glorious new High Blantyre School, built of similar design, of stone at Hunthill Road. Both were opened on the same day.

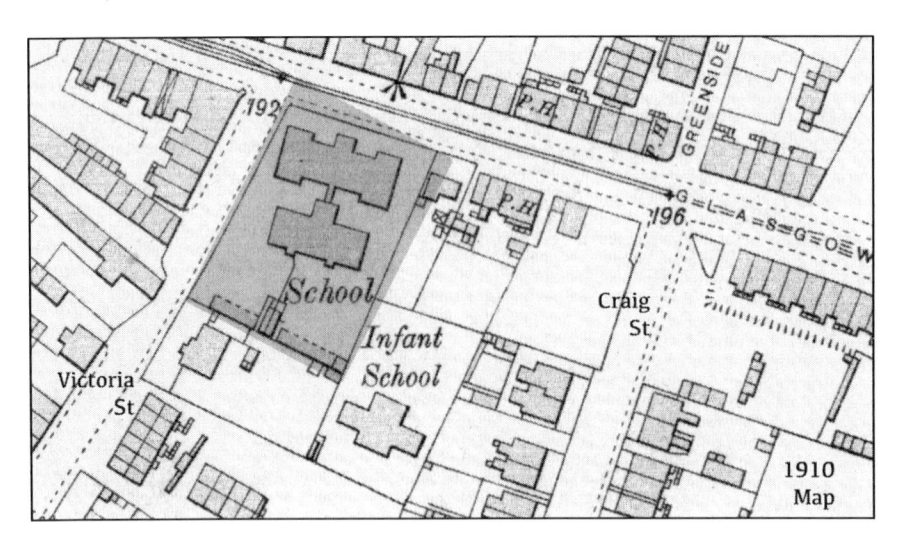

Figure 246 Stonefield Parish School, (or Ness's School) on Glasgow Road 1910 Map

Coalmining was big business by the mid 1870's and the population was expanding rapidly and Blantyre had a great requirement for the schooling of junior pupils. These schools were built to the same design by Andrew J Smith and were built to "future proof" that expansion and provide state of the art facilities. Stonefield Parish School, sometimes referred to as Low Blantyre

School had address 205 Glasgow Road and was located on the eastern side of the junction of Victoria Street and Glasgow Road. 1875 was certainly an important year for this area as a whole with several new buildings built on Glasgow Road including Hart's Building across the road.

Figure 247 Stonefield Parish School 1907, Victoria Street & Annfield Terrace in background

On the school opening day, the pupils assembled in procession (having previously met in the Old Works Schoolroom at 9am) and been given a short address by the Headmaster, John Ness. As they marched up Station Road, they sang, "Auld Land Syne" and were met at the new Glasgow Road School by the Rev. Stewart Wright, chairman of the Blantyre Parish School Board, who occupied the chair for the opening ceremony at 10am. (The ceremony at High Blantyre took place at noon that same day, although that school was not ready for occupation).

The opening ceremony is further described. The School Board and Parochial Board members lined the entrance to the Stonefield Parish School on Glasgow Road, along with the local ministers. Rev. Doak opened the proceedings with a prayer. The school chairman (Rev Stewart Wright) then said "These schools have been erected at no small expense – an expense to be borne by the ratepayers for many years yet to come. But the School Board can truthfully say the expense has not been extravagant.

They have studied economy; whilst at the same time had a proper regard to the great requirements of a fast and steadily growing population."

He continued, "The two schools have cost but £4,500 or £5 for each pupil, by comparison to the £10 per head unnecessarily spent for Glasgow schools. The 2 schools are capable of receiving 400 pupils each, governed by the recent Act of Parliament and assessed during the census a few years ago. However, Blantyre is receiving such an incoming number of people that already the information is outdated. In a census taken just the other day, it shows 900 children in Blantyre of schooling age between 5 and 13. It is sad therefore and cannot be said that in erecting these edifices we have exceeded the requirements of the Parish. More schools in Blantyre will need to be built."

The school was then declared open followed by further addresses by the eminent men on the Board. The Board then walked the short distance to the High Blantyre School, and gave a similar opening ceremony.

It may seem slightly negative and "not the right thing to do" in giving an opening speech about the inadequate capacity, but it was done purely to alleviate the complaints made by older residents of the village who thought the schools were massive and too large. Rev Wright confirms this in his Annals of Blantyre book.

Figure 248 Pupils and Teacher outside the school in 1896

In 1879, according to Naismith's Directory, the headmaster was John Ness and the mistress was Mrs. Margaret Murdoch. Ness was headmaster at the Low Blantyre School for 32 years, on top of the 18 years he had previously spent at the Village school. In 1875, he was given an initial salary of £120 a year or £10 per calendar month. We'll come back to John Ness shortly.

By 1881, as predicted, there was severe overcrowding in the School and on 16th January 1882, Mr. A.J. Smith the Architect had prepared plans for an addition to the southern rear of the building, with a permanent connection between the two. The new extension was commissioned quickly with workmen underway on site in October 1882. The Inspector's report for 12th February 1883 stated the new classrooms were ready to accommodate 250 more pupils and formed a handsome addition to the School, by then one of the largest in Lanarkshire.

In the front building on Glasgow Road was a main room, to the west, infants room and classrooms. In the rear building were a series of classrooms separated into West, East and Mid areas.

Indeed, in 1883, two large extensions were added to both schools to accommodate more pupils, taking attendance then to over 1,200. By comparison only 50 years earlier, only 50 pupils attended Blantyre works school and 100 in the High Blantyre's School Lane. It was hoped that out of the doors of these new schools, would come gifted individuals, just as had done in previous Blantyre schools.

In 1885 Rev Wright wrote about these schools, saying, "May our children unto many generations be able to bear even a better testimony to the great value of our imposing national schools. Their present efficiency is certainly a good guarantee of their efficiency."

School life was strict and like other schools of the time, attendance not the best, with pupils often deciding to abscond or "bunk off" for the day. This could result in parents being reprimanded and in those early times, it could affect employment prospects of parents if they were known to have unruly children, prone to non attendance.

By 12th October 1891, with a population boom in Stonefield taking place, there was much overcrowding in the infant room in the front part of the building. The Board's solution to this matter was to procure a new Infant School altogether, opening in 1893, alleviating the problem of overcrowded infant classes, and freeing up a further classrooms for older pupils. This also offered familiarity for the infant pupils when they made the transition to the junior school nearby already in an area, and sometimes with teachers they knew.

Figure 249 Stonefield Parish School Pupils class of 1911

On 29th November 1922, the old Blantyre Works Mill bell was hung in the belfry of Stonefield or Low Blantyre School gifted by Stonefield Parish Church, which by then had lost its steeple due to subsidence. An agreement was made that it could be returned whenever needed. The formal installation of the bell by Sir Henry S.Keith took place at 2pm on 11th December 1922. The bell was only there for 11 years, for by April 1933 it had been replaced by a new one, which allegedly often did not work properly or got stuck. The reason for the original much travelled Mill bell's departure from Stonefield, was to accommodate the newly opened David Livingstone Museum, placing the bell back near to its original location. The bell can be seen today on the North gable of Shuttle Row at the David Livingstone Centre but may yet again see a move soon with the imminent modernization and renovation of the museum.

William Smith, whose son was injured in WW1 was the headmaster from 1908 following he death of Mr. Ness. James Aitchison was schoolmaster from the early 1920's. In 1928, James was still headmaster and on 1st June that year was considered for transfer to Whifflet Primary School in Coatbridge. However, this did not come to pass. For many pupils, the school was affectionately known as "Ness's" school after the former headmaster and the school's nickname was well known and continued through the 20th Century, decades after Mr. Ness's death. It was nicknamed 'Ness's' School, not 'Nessie's.'

According to the 1930 valuation roll the County Council of Lanark owned the public school, James still headmaster. The school was always complimented by the previous addition of the separate and adjacent "Stonefield Infant School." Two rooms had to be vacated on 26th August 1932 set aside for the use of Calder Street pupils and this continued throughout the remainder of the school being open. In the 1940's and 1950's Miss Neilson taught Class 1.

Figure 250 Ness's School pictured in 1946, Victoria Place in background

Stonefield Parish School closed to junior pupils on 28th June 1957 with the opening of the new David Livingstone Memorial Primary School in August of that year. The old Stonefield Parish Primary school then became Blantyre's labour and employment exchange, right through the 1960's and into the 1970's, a source of employment itself for dozens of people. Part of the building, as well as the Infant school continued in use as an Annex for Calder Street Secondary and subsequently Blantyre High School and some pupils may remember the short trip between lessons, having to go from school to school.

The Stonefield Parish School, especially the name of 'Ness's' is fondly remembered in Blantyre and had been a place of education of many thousands of people from its opening, until the middle of the 20th Century, then latterly also a place of employment for many people until its complete closure in May 1977. The school was demolished later that year, surviving around 102 years, paving the way for the planning phase of the western side of Clydeview Shopping Centre.

By Paul D Veverka

Figure 251 Pupils in 1951, with happier faces than previous decades

Blantyre Project Social Media:

Sheena Thomson: "I went to the wee infant school behind it in the 1950's. I only went to Ness's school for a year before moving to David Livingstone Primary School. I'm sure my teacher at Ness's was Mrs. Neilson."

Christine Forrest: "The children look so smart in these old school photos."

Anne Quinn: "My parents, 2 sisters and I stayed in the 'Honeymoon (Victoria Place) immediately behind the school playing ground. It was really handy for the school."

Moyra Lindsay: "The first time I went through that front door, it was no longer a school. I was picking up my 1 year passport. It was cardboard, a simple piece of paper, not anything like the complicated passports of today."

Etta Morrison: "I remember Calder Street School using Ness's as an Annex. I can't remember which subjects were taught in the annex though."

Helen Lawson Taylor: "I have memories of being in trouble for talking whilst in those classes in the Annex!"

John Boyd: "Bloody freezing building. A childhood of colds and runny noses were caused by being schooled in there!"

Major John Ness, headmaster

During the late 19th Century in Blantyre and surrounding districts, there was no better known gentleman – and, we venture to say, no more popular than Major John Ness, the veteran and beloved headmaster of Stonefield Parish School. A special favourite with all classes, his services were in great demand and at public of Masonic functions, the Major could always be relied upon to take an active part, either as chairperson or speaker and no better orator could be found. A military man, known to administer discipline in a balanced manner with pupils, whilst continuing to be liked and respected.

Figure 252 Major John Ness 1890's, (b1830-d1908), former headmaster

He had a fluency of speech that could rarely be excelled, which combined with the general understanding of the subject he was speaking about, he had the happy knack of being humorous in the extreme, making him a favourite with audiences.

John Ness was born in Glasgow in 1830 and educated in St Enoch's Parish School, Glasgow then later in St Matthew's, Glasgow. His first success was in gaining a Queen's Scholarship in the Training College after which he emerged a duly, qualified teacher.

Opportunity arose when Monteith, owner of the mills required the services of a new headmaster in Blantyre Village Works at his small school. John Ness took up the position coming to Blantyre in 1856 and became teacher of Blantyre Works School on 1st June 1856.

In 1857 John Ness, knowing his personal friend and Explorer David Livingstone was back in Britain, wrote to Livingstone to ask if he would come back to his birthplace at Blantyre to attend a soiree, celebration of the explorer's accomplishments. Livingstone was not keen, due to the weather and had intended to stay in London. John Ness persisted and wrote to Livingstone's mother at Peacock Cross in Hamilton asking if she could perhaps persuade him instead. Livingstone mother duly wrote the letter, referring to all of Livingstone's Scottish rallying friends and Livingstone despite his reservations, came back to Blantyre in 1857 to visit. This much celebrated event was publicized far and wide and great accounts exist in detail of what took place at the soiree. Having been in Africa for 16 years, Livingstone told his audience he had hardly seen a white man for all that time and had started to forget English. At times in his speech, Livingstone would pause and gaze ahead. Heckler shouting out, "Spit it out Livingstone!" and apologies were offered explaining at times he would forget larger English words in mid sentence. It is said Livingstone had no real great desire to relearn English, his heart truly belonging to the "Dark Continent".

He's recorded as being at the Blantyre Works School in the 1862 Handbook of Hamilton, Bothwell and Blantyre & Uddingston Directory. He remained at this school until 1873, the year his friend David Livingstone died. His decision to leave really was outwith his hands when, by the unanimous vote of the ratepayers, who petitioned the newly-formed School Board for the purpose, he was chosen headmaster of the proposed Stonefield Parish School and asked to oversee its construction. During this time in 1874, he was admitted a Fellow of the Educational Institute of Scotland.

Up until 1875, he lived at Waterloo Row, near the mills of Low Blantyre, was married and had 5 children. He was a very strict man and discipline came naturally, overhauling the rampant disobedience that existed when he first came to Blantyre schools. His word counted at all times. This was true for parents too, who if they dared complain about the punishment their children were receiving at school, were likely to face possible dismissal themselves at their own employment!

On 26th October 1875, he became headmaster of the Stonefield Parish School which opened that day, prompting also a house move to the adjacent Schoolmasters home at Victoria Street. In 1875, he was given a salary of £120 a year or £10 per calendar month. School children had a playground chant, "The Ness's School is a great wee school, built wi' bricks an' plaister. There's wan thing wrang wi' the Ness's School, it's its baldy heidit maister!"

Outside of his duties the Major had one or two hobbies and as a Volunteer and Freemason, he showed much enthusiasm. He had only been in Blantyre a short time when he raised the Volunteer Company and man ever did more to install a love for Volunteering into the minds of Blantyre youths than John Ness. Following out his military career, he was a sergeant up until 1865, when he was a appointed a colour sergeant; then ensign from 1870 until 1873, lieutenant for a period of 9 further years and captain up until 1886, at which time he received the honorary rank of Major. In November 1887, he resigned from military service in the Blantyre Volunteer Company, carrying with him the privilege of retaining the rank and wearing the uniform of the regiment. He was one of the few officers entitled to wear the Volunteer Decoration after leaving. He was present at the reviews of 1860 and 1881 on the latter occasion in command of the East Kilbride Company.

As a Freemason, the Major was one of the most popular members of the Craft, for 4 times holding the office of R.W.M in "Lodge Livingstone 599" and attended the opening in 1904 of the nearby Masonic Halls on Glasgow Road. In the Provincial Grand Lodge he occupied many important offices. A stained glass window was installed in the lodge in his honour and in Hamilton, a whole Lodge named after him, "Major Ness Lodge 948." He was also a prominent member of the "Clark Forrest R.A. Chapter" . He also held office in Bothwell U.F church for close to 50 years.

The Jubilee of Headmaster John Ness F.E.I.S.V.D was celebrated in Blantyre Works Old School on 1st June 1906 where he had started his duties in 1856. Flags were hoisted on the school at Stonefield and there was a fine display of bunting in the village.

In 1907 John Ness became ill forcing retiring from his headmaster's position. Ness was headmaster at the Low Blantyre School for 32 years, on top of the 18 years he had previously spent at the Village school.

John Ness died on Saturday 23rd May 1908 aged 78 with 52 years service for the community.

On 13th January 1909, a granite obelisk was unveiled in the Cemetery at High Blantyre to his memory. Commissioned and laid by his fellow Masonic members, the memorial is a fitting and impressive gravestone.

Such was his renown, that the Stonefield Parish School became known as "Ness's School" even in later years after his death. The position in the Cemetery reserved for more prominent figures of Blantyre's history. Next to him on the right is the Rev Burleigh's smaller obelisk.

Figure 253 Ness Obelisk in Sep 2017

James Aitchsion, headmaster

James Aitchison was another former teacher of Stonefield Parish School. He was born in Cambuslang on 6th September 1873, the son of John and Jane Millar. For the early part of his life, he lived on Cambuslang Main Street with his parents and many siblings including aunts and cousins at the same house.

By 1891, at the age of 17, he was engaged in education as an elementary teacher. His father John passed away in 1899 at the age of 56. By 1901, he was employed as a School Anchor news correspondent for the Greater Glasgow Area. It seems likely he came to Blantyre between 1920 and 1925, for according to the 1925 Valuation roll; James was occupying the Schoolhouse at 1 Victoria Street, adjacent to Stonefield Parish Primary School. James was the schoolmaster of the nearby Stonefield Parish School and was renting this house from the Education Authority of the Council of Lanark for the sum of £25 per annum. On 1st June 1928, Mr. James Aitchison, according to local news reports was being considered for transfer to Whifflet Primary School in Coatbridge. However, this did not come to pass, and James was still the headmaster at Blantyre in 1930, living in the same schoolhouse at Victoria Street, teaching nearby for some time afterwards.

Clydeview Shopping Centre (West)

In 1980, Clydeview Shopping Centre's western block opened on the former site of Central garage, Nimmo's Land, Bloomfield Cottage and the Stonefield Parish School.

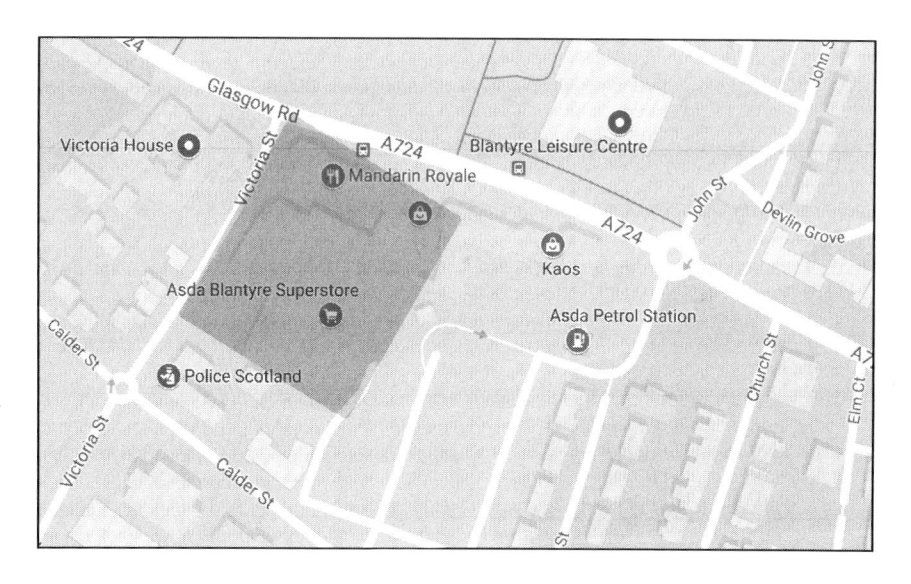

Figure 254 Modern Map showing location of Clydeview Shopping Centre – West block

Built of brick and slate in similar style to the adjacent joined ASDA supermarket, the shopping centre at this location has seen slightly more retail stability through the subsequent decades, perhaps due to its linkage with the actual store. However, it is undeniable that many, many businesses have traded for short times then gone.

We have identified 36 businesses to have traded there, some of them still there to this day. Asda, Asda Café, Citizen's Advice Centre, Cheque Centre, Oliver's Shoe Shop, Shoe Zone then Tandem Shoe Shop, Lightbody's Bakers, Auld's Bakers, Botterils Shop, Spar, Post office temporarily, Blantyre Special Initiative and New Routes regeneration, employment and training initiatives – occupied the large corner unit between 1986 – 1992 then Salvation Army Trading Co, Lorraine Harkin Hairstylist, Stefano's Pizza Shop then Pappys Traditional Smokehouse, Glen Travel, Remax Estate Agents, Eddie Coyle Opticians, Weavers Wines, Victoria Wines, Optical Express, 'Small pound shop, The Laundry' Launderette, Mandarin Royale (Cantonese Restaurant), Ladbrokes then Mecca Bookmakers above the Mehran Tandoori Indian Takeaway early 90's then Bombay Nights Indian Takeaway, Community Links, NHS Lanarkshire, Rascalz then Casper's Nightclub and finally Blantyre Library at the Glasgow Road corner of Victoria Street.

We would need another book to write about the history of all of these businesses, so once again, let's pick a few of the more well known and prominent businesses on the west side of the Shopping Centre.

> Blantyre Project Social Media:
>
> **Michelle McNeil:** "Lightbodys! Best Chips ever!"
>
> **Allan Love:** "Tandem's, shoe styled handles, stayed on the front door of the shop, long after it had actually closed down."
>
> **Linda Pemberton:** "I got great Pakora out the Mehran Takeaway after Caspers Nightclub on a Friday and Saturday evening."
>
> **Elizabeth Freer:** "The NHS Lanarkshire at shared offices with Community Links. They moved out recently either late in 2016 or early 2017."
>
> **Matthew McGuigan:** "Never have I known a town so decimated by the opening of one large superstore. Personally, I think ASDA killed off the local businesses trade and then raised their rents for the retail units, deliberately to avoid competition. Whilst this may be controversial, I'm surprised no other supermarket has arrived in Blantyre to compete. "
>
> **Marian MacGuire:** "I wouldn't miss ASDA if it ever left Blantyre."
>
> **Ray Couston:** "Being born in 1989, the idea of nightlife and nightclubs in Blantyre is somewhat alien to me. Saturday's can be good in the right pub with good company but the night always comes to an end at midnight now. The 'Roc' in Hamilton is the only place to go if you want something to drink until 3am with some late live night music, else its taxis to Glasgow. It would be great again to see somewhere in Blantyre open up until 3am. Young people need somewhere decent to go."
>
> **Marie McVey Crossar:** "I remember Diamond Blush at the bar in Caspers and also K Cider!"
>
> **Abigail Mullings:** "I loved Caspers. So many excellent memories of a fun place. Long Vodkas and Redstripe were my drink of choice at the time."
>
> **Collette MacGuire Gardiner:** "Darting back and forth between Caspers and Ziggy's across the road. Two nightclubs and spoiled for choice in the late 1980's. Great times with friends."
>
> **John Boyd**: "Never been sure about the library there. I just cant see people parking to go and walk over to it. Maybe a sign of the times, but its always empty anytime I walk past. It would be a shame if this is the start of the end for books!"

Asda Supermarket

Asquith and Dairies (ASDA) submitted plans in 1978 to open a new supermarket in Blantyre. Construction commenced in 1979 at a cost of £3m and they opened their massive supermarket new store in October 1980 to divided reactions.

The company had its origin even back to 1920's as Associated Dairies. On one hand the boarded up premises along Glasgow Road had been demolished and a new, modern commercial hub had appeared in Low Blantyre. On the other hand, some businesses and individuals, including homes, were casualties of that development, either having to relocate or retire. Many shopkeepers however, could not relocate and felt that they would not be able to compete with such a giant coming to our town.

Part of ASDA's development included the building of Clydeview Shopping Centre on redeveloped land between Logan Street and Victoria Street. Whilst some successful businesses have thrived in the location, there are many empty retail units in the shopping centre, primarily due to excessive rates; way beyond most local small enterprises would pay.

The large supermarket is open plan and has attached large warehouses, stores and upper offices and staffing rooms. Of course, rather than condemning ASDA, which many people do when they talk of Blantyre's history and lost character, remember too, that ASDA have been a source of employment for thousands of people over the decades in Blantyre and still attracts many residents for their weekly shopping and fuel.

Asda became part of the Walmart chain in July 1999. In August 2009, Walmart "sold" Asda for £6.9 billion to their Leeds-based investment subsidiary Corinth Services Limited. Asda originally had a "simple and fresh" store format, which under Director Archie Norman's team and the focus on a Walmart style strategy became more apparent. The stores are generally white and green, with simplistic layout but built on a Walmart larger footprint format – Asda's average store is almost 20% bigger than its rivals. In 2004, it introduced its George brand of clothing to the store. It is estimated ASDA alone have approximately 17.5% of the overall UK retail market share for food.

Even until only a few years ago, the ASDA Blantyre Petrol Station had a kiosk and was operated by staff, rather than the self-service we're used to now. For staff working in the petrol station, it was an early start at the weekends, even before the store opened and no sign of any kind of self-service payment. Similarly there appears to be a trend towards self-service in the store too with several self-checkouts installed between 2011 and 2014 around the time of 24 hour opening, a first for any shop in Blantyre. Who would have thought in 1980, we'd one day be able to walk into a store and have technology trust us enough to pay without an operator?

Glen Travel

Glen Travel is a contemporary business formerly located at Clydeview Shopping Centre. David Glen of Station Road established the Blantyre Travel Agency in 1973 with premises in Bellshill and Blantyre and along with staff moved into Clydeview Shopping Centre in the early 1980's. Since then, their successful business has prospered and with many more staff now employed, it was time for them to seek larger premises. Staying in the local area, a brand and name we're all familiar with, Glen Travel in Springtime 2017 bought and renovated the former Clydesdale Bank building, which closed in August 2016. The travel agents moved in November 2017 to their new location at the top of Station Road. One hurdle overcome in Summer 2017 was the removal of the former large bank vaults, which were removed entirely. These new premises are spacious, are tastefully decorated and offer prime advertising space.

Caspers

Casper's Nightclub was a former nightclub located at the corner unit of Clydeview Shopping Centre at the junction of Glasgow Road and Victoria Street during the late 1980's and early 1990's.

Prior to 1987, it was called Rascalz. When Caspers first opened it provided meals but only very briefly. It was in the building that is now currently Blantyre Library. It cost just £3 to get into the club each evening, free at weekends if you were in before midnight. It had an upper balcony overlooking the dance floor; sticky dark blue carpets wet from spilled drinks and a cut out of Casper the Ghost above the entrance.

The bouncers or security were notoriously difficult to deal with, not permitting entry with trainers. They were known to keep baseball bats in amongst the pot plants in the foyer. Also at the entrance was a full size replica telephone box.

Inside the club, the décor was blue velvet walls and seats and mostly carpets. The bar was located on the upper part near the balcony at the back of the building and had black and white tiles on front. It was often 3 or 4 people deep. The club could get so hot from being packed out, that condensation would drip from the mirrored walls and neon light fittings. The upper floor also had comfortable seats around the back walls and a staircase leading down on to a sizeable dance floor. During the late 1980's, Geraldine McLaughlin was the manager who ran it very well.

The DJ box was elevated and located in the corner not far from the door. The DJs all worked for Mastercraft discos and included Chic McGuire, Chic Devine, John McDonald & Tom Crawley. Another local DJ, Davie Clegg was popular. Ross King and Gary Marshall, Radio Clyde DJs also did brief stints on the decks. The staff members were usually all local.

Figure 255 Inside Casper's Nightclub in 1990 looking over to DJ booth

There was an under 18's evening on a Saturday prior to adults arriving, but it was stopped due to too many fights. Popular drinks, served when adults arrived, were pints of Snakebite and Blackcurrent (or commonly known as a Diesel), which cost £1.25. Long vodkas were another popular choice.

The music in the late 1980's was 50% Stock, Aitken and Waterman (More Kylie, Jason, Sonia, Hazel Dean), but in 1990, it was turning more towards more mainstream dance and soul era, with Technotronic, Rebel MC, Soul to Soul etc. Musical artists played week on week from the DJ box in this club included Big Fun, Betty Boo, Black Box, Adamski, MC Hammer and Neneh Cherry. Of course the occasional howler like Jive Bunny was thrown in, as well as old classics like "Dignity" from Deacon Blue and The Waterboys, "Whole of the moon". The last song was a "smoochie" or slow dance, almost always, and usually a time when people 'hooked up'.

DID YOU KNOW?

On one occasion, when a fight started, Jude Lewis got locked in the cellar! Many clubbers would make their way to the adjacent Indian Takeaway for Pakora or a Pizza after the club closed at 3am, despite the late hour. Ex Celtic player Joe Miller was eventually the owner buying from former owner, Gerry around early 1990 and customers were excited to see him upon his debut, welcome night.

When Joe bought it over, all the previous staff left. Caspers burned down, some still say to this day done deliberately by disgruntled staff in 1991 and it lay empty for many years before becoming the Council's 'Blantyre Library'.

Blantyre Project Social Media:

Linda Marshall: "I hated working in Weavers Wines. Needs must. You felt like you were working in a cage, behind the security large black bars."

John Cornfield: "Aye when Rascalz opened, it was a new concept for Blantyre. During the day serving food and drink and at nights it was a nightclub! We had one of the trendiest clubs in Lanarkshire at that point in the early 80's"

Paul Veverka: "I worked in the ASDA petrol station kiosk in the late 1980's. What started out as a Saturday morning job turned into a full day as nobody liked opening up at 6am and working until 6pm. I didn't mind the overtime and it let me have enough money to go out to Caspers at weekends. Twice I was interviewed by Police for accidentally letting cars go through without paying in the days before proper technology controlled that. I was moved to checkouts and soon learned that as an 18 year old, I could flirt with the 30 something year old female managers and often get a Sunday double time shift! There was more than one occasion a pretty ASDA manageress got a drink bought for her in Caspers!"

Margaret Farmer: "I left Blantyre before many of these changes, but I will always remember the good service I got from Glen Travel. I used their services many times for holidays."

Stuart Tremble: "Asda weren't the innovators in 24 hour opening. Scotmid, as Spar at the bottom of Stonefield Road did this through a small hatch window during the mid 1990's. However, you couldn't buy alcohol from it after 10pm."

Marianne Stark Aitken: "I remember those early shifts in the petrol kiosk, which opened so much earlier than the store. I worked there with Margaret Douglas. We had some good times."

Figure 256 ASDA Entrance in 2017

Figure 257 Salvation Army on Corner 2016

Figure 258 Glen Travel Agents in 2015

Figure 259 Lorraine Harkin Hairdressers

By Paul D Veverka

Figure 260 Mehran Takeaway 2010

Figure 261 Blantyre Library, (Caspers) 2016

Figure 262 Asda Petrol Station pictured in 2017 not far from corner of Logan St

CHAPTER 12
GLASGOW ROAD SOUTH
VICTORIA ST TO PRIORY ST

Origins of Victoria Street

Unlike the other streets leading south we've explored so far and with exception of Auchinraith Road, Victoria Street joined Low to High Blantyre, cutting right through Blantyre and has many homes and public buildings.

During the 19th Century until the mid 1870's, small track led up a slight gradient from the Glasgow to Hamilton Road, up towards the Stonefield Farm ending at that property. The farm was elevated overlooking fields at that time and the small, expanding village hamlet of Stonefield (itself then only a few homes and shops.) This track was extended during the 1870's and 1880's leading up to what is now the crossroads at Calder Street, providing easier access to Netherfield Place and Dixon's Rows. The track was known as "the Clay Road", a good indication that it likely did not have a good surface.

During the late 1890's, Blantyre was still going though rapid population growth due to the coalfields. At this time, upgrading the narrow paths and thoroughfares was an important reinforcing of infrastructure. The Clay Road was then further extended during the 1880's and 1890's from the crossroads right up to Main Street on High Blantyre to the South. The track generally inclined upwards the further south you travelled as it does today and was narrow, muddy and frequently used by miners as short cuts.

The track had previously simply been a field boundary for Stonefield Farm. It was essentially a route over fields, with no buildings at any side. Likely to have simply had the topsoil and turf taken off. In the first decade of the 1900's, the Clay road was widened and constructed over with a more permanent surface forming what is now Victoria Street. A section of the original Clay Road still exists today at the very top of Victoria Street at the junction of High Blantyre Main Street. The road at that point significantly narrows back to the size it was then which was not much larger than the width of a horse and cart. It's for that reason cars cannot exit off Victoria Street directly on to Main Street.

Victoria Street was named so, following the death of the Monarch Queen Victoria in 1901, coinciding with a new century and the 'Clay Road' name abandoned, it had been given the name "Victoria Street" by 1910.

Buildings on Victoria Street

During the late 19th and 20th Centuries, some very prominent and public buildings existed on Victoria Street, some still do! On the eastern side behind the school was the Schoolmasters house and the Police Station near Calder Street Junior Secondary School. Also ASDA warehouses. On the eastern side there were shops, Health Institute as well as a Hospital for Infectious Diseases. These properties are explored fully in other Blantyre Project books.

However, it is perhaps the homes and number of families that lived in Victoria Street that defined it as a popular place. Alongside the schoolmasters house and Victoria Place (tenement houses for miners nicknamed 'the Honeymoon' behind Stonefield Parish School), there were privately built stone homes and huge expansive council estates built in the mid 1920's.

Figure 263 Victoria Place (The Honeymoon) in 1946

Blantyre Project Social Media:

Thomas Dunsmuir: "I was born in 1930, an address at 3 Victoria Street, a row of Miners Raws which went under the name 'The Honeymoon'. There was a wall to the north which surrounded Ness's School from the squalor of the raws. This wall came in handy for us to kick our ball up against and we used it for other activities. Some of the Honeymoon kids attended the school so any playthings lost over the wall were usually returned to us. Like all raws in Blantyre, ours being one of the oldest, it was a mess."

Elizabeth Weaver: "We lived three quarters of the way up Victoria Street near where the road went under the Railway bridge. We'd often watch the trains go by our home on the elevated embankment. Very handy throwing school bags out the train window into the garden, so you didn't have to carry them home when you got off at the station! In the 1950's, under the bridge were wooden panels which children would often play against."

Stonefield Farm (Hastie's Ferme)

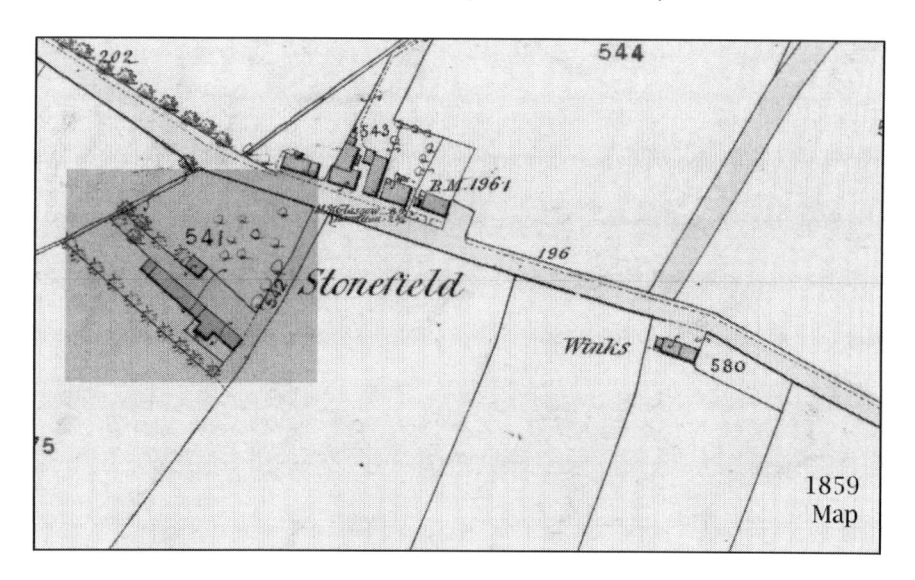

Figure 264 Stonefield Farm in 1859 with track which would become Victoria St

The former farm of Stonefield is more commonly remembered in modern times as being "Hastie's Farm", but its roots go back further than the Hastie family. Constructed in the 1810's, the farm is later than some other older farms like Blantyre Farm, Auchinraith (Burnbrae) Farm, Coatshill, Croftfoot or Calderside.

The original owners were the Forrest family, acquiring the land from Lord Blantyre and buildings are first referred to at Stonefield on William Forest's Map of 1816. (of no relation to the Forrest family who owned the farm.)

Built of stone with slated roof, the farm buildings ran east to west and were location in an elevated position above some poorly drained fields. The inadequacy of the fields would have required tremendous effort to make them suitable for farming and it is here we find the likely source of the name "Stonefield", the small hamlet that grew around the farm.

By 1832 as shown in John Thomson's Atlas of Scotland, at least a half dozen small homes and businesses and been built on the north side of the Glasgow to Hamilton Road and the name of this little hamlet already established as "Stonefield". These were the humble beginnings of the a district that would later than century become extremely populated.

In 1855 the only land and property in small, rural Stonefield belonged to the families Craig, Hill, Rintoul, Monteith and of course Forrest.

Following fierce competition, William Forrest bought Stonefield Farm in October 1851 with 59 acres for the price of £2,750, including a tile works to the north, which was let out. William certainly was a prominent landowner and there is good evidence that Stonefield Farm fields occupied much of the land to both north and south of Glasgow Road in those early, sparsely populated times. William Forrest also owned a quarry at Blantyre Moor, the larger farm of Auchinraith (Burnbrae) occupied by James Scott as well as further homes, shops and a blacksmith around early Blantyre. However, William was a remote owner of these properties, not living in Blantyre, but instead letting them out. James Williamson was the farmer of Stonefield Farm in 1855, renting from William Forrest for £83 per annum.

In 1857 upon the death of William Forrest or Forest, the farm passed to two other family members. Part of the farm went to William's son, John Clark Forrest and the other part to his son's wife, Janet Clark Forrest (nee Logan). It may be that the whole was inherited by John and he sold or gifted part to his wife.

Stonefield Farm is described in 1859 as, "A Farm Steading. The property of Mr. Forest J.P. [Justice of the Peace]. This name also applies to several feued (houses) between "Blantyre Cotton Works T. P. [Turn Pike]" & "Winks."

John Clark Forrest

One of the most eminent men to come to Blantyre was Stonefield Farm owner, Mr. John Clark Forrest. Born in Shotts on 17th October 1832, John had strong connections to Blantyre. His mother was a Clark whose family had farmed Auchinraith Farm for centuries beforehand, with his grandparents buried in the High Blantyre Kirkyard. A military man at heart, he rose through the ranks to become the Captain of 16th Lanarkshire Rifle Battalion.

However, it was his other pursuits that interested and impacted Blantyre. He was an active member of Blantyre's Parochial Board, responsible for making important decisions such as the funding and building of schools and churches, the clean up of the town and installing permanent water supplies. Although strict, he was well respected and could influence many civic decisions about Blantyre. He strived for betterment, cleanliness and progress. A family man too, marrying his love Jane Logan, five years his junior.

His life wasn't without tragedy. On 9th June 1866, at just 29 years old, Jane (or Janet) sadly died. Despite being only 34 years old, John was inconsolable and chose to devote the rest of his life to work and career, never remarrying again.

Following the demolition of the tired miner's row housing throughout Blantyre, and as a result of upgrading Blantyre's homes and streets, John and Jane's influence gave to the naming of several new streets along Glasgow Road. Some are still there today on the north side, namely names were; John Street, Clark Street, Forrest Street and on the south, Logan Street, are all within his beloved Auchinraith/Stonefield.

Figure 265 John Clark Forrest owner of the farm

As Provost of Hamilton from 1875-1881, he welcomed the Prince of Wales to Hamilton Palace in 1878 and later Prime Minister Mr. Gladstone in 1880. He was also the honorary Sheriff substitute in Blantyre from 1879, in which position he read "the riot act" in Blantyre during 1887. In 1888 he became Lieutenant Colonel of the 5th Volunteer Battalion Scottish Rifles in Airdrie.

On 28th August 1893, at the age of 61 John passed away at his Udston Home. After Auchingramont Church service and further small service at his home, this public figure then had a funeral service the likes of what Blantyre had never seen before. It was by no doubt the largest funeral procession the town had seen.

His coffin was oak clad and lined inside with lead. Placed on a gun carriage with his military helmet and sword on top, the carriage was pulled by six magnificent black, plumed horses. His favourite Charger followed with his solitary boots, attached and reversed in the stirrups. Next, followed the Burgh Council and magistrates followed by over 1,500 local Blantyre mourners. The Burgh Police had to unusually attend the funeral if only for crowd control. The procession is reported to have tailed back a mile and was ceremoniously handed over to the Lanarkshire Constabulary at the border of Hamilton and into High Blantyre.

Along Main Street the procession arrived at the Blantyre kirkyard. The stone walls of the kirk graveyard were lined by volunteers standing two deep in their bright red uniforms. His regiment carried the coffin down from the carriage, up the cemetery steps and to the prepared lair. (near the back left of the kirkyard). The nearby Church bells constantly chimed a slow, funeral dirge. People congregated in Douglas Street and Main Street and there was reputedly not a place to stand. Then, having been laid to final rest amongst a mountain of flowers, a firing party 300 men strong (5th Volunteer Battalion) discharged a volley of shots to the air.

Becoming Hastie's Farm

John Clark Forrest owned Stonefield Farm for 36 years between 1857 and 1893 although of course never farmed it himself. After James Williamson stopped farming the land as tenant in 1872, a young contractor by name of David Hastie took up the rental of the farm. From that time onwards, the name 'Stonefield Farm' was used less often and suddenly stories appear in local newspapers as being 'Hastie's Farm'.

Eventful night at Hastie's Farm

A good deal of excitement was caused in the wee small hours of Saturday 21st August 1875. The people residing at Hastie's Farm were awoken by some violent knocking at their door. On going out to find out what was going on, they were confronted by a giant of a man who was clearly drunk. The man repeatedly said he "wanted to get into his bed", much to the alarm of the farmhouse owners. After some time, they managed to get rid of him, by calmly talking and the man seemed to go back towards the (Glasgow) road. They went in, but were on guard and listened for his return.

Figure 266 Hastie's Break in

Some time later, they again thought they heard somebody about the place, although this time with fear as the noises were coming from the house itself. They walked carefully into one of the unoccupied bedrooms and were alarmed to see the tall man laying comfortably in bed amongst their good, clean sheets. The window was ajar which had obviously been his point of entry. Upon being discovered, the man rolled over and promptly fell out the high bed to the floor in his stupor. Being near to the Police Station, one of the Blantyre constables was fetched who quickly detained the intruder, took him to the station and later on to jail. The giant man was Alexander Craig, a navvy living in nearby railway huts. Spending his wage on a night at Blantyre's taverns, his eventual condition obviously led him to mistake the large farmhouse for his own railway hut lodgings. However, there is more to this story.

Whilst the police were being fetched and Alexander lay on the floor of Hastie's farm, Mr. Hastie had to run outside as a call of "fire" was heard. Whilst the Alexander story unfolded, a secondary commotion took place. One of the farm carts was ablaze. A number of neighbours soon turned up to put out the fire but were unable to save the cart and its contents, which belonged to Mr Wright, a farmer at Spittal. The cart was believed to be insured. Alexander had been the only person seen in the yard, but with no witnesses, he was never charged.

Once the police had left with Alexander in custody, Mr Hastie and the kind people of Glasgow Road residences had managed to put out the fire. Thankful that it hadn't spread and beyond sleep, Mr Hastie decided to sit in his scullery and treat the makeshift firefighters with some of his own whisky which is reputed to have been consumed in significant quantities. (Hastie had a fine sideline going in selling whisky to locals)

Around 5.00am as the sun came up and after 3 or 4 hours solid drinking, the 3 remaining locals who had helped, set off from the farmhouse for home. However, as Mr Hastie bade them farewell from his door, to his surprise the men started fighting amongst themselves at the nearby road. Punches and kicks, 2 of them set about the third, robbing him of his boots. Mr. Hastie stood by the door, watching and later reported to Police, he had sighed heavily and said out loud to himself "Blantyre. I don't have the strength!"

Remainder of 19th Century

In 1879 within Naismith's Directory, David Hastie is noted as being the contractor at Stonefield Farm. In the 1881 census he is 39 years old living with wife Janet (42) and sons John (9), Peter (2) and daughter Helen (7). David was born in Carluke and came to Blantyre in 1872. All his children were born there. He had another eldest daughter, Margaret who died in 1943.

During the 1890's Daniel Henry owned a nearby house, stable and store adjacent to the farm. David Hastie that decade established the business, "David Hastie & Sons". John Hastie and his father bred Shire horses on the farm and kept them in the front field near the Glasgow Road, which had a small horse shed at the very corner of what would become Victoria Street. In 1905 he was selling off some of his "Draught Geldings" horses at auction.

Such beasts would have cost around £70 then and it is known they were sold direct fro the farm on occasion too.

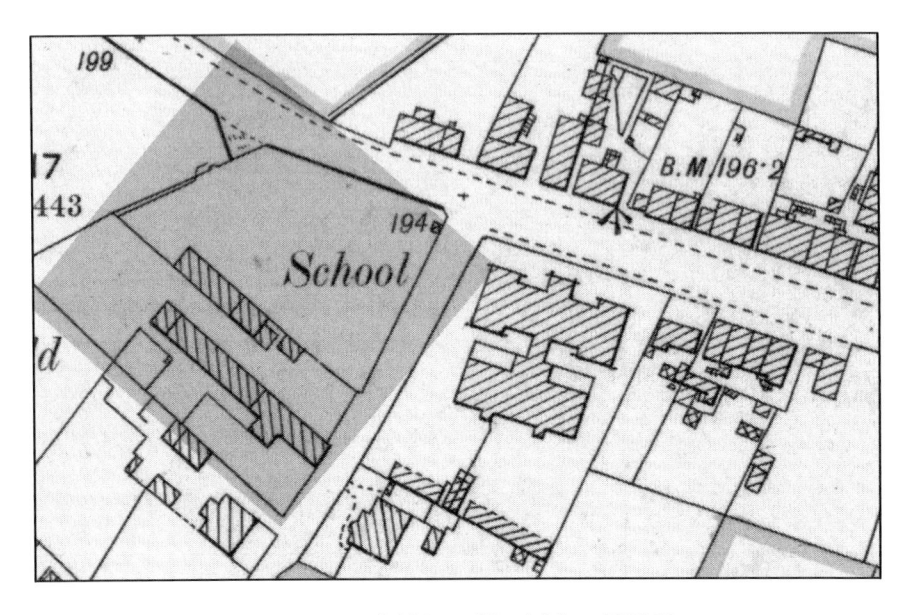

Figure 267 Stonefield Farm (Hastie's) on 1898 Map

David Hastie & Sons

Hastie's Farm may not have operated in the traditional sense of growing crops. It was more a working farm, for horses and base for David's contracting activities but did keep cattle for the dairy. His business David Hastie & Sons were primarily contractors and the farming activities may have become secondary by the 1890's onwards. For example in February 1891, David Hastie & Sons won the contract for the construction of Motherwell Waterworks for the considerable sum of £8,500 (£1.3m in today's money). Works took 3 years to build and would have been full time employment for the family business. The idea that the farm may have not been recognized as such around the turn of the 20th Century is further supported by the lack of any word of "farm" being mentioned in the 1905 valuation roll. David Hastie owning "a house, shed, byre, workshop, offices and ground."

By 1895, David Hastie was still renting the Stonefield Farm from the Trustees of John Forrest Clark, who died 2 years earlier. His large contract in Motherwell, likely gave him the cash and means to acquire and buy the farm buildings and land outright, something he did between 1895 and 1900. Concentrating on their contracting business, the Hastie family once acquiring the land, sold off some of their surrounding fields in 1902 and others would build upon them. E,g. Annfield Terrace hemming in Stonefield Farm.

In 1905 David Hastie & Sons won the contract for filling up the old pit shaft at Barncluith and Silverton(hill) including landscaping the pithead.

Away from work, the Hastie men (David and sons John and Peter) were good curlers and helped form a team in Hamilton. David certainly was a noted sportsman. In 1912, son John Hastie played for Scotland in an International match with England. He was a sporty type and also played football. Other son, Peter Hastie won accolades for curling up until the late 1930's. Daughters were musical and often gave performances.

During WW1, David's health was failing and in his 70's he passed the farm to daughter Miss Margaret B Hastie. She's noted in the 1915 valuation roll and owning the farm, leasing out to her retired father and working brothers 'David Hastie & Sons' for £70 per annum. By this time the sons had established a sand quarry at Ferniegair and were advertising for carters. Margaret owned the farm outright until 1944.

Figure 268 Hastie's Whisky Bottle (unopened!)

In March 1917, many surplus farming tools were auctioned off from the farm. Also auctioned was a lorry with 'rubber tyres." In December 1917, David Hastie & Sons were selling 5 cart yokes from their farm having previously acquired them from Ferniegair Sand Quarry. By this time, Stonefield or Hastie's Farm (as it was becoming more known by) had address 16 Victoria Street. Whilst this is not Glasgow Road, such a prominent, important building for Stonefield and the frontage it had overlooking Glasgow Road and the fact nobody seems to have explored its deeper history before, deserved to be told here.

In 1920, David Hastie died, aged 78. Whilst David Hastie & Sons would continue in name, the sons would go separate ways with Peter in Blantyre at the farm and elder John continuing to love at Eddlewood Farm, Hamilton (which the business also owned since 1901).

End of the Hastie Era

DID YOU KNOW?

On Tuesday 2nd May 1932, In the early hours of that morning, a large garage situated at Hastie's Farm owned by Mr. Peter D. Hastie, was burned out, and the owner's car and another car belonging to a commercial traveller were destroyed. The damage was estimated at £2,500.

On Friday 18th November 1932, the funeral took place in Blantyre of John Hastie, the eldest son of the late David and one half of the business, "David Hastie & Sons". It was attended by a large gathering of agriculturists from all over Scotland. John was 61 years old.

John had retired from the business in 1930 owing to failing health and of course had been living in Hamilton, leaving the Blantyre property to his brother. Trained by his father, a capable judge, it was only natural that he inherited rare and sound judgment. He was noted as being one of the most accomplished breeders of Clydesdale horses in all of Scotland with some of his champion breeders being exported to New Zealand, Australia and Canada. He had been a Director in Glasgow Agricultural Society and we've already touched on his ability as a curler. Mr Hastie left behind a wife, one son and five daughters and at the time of his death had been spending some time at Largs for the sea air.

Figure 269 Hastie's Farm entrance on Victoria St in late 1960's

In an article upon his death, the Hamilton Advertiser reporter wrote that, "The name Hastie became known amongst Scottish breeders and farmer. As a judge of Clydesdales, Mr. Hastie may even have exceeded his fathers popularity all over Scotland. His duties took him to the farthest points of Scotland and at all the principal shows his cheery personality was always welcomed."

Peter Duncanson Hastie, the remaining son of the late David and brother of John, died on 23rd June 1944 as the result of an accident at Hamilton, survived by wife Annie McLennan. He left £10,309 in his will (a sum of half a million pounds in today's money). It is noted at this time David Hastie & Sons had still been operating in Blantyre. However, the death of Peter Hastie, the remaining partner of the firm, prompted selling off Stonefield Farm buildings in Summer 1944. The Hastie family had lived and worked on this property for 7 decades, which coincidentally is also how long in earlier times, the Forrest family members had owned it.

Hastie's Farm (Post World War II)

At the end of 1945, with inheritors living in Hamilton, Stonefield Farm ceased operating as a contracting business and was sold to a new owner. Mr. Arthur Cunningham bought the farm from the Hastie family and operated a motor hire business from this location at 16 Victoria Street. His telephone number was Blantyre 50 and he hired out wedding cars for functions and weddings.

In July 1950, Arthur Cunningham family put the property up for sale. He owned the building only a short time following two generations of Hastie family members before selling to John and Mary Cunningham who owned and farmed the land again for many years until 1963.

Arthur had offered the premises to the County Council to use the outbuildings as storage for their scavenging vehicles, for repairs and to make use of the car pit and garage space. The annual rental of the extensive grounds was £95. It was then used as a National petrol station and service garage, the cobbled yard at the rear being useful for vehicles.

In the early sixties the Royal Mail at Blantyre filled their vans with petrol there, which as you can imagine they were filled often! The garage however was not to last. The disused pumps and small glass office were still there years later. You had to drive through them into the back parking lot.

Fortunes changed for the building, when in 1963, Mr. Bobby Brown bought Hastie's Farm Buildings. Bobby Brown kept pigs, chickens and a donkey at the end of the yard. An elderly gentleman named Charlie tended to the animals and he and Bobby also kept a small greenhouse too. Bobby took the decision to lease out the farmhouse and an adjoining building to a taxi company in June 1964. He was a local building contractor and deployed his skills and manpower in going about renovating the front part of the building facing on to Victoria Street, as a small café which had the luxury of providing live music to his customers. The name? Why "Hastie's Farm" of course!

In 1967, seeing the success and potential of his café, and being forever the businessman, Bobby decided to cease the lease of the taxi company and convert the old farmhouse building, into a larger restaurant, complete with a bar, which would all be quaintly set amongst the old interior stone walls of the farm building. It was suitably decorated with oak beams and brassware on the walls, in keeping with its former farming heritage. How the crowds flocked. The taxi company would later resurface in Glasgow Road known as "Hasty Cars" not be confused by the contemporary Hastie Cars.

The restaurant quickly became a popular venue for many people when it was first granted a food and drinks license in 1967. Bobby Brown fed the pigs with all the leftover food and beer slops from Hastie's three kitchens and bars. The restaurant was a culture shock for Blantyre when it opened. Teachers, attracted by quality meals at discounted prices, ate well at lunchtimes, 1970's favourites like chicken in a basket being popular. The hall was very popular for parties, functions and wedding receptions and was still being used for that purpose in the 1970's. Blantyre couples had their reception there in the late 1960's and throughout the 1970's.

When nearby Annfield Terrace was demolished in the early 1970's, the field in front of Hastie's became the property of the County Council who would host a Tuesday market at that location.

Sunday afternoons were singalong afternoons at Hastie's and it was known that some people hurried away from mass to ensure they got a good table. The hypnotist show was popular too. Mary and Elspeth Gilmour worked as waitresses as did Greer and Kathleen McGuigan. Mr. McNamee played piano. Thursdays and Saturdays were big singalong evenings, where bands like Jon Doc Trio played and singers like Bryce Sloan and Pete Bolton. Indeed much of Blantyre's talent matured when first given an airing as the entertainment at Hasties. An anonymous local man commented, "On the night of the 25th May 1967 I sat in Hasties Farm with my mates Joe Ayres, Jimmy McGuigan (Greer's brother), Brian O'Hara and Jimmy McFaulds and watched Celtic win the European Cup. I woke up alone in the Blantyre Public Park at 3am the next morning."

In 1975, Hastie's Farm burned down. Bobby Brown, wishing his business up and running as quickly as possible diverted labour from his business to ensure the place was fully rebuilt, which allegedly was done in under 3 weeks.

Figure 270 Hastie's Farm was renovated in 1975 in modern style. Photo 1977

However, the rebuild was modern and the place lost much of its character and with it some of its older customers. The entire roof was rebuilt too. A younger crowd, intent on going out each and every weekend frequented the new place and the business continued to prosper, as did Bobby himself. Bobby was known to be a kind soul and on occasion even known to run workers home in his Rolls Royce, his pride and joy.

By 1979, prompted by the extreme redevelopment of Glasgow Road and faced with his business looking out upon a forthcoming large Asda warehouse, Bobby decided to retire. It was the end of an era for him and wife Kathy and indeed the end of an era for Glasgow Road itself. He left on a high though, for in 1979, Hastie's had achieved a reputation of being a showplace for amateur musical talent.

Two gentlemen, now sadly passed on are well remembered for being on the door. Mr. Terry White and Mr John Rodwell. Some memories people still talk about are the smell of the oak beams, the food, not to mention the big chunky pint tumblers with handles. Hasties Farm was also written in huge letters on the Glasgow Road frontage looking down upon Glasgow Road. The pubs closed at 10pm back then, but Hasties' bars were open until 11pm, on account of it being a licensed restaurant. There was always a late rush of new customers for that last extra hour of drinking. Even after 11pm you could still get in if you were a friend of the various doormen, and Hasties was notorious for after-hours drinking. The sign on the door said "oot" instead of "exit!"

Figure 271 Bobby Brown of Hastie's Farm sponsoring Boxers in 1975

Change in ownership

So it came to pass, that on 1st July 1979, Bobby sold Hastie's Farm and the successful business to new owners Sam Plotnikoff, an incomer from Glasgow and his business partner, Graham Gordon.

Sam was then a young man and together with Graham, their vision for Hasties was destined to be incredibly respectful and ensure the business continued with high standards of excellence for food, drinks and entertainment.

Putting a mark on things, the frontend café of Hastie's Farm Restaurant was sectioned off and became 'Bananas Disco'. It was incredibly popular and always very busy. In 1979, full of enthusiasm for Hastie's future Sam told reporters, "The atmosphere we're determined to create is casual, informal, and relaxed."

"It's not a dinner dance, and we don't have a cocktail bar," he stressed.

Graham added: "When we took over, there was a long list of exotic drinks at the bar, some of which weren't asked for more than once a year. We pruned that and, apart from the usual drinker, we only have six or seven "specials." One of the first moves the new owners made was to approach John Doc, the well-known Lanarkshire musician, and lure him and his trio back to Hastie's, a move that proved very popular. Doc and his Trio was the resident band at the time. They launched an EP called 'John Doc At Hasties Farm', logically enough. The tracks on it were 'Everybody Knows', 'My Way', 'Nobody Wins', and 'Sweet Caroline', suggesting that it was a standard Club / Cabaret record. The catalogue number was HF-101.

Figure 272 Blantyre Mothers on Night out at Hastie's 1974

During the early 1980's, John Doc played at Hastie's from Wednesday to Sundays, and on some of these evenings there was dancing. Monday was a quiet night down at the Farm, with the bar open for customers. Sam used his connections in the entertainment industry to bring some well-known names to Blantyre to his club.

The late Blantyre historian Jimmy Cornfield once commented on this saying, "Some of the celebrities, actors and artists who came to Hastie's at that time, not all to perform, but just to see and be seen were, Matt Munro, Ruby Murray, Frank Ifield, Vince Hill, Marty Wilde, Jiminy Cricket, Alistair McDonald, Russel Hunter, Neville Taylor, Brian Taylor, The Dutch College Swing Band, The Livingstones, Christian, John Cairney, Aker Bilk, Andy

Cameron, Hector Nicol and Jock Stein. Many of the Celtic, Rangers and other Scottish Football teams players were seen from time to time."

Tuesday was disco night. Sam and Graham were worried that folks would think they'd turned the place into a disco joint, but that's not the case at all. Although the bar had been done up and converted into a young people's bar, the Disco was only held on Tuesday evenings in the restaurant. The disco evenings kicked off with Radio Clyde's Dougie Donnelly and the Clyde Disco Road Show.

On other nights of the week, Hastie's provided a good three-course meal and coffee for £3.75. The catering was under the eye of Graham's wife Irene who, like her husband and his partner, had entered the business with tremendous zest. Visitors come from far an wide and the visitor's book showed entries from as far afield as Romania, Australia, Canada, U.S.A, Iraq, Thailand, and South Africa. Speaking shortly after opening, Sam said: "We're quite a tourist attraction, People bring their friends and relatives to show them typical Scottish entertainment."

Saturday was just one evening when all the good amateur singers came to take their turn at the microphone. Sam said: "There is a core of regulars, but new talent appears all the time. Some are every bit as good as you would hear on the T.V."

Group outings were also welcome at Hastie's Farm. They received parties of all sizes for every evening, with busloads of people even coming from Glasgow. By the early 1980's, booking was strongly advised, although the restaurant could seat 180 people. Advance bookings for the following year were common. After all, there's no local competition", Graham said in 1979, "and we're in a very handy location just 20 minutes from Glasgow. The bus loads come from all over, Ayrshire, Stirlingshire, and even further away."

Still concentrating on local amateur talent, a Sunday afternoon singalong was again started up. That began on August 5th 1979 and with some 25 singers taking the stage, which proved a great success. Snacks were on offer at the singalong with lunches in the other part of the complex. On other days lunches were also available. Although there was a waitress service, the idea was to provide a "Pub Grub" style of menu. Lunch at Hastie's with a quiet drink was expected to increase still further in popularity when the giant new Asda store, adjacent to the complex opened that following year.

All this was keeping the partners busy for 18 hours a day. But they didn't mind and were determined to build Hastie's back to its former glory, something which was always their intention.

However, by the mid 1980's, several nightclubs had opened up in Hamilton and in other nearby towns. Blantyre residents suddenly had more choice and were not limited to going out in just one small club in Blantyre with the same neighbours, friends and familiar faces. Stylish clubs like the Rococco in Hamilton attracted youngsters away from Blantyre at weekends, and by 1985 Sam was noticing a dip in trade. Trade was also further affected by the arrival of fast food chains like Wimpey, MacDonalds and more affordable eating out in pubs and restaurants in nearby towns and in Blantyre itself. Trade may also have been affected by the nightclub opening across the road, called Rascalz. Youngsters wanted bright neon lights, dark nightclubs with booth seating, state of the art lighting and larger dance floors. The appeal of the old farm building and its brass horse memorabilia hanging from the walls was fast waning.

So, in 1985, Sam decided to focus on other business interests, chiefly his snooker clubs and put Hastie's up for sale, creating quite the talking point in Blantyre. A company named Lanarkshire Holdings briefly took over the business but they were remote, and did not share the same enthusiasm as Sam or Bobby.

'Ziegfield's' and the end

Figure 273 Zeigfields Advert from 1986

What was needed was the input of somebody who knew all about nightclubs. Somebody who knew what youngsters wanted. Nightclub owner James Mortimer (b1946) then in April 1985 changed the rear Hastie's Restaurant into 'Zeigfields Disco' and the front, former Bananas Disco, into 'Barnums'. Other facelifts included changing parts of the building to Panama Jacks and Happy Jacks.

However, despite special offer nights, (like Zeigfields 50/50 night on a Thursday where it was

50p to get in and 50p a drink), trade continued to decline, and even more so when a Celtic player opened up neighbouring Caspers in 1988. The whole complex including Zeigfield's (Ziggy's) closed for good in early 1990.

A year later on 31st December 1990, just before the New Year Bells, a fire was discovered in the roof of the derelict Hastie's Building. The courtyard was being used as a taxi pick up point for Caspers nightclub opposite and the taxi drivers phoned for the fire brigade. Despite arriving promptly, the main roof was damaged to such an extent that it was condemned in January 1991 as being unsafe and was demolished a few years later.

Blantyre residents still fondly remember everything about their entertainment at 'Hastie's Farm' and it remains one of the most powerful and popular memories for many people in this town.

Blantyre Project Social Media:

Len Northfield: "I was working in Hastie's petrol station, clearing out the bars in the mornings and peeling potatoes for the kitchen (when I wasn't at school!), all for 25p per hour."

Julie Tabor: "My grandfather worked at Hastie's. His name was Charlie Brown. So many family memories here."

Lon McIlwraith: "My grandpa Bob Brown had 2 daughters. Rena (mum now gone) and Moira who lives in South Africa. Auld Charlie done a bit of everything around Hastie's. He was quite the character. Going back to Bob Brown for a moment, he was a brickie by trade and in WW2, he worked hard at Motherwell Steel works. After the war, he opened a brick making business at Bog's Brae near Bellshill. Bob distrusted banks and the taxman and kept his money with lawyers. He later worked a deal to swap his Calder Street house for the house next to Hastie's and his National Petrol Station. Hastie's Farm made my grandfather rich. He left quite the legacy and mystery. Upon Bob Brown's death in 1982, my grandmother found no explanation for where the money had gone. He had remortgaged the house a few months before his death. His boat was away from the marina, businesses untraceable and my grandmother was left in poverty."

Graham Elder: "Who remembers the big plough that sat outside the front of Hastie's to advertise?"

Maureen Downie: "One night in a thunder and lightning storm, I got a run home in Mr. Brown's Rolls Royce."

Colin Pitcairn: "50/50 night in Zeigfields on Thursday evenings! Many a Friday hangover at work."

Bobby Brown

Figure 274 Bob Brown with 'Sally' the dog in Front room at Hasties

Bob Brown was a bricklayer to trade, and during the Second World War he worked at the Motherwell steel works. His job was to replace the refractory brickwork inside the blast furnaces (when they had cooled down, of course), and this occupation exempted him from military service. Incidentally, he was a coal miner, which meant he was exempt too.

Sometime after the war, Bob Brown opened a brickmaking business at Bogs Brae near Bellshill which certainly existed in the 1950's and 1960's. He later had a building business which he ran from offices and the yard behind his home in Calder Street, directly opposite the present sandwich shop. He left the building business when he opened (or bought) the National petrol and service station, at Hasties Farm. Of course, he kitted out the Victoria Street end of the old barn building opposite the petrol pumps to open the café, later licensed restaurant, and the rest is history.

As Hasties Farm became more and more popular, Bob worked a deal to swap his house in Calder Street for the home beside the National petrol station, meaning he now lived right beside his business.

His grandson Lon, added "As I worked between the bars I soon found out what the regulars and staff were up to. There was rampant thieving, which culminated in a fierce 'all staff' meeting where Bob laid out the truth, and a few people were outed and fired on the spot. There were quite a few affairs and other personal shenanigans over the years, and a few tragedies as well.

There were two lovely waitresses whose faces I can clearly see. One was quite tall with dark hair; the other quite short and with a slight speech impediment. They both had young children. One evening when they were both working, their kids had been left with a babysitter (or relative) in one of their homes in Burnbrae Road or a nearby street. There was a fire and all the children died. I still remember the scenes in Hasties, as everyone was in shock at this terrible tragedy."

Blantyre Project Social Media:

Lon McIlwraith: "Bobby Brown was my grandfather, my Mum Rena worked there as a waitress for years, and I also worked there from age 12, cleaning and re-stocking the bars on Saturday and Sunday mornings. From age 15 I worked in the evening bars, restocking and cleaning the glasses, then eventually serving the booze too. Monday and Wednesday dance evenings I played guitar in the back room band. Bob's sister, my Aunt Isa, worked in the middle room, selling cigarettes and tending the cloakroom. We were all dragooned into working for Bob - there was no escape. I know almost all the characters mentioned from the mid-60s till the around 1978. Most of them are dead now. I don't know anything about the place after my grandfather sold it. I emigrated to Vancouver, Canada in May 1980. My brother Steve has the Hasties Farm visitors' book from the years my grandparents owned it, and it confirms that there were visitors from all over the globe, especially Canada and the USA, but surprisingly a lot from Africa too. Even a few Russians were there, back in the USSR days (must have been spies!)"

Hasties Farm made Bobby Brown rich, although none of his family saw any of it. He was a hard taskmaster and didn't believe in anyone getting handouts, although many of the 'hingers-oan' that surrounded him borrowed lots of cash from him. He distrusted the taxman and had most of his money in care of his lawyer, not the bank. He also thought that insurance was a scam, and would have nothing to do with it, which leads to the most common rumour people talk about Hasties… that he deliberately burned Hasties down for the insurance money. This myth is disproved here. There was no insurance policy. Bob rebuilt Hasties Farm with his own money, and using his many contacts in the building trades to get the job done quickly. There was no obvious motive for the fire, it was an accident. Hasties was as busy as ever after the fire, but Bob's heart had gone out of it. He opened a fish shop in Glasgow, and also had a mussel farm somewhere doon-the-watter. He would disappear for days then return home with great rolls of cash. The family were astonished by how much money he carried around.

Figure 275 Hasties Pre 1975, before the fire destroyed this room

Bob was also famously known in Blantyre for his Rolls-Royce cars. He had three in succession. The first two were second-hand, but the third was ordered brand new, painted gold. One night he was visiting his 'fancy piece' in Glasgow, and thought his gold roller would be safe if he parked it in the grounds of a nearby church. He returned to find it a burned out wreck the following morning. This event, more than anything else, sickened him of everything.

It was shortly after this that he sold Hasties Farm, for close to £250,000, a fortune in those days. (about £1.5m today.) Bob and Kathy bought a house in Inverkip, overlooking the Clyde and they seemed very happy there. His cabin cruiser Hasties was moored in Kip marina.

Bob died in 1982. He checked into hospital in Glasgow to have an aortic aneurysm repaired. He even drove himself there in his Volvo estate car, thinking to drive home, a new man, a few days later. He never came out. Cardio-renal failure, followed by brachopneumonia, carried him off. His wife was devastated, but there was worse to come. He had paid cash for their Inverkip home, and there was plenty left over, so she thought she would be quite comfortable. Her daughter was staying with her during that time, and what she discovered next destroyed everything.

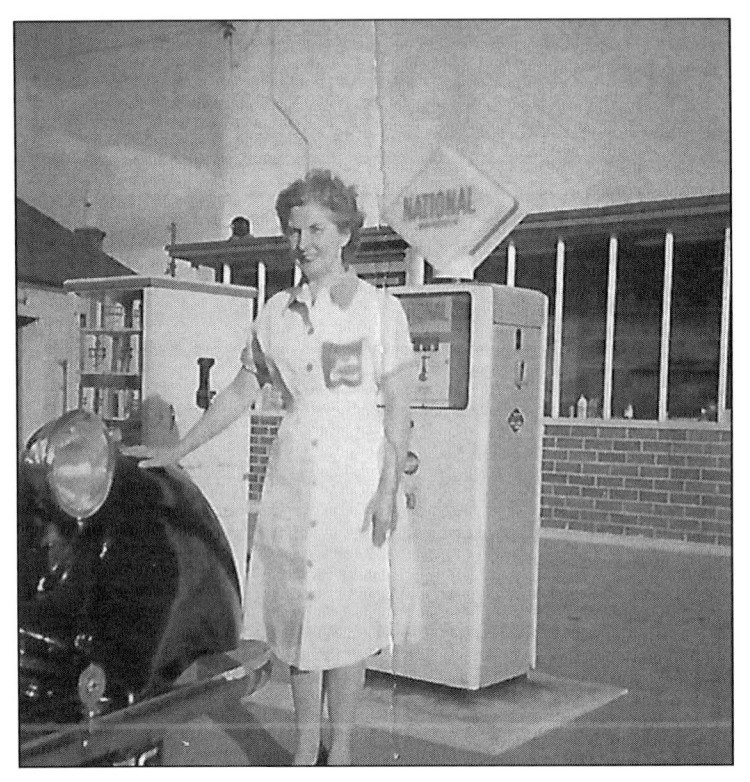

Figure 276 Kathy Brown, Bob's wife at Hastie's Petrol Station 1962

Bob had mortgaged the house almost entirely a few months before he died. His daughter went to see Bob's lawyer to find out what was going on. He informed her that there was only about £15,000 left. The lawyer had no explanation for where all the money had gone (no paper trail). Mrs Brown and her daughter could prove nothing.

Also, his Volvo had disappeared from the hospital car park, his boat vanished from the marina, the fish shop and mussel farm were untraceable. Instead of retiring happily, Kathy Brown was left in poverty.

In the words of his grandson, "That's the legacy Bob Brown left behind."

Annfield Terrace

Annfield Terrace was a former 20th Century, two storey tenement at the western corner of the junction of Victoria Street and Glasgow Road. It should not be confused, as others have done with the older 19th Century 'Annsfield' or 'Annsfield Place', which was further away at Stonefield Road.

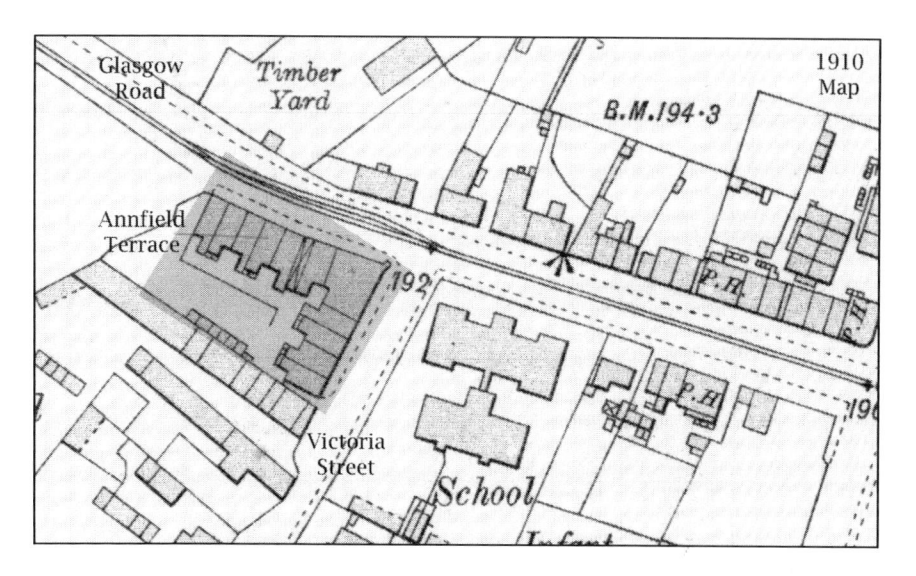

Figure 277 Former Annfield Terrace shown on 1910 Glasgow Road Map

The field belonged to Stonefield Farm during the 19th Century belonged to the Forrest family, for the best part until 1893 belonging to John Clark Forrest. In 1902, Mr. William Nelson of 190 Great Eastern Road, Glasgow bought the field from David Hastie, whom by then had only recently bought Stonefield Farm.

The name 'Annfield' is interesting and the source of the name was exclusively discovered whilst researching this book. David Hastie's son Peter had married a woman named Ann, but this wasn't until much later in 1933, so couldn't have been how the field got its name. Next for investigation, other son John was looked at, but his wife was Margaret, and David Hastie's wife was Janet. There were no connections within the Hastie family to suggest a reference to "Ann". Next William Nelson the builder and owner of the property was looked at, but his wife was Margaret and again no Ann connected to the family. Deeper research took us back to 1866 at a time when John Clark Forrest owned the farm and in that year his wife Jane Logan died, aged 29 on 9th June. She died at home in Allanton Farm, Hamilton from being weak at childbirth combined with scarlet fever. Her surviving child, a daughter for John Clark Forrest, named Ann (or Annie) Logan Forrest, born a few days earlier on 5th June 1866. We have our connection and the writer proposes here that the vacant field, used for horses was called 'Annfield' after the daughter of the farm owner.

Figure 278 Birth Certificate of Annie - Logan Forrest 1866

When William Nelson started constructing his L-shaped stone tenement, there already was a "Nelson Place" in High Blantyre and so another fitting name would have been required. Naming his building after the land it sat on would have appeared logical, just as much as it does today and "Annfield Terrace" was built by 1903.

Figure 279 Former Annfield Terrace on the right, 1910 Photo looking east

It sat on the south side of Glasgow Road, directly across from older small single storey buildings on the north side (not the toll house as others have written, which was actually at the corner of Station Road). Annfield Terrace was rather remarkable in appearance by comparison to more traditional 2 storey tenements for it had bay windows on both lower and upper floors, meaning parts of the building protruded along the frontage of Glasgow Road.

The upper storey was accessed by 5 sets of steps at the rear of the property. Access to the rear yard was via a small entrance at Victoria Street next to Hastie's Farm and also through a pend close on the Glasgow Road side. The field at the back was sloping, so a retaining wall separated the field from the yard. The building was stepped slightly as it rose up an elevation at Victoria Street, but sat in a dip on badly drained land at Glasgow Road, sitting away from the start of the Toll Brae further westwards.

These were primarily homes for miners to rent. When it was completed some miners from Craighead Rows and others from nearby Rosendale moved home to the 25 new homes at Annfield Terrace, 12 of which were on the Victoria Street side.

Homes were more spacious than miners' raws and likely desirable due to their proximity to the school and more rural, un-built setting removed from the shadow of any pit bing. Only one shop existed in the building at any one time, which was located on the corner with a unique, oblique entrance door, across from Stonefield Parish School.

William Nelson

William Nelson was a horse dealer from Glasgow. He never lived in Blantyre and his addresses at Great Eastern Road, then later at Gallowgate would suggest he was a wealthy man. Being in the equestrian industry is of no surprise and he would have likely been well known to the Hastie family, themselves renowned for breeding horses of a first class pedigree. Indeed the whole acquisition of the land, may even have been around some expansive business venture between Nelson and Hastie. Being absent, William Nelson entrusted the factoring of his new rented homes to William Wilson, of Hyde Park at High Blantyre. William Nelson would own Annfield Terrace for just over 2 decades.

Tenants and the shop

Having only 1 shop makes this building much easier to explore. Throughout the life of the building, it always had 25 homes and 1 shop. The shop had address 207 Glasgow Road and also 2 Victoria Street. There was 1 house at 209, 211, 215, 217, 219, 221 and 223 Glasgow Road and 6 homes at 213 located on the upper level. There were also 4 homes at 4 Victoria Street, 1 home at each of 6, 8 and 10 Victoria Street and 5 homes at 12 Victoria Street next to the farm.

According to the 1905 valuation roll, the initial tenants were Mrs Martha Rankine, a grocer in the corner shop at 207 Glasgow Road. The other tenants were all rented residents namely George Stein, Joseph Moore, Robert Mackie, Adam Stewart, Hugh Nimmo, Gavin Watson, William Carberry, John Batters, James Crawford, James Kirkwood, Daniel Broadley, William Morris, James Reid, John Walker, Cecila Harkins (w), James Gilchrist, William Mathieson, Richard Price, Charles Russell, Michael McCue, Alexander Smith, John McKay, David Reid and Malcom Mitchell. 1 house was empty. Even allowing an average of 4 people per household, there were well over 100 people living at Annfield Terrace.

Figure 280 Annfield Terrace in 1936 after adjacent tramlanes removed

Rankine's licensed corner Grocer shop existed at this location for a long time. From the buildings construction in 1903 until beyond WW2 years, passing from Martha Rankine to Thomas Rankine at the end of WW1. It is safe to say generations of Rankine's worked there and in 1925 they were paying a rent of £38 per annum. Around this time Alexander Young Billposters were hiring gable space at the west end of the building.

Gallantry, Bravery and an Accident

In October 1917, another D.C.M. (Distinguished Conduct Medal) came to Blantyre, the fortunate recipient being Cov. Sergt Major James Fox, whose father, Mr. Frank Fox, resided at Annfield Terrace. The gallant Sergt. Major joined the 'Gordons' at the end of August 1914, and was sent to France in July 1915, and had been twice severely wounded, ending up in 1917 in hospital in England, recovering wounds sustained on 22nd August 1916. The D.C.M. was awarded for bravery in the field on the day he was wounded. Sergt. Major Cox was also the proud possessor of the French Medal Militaire, this honour having been awarded to him in May 1916.

Sergt. Major Cox at that time was 26 years of age, was married and his young wife lived in Cambuslang. Prior to joining the colours, he worked as a minor in Dechmont Colliery, and was an active member in Masonic circles and belonged to Lodge "Livingstone," No. 599, Blantyre.

In 1923, Peter French, residing at Annfield Terrace was visiting Motherwell dog racing grounds, but met with a serious accident. On stepping off a tram car, his dog escaped from the leash, and ran across the tram lines. French, in his endeavour to recover the animal, failed to observe the approach of a tram car, which knocked him down, dragging his for some distance. His friends ran to his assistance, and found that he was unconscious. He was conveyed in a motor car to the County Hospital at Motherwell, and his condition was regarded as serious. It is thought though that he recovered. A storm in August 1924 collapsed the chimneys at Annfield Terrace.

Latter Years

Between 1925 and 1930, William Nelson passed away and in 1930 the property was owned by his widow, Margaret Nelson until the early 1930's before passing to James Todd, an oil merchant. During the 1950's the shop became Gibson's Grocery then later a Sweet Shop, which must have thrived being sited so close to the school gates, perhaps not so much when the school became the employment exchange in the late 50's.

Blantyre Project Social Media:

Patrick Donnelly: "I can't ever remember these buildings being boarded up. One minute they were lived in, next minute you drove by they were down."

With so many modern quality homes built nearby to the south at the Burnbrae housing estate in the late 1960's and rumoured subsidence in the building, Annfield Terrace at Victoria Street was demolished around 1970, the part at Glasgow Road shortly after. By 1972, the site was entirely cleared and Annfield Terrace had once again become just a field, which was subsequently re-graded for use by the Blantyre market.

By Paul D Veverka

Blantyre Market

Way back in 1599, the weekly Blantyre market was fixed to take place on a Thursday and an annual fete was to be granted on 14th October "for buying and selling of flesh, fish, oxen, sheep, meal, peas, corn, barley, linen and woolen cloth skins and all other goods, victual and merchandise." This would serve Blantyre's 500 population and no doubt attract others from nearby villages.

In the 20th Century, Tuesday markets were held at ground in front of Logan Street and also from 1972 on the vacant, sloping ground in front of Hastie's Farm, where former 'Annfield Terrace' was once located, following the removal of the rear yard retaining walls and subsequent re-landscaping over the field.

In early November 1978, the council announced they were closing the market much to the dismay of traders and residents. The Hastie's Farm 1970's market was run by an English based company called "Spook Erections" and their market would open in Blantyre every Tuesday. It had a maximum capacity of 50 stalls and was a popular, lively and thriving place to do business. Traders of dozens of different types took part selling hot and cold food, clothing, vinyl records, music instruments, wool, sweets of all sorts, home made craftwork and promoting their goods and services. It was a place where you could also buy second hand goods, get your ears pierced, your hair styled, make up done, buy latest fashions and an excellent place for a good old 'chinwag' with traders, neighbours and friends.

Figure 281 Removal Retaining walls from 'Annfield' for the market early 1970's

Indeed, the market was doing so well and with dozens of people lined up, asking to be involved in outdoor trading that in 1978 Spook Erections applied to DOUBLE the market size to 100 stalls planning to use all the space in front of Hastie's farm right down to Glasgow Road.

Hamilton District Council turned down the application on the basis that nowhere nearby offered good parking for the market, something incredulous to people given Glasgow Road at the time, had so many vacant plots. The decision was taken by Councillors who visited the site and had already decided amongst themselves that an extended market would not be a good thing for Blantyre as plans were already underway to create a modern shopping centre. It was believed open air trading was a thing of the past and relied upon weather for successful trading. Hastie's Farm Market closed for good in March 1979 upon expiry of the final issued trading license.

Spook Erections who applied annually to renew market licenses, were not best pleased. From their English offices, in 1979, together with petitions from Blantyre people, they collectively voiced their protests to the Council and the market was moved briefly to space near Glasgow Road, (later Devlin Grove.)

Contemporary Markets

In the 20th Century, markets tend to be confined now to fetes, events and gala days. In 2012, the Blantyre Community Committee organised a successful Christmas market, one of the largest in Lanarkshire, which has become an annual event, attracting around 70 stalls each year, the largest Blantyre certainly has ever seen.

Figure 282 Blantyre Markets are back pictured 2013

Festive and Summer markets continue to this day although success is still very much dependent upon weather. The writer of this book is proud to be part of the little committee who brought sizeable markets back to Blantyre and in 2017 was also responsible for setting up "Blantyre Market" online on social media, allowing local craftspeople and those offering goods and services the ability to trade to large audiences at no advertising cost.

Pictured in 2013 is the festive Blantyre market, with a grass area behind it, across the road where the old Hastie's Market once was. Although infrequent, the market is well attended, the latest on Sunday 26th November 2017.

By Paul D Veverka

Victoria House Care Home

Figure 283 Victoria House Care Home in 2016

Today, situated on the corner of Victoria Street and Glasgow Road, on the former site of Hastie's Farm, Annfield Terrace and Blantyre market is the modern Victoria House Care Home.

Whilst this building has an entrance and address at 16 Victoria Street, its large, impressive frontage facing out on to Glasgow Road makes it hard to ignore in this book and deserving of being touched upon here.

Owned by private family run company 'RAM 217 Ltd', the care home was built in 1996 and has 50 rooms offering care and nursing services for the elderly and disabled. Each room has en-suite facilities and living spaces are a variety of sizes. Costs are around £500-£600 per week and residents are permitted their own furniture and pets by arrangement. The care home offers ground floor accommodation and a nice garden with good wheelchair access. Maria Guarino is the person in charge and Laura McFadyen is the current manager.

The purpose brick and block built complex also had 3 generous sized lounges, a laundry and even a hair salon! All staff are carefully selected for skill, motivation and their enthusiasm. Victoria House has its own mini-bus to allow the Residents to enjoy outings around Glasgow, Edinburgh, Stirling, Loch Lomond and all the local places of interest. Outings to the adjacent Little Tea Room are frequent to the delight of all residents.

Stonefield Burn

When the 59 acres of land was up for sale in Stonefield in 1851, including the farm steading and fields where the park is today, its starting price of £2,000 ended up at £2,750 due to keen competition. The buyers being the Forrest family. They may not have realized the extent of some of the issues on the land however, for much of the fields which would later become the public park, would never be built upon, poorly drained and with a burn running right through the middle.

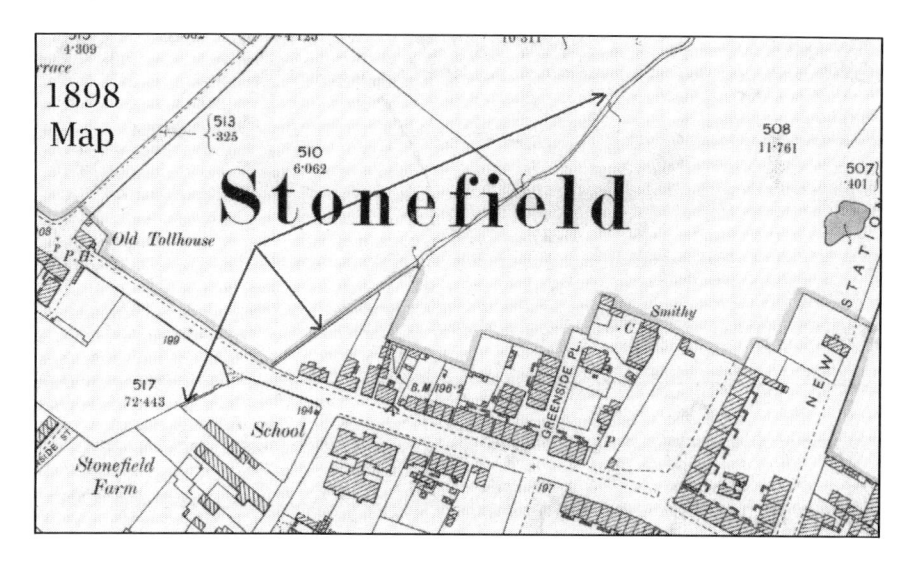

Figure 284 Stonefield Map of 1898 showing Burn crossing the fields

The burn rose far to the south off Stonefield Road, near where the Bowling club is today and ran north eastwards over fields, even determining where Dixon's Rows was built. It ran near Stonefield Farm and down to Glasgow Road, long before any tenements crossing, under the road at a low dip slightly west of where Annfield Terrace would later be built. No building would ever be built on that low dip just before the Toll Brae rose, not even to this day. North of Glasgow Road, the burn crossed the field, under the railway and to the Clyde. It may have had the nickname, "Christie's Burn" after John Christie in the 1865 Valuation roll as nearby landowner and weaver's agent.

In November 1962, to relieve flooding at Stonefield Road, Glasgow Road and Stonefield Public Park, a large outfall sewer was completed cross crossing through Blantyre. The sewer was dual pipeline and was of sufficient capacity to permit the capture of both sewage and stormwater from all the nearby housing estates at Stonefield Road and the surrounding district, ending up going through the Public Park and out towards the Clyde.

By Paul D Veverka

1930's Council Houses

Figure 285 Council Homes on Glasgow Road photographed in 2016

During the mid 1930's, the County Council throughout Lanarkshire was on a huge drive to clear old, condemned or poor quality slums from towns and villages. Blantyre saw hundreds of homes demolished in the early to mid 1930's no longer fit for purpose. These included homes at the Village, Springwells and nearby to Glasgow Road, the northern streets of Dixon's Raws. Whole streets at Stonefield were demolished to the ground including Carfin Street, Govan Street, Miller Street and Burnside Street. Of course this created a huge demand for new housing and the council took the opportunity to ensure homes were well built, spacious and with indoor toilets.

When Messrs Andrew Wright & Sons commenced construction of the new council homes 1935, the council already had a list of people who would accommodate them. The houses were ready in Springtime 1936, the first tenants moving in then, given addresses 223a, 223b and 223c Glasgow Rd.

Constructed in three large double storey blocks, homes were built of brick with slate roofs. The houses are stepped and terraced with front doors facing out to the A724 (Glasgow Road) offering access to each of 24 properties. They are constructed well and have accommodated hundreds of families, including generations of the same for over 80 years. None of these families ever saw trams going by their windows, for trams had ceased running by the time these homes were constructed. These are homes for "a modern age."

Toll Brae

From the start of the Council houses, directly opposite the public park entrance was the lower end of the "Toll Brae". This was a local name from the 19th Century for a short part of Glasgow Road for about hundred yards before the old Blantyre Cotton Works Toll Point (not to be confused with Monteith's Cotton mills). The toll building was not at the park entrance, but formerly sat at the corner of what would become Station Road. It would tax horses and carts upon passing that building, a prime spot for tax collection given the populated centre of Blantyre Works Village to the north.

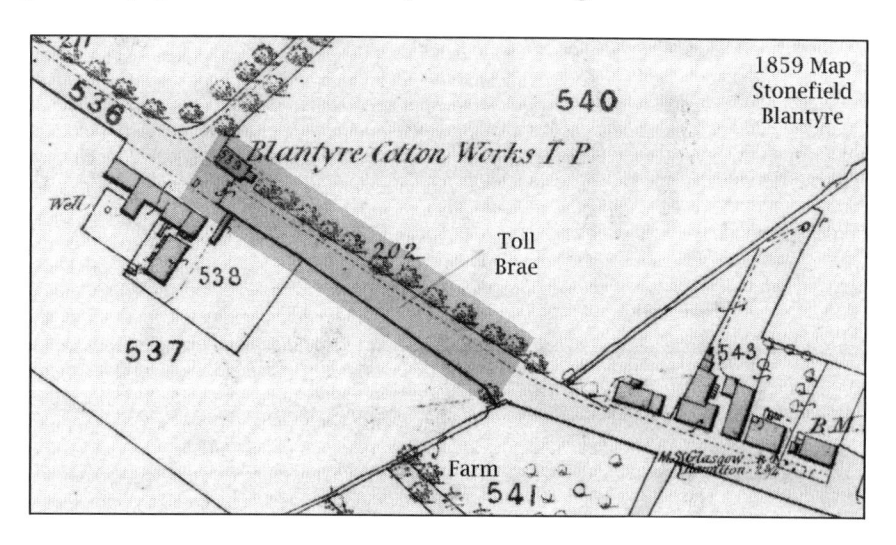

Figure 286 The Toll Brae highlighted on 1859 Stonefield Map

The collection of tolls was made illegal shortly after this map was surveyed in 1859, by local surveyor N Fleming. In the mid 1800's the toll collector was Blantyre man, Stephen Hunter. Rising on an incline the further west you went, this part of the road would later cause trams to slightly decelerate as the cars progressed up the hill. The "Toll Brae" name is now largely forgotten, a throwback to old generations and seems likely to disappear from memory.

Blantyre Project Social Media:

Steven Dolan: "I read online (at the old Blantyre's Ain site) that Clydesdale horses pulled carts up this hill? My great, grandfather said it was actually horses of all types and not dedicated for the toll house. Beasts were owned by local merchants all over Blantyre and not stabled for the toll house at John Street. As often happens on that old website, somebody has assumed and got it wrong."

Blantyre Project Social Media:

Thomas Dillon: "If you look real close on that 1859 map, you can see a feature on the Glasgow Road outside the Toll House. I think this was a horse trough, or somewhere to tie them, whilst taxes were collected and business was done. It makes sense that horses could rest in this area. There looks to be a paddock and small building across from the toll house which could be a stable"

CHAPTER 13
GLASGOW ROAD SOUTH
PRIORY ST TO STONEFIELD RD

Origins of Priory Street

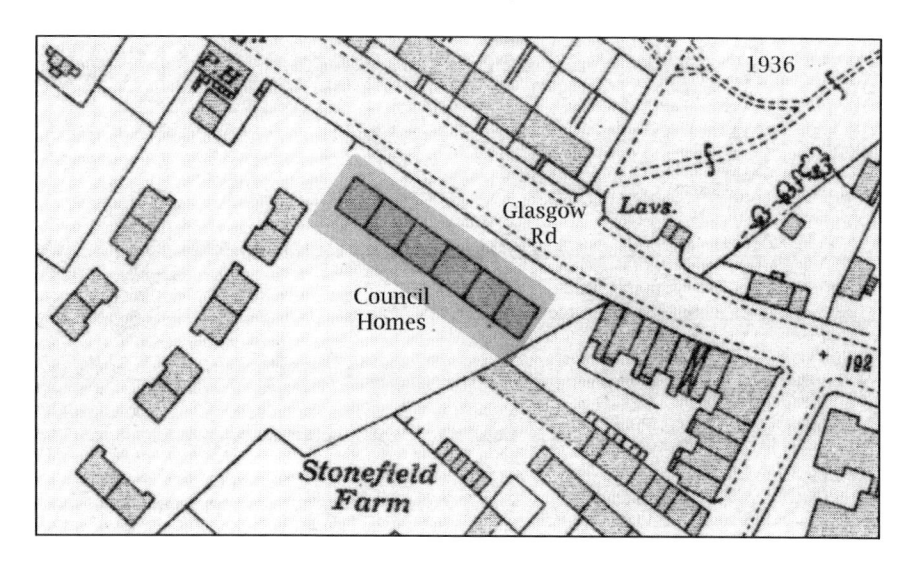

Figure 287 Council Homes & no Priory Street shown on 1936 Map of Blantyre

Priory Street dates from 1936 and runs in a northeast to southwest position linking Glasgow Road to Calder Street. At its junction with Glasgow Road, nearby stands the Stonefield Tavern. With the slum clearance of the mid 1930's demolishing many of the most northerly homes of Dixon's Rows, a County Council programme of 92 brand new homes was started on a site known as the 'Calder Street site.'

Delayed by adverse weather in January 1936, twenty of the homes had been built by that spring, along Glasgow Road and up what would become Priory Street towards the next proposed site at Calder Street. The 1936 map remarkably shows the houses built, empty with no Priory Street yet built until later that year.

The houses are made of brick, roughcast with slated roofs. They are double storey of three, four and five apartments and all them still stand today. At the time of construction, part of the ground was taken over from William Dixon & Co by the County Council who intended building the remaining 72 homes on the rest of the nearby Calder Street site.

The Priory Street council homes were built by local builders, Messrs Andrew Wright and Sons, who also had contracts to build 176 homes at Fallside in Uddingston. Priory Street named after Blantyre's most ancient ruin, once connected Calder Street to Glasgow Road, but is now a cul de sac, with access to Glasgow Road, now prohibited to vehicles. Postal addresses are odd on the east and evenly numbers on the west.

People may remember popular families like the Slaters at 1 Priory Street, the McGurks at number 3 or the Bevridges at number 11.

This treasured family photo was kindly shared by Duncan Slater and was taken outside 1 Priory Street

Figure 288 Slater Family at 1 Priory St in 1938

in 1938. In the photo is Duncan's mother with her children. Duncan is actually the baby and Sadie, his elder sister. Generations of the same family have lived at Priory Street. It was a busy junction on Glasgow Road during the mid to late 20th Century. Several popular opposing shops and the proximity to the pub and cinema made it a regular place to park.

A large bus stop and layby now blocks off the street at Glasgow Road, next to the Stonefield Tavern. In 1967 as political figures vowed for Blantyre votes, Mrs. Winnifred (Winnie) Ewing of Blantyre SNP campaigned at the corner of Priory Street, and as these wonderful photos show, youth listened!

Figure 289 Mrs Winnie Ewing (Blantyre SNP) campaigning on 1st November 1967

Winifred Margaret Ewing (b1929) is a Scottish nationalist, lawyer and prominent Scottish National Party (SNP) politician who was a Member of Parliament (Hamilton 1967–70; Moray and Nairn 74–79), Member of the European Parliament (Highlands and Islands 1975–1999) and Member of the Scottish Parliament (Highlands and Islands 1999–2003). Now 88, her by-election victory in 1967 was significant in Scottish political history and began a surge of support for the SNP. She was SNP President from 1987 to 2005.

By Paul D Veverka

Figure 290 Winnie campaigns for support at Priory Street corner 1967, near the Tavern

Blantyre Project Social Media:

Michael McDonagh: "Regarding Winnie, BBC Alba ran a fascinating programme about her a few years back. It was about the successful election she had and the sheer panic it caused in Westminster. I think it was Tony Benn who said Westminster set up a special committee to see if they could pay back what they owed Scotland for its oil if the SNP got into full power. Interestingly, Winnie in that programme said everybody treated her with respect except some members of the Labour Party."

Andy Callaghan: "My older brother Gerry (24 years old at the time) voted for Winnie. It caused a rift in our house. My parents, both long term labour supporters were scandalized. Even worse, my Grandpa, a lifelong supporter of Communism, threatened to 'cut the arse off him!'

Thomas Barrett: "Alex Anderson is top left in one of these pictures and the late Willie Quinn is beside Winnie."

Helen Grieve: "The wee girl beside the railing is Gina Hutchison."

Patrick Donnelly: "Winnie campaigned in Blantyre a few times. Engaging with youth, she knew that it would be difficult to turn older longterm Labour voters. Actually, when you look at that now, SNP now also adopt that campaign method, as seen in 2014, a driver in the movement for Scottish independence."

Wooden Office, Yard & Field

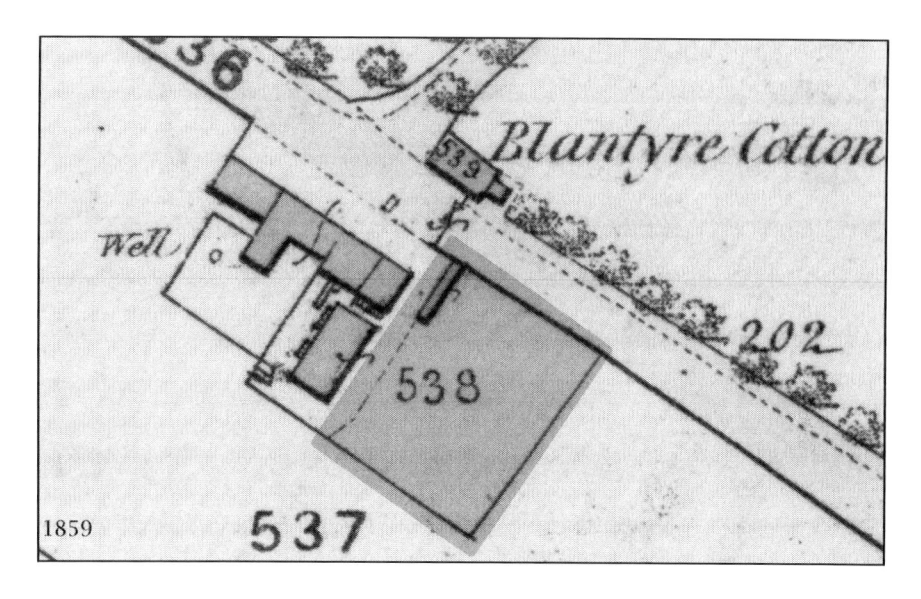

Figure 291 Wooden Shed and Field on 1859 Map

The suggestion that there was a stable or small field opposite the Toll House is an interesting one and needed further investigation. At a time before any elderly recollections and not previously written about, this book explores these old 19th Century group of buildings, which during the 1850's were the only buildings on the south side of Glasgow Road between Stonefield Farm and Stonefield Road!

The 1859 map does indeed show an enclosure, walled or fenced off, ideal as a paddock for horses at the opposite toll house. A small rectangular building, narrow on plan is shown where the entrance to Priory Street would eventually be, which could well have been for animals.

This was land belonging to John Coats of Blantyreferme. However, by 1898, the field and little building was rented to William Rinn of nearby Hall Street. It was an unimpressive building, made of wood and only had a rent of £1, 6 per annum in 1895. That year it was being used as a wooden office for Blantyre Miners Association. By 1905 it was being rented differently by Archibald Borland, a cattle dealer and it changed use again in 1915 when the building and field was used as an office with yard for William Jamieson, a slater of 38 George Street, Hamilton.

The wooden building was gone by 1920 and the last owners of the field prior to the Council acquiring it, was by Alexander P Smith of Hamilton.

Coats Buildings

Exclusively researched for the first time is the next building to the west. 'Coats Buildings' was a mid to late 19th Century census name for several buildings gathered in the same area on the south of Glasgow Road directly opposite the junction of Station Road.

The small populated centre highlighted is thought to be amongst the oldest known buildings along the whole of the Glasgow to Hamilton Road. They comprised of 8 tenement homes (at the corner of what would become Priory Street), included the Stonefield Tavern building, an adjacent separate 2 storey house and adjoining shop to the west with later additions to the rear. When first built, they were the only buildings on Glasgow Road between Stonefield Farm and Stonefield Road, sitting in isolation in farmlands. Let's look at each in turn.

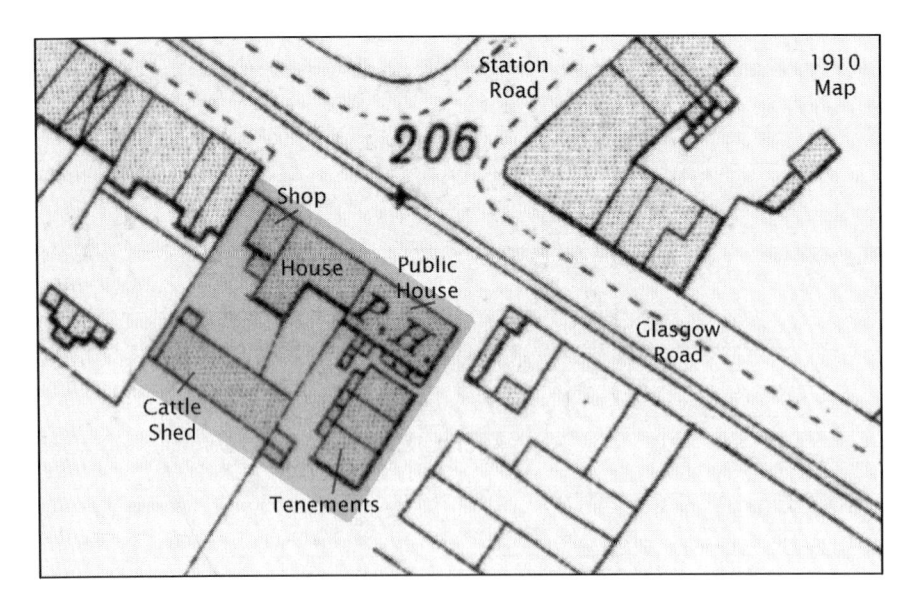

Figure 292 All these buildings were Coats Buildings. Shown on 1910 map

Coat's Tenement Houses

These former three 2 storey stone tenements were located behind the Stonefield Tavern building and had their eastern frontage on to a field (which later became Priory Street). Being so old and demolished for many decades, they're often forgotten about and largely unknown to people alive today. They occupied a north to south direction in 2 blocks, totaling 8 homes. Built between 1832 and 1859, they were constructed around the same time of the old tollhouse directly opposite. The upper storeys were accessed by steps to the rear and a small gap or lane separated the building from others.

The constructor is unknown but they may have originally been associated with nearby Woodhouse (near the top of Station Road) and used to service travellers at the toll stopping point. A firm history for these tenements however, can thankfully be traced from 1859 onwards, shown on the map of that era, with fields surrounding them in all directions.

John Coats

Born in 1834, John Coats was the son of local farming parents, John and Elizabeth Coats. John Junior grew up on Blantyreferme (much further to the northwest) on the banks of the River Clyde, often working on the family farm and indeed in the 1861 census was still living and working there, aged 27. Sometime between 1862 and 1864 not long after tolls were abolished, Mr. John Coats Snr acquired the tenements and the other properties beside them either through purchase or inheritance. It is from 1865 or so that we see these buildings collectively being referred to as "Coats Buildings", something that would continue for half a Century in official documentation.

Figure 293 Putting Former Coat's Tenements into modern perspective

The tenement houses were primarily let out to labourers and miners, workmen and their families. John Coats Jnr looked to have moved up to Stonefield with brother, Thomas in the early to mid 1860's looking after their father's interests but did not live in these tenements, opting instead to stay in a house to the west of the Stonefield Tavern building, also under his ownership.

In 1875, Coat's Buildings is noted as 10 houses (these 8 houses and 2 explored shortly). That year the tenants were Mr Boyd (a shoemaker), James Bruce, Mrs Henderson, John Virtue, Neil Greenhorn, Matthew Wilson, Robert Anderson and other unnamed tenants rents for less than £4 per year (perhaps several people temporarily in the one house). Thomas Coats died in 1877, his share, unsuccessfully advertised, then passed to John Coats Jnr, his brother in late 1877. 'Coat's Buildings' is in the 1881 Blantyre Street Index.

John Coat Jnr's ownership of these 8 homes continued until his death in 1890, aged 57 with his trustees continuing to look out for the Coats family interests until just before WW1. Prior to the outbreak of war, the 8 tenement homes were bought by Mrs. Jessie Rae, the proprietrix of the nearby Stonefield Tavern and she would own the tenements for the remainder of their time as homes. Merry & Cunningham (Coalmasters) had bought the mineral rights to dig below this area and by the time of the First World War, these tenements, (before Priory Street), had addresses 225 Glasgow Road, the same address as the nearby public house cellar.

DID YOU KNOW?

In the 1930's, the upper storey of Coat's Tenement Houses was removed, including part of the building to the south. We know the area was mined below so this may have been due to subsidence or perhaps simply due to the deteriorating age. However, a single ground storey was left, notably later that decade facing out on to Priory Street. Sometime after 1950, it was used as a store for the public house.

Figure 294 Aerial Photo lower part of Coat's Tenement in 1950 beside the Tavern

That single storey, once part of Coats Tenement houses remains today and was recently renovated by Nicola's Hair Salon in 2017, punching through new doors and windows to create her modern business from that excellent, busy location.

Nicola's Hair & Beauty Salon

Local lady, Nicola Gordon had a busy springtime during 2017 and as a result, there's a new business in town. Her unisex hair and beauty salon opened its doors for business on Friday 23rd June at 6 Priory Street, G72 0AY in the lower remaining floor of Coat's tenements. (which prior to the 1930s had address 225 Glasgow Road). The small property behind the Stonefield Tavern underwent a complete renovation, most notably with a new entrance and window installed near the junction of Glasgow Road.

When writing this book, Nicola commented upon opening, "I'm excited to open up a new salon in a great location in Blantyre. All the locals have been so friendly and helpful. Can't wait to see what the future holds, thanks so much x". This is a busy, popular location and it's fantastic to see these storage premises suddenly become a visible, viable, public business and being put to proper use again. Wishing Nicola and staff all the very best for the future.

Stonefield Tavern

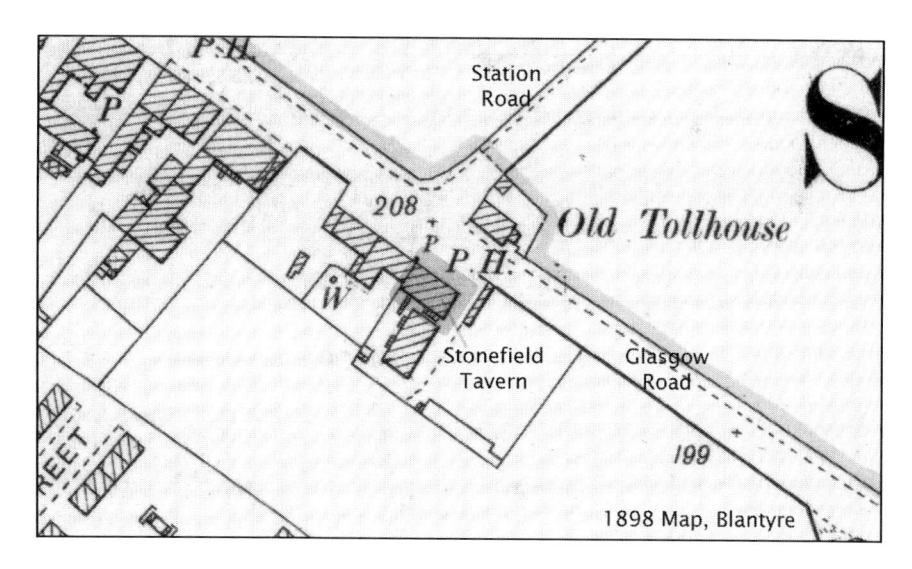

Figure 295 Stonefield Tavern on 1898 Map Low Blantyre

The Stonefield Tavern is one of Blantyre's best known pubs. Situated in a prime location on the south side of Glasgow Road, directly opposite the junction of Station Road, it has good frontage opening directly out on to the pavement and remains popular to this day. It may surprise you however, to learn that as an official 'public house', its late Victorian roots are relatively 'recent', from a similar era to the likes of the Westend Bar, Blakely's Pub and

Auchinraith Vaults, although of course nowhere near as old as the early Georgian era Blantyre pubs that still exist like the Hoolets or Village Bar. As a property with a slightly different use though, we can go back before Victorian times.

Figure 296 Stonefield Tavern on Glasgow Road in late November 2009

The building is noted on Forests 1816 map and was likely constructed around that time as part of the gathering of buildings around the old tollhouse, purposely built and sited to service passing travellers. Perhaps used first as an inn or place to rest. The proximity to a small paddock field made the building an ideal changing house. (A changing house was a place to rest, to feed and change horses, a place for the traveller to stay overnight, get something to eat and drink). The changing house was tied to an adjacent 2 storey house and shop further to the west and following 1832, also to 8 tenement homes immediately to the south behind it.

Built of stone, the changing house was 2 storey with a slated roof. It had 3 upper windows and was entered from Glasgow Road. The upper storey was accessed via 2 sets of steps at the rear yard. The lack of any 'P.H' marking on the 1859 map is telling that it was not recognised as a public house yet at that time.

Between 1862 and 1864, Mr. John Coats of Blantyreferme, then in his late 20's started managing the changing house for his father, the 8 tenements behind it and the house and shop to the west of it. For near 30 years, the business became part of several buildings known as "Coats Buildings". John was a farmer's son but by 1875, he is noted as being a spirit dealer. His younger sister, Elizabeth Coats (b1837 Blantyreferme) ran the changing house and is noted in census of that decade as being a hotelier or innkeeper.

It appears at some point in the 1870's, the name "Stonefield Tavern" was established, (most likely in 1877 when John Coats Jnr fully acquired the building from his brother Thomas who had died) and we first see the building being recognised properly as a Public House, a place for the general public to wander in for ale. This coincides with several other pubs being constructed along Glasgow Road. The dates also coincide with the construction of nearby Dixon's Rows. The tavern was just a stone throw from those miner's 'raws'. As the hamlet of Stonefield expanded rapidly in the 1870's and 1880's, its likely many a weary miner called into the tavern for a pint. It had and still has a long association with Tennents Caledonian Brewery (Wellpark) in Glasgow.

In the 1881 census, at 47 years old John Coats is still a single man, noted as a spirit merchant living in the adjacent house. His business may have initially drastically suffered when so many miners from the adjacent streets behind the pub were killed in the Pit Explosion of 1877, something like all in Blantyre, he would have been sympathetic to. In 1885, beside the tavern was an empty shop owned also by John Coats. Blantyre's population was rising sharply and business at the Tavern would have been steady enough, although so many other pubs nearby was soon to have an impact.

Change in ownership

In 1890, John Coats died and with no children, his bankrupted estate in 1891 was subsequently nursed and repaired up until WW1 by his trustees. Following his death, Mr. Thomas Rae a spirit merchant of McGhie Street, Hamilton rented the tavern, which in 1895 he did for £36/year. Thomas also ran the 'Old House' in Rutherglen. Born in 1862 in East Kilbride, his father had owned the Torrance Hotel. After eventually selling this inheritance, Thomas bought the County Hotel in Cadzow Street, Hamilton. His business interests were consolidated in 1895, when as a partnership with Mr James Craig (his sister's husband) they took over J&A Yuill in Broomielaw, Glasgow. He was a successful man owning many homes in the surrounding District and shareholder of multiple businesses including Hamilton Aerated Water Company. Thomas kept Mastiff dogs at the tavern to assist security.

By 1905, his wife Jane Rae rented the Stonefield Tavern as landlady. She came from the Craig family (spirit merchants in Blantyre who owned the West End and newly built Old Original Bar). Jane was also a spirit dealer living at Hamilton and would have been delighted to catch a tram car each morning taking her directly from her home to the exact location at a tram stop outside the public house in Blantyre. This short commute would have seemed very modern in those times. Renting the pub from John Coats Trustees, she also was renting a store for the pub in the nearby Co-op buildings not far to the west. Employed in 1905, was barman Frederick Pirie who lived nearby at Coats Tenements. He later kept chickens and sold eggs as a WW1 sideline. Another barman, Malcolm Mitchell was from nearby Annfield Terrace.

Burglary at Stonefield Tavern

DID YOU KNOW ?

Just over 110 years ago, John Davidson, a miner living at adjacent Coats Tenements and Daniel McGuire, miner, of nearby Dixon's Rows were charged at Hamilton Sheriff Court with attempting to break into the Stonefield Tavern on Tuesday morning of the 6th August 1907. Evidence showed that the masonry of the window sill had been smashed with a causey-set, a stanchion torn away and glass broken. The accused were disturbed and ran away without entering the premises.

Sheriff Thomson sent each of the accused to prison for 60 days. This would have been highly embarrassing for the families of these young adults, living so close by to the scene of their crime.

Post WW1 Years

By 1915, postal addresses had been allocated to Glasgow Road and Stonefield Taverns' cellar was 225 Glasgow Road, with the Tavern known as 227-229 Glasgow Road, something still maintained today. By that year, the pub and 8 tenement houses behind it had been bought outright by the Rae family.

Mrs. Jessie Rae, a spirit dealer from Hamilton owned and managed the pub right up until WW2 one of the longest serving owners, far surpassing Thomas or Jane Rae. As proprietrix, she kept a watchful eye over her bar staff and ran a 'tight ship'. The pub was also known shortly after locally as Fred Rae's, under George Younger & Sons Ltd.

Figure 297 Tavern in 1910

Sometime in the 1960's, the upper storey was boarded up and used for storage. People may remember the large advertising billboard that adorned the gable end. In the second half of the 20th Century other owners and landlords included Teddy McGuiness in the 1960's, which gave the pub its familiar nickname "Teddies". During the 1970's May Maxwell was landlady, her parents Sammy and Maimie Maxwell managing the business before her. Other landlords and ladies included couple, Ivor and Josephine. Jim Queen was another owner and Katie Ferry managing. The Saloon Bar entrance was then on the Priory St side.

Recent Years

In post Millennium years, the Tavern was owned by 'Punch Taverns', but closed in 2007. In 2008, a Blantyre man teamed up with former Rangers and Scotland goalkeeper Andy Goram to buy the pub. James 'Stan' Gordon (44), has a strong connection with the Ibrox club, and intended to create a Rangers theme for the popular Glasgow Road hostelry, which he opened with a weekend of celebrations on 4th and 5th of October 2008. Stan enlisted the help of best friend John 'Bomber' Brown, the former Rangers player, and initially hoped to get other Rangers stars, such as Ally McCoist and Ian Durrant, involved.

Figure 298 Davy pulling pints at Stonefield Tavern 2016

Stan told reporters at the time, "John Brown is my best pal so through him I know most of the Rangers players, and got friendly with Andy Goram. Andy and his missus, and me and my girlfriend, regularly meet up, and we got talking about going in for something like this. I'm a Blantyre man and I was a regular at the Stonefield Tavern but it's been closed for about seven months, so we spoke to Punch Taverns and agreed a deal for the lease." Goram, a part-time coach with First Division club Clyde at that time, where Brown was manager, was expected to spend more time in the bar than Stan, who intended to continue in his offshore job.

Stan said: "Andy's part-time at Broadwood so he has more time than me, but he's also more experienced at running a bar. Even with that, we're going to get people round about us who know exactly what they're doing, and we'll appoint a bar manager. Our object is to make money from the bar but we're not looking for millions. We're hoping to get after-dinner nights going, with people like John Brown, and nights for ex-players. We want to make it a Rangers theme bar and get players to come down quite regularly, so that if people go to the Stonefield Tavern there's a good chance of meeting them. Everything's looking good at the moment."

The pub is currently managed by company "Teddies Two Ltd" and still has strong connections to Rangers even now in 2017 following a troublesome few years for the football club. Many regulars are loyal supporters. There are regular karaoke evenings, quiz nights, a darts team and charity evenings like race nights. Ex Rangers players visit often, especially on charity nights. The pub has a friendly, pleasant atmosphere and the days of brawls, seem to be long gone. Staff are polite and attentive. Despite the sign outside saying Stonefield Tavern, it is known primarily today for its former owner and Rangers nickname, 'Teddies'. The name spelling with "ies" rather than "y" as confirmed by the business social media website.

Blantyre Project Social Media:

Patrick Donnelly: "Mrs Rae renovated and extended the Tavern in 1906."

Janet Saunders: "The wee man pictured is my da. The best in the business!"

Betty Brown: "I was a cleaner back in the 1970's."

Margaret McLaughlin Russell: "I worked in Teddies in the late 1970's and 80's. It was a great pub. Never a trouble makers pub."

Anne Grogan: "My brother David Scott is in that pub so much, I'd swear he has shares in it!"

Anton Le Grandier: "My favourite memory by far is Eddie Conn, nursing a beer as his wife walked in and slammed his cold dinner right into his face!"

Coats House & Bake-house

Sometime between 1832 and 1859, a 2-storey house was constructed westwards and adjacent to the changing house (later Stonefield Tavern). L-shaped on plan, it was distinctive in its appearance from other early buildings at this location for the stonework was whitewashed and with no pavement outside it, painting would have been something required often due to the mire and dirt on the 19th Century Glasgow Road.

Of slightly lower height than the Stonefield Tavern, it was tied to the adjacent building and had a small shop to the west. To the rear was a yard with a well, fenced off from the surrounding expansive fields of Stonefield to the south.

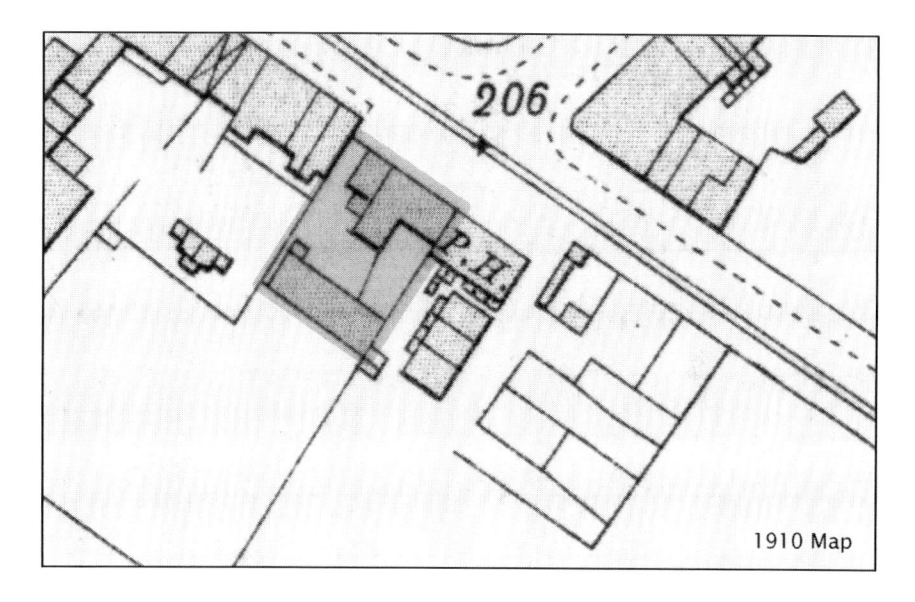

Figure 299 Coats Double Storey L shaped house & shop on 1910 map

Between 1862 and 1864 John Coats acquired the building and it is known his brother Thomas and sister Elizabeth Coats lived in this house along with him. The siblings, who grew up on Blantyreferme would be involved with the early formation of Stonefield Tavern as a proper public house and living at this location next door would have been ideal. Dixon's Rows would then be built behind the property, further back to the south.

Coat's House was occupied by John Coats in 1881 and that year he was only sharing with Archibald Boreland, a cattle dealer utilising a nearby field belonging to Coats. Boreland would live and work there for around 3 decades building a large, wooden cattle shed to the rear of the house. He was initially a carter and rented the house for £15 per year. The shed was there in 1910 but demolished by the 1920's.

In the 1870's Coat's shop was situated at Glasgow Road, directly opposite the track and junction that was to become Station Road.

Adjacent to his house, the shop that decade was occupied by Mr. M.C Young and used as a grocers. However, on 17th February 1882, John Coats advertised in the Glasgow Herald for a new tenant for the shop. This was responded to by the newly established Stonefield Independent Co-operative Society in 1884, who wished to run their first bake-house.

Figure 300 Co-op Bake-house opened in 1883

By 1885, a kiln for the Co-op bake-house was situated in the rear yard and the shop, formed a frontage for selling the Co-op bakery products to passers-by, one of the very first Co-op shops in Blantyre. This arrangement would continue only for a few years for the Co-op expanded rapidly and soon had a bakery and bake-house on their own land with no requirement to rent or use these premises.

Owner, John Coats died aged 57 on 28th September 1890 his affairs in a poor state. This little shop, would however, continue as a bake-house for others although the shop and bake-house was reduced in size to make way for the building of the large, tall Co-op premises further west. The little shop was left a ruin by the 1910's when Mrs. Jessie Rae took ownership of all of the former Coat's buildings, including the adjacent Tavern.

Prior to WW1, this created a property gap on Glasgow Road between Coats whitewashed house and the Co-op's 3 storey dedicated taller building to the west. The gap was a prime spot for billboards being erected, offering good advertising space and is seen in the following excellent photo.

Coats whitewashed House was completely demolished in the late 1920's, along with the ruinous shop, which had existing for 7 or 8 decades. The entire site between the Stonefield Tavern and the Co-op Building was cleared and leveled by 1936, perhaps as a general tidy up of the area upon the building of Priory Street nearby. This site would not be built upon again until the 1950's when the Co-op expanded by building their popular 'Emporium'.

Figure 301 Glasgow Road looking west. Coats Buildings on foreground left 1910

Co-op Emporium

After being vacant for over 2 decades, the space between Stonefield Tavern and the Co-op tall building was built upon again when the Blantyre Co-operative Society expanded their existing premises to the immediate west.

By 1954, the Co-op had acquired the vacant ground formerly the site of John Coats house and bake-house and their plan was to extend their Co-op building adjacent. It was to be a modern, brick and timber constructed building which would become known as the 'Co-op Emporium'. The modern facade incorporated 9 distinctive circular porthole type windows, a unique feature unlike anything in Blantyre. The upper storey had mainly glass windows, which in subsequent years would be boarded up.

When it opened in 1954, crowds of people flocked to see the new building and a small ceremony was conducted by Daniel Morrison, the manager of the nearby Co-op. The event coincided with the formal end of remaining rationed items and the timing close to a few other co-op shops becoming self service, or more like modern supermarkets.

In the following picture, Daniel addresses the crowd upon opening. Others have incorrectly suggested this was Gordon Jackson, the famous actor at the ceremony. It was definitely not, although he does have resemblance.

By Paul D Veverka

Figure 302 Construction Co-op Emporium 1954, viewed from Station Rd

Figure 303 Opening of Blantyre Co-op Emporium 1954

The photos show the pitched, timber roof trusses being constructed in 1954 on Glasgow Road, from the nearby vantage point of Station Road. Gordon Cook who kindly shared this photo added it may even have been on his first visit to David Livingstone Centre.

The Co-op Emporium was very much part of the series of Co-op Buildings in this location. It could also be accessed from the adjacent Co-op funeral parlour. It was to serve Blantyre well. During the 1960's and 1970's, it sold furniture, ornaments and haberdashery, ladies, men and children's clothing and was the place to go to get school uniforms. By the early 1970's the upstairs sold vinyl records, radios and radiograms. The address was 227 Glasgow Road, even although the Tavern next door is 225-229.

Upstairs also had a payment desk where people could pay for their hire purchase goods or spend their collected "divi". The idea of co-operative trading revolutionised retailing with the dividend, often known as "divi", and the "divi number" became a part of British life. Many Blantyre residents remember their divi number, some still using it for modern banking pin codes. The way in which co-operative retail societies run on behalf of their members sets them apart from their modern-day competitors. The dividend was and still is a financial reward to members based on each member's level of trade with the society. The distribution of profits on the basis of turnover rather than capital invested is a fundamental difference between a co-operative and most private sector enterprises. Co-op points cards currently today pay a 4% divided.

By the late 1970's, the Emporium like many of Glasgow Road's buildings was boarded up in 1980 and was still vacant in 1981, until shortly after in 1983 when the Clydesdale Bank moved in.

Blantyre Project Social Media:

Serge Mikkleson: "Did you know the bank's pitched timber trusses were such a small, shallow angle, they gave the appearance of looking like a flat roofed building. Modern photos illustrate this well, especially if taken from the ground by comparison to the steep pitches of Stonefield Tavern and the Co Buildings."

Drew Fisher: "I remember they sold records in the upstairs section. In the early 1960's, it was one of only 2 places in Blantyre that sold records, the other being McClenaghans near the bottom of Craig Street."

John McCourt: "I worked there driving the Furniture van and also in the Gents Department. Mr. MacMillan was the manager along with Davie Dickson. The Gents Dept Manager was Robert Clelland."

Clydesdale Bank

By 1981, the Emporium was lying vacant and derelict, awaiting another use. It attracted the interest of the Clydesdale Bank in the early 1980's, who were to move from their location further westwards to this more modern building in 1983. For nearly 4 decades, the Clydesdale Bank became a well-known feature in Blantyre at this location directly across from Glasgow Road.

Figure 304 Derelict Emporium in 1981 before Clydesdale Bank moved in

The Clydesdale Bank is known to have been in Blantyre since 1879. By

1909, it was one of two banks in Blantyre. In 1930, according to the valuation roll, the Commercial & Clydesdale Bank was leasing the lower floor of 301 Main Street within the Gardiner Place building at High Blantyre. It was renting from John Allan McKillop. During the 1950's and 1960s, if a woman worker got pregnant, she had to leave the banks employment for good. At that time also, it was a branch of the British Linen Bank, changing to the Clydesdale Bank as we know it today around 1969/70.

In 1986, Ernest Barrie was convicted for armed robbery at Blantyre's Clydesdale Bank. The bank was robbed again by others around the Millennium.

Rather than dwell on that, let's note importantly that it was a good source of employment for many people in the local area over the years and a vital service for all customers. In the latter 20th Century, it was largely a choice between Clydesdale and RBOS for banking in the town.

Figure 305 Clydesdale Bank in 2015, situated in the former Emporium building

On Wednesday 13th April 2016, Clydesdale Bank issued a statement advising that their Blantyre branch would close between July and September 2016, along with 8 other Scottish branches, stating it was necessary due to changes in the way people bank and the popularity of online banking. Needless to say many customers were angry and disappointed. It meant having to bank elsewhere or being forced to learn how to bank online.

The bank actually closed for the last time on Glasgow Road on Tuesday 23rd August 2016, the signs removed and fittings stripped out on Wednesday 24th and Thursday 25th August 2016, immediately after. It sat derelict for a few months before an announcement that Glen Travel were to relocate from Clydeview Shopping Centre.

DID YOU KNOW? Throughout all of 2017, Glen Travel have been renovating the former Co-op Emporium / Clydesdale Bank. The large vaults inside have been removed, the ATM is away and the travel agents will soon have impressive frontage on to Glasgow Road in a prime advertising spot. The shop opened their new premises in the former bank building on Monday 30th October 2017, putting up their brand new prominent sign on 12th Nov.

> Blantyre Project Social Media:
>
> **Henry Hambley:** "I have my first bank account with the Clydesdale Bank. I think the manager was Mr. MacAusland."
>
> **Serge Mikkelsen:** "After the High Blantyre Pit Disaster Memorial was built in 1977, there was some money leftover, and a record of it was publically put on display in the Clydesdale Bank for all to see. The remaining money was put in trust to look after it in future years, I think governed by the minister John Silcox"

Alarming Break ins

An alarming incident happened on 22nd and 23rd September 1928 in a nearby shop. A theft occurred at a sweet shop belonging to Messrs Maxwell. However, this was no theft of penny caramels. The young lady in charge, working on that weekend was locking up in the early evening. She locked the glass door and was pulling down the iron grilles, when from behind some youths attacked her in Glasgow Road, snatching her handbag from her.

Police later determined that the thieves likely expected the shop's takings to be in the bag but would have been bitterly disappointed to find only the lady's 1 shilling bus fare to get her back home to Glasgow where she lived.

Elsewhere that weekend the Boot Department of Blantyre Independent Co-op was broken into. Entrance was gained by breaking a pane of glass and pushing back the snib on the back window, which was heavily protected by iron stanchions. The burglar raised the bottom half with a crowbar. 20 pairs of boots which had been hanging in the shop window were stolen.

Stonefield Independent Co-op Buildings

To the immediate west and joined to the Co-op Emporium were 2 separate Co-op buildings. A 3 storey tall tenement and a 2 storey tenement further west, the original Co-op older building. Lets look at each in order of their addresses, starting at 235-239 Glasgow Road, the 3 storey tenement.

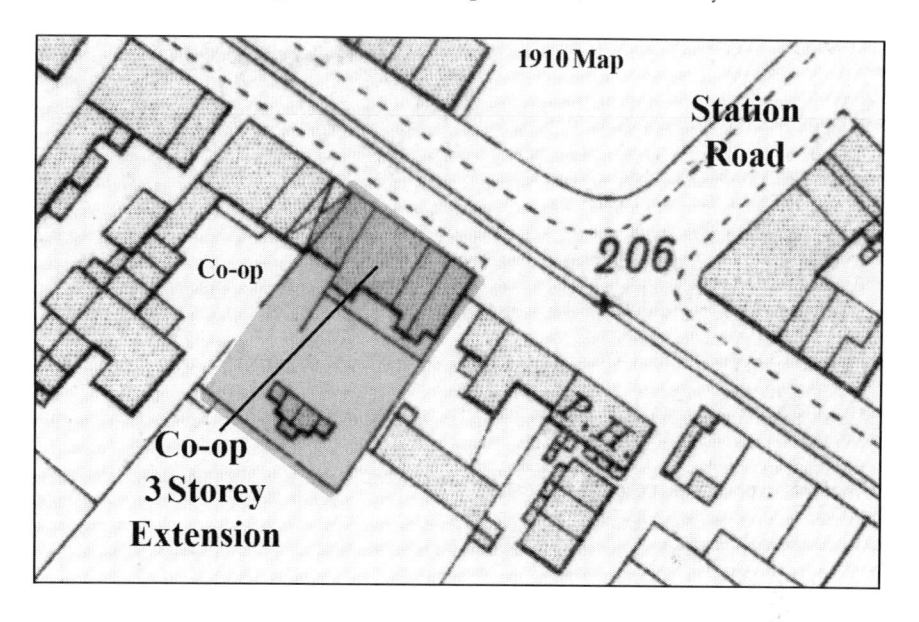

Figure 306 Stonefield Independent Co-op Buildings on 1910 Map

These buildings were owned by the Stonefield Independent Co-operative Society, a separate company and different from the Blantyre Co-operative Society who owned other Co-op buildings in Blantyre. The two should not be confused, especially looking at these early beginnings, as is often the case.

The Stonefield Independent Co-operative Society (SICS) was formed in 1884 when they first opened their bake-house nearby. It served as an alternative (but similar) to the larger Blantyre Co-operative Society, who had opened a year before them at Station Road.

In 1891, the SICS built their own 2 storey premises to the west of this location, which we'll explore shortly. Their success meant expansion was required and in 1907, the SICS acquired land to build a larger, more impressive building facing out on to Glasgow Road not far from the junction of Station Road. Constructed of stone with slate roofs, the building was well built and remains standing today, shops on the lower ground floor, homes above. In later years the gable would be reinforced in brick.

Remember, the 3 storey building was an 'expansion' of the original adjoining to the west. The building is symmetrical and upper homes have bay windows. Large stone chimneys still stand, unusual for remaining Glasgow Road tenements. On the upper storey, the crest of the Stonefield Independent Co-op and dating stone can be seen near the top gutter.

Figure 307 The 3 Storey Co-op Expansion, pictured In 2015

The original shops were the Co-op Bread shop and Drapery at 233 Glasgow Road. These included an office, 2 homes above and a stable at the rear as shown on our 1910 map. Horses were used to pull several delivery carts, the vehicles themselves stored in the outbuildings at the back of the original co-op next door.

235 Glasgow Road had 4 houses with ground at the back and at 237, a further 5 houses. The Co-op would advertise often for staff and workers and in 1916, a Co-op baker was getting paid 44 shillings with a 1 shilling bonus/wk. The configuration of these shops remained like this right through until post WW2 years although the stable had gone by 1930's as mechanized vehicles became the norm.

In 1925 the SICS acquired the Bethany Hall across the road on the north side at 266 Glasgow Road. This was to be their hall for dances and parties, but the trade depression of the 1920's and difficult trading conditions saw them sell it in 1931 when it became the unemployment exchange. Selling assets was a sign that things were not well and competition with the larger, more successful Blantyre Co-operative Society was having an effect.

Merger

By 1929, Thomas McCool was Secretary of the Stonefield Independent Co-operative Society and he had a few tough years ahead of him steering the business into trying to be more successful, to no avail.

After 48 years of operating, and much deliberation, on the evening of Saturday 30th April 1932, the Stonefield Independent Co-op Society ceased trading independently and merged with the larger Blantyre Co-operative Society. The properties and shops owned by SICS were valued at £11,000 and incredibly were taken over by the Blantyre Co-op for a mere £2,500, a bargain. Members of SICS were enrolled into the Blantyre Co-op automatically, their debts and orders taken on board, like for like.

SICS was most likely unable to compete with so many shops that Blantyre Co-op had and perhaps was a victim to private enterprise and growing commerce all over Blantyre as a whole. At the time of the merger, their membership was only 270 people, yet the Blantyre Co-op had over 3,000 customers. The merger however was ultimately successful and the Co-op would continue to dominate Blantyre's shops in the 2nd and 3rd quarters of the 20th Century, hugely extending the premises to the rear.

Later Years

Blantyre Co-operative Society continued to let the 11 homes in this block out to miners and their families. With Blantyre Co-op already had Central Number 1 premises to the east near Herbertson Street, following 1932, the buildings acquired at 233-239 Glasgow Road became known as "Blantyre Co-op Number Two".

Following 1972 when the Co-op was Nationally rebranded and integrated into SCWS Retail Group, the localized nature of Co-ops was somewhat diminished and parts of the building were let out to others.

233 Glasgow Road was retained as the Co-op Funeral Parlour, a place for arrangement funerals, which still exists today. For several years, the late Elaine Campbell McQuade was the manageress of the shop. 237 Glasgow Road became 'J Estees' Furniture then from 1987, Video Vision and 90's 'Clyde Star', which was a grocers, stationers and video shop. Around the Millennium the Post Office sited temporarily at Clydeview Shopping Centre, moved to the rear of the supermarket, now occupied by 'Londis' since 1994, still trading today. The last shop to the west, within the tall Co-op building became the Leeds Building Society, lawyers, Old Mill Barbers then Agnew's Café, still a popular shop today, especially amongst school children at lunchtimes.

By Paul D Veverka

Co-op Original Building

Adjacent to the 3 storey Stonefield Independent Co-op Society's (SICS) Building to the west is the older 2 storey premises. It still stands today. This was the Stonefield Independent Co-op's original fully owned premises.

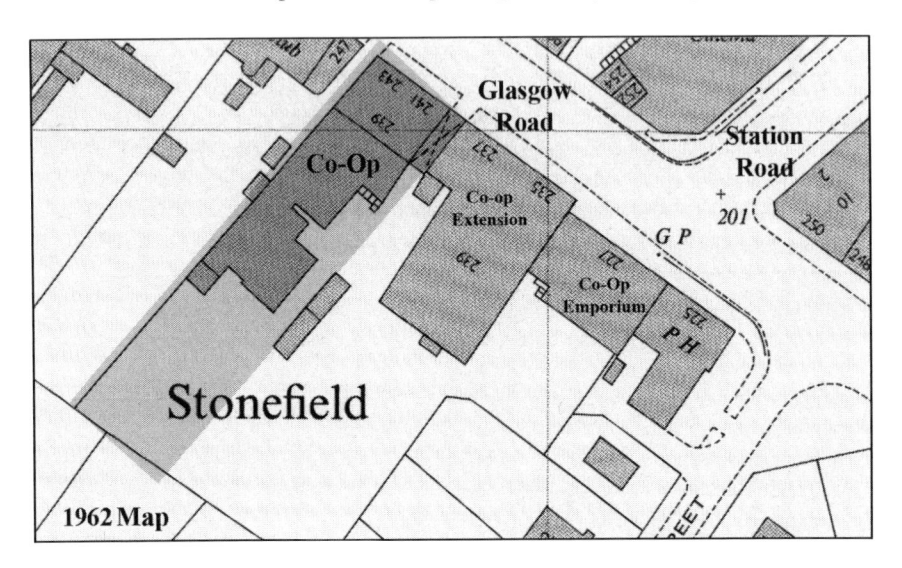

Figure 308 Original 2 Storey Stonefield Ind. Co-op Building on 1962 Map

Again, the beginnings of this building are associated with SICS and not Blantyre Co-operative Society. Constructed in 1891 from stone, the 2 storey building was built with a pend close, leading through to the back. This was a typical design detail of the era as it permitted buildings to later be built next to it, without closing off access. The Stonefield Independent Co-op had a large rear on a long, rectangular plot of land, with Dixon's Raws to the south. Dating is easy for this building as there is a huge "1891" carved into the masonry on the façade facing on to Glasgow Road, easily seen today. These premises would later be allocated postal addresses 239 - 243 Glasgow Road.

The SICS formed in 1884 at the nearby rented bake-house. Mr F McDade was instrumental is steering the Co-op in these early years and indeed in 1889, was presented with a gold watch for his achievements. Such wonderful gifts were reserved for deserving staff members. The actual watch is pictured, having been sold at auction in 2017 in England for a considerable sum.

Figure 309 McDade Watch

More notably was Thomas Carrigan, a salesmen for the Co-op from its humble beginnings and would go on to become the longest serving Co Manager for 33 years before retiring in 1927. Thomas lived in the new premises from 1891 and in his career would notably have to pilot the society through trade depression in the 1920s. His wife was mistress of Auchentibber RC School. In 1889, Thomas also received a gold watch, particularly for increasing numbers of customers.

Shops & Tenants

In 1895, it is noted that there were 2 shops, a bake-house and 4 houses. The original tenants were Patrick Quinn a labourer, David Kerr a justiceman and also Secretary of the SICS, James Canning a miner and aforementioned Thomas Carrigan. The 2 smaller homes were let for £6 a year, the 2 larger for £9. All homes were on the upper floor.

In 1905, nearby spirit merchant Jessie Rae of Stonefield Tavern was renting a small store at the back yard. The Stonefield Independent Co-op was taken over by Blantyre Co-operative Society in 1932. Both the 3 storey and 2 storey buildings they acquired are shown in this photo from 1979, courtesy of local man, James McGuire.

Figure 310 Blantyre Co-Op 2 - 3 storey & 2 storey looking east in 1979

241 Glasgow Road lower shop in this building next to the pend close, was the Co Drapery & Boot shop, but by 1915 had become the Co Butchers, where it would remain right up until near the Millennium, before becoming the current Peters Family Butchers.

243 Glasgow Road, the original Co Hardware and Grocery shop remained as such until the 1950's when it became self service, effectively turning into a small supermarket. How Blantyre families would marvel at being able to actually touch the goods! The shop in later years became MacKintosh Carpets & Furniture, which closed in September 2010. Today, located at the western end of the building, it is now the St Andrew's Hospice Charity Shop.

Figure 311 The Co-op Buildings in the 1990's

The old outbuildings were demolished at the back sometime in the 1950's and the Blantyre Co-op extensively extended the premises to the south. In 1967, several windows were often smashed in a spate of vandalism.

This wasn't the only renovation that took place. Along with several other buildings at this location in Glasgow Road, both on the south and north sides for the Millennium, shops were given similar makeovers, when dark green shop signs and white, black or silver embossed signage. The idea was to bring back some character and uniformity to the street, but within a couple of years, desire for own logos and signs, saw shopkeepers settle back into providing their own signage and putting their own stamp on their premises. As seen by the comments, the Co Buildings are fondly remembered by all.

J Estees Furniture Shop

Estees was a former furniture shop and convenience store located in the 3 storey expansion of the Co-op. During the 1980's, they occupied both shops where the funeral parlour and Londis/post office currently. You could walk from one part to the other at the middle. It had a hairdressers in the back of the shop. It sold pretty much all sorts of items for the house and notably had a large wicker chair in the window for several years during the early 1980's. It sold gifts, stationery and offered a photocopy service. Jim and Margaret Taylor were owners. Video Vision took over both shops after Estees moved out around 1987, then later split to the Co Funeral Parlour and Clyde Star.

Blantyre Project Social Media:

Matthew Neil: "I see Police car is a 3.0 litre Capri! The Allegro car in the picture is my ex wife's."

Stephen Crowe: "I was sure there was a shop called 'Carousel' there in the early 1980's too."

Caught Faking Cheques

In February 1932, American immigrant, William Reid had only been in Scotland for 4 weeks, when he was imprisoned for 1 year for faking cheques. Starting out his new life in the worst possible away his methods were cunning in obtaining £31 from 2 banks in Larkhall and Blantyre by means of faked documents and cheques. It took the canny staff at the Blantyre branch to catch him out. He first obtained a cheque from the bank by means of a faked document purporting to be the Secretary of a Friendly Society. He thereafter produced cheques to a total of £31 at various banks and stated he was entitled to the money for funeral services.

When he presented the cheque at the Glasgow Road bank in Blantyre, the agent asked Reid to get authentication. He left the bank and later a telephone message purporting to be from the manager the local nearby Co-operative Society's shop was received at the bank. The message was to the effect that everything was in order. The manager was then requested to pay the cheque and the bank would give payment the following day.

The man thereupon went to the bank and cashed the cheque. Later, it was found that the manager of the Co-op shop knew nothing about the telephone message and police were called.

Clydeview

'Clydeview' is the name of a former 3 storey tenement located at 245 to 251 Glasgow Road, of which only the ground floor remains today. It should not be confused by the shopping centre of the same name and of later build much further east.

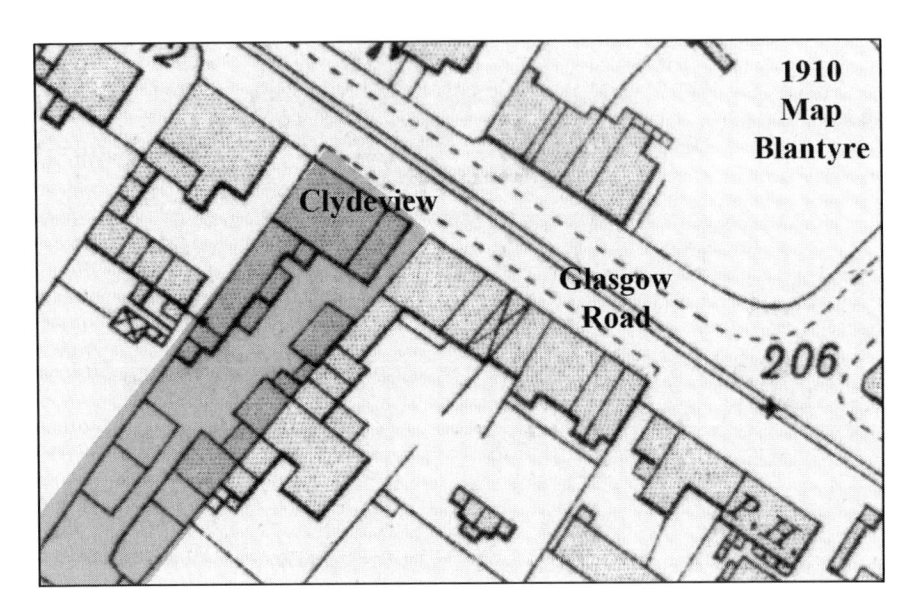

Figure 312 Clydeview located on Glasgow Road directly across from the Bethany Hall

The building has had other nicknames throughout the 20th Century including Cameron's Buildings, Blantyre Social Club, The Post Office and Knights of St Columba, businesses located on the lower floor at one time or other but the building has primarily been called on all official census, valuation and documentation, simply "Clydeview". It's had a complicated, interesting history of changing use, which we fully explore now.

'Clydeview' was built in 3 storeys in 1880. Constructed of stone, shops were on the lower storey with up to 6 homes on the above 2 storeys. Opening out on to Glasgow Road pavement, it was built on a slight, rising incline heading up to the west, and therefore the doorways were stepped.

The constructor and original owner was Mr. Duncan Cameron, a flesher and spirit merchant whom in 1879 had been living at Woodburn Place. The 1881 census has Duncan aged 25 living with wife Margaret at their new buildings, let out also to others born outwith Blantyre. On the lower floor were 3 shops and in 1885 these are confirmed as Cameron's Spirit Shop, Joseph Lister Barbers and the Independent Co-op shop. However, Cameron's

Buildings (as it was known in the 1881 Street Index was short lived under that ownership and by 1884 had been sold on.

New owner, Mr. Patrick Masterton, a spirit merchant (who did not live in Blantyre) is the likely source of the long standing name, "Clydeview" and likely responsible for not calling it Cameron's Buildings anymore after 1884. Born in 1841, Patrick lived in Paisley and would let out these buildings as businesses and homes for others. They appear to have been built around the time of the miner's riots in Low Blantyre.

However, much of the lower ground floor was kept aside for his own use and by the time the buildings were constructed in 1888, he was running his own Public House from the premises. The name of the pub is unknown but Masterton's Pub may have been called "Clydeview" the same as the whole of the building. With such a tall building and facing northwards, the upper floors may have indeed provided a nice view over to the Clyde Braes and beyond.

Figure 313 Location Line drawing putting Clydeview into context, & what remains

In November 1889, Patrick Masterton sought to renew his annual license at Hamilton Sherriff Court, a good indicator that he had been there at least a year. He is noted as being the Proprietor of the Public House. Clydeview also comprised of a small, narrow 2 storey part to the building on its east, with a narrow lane separating from the 1891 Co-op building. As such Clydeview is earlier than the Co buildings.

19th Century Tenants and Shops

Amongst the first tenants were David Green, William Currie, David Archibald and Patrick Clark. In 1893, Patrick Masterson in recognition of the growing population, was amongst one of the prominent businessmen of Glasgow Road who would sign a petition asking for Stonefield to be made into a Burgh in Blantyre. However, this failed to happen and we're left wondering what advantage this all was to the businessmen or their customers.

In 1895, the small shop in the 2 storey part was occupied by Thomas Henderson, a plumber. Patrick occupied the spirit shop and cellar and at the far west of the building on the lower 3 storey part was Henry Montague, a shoemaker who operated there only a short time until 1898.

In 1895, Patrick also occupied Naismith's pub in Auchinraith. In March 1898, about 10 years into ownership, Patrick decided to sell. The reason is unknown, but he was financially ok. On 23rd March that year he placed an advert in the Glasgow Herald selling his pub and the tenement houses above it, stating it had a rental potential of £117, 10s per year. It sold quickly and in July 1898, Patrick left Blantyre for good to run a hotel in Broxburn.

The next owner of Clydeview, was Thomas H Bennett & Co Ltd, a business of well known spirit merchants in Glasgow. Thomas and his son Thomas Junior owned several pubs in Glasgow at the time. However, they ran into an immediate problem upon acquiring Clydeview. The license was not permitted to be renewed. So, they would let out the building and 5 homes but as of 1898, there would never be another public house here. They also owned the buildings at Main Street, High Blantyre near the Auchinraith Vaults.

Thomas Henderson would continue to rent his little plumbers business from the small shop, something he did until just before WW1. The large ground floor shop, formerly the public house, was taken over in 1898 by Piscina Guiseppe, an ice cream manufacturer. This was a large ice cream parlour occupying the whole ground floor at 249-251 Glasgow Road and Piscina rented for £30 per year also up until just prior to WW1. It is observed that Blantyre had many ice cream parlours at the turn of the 20th Century, most all owned by Italian incomers, a trend that would continue for a couple of decades.

20th Century Shops and change of use

The trigger for the businesses changing use prior to WW1, wasn't war itself, but was the liquidation of Thomas H Bennett & Co Ltd, which happened between 1910 and 1915. (The liquidators of this company however, would continue to own Clydeview right up until WW2 years.) When liquidation happened, the little shop at 247 Glasgow Road became Joseph Britton Painters, and would remain there until the early 1920's. The Valuation roll of 1915 also noted 6 houses in the building occupied and an empty stable at the rear. By the time WW1 had started, Blantyre Social Club occupied 249-251 Glasgow Road in the 3 storey part of Clydeview, with John Berry their secretary. Blantyre Social Club would remain there until the late 1920's before relocating elsewhere.

Blantyre Social Club

Originally from just before WW1 at 249-251 Glasgow Road in the 'Clydeview' building, they were forced to move premises in the late 1920's when the main Post Office relocated from Stonefield Road to Clydeview.

However, they didn't move far relocating to 253 – 257 Glasgow Road next door. When they moved, they bought the adjacent building for address 253 Glasgow Road was owned and occupied by the club outright. The premises were licensed. Managed by a committee of 12 people in the early 20th Century, the notable characters being Mr. Thomas Price (president), Mr. John Clements (Vice president), Mr. Thomas McGuire (Treasurer), Mr. Thomas McCool (Secretary), Mr. William Corrigan, Mr. Terrence Mulvaney, Mr. George Stein, Mr. Peter Quinn, Mr. Patrick Taggart, Mr. William Weir, Mr. John Davie, Mr. Michael Duffy and John Crookston. They may have had their own quoting club of the same name.

Sheriff Boyd Berry in Glasgow refused the renewal of their club license on 5th June 1931. Almost a month later on 30th June these 12 members were in front of the court charged with being the persons responsible for a club which was kept mainly for the supply of alcohol in respect that intoxicated people were frequently seen to leave the premises. The accused all pleaded guilty and fined 20 shillings or 10 days imprisonment. Their new building later became the Y.M.C.A under ownership of Alexander Thomason merchant of Perth.

Pre WW2 years

There were several outbuildings to the rear, most likely washhouses and toilets as well as storage for the businesses. In 1925 M. Campbell & Co had taken over the small shop at 247 Glasgow Road but only for a short time. It is unknown what their trade was, despite searching.

In the late 1920's Clydeview lower floor at 249-251 Glasgow Road became the Blantyre Post Office and it would remain there until 1954 before moving to their new, larger premises at the corner of Logan Street. The Clydeview

Post Office was apparently very cramped and unsuitable for the type of work being carried out by the postal authorities, conditions that they had suffered for years. It was woefully inadequate and workers delighted in being moved.

In 1930, there were 6 upper houses continuing to be rented from the liquidators of Thomas H Bennett & Co Ltd and the small shop at 247 had become Umbeto Schivone's Ice Cream Shop, which existed only a short time until 1935. Tenants of the house above the small shop had to make a hurried escape, when fire broke out in a new fish and chip shop at 247 Glasgow Road on Friday 11th October 1935. Within a few minutes the inside of the shop was a raging furnace, the whole building owned by Alexander Thomson.

The property and house above was occupied by a Mr Thomas Rusk, a widower, and his family. They made a hasty retreat with no time to remove any belongings. The No. 2 branch premises of Blantyre Co-Operative Society was only separated by 8 feet from the fish shop. Employees tackled the flames with extinguishers, and assistance was given by men carrying pails of water. The flames were held back until the arrival of the Lanark County Fire Brigade. The fish shop, which has been closed for several months, was to have been opened that day by Mr. Charles Gray, Halfway, Cambuslang. It was completely gutted, but the house above was saved, although damaged by water. It wasn't the first time a chip shop would go on fire at this location. When Gray's fish shop became Pat McNally's Fish & Chip shop, it went on fire again in the early 1970's, as this dramatic photo shows.

Figure 314 Fire at Clydeview during the early 1970's, with permission A Smith

The shop in the eastern end would change use a few times in the 1960's and 1970's. In the late 1960's and early 1970's it became the "Pat McNally's Fish and Chipshop" then a chip shop owned by Maggie Bell. In 1976, for short time, the "Shat In Chinese Takeaway." Ariel & Art Cabs occupied the west shop in the 2 storey part during the mid 1970's. It does not appear that the upper storey (within the 2 storey part) of the building was used by that time, the window bricked up.

Copper Kettle

The Copper Kettle was a former café located at 249 - 251 Glasgow Road in late 1960's to early 1970's and still there in 1973. It was run by Mrs Watson and sold sandwiches, coffees and teas, cakes, biscuits and the like.

Shat In Chinese Takeaway

The Shat-In was a former Chinese Restaurant and takeaway, one of the first to arrive in Blantyre during the early to mid 1970s. The 'unfortunate' sounding business name is named after the Hong Kong racecourse of the same name, and was a common name for takeaways all over the UK at the time. It was located at 249 Glasgow Road.

You could sit in to have a meal or takeout. The Shat In was originally located further along Glasgow Road near Herbertson Street but moved to the 249 Glasgow Road location at Clydeview in 1976. The takeaway was on the left, the restaurant on the right to the west. The restaurant became the Sun House Cantonese Takeaway in 1976.

Knights of St Columba

When the Post Office moved out of Clydeview in 1954, the ground floor on the 2 storey part was split and became Ashley F Mack joiners business, which had telephone number 341. The other side was Robert White Plumbers & Electricians, with telephone 380.

By the end of the 1950's, both these shops combined again to become the 'Knights of St Columba'. This social club would remain at this

Figure 315 Clydeview 1981

location before moving to dedicated premises at Carlowrie Avenue in Coatshill in 1975. It was a popular club, liked putting on entertainment and was heavily involved in charitable work for the community. They subsequently became 'The Columba Club', which closed on 8/10/17.

By the 1980's, the 3 storey building started to have a dangerous lean, as this photo from 1983 shows. At almost 100 years, it was becoming dangerous and later that decade something drastic was done to make it safe. The trigger for this was a storm which caused the stone chimney to come crashing in through the roof of Ariel & Art Cabs, forcing them to move to the Industrial Estate.

The upper 2 storeys were removed very carefully, some say stone by stone, hand by hand. Contrary to what others have written it was not entirely demolished and rebuilt, but actually the lower ground floor of the 3 storey part was retained. The 2 storey part completely demolished. Receiving a new pitched roof and render roughcast over the gables, it re-opened again as the Sun House Chinese Takeaway in the 1980's, which still trades under that name today.

Phew! We told you this was a complex building! One which has seen businesses change frequently and we're not quite finished yet…..

Figure 316 Stonefield at Glasgow Road South looking west during 1983

Sun House Chinese Takeaway

Takeaway and offsales. The Sun House is a contemporary Chinese takeaway with address 249-251 Glasgow Road, G72 0YS. The business established in 1976 and was initially located further east on Glasgow Road not far from Herbertson Street. By the 1980's, following Glasgow Road redevelopment, it was at this new location. Sun House also delivered cigarettes and alcohol, and indeed people of Blantyre are known to order just 1 bag of chips to validate their delivery of booze and fags too. Indeed, it was noted that by ordering food with the alcohol order, it arrived faster to ensure the food didn't get cold! The curries are reputed to be very good. Mrs. Lee owns the Sun House, at one time owned another takeaway across the road, but not anymore, retaining only the Sun House.

In February 2017, planning permission was given to change the use of the Sun House to become a café, sandwich shop as well as takeaway, something that as of Deceber 2017, has not yet happened.

Blantyre Project Social Media:

Andy Lynch: "I was sorry in October 2017 to hear of the permanent closure of the Columba Club on Carlowrie Avenue or the Knights as we all knew it by. So many fond memories of the Club. There was a time when my dad, Wullie Lynch and I decided to buy a dog from somebody in the club. We were a wee bit drunk and although my sisters were happy, mum Ella was not so much. However, in later years the dog would lie out in the garden, let out by Ella and would wait for me to come back from the club."

Serge Mikkeson: "I often get my sandwiches out of Agnew's Café. They have good portions and its not expensive. However, I would avoid going in at midday. School lunchtimes can be very busy as pupils of all ages descend upon the shop with lengthy waiting times. It's a great wee shop I'd like to survive."

"Read More about **Clydeview** online. Scan our handy QR Code for more narrative and photos at Blantyre's History Archives.

Further information, photos and commentary from readers are added from time to time. Learn about QR codes at the beginning of this book."

Grays Buildings (YMCA)

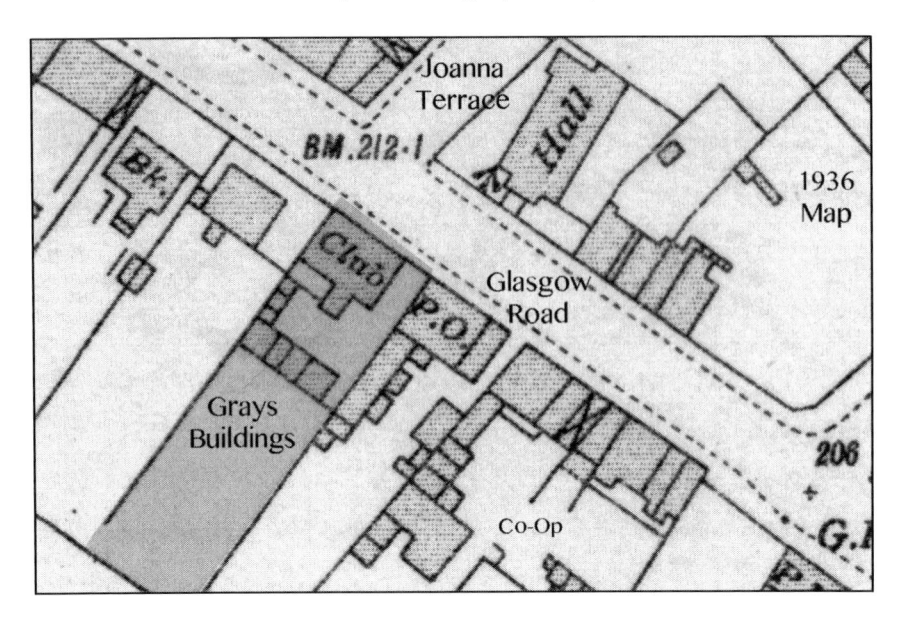

Figure 317 Grays Buildings on 1936 map. Building still exists today

We next arrive at interesting tenement which still stands today. 'Grays Buildings', or more recently known as the YMCA building, directly across Glasgow Road from Joanna Terrace.

However, before we delve into the detail, we're going to tell a nice little story to set the scene, a story belonging to the 'Gray family' the original constructors. The tale was first offered to the late Blantyre historian Neil Gordon in 1979 perhaps as a myth, but it is retold below after our correction of dates and providing facts exclusively related to the event.

Mary Blantyre

At Barnhill on the western side of Blantyre on Bardykes Road stands a cottage known as Brownlie cottage, named after a family who lived there for many generations. One day in 1813, the same year explorer David Livingstone was born, Mr Brownlie was leaving his cottage and shocked and surprised to find an abandoned new born baby girl in a basket, which was sitting on his doorstep in the lane that now leads on to Glenfruin Road. A note was pinned on the shawl, asking the Brownlie family to take the child in and raise her as their own and requesting specifically that the baby be called Mary.

Now, just a week before this, Mrs Brownlie had given birth to a baby girl of their own, whom , by co-incidence and in fashion with the day, they had already named Mary. Still, the kind soul she was and unable to trace parents, she took the newly found baby in and raised the child as her own.

She was keen to grant the request regarding the child's Christian name but she could not possibly consider raising two children with the same name, Mary Brownlie. So she gave the baby another surname and had her christened as Mary 'Blantyre.'

Figure 318 Little Mary Blantyre in 1813 at Barnhill

A heart warming tale and one which has relevance to our book, for little Mary Blantyre would grow up and marry Robert Gray, an incomer to Blantyre ,a grocer born in Lanark in 1808.

Robert and Mary Gray (Blantyre) settled down in Stonefield in the mid 19th Century and it is known they were living at Coats Buildings in 1865, with their grown up family. However, by the 1871 census, they were living in their own building, "Grays Building". It was constructed in 1868 and 1869 and opened in Autumn of that year, a license provided in October for Robert's new grocers shop. This makes it, with exception of the Stonefield Tavern, the oldest existing building on all the south of Glasgow Road.

The early years

Built on a long, narrow strip of land, this building may have sat alone in fields with nothing around it when first built. The 2 storey, detached tenement had shops on the ground floor and homes on the upper. The property and yard was entirely fenced off with stone gate posts to the east side providing a wide entrance to the back.

The pillars still exist today. Built of stone with a slate roof, there were 5 upper windows on the front facing out to Glasgow Road, with 1 window on either gable side offering at the time views up and down the road. There were 2 doors and three large windows on the lower floor. One, large central stone chimney towered above Glasgow Road with gable chimneys either end.

To the rear was plenty of space in the back yard, which was put to good use. Several buildings were constructed at the back including a granary, a stable, a hayloft and a slaughterhouse. Beyond that to the south was a large plot of land used for growing vegetables for sale in the front grocers shop. A water pump was situated in the rear yard and small glass or greenhouses, although these had been cleared by 1930.

Figure 319 Gray's Buildings in 1981 in foreground. Looking east.

Robert Gray became a master grocer in his lifetime. The 1875 valuation roll has him owning and occupying the house above, as well as licensed grocers shop on the lower floor, and of course, the aforementioned buildings to the rear. However, Robert Gray's ownership of the building was fairly short lived and when he died in 1879, aged 71, it passed to his wife Mary Gray who was by then 66 years old.

In 1881, Grays Buildings are noted being called as such in the Street Index and that year the shops were a butchers, a licensed grocers and a drapers. These were being run by the 2 sons and a daughter of Mary Gray. In the house above that year were Mary (68), daughter Mary (42) and son Arthur

(28). Another son John Gray lived in a small cottage named "Milne", immediately next door.

Their businesses would have thrived in those early times, but faced more and more competition as further buildings sprang up around them, competing with their drapers, butchers and grocery businesses. By 1895, elderly Mary was 82 years old and the businesses were run by "J&A Gray", most likely standing for John and Arthur Gray, brothers, and the sons of Mary.

Mary Gray (Blantyre) died on 21st October 1901, aged 88 and 'Grays 'Buildings were inherited by her oldest son John Gray.

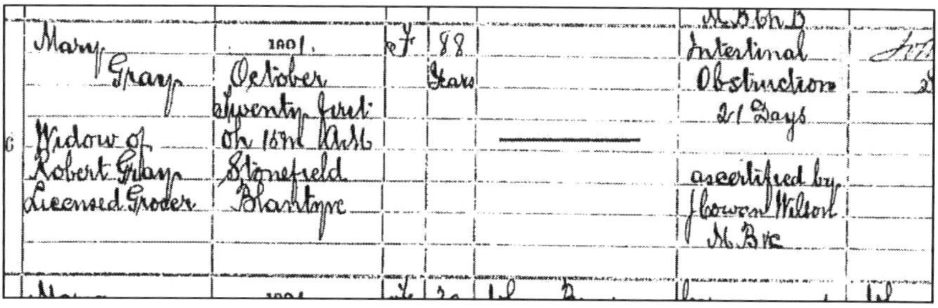
Mary Gray
Widow of Robert Gray Licensed Grocer
1901. October twenty first 0h 10m A.M. Stonefield Blantyre
F 88 Years
Intestinal Obstruction 21 Days
as certified by J Cowan Wilson M.B. &c

Figure 320 Death certificate of Mary Blantyre in 1901 shows NO parents

John Gray was a master grocer and wine merchant, born in Blantyre in 1844, the son of Robert and Mary Gray. During his life he married Agnes Semple Murdoch and had a son whom he named Robert junior. In 1901 he took ownership of his parent's legacy in Grays Buildings. He moved from his nearby cottage into the upper floor of Grays Buildings and let his son Robert rent the cottage from him.

By 1915, Grays Buildings had address 253, 255 and 257 Glasgow Road, the house being 253 with a rated value of £30 per annum. He would continue to run the granary, hayloft and stables for the rest of his life, as well as the licensed grocers shop. Tenants of the slaughterhouse in 1925 were liquidated.

On 1st January 1928, just shortly after the New Year Bells, John Gray died at 253 Glasgow Road, aged 84. He had been suffering from dementia amongst other things and his son, Robert was present. It was an end to the name "Gray's Buildings", having existed for over 6 decades, but not of course to the building itself, which was about to go on to serve an important function for the community as a whole. The Blantyre Social Club moved in during 1928, and found themselves in trouble with the law over licensing laws relating to the sale of alcohol. Joseph McCool was secretary. Between 1936 and 1938, the Blantyre Social Club closed at this location, becoming the Y.M.C.A.

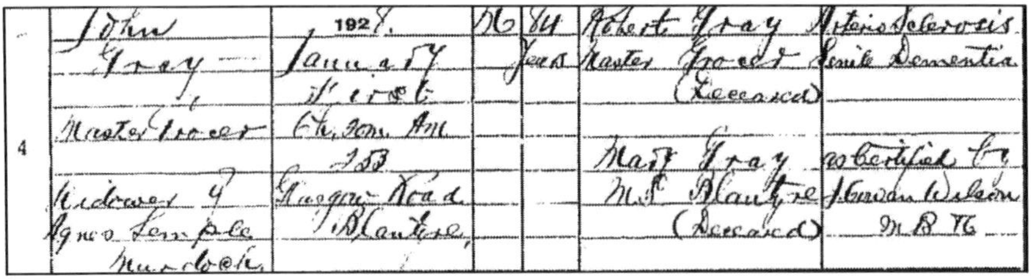

4	John Gray Master Grocer Widower of Agnes Semple Murdoch	1928. January First 6h. 30m. Am. 153 Glasgow Road, Blantyre	M	84 years	Robert Gray Master Grocer (Deceased) Mary Gray M.S. Blantyre (Deceased)	Arteriosclerosis Senile Dementia as certified by Gordon Wilson M.B. Ch.

Figure 321 John Gray's Death Certificate in 1928. The end of an era

Between 1940 and 1945, the Y.M.C.A building, under new owner Thomas Melville was used as the "Home Guard" training headquarters. Behind it, the former slaughterhouse and granary used also for wartime training as volunteers practiced attack and defend war-games, adjacent to some home made trenches. For a short time following the war, children would sneak in when the YMCA wasn't holding functions or classes on and play soldiers in those trenches. Post WW2, the Thomson family moved in above the hall.

Shelter for Homeless Families

During 1948, ten families were rendered homeless when fire ravaged through their Watson Street homes in High Blantyre. Almost 40 people lost their homes and most of their possessions, being forced to stay temporarily after the fire in the YMCA on Glasgow Road. The fire had started early one morning at 12 Watson Street and destroyed the two-storey building. Temporary repairs were carried out at one end of the building to ensure the families adjacent were protected and could remain there. The fire was believed to have originated in the upper storey in the home of Mr. and Mrs. McNulty and their four children. Within half an hour the roof the building was on fire, as was the two shops on the lower floor, burning furiously. Mrs. McNulty's cries for help caught the attention of her neighbours who raised the alarm. Householders made a vain attempt to put the fire out with buckets of water but were unsuccessful. Similar attempts were made to rescue possessions.

Blantyre YMCA

YMCA is sometimes perceived to be primarily a place for homeless young people; however, it offered a broad range of programmes such as sports, personal fitness, child care, overnight camping, outings, employment readiness programmes, training programmes, advice services, immigrant services, conference centres, and educational activities as methods of promoting its values. There is no doubt that from as early as 1938, this was an important organisation for Blantyre, in the days before proper community centres. Financial support for local associations was derived from programme fees, membership dues, community chests, foundation grants, charitable contributions, sustaining memberships, and corporate sponsors.

Children took great delight in escaping the tensions of the war years by being able to go on organized trips and outings. These 3 teenagers were on a Blantyre YMCA outing in 1945. On the left Blantyre youths, Tom Ashbridge, in middle an unknown handsome chap and on the right Thomas Buchanan. How smartly these young men were dressed for this exciting field trip.

Figure 322 The Blantyre YMCA field trip during 1945

We have to note just how much the YMCA was used. A small café was located inside the centre, and the halls held different kinds of classes for many decades right up until the 1990's. Gymnastics, Tap Dancing, The Red Cross and many youth discos. During the 1960's the Blantyre Discussion Group would meet there.

Between the 1940's until 1960s the upper storey remained as homes and it is known Andrena Black a local lady was born there in 1961 and the Geddes family occupied it. At the vacant plot at the back of the yard, by the 1960's a small woodland had sprung up between the outbuildings and Calder Street.

Blantyre YMCA Football Club was also based there coached by Tommy Chassels. They started out as "Cherrytree United" but were allowed to change name in June 1952. The Blantyre Miners Welfare held a gala day in Blantyre up until 1960 but stopped when the larger YMCA and Community Council events started in the public park. However, the Welfare would resume galas in

1978 and suddenly Blantyre often had TWO gala days each summer!

In the early 1970's, the upper storey was made use of as halls also. By this time the building had no permanent residents. It meant dances downstairs in the hall, could also be held upstairs, even at the same time! Mr Park of Fernslea Avenue did a lot of charitable work for the YMCA as did many volunteers in Blantyre.

Figure 323 Derelict YMCA Building 2010, in need of development

The Roxy

From 1972 until the late 1970's, YMCA discos were a popular event in Blantyre. It was the place to be if you were between 9 and 13 years old. Youth discos occurred every Saturday night from 6pm until 8pm the children naming the disco, "The Roxy". Mr. Sandy Nisbet was responsible for supervising the kids along with his then girlfriend, Alma. Local man, Jimmy Whelan remembers the "Roxy" by his poem of the same name, kindly shared here:

"Doon the Roxy on a Saturday night,
Dressed to kill oh what a sight,
Struttin oor stuff oan the dance flair,
The whole of Blantyre seemed to be there.

Two bob tae get in or a tin a beans,
Ten bob for sweeties that was yer means,
Music kicks aff wae some rock n roll,

Smoochin some burd tae a wee bit of soul,

Smelly toilets and flaking paint,
Fae oor crowd ye got nae complaint,
Loads of great memories in that wee hall,
Generations of people having a ball.

Another memory to be wiped away,
Gone forever the Y.M.C.A.
At least there calling it a fancy name,
But the Spice of Life just is'nae the same."

J.J.Whelan 2010

Kids had a blast, especially around annual parties like Easter, Christmas and Halloween, where apple bobbing was especially fun!

Figure 324 Halloween Parties were fun, especially apple 'bobbing'

During the 1980's for a time, although the YMCA continued to be in use, a Health & Lifestyle centre was based there, a kind of home help for elderly people within the community. However, by the 1990's the building was used less and less and in 2007 became closed and started to become derelict. Even as late as 2010, some of the windows were boarded up, security cameras installed and warnings to trespassers adorned the façade.

By 2013, however, the building got a new lease of life. Shops on the lower floor were renovated by new owners, former homes on the top, given new windows and a makeover. The Spice of Life Indian Takeaway moved into the eastern shop and William Hill bookmakers into the west at 253 Glasgow Road. This configuration still exists today and as of time of writing in 2017, it may surprise many to know that little 2 storey building is currently almost 150 years old!

Before we leave Gray's Buildings, a note for just some of the many businesses that were located out of sight, at the rear yard. Mr. William McSeveney owned a coachbuilders shop in a small garage/ workshop at the back of Blantyre YMCA in the late 1950's and 1960's. Previous to this he had run the garage further west beside the Old Original Bar. In 2009 it was G Valets and following 2010, became Stoddart's Accident Repairs and a carwash. As you see, Gray's Buildings certainly had a packed and interesting history.

Blantyre Project Social Media:

Laura Gaffney: "I danced in the YMCA with Young & Aitken Dance School for many years. Lots of great memories."

Thea Boreland McNamee: "My work was based in the YMCA in 1985. My boss was Austin Kerrigan and our group went to the elderly and infirm in their homes, like shopping etc. It was like a home help kind of service."

Andrena Black: "We lived in the 2 rooms above the YMCA. I think my parents Ronnie & Mary Geddes moved in during 1958 or 59. My dad was caretaker. We moved out in 1964. Dad was from Blantyre, my mother from Barra."

Bridget Irwin: "Robert and Elizabeth Chatham also lived in the YMCA building with their children Jean and Victor."

Elaine Speirs: "I remember going to Roxy's in a sky blue Lurex dress and white platform shoes. I thought I was all that! I went to the Guides in that building which were run by Maureen Ireland."

Karen Sweeney: "Great memories of the YMCA Gymnastics run by Sandy. The Gala days and the discos right into the mid 1980's."

Catherine Sneddon: "I used to love going here. I'd always call into the nearby chippy on the way home, with great memories."

Broomknowe Cottage

There's a little one storey, detached cottage, which still exists to this day at 259 Glasgow Road. Sometime between 1876 and 1880, the Gray family who had already built their neighbouring tenement constructed a small cottage, as home for their son, grocer John Gray. His first child was due in 1878 and the cottage may have been built in time to coincide with that life event.

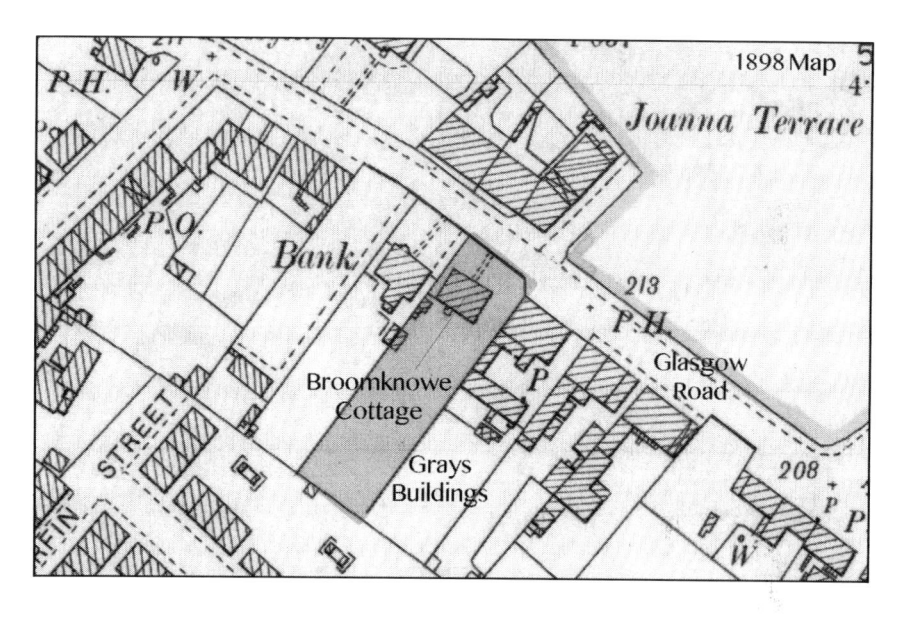

Figure 325 Broomknowe Cottage on Blantyre's 1898 Map

Original ownership and the likely constructor was Mr. Robert Gray, the father of John, who initially called it "Milne Cottage". The name would change in that first decade to become "Broomknowe Cottage", a name that is still even today the official name of the building.

The cottage was set back slightly from Glasgow Road, but still opened out on to it. Situated on a long, rectangular plot, it had a path leading from the road up to the doorway, with plenty room at the back gardens. Being a family of grocers, this land would have been put to good use and it is telling that during their occupancy, the back gardens were never built upon. They would have provided an ideal place to securely grow vegetables for sale in their shop at nearby Gray's Buildings.

In 1881, the occupants were John Gray (36), wife Agnes (35), son Robert (3), daughter Agnes (2) and domestic servant Jane Hamilton (18). John is noted in that census as being a grocer employing 1 man and 1 boy.

Following the death of Robert Gray in 1879, the cottage passed to his widow, Mary Gray who continued to rent it out to her son John right up until her own death in 1901. In 1895, the rent was £18 per annum.

In 1901, John Gray, who had been living and renting this cottage for over 20 years, inherited it. He was still living there in 1905, but before WW1, as he became older, (perhaps to retire) he moved next door to the upper flat at Grays Buildings. His son Robert junior then rented Broomknowe Cottage. By 1915, Robert Gray (37) was an electrical engineer, considered in age to be 'too old' for the wartime initial draft and so in those rough years, he continued to rent the cottage for the modest rate of £18 per annum and conducted his grocer business, established by his grandfather 2 generations earlier. Robert continued to live at Broomknowe Cottage before moving away.

Figure 326 Broomknowe Cottage in 1981

During World War Two and immediately after, the Aitkenhead family lived in the cottage, occupying it solely as a house.

In the 1950's and 1960's, Mr. Felix McLaughlin, a car hirer conducted his business from the building, which had now become a business for the first time. Felix would go on later to establish a funeral parlour and had telephone number Blantyre 373.

The little garden once at the front was landscaped over with hardstanding to accommodate parked vehicles for the business. Metal railings were erected in the 1970's to fence off the street and pedestrians.

In later years it continued as a Funeral Parlour, taken over by Joseph Potts and has had that use for many years now at time of writing in 2017. Premises at the back have been, in post Millennium years occupied by Kennedy Travel, then from 2015, Kennedy Coachworks.

Figure 327 Broomknowe Cottage in 2015 now Joseph Potts Funeral Parlour

> Blantyre Project Social Media:
>
> **Fairlie Gordon:** "Felix McLaughlin was my grandmother's younger brother. He was born in 1915, the youngest of 5 children. His parents were Charles McLaughlin and Elizabeth McBride, both from Fermanagh, Ireland. They came to Blantyre to live in the late 1890's. Felix married May Cassidy, a Blantyre girl and they had 2 sons, Brian and Gerard, both of whom would follow in the family business. Brian moved to the Dumbarton area when the business folded and had worked in the same line as the Co-op. He sadly died a couple of years ago. Gerard was in the Bothwell area, I think going into the license trade."

"Read More about **Broomknowe Cottage** online. Scan our handy QR Code for more narrative and photos at Blantyre's History Archives.

Further information, photos and commentary from readers are added from time to time. Learn about QR codes at the beginning of this book."

Figure 328 Broomknowe Cottage in 1979

Figure 329 Clydesdale Bank 1979 to the immediate west of Broomknowe

You'll notice the configuration of the doors and windows has changed.

Clydesdale Bank Building

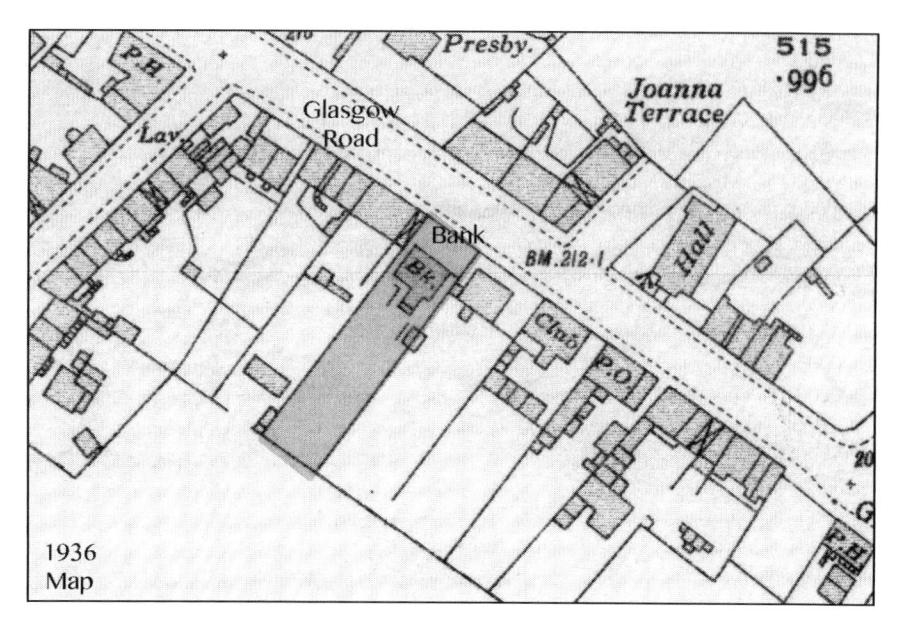

Figure 330 Clydesdale Bank on 1936 Map not far from Stonefield Road

Known to be in Blantyre since at least 1879, the Clydesdale Bank was not in the 1875 valuation roll, but was in Naismith's Directory of 1879, meaning a likely construction date between 1876 and 1878. Then known as the Clydesdale Banking Company, the business was founded in Glasgow in 1838 and became limited in 1882.

The detached house, garden and bank office has been wholly owned by the Clydesdale Bank for most of its lifetime. An early, small outbuilding at the back may have been a store for the bank manager's garden. The first agent was Mr. Hugh McCallum, who would be manager until the late 1880's.

The building is quite distinctive and unique for Glasgow Road. Not built in a traditional tenement style, this property has a pitched roof above bay windows on the west side and is 2 storey high. Constructed of stone with a slate roof it has a central doorway, a double window on the east and bay windows and single window on the west. An attic room above the bay windows gives the tall building an impression of being 3 storey on one side. Wooden soffits are ornately carved in curves and spirals and still exist today, suggesting the initial good choice and use of quality hardwood timbers. These wooden features make the building instantly recognizable to locals, as no other building on Glasgow Road has that unusual style. Perhaps it was the Bank's way of showing the importance and uniqueness of this property.

By 1895, the next bank manager was George Campbell who would manage the bank until the end of the First World War. The rent value of the bank prior to the war was £70 per annum, but only £60 following the war as the country struggled to piece back normality. The bank manager lived in the building in the upper house and would work downstairs in the office, overseeing clerks and early tellers.

The building would be given address 261 Glasgow Road prior to WW1 and by 1920, the next manager and agent was J. Thomson who would manage the bank well into the late 1930's.

Figure 331 Bank in foreground, Glasgow Road looking east in 1981

Clydesdale Bank was sold in 1920. However, it continued to operate independently under the same name and was always referred to as an affiliate, not a subsidiary. The Glasgow banks suffered more than others in the depressed economy of the inter-war period and from being the largest lender in Scotland in 1920, it fell to fifth place by 1939. Despite this, the Bank continued to open branches, particularly in areas enjoying export growth, and the network increased from 158 in 1919 to 205 branches in 1939, one of which was still Blantyre.

Midland Bank had acquired the North of Scotland Bank in 1923 but the management had fiercely resisted any attempt to merge with Clydesdale. However, the changed competitive market after the Second World War meant that the two banks could not remain separate and in 1950 this was reconsidered and they were amalgamated to become the Clydesdale and North of Scotland Bank (soon shortened to Clydesdale Bank).

Post WW2 Years

The resident Bank Manager in the 1950's was Mr Blaikie. The downstairs were all tellers and the safe and secure area where a large locked safe occupied a large part of the floor. Upstairs as well as the bank managers home were old ledgers and document storage. Another manager was Mr. McAustin. This was an era when all transactions were hand written, even into the 1960's with fountain pens. Clerks would get annoyed at this practice as it would often be messy.

Another bank manager was Mr. Cummings who lived with this wife and 3 sons in the upper storey. However, after his son David, drowned in the River Clyde, Mr. Cummings moved away. Around that time, Mrs. McQuade was a cleaning lady on the premises.

By 1969, mergers elsewhere had reduced the number of Scottish banks to three with Clydesdale Bank now being the smallest.

In 1983, the Clydesdale Bank moved location further eastwards to the former Co-op Emporium Building. It was a more modern building and more functional for the bank, who was by then up against competition in Blantyre not just from Royal Bank of Scotland, but also the arrival of the 'Abbey National' at Clydeview Shopping Centre.

261 Glasgow Road then became a bookmakers and the external stonework entirely whitewashed in the mid 1980's completely changing the look of the building. Ladbrokes continue to operate their business from the lower ground floor. The upper floor had become 'Crawford Mason Layers' and remained there until 2013 when the lawyers became 'Lanarkshire Law Practice.'

Blantyre Project Social Media:

Moyra Lindsay: "Mr Blaikie's daughter taught at Auchinraith School in the early 1950's. She had reached Priory Street each morning in her full make up and high heels, just as my dad's car passed by from Station Road. We would give her a lift and I would sit and cringe in the back as she sat in the front. It still didn't stop her berating me in front of the whole class for adding instead of subtracting. I went to my grannies at lunchtime and was tested for Polio by the doctor who realized I was still upset by the telling off. My mother marched down to the school to tell her off for giving a sickly child a row. A lasting memory of the Blaikie family, of course which may have just been me."

In 1989 National Australia Bank bought the Clydesdale bank for £420m with bank branding changing. In 2016, the Clydesdale Bank announced their departure from Blantyre after being there for nearly 140 years. Their building next to Broomknowe Cottage still looks in good condition and is well used.

Figure 332 Former Clydesdale Bank Building, now bookmakers & Lawyers Office 2015

Dervoch Cottage

West of the Clydesdale Bank was Minto's Land. Initially in the late 19th Century, this was just one cottage but the Minto family later in the 20th Century expanded their ownership by building tenements in front of it.

The former cottage was stone built, of single storey and sat off Glasgow Road, at the southern end of a long, rectangular plot. The Constructor and original owner was William Minto, a warehouseman who also owned other Blantyre cottages by name of Belmont, Mossgiel at 306 Glasgow Road and Castleview near Coatshill.

William Minto was born in Blantyre and lived at Castleview Cottage, Blantyre during the 1880's. He was the son of James Minto a Blantyre coachman. Sometime between 1882 and 1884, William bought a vacant plot of land not far from the corner of Stonefield Road and built a cottage for his son Robert S Minto. He initially called it "Stonefield Cottage" and it is noted as that name in the 1885 Valuation roll situated right beside the bank, however, later in that decade, the cottage was renamed to 'Dervoch Cottage', sometimes "Darvock", perhaps due to confusion caused by another property called Stonefield Cottage further west along Glasgow Road.

In 1885, Robert S Minto, was a 28 year old watchmaker renting his father's cottage in the district of Stonefield. Robert conducted his business in the adjacent tenement building, "Broompark Place". Robert lived at Dervoch Cottage until mid 1893 with his wife Annie and a teenage servant girl, Jessie Skinner.

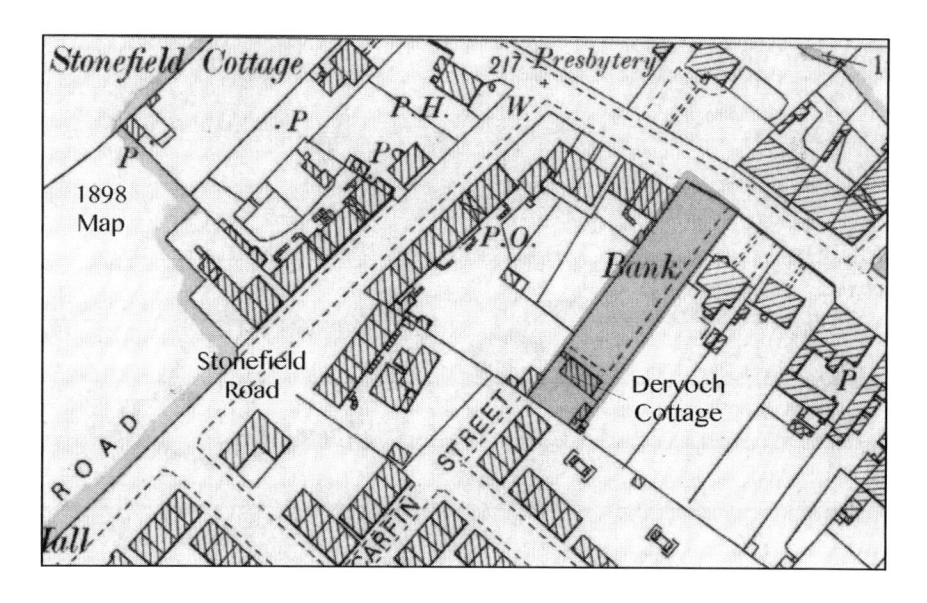

Figure 333 Dervoch Cottage on 1898 Map in Stonefield District

William Francis Benham

The next tenant of Dervoch Cottage in 1893 was Mr William Francis Benham, a travelling salesman. Born in Edinburgh, William Francis (Frank) Benham arrived in Blantyre that year with wife, Lizzie Craig & 3 daughters.

His initial time in Dervoch Cottage was likely sorrowful, when the couple lost a child, William Junior in 1895. This may have prompted a move from Dervoch Cottage which they were renting from William Minto for £17 a year. The couple moved shortly after, but remained living and working in Blantyre.

William Francis Benham would go on to form his own shop nearby at 11 Stonefield Road, the family becoming well known in Stonefield. He took ownership of the Old Original Bar in 1917 for a short time, living at both Station Road then later, 'Craigrock' on Glasgow Road. William died in 1925.

By 1905, joiner John Hunter was renting Dervoch Cottage for £15 a year, and this tradesman was perhaps a good contact for William Minto, who constructed large, new tenement buildings at the front of the cottage around this era, the cottage losing its large front garden. The cottage was accessed via an eastern path leading down the whole length of the plot, alongside the bank.

By WW1 years, Dervoch Cottage had an address of 263 Glasgow Road and William Minto had been living at Vale View, East Finchley, in London until his death in 1918. Peter Muir, a stableman was the rented tenant in the years immediately before and after the death of William Minto. Peter Muir lived there until the early 1920's.

Dervoch Cottage was inherited in 1918 by William Minto's son, Martin Orme Minto, who owned the cottage, along with others in Blantyre until World War 2. Tenants changed in these intervening war years too. In 1925 William Pretsell, a general builder was renting, then James Stewart, a retired man by 1930.

Behind the cottage was Carfin Street, part of the Dixon's Miner's Raws and at one point there was a back entrance to the cottage from the raws. In post WW2 years the cottage passed to Michael (Mick) Devlin, a popular and well known man in the area.

However, due to the creeping age of Dervoch Cottage, it became unfit for purpose in the late 1950's and by 1960 had become a ruin, something confirmed by 1962 maps. The building lay derelict in a partially collapsed state until the 1990's when it was cleared to make way for modern, contemporary houses named Valerio Court.

Electric Street Lights

Electricity started to replace gas street lamps in the 1920's throughout Blantyre. However, it wasn't without its problems. On Saturday 28th January 1922, in the middle of Winter and long dark nights, inconvenience was caused to Blantyre residents through the failure of electric street lights. We take street lighting for granted these days and outages are very rare. However, on this dark weekend in 1922 a leakage in the cable, caused the failure of the newly installed electric lights in Glasgow Road. The main thoroughfare, got dark around 3.30pm and on a busy Saturday, locals were left fumbling along the pavements in the complete dark. However, it was the shopkeepers who felt the inconvenience. They had only just weeks before discarded their gas equipment in favour of this new technology. Light was restored to the town the next day.

Minto's Buildings

Minto's Buildings was a former 3 storey large stone tenement at 265 Glasgow Road, situated immediately adjacent to the Clydesdale Bank and the 2 storey Broompark Place. The property was situated not far from the eastern side of the junction of Stonefield Road.

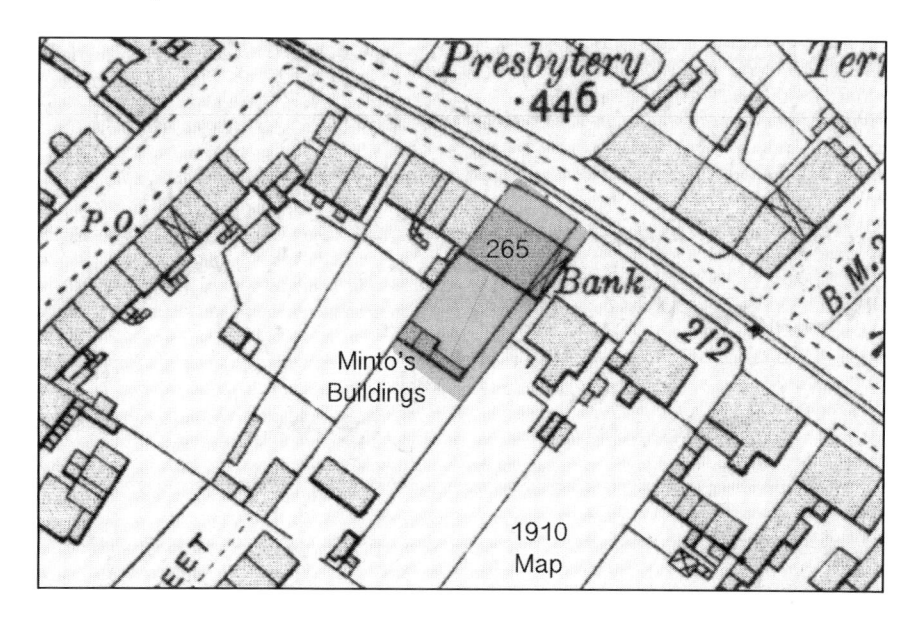

Figure 334 Minto's Buildings shown on 1910 Blantyre Map

The tenement was built between 1902 and 1903 on Minto's Land, a long, rectangular plot of land that already had a cottage named "Dervoch Cottage" on it, also owned by the Minto family. A small wall and a few trees were removed upon construction of the building. The little front garden was fenced off by a wooden fence, blocking off the pavement in front of it. Opening out on to Glasgow Road, the building was imposing at 3 storeys, being even taller than the fairly tall bank next door. An internal stair let to the upper 2 floors.

With Dervoch Cottage situated at the rear, access was required to be maintained, so a large pend* close was built on the east of the building, allowing through access to Minto's rear yard and of course leading down to the cottage. These were spacious homes by comparison to other tenements with only 8 homes in all of the 3 storeys. There were no shops in the property.

- Note: 'Pend' is a Scottish architectural term referring to a passageway that passes through a building, often from a street through to a courtyard or 'back court', and typically designed for vehicular rather than exclusively pedestrian access. A pend is distinct from a vennel or a close, as it has rooms directly above it.

By Paul D Veverka

Figure 335 Minto's Buildings in 1950, immediately adjacent to the bank

The original owner was Mr. William Minto, a warehouseman of Castleview Blantyre, who would later live in London following WW1. In 1903, the completed building attracted families from nearby, upgrading their rented accommodation. Amongst them John Hunter and Peter Clark who moved from nearby Calder Street and also Alexander Christie, a tailor who moved from Central Buildings.

During WW1, the 8 homes were rented out for rents between £10, 5 shillings and £13, 10 shillings. William Minto's tenants were families Trainer, Forrest, McCutcheon, Carmichael, Nimmo, Steele, Crombie and Duncan.

When William died in 1918, Minto's buildings remained in the family passing to Martin Orme Minto, who was absent, living in Michigan, USA.

Ownership of Minto's Buildings would remain in this family for some time. In the 1960's families including the Ross and Steele family lived in the building. It would take until the 1970's for the building to be demolished, no longer fit for purpose in the modern era and in desperate need of repairs, rewiring and plumbing.

DID YOU KNOW ?

When Minto's Buildings were demolished, it created a gap between the bank and Broompark Place, a gap which still exists today. Grassed over, a couple of trees planted in the 1970's are now quite tall. Today, the rest of Minto's Land, where the yard and cottage once were is now modern day Valerio Court, with at least 4 of these modern homes on the plot.

Our location line drawing below shows how it once looked against a modern context. How much simpler a building's history is to tell, when it didn't change hands often and contained no shops!

Figure 336 Location Line Drawing showing Minto's Buildings in modern context

Broompark Place

Near the eastern corner of Stonefield Road at Glasgow Road junction was a former 2 storey tenement officially called, 'Broompark Place'. The name certainly sounds strange in a modern context, a name that many people would more associate with High Blantyre, which in itself may have been a reason the name fell out of existence through the lifetime of the building.

Broompark Place was constructed of stone with a slate roof and had a large central close running north to south right through the building leading from Glasgow Road to its rear yard. Built in 1888 into 1889, it consisted of 1 shop to the east of the close, 2 shops to the west and with 2 houses on the upper floor. Access to the upper homes was through the close and up a stair at the rear yard.

The property was initially detached, but later neighbouring Minto's Buildings would be built up against it. It had a prominent position directly across from St Joseph's Presbytery (later the entrance to St Joseph's School) and would also have enjoyed good views across to St Joseph's Church.

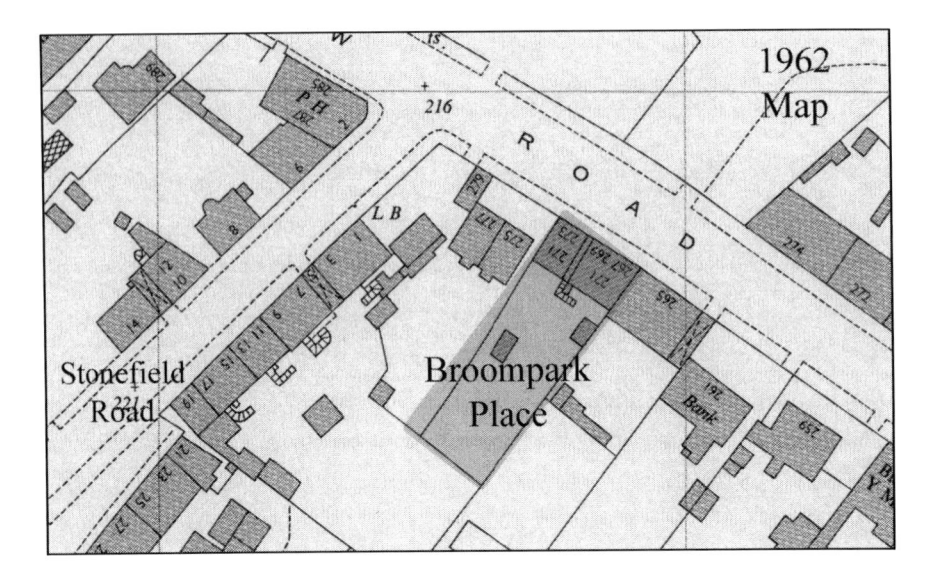

Figure 337 Broompark Place, 2 storey tenement on 1962 map, Blantyre

The name 'Broompark' was certainly popular in the 1880's. Indeed, in 1885, there already were another two 'Broompark Places' in Blantyre! A building at Larkfield with several shops and homes and another building on Stonefield Road with 9 houses, should not be confused with this article. When Broompark Place was constructed on Glasgow Road, it may have taken the name from the Stonefield Road property demolished around the same time.

The original constructor appears to have passed away between 1889 and 1895, for the first recorded owner in valuation rolls in 1895 was a Mrs M.W.D Cruickshank of Polockshields, noted as being the bondholder in possession. Mr. George Campbell of the adjacent bank was factor. In the houses, Mr George Pate and Mrs Arabella Arbuckle were first tenants.

James B Dall

Broompark Place was a building which would have a long retail tradition of being associated with clothing or drapery. The first shopkeeper occupying all three shops on the lower floor was draper, James B Dall of nearby Brownlie Cottage. He was advertising looking for drapery staff in 1889 at newly constructed Broompark Place, having moved from Gilmour Place on the north side of the road presumably for this opportunity. In 1891 James was 37 years old, married to Margaret and had 6 sons and an infant daughter. The Dall family moved away from Blantyre by 1901, perhaps due to drapery competition from the Co-op and several other private retailers. However, it was far from the end of drapery businesses at Broompark Place.

In 1900, another draper arrived in Blantyre for the first time and moved his business into the 3 shops, i.e. the whole lower floor. Henry R.S. Oliver was to be a long term occupier operating his business there for several decades and was to be one of the longest established traders on Glasgow Road.

Oliver's Building?

Others have incorrectly assumed and called this building 'Oliver's Building'. However, it was never called that. Not in any census, any valuation roll or official documentation. Oliver rented the building at all times and at no time was it ever his building, never owning it. There's no doubt though that Blantyre residents knew where 'Oliver's Shop' was being there for so long.

Henry R.S. Oliver

Henry Russell Stewart Oliver was born in 1867 in Alloa, the son of James Oliver a master baker and Mary White. He was 33 years old when he came to Blantyre in 1900, but was already established as a draper. He was married to Irish woman, Isabella Holland. The Oliver family lived nearby at Brownlie Cottage and it is known they had at least 1 son who went into the family business. The Olivers would rent the lower 3 shops at Broompark Place for an incredible 46 years until his death. Henry's died on 11th March 1946 at Homeland, Glasgow Road, Blantyre.

Figure 338 Death Certificate of Henry Oliver in Blantyre in 1946

Tenants in the upper storey would change over the years. In 1905 Hugh Davidson a roadsman and Gilbert Harper Junior, a mechanic lived there. Alexander Russell, a roadsman lived there from prior to WW1 until the late 1920's. Sometime between 1920 and 1925, the 2 homes upstairs were reduced to just one, as one side of the upper storey became a storeroom for the shops below. The house was occupied by James Devine from the late 1920's.

The name 'Broompark Place' was used less and less following WW1 for this building, even more so when it was allocated postal addresses 267, 269, 271 and 273 Glasgow Road. The shops were 267, 269 and 273 and upper homes was 271 Glasgow Road, a configuration that continued throughout the 20th Century. Olivers may have flourished especially at this location being so near the tram terminus at Glasgow Road, offering shoppers convenience.

Figure 339 Glasgow Road 1903. Minto's Buildings & Broompark Place on the left

It is little wonder that this charming postcard was commissioned in 1903. Looking east along Glasgow Road, as well as celebrating the arrival of trams to Blantyre, it must have represented modernization at the time. The newly built Minto's Buildings on the left foreground with its wooden picket fences, next to it the older Broompark Place with iron railings. (Railings were not removed during the 'Iron Drive' in World War 2 but removed earlier in 1930 when the road was widened.). Elsewhere other relatively new buildings of the era like Mayberry Place and the Old Original Bar feature.

As well as clothes and textiles, Oliver's sold curtains, bedding and other decorative soft furnishings, some of which may have been considered as luxury goods for any humble mining family. In WW1 years Oliver's rents to Mrs MWD Cruickshank was around £8 and 10 shillings. Mrs Cruikshank lived in Liverpool by that time, still owner, bondholder in possession of the entire property right up until the end of World War One. Ownership then passed to John Jackson Coats from 1918 until the early 1930's and subsequently before 1935, to AJ & A Graham, as bondholders beyond World War Two.

Following 1946, shops changed use and in the late 1940's for a short time into the 1950's the end shop at 273 became Dr. Terris's surgery. When he moved to High Blantyre in the 1950's the surgery became Dr. Harkins practice then Dr. Church's surgery then Batters, Malone & McKay lawyers.

Post WW2, the other shops were also well used. Many Blantyre residents remember Pat Hughes Photography throughout the 1970's and 80's. Pat lived in Victoria Street. His shop was small with a single room studio, but it was well used and photography services could be called upon away from the shop too. It moved westwards to Westend Place in the early 1980's.

The other middle shop was Paton's Ladies & Gents Hairdressers. Willie Paton, his wife and daughter Margaret were well known in Blantyre throughout the 1960's, 70's and 80's. Willie's nickname was 'Scooby' and he had a pleasant manner about him. Although only 1 public room for each of ladies & gents, the shop was always busy, with loads of chatter and gossip.

Blantyre Project Social Media:

Arlene Green: "My mum remembers Pat Hughes Photography shop as being an old fashioned type shop with a simple counter. Next door was Paton Hairdressers. Willie Paton's daughter Margaret worked there as did a girl called Grace Brown. I got my hair done in Paton's. The 'Purdie' was a famous cut in the 1970's and then frizzy perm in the 1980's."

Martin Smith: "Pat Hughes did live on Victoria Street. He was good friends with my father."

Sharon Morrison Doonin: "Hughes Photography was still at the Westend in the mid 1980's. I remember getting my photos there."

Elaine Spiers: "I had my first communion photo taken at Hughes. The hairdressers next door was where mum got her hair done. It was a noisy room with big 'sit under' hairdryers and always with a smell of hairspray and perm lotion. I watched people endlessly getting their rollers put in. In 1978, I had hair so long I could sit on it, but I wasn't allowed to get it cut until I was 12. Even then, Margaret Paton refused to cut all that lovely hair so short, so we had to go elsewhere."

Patrick Donnelly: "Don't forget, in this building, there was also a lawyers office called 'Batters, Malone & McKay during the late 1970's. It was a busy wee office and well used, existing right up until 1993."

Broompark Place was completely demolished around 1993 and is now the site of several homes belonging to modern Valerio Court.

By Paul D Veverka

Figure 340 Hughes Photography and Paton's Hairdressers 1979

Figure 341 Broompark Place in 1979 few years before demolition

We're sure these pictures will evoke lots of memories for Blantyre folks, still to this day amongst the most fondly remembered Glasgow Road shops.

Blantyre Project Social Media:

Irene Berry Milligan: "The front of Paton's shop was the barbers and the back was ladies hairdressing. I worked there many moons ago and have lovely memories. There were some characters that came in!"

Jim Canning: "A family tragedy happened in the upper flats above the shops during the 1950's. A Gas leak killed my Aunt Catherine Doran. Her husband Robert survived as did the 2 children. The babies survived asleep in the cot beside the mother. Robert was never the same, the gas and grief affecting him. He died recently in Blantyre in a care home.

Lisa Martin: "My gran, Ethel Martin worked in the hairdressers."

Eleanor Cockburn: "I got married in 1972 and Hughes took our photographs in East Kilbride. I was so happy with them."

James Rouse: "When the end shop was Dr Church's surgery. You left by a door that entered the close. I'm sure Crawford Mason lawyers used this office for a time after Dr Church moved to the Health Centre, before Batters, Malone & McKay took over it."

Ann Hartman: "My wedding photos were done by Hughes in the early 1970's/ Bought and paid for colour, all delivered in black and white with no apology or refund. Mistakes happen I suppose, but I didn't use them again."

Gerald Kellachan: "The lawyers was a Satellite office of Batters, Malone & McKay of Sauchiehall Street, Glasgow. McKay was the brother of well known St Joseph's teacher, Archie McKay. The original office was in Kelly's (Henderson's) Buildings at the other end of Glasgow Road. Doctors Harkins and Church were both heavy smokers. The surgeries reeked of smoke, their ashtrays on their desks always full and invariably always had a lit cigarette sitting in them!"

Valerie Krawczyk: "John Batters was part of the lawyer's group. His parents had the ironmongers on Glasgow Road. He lived in Church Street."

Elaine Burns: "I worked in Batters, Malone & McKay from 1988 until 1993. I remember it well and having to work hard."

Daniel Anderson: "I remember getting my haircut in Hughes barbers. As a child, I was placed on the board spanning the seat handles, so I was tall enough to avoid the barber bending down. A lasting childhood memory!"

Margaret Liddle: "Hughes did our Wedding photos in November 1975. My brother worked next door in the barbers for many years."

Jim Brown: "Jim Paton lived at Waverely Terrace and living nearby, we got regular crew cuts at his house!"

By Paul D Veverka

Clyde Cottages

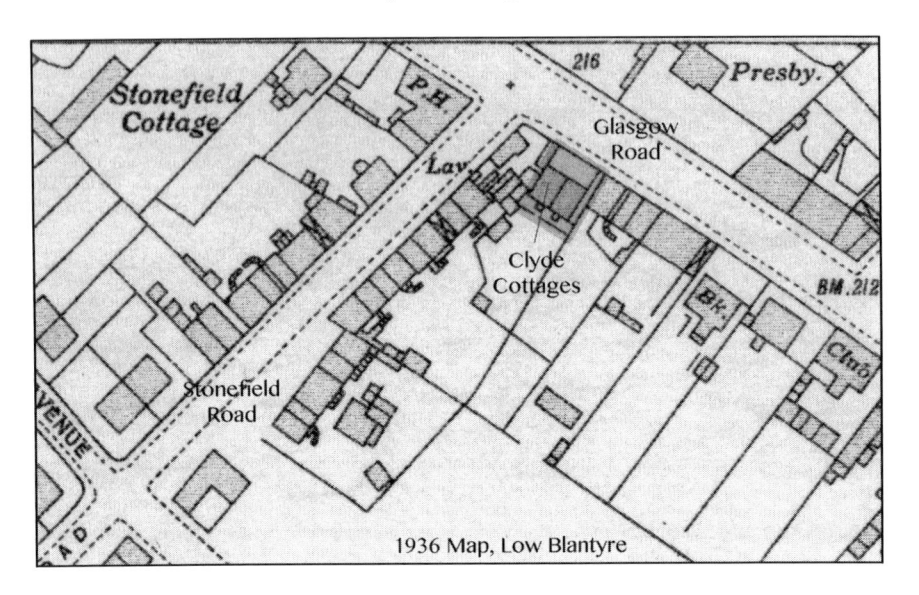

Figure 342 Clyde Cottages shown on 1936 Map Low Blantyre

Clyde Cottages were two former semi-detached homes at 275 and 277 Glasgow Road near the corner of Stonefield Road at Glasgow Road junction. They should not be confused with Clyde Cottage in Auchentibber. The cottages accessed by one central path, appear to have been well built lasting nearly 120 years and served as homes for many different families.

In 1865, Mr. Robert Clyde Lindsay constructed the cottages, giving them his middle name, which was also the maiden name of his mother. As such, the name Clyde, although popular and relevant in Blantyre due to the nearby River of the same name, is attributable in this case to a person's heritage.

Born in Glasgow, Robert lived in Denholm Cottage in Kilmalcolm prior to coming to Blantyre and is noted in the 1871 census. The Lindsay family initially moved in around 1866 and also owned an adjacent blacksmiths shop, yard and corner ground which they let out to Messrs Mitchell & Forrest. Also in 1866, eldest son David Lindsay a joiner, got married at the new cottages, the event noted in the local newspaper and the cottages named specifically.

The Lindsay Family

There is good evidence that the Lindsay family initially lived at Clyde Cottages from 1865 until around 1871. In 1867, James Lindsay, the brother of Robert was a road surveyor, who was looking to learn more and take part in

Architecture classes, even advertising asking if there was any nearby. He would later go on to own land at Stonefield Road named Pilot Acre.

On 4th June 1868, Robert Lindsay married Alison Mitchell and the same year his sister Margaret Smellie Lindsay married at Clyde Cottage to William Pollock. Robert and Allison had a child Robert Lindsay Junior born in 1871 who would live until 1929. It is known Robert and Allison Lindsay had at least 4 children, all of them having the middle name 'Clyde'. It was therefore a place that saw several family weddings, the cottages being comfortable enough for the weddings to be held and for births of family members. They may only have occupied one side of the Cottages, for in 1871, a lady named Janet, the wife of a William Adam died at Clyde Cottages.

The Lindsay family had moved out by 1875 although continued to work in Blantyre. Robert Lindsay was involved in the construction of Allison Place in Springwell in 1878, hired by Ann Allison Heriot. New tenants were then renting Clyde Cottages from Robert Lindsay Senior. In 1875 Thomas G Brown and John Waugh rented the property for £18 per annum.

By 1881, Robert Lindsay Senior after living next at Brownlie Cottages, had moved away from Blantyre. It is unknown why he left but the fact that his furniture was auctioned and that the bank took full ownership of Clyde Cottages, is telling that all may not have been well financially. Despite this assumption, there are no records of any liquidation, so the reason for the departure may well have been unremarkable enough, perhaps just a change of scenery. On 31st July 1882, the furniture of Clyde Cottages in its entirety including all the kitchen equipment for both cottages was sold at Smellie's Auction House in Hamilton. The Hamilton Savings, Investment & Building Society took ownership of Clyde Cottages in the same year.

Tenants changed again. In 1885, Mr. Greenshields a warehouseman occupied one of the two houses, and Mrs. Hogg, widowed wife of James Hogg occupied the other. James was a stationer who died in 1884, and also a military man, a quartermaster-sergeant in the 74th Highlanders. Rents were being paid to Hamilton Savings, Investment & Building Society and the houses were both factored by Angus McQuarrie, a grocer at High Blantyre.

In 1895, tenants were David Thomson, a warehouseman and Mrs. Jane Simpson. In 1905, the houses were occupied by James Galloway, an Inspector of Drains and Mr. James Smith, a joiner, renting for £14, some £4 less than the rents had been 20 years earlier! A sign of the rented accommodation competition that may have prevailed in Blantyre at the time. The Smith family would live at this address for some time and James's woodwork skills may have become especially handy as the family business of undertakers took off.

Sometime between 1898 and 1910, the toilets at the outside were rebuilt adjoining and part of the cottages at the back of the building. Likely feeling more modernized this would have saved a walk out in the cold winters to get to the loo.

By 1915, Clyde Cottages had been given addresses 275 and 277 Glasgow Road, the Smith family living at 277. Each were rented for £15 and the location may have seemed ideal as an abundance of shops sprang up at Stonefield Road and the previous decade had seen modern buildings like the Old Original Bar, the Church be built nearby. The proximity to the tram terminus would have been welcomed too. At 275 that year were Hugh Anderson a miner although he died in 1916 a year later. His widow, Mary would live there until the late 1920's. Next door at 277 was Andrew Smith, a funeral undertaker, and son of James, who lived there well into the 1950s.

In 1930, at 275 William H Young, a confectioner was tenant and by 1935, the house had changed rental again, occupied by John Young, a fruiterer. In post WW2 years, this house would be occupied by Tommy Valerio, a well known shopkeeper who ran the Café De Royale, or "Mickey's Café" situated very close to the back of Clyde Cottages. Interestingly, after 1930 Clyde Cottages became referred to as "Clyde Cottage", i.e. in the singular, the name from then on only applying to 277 Glasgow Road, the home of the 'Smiths.'

Injuries caused by a wheel

DID YOU KNOW ?

Dan Connor (73), was injured in a peculiar road accident on Monday 3rd August 1931. He was standing at Clyde Cottage, near the junction of Glasgow Road and Stonefield Road when one of the wheels of a passing motor car (which had been forced to swerve avoid another vehicle), became detached from the axle and dashed against him, knocking him down with force. He received facial injuries, including a broken nose.

Smith Undertakers operated under the name "J&A Smith Funeral Undertakers" and worked from their yard at 277 Glasgow Road adjacent to their Clyde Cottage home. With Telephone number Blantyre '44', however, their main business was at Victoria Garage in High Blantyre.

In the 1950's and 60's large trees adorned the back gardens of Clyde Cottage, at the back of Mickey's Café. The Carruthers family latterly lived there. Both homes were eventually demolished in the early 1980's, as part of modernization of Blantyre. It is safe to say that many families had occupied these unassuming homes, often missed being set back from Glasgow Road.

Figure 343 Clyde Cottages in 1979

Figure 344 Stonefield Road Junction at Glasgow Road 1979

The configuration of the corner of Stonefield Rd has changed a few times.

Workshops & Yard

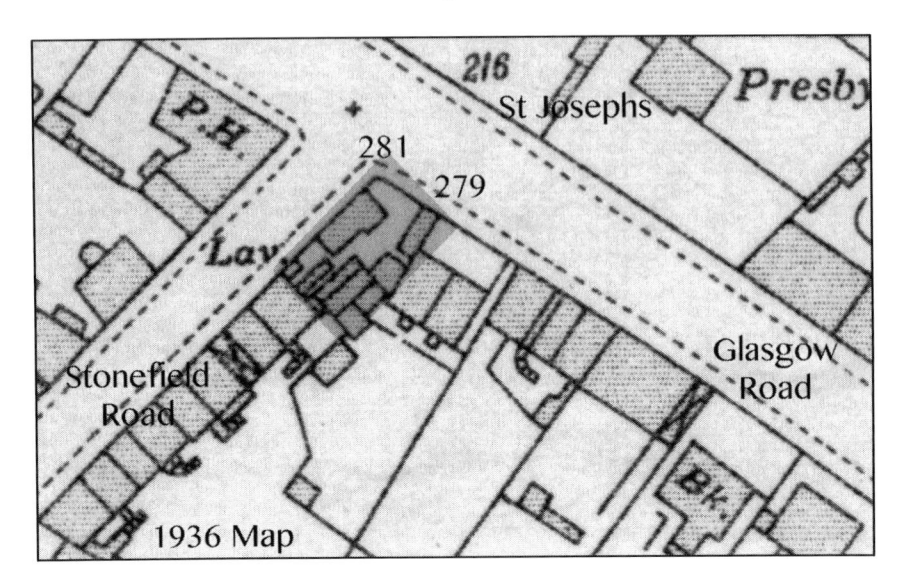

Figure 345 Joiners Workshops & Yard at corner of Stonefield Road

On the eastern corner of Glasgow Road at the bottom of Stonefield Road was a couple of workshops and a yard. The earliest workshop dated back to 1865 when constructor Robert Lindsay built it and let it out to Mitchell & Forrest, local joiners and blacksmiths.

This commercial relationship existed even after 1881, when the Lindsay's left Blantyre and John Mitchell, a joiner continued to rent with his business partner for around £9 per annum. In 1895, John lived nearby in Stonefield Road and rented from new owners, the Hamilton Savings, Investment & Building Society, who also owned most of the buildings at the corner of Stonefield Road also.

Around 1900, a second joiners workshop was built in the yard, facing out on to Stonefield Road, which was initially rented by John Reid, a joiner. John would operate from this workshop and yard until the end of the First World War, by which time it had address 281 Glasgow Road.

Also around 1900, the older workshop expanded with a new small pitched roof single storey workshop facing out on to Glasgow Road. This would have address 279 Glasgow Road and was situated between Clyde Cottage and Reid's joinery workshop. This was to be the rented workshop of the Smith family for several decades. The workshops would have been a common sight as passengers alighted at the nearby, new tram terminus in 1903.

In 1905, the pitched roof workshop at Glasgow Road was rented by James Smith, a joiner. By 1915, Andrew Smith occupied the workshop.

The Stonefield Urinal

DID YOU KNOW?

Yes, you read that right! By 1915, space at 281 Glasgow Road, directly on the corner had been reserved for a public urinal. It was noted in the 1920 as still being reserved and constructed during the 1920's. It was likely sited there due to the proximity of the Old Original Pub across the road. The urinal was an 'iron duke' type and despite having a Glasgow Road address, opened out on to Stonefield Road. Under ownership of the Middle Ward District Committee (part of the County Council), it was still there in the late 1930's, but demolished after WW2.

Workshops Post WW1

Andrew Smith joinery business rented 279 Glasgow Road, the little pitched workshop right up until the early 1930's, until such a time the business was renamed as "J&A Smith". In 1935 their business as joiners and carriage hirers was flourishing and as undertakers, business was good. Smiths undertakers however, were still renting the workshop and yard from the bank who remained owners for most of the 20th Century.

The large hut in the yard was used to make and store coffins, the workshop used as an office and nearby at 5 Stonefield Road, certainly in 1920, their salesroom shop. J&A Smith kept their carriages in a large wooden building at 10 Broompark Road. Several other wooden buildings, huts and stores sprang up over the years within the yard for the purposes of Smiths, some being immediately adjacent to Valerio's Café de Royal on Stonefield Road.

The other workshop at 281 Glasgow Road facing on to Stonefield Road was occupied by Stewart W Allison, joinery in 1920 right up until the immediate post WW2 years, passing to Alexander C Allison , a joiner sometime between 1930 and 1935.

Fisher's Yard & Latter Years

Contrary to popular belief, the corner of Stonefield Road and Glasgow Road was not Mickey's 'Café de Royale' which was actually nearby further up Stonefield Road during the 20th Century. In post WW2 years, the corner of this junction was David Fisher's Yard.

David manufactured wrought iron gates, fences and offered general blacksmith (smiddy) services. The main office and showroom faced out to Glasgow Road at number 279 in the small pitched roof building similar to the current hairdressers shop at Larkfield. The yard was narrow and long, running from the Glasgow Road to the gable end of Valerio's, with its entrance at the bottom of Stonefield Road. David Fisher's company was there well into the early seventies. After he retired the little showroom became a different kind of showroom selling interior light fittings, tables lamps etc.

> Blantyre Project Social Media:
>
> **Robert Stewart:** "For years an old double decker bus sat at the right hand corner of the yard next to Valerio's. I remember being in the yard with my dad and I'm sure it was used for storing strips of steel. Silly the things you remember from youth!"

Fisher's Yard looked likely to have been cleared when the other buildings were demolished around 1979 and 1980. Prior to that around 1975, the yard was fenced off and a gravel path was constructed on the small triangular plot of land offering a bench to sit on and a few shrubs cordoned off by some modern red 2 foot high tubular railings. A tiny little park no less at that busy junction with good advertising space on the billboards on Valerio's Stonefield Road gable.

> Blantyre Project Social Media:
>
> **Drew Semple:** "I remember that plot of land at the corner. At the end of Fisher's Yard was a corrugated fence with a cigarette machine built into it. Needless to say, it got emptied a hundred times by locals."
>
> **Moyra Lindsay:** "I remember David Fisher. He made our railings for our verandah in 1971. He had a white poodle, which went to work with him and he cut the doghair himself, it was a right sight! I'm sure he was bit grumpy."
>
> **Moira Hutchings:** "In the early sixties we went to Mickey's once a week to use the payphone to speak with my Dad who was working in England. Sometimes we even got an ice cream! Across the road was the grocers, where my Aunt's friend Janet worked. Butter was still sold from a massive block from a barrel and had to be patted when you bought it. Next door was the butchers."
>
> **Stewart Dennings:** "In the 1970's, I recall Jeannie Scratcher (a nickname obviously). She used to sit on the wee bench at the corner, her affliction causing her to touch her face often. Not nice name on reflection. Hope she lived long."

Valerio Court

Following demolition of Minto's Buildings, Dervoch Cottage, Broompark Place, Clyde Cottages, the workshops on Glasgow Road and the tenement houses and shops at the bottom of Stonefield Road, a new housing estate sprang up at the corner around 1993/94. The estate was named to remember the Valerio family who had traded at the former popular Café De Royal (Mickey's Café) rented nearby on Stonefield Rd, run by 'Valerio & Co'.

Why not named after other well known traders of the area? Benhams? Pates? Or the property owners themselves? Well, clearly the chosen name of Valerio not only honoured the Valerio family for conducting business there for so many decades, but also acknowledged their presence in Blantyre since as early as 1900, in other parts of Glasgow Road. Councilors named the housing estate well, for this had been a well known family throughout Blantyre for many generations.

Figure 346 'Cafe De Royal' latterly nicknamed Mickey's Café, run by Valerio & Co

The detailed Valerio history and that of the Café is reserved for exclusively telling in another Blantyre Project book covering Stonefield Road.

Valerio Court is today centered around a small mini roundabout, accessed off Stonefield Road. Around it are 2 storey beige and brown brick houses in an L shape with frontage on both Stonefield Road and Glasgow Road. (hence inclusion of Valerio Court in this book). Bin stores and sheds are kept at the back. The opposing part of the court is a combination of bungalows, one and 2 storey homes. All homes have good access to local amenities.

Valerio Court is still today a well maintained, neat and modern housing estate but the days of many, many shops in this area are long gone.

Figure 347 Bottom of Stonefield Road in the 1920's

Figure 348 Valerio Court in 2016 at the bottom of Stonefield Road

CHAPTER 14
GLASGOW ROAD SOUTH
STONEFIELD RD TO BARDYKES RD

Exploring Stonefield Road

Figure 349 Stonefield Road looking to junction of Glasgow Road 1915

Stonefield Road takes its name after the old district of 'Stonefield' in Blantyre, which in the early 20th Century actually extended from this point southwards up to Larkfield and as far east along either side of Glasgow Road towards Auchinraith Road.

The road, initially a track connected Larkfield down to the Glasgow to Hamilton Road and may have been formed properly when the Free Church was constructed midway up the road. It offered a good way for people to walk from Glasgow Road up to Larkfield and branch off to Barnhill or Causeystanes at High Blantyre.

At the lower northern end of Stonefield Road, a cluster of several houses and a public house were the only buildings in the mid 19th Century in this area. However, like the rest of Stonefield, rapid growth in the 1860's to 1890's saw many other homes built with shops on the lower levels.

Prominent buildings like Commercial Place, Dixon's Rows and the important tram terminus would define the character of this area, with the majesty of the School Chapel and later St Joseph's Church looking down on them. This was a thriving, popular area of Blantyre with fleshers, bakers, cafes, grocers, public houses, church, a post office, cobblers as well as many other trades.

Popular former shops are embedded in the memories of Blantyre residents. Certainly some of the most talked about are amongst the following:

- Mickey's Café De Royal,
- Scobie's Bakery,
- Cameron's the Butcher,
- Sweenie's Confectionery,
- Gilbert the Baker,
- Black the Baker,
- McCorgary's DIY,
- Chalmers Emporium,
- Smart the Butchers,
- Benham's Newsagents,
- Geoff Pate's Newsagents,
- Lightbody's Bakery shop
- The Red Lion Pub,
- The Old Original Pub,
- The Black Hole,
- Clyde Star Video,
- Loughlin's Cobblers,
- Scotmid Chemist,
- KG Copystat,
- Tan Unique,
- The Launderette,
- The Priory Inn,
- Mecca Bookmakers,
- William Hill Bookmakers,
- Hair by Brogan,
- Melanie Brown's Salon,
- Spar,
- Stonefield Newsagents.

Perhaps the most commercially astute was the Valerio family. The Café De Royal (Mickey's) established in 1906 will be fondly remembered by many people, even right into the 1980's. Mickey Valerio cleverly penned the slogan on his adverts, which catered for all weather, "Do you feel cold? Try a coffee now. You feel hot? Have an Ice."

This was a great shopping area for more than 100 years, but now, since the 1990's only has shops on the western side near the junction.

Not so much "everything you will need in one place", but now more like "some things you may need (from time to time!)"

Clive Place

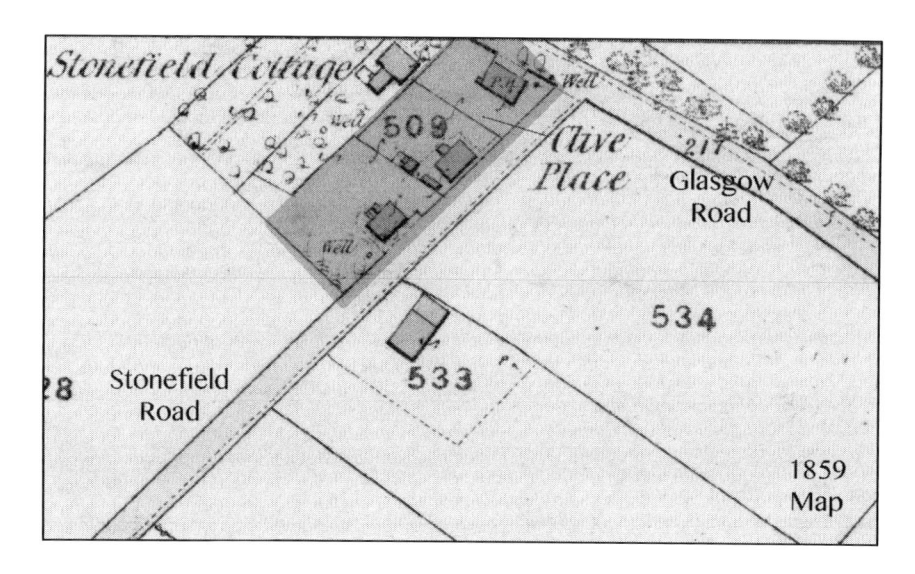

Figure 350 Clive Place Public House & Houses on 1859 Map

In the early 1800's a popular and well known public house existed at the western corner of Glasgow Road and Stonefield Road called 'Clive Place'. The exact spot of this former pub also used an inn, was where the 'Old Original Bar' is today.

The name 'Clive Place' incorporated not just the pub, but also a couple of small homes too, nearby on Stonefield Road. The origin of the 'Clive' name, dating back to the early 19th Century is unknown, perhaps a person's surname or place, now forgotten to time. The surname is not in early census information for Blantyre.

The original owner and constructor was Mr. George Bruce. Born in 1796, George is first noted in Blantyre census information in 1841 as being the owner of houses at Clive Place. George was a 'wright' or blacksmith, a profession that would have assisted in attending to horses at his inn. During the 1850's George owned nearby Stonefield Cottage. He also owned the one and a half storey detached house with dormer windows at 8 Stonefield Road (named 'Clive Cottage'), right up until his death in the late 1870's.

The single storey, detached public house was modestly made of stone with a small lavatory to the western side. Latterly with a slate roof, it may have originally been thatched in the first half of the 1800's. It is thought to have dated back to the 1830's. Like 'Winks' and 'Stonefield Tavern' further eastwards along Glasgow Road, it may have originally been a changing house or inn where weary travellers could rest and get their horses attended to. Situated on the most western extremity of the hamlet of Stonefield, the public house was well used, popular and one of the best early public houses. During the 19th Century, upon exiting the building, you would have looked over towards a small woodland, where now St Joseph's Church stands. The public house at Clive Place sat isolated at that time, existing long before most Glasgow Road buildings.

Figure 351 Clive Place Public House in 1890's (now the Old Original Bar)

The public house opened out on to Glasgow Road and had no windows in the gables. On the Glasgow Road side of the building were 2 large windows and a central large door, illuminated by overhanging gas lamp, with space above for signage. It was heated by coal fires at either end of the building. Nearby two modest sized trees are shown on the 1859 map and on the only known photo of the building. The trees at the back of the photo were in the grounds of nearby Stonefield Cottage. The property including a small paddock for horses, was enclosed by waist height wooden picket fences. A well was located at the junction serving the property.

Craig Family Ownership

Between 1851 and 1854, Thomas Craig, a spirit dealer from Bothwell moved over to Blantyre with his wife, Helen, young daughter Margaret and their new infant son, Robert. This family would become synonymous with Glasgow Road Public houses until the end of the First World War. Born in 1817, Thomas Craig was the son of George Craig, spirit merchant of Bothwell and Janet.

Thomas Craig and family initially in the early 1850's rented a house at Clive Place from George Bruce, and Thomas would run Clive Place public house. In 1859, the name book for the Parish hints at how established this public house had become, describing 'Clive Place' as "A Public house on the side of the Hamilton to Glasgow Turnpike Road. The name is well known throughout the Parish."

Opportunity arose in 1861, when George Craig, Thomas's father died, a situation which resulted in Janet Craig, Thomas's mother buying Clive Place Public House outright from George Bruce. So it came to be in 1861, at the age of 43, Thomas was still running the pub as he had done for the best part of 10 years, albeit now for his mother Janet Craig, whom by then was absent from Blantyre running her own inn, at Kirkintilloch.

By 1865, at a time when coal was being discovered in and around Blantyre, and more people arrived, Thomas Craig and family were living at Clive Place, running the public house.

DID YOU KNOW In 1865, George Bruce had let out a nearby house within Clive Place to the Blantyre Co-operative Society, although only for a short time. It dispels the myth that the Co-op first arrived in Blantyre in the 1880's and is a full 18 years earlier than previously recorded. The Co-op may have failed in the 1860's, due to lack of population or presence but would flourish considerably when established again in 1883. By 1875 John Mitchell and 2 other tenants were renting that house instead.

In the 1871 census, Thomas Craig and wife Helen were in their mid-50's and together with son, Robert (20) and daughter Margaret (24), they all lived at Clive Place operating the family wine merchant's business, on behalf of Thomas's mother, Janet Craig, the owner.

In 1877, the year of the Blantyre Pit Disaster, Robert Craig was 26 years old and saw opportunity in establishing his own public house, at a sufficient distance away for business to be successful, non-competitive, yet close enough to be near his home and family. License was sought for establishing a public house at Westend Place, on the corner of Bardykes Road at the western extremity of Blantyre. The license was granted and Robert established himself at that location, along with his sister, Margaret made their own way in the world as wine and spirit merchants, just like their father, Thomas still running Clive Place.

Trade at 'Clive Place Public House' may have drastically dipped in 1877 following the Pit Explosion on 22nd October 1877, with so many of the dead miners previously living nearby at Dixon's Rows. In 1885, Thomas Craig died aged 68 and the running of Clive Place was taken over by his widowed wife, Helen who was by then 70 years old. Janet Craig, mother of Thomas outlived him and in 1885, it was all change within the Craig family.

Robert Craig

Robert Craig, son of Thomas and Helen was born in Cumbernauld in 1851, coming to Blantyre as an infant. Living at Clive Place, he grew up around the wine and spirit merchant business and would have known the trade well by the time of applying for his own license at the age of 26. When his father died in 1885, his grandmother Janet gave up her ownership of Clive Place, over to Robert, who would become the owner outright from that date.

By the end of 1885, Robert Craig owned, not just his public house at the Westend, but also Clive Place. Indications of stretched working life are apparent for Helen Craig (80), Robert's widowed mother was running Clive Place by 1895, whilst as owner, he was also 'hands on' at the Westend. There is no doubt he would have been running between both businesses, overseeing the interests of each. Robert would establish his own mark at Clive Place following 1885. A gable sign erected, noted 'Robert Craig's' wine and spirit merchant business with established date of 1832, going back to the days of his father and grandfather, something he would have been proud of. Local people may have shortened the name, referring to Clive Place simply as "Craig's Pub". Robert's sister, Margaret died in 1895, leaving her share to him.

By 1895, the other homes at Clive Place were owned by John Virtue and the Craig family no longer living there. Success of having two pubs meant Robert Craig could afford to live in one of the new large villas on Glasgow Road. By then, a single man, he moved to "Craigrock" a semi-detached villa at 312 Glasgow Road midway between Clive Place and the Westend.

He married once in 1899 to a woman named Margaret Thomson Roxburgh (who died young, aged 49 in 1914). In the 1901 census, Robert is 50-year-old, living there with his 86-year-old retired mother Helen. He took part in many community engagements and functions and was well known. He had a son, young Robert in April 1904, who would later move to Australia.

Figure 352 Closer photo of Horse & Carriage at Clive Place 1890's

When Helen Craig died in 1903, aged 88, her grandson, Robert was the rightful inheritor of the Craig Estate. Likely coming into money, Robert would seize the opportunity for a fresh start. At the age of 52, as trams commenced directly outside Clive Place, and the opposing St Joseph's Church construction got underway directly opposite, Robert took the opportunity to demolish the aging Clive Place Public house entirely, making way for a modern, ornate corner tenement building. He may have felt a growing pressure to keep up appearances and modernization given the amount of pubs and new building springing up nearby around this time.

From Robert's perspective, his own pub had always been the Westend, and Clive Place was the 'Old Original Bar' belonging to the family. The name was a logical choice for his new public house at 283/285 Glasgow Road. Located on the corner of his modern tenement in 1903, he named the pub exactly that, i.e. "The Old Original Bar" in honour of his family's legacy.

The name 'Clive Place' however would not totally disappear at that time. The upper homes within the new corner tenement with address 287 Glasgow Road would officially continue to be called "Clive Place" for several decades, as would the cottage at Stonefield Road. However, the name 'Clive Place' looks to have vanished by WW2, the former pub itself, now an impossibility for any living person's memory or recollection.

This was truly one of Blantyre's forgotten old buildings.

The Old Original Bar

1903 was a year of significant change at the Glasgow Road junction of Stonefield Road. Leading that evolution was the construction of the tall and impressive St Joseph's Church on the north side, so distinct in style by use of its red sandstone, by comparison to other grey stone used in Glasgow Road. Trams had started running along Glasgow Road with the terminus directly outside Clive Place, the former public house directly opposite.

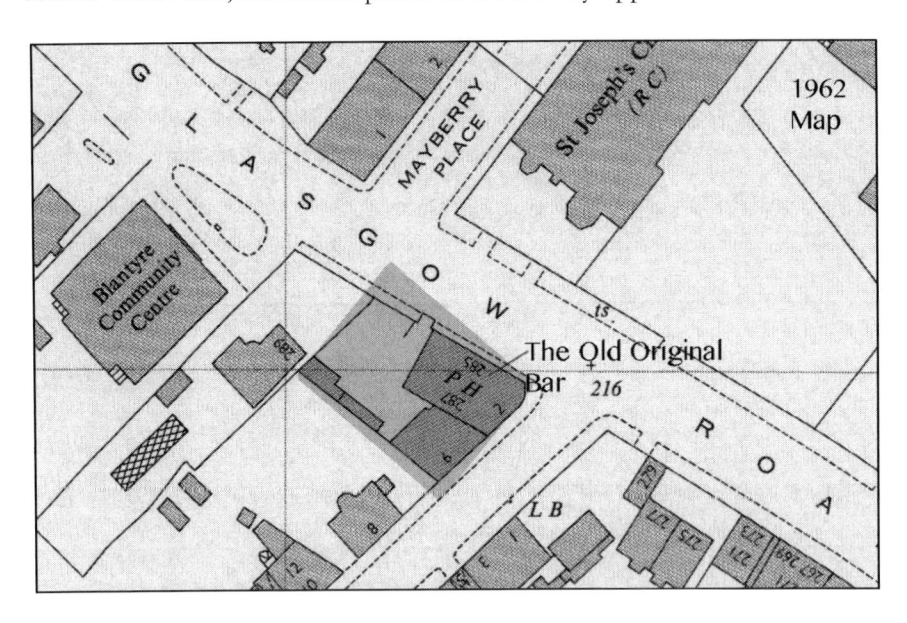

Figure 353 Old Original Bar and adjacent owned shops on 1962 Map, Blantyre

Robert Craig, in 1903, was a 52-year-old Blantyre wine and spirit merchant, whom after acquiring the Craig family inheritance following the death of his grandmother, built the 'Old Original Bar'. Robert had owned Clive Place since 1885 and was also owner of the Westend, a public house he established over 2 decades earlier. Clive Place had been the family's 'Old Original Bar', hence the fitting name for his new venture.

'The Old Original Bar', is of tenement style with frontage on Glasgow Road and Stonefield Road, initially with 2 or 3 shops on the ground floor on Stonefield Road. There were homes above the public house. Robert's chosen design may have been inspired from seeing a similar public house constructed in High Blantyre at Broompark Road by Arthur Blakely some 9 years earlier. However, it looks more certain to have been influenced by the tall church being built across the road to the north. Indeed, his chosen red sandstone matches the colour of the church exactly, dare we even suggest possibly from the same quarry, obtained and hauled to Blantyre at the same time?

The religious influences witnessed daily during Robert's construction, may also have influenced the design of his pub. Three large arched doorways, faced by red sandstone, quoin blocks adorn the ground floor of the pub, of similar design to the church doorways, opening out on to the pavement. It appears Robert's Architect had put some thought into the design to ensure a complimentary appearance to larger, nearby emerging structures.

There's no doubt Robert Craig would have been proud of his modern, new public house and setting nostalgia aside for a moment, perhaps he was glad to see the old Clive Place building, no longer fit for purpose. Certainly, in 1903, Robert must have witnessed many Blantyre public houses being upgraded or built in the previous decade and this would be his further imprint upon Blantyre.

Figure 354 Old Original Bar in 2009, Glasgow Road on right

At 2 storeys and L-shaped on plan, there's a door on each of Glasgow Road and Stonefield Road as well as the corner itself. The corner is ornate, especially the upper part, which features 2 large column turrets and 2 smaller. Upper windows have small "French" style railing balconies. Cellar access was via hatches in both Stonefield Road and Glasgow Road pavements. The roof has always been slate covered.

Inside was, and still is a large central island bar, enabling bar-staff to serve in full 360 degrees. Some of the original interior features remain in the pub, including woodwork and plaster architraves.

Taking time to commission a '1903' date stone at rain gutter level facing on to the Church, Robert also included an ornate and impressive carving containing his overlapping initials 'RC' directly above the central, corner doorway.

There would be no doubt. This was 'Craig's Pub.'

Figure 355 Date Stone showing '1903' facing Church

'The Old Original Bar' would have had a regular clientele, primarily of miners and the proximity to the miner's homes of Dixon's Rows is noted. It's highly likely the regulars of former Clive Place Public House came to frequent the new 'Old Original.' From the time of his marriage in 1899, Robert Craig lived at "Craigrock" at 312 Glasgow Road, a short distance away. His wife died young in 1914, aged 49. Business consumed Robert's life, not married until 49 years old. He was driven to make his pubs as successful as they possibly could.

By 1915, 'The Old Original Bar' had address 283/285 Glasgow Road and the homes above 287 Glasgow Road, the homes referred to as the resurrected name, 'Clive Place' until WW2. In later years, the cellar at 283 was dropped from addresses to give 'The Old Original Bar' its modern address simply 285 Glasgow Road.

Figure 356 Robert Craig's death certificate in 1917

Robert Craig died during WW1 on 28th March 1917 aged 66 from prolonged bronchitis. 'The Old Original Bar' had been his pub for only 14 years. With one underage child, his estate was to be held by trustees.

William Francis (Frank) Benham

After Robert's death, his good friend, tenant, cousin-in-law and trustee of his estate, Mr. William Francis Benham expressed an interest in owning the bar. William Francis (known as Frank) Benham had attended Robert's house just before his death and had been there at the time.

When William Benham took over 'The Old Original Bar' in 1917, he lived at 'Craigrock' villa at 310 Glasgow Road, next door to Robert Craig at 312. He would live there with family for the rest of his life. On 7th April 1917, Frank Benham applied for a alcohol license, which was granted by authorities.

Figure 357 William Francis (Frank) Benham outside his Stonefield Road shop in 1921

We've dated this photo of Frank as being definitely 1921 according to worldwide news posters which were on the side of the shop, on the rest of the picture. (not featured). Frank Benham was too old for war, but was a known character in the area.

Born in 1857 in Edinburgh, he moved from Glasgow to Blantyre in Summer 1893, initially living at nearby Dervoch Cottage as a booksellers assistant, with wife Elizabeth (Lizzie) Ann Pearson Craig and his 3 daughters, Elizabeth Jackson Benham (Bessie), Margaret Ann Benham (Meg) and Jane (Jean) Craig Benham. His only son died in 1895 as an infant, prompting a house move, this time to St Clair Cottage in Rosebank Avenue by 1901. The family moved to Glasgow Road by 1911.

Frank rented and ran a popular newsagent shop, adjacent to the large pend close at the bottom of Stonefield Road at number 11, between Valerio's café and Blantyre Post Office, his full story covered in another Blantyre book.

He died on 13th December 1925, at his home at Craigrock, his will read on 8th April 1926 with eldest daughter Elizabeth Jackson Benham inheriting £901, 13 shillings and 6 pence. (Around £50,000 in today's money). However, Craigrock and the shop at 11 Stonefield Road were rented and did not form part of the estate. The Old Original Bar was however part of the estate and would be sold on. His barmen at the time were John Gibson and Felix McBride.

The next owner of the Old Original Bar from 1926 until into the 1940's was Mr. James Jones, a traveller of 30 Calderwood Road, Rutherglen. He kept on Felix as barman. He also took ownership of the adjacent shops at 4 and 6 Stonefield Road, which once were part of the Old Original building. Elizabeth Benham and her sister Meg would continue to run their fathers old shop at 11 Stonefield Road.

Throughout WW2, 'The Old Original Bar' was still a real miner's pub. Dominoes, darts, talk about sport, the hardships of work and war, a pint after work type of place. Some of these old miners would frequent the premises well into their elderly years, long after the pits closed.

During a fierce storm in January 1968, residents in nearby Stonefield Cottage were woken by an almighty crash as the chimneystack on the gable of The Old Original crashed to the ground. It is alleged the same thing happened across the road at Mayberry Place.

A poem by the late Blantyre historian, Jimmy Cornfield, all about the Old Original Bar and its characters remembers the past. The poem is accompanied by a very suitable photo, courtesy of the Cornfield family. As follows:

Figure 358 The Old Original Mob photographed early 1970's (c) J Cornfield

The "Old Original Bar" Mob
(Craig's Tae You An Me)

A bunch O the boys were whopping it up outside Craig's Auld Original Baur,
They had all been in and had a good sup, now they were home for the war!
Whilst standing in the cold rain, a photo was taken by McGuire,
The ale had given them Dutch courage, to face she who sits by the fire.

Up spoke a voice from within the bunch,"I'm hame for the trouble I'm intae"
The rest looked in awe at this brave man, whose name was Jim McGinty.
Cousin Hugh then spoke, but he was alright, for a bachelor man was he
Not for him, the fear O` a woman, he was a gentleman and fancy free

James McFauld and Todd were another two, both single the same as Hugh
Not for them the wrath o` a woman, so they drunk the whole day thru.
McBride McGaulley and Morris, Coulter, Cummiskey and Finnegan
Cowardly looked at each other, then turned and went back in again.
I look at this photo now and again, taken in days O` lang syne,
The reason I'm not in it? I was in the loo at the time!

"Now the moral of this tale, is never be a liar
Don't get a photo taken outside a pub in Blantyre"
Just be like me and go for a pee and never tell McGuire……..

By James Cornfield 2008

Amongst those who latterly worked there are John Rundell, Davie McKean. A couple named Bernie and Bella worked there from 1968 for a few years. Other workers included John and Mary Welsh and their 3 daughters Ann (who married Bobby Rooney who also worked in the pub), Mary and Josephine (who married into the Mooney family). Also Brenda McGuigan. Other bar managers were Katie O'Brien Anderson managed the pub for many years, living above it in the corner flat. Donald Storrie owned the Old Original for a time, employing Sam (Sammy) Johnston as his barman in the 1980's. Jim Quigley, another manager. Upper flats lay empty for 20 years until 1990.

Figure 359 Old Original Bar with Glasgow Road on right in 2015

The pub went up for lease again in 2013. In 2015, Punch Partnership held the license for trading and still own it, under the watchful eye of current landlady, Betty. When it was taken over by Punch, they painted the exterior signage bright red, as opposed to the black which had been there for many years prior. Visiting in November 2017, we took the next photo of the interior, on one of the quieter days.

Blantyre Project Social Media:

Bill Hunter: "During the 1960's and 1970's there used to be an old alcoholic gentleman who would frequent this bar (no names given). He was refused entry often and when denied, would lift any object outside the pub smashing as many windows as possible. It happened many times!"

Figure 360 Interior of Old Original in November 2017

In the flat above the corner door a family by the name of Forrest lived there. Three sons Charles, Jim, William and a daughter Lynn. The other two flats facing Glasgow Road, one was occupied by Mrs. Bell and her son Jim, and the other by Mrs. Bell's daughter.

Today, the rear yard is accessed by a path to the west of the building. There is an open space behind the pub which seems largely unused. The pub itself, remains open with tidy neat signage, clean paintwork although the stonework has seen better days. A sign of the times are the multiple satellite dishes on the upper floor, not just for the pub, but for resident's homes. A line of artificial grass adorns the façade midway up, containing anti bird roosting equipment, preventing Blantyre's birds from doing their business. From what we witnessed on our visit, staff are attentive and engaged in playful banter with all the punters whilst going about their job. You won't get to the bar without somebody telling a story.

As with all pubs in Blantyre, it has its own set of regular and loyal customers. It is safe to say at time of writing and at 115 years old in 2018, 'The Old Original Bar' is one of the few pubs left in Blantyre which still retains an interior with the old, nostalgic charm and a character people look back fondly upon.

Stonefield Cottage

Immediately adjacent westwards to Clive Place (later The Old Original Bar) was a former detached house, named Stonefield Cottage.

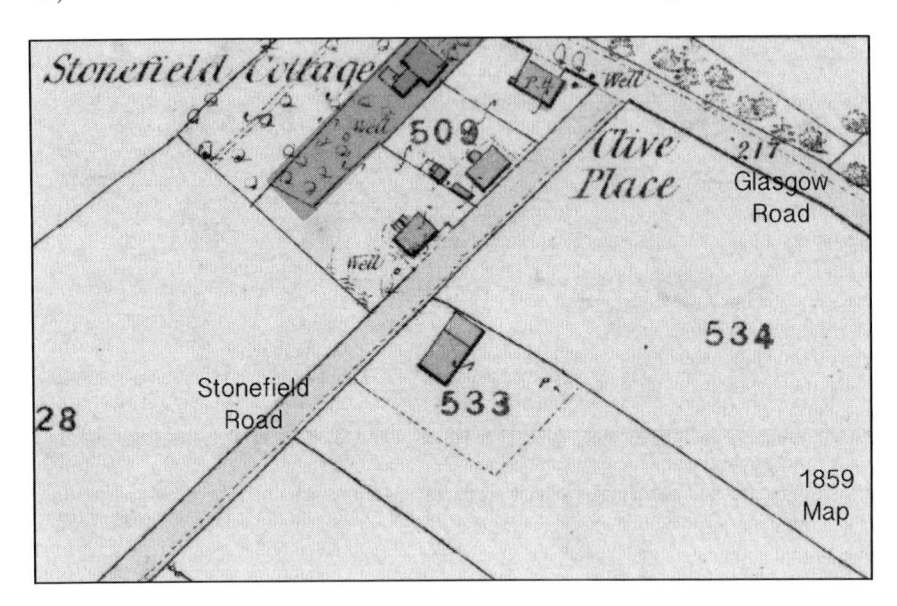

Figure 361 Stonefield Cottage highlighted on 1859 Blantyre map

This little house was important for the area of Stonefield on its western boundary and indeed was one of the first buildings within the hamlet of Stonefield itself. Dating back to the 1830's, it was situated in open fields, directly facing out, but set back from the Glasgow to Hamilton road on a long, rectangular, but narrow plot. It was of similar design to the adjacent Clive Place, something confirmed by a former resident of the cottage.

Thought to have been constructed by the Coats family from Blantyreferme, (who also were constructors of the Stonefield Tavern buildings), it was called 'Stonefield Cottage' and initially rented out to others. In the 1850's, Mr. Charles Ford and his wife were renting the cottage fro the Coats family but tragedy would strike on 19th April 1857 when their infant daughter was born but only lived a few hours, passing away at the property.

It would have perhaps felt very rural in those days. There were no buildings across the road and cattle would have been a frequent sight on the Wheatlandhead Farm fields to the rear. A central path led up to the front door from the Glasgow Road. With trees in the small front garden and woodland at the back containing a well during the 19th Century, such sparsely sited early Blantyre buildings quickly became well known to others.

The 1859 name book for the Parish describes Stonefield Cottage as "a neat cottage between 'Woodneuk' and 'Clive Place'. The name is well known." (Woodneuk was a property immediately to the west.)

Early Owners & Tenants

The Coats family would own Stonefield Cottage for the remainder of the 20th Century, passing between family members Elizabeth, John, William and Margaret. Tenants changed fairly frequently too.

In 1875, John Clark was renting the cottage. By 1885, Robert Gray (the grocer) rented although he would go on to build his own buildings further east. By 1895, Elizabeth Coats was occupying the cottage, as well as being owner, leasing out the nearby grasspark to Archibald Boreland, a cattle dealer, who lived near the Stonefield Tavern.

As the 20th Century dawned, the 1901 census has Margaret Coats (62) and widowed sister Elizabeth Coats Smith (62) and brother William Coats (55) living at Stonefield Cottage, the siblings also having ownership of other properties in Blantyre. By 1905, only William Coats was there, perhaps feeling lonely or the house was too big for just him, for he shared the house with a miner, Alfred Brooks. It would have been a time of great change for William Coats. Losing his sisters, now living alone, seeing trams stop outside his property and large buildings popping up around his cottage like the Old Original and opposing St Joseph's Church.

By World War One, the siblings all had passed on and the cottage belonged to Miss Isabella Jackson who owned and let it out to Arthur Beattie until the early 1920's. By this time, official address was 289 Glasgow Road.

During the early 1920's, shopkeeper Mrs. Annie McGeachie bought Stonefield Cottage, directly opposite Mayberry Place. She let it for a short time to family member James McGeachie whom by then was retired. Annie, then in the late 1920's moved in as owner and occupier and lived there until the 1940's.

Following WW2 in 1949, a Mr. Stewart bought the cottage, which by then was nearly 120 years old. After years of trying to repair it, he eventually gave up in 1959. In July, at the Glasgow Fair Weekend of that year the old cottage was entirely demolished and a new one built from scratch.

During its construction the Stewart family lived at Barnhill Farm on Bardykes Road. Mr. Stewart's young son, Robert is pictured in the next photo in August 1959, whilst the foundation work got underway.

The photo was from a slide, and whilst not of best quality, it does capture the moment perfectly. One can just imagine the young Robert Stewart excited to see his new home being built.

The building to the left is still there today, as is the Co-Op on the right.

Back then those buildings in the rear on Stonefield Road housed Norris Grocery. Living in the flats above were the Robertsons on the left, Mrs Clements on the right and in the shadow, the door to the shared outside toilet. The low building in the centre was Tommy the Cobbler's shop with another two flats above. During the 1960's, a long greenhouse was out the back, centrally located in the rear of the plot.

Figure 362 Robert Stewart at Stonefield Cottage August 1959

The new house was also named Stonefield Cottage and was sold by the Stewart family in 1983. Today, as the following modern photo shows, the cottage and front garden have a rather minimalist appearance, although the house itself is well maintained and has been extended at the front including new windows and doors. Surrounded by modern flats, it's a far cry from the rural location initially, but we should always remember that part of Stonefield had its roots at this little plot of land, lived on now for over nearly 190 years!

Figure 363 The Current Stonefield Cottage in 2015 (built 1959)

Westneuk Concert Hall (Stonefield House)

When looking back at Blantyre's history, perhaps one of Blantyre's least known and hardly explored buildings was the 'Westneuk Concert Hall' on Glasgow Road. Incredibly this plot of land devoted to public entertainment would later become a house, then in future years once again serve the community for purposes of their enjoyment.

The humble beginnings of this Victorian concert hall date back to the 1840's when Hugh McPherson, a merchant of Haughhead, Blantyreferme bought a long, rectangular plot of land on Glasgow Road, directly opposite some dense woodland. The plot was situated not far from the junction of what would become Stonefield Road and was near Clive Place and immediately to the west of Stonefield Cottage. It was on the western extremity of the hamlet of Stonefield, its western corner, and naming would have been easy with the word "Westneuk", quite literally meaning the 'western corner.'

Hugh McPherson was born in 1800 in Shotts and was in his 40's living in Blantyre with family by the time he constructed the concert hall. Built of stone, detached and 2 storey, it may have had intricate stonework features that set it aside from other buildings in Blantyre. At the rear, a small house was constructed separately to accommodate the hall manager or licensee.

Westneuk was initially built as a Public Entertainment Building, hosting plays, live music and recitals. It must have been a welcome retreat for the hard working people of Blantyre and somewhere to let off some steam! When Queen Victoria took to the throne, Scotland was undergoing a period of critical change. The industrial revolution led people to move from the country to the emerging villages and towns in search of work, resulting in the adaptation and rejection of rural traditions. Like the village pub, the urban public house became an important social space. By the mid nineteenth century, village life offered an increasingly wide range of leisure activities including sporting events, music and exhibition halls meant to cater for the tastes of the working and middle-classes who valued and were prepared to pay for their entertainment.

Figure 364 Victorian Concert Halls were popular throughout the country

The new audiences wanted music, dancing, spectacles and excitement, and many theatres such as Westneuk began to meet public demand offering alcohol on the premises. In the mid nineteenth century, such venues presented musical concerts, ballets, gothic dramas, melodramas and pantomimes. It would have been a noisy, rowdy place at times and not a place women would have frequented. The location was likely chosen carefully, at the corner of Blantyre, next to open fields with nothing westwards, at the time of its construction on Glasgow Road until you reached Blantyre's boundary at Priory Bridge.

Hugh McPherson's ownership of the concert hall was short lived. He died in the early 1850's and Westneuk would pass to ownership of his Trustees. Around 1855, the McPherson family let out the concert hall to incomer,

Gavin Muirhead, who acquired a license to sell alcohol on the premises.

Born in Bothwell in 1815, Gavin Muirhead, a grocer came to Blantyre around 1855 and rented the house and garden behind the hall at Westneuk for £18 per year. There, he lived with his wife Sarah, some 16 years his junior and their young family. However, the important short, few years between 1855 and 1859 would seal the fate of Westneuk.

The End of Westneuk

It would appear Gavin Muirhead was simply 2 decades too early for his concert hall. In the 1850's, Blantyre's population was still relatively small and business was not good. Neighbours complained of the noise, the disorder of regulars and for unknown reason, whether through lack of custom, mismanagement, or excess, Westneuk was not the thriving place it was intended to be.

In March 1858, only 3 years after taking over the concert hall, Gavin Muirhead had other problems brewing in the form of mounting pressures and complaints from neighbours.

For example, Charles Ford renting next door at Stonefield Cottage had recently lost an infant child. Perhaps wanting peace, he was fed up of the entertainment public house next door and disorderly behavior emanating from it at all hours. Charles involved others and it went to court.

The Edinburgh Evening Courant reported the case. MUIRHEAD V. FORD AND OTHERS states, "The pursuer sells whisky and other liquors at Westneuk Blantyre; some of his neighbours petitioned to Justices that he might not get his license again, as he kept a disorderly house, Ford raises action against Muirhead. On Thursday 11th March 1858, the Court held that there was no necessity for issue of 'veritas convicii' (an excuse) but that the truth of the complaint was in malice and want of probable cause. In other words, Muirhead got away with it, and Charles having to retract complaint.

This was no victory though. Neighbours ill feeling and falling or inadequate custom did not make a successful business.

By December 1858, only 3 years after coming to Blantyre, Gavin Muirhead was declared bankrupt, forcing a move out. He left Blantyre for good sometime shortly after 1861.

With the closure of Westneuk concert hall for good at the end of December 1858, so too, the name 'Westneuk' would permanently disappear.

Stonefield House

However, Westneuk's story does not end there. The building after all still existed in 1859. The name-book for the Parish that year describes the property as "a superior home formerly used as a public house of entertainment. The property of Mr. McPherson."

Westneuk was renamed in 1859 to 'Stonefield House' perhaps to compliment the adjacent 'Stonefield Cottage.' The building's hall would be renovated and split into functional homes, indeed enough for 2 spacious homes, 1 on the lower floor, 1 on the upper, accessed by stone steps at the back. A central path led from Glasgow Road up to the front doorway.

Figure 365 Location Line Drawing putting Westneuk into modern context

The houses continued in ownership by the McPherson family from 1859 let out to miners until they changed hands, bought over by Hamilton Brendon McDougall, of Hamilton Villa, Park Road, Kirn during the 1880's. This family would own Stonefield House for the rest of its years well into the 20th Century. Around the time they acquired the property, the opposing David Livingstone Memorial Church was being built on the north side of the road, directly across from the 2 houses, still with wide open Wheatlandhead fields to the south and west.

It is known the Harvey family were renting in the 1880's, a daughter born to William Harvey on 9th February 1884 in one of the homes. The Harvey family shortly after moved eastwards to rent at Henderson's Buildings.

It is thought also that during the mid 1880's, William Small, the prominent Secretary of the Miners National Federation may have lived there a short time between censuses, before moving to Forrest Street. By 1895, James Powell a flesher and James Malone, a mining Contractor were renting from Hamilton Brendon McDougall for £16 and £14 per annum respectively.

At the turn of the 20th Century, as with many properties in Blantyre, the property was further sub-divided to maximize rental potential. The 2 homes became 4, with two on the lower floor and 2 on the upper. In 1905, one house was empty, two were occupied by miners William Stewart and Adam Yanker. The remaining house and stable to the rear was occupied by Thomas Reid, a fruit dealer. The stable would have been used to store his horse and cart for his deliveries. Thomas Reid was in the news a couple of years earlier.

In July 1903, Lord Kyllachy heard evidence in an action of divorce by Thomas Reid of Stonefield House against Mary Stirling or Reid, Lochore Bridge, Lochgelly, Fife. Thomas, the person who raised he action was a blind man. He said he had married on 14th April 1876, and there were three surviving children. He had been a miner, but in 1883 he had an accident, by which he lost his sight. Since then he had been hawking fruit and tea. Four years after the accident his wife deserted him, and he had learned that she had gone to stay with a miner named Phillips at Lochgelly. Other evidence was heard and the divorce decree was granted.

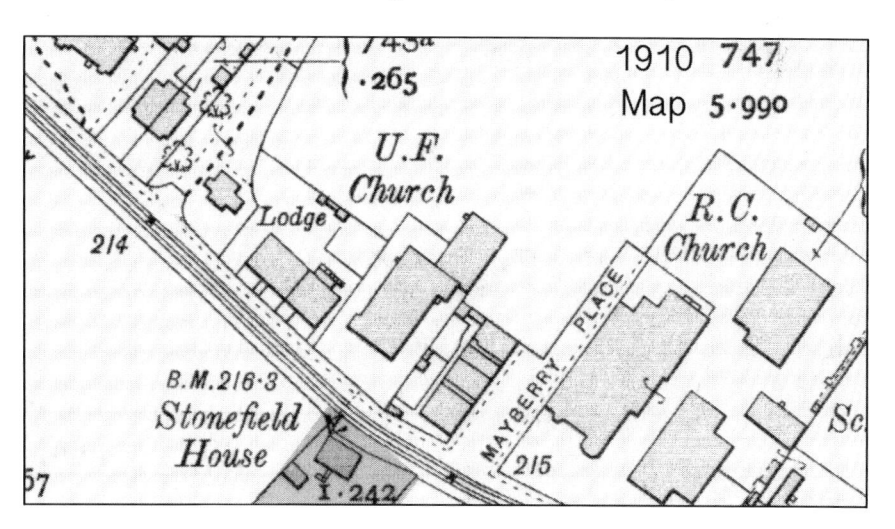

Figure 366 Stonefield House on 1910 Map, directly opposite the Livingstone Church

By 1915, the name Stonefield Cottage was being used less and indeed does not appear in valuation rolls after that time, replaced simply by 291 and 293 Glasgow Road.

In the 1910's to 1930's, the 4 homes within Stonefield House were let out to miners and their families, all under the ownership of Hamilton Brandon McDougall, although by 1925 Nellie McDougall, a family member took ownership through inheritance. Rents in 1925 were £14 per annum. The stable was gone by that year too.

In 1935, all 4 houses lay derelict and empty, condemned by the council and were subsequently cleared as part of the slum clearance later that year. Stonefield House does not appear on the 1936 Blantyre map, a time when the County Council took ownership of that plot of land.

The ground lay empty for a few years, before being used again when a Public Entertainment building was built, in the form of a brand new, Council owned, Community Centre, itself now long since demolished.

Today, there's no trace of Westneuk, Stonefield House or the Community Centre. The site, today accommodates modern flats at Mayberry Grange, which were somewhat sympathetic in design by adopting a similar footprint, certainly at Glasgow Road as the old "Westneuk".

Community Centre

When Stonefield House, (formerly Westneuk Concert Hall) was demolished in 1935, the plot of land lay vacant for a couple of years whilst the council decided upon what they should use it for. A community centre was decided upon, which was to benefit all of Blantyre. There is a little urban myth that this community centre opened on the same day as the David Livingstone Memorial in 1929, which wasn't the case.

We turn our attention to 1938, by when the new community centre had been built. The Earl of Home was the president of the new Centre and Mr W. G. Dow was the chairman; the vice-chairmen were Rev. James Gibb and Mrs M. Robb, Mr R. Paton was its honorary secretary; Mr Quintin Smith (well known local teacher), was the honorary treasurer, and a Mrs Douches and Mr R. Neill represented the men's and women's sections.

The Centre had facilities for making furniture and for cobbling (a roaring trade at the time), and for a while there was a library with reading room, a dressmaking room, and other recreational activities.

Attached to the Centre there were nearly 50 allotment gardens, again a popular pastime for many. The Centre also had a large kitchen, a games room and it even had public baths for both sexes!

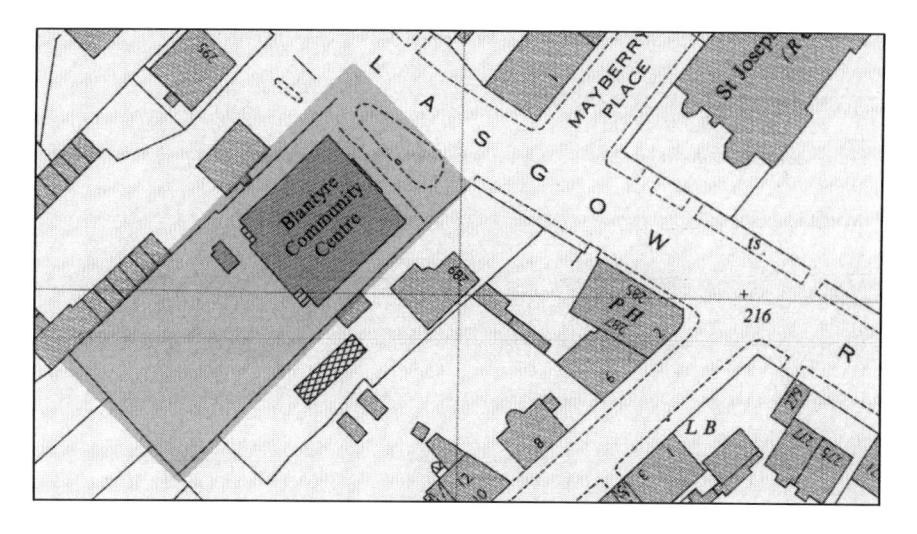

Figure 367 Blantyre Community Centre on Glasgow Road 1962

The Glasgow Road Community Centre was opened on Wednesday 13th April, 1938, by Lord Nigel Douglas Hamilton (Commissioner for Special Areas in Scotland), and was designated for the Blantyre Mutual Service Association, (it was a government scheme, funded entirely by the government to help deprived districts).

Others present that day were Mr. Allan Chapman M.P., for Rutherglen, Captain Watt, Chairman of Lanark County Council, and Robert Bryce Walker, who was the County Clerk. The County Director of Education, C. T. Mair was also there and Councilor Edward Daly present too, although he wasn't mentioned in the news report.

Mrs. John Dunsmuir of High Blantyre, on behalf of the women members, presented Lord Nigel with a Douglas tartan scarf, and Mr. John G. Dunn, the architect, on behalf of the contractors, handed over a cheque to the president for the local funds raised to get the centre underway.

Heart of Community

The building was one storey, opening out and with frontage to Glasgow Road. It certainly had architectural features of an art-deco style, typical of public buildings in the 1930's. The high raised arched window of the large hall, gave the building an appearance of having further storeys.

During the fifties, 3 large allotments at the rear still remained. One was worked by Jimmy Burgess, one by Jock & Robert (Rab) Jackson, and the third by Mr. Stewart of nearby Stonefield Cottage.

Figure 368 Blantyre Community Centre in 1995, not long before it closed

The Centre's youth Club, held on Monday evenings was host in 1973, when it received a visit from Comedian, Sir Billy Connolly. (although at the time, he was very much an emerging comedian, folk singer!)

Pictured here in May 1978 in this unusual scene are 50 enthusiastic individuals who regularly attended a dedicated YOGA class in the centre.

Keeping fit was the name of the game!

Figure 369 Yoga Class at Community Centre 1978

The event was part of a full day of fitness activities for men and women. Mrs. Mary Wilson, of Wolcott Drive, who was a yoga teacher and organiser of the event hailed it as a great success. She told reporters, "At our normal yoga classes, we don't have enough time, so we booked a full day, so we didn't have to rush things."

Mrs Patti McTavish, Vice chairperson of the Scottish Yoga Association came along and provided a lecture and expert demonstration. Classes were made up of new starts and experienced individuals.

Figure 370 Children of 1978 Play-scheme at the Community Centre

Pictured in 1978, these are just some of the many Blantyre kids who enjoyed a summer of fun at the Blantyre Community Centre. It marked the start of 4 weeks of summer school holiday fun which got off to a great start, despite earlier fears that the events may not go ahead due to lack of supervision.

The Playscheme events were dually run by The Elizabeth Scott Centre and the Glasgow Road Community Centre and they attracted youngsters in their droves! The idea was to stop children being bored in summer, but still give them something interesting to do in the company of many friends.

Jimmy Coulter was the Caretaker, Jim Sweeney manager and Una Mason Hynds oversaw the Cafe with her sister-in-law, Sheena Mason from 1989 until 1991. Una's husband ran the drama group and was instrumental in the protests against the building being closed down.

Following 1997, the Blantyre Community Centre at 291 Glasgow Road lay derelict for a few years well into post Millennium years. In 1994, it was completely demolished and the land lay vacant again for a few years. It is now many residential flats at modern Mayberry Grange.

By Paul D Veverka

Figure 371 The Community Centre derelict in 2001, now Mayberry Grange

> Blantyre Project Social Media:
>
> **Robert Stewart** "During the 1950's and 60's the centre was known locally as the TocH. A popular wedding venue, the Old Original pub nearby always did well at weddings as licensing laws didn't allow the hall to sell alcohol at public halls. They was a popular playgroup there in the 1990's."

Mayberry Grange

Mayberry Grange are modern flats constructed on the site of the former Westneuk Concert Hall, Stonefield House and Blantyre Community Centre. Built in 2006 and 2007, the Electrical contractors 'Core' led in the power cables in August 2007. By winter, some were ready and Kayleigh Finnigan was one of the first people to rent the properties, moving in around November 2007. Residents had to wait quite some time before they were given addresses.

Figure 372 Mayberry Grange, residential flats in 2015

Blantyre Trams

From 1903 until 1930, trams were a vital part of Blantyre's infrastructure, welcomed by almost everybody, and brought jobs and good transport links to Hamilton, Cambuslang and Glasgow, Motherwell and Wishaw. They 'opened doors' for business and trade, made it easier to visit relatives and friends and provided, linked easy access to Central Scotland for exciting, day excursions.

Lanarkshire trams have a long, detailed story which deserves attention and is consequently the subject of another Blantyre Project book.

Figure 373 Blantyre Trams

However, one cannot write a defining book about Glasgow Road without at least touching upon trams and their impact upon Blantyre. Knowing others have incorrectly published dates and information, this brief synopsis is available as fact.

Proposal

On 7th and 22nd November 1898, the Hamilton, Motherwell and Wishaw Light railway company made an application to construct a 'light railway', 3 foot 6 inches wide from Blantyre near the junction of Stonefield Road, eastwards along the entire length of Glasgow Road, into the Burgh of Hamilton and Burnbank, then on to Wishaw. However, the Provost and Magistrates of Hamilton objected, on the basis that it would be unsightly, carriages and carts used for transporting manure, coal and animals and the narrow width could not safely accommodate passengers. The plan was shelved.

However, the Middle Ward of the County was expanding fast and the idea of being able to easily travel between populous centres was a good one. A year later, on 10th November 1899, the idea arose again and was proposed at a meeting by Hamilton Town Council. Extending the scheme to Larkhall was decided as being too expensive, but contractors were invited to tender on the basis that it used new electric power, rather than dirty steam and coal and of course that animals would not be permitted. Trams were to be wholly, a passenger transport service.

Figure 374 Blantyre Tram Cars 3 & 6 on opening day 22nd July 1903

The Arrival of Trams

Blantyre's line was to be part of Tramway Lane 1 of 3. The main line leading into Hamilton onwards to Wishaw at 8 miles and 5 furlongs. The tramlines were designated to be 4 foot 7 and three quarter inches wide, to comply with other tramlines in the Clyde Valley. Construction commenced in June 1902, but at the opposite side at Motherwell. Work teams also shortly after commenced in Hamilton and Blantyre, opening up the roadway, which in those times was still relatively clear of any services or pipes.

The soft, dirt tracks of the era made the digging relatively simple and residents were delighted to gain the added bonus of granite setts, a hard road no less being laid throughout the route. People were thrilled to see for the first time, a 'modern' road emerging, that could be walked and travelled upon without getting muddy, a first for Blantyre. Separate crews throughout 1902 and 1903, worked tirelessly erecting pole after pole at the roadside.

Poles and standards along the route were ornate to beautify the network.

The tram workshop, store and garage was named 'the powerhouse' located at the terminal in Motherwell. On 19th June 1903, Tram Car 20 left the powerhouse to make a trial trip. Passengers were not permitted on board but the car drew crowds of spectators as Hamilton, Motherwell & Wishaw Tram Company trained its drivers and tested the tracks and wires.

Figure 375 Motherwell "powerhouse", repair workshop & central offices 1903

On Tuesday 21st July 1903, Car 3 and Car 6 left Motherwell with the Board of Inspection. Car 3 travelled the whole line to the Blantyre end to inspect the track and as such, it is that day, not the reported 22nd that trams first ran and were seen in Blantyre. All was well and the following day, 22nd July 1903 would be the turn of paying passengers, with all the cars brought from the powerhouse on to the network.

The Motherwell Times reported that opening day, "Thirty thousand passengers it is estimated travelled on those cars in that first day. Although all the places of business were closed it being the merchant holiday (Fair holidays), the town seemed very busy. From early morning until 11pm, the cars ran merrily. There was nothing but praise for the handsome and commodious structures. The July weather was glorious and the novelty of the outing appealed to all. People clearly opted for a ride on the cars, rather than heading to the coastal towns and beaches. The whole thing went without a hitch."

A Vital service

Despite Glasgow's long established tram network being so nearby, for many, the arrival of trams in Lanarkshire was the first time they had seem them up close. Along the route were 32 tram stops, marked simply by names on the poles, at quarter mile intervals and the tinkle of the car bells became a familiar noise, one ring for stop/start, multiple rings for alarms. The fare for the whole journey between Blantyre and Motherwell was 5p, the other fares being just under a penny a mile, making it affordable for all. It was a service for people of all ages, all walks of life, all backgrounds.

Cars 1 – 25 of the network also had upper decks and had a livery of light blue and off-white initially but were later coloured green.

Upon opening, 'Lanarkshire Highways Tram order of 1903', further subdivided the lines into 11 manageable sections. Blantyre's tramway from the terminus 75 yards past Stonefield Road junction, (directly opposite David Livingstone Church) heading eastwards to Springwell was officially on timetables as 'tramlane 2'. Tramlane 1 was reserved for the future between the Stonefield terminus and Priory Bridge, in the hope one day Lanarkshire's trams could be connected to the Glasgow Network at Cambuslang.

Figure 376 Lanarkshire Trams waiting to be deployed in 1903

It is safe to say trams were well used. In the New Year holiday period in just a few days in 1903/1904, over 106,000 people used the trams, bringing in around £200. Inevitably, there were accidents. Small claims against the tram company were numerous, usually from injured horses and damaged carts.

However, in May 1906, a first occurred when the tram company sued a private owner for reversing his bakers van into one of their cars.

Extension of Blantyre Network

Given the nature of a miner's work, trams started early. On weekdays, the first car ran from Blantyre at 4.37am and left at 11.22pm. After that, you were going to be stuck, unless you wanted a long walk!

Glasgow Road from the Livingstone Church westwards to the West End was subject to heavy disruption from May 1906, when the Blantyre extension of the tram network commenced. Squads of workmen lifted parts of the road and laid rails from the terminus to create a new terminus further along at Priory Bridge, an area which caused the company considerable concern due to the narrow bridge and curvature of the road. Dunallan Loop on Glasgow Road near Coatshill, was a passing point and not as others suggest, a terminus.

On 20th January 1907, the extension opened allowing Blantyre passengers to board before Stonefield and be taken to Cambuslang.

The two different tram networks would never fully run through and join. However, a terminus and change point was located at Priory Bridge, which had to be renovated to accommodate the cars. It was a dark, dimly lit area and did not make a comfortable or welcoming place to alight and change.

This wonderful postcard of 1907 demonstrates the sentiment in Glasgow as passengers contemplated being able to travel by tram into Lanarkshire.

Figure 377 In 1907 Glasgow passengers rejoiced connecting to Lanarkshire

By Paul D Veverka

The outbreak of World War One in 1914 didn't affect the running of the trams, but when the war "hotted up" in 1915, many conductors and drivers volunteered for duty and left the tram company with a severe shortage of manpower. This resulted in June 1915, women being employed for the first time. Within 6 months however, police were deployed on occasion on to the cars, for children filled with cheek and hope of a "free hurl" were somehow able to talk back to the women drivers in a way that the men had previously not tolerated. Thankfully such intolerance was only short-lived and women of strengthened, more confident character were employed who could put those 'imps' into their place and remove the public police presence!

Stop also to think for a second of how the tram drivers task in winter must have been a grim one. Steering in snow, hail and rain in an open front car, a little windshield offering little protection, it is something many of us forget these workers had to endure.

Cars were sometimes used for different purposes. A funeral car in black carried the tramway managers, who passed away. A recruitment car adorned in posters during World War One advertised the need for more men to fight. Cars were sometimes also given names. Playful names of places and people than were more recognizable from a distance than saying, "here comes car 3".

1918 was a problematic year for the tram network. A strike by women's workers over pay stopped trams temporarily in August. Also, the introduction of more expensive fares was not met with any sort of gratitude! Indeed, many who used the cars simply to get to and from work, took to walking and for the first time since launch, 1918 was a year where passenger numbers dropped.

In 1921, parts of the Network were bought over by the County Council for over £60,000. 1922 and 1923 were years of heavy litigation with many claims made by individuals for accidents and damage to their vehicles, perhaps coinciding with the growing number of motorized vehicles and lack of road safety laws.

On 10th March 1926, the Hamilton to Uddingston tramway closed for good, meaning part of the circular route was severed. For some it meant longer journeys and that prompted the use of local privately run bus services, which were springing up in great numbers.

Writing on the wall

In 1928, the writing was 'on the wall' for Lanarkshire Trams when the company asked a hypothetical question to the County Council, if they would be recompensed if they withdrew their trams from Lanarkshire, but left their cobbles and hard standing setts within the road for the use of the council. The reply from the council was shocking in that they asked for the tramway company to make good all the roads, something estimated as costing £98,000. This would have liquidated the company, so eventually a deal was sorted where for £12,500, the Tramway company would amend all roads, lifting rails and putting a hard surface down, having 5 years to pay for it, work to be completed by 1933.

With the closure of other parts of the route, the company renamed itself to "The Lanarkshire Traction Company" and combined a use of their tramcars with their own bus services, a transitional period in 1929 and 1930 to oversee the winding down of the tram era. Blantyre trams ran for the last time on Monday 6th October 1930 the service between Hamilton and Cambuslang then terminated abruptly. It was truly now the age of bus public transport.

Figure 378 Lifting Glasgow Road's tram Cobbles outside Old Original Bar 1930

In December 1930, restoration of Glasgow Road commenced, the cost ending up at £26,500. The granite cobbles and rails were lifted and the county council took the opportunity to widen Glasgow Road between the Stonefield and Priory Bridge Terminus. This meant compulsory purchase of the front gardens of many Glasgow Road houses. Buildings including the Parkville and Livingstone Memorial Church lost much of their large front gardens as new pavements and a wider road were formed, enough for 2 passing vehicles. Walls and railings were re-erected around the smaller gardens. It was a significant change and one not always welcomed until the appropriate compensation was attained. The last tram in Lanarkshire ran on Valentine's Day, 14th February 1931.

Roselea

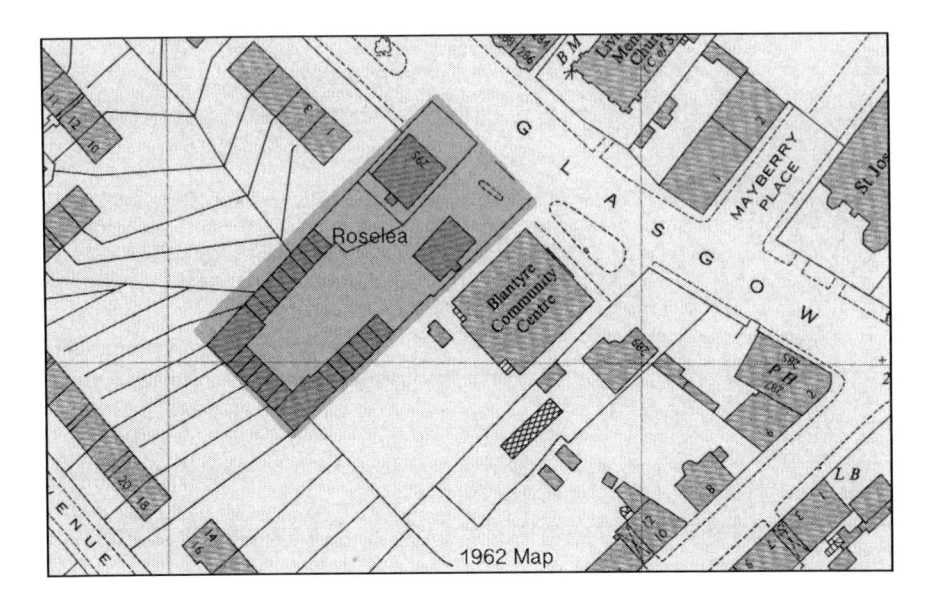

Figure 379 Roselea House and Garage on 1962 Map, beside Community Centre

We next arrive at 295 Glasgow Road at a property used to this day for both residential and commercial purpose, named 'Roselea', the original constructor and owner being Mr. John Richardson.

John Richardson was born in Rutherglen in 1871, one of 13 children. As a young man, he worked at the Greenfield Colliery on the outskirts of Blantyre. Initially a coal miner, he changed profession and became a general dealer living midway along Glasgow Road at 41 Greenside Street.

Following World War One, he had moved home and was renting 'Glenpark' a house at 33 Station Road. He was also renting a nearby stable yard at that address in connection with a barrel business.

Things were to change, when after some success, he acquired and bought a long, narrow rectangular plot of land at Glasgow Road adjacent to Stonefield House, directly across the road from the David Livingstone Memorial Church. Like many people, he may have been invigorated and excited by the arrival of mechanized vehicles to towns and seeing opportunity, he built Roselea Cottage, a one storey bungalow and a small garage directly facing on to Glasgow Road. His construction and move happened between 1921 and 1924 and he made further use of the land by building sheds within the yard at the rear. He is noted in the 1925 valuation roll living at Roselea.

During his life, John married twice. In the 1940's, he became a councilor and is pictured here at a Police dance, perhaps supporting his police officer son-in-law at that event. His daughter Christina is on the far right.

Figure 380 Councilor Richardson at a Police Dance one November during 1940s

John Richardson passed away in July 1956, leaving the old Roselea garage and adjacent house to his daughter Christina (Chrissie) Dyer and her husband Jimmy. At that time, the garage and yard was being rented out in the mid to late 1950's to McSeveney's Coachworks, a panel beater from High Blantyre before they moved eastwards along Glasgow Road.

However, after 1956, the garage would change hands again back to the Richardsons, when John's son, John Junior, (known as 'Jock') bought Roselea Cottage and the old garage and yard, back from his sibling, Chrissie.

Jock was born at 41 Greenside Street in Blantyre in 1906. He 'got his start' working in the Co-Op butchers and his father's garage and initially repaired butter barrels from the premises. As a teenager, he moved to Glen Park with his family although by the time he married in 1937 he was at Bruce Terrace. After the death of his father John in 1956, Jock moved up to Roselea Cottage on Glasgow Road. The old garage acquired from Chrissie was subsequently knocked down and he built the modern, current garage that year, set back off Glasgow Road, with enough room for a forecourt. (The previous garage & petrol pumps had been situated where the forecourt is today.)

Richardson's Garage & Business

John (Jock) and Jean opened their new garage in the late 1950's, (branded Fina fuel) and subsequently removed some of the old sheds and building and renting out lockups at the rear of the garage. Jock was a popular, well known man who owned a butcher's shop on the north side of Glasgow Road opposite Elm Street, another butchers at Stonefield Road and one in Hamilton. Indeed, Jock may have been more well known as a butcher in the 1960's and 1970's, than as a mechanic or garage owner.

Richardson's had 2 delivery vans which went around Blantyre, one operated by Jock's son James, the other by another son, Robert. Jock had 4 sons. In the early to mid 1960's, the Richardson's kept a large Great Dane in the forecourt. The dog, named Roy was huge and remembered by many.

Figure 381 Early 1970's Jock and Jean Richardson outside Roselea Cottage

In the early 1970's, Mr. Innes rented a shed from the Richardson's at the rear of the garage, where he ran a small blacksmiths business. He also made and erected the large, current front canopy to protect customers from the weather which is still there today. According to Jean Richardson, her grandfather Jock died in July 1978 and his wife Jean in August 1983 and it is clear from the family how much they are missed.

DID YOU KNOW? Jock's four sons were not partners in the business but continued working the shared, various parts until the death of Jock's wife in 1983. The sons continued then working in separate shops and the garage and the family home was sold to "Jimmy Maxwell the Janny" from the High School around 1986. Men who worked in the garage over the years included Mr. Tremble and Willie McNulty although dozens of people over the years have been there.

Finally, 'Roselea Garage' was acquired by Jock's other son, George Richardson, a likeable, friendly man, whose hard working son Kenny, still works there today. Kenny is the fourth generation of this family to work at that same location, something rarely seen these days elsewhere in Blantyre!

Blantyre Project Social Media:

Fraser Cosh: "I remember as a boy regularly being sent up to Richardson's for 2 gallons of paraffin. Loaded them on to my 'Boagie' and towed it back home. We would have been 7 or 8 at the time. Don't imagine parents would get away with that these days."

Drew Fisher: "I seem to recall Richardson's sold 'Fina fuel' and were the cheapest filling station in Blantyre. Fifty pence would half fill the tank of a Mini in 1972 – changed days now!"

Ann Hartman: "A big Great Dane would stand outside the old Community Centre nearby to the garage. On a Saturday morning, when I came out of Mrs. Brown's dance school, it frightened the life out of me. It was a the size of a horse, this was early to middle 1960's."

Patrick Donnelly: "I remember that Great Dane dog. A local myth in the Old Original was that Jock went to buy a dog coat for it in winter but pet shop couldn't supply one large enough to fit, so he bought one for a pony instead!"

Julie Bruce (nee Richardson): "Robert Richardson is my dad. All the grandkids used to play out the back of the garage in times when health and safety didn't really matter! During the mid 1980's, I worked in the garage on a Sunday. George paid me 15 pounds and a few Wispa chocolate bars. I loved working there and was probably around 14 years old at the time."

Figure 382 Roselea Garage and Roselea Cottage as it is today

Rowan Place

Figure 383 Rowan Place on 19th May 2015. Photo by R Stewart

Although the houses at Rowan Place do not have Glasgow Road addresses, they require to be included in this book due to having frontage along a proportion of Glasgow Road. Situated across from the entrance to the 'Dandy', these 12 single storey houses were constructed especially with pensioners in mind. They are numbered 1 – 23 Rowan Place, all odd numbers.

Built in the late 1950's as part of the 'Orlits' housing scheme (homes behind and to the south at Fernslea Avenue), they are set back off Glasgow Road, offering good parking, single storey, unlike the other houses in the estate behind.

During research of this book, it was learned that they were cruelly nicknamed originally as 'Death Row', a name that thankfully does not exist in discussion anymore. Rowan Place looks to be well maintained with good sizeable gardens to the rear and have served families well over the last 60 years. The name 'Rowan' continues the woodland theme of Fernslea.

> Blantyre Project Social Media:
>
> **Patrick Donnelly:** "On 15th November 2017, an elderly gentleman motorist took a heart attack whilst driving, crashing his car into a lamppost at Roselea. Two passing women bravely conducted CPR, but the man was pronounced dead when the ambulance services arrived. Such heroism is still worth noting here."

Before the construction of Rowan Place, this plot had been the open fields of Wheatlandhead Farm, which in this particular plot, had stretched right down to Glasgow Road itself. The farm was also known as "Russell's."

Figure 384 Wheatlandhead Farm fields 1940's (later site of Rowan Place)

Contrary to writing by others, Glasgow Road west of this point was not all farmfields in the 20th Century. Indeed it was very much built upon, primarily for residential purposes. The last 150 years west of this point has seen some impressive houses being built. Let's take a look at these quality built villas….

Glasgow Road Villas

The homes westwards of Rowan Place are mostly large semi or detached houses, built in early 20th Century, although 4 of them were built much earlier in the 19th Century. Furthermore, every now and again, there are a couple of modern bungalows, built as plots have became available. For the best part, many of these old villas, that afforded such quality accommodation are still standing. Almost all of these prominent Glasgow Road houses have their own separate identities, or house names given to them by the original constructors.

Numbering and addresses along this stretch of Glasgow Road is a complex subject for whilst postal addresses (numbers) were allocated around 1910, the homes received entirely new numbers after the road was widened in the 1930's, renumbering an unusual move, but not unique by any means. Our table below summaries some basic information about these properties and unravels the complexities of the numbering system. Blocks of early tenements further West before the Westend are not included here but explored later in the book. Similarly Springfield Cottage which is accessed by a lane, a little distant from Glasgow Road is not explored in this particular book.

Glasgow Road South – Villas [c=approximation, >=after, <=before]			
House	Constructed	Original Address	Post 1930 Address
Bungalow (eastern)	1950's	None	313
Arnot	>1906<1909	None	315
Bungalow (western)	1950's	None	315a
Springfield Cottage	C1820	None	317
Brownlea Cottages (LHS)	c 1869	297	319
Brownlea Cottages (RHS) Originally Jeanfield Cottages	c 1869	299	321
Korek (originally Brownlie)	c 1869	301	323
Blairhoyle (orig. Brownlie)	c 1869	303	325
Clifton / Hilden / Moraig	>1902<1904	305	327
Laurel Cottage	>1902<1904	307	329
Oakbank (LHS)	>1902<1904	309	331
Oakbank (RHS)	>1902<1904	311	333
Campsie View	1903	313	341
House & Glasshouses	1903	315	343
Daldorch	>1907<1909	317	345
Dalveen	>1907<1909	319	347
Dunedin	>1907<1909	321	349
Orwell	>1907<1909	323	351

Bungalow (Eastern)

Figure 385 One Storey Bungalow adjacent to Rowan Place pictured 2016

Constructed: 1950's
Constructor: Unknown
House Type: Bungalow

Other Names: Unknown
Original Address: 313 Glasgow Road
Current Address: 313 Glasgow Road

Brief Summary: This plot of land was previously not built upon until the middle of the 20th Century. Originally farm-fields of Wheatlandhead Farm, the plot is adjacent to a council owned lane to the east, which accesses the 'Wheatland Orlits' housing estate behind.

The small, detached bungalow was constructed in the 1950's with 2 bay windows at the front and the main door unusually to the side. A separate garage is located to the east and there is a modest sized front and back garden. Mr. Jimmy French lived there in the third quarter of the 20th Century. His Burnbank shop specialized in Singer Sewing Machines. Jimmy's son Gordon died in a vehicle accident remembered by many people. There are no complexities of addresses at this location due to 'modern' construction dates. The cottage is today well maintained, whitewashed and desirable, being not far from the Parkville Restaurant and other amenities in Glasgow Road.

Blantyre Project Social Media:

Tina Riley: "All these homes from this point all along Glasgow Road are beautiful. We tried very hard to buy one in the 2000's after setting our heart on it, but it wasn't to be. Stiff competition and very derisable. Good to see them appear also in this book."

Arnot

Figure 386 'Arnot' constructed between 1906 and 1909

Constructed: >1906<1909
Constructor: William Coats
House Type: Detached Villa

Other Names: None
Original Address: Name only
Current Address: 315 Glasgow Road

Brief Summary: William Coats of nearby Stonefield Cottage obtained this vacant plot of land sometime between 1906 and 1909. He constructed a well built, stone detached cottage of one and a half storeys. As the picture shows there are certainly some tudor influences in the design. His build was likely to allow family members to live close together. The Coats family of Blantyreferme were responsible for building several buildings on Glasgow Road including those around the Stonefield Tavern and were one of the most prominent property owners on Glasgow Road during the late 19th and early 20th Centuries.

Despite sounding slightly French, 'Arnot' has its roots in Scottish origin in Kinross-shire. The name most fitting to Coats purchase of Wheatlandhead Farm fields, for in Gaelic it translates as "the place where barley is grown."

Margaret Coats, a spinster and sister of William, would live at this address which was always 315 Glasgow Road until her death in the early 1920's. The house went to her trustees, letting out to Peter Craig, a grocer in the mid 1920's. In 1930, this handsome house was empty as sale was progressed to Helen and Margaret Weir, who bought the house for their retirement. In later years, Mrs Young and Gilmour family lived there. The cottage is today, well kept, pretty in appearance and is unique in its design and charm.

Bungalow (Western)

Figure 387 Relatively modern Bungalow at 315a Glasgow Road

Constructed: c 1960's
Constructor: Unknown
House Type: Single Bungalow

Other Names: None
Original Address: 315a Glasgow Road
Current Address: 315a Glasgow Road

Brief Summary: This cottage has a similar history to the other one of the same era just 2 houses up to the east. A modern, single storey bungalow clad in stone with a slate roof, sits back from Glasgow Road offering modest front and rear garden space. Initially tied to the Averell family at Arnot next door. Margaret Averell was the neice of Mrs Young who took over Bowies fruit shop. This bungalow was built on land once within Arnot's boundaries.

Built in the 1960's on the former farmlands of Russell's Farm at Wheatlandhead, the cottage has an unusual address of 315a. When given its address it could not have 315 which belonged to 'Arnot' next door and could not be given 317 Glasgow Road, as this belonged to Springfield Cottage, set back off Glasgow Road, but thought to be the oldest house with a Glasgow Road addresss, accessed by a nearby lane. 315a bungalow was owned by the Averell family (Eric, Tom, Margaret & family) from construction until today.

> Blantyre Project Social Media:
>
> **Robert Stewart:** "The adjacent lane west of this cottage led to Springfield Cottage, former home of Mr. C. Innes Reid, the father of John Reid the printer".

By Paul D Veverka

Brownlea Cottages (Jeanfield)

Figure 388 Brownlea Cottages, oldest surviving residence on Glasgow Road South

Constructed: c 1869
Constructor: Robert Lindsay
House Type: 2 storey houses

Other Names: Jeanfield Cottages
Original Address: 297/299 Glasgow Road
Current Address: 319/321 Glasgow Road

Brief Summary: Incredibly important building for our heritage, as this is the oldest surviving house with frontage on Glasgow Road South between Springwell and the Westend! Built in 1869 by constructor and bookseller, Robert Lindsay (who lived nearby at Clyde Cottages and would later build Allison Place), it was originally called 'Jeanfield Cottages'. One side in 1875 was owned by Hugh Montgomery. By the early 1880's, Robert had moved away from Blantyre and the property was bought by Penelope Galt Renfrew, of Muir Street, Hamilton, who owned it and let it out until her death in 1900. On 12th October 1912, the Thomson family renting here lost a baby son (aged 10 month), named Wee Bunty. In 2 separate homes, it was twinned with an identical separate building to the west, and renamed 'Brownlea Cottages' although it is not connected in any way to the Brownlie's of Barnhill. Of solid, functional 2 storey construction it is short on ornate detail. By 1905 John G Johnston of Glasgow was the owner, although he had died by WW1. Tenants included Henry RS Oliver, draper and Thomas Devaney, a publican. Owners changed often. Joseph Hughes in 1920, Alexander Struthers by 1925 and by 1930 subdivided into private homes, one belonging to Struthers, the other to Thomas Little a works manager. The Bennett family have lived there now for over 35 years. At almost 150 years old, we see no reason why this won't still be standing and occupied in another 150 years. Lovely, quality family home!

Korek

Figure 389 Korek, was originally Brownlie House, built c1869

Constructed: c 1869
Constructor: Robert Lindsay
House Type: 2 Storey Houses

Other Names: Brownlie House
Original Address: 301 Glasgow Road
Current Address: 323 Glasgow Road

Brief Summary: The name 'Korek' may have Polish origins, although there is no immediate connection to constructor Robert Lindsay, who built this twinned property in 1869. Similar to adjacent Brownlea Cottages, the original name appears to be Brownlie House, although was quickly changed perhaps due to the similar name in Barnhill. The 1875 valuation roll has upstairs empty.

It is identical to its neighbor and shared a similar history of ownership with Penelope Galt Renfrew of Hamilton owning it from the early 1880's up until 1900. John G Johnston let it out to 2 tenants, one of which was Thomas Oliphant, a solicitor. By 1920, John F Dott owned the property and by 1930 it had changed hands to Mary Cumming Izett, a spinster newsagent, who sold in 1941 for £340 to family members, Sunday Post journalist William Izett & his wife, who lived there beyond WW2 years. 'Korek' is semi detached, only noted separately here as ownership of the other half took a different path in the early 20th Century. Again, it's an important building for Glasgow Road South, with exception of Springfield Cottage, being jointly the oldest house.

Blairhoyle

Figure 390 Blairhoyle, jointly oldest surviving house on Glasgow Road South

Constructed: c 1869
Constructor: Robert Lindsay
House Type: 2 Storey Houses

Other Names: Brownlie House
Original Address: 303 Glasgow Road
Current Address: 325 Glasgow Road

Brief Summary: 'Blairhoyle' no doubt takes its name after the beautiful, scenic place of that name near Callendar in Stirlingshire. Semi detached, with a garage it together with 'Korek' attached forms a property built in 1869 by Robert Lindsay. A slightly different ownership from 1895 to its neighbor, when Penelope Galt Renfrew sold it to Mrs. Young of Cambuslang who let it out that year to Rev Robert Paterson, a retired minister.

John G Johnston acquired it prior to 1905 and a family member was letting it out to Dennis McLinden, a draper by 1920. Mrs Jean G Smith was owner from the early 1920's until beyond WW2 years. Her husband, Quintin was a notable school teacher at Auchinraith Primary School.

In 1940, Quintin was cleared of assaulting an 11 year old pupil, John Cook who had been misbehaving in the playground. Quintin had taken the boy and strapped him as corporal punishment, away from the sight of others, the boy making out his punishment had been more severe than had been. It is understood the boy whilst being strapped had threatened Quintin saying, "My dad will get you for this, think twice before doing it!"

Clifton (Moraig / Hilden)

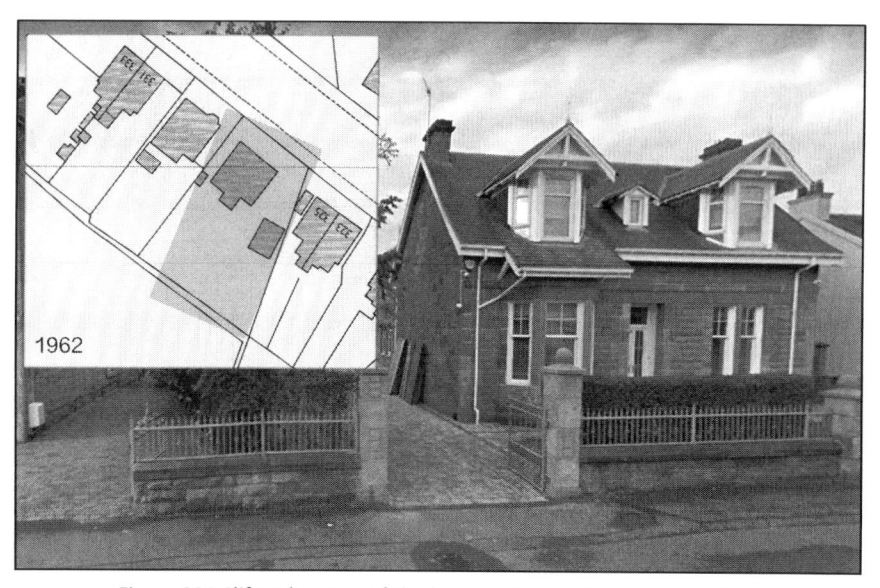

Figure 391 Clifton has one of the largest Glasgow Road rear gardens

Constructed: >1902<1904
Constructor: W.G Robertson
House Type: detached Villa

Other Names: Moraig, then Hilden
Original Address: 305 Glasgow Road
Current Address: 327 Glasgow Road

Brief Summary: Constructed by William G Robertson sometime between 1902 and 1904, Clifton is an impressive detached villa with one of the largest gardens and garages on Glasgow Road. William was a bricklayer and worked in South Africa for a time letting his house out to family member, Elizabeth Robertson. The house was originally called 'Moraig' but when passed in ownership to Thomas Devaney, a spirit dealer before the First World War, it was renamed as "Hilden". At that time it was let to Michael J Harkin MD. During Springtime 1917, Robert Colquhoun a draper bought, owned and occupied the house for a short time, selling to Dugald M Norris, the grocer by 1925. It had 2 public rooms, 4 bedrooms, a washhouse, pantry, tool store, bathroom, kitchen and scullery. This was luxury for the era, a far cry from the 'miner's raws' dotted all over Blantyre. It would take a successful person to afford and live in such a home. Norris the grocer lived in this desirable villa until around 1936. It changed hands again in 1943, after which it was bought by popular Doctor Stewart. In post war years, the house was renamed for a third time to "Clifton" as it is still currently known today. Robert Reid & Son, timber merchants & builders were based there in the 1970's. At one and half storeys, with dormer windows, it is well built and maintained, its architecture and design standing the test of time.

Laurel Cottage

Figure 392 Laurel Cottage, a charming, detached villa

Constructed: >1902<1904
Constructor: Richard McCall
House Type: detached Villa

Other Names: None
Original Address: 307 Glasgow Road
Current Address: 329 Glasgow Road

Brief Summary: Richard W McCall was a builder from Auchinraith Road whom, when trams arrived in Blantyre, wanted a taste for himself of owning a superior home near the Glasgow Road terminus. Between 1902 and 1904, he acquired a long, rectangular plot of land and built a stone cottage of one and half storeys.

Richard would only live in the house for a short time, opting to rent it out to others by the First World War. His first tenant was Thomas Robertson, a relative of neighbour W.G Robertson next door. Thomas was an Architect and we cannot rule out he may have been involved designing the house he ended up living in.

In 1918, Richard's son, Donald McIntyre McCall was killed in action in France during the war. The cottage would remain in the hands of the McCall family until the late 1920's, always let out to Thomas Robertson during that time.

By 1930, John G Johnston, a Blantyre draper bought and occupied the cottage. John, a keen fisherman lived there for many years and was selling a 4 berth caravan from the rear of the house during 1930. In later years, a garage was added. The cottage is distinctive as it has a hedge in front rather than any wall or fence. It is attractive, well kept and remains most desirable.

Oakbank

Figure 393 Oakbank dates from the early 20th Century. Now at 331 and 333 Glasgow Rd

Constructed: >1902<1904
Constructor: T. Crombie
House Type: Semi detached

Other Names: None
Original Address: 309 & 311 Glasgow Rd
Current Address: 331 & 333 Glasgow Rd

Brief Summary: 'Oakbank' is a semi-detached stone cottage of one and a half storeys. Situated on a long rectangular plot, in front of the modern St Blane's Primary School, it has 2 small bay windows and 3 upper dormer windows. It is noted in the early valuation rolls as having a garage.

Built between 1902 and 1904 by miner, Thomas Crombie of Auchinraith Road, the east side initially had address 309 (later 331 Glasgow Road) and served as his home. The west symmetrical side was rented for over 2 decades to Andrew Arbuckle, a butcher.

Thomas Crombie's time living there was short lived and the whole property passed to his widow, Hannah, when he died on 13th August 1910. Hannah Crombie owned 'Oakbank' until her own death in the early 1920's. Samuel, their son moved to Auchinraith Road near Welsh Drive. By 1925, the whole building was bought by John Stirling McCallum, a merchant who operated from the bottom of nearby Stonefield Road. John lived there only a short time and by 1930 had sold the east side to James Pate, a surface foreman who would continue living there with wife, Meg Fisher although he died in 1945. The remaining family emigrated to Australia shortly after the war. The west side, John McCallum retained for his own home, retiring there in the house previously rented by Andrew Arbuckle. Today, 'Oakbank' sits opposite a traffic calming island in Glasgow Road and at over 115 years old, is tidy and well maintained.

Modern Homes

Between 'Oakbank' Cottage and 'Campsie View' on the south side of Glasgow Road was an unusual gap of around 28m throughout much of the 20th Century. Part of this gap was occupied in the first half of the Century by the Bowie Family's Market Gardening sheds and stores.

In modern times, a semi-detached 2 storey house at 335 and 337 Glasgow Road has been built. The stone is light in colour and sympathetic to surrounding villas but at 2 storeys it is higher than the adjacent homes after modern planning required it to be relocated further back set off Glasgow Road and out of alignment of the existing villas. As such, it has a large front garden which is currently graveled with iron railings. To the rear on land formerly by the Gray family at 333, a garden faces into St Blane's School.

Figure 394 Modern Homes on former ground of Bowie's Stores & Sheds

Also, to the west of this gap is now a one and half storey modern detached house at 339 Glasgow Road. Built of red brick and concrete tiling, it has a large front garden offering a good monoblocked, driveway and like its modern neighbour, is set back off Glasgow Road.

The house is built in the same style as the lovely homes on the extended, Poplar Place to the rear. In the last decade, conifer hedges have grown taller, threatening to obscure the house from being seen from Glasgow Road, but all these homes in this article are certainly, quality & desirable family homes.

Campsie View

Figure 395 'Campsie View' initially was on a huge plot of land

Constructed: 1903
Constructor: George Bowie
House Type: Semi detached

Other Names: None
Original Address: 313 & 315 Glasgow Rd
Current Address: 341 & 343 Glasgow Rd

Brief Summary: Built in 1903, Campsie View is a semi-detached stone villa, the first to be built in this area by the Bowie family. This was the beginning of a large, market gardening 'empire' in Blantyre which would still be prominent into the 3rd quarter of the 20th Century.

George Bowie and son, James Bowie were the constructors, each taking one side of the property as their own family homes. The building was named Campsie View, for obvious reasons looking across to the hills on the horizon to the north. Initially with a garage, it had large tomato houses to the rear.

The Bowie family grew their own flowers, fruit and vegetables to sell in their Blantyre shop at the Masonic Buildings. Initially with address 313 and 315, 'Campsie View' later after the 1930 road widening, became 341 and 343 Glasgow Road. George Bowie died in 1906 and his wife Williamson Bowie inherited the eastern home living there until her own death in 1931. Son, John Bowie then inherited that side, letting out to other family members.

James Bowie on the western side, a miner turned florist lived there until the 1930's, before moving away to Bardykes Road to Greencroft. In 1935 he was letting his side of Campsie View out to James Mitchell, a joiner.

During the 1960's, a large building in the western part of the rear garden was used as a fruit store for bananas and oranges. There was also a potato machine kept in this store. Lorries drove into it to get loaded. An adjacent building was another store. A central storage building in the rear garden, located in the middle was where the potatoes were packed into different sized bags. The small shed to the back of it was utilized for making beetroot and the other small one was a boiler house. The long buildings on the eastern wall of the garden was a garage and offices. Large wooden framed glasshouses were located to the rear, then long rows of cold frames to the west of the glasshouses. In the mid 1960's, aluminium greenhouses were built on the vacant field but were ruined in the great Scottish storm of January 1968.

A tree in the small front garden has doubled in size in the last 10 years. The original stone wall still exists today. Old postcards show this location originally had high hedges in the front gardens, perhaps to mask from nosy passengers on the 1907 expanded tram network. Bowie's still lived here in the 1950's and 1960's followed by the McIntyre family from 1962 until 1983. To the rear is the Loretta Housing in Poplar Place, built in 1989 and 1990.

George Bowie

George Bowie, the constructor of 'Campsie View' villa on Glasgow Road, was born on 10th February 1856 the 6th child of ten by parents James Bowie and Margaret Moffat of Wanlockhead. His elder brother John Bowie, born 22nd May 1846 was one of the rescuers in the Blantyre mine disaster of 1877 and indeed is the great, great grandfather of the author of this book.

Figure 396 George Bowie 1856 - 1906

This large family was not without tragedy, especially referring to his siblings. Elder brother William (b1844) died aged 25. Elder sister Agnes (b1848) died aged 24. Elder brother James died only aged 8 and even when the family had another son, naming him James too in 1860, he also died aged 8. His elder sister Mary Bowie (b1853) married William Little, whose son James (b1878) would go on in life to be a major Blantyre property owner including the Crossbasket Estate in the 1930s.

George was a leadwasher at Wanlockhead marrying Williamson Watson (b1855) on 20th July 1877. The couple lived with George's father in Wanlockhead and sadly their two infant daughters died less than a year old. The couple came to Blantyre between 1886 and 1889 to start their own family. One of the first things he did whilst living at 5 Hall Street in Dixon's Rows, being a miner, was to buy a lair in the Blantyre Cemetery.

By 1891, George was a coalminer living at Larkfield at Maxwell's Land and by 1901 he had moved to Broompark Cottages. By 1903, he was working at Spittal Colliery, aged 47 and it is in that year along with son James, they built 'Campsie View'.

George died on 15th June 1906, aged 50. George's death certificate showed he died of dislocation of shoulder and heart failure but an inquest changed this to "Injuries received in the month of September 1905, by falling from an engine house at Spittal Colliery, Cambuslang, when stripping the slates from the roof.

His wife, Williamson, who then became the matriarch of the growing fruit and vegetable empire, outlived George until her death on 13th June 1931.

It was the children of George and Williamson, and indeed their grandchildren who opted out of a mining life and would establish the market garden, florists, fruit and vegetable business that prospered so well in the early 20th Century.

As will be seen next, Williamson also became the owner of further adjacent properties built for her large family, following the death of her husband.

Figure 397 Williamson Bowie b1855-d1931

Blantyre Project Social Media:

Rhona McIntyre: "We lived in Campsie View from late 1962 until 1983. I have such happy memories of living on Glasgow Road. We didn't move far, in the 80's moving across the road to 330. Mum got married in March 1963 and my parents had the house just before that. I loved living there. "

John McLean: "In the 80's, mum worked for 'Clean Walls' near 339."

Daldorch

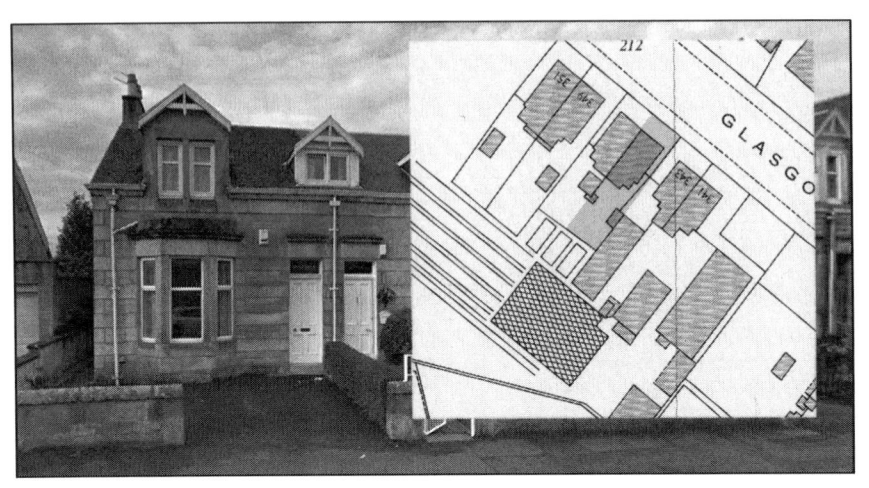

Figure 398 Daldorch provided homes for the Bowie's Gardeners

Constructed: >1907<1909
Constructor: W&J Bowie
House Type: Semi detached

Other Names: None
Original Address: 317 Glasgow Rd
Current Address: 345 Glasgow Rd

Brief Summary: 'Daldorch' is the eastern side of a semi-detached stone Glasgow Road residence 1.5 storeys high. (the western side being 'Dalveen.' Built between 1907 and 1909 by Williamson and her sister in law, Jane Bowie, it appears to have been constructed following the death of Williamson's husband George, in 1906. Initially 317, it became 345 Glasgow Road after 1930. This house was constructed as a business opportunity to let out to the Bowie's employees.

Daldorch looks to be named after a place in Ayrshire, perhaps once a favourite of the Bowie family? The house was initially let out to William Sillars, a gardener employed by the Bowie's to tend to the many glass houses and expansive vegetable plots to the rear of the house. Even after Williamson Bowie's death in 1931 and as the house passed to her son John Bowie, a fruit merchant, the Sillar family continued to rent here into the WW2 years. Mary Sillars was a schoolteacher. The Bowie family moved soon afterwards to Greencroft at Bardykes Road, and Daldorch continued to change hands to private owners. The Bowies were well known in Blantyre. Their family business grew successfully and many members of the family were involved as gardeners, wreath manufacturers, vanmen, florists and salespeople. Today, it is one of the few villas on Glasgow Road which still has the original cast iron guttering and downpipes. The small, front garden is entirely covered in tarmac for low maintenance.

Dalveen

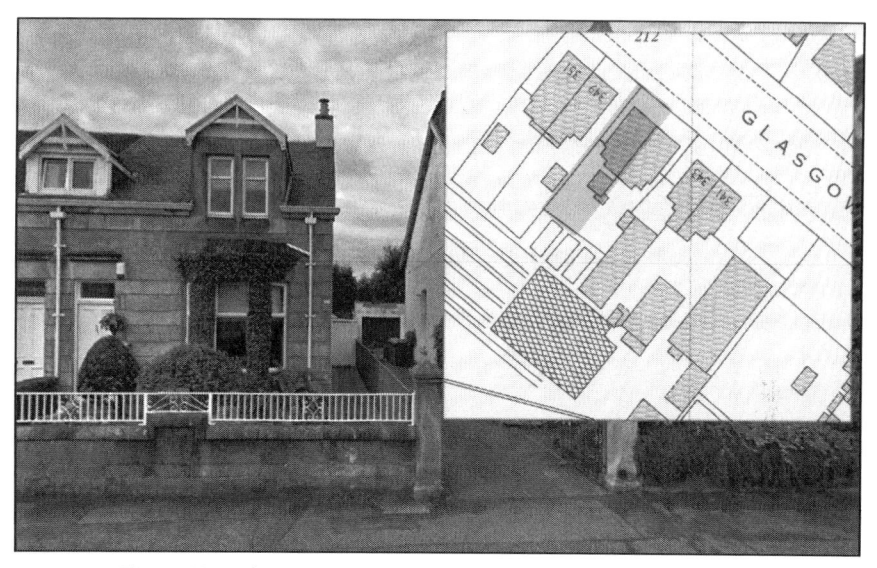

Figure 399 Dalveen at 347 Glasgow Road, constructed around 1908

Constructed: >1907<1909
Constructor: W&J Bowie
House Type: Semi detached

Other Names: None
Original Address: 319 Glasgow Rd
Current Address: 347 Glasgow Rd

Brief Summary: 'Dalveen' is the western side of the semi-detached 1.5 storey stone residence, the other side being 'Daldorch'. Dalveen, originally numbered 319 is now 347 Glasgow Road. The story of ownership is identical to Daldorch's up until the 1940's. Constructed around 1907 by Williamson and Jane Bowie, their second property around this location, it served the purpose for renting out to others. An early tenant until the late 1920's was William Inglis, a miner.

By 1930, John Bowie a fruit merchant was the owner and lived there right up until World War Two. The large glass houses and vegetable and flower plots to the rear of the house would have kept him and the rest of the Bowie family very busy. There are stories in Blantyre of how the Bowie family would go up to the high elevated fields above Blantyre in Winter and collect moss to make wreaths and garlands.

Today, Dalveen is a private home and recognition should be given here for its well-kept garden and good maintenance. The house has green ivy climbing up the stone walls around the bay window, hedges are well trimmed with neat, white railings above the little wall at the front. Some of the Ivy has been cut back during the last decade. Altogether, it looks a beautiful place to live.

Dunedin

Figure 400 Dunedin, constructed by Auchinraith Builder, Gavin Semple

Constructed: >1907<1909
Constructor: Gavin Semple
House Type: Semi detached

Other Names: None
Original Address: 321 Glasgow Rd
Current Address: 349 Glasgow Rd

Brief Summary: 'Dunedin' and its semi-detached neighbour 'Orwell' have a unique appearance. The stone built villas are symmetrical with bay windows and upper dormers like their neighbours but are distinct in that the pitches above the dormers are very tall by comparison to homes nearby. As such, the villa has an individual charm.

Mr. Gavin Semple, a builder formerly of Springwell was responsible along with his brother for the building of much of Auchinraith Road at the turn of the 20th Century. His family had built many homes in Springwell in the late 19th Century and they had close ties with New Zealand giving names to their homes associated with that country like Melbourne Place and Dunedin.

Prior to WW1, sometime around 1907, Gavin bought a plot of land beside the Bowie family on Glasgow Road and constructed his property rising out the ground by 1.5 storeys. The right had side, he sold off, perhaps to partially pay for the venture. A successful and well known builder, Gavin Semple and his family occupied 'Dunedin' until the early 1930's. The next owner by 1935 was Mr. William S Hamilton, a newsagent who brought up his family at this address (by then 349 Glasgow Road) for the next few decades. His daughter, Mary married there in 1948. In later years, a garage was added at the rear.

Today, the original wall and pillars enclose the small front garden, a mixture of heathers and conifers, some of which have grown rapidly these last

10 years. Aside from some minor signs of age on the ornate details on the timber dormers, the property still has a grand, old appearance. There's no doubt that when this house was built, it was a sure sign of business success and as far removed from the abundant miner's rows and pits as any house could be.

Orwell (Larchmont)

Figure 401 Orwell, the last villa on Glasgow Road south, now Larchmont

Constructed: >1907<1909 Other Names: Larchmont
Constructor: Gavin Semple Original Address: 323 Glasgow Rd
House Type: Semi detached Current Address: 351 Glasgow Rd

Brief Summary: The final most western villa is 'Orwell' at 351 Glasgow Road, which is the other semi-detached side adjoining 'Dunedin' to the east. A large house, extended at the back, it was built by Auchinraith builder, Gavin Semple sometime around 1910, who immediately sold this side to Grace McCallum, a widowed spirit merchant. By 1920, Grace had remarried to David Livingstone Harley, an oil blender and along with her new husband, she continued to live at 'Orwell' right into the 1940's.

At some time in the mid-20th Century, the house changed name to "Larchmont", a name still above the door today.

By Paul D Veverka

DID YOU KNOW?

There's an interesting story about the Harley family that took place in 1937. During the 1920's and 1930's, David Harley was the proprietor of the Clydesdale Oil Company, based at 170-174 Station Road. Initially enjoying some success, his family home had been at 'Bythorne' an impressive, grand house not far from Farm Road. His elderly mother still living there in the 1930s. When she became widowed, she found she had no means to support continuing to live at Bythorne and called upon David, her son to support her. The sharp, 85-year-old lady however, had been estranged from her son and when that financial support did not come as readily as she hoped, she decided to legally sue her son through courts with assistance of lawyers. So, it came to be in 1937, eighty-five-year-old Isabella Thomason Harley stood up in court, stating she was about to be made destitute and asking for David Harley to support her with a weekly allowance of £2. By this time, David and his oil company were struggling financially and operating at a loss. However, the court, discovering entitlement of some sort, awarded his mother the sum of 15 shillings per week, to come directly from the ailing company. It was the 'nail in the coffin' with the Clydesdale Oil Company closing for good several years later.

Dunallan Loop

Up until 1910, there was nothing on the south side of Glasgow Road for 500 yards between the villa 'Orwell' (today called Larchmont) and the next tenement further along to the west. A small, wall or fence separated the fields of Wheatlandhead Farm and the main Glasgow Road. From 1907 until 1930, running along this length on the main carriageway was a passing place for tramcars, known as Dunallan Loop.

The name is derived from a nearby villa on the north side of the road at this location. The tracks split at either end of this length into double tracks, allowing cars to stop, wait for other cars, or to let other cars pass by safely. The loop also acted as a tram stop, but never as an end terminus. It was part of the extended tram network built in 1907 and included a platform for alighting and disembarking.

On 15th February 1915, Mrs. Mary Watt of 14 Bardykes Road was disembarking from a tram that dark night and as she stepped on to the platform with her child, the tram pulled away too quickly, throwing her and the child to the ground sustaining bruising. In December, she successfully, with the aid of witnesses, sued the tram company for £200.

The name 'Dunallan Loop' however did not disappear when the tram-tracks were lifted in the early 1930's. It survived for at least another decade as an official name for one of the bus stops.

On the morning of Saturday 20th July 1935, five persons had a miraculous escape from serious injuries in a remarkable bus accident near Dunallan Loop. A Central S.M.T. bus proceeding from Glasgow to Hamilton turned over on its side after coming into collision with a tramcar's redundant electric standard. The bus was thrown over on its side and badly wrecked, both sets of wheels being wrenched off, while the standard was demolished. The accident happened outside a 2 storey building on the south side of Glasgow Road opposite now what is the junction of Coatshill Avenue.

The driver, Andrew McCusker, of Motherwell, was imprisoned in the wreckage of his cabin, but escaped with slight injuries. A passenger on a passing bus, Henry Connor (28), 564 Gallowgate, Glasgow, had his left leg lacerated when attempting to rescue Andrew. The conductress of the damaged bus. Miss Cathie Reid (23), Orbiston, Bellshill, suffered from severe shock. Quite understandably as our picture shows.

Figure 402 Bus at Dunallan Loop 1935, facing south west. Walkers Building at back

Fortunately the injuries to the passengers, caused mainly by broken glass, were not of serious nature, and they were able to proceed home, as were also the driver and conductress. It was little short of miracle that those travelling in the vehicle did not receive injuries of a more serious nature. Eye-witnesses stated that the 'bus was not travelling at a quick pace and that prior to the accident the framework of the vehicle quivered visibly, the rear portion rising about foot from the ground and then toppling over.' There were only three passengers in the bus. Miss Nancy Welsh. Craigrock Cottage, Blantyre, sustained a bruise over the eye and suffered from shock. Mrs M'Lean, 16 Braeside Avenue, Rutherglen, had injuries to arm and shoulder and shock, and Miss Jessie Kirk. 18 Park street, Cambuslang, suffered from leg and ankle injuries.

Modern Flats

At 353 – 367 Glasgow Road in front of a contemporary bus stop are 8 modern flats, located in two identical blocks of same shape and size. A small lane, inaccessible to vehicles separates them in the middle, linking Glasgow Road pavements to Poplar Place behind.

Figure 403 Modern Flats at Glasgow Road modeled on Dunedin / Larchmont

The site they occupy was once greenfield, never previously built upon until their construction. Brick built by private developers Loretta Housing in 1990 partly for council waiting lists and partly for people with special needs, the flats have secure entrances, once had a dedicated matron and were modelled on the adjacent older properties Dunedin and Orwell (now Larchmont). Kerry Hutcheson was first tenant at number 363 in July 90 followed by Billy Miller, Karen and Ann Maire McQuade. For 'Care in the Community' initiative, the homes feature the same high pitched roofs with matching timber ornate details at the upper reaches of each ridge. Initially you had to apply via Church of Scotland and RC Church to be offered a home here. Whilst pleasing in design, they somewhat lack the charm of the older stone villas adjacent, but are still kept tidy, well maintained and offer excellent family accommodation.

Walkers Building

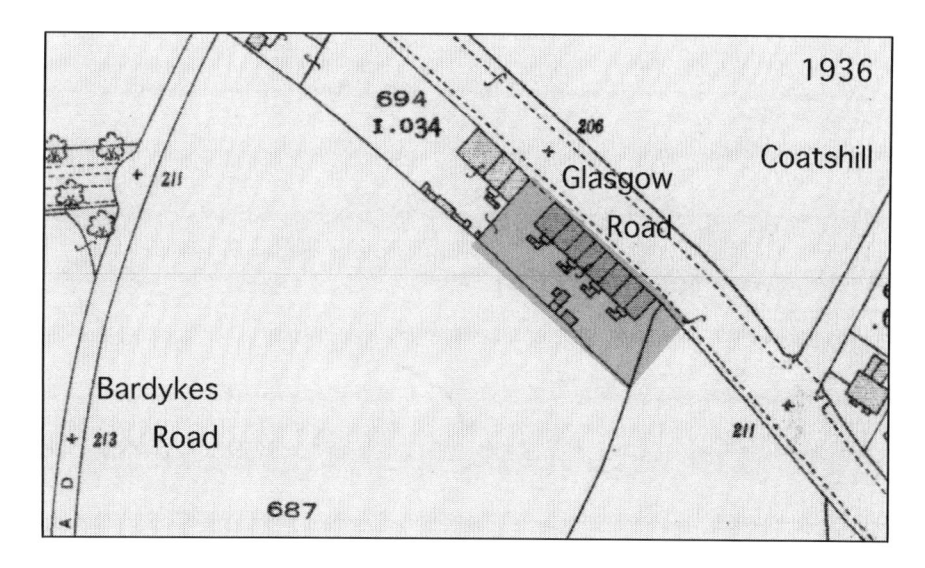

Figure 404 Walker's Tenement Buildings shown on 1936 map

'Walkers Buildings' were named after constructor James Walker, who was one half of a former joinery partnership named "J&J Walker (based in Larkfield)." James Walker born in Motherwell in 1843 lived at the bottom of Stonefield Road, the neighbour of the Craig family and was a joiner by trade.

Around 1877, the year of the pit disaster, his business bought a long, narrow plot of land from nearby Mr. Jackson of Barnhill, situated in an open field, but with frontage on to the developing Glasgow Road. Situated near the Westend, 'J&J Walker' halved the plot for 2 different buildings and on the eastern side built 2 storey tenements, which would be named appropriately, "Walker's Buildings". James was married and had 6 children under 16 at the time.

The venture was to be an investment. Walker built the homes and retail space to sell outright to others. Seeing potential to maximize their sale, they subdivided Walker's Buildings into 2 district properties, although the whole situation was adjoining and terraced. The whole block was constructed of sandstone with slated roofs. 2 storeys high, upper floors were accessed from steps at the rear, where also the washhouses and outdoor toilets were.

Walkers Building looks to have been completed in 1877 or 1878 and went on the market, the Walker family hoping to make a good return on their investment. It wasn't long before 2 separate buyers showed interest, each acquiring outright ownership of different parts of the building.

By Paul D Veverka

Walkers Building – Eastern Side

At the far eastern side, 12 homes, all double storey were bought in 1878 by Adam Thomson who would remotely own and rent them out his home in Castle Douglas. This part of the building would initially have address 321 to 329 Glasgow Road, with 321 having 8 of the 12 homes!. (Following road widening in 1930, they would be re-addressed as 401 – 423 Glasgow Road.)

The first tenants were mostly miners including William McCall, William Sharp, James Gibson, John Smith, Pat McEwan and Rob Sneddon. It is noted James Walker Jnr, the son of the original constructor lived there initially too. The 12 homes would always be let out to miners and around the late 1880's, rents of just £4 per annum were common.

Adam Thomson however died and by 1895, the 12 homes passed to his trustees, firstly to Robert McVane, of Academy Street, Castle Douglas. Robert continued to let out the property with John Sneddon of nearby Springfield Cottage, being factor of the homes as collector of rents.

Between 1920 and 1925, Robert McVane also died and a secondary trustee of Adam Thomson, namely John McLellan, also of Castle Douglas became the owner. John continued to own the property for several decades.

In 1930 upon the road being widened and allocation of new addresses, Walker's Buildings lost their front garden space, and subsequent construction of south pavements thereafter meant the doors of these homes then opened directly out on to the Glasgow Road pavement.

There were never any businesses or shops in this particular part of Walker's Buildings, with homes situated also on the ground floor.

By the 1940's, Walkers Building was perhaps starting to show its age, and it is noted that during the war calls were made for its modernization. For over 6 decades it had served as homes for many families, including generations of the same family. Rents around this time varied depending on the quality of homes and ranged from £8 to £16 per annum. The end was in sight.

Walkers Buildings were bought over by the county council in the early 1950's and subsequently demolished to make way for the council's modern homes of Cloudhowe Terrace.

We next explore the western side of Walker's Buildings, which certainly for the purposes of this book, we think has rather a more interesting tale to tell and one which definitely had a much more public use.

Walkers Building – Western Side

In 1878, the western part of Walker's Building was sold outright to Bathgate teacher, John Whelan (or Wheelan). A smaller part of the overall building, it comprised of 6 houses spread over 2 storeys and 2 ground floor shops, one of which was fairly large. It was adjoining 12 homes to the east.

John Wheelan would rent out the 6 homes to miners and their families and would own this building for many decades. By 1879, tenants were found and one of the shops was being rented by Duncan MacFarlane, a grocer. The other shop was opened as a public house, " The Cross Guns", with license holder, Mr. William Roberts a spirit merchant occupying it. Naismith's Business Directory of 1879, confirms the existence of the public house and the license ownership of William Roberts at that time.

This part of Walker's Building initially had address 337-351 Glasgow Road but following road widening and new addresses in 1930, it became 425 to 441 Glasgow Road.

In 1895, the grocers was owned by Janet Paterson renting for £13 and the public house had changed license holder, explored separately next in this book. By 1905, Elizabeth Smith was the grocer and again the license holder of the neighbouring public house had changed. Two of the homes were empty that year. The public house then became known as "The Volunteer Arms."

By 1915, James McCartney was renting the grocery business and the landlord of the pub was absent in combat during WW1. A temporary landlord ensured the continuation of business in the public house.

Between 1920 and 1925, owner John Wheelan retired but continued to let out the building in his elderly years. By 1925, grocers had temporarily become a blacksmiths shop, owned by Robert Craig (the son of the former Westend Bar owner). By 1930 Morris Grocers occupied one shop and the pub was by then empty, later to become a hall or meeting room. An address change saw Richard B Morris's Grocery at 427 Glasgow Road, the hall at 435/437.

Walkers Building was entirely demolished in the early 1950's prior to 1953 after being bought over by the County Council, the site cleared to make way for new council housing at modern day Cloudhowe Terrace.

With the 'Volunteer Arms' Public House so little known about these days, largely forgotten by all alive, and never previously written about, it is worth exploring its rise and fall separately, something we endeavour to do in the next page of this book.

Volunteer Arms (Cross Guns)

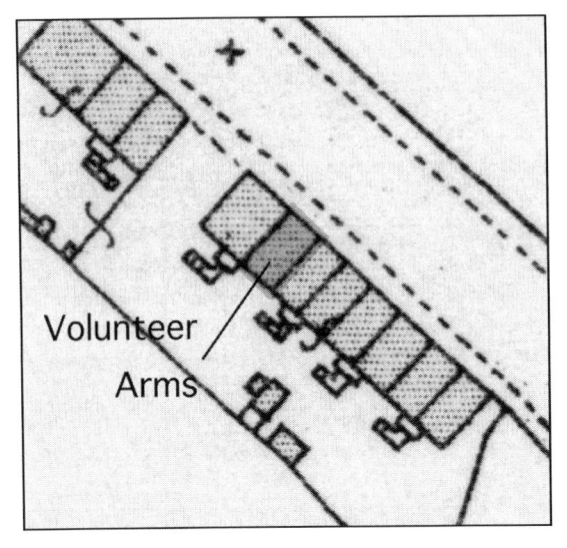

Figure 405 Volunteer Arms Public House

'The Volunteer Arms' is a former late 19th Century, early 20th Century public house on the south side of Glasgow Road, located in the western part of Walker's Buildings, a double storey tenement on Glasgow Road, not far from the West end. The site would now be the front gardens of Cloudhowe Terrace.

Constructed in 1878 by J&J Walker, part of the building was sold off to Bathgate teacher, John Whelan (or Wheelan) as 6 homes and 2 shops, 1 of which immediately was to become a public house.

Initially with address 345/347 Glasgow Road, the address of the pub would change after 1930 to become 435/437 Glasgow Road. Situated on the ground floor at the western end gable, the public house was large by comparison to the other shop and homes adjacent and above it.

Mr. William Roberts, a spirit merchant was the initial license holder, perhaps as early as 1878 and the pub was named 'The Volunteer Arms", likely a connection to William's strong association with the Rifle Volunteers.

Figure 406 Rifle Volunteers during the 1870's

The Roberts family were well

known in Blantyre at the time as builders and spirit merchants. His son, John Roberts would later own the 'Priory Bar' further eastwards along Glasgow Road. The Roberts family lived in neighbouring 'Causeway Shott Place', a former tenement between 'The Volunteer Arms' and Westend Place to the west.

There is no doubt that the pub was in direct competition with Robert Craig's neighbouring 'Westend Bar'. Attracting the custom of miners and agricultural workers in the area would have been paramount to the success of each business, and perhaps the locality and fact that Bardykes and Priory collieries were not far, helped this goal.

In October 1891, a newspaper report recorded that the Volunteer Arms was renewing its licensing certificate. By 1895, Archibald Jamieson, a spirit merchant was renting it for £39. Archibald started trading there in 1891. "Volunteer Arms" is shown on the 1898 map of Blantyre. The map also shows the front of the pub had a small yard or garden between it at Glasgow Road, although this would change in 1930 when the pub opened directly out on to the pavement.

In 1901, a Mr. Charles Angus McGaughey, a 28-year old Irishman was living at Walkers Building and is noted as a spirit merchant. The census reveals he was there with wife Margaret, their 2 little children and a live-in domestic servant by the name of Elizabeth McGhie. He was still the license holder in 1905. In 1907, tram cars started operating past the pub.

Charles & Annie Cook

In the years prior to WW1, Mr. Charles Cook (b1887) was the license holder of the pub. Charles was a spirit merchant by trade and commenced renting his pub from owner John Wheelan in 1909, running it with his wife, Annie Cummings.

Now, Charles it would appear like Archibald and William the license holders before him, was also a keen military enthusiast and a member of the Rifle Volunteers. The men were likely known to each other through that circle and the idea of volunteering and training for military duties, common to them. Looking westwards along Glasgow Road from the public house would have given a good view of Dechmont Hill, where their firing range and practicing took place.

When Charles volunteered for active duty in WW1, he was incorporated into the Royal Scots and headed off to the Mediterranean in combat. To ensure continuation of his pub, his wife took charge of operations. 'The

Volunteer Arms' pub, should not be confused with Mr. Bruce's 'Volunteer Bar' at High Blantyre, which was a different pub entirely but conducted business around the same time during WW1 years.

A terrifying situation arose in 1917 for Annie Cook, compounding further her personal worry of her husband being away at war. In early May 1917, whilst Charles was away, the pubs license was suddenly withdrawn by authorities and Annie, not permitted to trade, her great worry being it was her only means of income. The case went to court that month.

An appeal was made by Annie on behalf of Charles Cook whose certificate had been withdrawn by the lower Court. It was first recorded that Charles had held the license for eight years without complaint. The appeal continued showing how Charles was now military service, was married, and had a family of three, and this license was practically their only means support.

Unfortunately, he had recently had two convictions against him but in the more serious of these, the offence had actually been committed by an employee directly against Mr. Cook's explicit instructions to obey the license regulations. The Fiscal (Mr. Weir) said that suspicion had existed regarding the conduct of this house before the convictions were obtained, and Mr. Cook had a complex system of reliable scouting which practically prevented the police from getting at the place unobserved.

Mr. Cook had been at the premises when the latter offence occurred supplying two men with drink out-with hours and he had previously been fined £20. Mr. Montgomery moved that the appeal be sustained as he was sympathetic to the thought of taking away the house of a man called out an currently on military service. Mr. Hamilton seconded, remarking that it was not fair to withdraw the license from a man who was not there to defend himself and was fighting for ones country. Mr. Lambie, however was adamant for the prosecution pointing out that Mr. Cook had been 'on premises when the offence was committed', and therefore did not think it was fair to 'introduce appellant's absence on military service'. Besides, Cook was only on service because 'he couldn't help it.' Lambie continued, 'Cook had got conditional exemption from the war and that had been withdrawn, forcing him to go and fight.' But the main fact was that he had been on the premises when the offence happened. A division in opinion formed but the licensing committee overwhelmingly voted to uphold the appeal with 7 voting to reinstate the license and just 3, including Lambie against it. Mr. Jackson of nearby Bardykes chose not to vote. The license was therefore restored.

However, news of the successful win did not last long when communicated to the front. Charles died young, aged 30 on 2nd November

1917 whilst fighting Ottoman (Turks) and Germans in the third battle of Gaza in Egypt during World War One. Although an Allied Victory, some 2,696 people died that night alone. On 3rd February 1918, almost exactly 3 months later, news officially was communicated to his grief stricken widow, Annie. Of their 3 children, they had one daughter who lived her life in Blantyre, Mary Maxwell Cook b1911-d1978.

Figure 407 Ottoman (Turkish) Troops with machine guns train them on British 1917

In April 1918, a license application by Mrs. Annie Cook, widow of Charles for the pub was granted to continue running the pub. Dealing with grief and having 3 small children as well as running a pub likely took its toll and by 1920, Mary Cook, Charles mother had taken charge. It was a situation which sounded a little out of control and difficult.

Just a year or so later, Annie Wilson and her son Andrew Wilson who lived above the pub were the new license holders, an arrangement which existed in 1925. The Pub thereafter became known as the Cross Guns Public House. It is said, 'The Volunteer Arms' had rifles crossed over the fireplace and as a result often also went by the name "The Cross Guns." By 1930, the Wilsons were no longer there and the pub was empty. They were the last license holders, the pub only lasting half a century. Given new address 435/437 Glasgow Road, the premises then became a hall, although it is unknown for what use. Walker's Buildings, including this former pub was demolished in the early 1950's prior to 1953 to make way for the Council's housing at Cloudhowe Terrace.

> Blantyre Project Social Media:
>
> **Alex Rochead:** "Young Robert Craig, the son of Robert Craig Westend Bar owner would late move away from Blantyre to Australia"

By Paul D Veverka

Causeway Shot (Douglas Place)

Causewayshott, Causewayshot or 'Causeway Shott Place' was a former 2 storey tenement situated between Walker's Building and the Westend. Its location today would be in the front gardens of modern Cloudhowe Terrace.

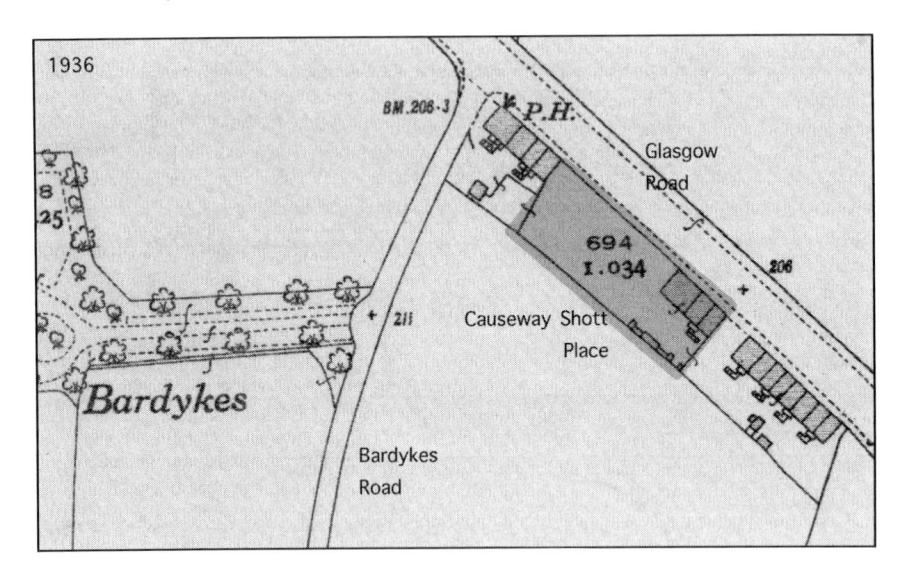

Figure 408 Causewayshott Place, shown near the Westend on 1936 map

Original constructors were J&J Walker (joiners of Larkfield) who in 1876 acquired the land from Mr. Jackson of Barnhill. Initially 6 homes, they were sometime in the 1880's later subdivided into 11 homes.

It is known the building was completed by April 1877, as a publican, Thomas Geddes Junior applied for an alcohol license there that month. He was refused by the authorities, perhaps on the basis that other pubs were already nearby. J&J Walker appear to have sold the building by 1877 entirely over to new owner, Walter Wheeling, a manufacturer at 30 Cadzow Street, Hamilton who would let the houses out from afar.

In October 1877, just a week before the Blantyre Pit Disaster, Walter applied for a license himself from the authorities. Later valuation rolls indicate he was also not successful in that application. Some of his initial tenants by the mid 1880's were Peter Scott, James Todd. Michael Murphy and John Jackson. Access to some of the upper homes was via rear steps.

During the early 1890's, Walter sold Causewayshott Place to David Orr, a grocer of 3 Low Patrick Street, Hamilton. It is thought David was the instigator of changing the name to "Douglas Place", perhaps to avoid any confusion with the existing name Causeystanes, part of High Blantyre. Certainly by 1901, the homes were now 12 in number, spread over 2 storeys all with the name "Douglas Place". Valuation rolls of 1895 and 1905 confirm this is indeed the same building as formerly named Causewayshott.

By 1915, David Orr was letting Douglas Place out to 14 miner's and their families, maximizing the space in the building for the highest rental potential. There were never any businesses run from this property. In those early times it had address 353 to 357 Glasgow Road, but this would change after 1930 and the subsequent road widening to become 443 - 457 Glasgow Road.

Miner's Prosecution

DID YOU KNOW ?

In 1915, one match found in possession of Walter Sneddon, miner of 6 Douglas Place was found in No. 2 Pit, Udston Colliery (where, safety lamps are required). Walter was prosecuted at Hamilton Sheriff Court where he admitted the charge and was fined 10s, or three days' imprisonment.

David Orr moved his own business around in Hamilton between Townhead Street and eventually to Quarry Street, renting out Douglas Place in Blantyre in retirement. Put up for sale on 29 April 1924, it didn't meet reserve so he held it until his death in the late 1920's, followed by his trustees.

Tenants in 1935 were mostly miners and it is very prudent to suggest that these men were mostly likely working nearby at Priory or Bardykes Pits not too far off from these homes. Tenants included the Robertsons, Feeneys, Logans, Cassidys, Kanes, McCluskeys, O'Briens, Smiths, McDades, Kennans and Tooles. 'Douglas Place' was demolished in the 1940's, the site cleared by 1945 evident in aerial photos of that year.

Before we leave the story of Causewayshott / Douglas Place let's go back again to constructors, contractors J&J Walker. The partnership was between James Walker, joiner who lived at the bottom of Stonefield Road and his son James Walker Junior, residing at nearby Walker's Building. Both men were joiners. The business appears to have been subjected to bankruptcy in the late 19th Century, with James Senior residing at Glebe Cottage in High Blantyre, then afterwards at School Lane. Competition from local joinery and sawmill businesses from the Adams, Roberts and Warnock families, would likely have made trading more competitive. By 1905, James was at Athole Cottage, his own house at High Blantyre. His son would own homes in Calder Street, a return to house ownership. There are no entries for the family after 1930.

By Paul D Veverka

Cloudhowe Terrace

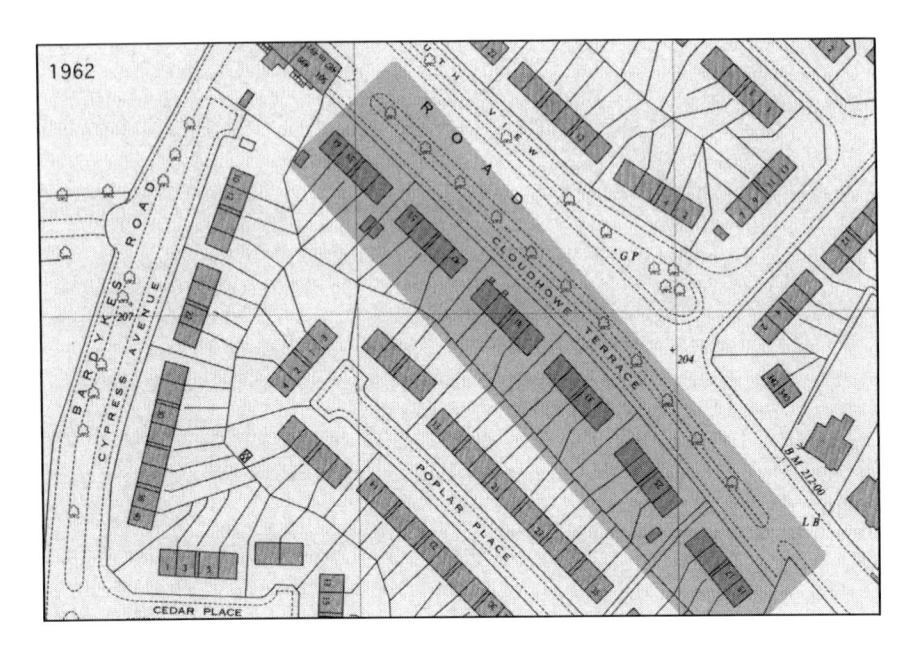

Figure 409 Cloudhowe Terrace on 1962 map, near Westend, opposite Coatshill

Cloudhowe Terrace are 'modern' council built houses situated on the south of Glasgow Road across from Coatshill and adjacent to the Westend.

Figure 410 Cloudhowe Terrace in Summer 2016

Built in 1952 and throughout 1953, the first tenants moved into these desirable homes of the time in Summer 1953. Set back off the Glasgow Road on the former site of Walker's Buildings, demolished a year or two before and on the site of former Douglas Place, these were to address and compliment and expand the large Wheatland Orlits estate beyond the rear gardens. Our map of 1962 above shows just how extensively Blantyre was being added to. Of 2 storey brick construction, these family homes afforded tenants large spacious gardens to the front and rear, particularly nearer the Westend and provided good, off-road, safe parking.

Six blocks, each with four homes meant 24 new houses were built at Cloudhowe Terrace. It is not known why this name was given to the street, but it may have been a reference to the popular Scots book of the same name.

Houses don't have Glasgow Road addresses. They are numbered all oddly from 15 – 61 (odd numbers only), with 61 being adjacent to the Westend. The fact that 1-13 were missing in other circumstances may have meant something had been demolished, but not in this case. 1-13 has never existed, the council choosing to begin numbering at 15, in the hope that the spare and vacant ground during the 1950's to the east of this belonging to the Bowie Market gardeners could be bought. It seems the council intention had been to construct further blocks and assigned the postal addresses on the basis of that plan. However, it never came to be, the Bowie's selling to private developers presumably for offers of a higher magnitude than the council was prepared to pay. An indication of the council's former plan for this still remains today at the end of Cloudhowe Terrace abruptly stopping where it had once been hoped to continue the blocks.

Figure 411 Cloudhowe Terrace abruptly ends at East side as other blocks were planned

In 2015, a resident, a cancer patient fell in potholes outside her home breaking her arm at Cloudhowe Terrace, prompting council action in making urgent repairs to the road. Today, many of the council homes have been bought over by private owners and each house has taken on a distinct separate appearance, with different walls, fences, colours and landscaping apparent. They remain well kept and we're told, have a neighbourly community spirit.

Westend Place & West End Bar

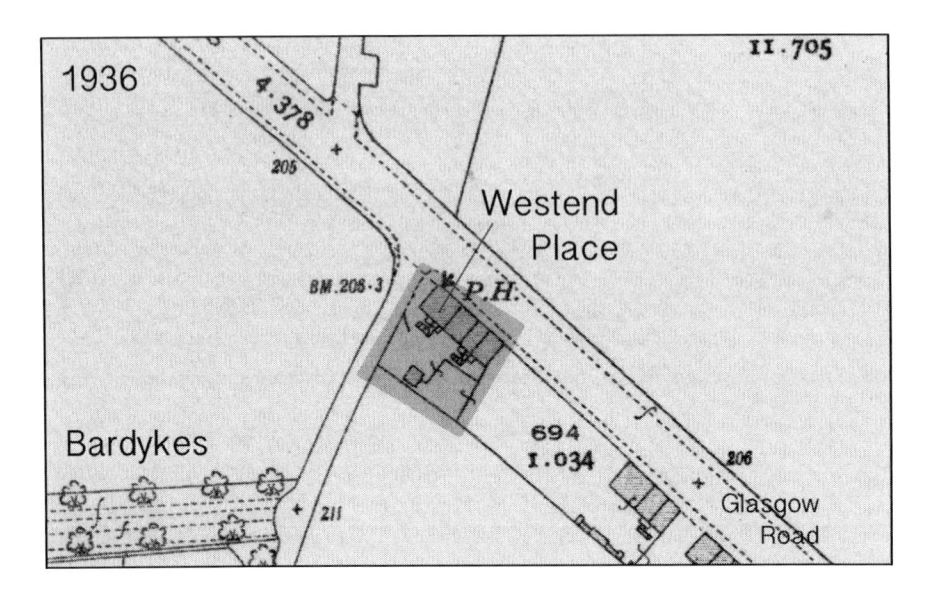

Figure 412 Westend Place, the 2 storey tenement on 1936 map

The 'Westend' is a current 2 storey stone tenement building located at the eastern corner of the junction of Glasgow Road and Bardykes Road. When looking at it historically, it should not be confused with 'Westend House' in Auchinraith, High Blantyre. The 'Westend' name in modern times tends to refer to the Public Bar at the corner of this building, although the name is applicable to the whole building, including the homes and shops. Such a prominent, well known building in Blantyre, we have explored this in detail.

The Beginnings

On 12th May 1876, a contract of sale was drawn up between Robert Craig, spirit merchant residing at Clive Place, Stonefield Road, Blantyre, his sister Margaret Craig and with Mr. John Jackson of nearby Barnhill who owned the land. John Torrance Weir of Blantyre Park was witness. Mr. Jackson sold a long, rectangular corner plot of land to the Craig siblings (grown up offspring of Thomas Craig) with good frontage on to both Glasgow Road and Bardykes Road. It is described then as such, '1 Rood 8 yards of ground, bounded on the west by the Road from Barnhill to Cambuslang Turnpike Road and on the north by said Turnpike Road, being part of the lands of Barnhill, in Parish of Blantyre.". Previous to this contract Robert Craig had been a wright, or blacksmith at Stonefield, a profession his own son would later adopt. The acquisition of the land saw Robert become a spirit merchant. Contrary to others assumption, the building was never a wholesale grocers and the public house has always been a public house since construction to the present day.

The Craig's neighbour at Stonefield Road was Mr. James Walker, joiner and family friend and as such may have been Mr. Walker who built the Westend building, employed by Robert and Margaret. Further information supporting this was the fact that Mr. Walker certainly built the 2 former adjacent buildings of Causewayshott Place and Walkers Buildings.

In April 1877, Robert Craig applied for a license to sell alcohol, clearly thinking ahead to his building being completed. Interestingly, the license was made for 'Craighall Place', Blantyre, which appears to have been the original intended name for the Westend Building. (It's easy to see how Robert and Margaret Craig arrived at the name 'Craighall'). However, the application was refused and in October 1877, just before Blantyre's Pit Disaster occurred, he applied again. This time his license was in the chosen name of 'Westend Place', the official name for the whole proposed tenement. Feu disposition documentation eludes that Robert and Margaret may have had access to the land since 1875 or been planning the building since then, although could not start their venture until the feu disposition was drafted.. The document was a contract of co-ownership drawn up between Robert and his sister Margaret, dated at 10am on 3rd October 1877. It asked for a hedge to be put up around the whole plot, for it to be maintained and within the space of 1 year, for a substantial building of stone, lime and slates to be constructed with a value no less than £200. Construction of Westend Place was therefore between October 1877 and October 1878.

The building had shops at the lower eastern end and the Public house was located on the western corner, as it is today. Above the shops and pub was a sign saying "Robert Craig – Wholesale Spirits". Robert Craig was never a grocer as has incorrectly been assumed in the past. Above the signs were homes, flats accessed by stairs to the rear. Six sets of double windows face out to Glasgow Road, with a diagonal corner single window on the western side.

The County of Lanark search sheets 89-606 and 89-607 provide the details of ownership and sale (deeds) for this property, which has proven to be instrumental in forming this article.

In 1885, Robert Craig took ownership of Clive Place, the family pub of his grandmother, further eastwards along Glasgow Road. By the mid 1880's Robert was managing two pubs. In those early days, the West End Bar was often being frequented by miners and agricultural labourers, a public house being used as a farmers club. During the 1880's, Westend Place was not just a public house, but also 9 homes. There were no other shops at that time. Tenants may have been chosen carefully by Robert. Some were blacksmiths and metalworkers, a profession Robert was in prior to becoming a spirit merchant. Other tenants included a teacher and engineers. This wonderful photo exclusively obtained and shared here for the first time in print shows the Westend homes and public house during that era.

Figure 413 Westend Place Homes and Public House during the late 1880's

Public House break in

On Saturday 6th October 1888, Robert Craig closed his pub at Westend Place for a short time during the afternoon. On returning after a quarter of an hour, he found his back window open and his place had been ransacked. The thieves were Thomas MacKenzie and Edward Smith miners of Larkfield. They had been found that evening in a pub in Larkfield celebrating their haul. Stolen was three bottles of whiskey, £2 of money and a revolver. They were both sentenced, guilty.

By 1895, tenants at Westend in the 9 homes were all metalworkers with exception of Andrew Clelland, a cattle dealer and Duncan MacFarlane, a waiter.

Margaret Craig

On 26th April 1895 Margaret Craig died of cancer, aged only 47. The daughter of Thomas Craig and Helen Roxburgh (who outlived her), she must have been very ill, for just 2 days before, she wrote out her intention to transfer her share of Westend Place over to her brother, Robert. This was officially recognized legally on 15th August 1895 and from that date onward, Robert Craig was the sole owner of Westend Place. Robert had been with Margaret at the time of her death at her home at Clive Place. Her death certificate confirms her cancer of the breast, stomach and liver, something she had lived with for nearly 9 months.

Figure 414 Margaret Craig's Death Certificate 1895

Margaret Craig left absolutely everything she owned to Robert, even her clothes valued at £5 and £10 cash in the house. Her total estate came to £670 and 6 pence, and when medical bills were deducted and the property share added, she had left £1,270, a sum worth nearly £170,000 today.

Tenants however, were largely unaffected and the miners and metalworkers living at the Westend would continue to rent from Robert Craig.

Figure 415 Miners on Glasgow Road at Robert Craig's Westend Pub in 1880's

By Paul D Veverka

Robert Craig

We've explored Robert Craig's life a little earlier in the book under the article about his other pub, "The Old Original", but it is certainly worth touching upon further details given the West End Bar had been his outright, somewhat longer.

Robert Craig married Maggie Thomson in Paisley in 1899 at the age of 48 and together they would have a young son, Robert Junior in 1904. Robert Craig was a wealthy man. As well as being a successful businessman, his inheritance from his sister in 1895 and then from his mother in 1903 only bolstered his financial standing further. During 1903, Robert used this new added wealth to demolish Clive Place and build the current pub, 'The Old Original.'

Robert based himself at the Old Original Pub from 1903 and solved the problem of running the West End Bar, by employing James L Bennett, a spirit dealer to do that. James Bennett, who lived above the pub, held the license from around 1903, but would never own the pub, nor would it be called his. James was killed in action on 26th April 1915 near St Julien during WW1, and Robert Henry Clark took over the license, renting from Robert Craig.

Another important worker that Robert Craig relied upon was Walter Stewart. Walter was the barman at the Westend Bar during 1900 and certainly still there in 1905. He was employed by Robert Craig and looked after Westend Place on Glasgow Road also as watchman. Following 1905, Walter's time in Blantyre was short lived and eventually he moved to Perthshire as a gamekeeper, a job amongst many he had in his life.

It was said Walter's mother went into labour in the old Westend washhouse, which possibly is the old garage (or other outhouse in the yard). Walter Stewart used his spare time to write about and undertake his other passion of bird watching. He was a noted ornithologist and some of his stuffed birds ended up at the Hoolets Nest Pub on display in glass cabinets in the 1970s and perhaps also at the pub in High Blantyre which became Matts Bar.

One evening around 1900, someone had broken into the West End Bar whilst Walter and his young family were asleep upstairs. He took his gun from the cupboard and went out onto the external backstair where he spotted the thief bending down in the road – he took aim to shoot the thief in the rear end, however things went terribly wrong and the thief stood up and the bullet hit the intruder in the spine, crippling the intruder for life. However, Walter was cleared of any criminal wrongdoing when it went before the court.

At the height of WW1, on 28th March 1917 Robert Craig died aged 66 at his home at Craigrock, Glasgow Road, Blantyre. However, his son young Robert Craig was only 13 and could not inherit anything from the Craig Estate, strictly as per will agreements, until he turned 25 years old. Young Robert would have to wait until 1929 and meantime the property would be held in trust for him. If they so desired, the will also permitted the trustees to retain their interest partially on the properties, strictly with agreement from young Robert Craig at the time of his succession.

Robert's inventory and will following his death makes good reading. He held stocks and shares and was perhaps distrustful in banks, holding just as much in cash at his home, as he did in the bank! He held life insurance and his possessions also had considerable value, indicating he may have like the finer things in life. His estate was £2,143 less £679 debts and funeral expenses plus £4,450 property for Westend Place and Old Original. It totaled a whopping £5,913, 16 shillings, which if compared to an equivalent £500,000 today, had been devalued hugely by the economic strife caused by WW1. It was still a huge sum and responsibility to leave to trustees.

Robert Craig Senior had owned Westend Place for 40 years, which to this current date, is still the longest ownership of this building for any one individual.

Robert Henderson, Tenant of Westend Place

Mary O Neill, shared this photo of her great grandfather, Robert Henderson who resided above the West End Bar for 50+ years.

This photo was taken about 1949-50 and he would have been approx. 85 years of age. He was born in 1865 in Clelland and the Henderson family moved to Barnhill when Robert was a young boy. The Henderson family lived in an upper apartment at the Westend from around 1900 – 1953.

Robert worked initially as a miner, then as a gardner for the Jackson family at Bardykes House on Bardykes Road, nearby to his home. Apparently Mrs Jackson's eyesight wasn't the best. One day, Robert and his son John were walking towards the Bardykes House and Mrs Jackson pointed her rifle at them shouting at them to stop. Robert shouting back 'it's alright Mrs Jackson it's only me Robert and my son John'. She sounds like a lady not to be messed with! His wife Elizabeth Mary Neillans was killed in 1943 when she was hit by a chieftain bus on Glasgow Road. They lived in the end apartment furthest from the door to the bar. Samuel Henderson, Robert's father worked for the blacksmith John Templeton at Barnhill, who was also his brother in law Samuel maybe helped build parts of the infamous "early aeroplane" as he worked there about that time. Unfortunately Samuel died suddenly in 1868 after a drinking session in the Barnhill Tavern, when he fell down some stairs.

Figure 416 Robert Henderson (b1865) in 1950, Westend tenant

OK, let's get back to 1917 and Robert Craig. Upon Robert's death, William Francis Benham of Stonefield Road took over ownership of Westend Place. As a trustee William Francis (known as Frank) was the cousin of Robert

Craig's wife and had been a neighbor and trusted friend. He had been added to Robert's will in 1910 when one of his trustees had died suddenly that year. Frank already had business interests in his own shop at Stonefield Road but stepping up to the Craig legacy, he continued to let the nine Westend homes and the Bar out to Robert Henry Clark of Langside.

In December 1921, the license holder Robert Henry Clark was charged with selling alcohol in a vessel which was neither corked or capped to a child under 14 years of age. He was fined £2 which was paid.

A minor boundary clarification in April 1924, resulted in Robert Craig's trustees having to pay another 6 shillings, 7 pence per annum in feu duty to the Jackson family of Barnhill, which looks like it was resolved quickly.

In 1925 William Francis Benham died, then John Anderson Gray, another trustee took over as proprietor of both the Westend home and the Bar.

Gray & Craig Ownership

On 14th August 1929, coming of age, young Robert Craig officially inherited 50% of Westend Place, the other 50% remaining in the hands of Robert Craig senior's surviving trustee, John Anderson Gray. Young Robert was living at 275 West Princes Street, Glasgow at the time. This may have been a complex transition for the pub and indeed the shops rental income and for the homes would now need to be divided. Young Robert may have conflicted with his older business partner in what was best for the pub or perhaps which landlord should occupy it, for just 3 months later, the pub was empty, lying vacant. The 1930 Valuation roll confirms that in Springtime that year, the Pub was still empty. John Anderson Gray and Robert Craig, as owners needed a new landlord, somebody to run the West End Bar, which was rated that year as being worth an annual rent of £50. It's noted in 1930 that 'Westend Place' had address 487 to 497 on the lower floor, pub was 497. Above, the homes were 499 and 501 Glasgow Road.

Although the whole building is Westend Place, the public house is written as "The West End Bar", the words 'west' and 'end' separated as it is on the title deeds and original MacNeil sale documents. However, it is often written as 'Westend Bar', primarily on social media and in modern advertisements, indicating both are used and equally acceptable.

The pub was then empty for 3 or 4 years, but not for long. Fortunes favoured the continuation of the public house, when in 1934 following lowering rents to £30, dedicated new license holders were found in Joseph MacNeil & his wife, Elizabeth.

By Paul D Veverka

MacNeil Era

Joseph MacNeil was born at Mingulay just south of the Isle of Barra in the Outer Hebrides. When he was 17 he came to Glasgow and joined a merchant steamer, serving as the chief officer in WWI on an armed trawler and saw some action. In 1920 he gained his Captain's certificate, but four years later he got a really bad hand injury that forced him to quit the sea.

Retired from service, he came to Blantyre in late 1925. In 1926 he was renting a pub and house above at 346 Main Street (near Kirkton Cross). He had renamed it, "The Caledonian Bar", locally nicknamed by customers as, "The Heilandmans" for obvious reasons. Rents were paid to Mr. Pearson, a trustee of Mr. William Barr, (a retired shoemaker and pub owner.) Joseph MacNeil never bought or owned the pub in High Blantyre at any time. However, in 1933, Captain MacNeil received some unwelcome news that the building he was renting at Main Street was subjected to compulsory purchase order by the county council so that the road could be widened and was to be demolished. Having no control over this, he was forced to find new premises and the vacant public house at the corner of Bardykes Road seemed ideal.

At the end of October 1933, Joseph MacNeil applied for a license at the Westend, which was granted and he commenced trading there in New Year 1934 moving home too. People in High Blantyre may have been sad to see this spirit merchant move after being there for just over 7 years. At the time Joseph moved to his rented pub at the Westend, John Anderson Gray and young Robert Craig were still the owners.

The MacNeil's initial years at the Westend were touched by tragedy when Joseph and Elizabeth's daughter Margaret MacNeil died on 12th September 1936.

Naming the pub, the "West End Bar", Joseph & Elizabeth MacNeil continued to rent the pub right through the 1930's and into the 1940's from owners Gray & Craig. When Joseph died on 4th September 1941, Elizabeth continued to rent and run the pub, renewing each license upon their expiry.

MacNeil Ownership

On 4th December 1947, William Anderson Gray inherited his father's 50% of Westend Place. In those immediate post WW2 years of change, fresh starts and looking to the future, both William Anderson and Robert Craig (by then living in Sydney, Australia) decided to bale out and sell Westend Place. It took just 3 months for a sale to complete and on 28th February 1948 a new owner was found. Just £500 was paid for the whole building, a bargain worth around £20,000 in today's money due to the fragile and recovering economy, the sum also indicating a quick sale and goodwill to the new buyer. That same day, the Craig era of spirit merchants in Blantyre, that had existed for 4 generations spread out over 100 years came to an abrupt halt.

The new buyer? It was Mrs. Elizabeth Currie or MacNeil, from the family who had been renting the pub for the previous 14 years. MacNeil outright ownership commenced in 1948 and would continue in one form or other with family members right up until 2008, some 60 years later.

By the 1940's, Elizabeth was already an established wine and spirit merchant. She would own the entire Westend building, all shops, all homes and of course her own public house. It is around this time we see the name 'Westend Place' being used less commonly and more referred to simply as 'The Westend.' The building was not known as "MacNeils Building".

In 1952 and 1953, the back yard of the Westend was used by contractors for their cabins and equipment whilst they built nearby Cloudhowe Terrace.

Figure 417 Contractors at the Westend, with Cloudhowe Terrace built 1953

Incredibly, Westend Place was held intact as one property for nearly 100 years following its construction until 8th April 1971, when Elizabeth Currie MacNeil decided to sell part of the building. The farthest part to the east, with address 487 Glasgow Road had previously been a hairdressers shop for many years during the 1960's leased by Margaret McGlynn. However, in 1971 it was sold by the MacNeil family to Ercole Di Vito of 1 Wallace Place, Hamilton, who rented it out to Jameson Newsagents and then to Hughes Photography for a few years before moving in himself around 1982, opening Di Vito's Fish and Chip shop, which still exists today. Hughes is now the Lounge in the Bar.

Elizabeth Currie MacNeil passed away on the 4th January 1979.

On 18th February 1981, the Westend Building including the pub was transferred by sale to the MacNeil's daughter Mary Josephine, who lived in the flat above the pub at 501 Glasgow Road. The exception to this was of course the part owned already by Ercole Di Vito.

When Mary Josephine MacNeil died on 8th February 1991, she was buried at Barra alongside her sister and parents.

Her will asked for her estate to be divided up amongst her immediate family. The document asked on 26th February 1992 that Christine MacNeil of Troon should inherit her house, the flat above the pub at 501 Glasgow Road.

The West End Bar would go equally on 9th March 1992 to Annie Winifred McGhie of 497 Glasgow Road and to Joseph MacNeil of Priory Bridge,

Figure 418 MacNeil Family Gravestone at Barra

Blantyre. According to the title deeds, on 16th January 1995, Joseph would sell his half of another upper house over to Annie, the details of that sale deliberately not written here to respect the privacy of the MacNeil family. As seen next, the rest of the building would go to the MacNeil family.

The remaining part of the building, essentially 'The West End Bar', a month later (on 6th February 1995) was sold with joint agreement of Annie McGhie and Joseph MacNeil to five other members of the MacNeil family for their legacy to continue. The Bar's new owners were equally Rosemary MacNeil, and Elizabeth Ann Campbell both of Priory Bridge, Catherine Clark of Calderglen, Mary Josephine McGhie of Halfway and Felix MacNeil of Jura Gardens. All living locally, the new owners were passionate about looking after the 'West End Bar' and building it into a thriving business.

Figure 419 The West End Bar in all its glory today at corner Bardykes Road

End of an era

Time was called on the MacNeil ownership in October 2008. On 8th November 2008, the Daily Record ran an interesting article on the MacNeil's time in Blantyre although incorrectly noted that Joseph had bought his High Blantyre Pub and overstated the length of his ownership. Otherwise aside from typos on the spelling of names, the article was first class, a dedication to the service of the MacNeil family and is reprinted here in full: "A Blantyre family have called last orders – after running The West End Bar for the past 74 years. In 1934, the MacNeils took over 'The Farmers Club', which is now known as The West End Bar. Since then, the pub has been run by several members of the MacNeil family including Donald, Mary, Ian, Joseph and Nan McGhie, who is now the last surviving member of the original family. Nan, who was the licensee of the pub, celebrated her 80th birthday in August. The third generation of the MacNeil family – Elizabeth Campbell, Kathryn Clarke, Mary-Jo Furlong and Felix MacNeil – continued to run the pub until October this year."

On behalf of the whole family, Mary-Jo commented: "Throughout the years, most of the family have continued to work and live in Blantyre. The pub has, and continues to be, a well-known landmark and is renowned for its support to local groups. It was a very difficult decision for the family to leave the licensing trade. So many of our patrons are extended members of our family. Generations of the same Blantyre families have journeyed with us through the years. But none of us have children and there was nobody to pass the reins to. We all have other jobs and Felix, who was the bar manager, is looking for a new career."

Figure 420 Interior of the West End Bar as it looks today

Today the pub has address 493 Glasgow Road. The pub has expanded a little over the years, the current lounge once a separate room and scullery. The traditional Scottish Bar sits at the heart of the community and a warm welcome awaits everyone who visits there. The West End Bar is open 7 days a week with a warm atmosphere. There's live entertainment many weeks with some top acts performing. People will remember gigs by local bands like the Rocksox. The Function Lounge is also used regularly for a variety events and is available for hire free of charge and is perfect for Birthday Parties, Engagements, Christenings and Baby Showers. The Men's Darts Team went unbeaten for nearly five years and have a fantastic trophy collection on show in the bar. Licensing hours are open until 1am on Saturday, and midnight every other evening. The McCormack family (Maura McLaughlin and brother Mick McCormack) have run the pub since 2008 as licensees for Greene King Brewing & Retail Ltd, their family once living at Cloudhowe Terrace and Belvoir Place.

This detailed article is dedicated to the hard work of all current and previous West End Bar owners and especially to the memory of Nan McNeil, who sadly recently passed away December 2017, aged 89.

Blantyre Project Social Media:

Margaret Duncan: "Mary MacNeil was the music teacher at St Joseph's Primary School and her mother owned the bar. They came from Barra originally and at one time lived at Hardie Street at the corner house."

Helen McGowan Munday: "I remember the Westend always known as Maw MacNeils."

Jim Canning: "The MacNeils let a newsagents where number 3 is."

Christine Forrest: "I remember the Hairdressers before it became the Newsagents, which also sold all types of food. I used to buy sweets before waiting for the bus. It was empty for years and I think became a fish shop at one time. My mother got her hair done at the hairdressers in the 1960's. I remember buying foreign stamps in the newsagents in 1967."

Catherine Davidson: "As of November 2017, Di Vitos has been there 35 years. Franco at Di Vito's Chip shop told me this only recently."

Stephen McCall: "The MacNeils I remember are Mary and daughter Christine. Joe married to Rosemary. Nan married Peter and had daughters Kathleen, Liz, Margaret-Mary, Mary-Jo, Annmarie. Iain was the father of Vincent and Felix. There may have been a son Andrew too."

Maura McLaughlin: "We have run the West End Bar since October 2008. We've heard many stories and tales over the years about the MacNeils time running the pub. She was well liked and very much respected. The pub still bears the family crest above the bar."

By Paul D Veverka

CHAPTER 15
GLASGOW ROAD SOUTH
BARDYKES RD TO PRIORY BRIDGE

Origins of Bardykes

Bardykes Road is a main road artery connecting Kirkton in High Blantyre, through Barnhill to the West End near Bardykes. It is today, a busy road bordered on the west by the Calder. Bardykes is likely taken from the word "Bar"- meaning 'low hills' and the Gaelic Dike, Dyk, as meaning "a wall of turf or stone". In the context of the early area around Bardykes Road junction with Glasgow Road, it is a fitting description for this lower part of Blantyre that would have had many stonewalled farm fields.

The Jackson or Jacksone family were in possession of the lands of Bardykes, (or Bardykis as it was then known) officially from 25th October 1525 although former Blantyre historians have suggested it may be as far back as 1502. Incredibly, with the exception of the Miller family at Milheugh, they are the longest family to have owned land in one place in Blantyre, occupying and owning the land at Bardykes on the fringes of Blantyre Parish for the best part of 400 years.

Owning mineral rights on their lands, some wealth was accumulated from their nearby estates at Hallside and Spittalhill. They also owned lands in High Blantyre at Greencroft, Barnhill and are responsible for being early inhabitants of Springwell. Their wealth was reinforced in later centuries deriving from their vast tea plantations in Sri-Lanka (formerly Ceylon), conducting their business as merchants Messrs Jackson, Buchanan & Company in Glasgow. They went on to become one of the largest wholesale tea dealers in Scotland.

Being such a prominent family and as heritors of Blantyre, they owed a duty to Walter Stuart of Minto, the Commendator of Blantyre when he was given ownership of much of the Parish land on 18th January 1598. The land was noted as "Bairdisdykis" as well as other established areas. In 1606, when he became Lord Blantyre, as a gesture and a departure from paying taxes, the Jackson family presented an annual red rose to Lord Blantyre instead as a reddendo.

A John Jackson died in 1707, his will showing all belongings passing to his family of the same name. By this Century the family were marrying into other large farms in the area, occupying other Blantyre farms like Park, Coatshill, Croftfoot and Old Place. Prior to the current Bardykes House being built near the Westend of Blantyre, a good-sized farm steading was all that was on this land. The Valuation books for 1859 state, "A good Farm Steading. The property of Mrs. Jackson." Bardykes House today is the home of the Wilkie family. 1871, saw a fundamental change where Bardykes Farm was demolished and the construction of Bardykes House commenced.

The new sandstone house was to be 2 storey and accessed via a long tree lined avenue, that led off of Bardykes Road, the entrance located near the west end on Glasgow Road. A grand turning circle was created at the entrance and all former farm buildings demolished.

On 5th April 1957, the Wilkie Family moved to Bardykes. Peter, Margaret and their 3 children, all under 5 years of age flitted from High Blantyre to Bardykes for the first time, in the horse pulled milk float. With them was 'Dinky' the Alsatian dog and 'Minky' the cat.

We leave you with this beautiful verse taken from Revelations in the Bible chapter 14 verse 13, which served the Jackson family well. It's inscribed on the stone Obelisk memorial on their family graves, which can be witnessed in the Kirkton graveyard. "Blessed are the dead who die in the Lord. They rest from their labours and their works do follow them". Simply put, it means have faith in the Lord, work hard and your efforts will be remembered. By the very fact that this is being reprinted here, the motto has proved its worth and the statement is also very fitting for all the hard working people of Blantyre.

Today, Blantyre residents still know Bardykes House more commonly known as Wilkie's Farm. It is officially known however as "Bardykes Farm" and today incorporates "Bardykes Farm Nursery School". The Wilkie family are still very well known and respected in this town. They are noted too for charitable work, being involved in the fundraising for many community campaigns, including hosting the fondly remembered Blantyre Highland Games from their fields from 1987, with their association with Blantyre Round Table.

Not actually on Glasgow Road, the house is accessed off Bardykes Road and its detailed history is told in other Blantyre Project books.

Bardykes Grove

To the west of the Bardykes Road junction at Glasgow Road and beyond the Westend was until 1994, just farm fields, not built upon until that time. The fields belonged to the Wilkie family and prior to them amongst other owners, the Jackson family.

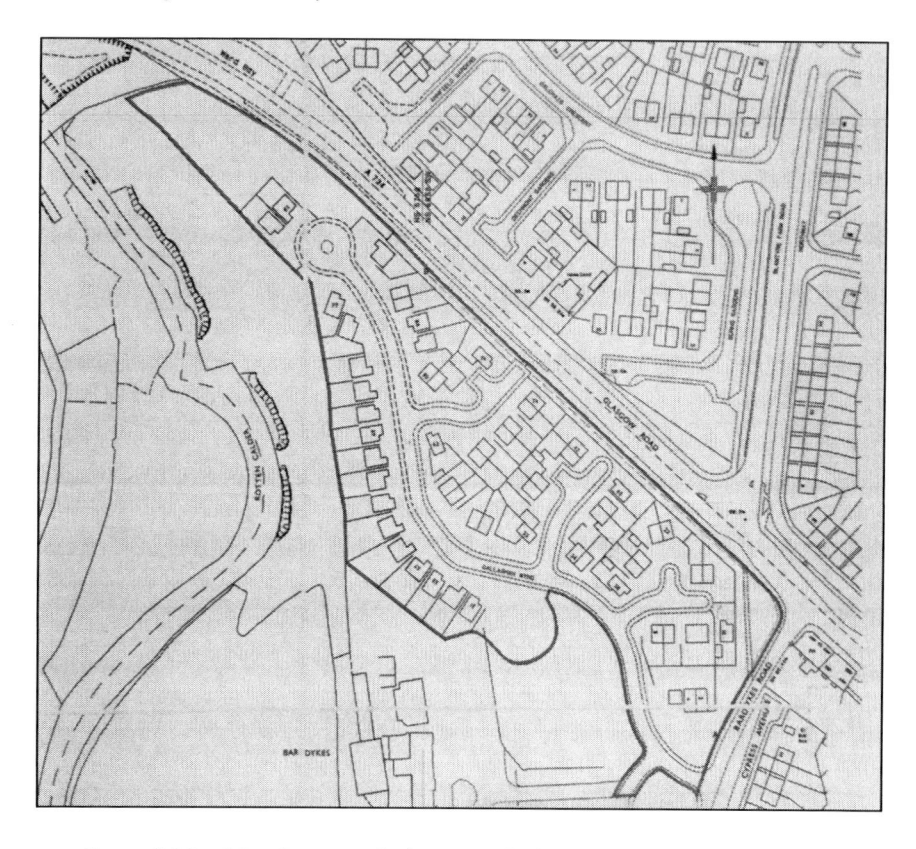

Figure 421 Bardykes Grove marked out on title deeds increasing size of Blantyre

On 26th January 1994, Alexander Wilkie (Sandy) with consent of the trustees of Wilkie Construction sold the field adjacent to Glasgow Road to Wimpey Homes Holdings Limited, well known house builders in Scotland. Wimpey commenced building a brand new housing estate, which was named Bardykes Grove. The estate consisted of one street, with 3 cul de sacs all to be named Callaghan Wynd. The street was named after Mrs. Cathy Callaghan, a long service teacher. Whilst researching this book, her daughter Margaret Mary O Sullivan added, " The street was named after my mum who spent most of her teaching career in Blantyre, teaching in Saint Joseph's, Blantyre and latterly in Saint Blanes - a job she loved. Like most people who came from a working class background, she appreciated the value of education in the fight against poverty. She was the eldest in her family and was ever appreciative of the sacrifices made by her younger sisters Bride and Theresa, who had to leave school and work in order to bring money into the house. She on the other hand being the eldest had the chance to continue with her studies. She believed that it was so important to give young people that opportunity."

Figure 422 Callaghan Wynd as it appears now. Neat, tidy, modern homes

It was a range of 3 bedroom semis and 3 or 4 bedroom detached houses which sold for a price range of between £52,000 to £85,000. Making use of almost all the field, a turning circle was located at the far western end. Alex Rochead was amongst first owners and moved into number 73 in November 1994. Arlene and James Green moved into 77 in December 1994. That winter was particularly harsh in Scotland with snow and temperatures down to − 15 degrees Celsius. Everything froze, including the pipes of the new houses, affecting many residents, some even having to move temporarily out.

Blantyre Project Social Media:

Arlene Green: "Callaghan Wynd was a super place for my family to grow up in. My 2 girls had plenty of friends. It had a playpark near the top end and was adjacent to the Wilkie's fields so very easy to feed the horses."

Gerald Kellachan: "Cathy was a labour activist. Her father Andy Fagan was awarded a BEM in the 1950's and Fagan Court in the village named after him"

Caldergrove

Although not directly on Glasgow Road, this next property is briefly explored here as the estate grounds fronted on to the road and had an entrance lodge house situated nearby. Caldergrove House was a large former detached villa in its own grounds by the Rotten Calder River. Situated just over the river in Cambuslang Parish, it was accessed by the private road, leading off Glasgow Road across the Priory Bridge and up into woodland, part of the Caldergrove Estate. The closest buildings to the stone built house was the West End Bar and Bardykes Farm.

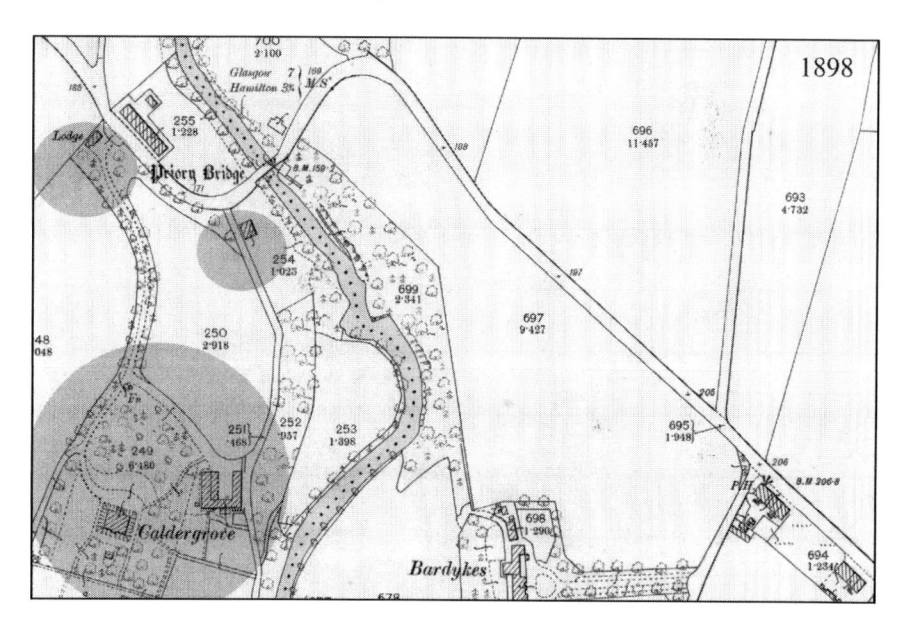

Figure 423 Caldergrove Estate, Offices and Lodge Houses 1898

It was built around 1830 as a private home and impressive it was too, with considerable land around it, sitting high up on the cliff ledge, overlooking the River Calder.

According to the 1859 Valuation Roll it was described as- "A superior and large dwelling house having offices a little last of it, and surrounded by young fir plantation. The property of and occupied by Mr. J, McCulloch." The River created the boundary between Blantyre and Cambuslang and with Caldergrove House on the West side, it sat firmly in the Cambuslang side, right on the fringes.

In 1875 a mansard roof and Ionic-style porch were added to give the house a more imposing façade. The interior was elaborately decorated in 1875 and at the height of Victorian fashion, the house was given all modern facilities, including refits of bathrooms, water supplies to inside and architectural adornments that gave the house a "wow factor". Many of the Victorian features and fittings inside lasted right into the 20th Century.

By the end of the 1890's, the house would have been a prominent feature in the area. The planted estate trees had grown to form the beginnings of the woodland we see today.

Ornate gardens were formed including a fountain, paths and a large Summer glasshouse, as well as routes created for strolling down by the river. Caldergrove House had evolved into being one of the grandest estate homes in the area.

Caldergrove gave over its residential use during World War One to be a local hospital. It was a convalescent home for wounded soldiers during those war years. A cast metal plaque on the exterior of the building was later inscribed: 'To record the use of this Building as an Auxiliary hospital during the Great War and the thanks of the Scottish Branch of the British Red Cross Society to the Generous Donors April 1919.'

Figure 424 Caldergrove Medical Staff during WW1 outside Caldergove (Hospital)

The equipment of the hospital was removed when the war ended and the interior was once again decorated in 1919, in a more "modern", art deco era. It once again became a secluded, private home. The house had lamps on cast iron posts flanking the stone steps leading up to the Ionic-columned porch. Above this an advanced bay led the eye up to the mansard roof with its ornate cast iron balustrade, which protected the roof terrace. This fine house had two gate lodges also situated in leafy grounds. It would have been a pleasant retreat for its wealthy 19th and 20th-century owners from the hustle and bustle of Glasgow.

In the post WW2 years, it was owned for several decades by 2 elderly ladies. Jenny & Bertha Waddell, daughters of Jeffrey Waddell were spinster sisters who ran a mobile Children's theatre, known locally in the area. They filled the house with antiques including a large collection of stuffed tropical birds.

Figure 425 Caldergrove Servant's kitchen in the Basement pictured 1982

Sadly, the house is no longer there. Its demise was relatively recent in 1983 when it burned down amidst suspicion, speculation and rumour about missing children! Rumours circulated soon after when one sister disappeared and the other was found dead, at the top of the Cliffside one October morning. The interior of the house was completely gutted by fire, resulting in the entire demolition of the house. Today, Caldergrove house is still there in name. However, it's now a modern building on the site, no sign of the old one and for a time until recently, was the modern head office of construction company, "Advance Construction". The detailed history of Caldergrove including many interior photos are explored in other Blantyre Project books.

By Paul D Veverka

Bardykes Mill & Mill House

Bardykes Mill, or more commonly known as The Black Mill or Priory Bridge Mill was formerly situated on the northern riverbank of the River Clyde immediately adjacent to the east side of The Priory Bridge. As you exit Blantyre, on the left, at the edge of the river, on the approach to Caldergrove, the ruined mill cannot be seen from the modern road, but certainly could up until the road realignment of the 1930's.

Figure 426 The Ruins of Bardykes Mill pictured in 2004, next to Priory Bridge

The mill can be traced and dated back to at least 1748 belonging to the nearby Jackson family at Bardykes. Built of stone over 2 storeys it was square on plan.

In the 1700's and 1800's, a condition existed, which was known as "Astricted Milling". This was a tri-party agreement between the landowner, his tenant miller and the tenant farmer on the land. It permitted that all the grain belonging to the landowner's tenant farmers was sent to the miller for grinding. The farmer would be paid by the miller, therefore providing the income for the farmer to pay his rent to the landowner. The Miller, in turn after working the grain, would be able to sell the product, allowing him a source of income and means to pay his rent to the landowner. The three parties, whilst independent upon agreeing their financial arrangements, were actually dependent upon each other to succeed.

This mill was formerly a flour or corn mill, and in the 1850's used for providing charred wood & coal dust, to make dross used for moulding purposes in Foundries. In some mills of this description coal dust was ground for putting in powder, & they were sometimes termed "Soot Mills". This was also commonly termed a Soot mill. The mills at Cambuslang of the same description as this, were called "Black Mills" so the Miller considered the term to be appropriate for this one too. The mill was one of 7 major mills in Blantyre.

This map from 1859 shows the location of Bardykes Mill which also hints even by then a nearby ruined lade running alongside the river.

Figure 427 Bardykes Mill and Millers House on 1859 Map

Nearby on the opposing north west side of the Priory Bridge was the miller's house. The house would have been the very last house as you left Blantyre Parish crossing over into Cambuslang Parish. It was inhabited property on the 1859 map, some 60 years later. A sketch by Jean Claude Nattes in 1799 shows this cottage as having a thatched roof. The 1859 map puts it in good reference and shows the house sitting in its own field with paths at the front of the property leading down to the waters edge and to the mill. In 1865 James McCracken was the miller, renting from Mr. Jackson.

The Hamilton Advertiser 5th October 1867, confirms the mill had a detached small house nearby with a small garden. The mill at that time was fitted out as a saw mill for which it was commented it had been very well adapted for. The machinery at that time included a saw and bench and was up

By Paul D Veverka

for sale as well as the mill house. Mr. John Jackson of nearby Spittal was showing the property at the time and the advert hoped to let out the still functional water powered mill.

The next occupier was Thomas Taylor who was still there in 1875 but gone by 1881. By 1885, there were no occupants in the mill, but the house was still occupied being rented by Mr. John Campbell.

Thomas Taylor

DID YOU KNOW?

Thomas (Tam) Taylor, was a man greatly in advance of his times. The Blantyre man, the last miller of Bardykes was also an inventor of one of the earliest reaping machines. Blantyre readers will be proud to know he attempted to make one of the First Flying Machines, a full 30 years before the successful flight of the Wright Brothers in 1903!

Born in Blantyre in 1846, Tam was by 1871 living in Bridgeton. Importantly, he's noted then, aged 24 as being a "Maker of Steam Boilers". It is alleged Thomas unveiled his great plans for a flying machine, which at the height of the industrial revolution, was to be powered by steam. Now Thomas had a great acquaintance in Mr Templeton, the blacksmith at Barnhill. The relationship was likely first a business one where Thomas commissioned parts for his inventions and Mr. Templeton would make and supply them. So it was no surprise that the flying machine endeavour, involved them both working together. Mr Templeton did indeed make the machine parts and assisted Tam in constructing their flying machine which was built in the barn at the old Barnhill Smiddy.

When completed, the flying contraption was taken out into the adjacent Larkfield field (now where the High Blantyre Primary School is) and the engine was stoked, ready for an attempted flight. The local inhabitants of Larkfield and Barnhill would have been naturally curious upon the sight. It is not recorded who piloted the flight, but it was likely Tam, given his investment and inventive nature. Varying accounts have this story in the 1860's or 1870's.

From an account written by Mr. Templeton's son, almost 80 years later, which says word for word, "The Smith's father made some of the parts of this machine over 80 years ago. The power unit was a steam engine. Tam and the Smith tried out the machine but just as it began to rise, the supply of steam gave out. The elements of success were there but the engine was not suitable. "I didna manage it", he said to the Smith, "but it will come yet whaever leeves tae see the day". A true prophet! The principles of flight were known even in 1860, but the problem lay in steam engines not generating enough speed and therefore the lift needed for takeoff. It would take the petrol engine to be invented and used in a flying machine in 1903 for successful flight to be established. People will remember Tam Taylor, the Blantyre born inventor. Regardless of the story taking place in 1860's or 1870's, Tam was a young man when he made this trial flight. By 1881, Thomas was married to Ellen Taylor and they were away from Blantyre living at Govan with a growing, large family, never to return.

In April 1872, Thomas Caldwell of Blantyre Works was convicted of maliciously removing tiles from the roof of Bardykes Mill on 24th March 1872.

The End of the Mill

Figure 428 Bardykes Mill Ruin in 2004

On the 1898 map, both the house and the Black Mill are shown as ruins and not lived in, concluding the final use of the house was between 1885 and 1897. The mill fell out of use earlier between 1876 and 1880.

In 1907, the fate of the Black Mill House was also sealed when the Parish authorities demolished it to extend the width of the road leading up to and over the Priory Bridge itself, to accommodate sufficient room for two trams to pass. It was the land to the North that was extended, the Mill itself left as ruins in-situ. The new widened road and tramlines are shown on the 1910 map.

In the late 1930's the area changed completely, when a massive earthworks embankment was placed alongside the roadway to realign the road. The first of several which forms the new and current Glasgow Road profile, the bend in the road at Priory Bridge becoming redundant. There is little hope of ever uncovering where the mill house was, as much of the realigned road and earthworks were placed in the field near the location of where it once stood.

Priory Bridge

The Priory Bridge is an iconic name and structure in Blantyre that exists to this day and yet it is still surprising how many people wonder where it is. Whilst the bridge has been entirely closed off to traffic for several decades, it still stands proudly as an old monument to Blantyre's history at the side of the new A724 re-profiled Glasgow Road to the South of the old Mavis Mill and to the North of Caldergrove Lodge. It spans the Rotten Calder River, which is the boundary between Blantyre Parish and that of Cambuslang. It's actually very close to Glasgow Road itself and you can easily drive past on the way to Cambuslang, not knowing it's there at the roadside within the woods.

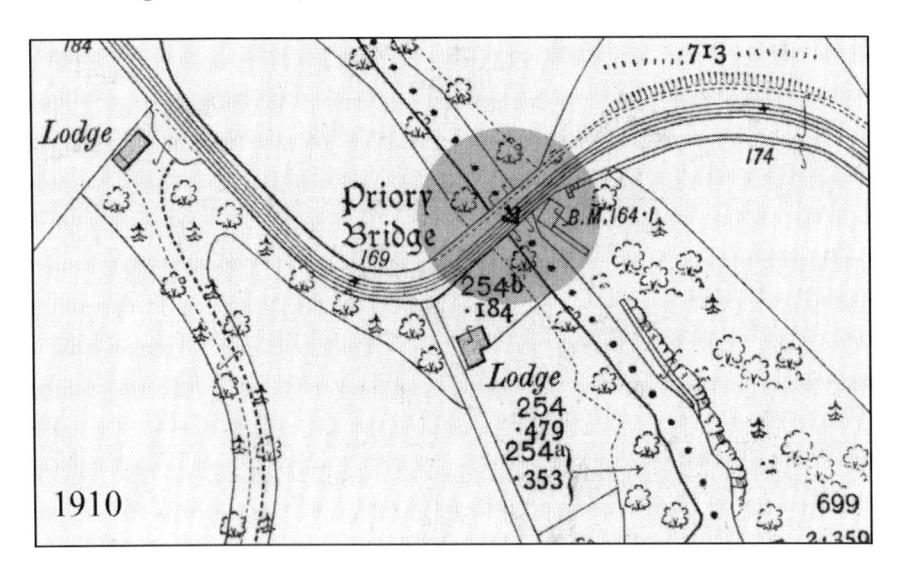

Figure 429 Priory Bridge shown on the 1910 map before road realignment

The bridge was sketched in 1799 by Jean Claude Nattes and is a fine example of stone vaulted arch construction. To the immediate North East side of the bridge was the Black Mill (Bardykes or Spittal Mill), which is now in ruins today.

Described in 1859 as, "A Bridge over the "Rotten Calder Water" — the Boundary of the Parish, on the T. P. [Turn Pike] Road between Glasgow & Hamilton. This Bridge is supposed, by the authorities given, to be as old as "Blantyre Priory." No authentic information can be obtained, relative to its date, or probable date in any accounts of the Parish or the neighbourhood. There is however, a tradition in the neighbourhood of the Bridge. — "That when the building of the "Priory" was finished the Masons employed there were so numerous, that upon each bringing a Stone from the Priory they were sufficient to form the Bridge, which, was built in one night." The Arch of this

Bridge is not as wide as the Road over it. The alteration in the width of the Road, as stated by Mr. Jackson of Blantyre Park, was made about 50 years ago. (1809). The construction of the Bridge, which is not seen until under the Arch, is supposed to be of a very old date. As stated by R. Ker Esqr. of Auchinraith House, the description given of the Arch, shows it to be similar to the construction of Bothwell Bridge, before it was improved. The oldest & best authorities in the Parish have been applied to for information.

The name "Prior" is a corruption of "Priory," supposed to have been adopted for sake of abbreviation. The Session Records of the Parish, are at present being searched for any clue to the age of Prior Bridge. If anything of importance [...] it will be immediately forwarded Tracing & Name Sheet of Cambuslang to be altered."

The account and suggestion of a 13th Century Bridge may be wishful thinking. It's unlikely the bridge is as old as the Priory (13th Century) and it is more likely in design and architecture, 17th Century, noted on a 1634 map, although an older crossing at that point may have been entirely possible. One has to assume fully the bridge was not built in one evening! It got its latter name of the Priory Bridge, instead of Prior Bridge by the end of the 19th Century due to Blantyre Priory, which despite a little distance away, was still one of the nearest, adjacent and ancient Blantyre landmarks.

Fatal Fall from Priory Bridge

On Saturday 21st June 1817 an open air stage coach travelling between Glasgow to Hamilton was involved in a fatal accident on top of the Priory Bridge at Blantyre. As the coach approached the bridge, an oncoming horse and cart startled the horses pulling the coach, and the passengers on top of the coach were alarmed as they were thrown from the side, as their coach toppled over. The coach didn't topple right over, but fell leaning on top of the high Priory Bridge parapet wall, with such a movement and jolt that several passengers fell from the coach to the bridge.

One passenger however, was not so lucky. A young man, named Bennie was thrown clear of the parapet right over the side of the Priory Bridge itself, and fell below in the River Calder. He was hurt so badly, he lived for only an hour afterwards. His body was so shockingly disfigured, for he had fallen a great distance from above on to rocks below. No other person was hurt, although there were several outside passengers on the coach. Mr. Bennie was a millwright who had been working at Camlachie and had been travelling to see his father in Blantyre, when the accident occurred.

Those who know Priory Bridge will realise just what a great height this bridge is. The next picture is a mock up of the scene created using an actual sketch of the bridge from a similar time period and showing a coach and cart of the day, poised ready for the accident to happen.

Figure 430 Coach passes over the Priory Bridge in 1817

Priory Bridge – The 20th Century

In 1906, a spate of crimes took place on the Glasgow to Hamilton Road near the Priory Bridge, the cause being people taking advantage of no light. It was pitch black at night. People were being robbed travelling between Halfway and Blantyre. When girls and women started to be violated by molestation, the authorities had to act. It was proposed that lights should be put up for the full stretch paid by each county council from the Westend to the Sun Inn at Halfway. The cost of this proved prohibitive and was put off when it became known that the tram network was to be extended. Authorities hoped the tram companies would simply put a light on each tram standard at intervals. However, the cost of this was eventually borne by both tram company and authorities, initially only lighting part of the way. Crimes continued in this area for many years afterwards.

When extending the tramlines from Blantyre to Cambuslang in 1907 this bridge represented a major obstacle. It was the source of a lot of expenditure to make the dual tram lanes run over it and connect with the nearby adjacent tram network. A passing line was also constructed next to the tram terminus, where cars could stack up and remain overnight without causing obstruction.

At this time, the bridge started to become known also as "The Spittal Bridge" a reference to the nearby area being mined. Contrary to other writings, the bridge was never widened beyond 1907, nor ever encased in concrete.

Its construction actually spans several decades and is a real mix of styles and type. From underneath you can see three clear stages of rebuilding or extension. In the centre is the early portion – a high single span arch of ashlar masonry, 3.3m wide. This original arch has the appearance of 17th or possibly early 18th century work. On either side is another extension constructed in approximately 1809 as outlined in the earlier account. This is furthered by the modern brick-and-girder extension of 1907 to accommodate tram and vehicular traffic. There is a moulded stone course round the arch of the original span. The top of the bridge is quite 'modern' dating from 1907.

Highway Robbery at the Bridge

In June 1910, a sensational affair was reported to the Cambuslang police. A man named Henry Kelly (28) visited his parents at 71 Main Street, Cambuslang. As he missed the last Lanarkshire tramcar at Cambuslang for Hamilton, he started to walk back towards Blantyre. He reached Priory Bridge about 1 a.m. Suddenly, he was accosted by two men, and asked for a match. Kelly complied with this request, and then his 'no-gooders' asked him if he "had anything on him." "Do you mean drink?" queried Kelly. "Yes," was the answer. " Well, I don't drink at all." "Have you any money ?" " Yes," answered Kelly, "and I mean to keep it!"

A desperate struggle then took place on Priory Bridge, but ultimately the taller of the two men pinned Kelly's arms, while the other turned out his pockets. Kelly still retained his watch and chain, and another fight took place over it. It was broken during the struggle. On Kelly demanding his money back, the taller of the two men lifted him and threw him over the parapet of the Priory Bridge into the river Calder, a drop of over 39 feet. How the unfortunate man got out he was not able to tell. When he recovered consciousness the murky water was running over his body. Kelly was able to reach home, but he was drenched to the skin, and covered with blood. The men were not caught and today, this crime would have been deemed an attempted murder.

The trams traversed this bridge until the late 1920's. Earthing guard wires were added to the tram network in 1923 between Priory Bridge and Springwell at a cost of £60. Various road realignments have also occurred in the 20th Century. The bridge was closed off to traffic and now also to pedestrians and has been so overcome by nature, there are trees actually growing on the bridge deck now in these post Millennium years. With the realigned road, Priory Bridge is a bridge to nowhere and consequently is not maintained. The structure is incredibly high and the steepness of the slopes immediately beside it, making it feel quite perilous to be in the area. Ivy trails over the side reach down almost to the water giving a romantic appearance to those adventurous enough to observe it from the river or steep embankments.

Figure 431 Priory Bridge in 2007 photographed by Jim Brown

Priory Bridge Tram Heist

Before we leave the Priory Bridge, let us tell you of a daring robbery at this location, the story worth telling here. Late on Saturday 9th April 1927, around 11.15pm, the last tramcar of the evening from Cambuslang was proceeding to the Power Station at Hamilton Road, Motherwell. To do this, it had to go through Blantyre as usual. Being so late, the car had only three passengers aboard, who occupied the inside of the car. It was around the Priory Bridge district (a quiet spot lying between Cambuslang and Blantyre) when three (it is alleged) young men stepped on to the parked tramcar and proceeded upstairs.

The night was dark, and it was the custom and duty that tramcar drivers proceeding to the depot on the last run of each evening required to switch off the street lighting. These were days when electric lights on roadsides were new. They were not controlled centrally, but instead operated manually by control pillars on each road. One switch would kill the streetlights. The electric lights on this particular roadside were being switched off at the time by the driver of the car who had stopped and got out to do so.

The fact that the lights on the roadside were out, coupled with the fact of the loneliness of the remote road, made the intentions of the men easier than if the lights had been on. However, the conductor, after the lapse of a second or so, proceeded upstairs to the open top-deck of his car to collect the fares from his three new "countryside" passengers who had boarded at an unofficial stop.

It was when he had reached the top that he noticed the three men had seated themselves in different parts of the car and were strangely not sitting beside each other, despite being previously observed chatting with each other. An uneasiness descended as the streetlights were put out adjacent to the car and the tram plunged into darkness. Approaching the nearest man, the conductor was informed that the tickets were being procured by the "other chap over there," meaning of course the passenger further along.

The conductor then proceeded to the next man and inquired about the tickets for all 3 passengers, and was in the act of punching the tickets when he was set upon from behind! A heavy blow being dealt on the back of his head by a blunt weapon of some kind or other. No sooner had the severe blow been received than the conductor felt a hand being forced over his mouth, whilst efforts were being made to pull his bag of money from off his shoulder. This was a robbery.

The conductor, however, appeared to have been stunned by the blow on the head, but he managed momentarily to free himself and in a brave moment, bit the hand which covered his mouth, biting his assailant's finger. With his mouth free, the conductor called out for help to the driver, all the time struggling against his 3 attackers in their desperate attempt to get a hold of his bag of cash. However, the driver heard the commotion upstairs, stopped his lighting duties immediately and ran back to the tramcar. Hearing his fellow-worker's call for aid, he shouted back he was coming.

The robbers now realised their "game was up," and knowing that the driver was likely now to be the scene at once, they made their escape fast as foot could carry them down the stairway at the opposite end of the tramcar and back into the darkness at Priory Bridge. The conductor appeared to be somewhat dazed, and was suffering from the effects of the blow his head. He had a nasty wound, which was bleeding profusely. Aid was summoned, and the local county police were informed of the untoward event. The bag was held by the conductor and it was later found that only 1s 9d was missing. The men were unknown to the conductor and it was not thought that any arrest was made.

Dr, Wilson in Blantyre, had been early on the scene, and attended the injured conductor who was later removed to his home. The conductor was James Wilson, a young Motherwell man. This was just a couple of years prior to the trams ending and we're sure would have prompted a lot more awareness against similar things happening.

Figure 432 Tramcar travels over Priory Bridge in 1910's

Road Realignment

In January 1927, plans were announced to upgrade the road between Cambuslang and Priory Bridge at a sum of £80,000. Further improvements were budgeted to bypass the Priory Bridge at a cost of £32,000 and to eventually remove the redundant tram standards. By May 1928, there had been complaints that the road was still not complete. Mr. A.B Maxwell (Councilor) of Blantyre stated that he saw no fewer than 3 buses per day stranded on the unfinished road that needed assistance to get moving again. Councilors agreed it needed to be expedited before the public made such observations.

In 1992 and 1993 the main road was given its most extensive upgrade, removing as many bends and dips as possible, with safety at the forefront. Despite this and the visible improvement, accidents have still happened.

Figure 433 Bad Bend at Spittal 1920's (road over Priory Bridge)

Spittal & Dalton Accidents

As well as bad bend in the road leading to Halfway, there were several dips, which caused the road to flood. In Winter, it would freeze over and caused a horrifying amount of vehicle accidents throughout the 20th Century.

Michael Duddy (58) of Northway was killed in January 1967 when his motorcycle collided with a car one Saturday night on Hamilton Road near Spittal Farm. We remember the many people killed on this stretch of road within this chapter. Amongst them, on Saturday 7th July 1928, two men riding a motor cycle travelling towards Hamilton were killed in a collision with a Glasgow-bound bus that night at Priory Bridge. The bridge was reached on both sides a steep "S" formation, and it was on one the curves that the accident took place. The motorcycle immediately burst into flames, but the men were extricated and immediate medical assistance was rendered. The men were terribly injured, one them having both legs broken, fracture of the skull, and severe injuries to the face. He was wholly unconscious, and the other, who suffered somewhat similar injuries, was semiconscious. They were conveyed to the Royal Infirmary, Glasgow, but died on the way. The men were Henry Mullen and Walter Duckenfield, both of Denny.

On Friday 10th November 1939, forty seven year old Alexander McFarlane was killed at Blantyre's Priory Bridge.

The man who resided at 21 Craig Street had been walking home and was killed outright when run down by a stray motor car.

By Paul D Veverka

We remember also two women and a boy who were tragically killed on Thursday 20th April 1967 when their car collided with a heavy lorry at Spittal.

The car had been heading towards Glasgow and shortly before noon it came off the road, killing all three people instantly. The car left the road at a downhill bend, ploughed through a fence and came to rest in a field.

The light blue Hillman Minx car was completely wrecked (as pictured), but the sorrow that day most definitely was learning that there were fatalities. Two ambulances and a fire engine were called out and all emergency services were deeply saddened to see the tragedy.

Mrs Irene Lillico (39), manageress of the Tillietudlum Hotel and her only child Archie (5) perished, along with Mrs. May Stirling of Netherburn a mother of 2 children. Both adults were in the front of the car, the child in the back, when it is believed the car became out of control and crashed into the path of the oncoming lorry, rebounding it towards the fence and field. William McGinlay, a lorry driver from Glasgow, aged 44 was uninjured.

Figure 434 Crash in 1967, left 3 people dead at Spittal

Other people who died on this road over the years include unfortunate souls remembered here from the Beaton, Chambers, Couser, Hendry, Gordon and Thomson families. These people and others who passed away here were all much loved and not forgotten. This stretch of road was notoriously dangerous and claimed lives right into the 1990's before being properly upgraded in 1992 and 1993, removing most of the dangerous inclines and bends. Accidents continued after the upgrade but were far less frequent.

Caldergrove Row

On the 1896 map, there is a curious block of 8 small homes, single storey all terraced directly opposite the Caldergrove Lodge House. What makes this curiously interesting is that they're not in the 1891 census nor the 1895 valuation roll or indeed in the 1901 census. Certainly not shown anymore on the 1910 map. As such they could only have existed sometime between 1896 and 1900, at the very most no more than 4 years.

Built on Marshall family land on the Caldergrove estate, they may have been hastily erected wooden or brick homes or huts as overspill for servants working on the nearby Caldergrove Estate, mansion house, offices and formal gardens. Servants tended to live in the Caldergrove House itself so these homes could have been temporary accommodation for contractors for renovation works or perhaps associated with nearby Spittal Colliery.

At the back of was another smaller block, most likely a washhouse or communal toilet. Another reason altogether may exist that explains these properties. No formal name can be found for these homes in documentation, their short existence little known about.

Today, the flat, gated field is still there, but there is no sign of any terraced buildings that once formed this little row at Caldergrove. A handful of small stones can be found amongst the grass, the remnants of small foundations.

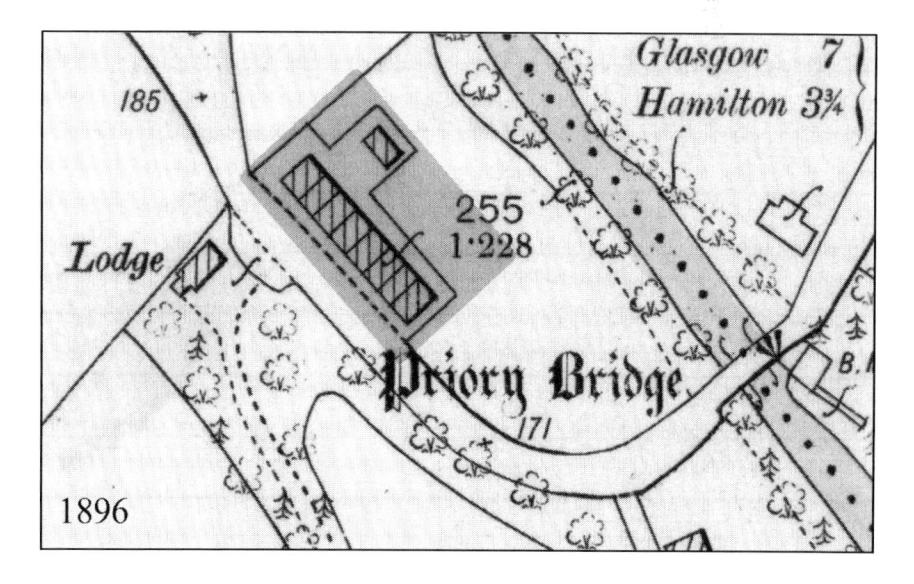

Figure 435 Short lived Row at Caldergrove on 1896 map

By Paul D Veverka

Archaeology at Dalton

Although slightly outwith Blantyre Parish into Cambuslang Parish, this next example of an archaeology find is interesting enough to tell here, and is good evidence of early habitation in this general area. In November 1930, two stone cists or and a cremation deposit were uncovered during the construction of Dalton School, Cambuslang. They are believed to be many hundreds of years old, predating Medieval times.

One cist, covered by a capstone measuring 1.1m by 0.8m, consisted of four sandstone slabs and measured 0.7m by 0.5m internally and 0.5m in depth. An upright Food Vessel was found on the floor, but there were no skeletal remains. The second cist, about 2m further W, had been disturbed, but also contained a Food Vessel; the capstone measured 1.4m by 1.1m. A deposit of cremated bones was discovered in a hollow dug about 0.6m into the ground at a distance of 2.1m E of the first cist.

The Food Vessels are now in Glasgow Art Gallery and Museum (Accession nos: '55-96). There are other examples of finds in the fields near Flemington and Dalton, perhaps an ideal place for early settlement due to the proximity to Dechmont Hill, believed to have once been an ancient fort.

Figure 436 The interesting find at Spittal in 1930

Our final picture below has a tramcar it is final years, heading towards Blantyre on the Glasgow Road, the turn off for Dalton and Flemington, on the left hand side. A snowy scene from the 1920's.

We're now of course sufficiently beyond Blantyre Parish boundaries in our exploration along Glasgow Road and as such, our fascinating journey on the South side comes to an end.

Figure 437 Blantyre Tramcar coming from Cambuslang, Dalton turn off on left (1920's)

CHAPTER 16
GLASGOW ROAD SOUTH
BUSINESS ADDRESS DIRECTORY

An unexpected but tremendously useful 'by-product' in researching this book has been the exclusive creation of a detailed home ownership and business directory for Glasgow Road. There is no doubt shops are still missing from this extensive list and it is in no way 'definitive' with gaps clearly to be filled in, perhaps more so in post WW2 years. However, it's previously unpublished, a first with unprecedented detail. With postal addresses in one place, it summarises and lists the business and house owners and for this whole complex subject, attempts to reconcile when they existed and where.

Numbers on the left refer to the odd number postal addresses on Glasgow Road only, e.g. 1,3,5 Glasgow Road etc. Shops and business are marked with a '*' and highlighted. Approximated dates are denoted by 'c'. No numbers if no known address were allocated. It is anticipated that this incredibly detailed piece of research, will be most useful for those researching Blantyre in future. For ref:

"Veverka's Glasgow Road South, Blantyre Directory"
Homes & Businesses – East to West
Compiled by Paul Veverka

No	Business	Service	Dates	Owner
*	Blantyre Lodging House	Hostel	1908-1975	Council, by subscription
*	Noel Kegg	Plant & Tools	1975-2010	Noel Kegg
*	Tool-Stop	Plant & Tools	2010-2016	Sons of Noel Kegg
*	Greenfield Foundry	Foundry	1877-1882	Taylor & Henderson
*	Greenfield Foundry	Foundry	1882-1900	Kesson & Campbell
*	Greenfield Foundry & Engineering works	Engineering	1900-1924	Campbell, Binnie & Co
*	Greenfield Foundry & Engineering works	Engineering	1924-1955	Campbell, Binnie, Reid & Co
*	Ireland's Scrap merchant	Scrap dealer	1955-1964	Charles Ireland, businessman

*	Ireland Alloys	Engineering	1964-now	Siegfried Jacob Metallwerke
*	First Buses	Bus Depot	1998-now	First Buses Transport Services
*	McLelland's Workshop	Carter	1891-c1915	William McLelland, miner
*	McLelland's Workshop	Joiner	c1915-c1933	Alexander Forrest, Joiner
1-5	McLelland's Buildings	3 houses	1881-c1933	William McLelland, miner
7-9	Welsh's Buildings	2 houses	1881-c1933	William Semple / John Welsh
11-17	McDougall's Buildings	4 houses	1876-1892	Duncan McDougall, miner
11-17	McDougall's Buildings	4 houses	1892-1916	George Speirs
11-17	McDougall's Buildings	4 houses	1916-1926	Thomas Speirs
11-17	McDougall's Buildings	4 houses	1926-c1960's	Robert & James McDougall
* 13	McDougall's Fruit & Veg	Fruit & Veg	1930-1960's	Robert McDougall
* 15	Alexander Lennox Workshop (McDougall's Buildings)	Shoemaker	1892-c1901	George Speirs, miner
* 15	John MacKinnan Fruiterer (McDougall's Buildings)	Fruit shop	1901-c1910	George / Thomas Speirs
* 15	Ice Cream & Sweet Shop (McDougall's Buildings)	Ice Cream /sweets	c1910-c1914	George / Thomas Speirs
* 15	Workshop (McDougalls Buildings)	Empty	c1914-1920	George / Thomas Speirs (demolished workshop in 1920)
*	Springwell Piggery	Pig Farming	1916-c1925	William McCallum
*	Springwell Piggery	Pig Farming	1925-1955	Robert McDougall
17-23	Smellie's Buildings	13 houses	1896-c1970's	Alexander Smellie / Lawson
* 21	Allan, the Tailor shop	Tailors	1896-1915	Alexander Smellie
* 21	Margaret Reid's shop	Unknown	1915-1920	Alexander Smellie
* 21	Jeanie Lawson's shop	Grocery	1920-1940's	Alexander Smellie
* 23	John Tenant's Corner shop	Flesher	1896-c1922	Alexander Smellie
* 23	David Berry's Corner shop	Unknown	1922-c1925	Alexander Smellie
*	Hayloft, stables and slaughterhouse	Slaughterhouse	1898-c1915	Alexander Smellie
*	Hayloft, stables & garage	Garage	1915-c1920	John Tennant, butcher
	McNair's Land	8 houses	1878-1905	James McNair / H. Craigen
19	McNair's Land	8 houses	1905-1935	Alexander Smellie
19	McNair's Land	8 houses	1935-1970's	Lawson Family
	Springwell Place	Cul-de-sac	1878-1927	Various homes as above
	Semple's Land	2 houses	1881-1895	William Semple Snr
	Semple's Land	19 houses	1895-1907	William Semple Snr
	Semple's Land	26 houses	1907-1915	Gavin Semple, mason
	Dalzell Place (Semples)	26 houses	1915-1929	Charles Easson / Thomas Bell
	Grasspark at Dalzell Place	Vacant	1929-now	County Council / SLC
25-33	Allison Place, Springwell	41 houses	1878-1907	Miss Ann Allison Heriot
25-33	Allison Place, Springwell	41 houses	1907-1921	A Heriot / Daniel Paterson
25-33	Allison Place, Springwell	41 houses	1921-1927	John Stevenson
* 27-29	John Miller's Grocery shop (Allison Place)	Grocery	1878-c1910	Miss Ann Allison Heriot
* 27-29	Robert McDougall's Grocery (Allison Place)	Grocery shop	1910-1926	Heriot / Paterson / Stevenson
* 31-33	Alexander Smellie Butchers (Allison Place)	Flesher	1878-1900	Miss Ann Allison Heriot

* 31-33	John Lees Sweet Shop (Allison Place)	Confectionery	1900-1912	A Heriot / D Paterson
* 31-33	John Crop's Shop (Allison Place)	Unknown	1912-c1920	A.Heriot / D. Paterson
* 31-33	John Bell's Shop (Publican) (Allison Place)	Spirit Shop	1920-1926	John Stevenson
*	Allison Pl Smithy & Stable	Blacksmiths	1878-1907	Miss Ann Allison Heriot
*	Allison Pl Lumber & Stable	Timber store	1907-1920	A Heriot / D Paterson
25-41	Springwell Houses	9 houses	1933-now	County Council / SLC
35-49	Gebbie's Buildings	10 houses	1879-1895	Francis Gebbie, Solicitor
35-49	Gebbie's Buildings	16 houses	1895-1902	Francis Gebbie, Solicitor
* 49	Robert Longmuir's Shop (Gebbie's / Miller's Building)	Grocery	1879-1895	Francis Gebbie, Solicitor
* 49	John English Dairy (Gebbie's / Miller's Building)	Dairy	1895-1902	Francis Gebbie, Solicitor
* 49	Samuel Moore's Dairy (Gebbie's / Miller's Building)	Dairy	1902-1915	David Miller, Solicitor
35-49	Miller's Buildings (Gebbies)	16 houses	1902-1931	David Miller, Solicitor
* 49	B.Fisher's Shop (Gebbie's / Miller's Building)	Cooper	1920-1925	David Miller, Solicitor
*	Blantyre Golf Club	Golf Course	1913-1918	Paterson/McGregor /McKenzie
*	William Tait's Poultry Run	Poultry Farm	c1925-c1937	Paterson/McGregor /McKenzie
	Eastern Railway Bridge 1	Railway Bridge	1882-1980	Caledonian Railway Company / LMSB
	Western Railway Bridge 2	Railway Bridge	1863-1977	Caledonian Railway Company / LMSB
51-59	Chamber's Land	17 houses	1879-1881	William Chalmers, joiner
51-59	Silverwells (Chambers Land)	16 houses	1881-1909	David G. Dunn (coalmaster)
51-59	Chambers Buildings (Chalmers Land)	18 houses	1909-1924	John Grant Sharp (Trustee of David G Dunn)
51-59	Chamber's Buildings	18 houses	1924-1959	Margaret Sharp & then others
	A725 East Kilbride Expressway	Dual carriageway	1967-now	Built in 3 stages by Hamilton & Strathclyde Councils
	Rosendale Place	47 houses	1896-1908	Adam Kirk, Joiner
	Rosendale Place	47 houses	1908-1922	Thomas Black & Son, trustee of Adam Kirk
	Rosendale Place	47 houses	1922-1950's	Mrs Annie Imrie Davidson or Carlton Miller
	Rosendale Place	47 houses	1950's-1976	District Council
*	Agnes Murdoch Shop at 6&7 Rosendale	Grocery	1896-c1908	Adam Kirk, joiner, Cambuslang.
*	Richard Pickering's Shop at 8 Rosendale	Unknown	c1896-1900	Adam Kirk, joiner, Cambuslang
*	Antonio Tracendo's Shop at 8 Rosendale	Ice Cream Parlour	1900-1908	Adam Kirk, joiner, Cambuslang.
*	Auchinraith Social & Recreation Club (Rosendale)	Men's Club	1919-1950's	Rented from Thomas Black & Son, then Annie Imrie Davidson
*	Auchinraith Fairground	Fairground	1910's-1970's	Laurences, Dan Taylor's, Irvins
61-63	Caldwell Institute	Hall, House	1900-1925	James Caldwell, MP

61-63	Caldwell Institute	Hall, House	1925-1926	Miss Elizabeth Caldwell
61-63	Caldwell Institute	Hall, House	1926-1965	Stonefield Parish Church
* 65	Shop in Caldwell Institute	Empty	1900-1915	James Caldwell, MP
* 65	Matthew Millers Shop Caldwell Institute	Shoe Repairs	1915-1925	James Caldwell, MP
* 65	Thomas McGurk, Shop, Caldwell Institute	Confectioner	1915-1925	James Caldwell, MP
* 67	Pasquela Lombardi, Caldwell Institute	Confectioner	1900-1911	James Caldwell, MP
	Springwell Farm House	Farm	1740's-1863	Herbertson family & others
	Springwell Farm House	Farm	1863-1876	Mrs Janet Jackson, of Spittal and later Old Place, Blantyre
69 - 95	Henderson's Buildings	36 houses, 8 shops, hall & public house	1877-1888	William Henderson, Builder
69 - 95	Henderson's Buildings	38 houses, 9 shops, hall & public house	1888- c1900	John Meek
69 - 95	Henderson's Buildings	36 houses, 12 shops, hall & public house	1900 - 1932	James Kelly, wine & spirit merchant
69 - 95	Henderson's Buildings (only 69-83 after 1940 fire)	Houses, shops & public house	1932-c1950's	Margaret Kelly and James Kelly Junior
69 - 83	Henderson's Buildings	Houses, shops & public house	1950's - 1979	Eddie McCrudden then Council
* 69 -73	William Harvey's Pub, (Henderson's Buildings)	Public House	1877-1888	William Henderson, Builder
* 69 -73	Horseshoe Bar (Henderson's Buildings)	Public House	1888 - 1932	John Meek then James Kelly
* 69 -73	Kelly's Bar / Kelly's Corner (Henderson's Buildings)	Public House	1932 - 1979	Margaret Kelly, James Kelly Jnr, Eddie McCrudden
*	Hall, Henderson's Building	Meeting Hall	1877 - c1905	William Henderson, John Meek then James Kelly
* 77	Empty shop (Henderson's Buildings)	Empty	1877-c1905	William Henderson, builder, then John Meek, James Kelly
* 77	McLuckie's Shop (Henderson's Buildings)	Unknown	c1905-1925	James Kelly, spirit merchant
* 77	McVey's Bookmakers (Henderson's Buildings)	Bookmakers	c1960s & 70s	Eddie McCrudden then Council
* 79	A. McWilliams Butchers (Henderson's Buildings)	Butcher shop	1877-1888	William Henderson, builder
* 79	William Young (Henderson's Buildings)	Unknown	1888-c1900	John Meek
* 79	Arbuckle's Sweet Shop (Henderson's Buildings)	Confectionery	c1900- c1910	James Kelly, spirit merchant
* 79	Elizabeth White's Shop (Henderson's Buildings)	Unknown	c1910-c1925	James Kelly, Spirit merchant
* 79	John Clarke Undertakers (Henderson's Buildings)	Undertakers	c1925-1940's	James Kelly, then J Kelly Junior
* 79	Archie McKays Shop (Henderson's Buildings)	Unknown	c1960's & 70s	Eddie McCrudden then Council
* 83	William Peters Shoe Shop (Henderson's Buildings)	Shoemaker	1877-c1900	William Henderson, builder
* 83	Love's Hairdressers Shop (Henderson's Buildings)	Hairdressers	c1900-c1910	James Kelly, spirit merchant

Address	Name	Type	Dates	Owner/Notes
* 83	McInally's Hairdressers (Henderson's Buildings)	Hairdressers	c1910-c1920	James Kelly, spirit merchant
* 83	Samuel Douglas's Shop (Henderson's Buildings)	Unknown	c1920-c1925	James Kelly, spirit merchant
* 83	Lawyers Office (Henderson's Buildings)	Lawyers	c1960's & 70s	Eddie McCrudden then Council
* 85	William Caldwell, tailor (Henderson's Buildings)	Tailor shop	1878-c1905	John Meek, then James Kelly
* 85	Mrs Kilgour's Shop (Henderson's Buildings)	Unknown	1905-c1910	James Kelly, spirit merchant
* 85	Walter Getty's Shop (Henderson's Buildings)	Saddler	c1910-c1918	James Kelly, spirit merchant
* 85	Joseph Barclay's Shop (Henderson's Buildings)	Unknown	c1918-c1925	James Kelly, spirit merchant
* 85	John Harrison's Sweet Shop (Henderson's Buildings)	Confectioner	c1925-c1940s	James Kelly then J Kelly Junior
* 87	Malcolm Reid's Shop (Henderson's Buildings)	Unknown	1878-c1905	John Meek then James Kelly
* 87	Stevens Sweet Shop (Henderson's Buildings)	Confectionery	c1905-c1915	James Kelly, spirit merchant
* 87	McSkimming's Shop (Henderson's Buildings)	Unknown	c1915-c1925	James Kelly, spirit merchant
* 87	Duncan Cochrane's Grocers (Henderson's Buildings)	Grocery Shop	c1925-c1940s	James Kelly, then J Kelly Junior
* 89	Thomas Lamond & Co (Henderson's Buildings)	Watchmakers	1878-c1905	John Meek then James Kelly
* 89	John Mathieson Jeweler (Henderson's Buildings)	Jewelry	c1905-c1915	James Kelly, spirit merchant
* 89	Ritchie's Sweet Shop (Henderson's Buildings)	Confectionery	c1915-1930	James Kelly, spirit merchant
* 91	Robert Docherty's shop (Henderson's Buildings)	Unknown	1878-c1905	John Meek then James Kelly
* 91	E.Kirkpatrick's Shop (Henderson's Buildings)	Unknown	c1905-c1910	James Kelly, Spirit merchant
* 91	Alexander Barrie's Shop (Henderson's Buildings)	Fitter	c1910-c1918	James Kelly, Spirit merchant
* 91	Joseph Dunn's Shop (Henderson's Buildings)	Unknown	c1918-c1930	James Kelly, Spirit merchant
* 95	Blantyre Co-operative Society (Henderson's Building)	Shop	1883-c1920	William Henderson, John Meek then James Kelly
* 95	Matthew Miller's Shop (Henderson's Buildings)	Shoemaker	c1920-c1930	James Kelly, spirit merchant
* 79-109	JR Reid Printers Ltd (previously further west)	Printers	1989-2009	JR Reid Printers Ltd
* 79-109	Gavin Watson Printers	Printers	2009-now	GT4 Group
97-101	Anderson's Buildings	2 houses & 2 shops	c1902-c1918	Thomas Anderson, Cycle agent
97-101	Anderson's Buildings	2 houses & 2 shops	c1918-1932	Matthew Anderson, pitheadman
97-101	Anderson's Buildings	2 houses & 2 shops	1932-c1975	James Botteril & Others
* 97	Ann Robertson's Grocery (Anderson's Buildings)	Shop	c1902-1905	Thomas Anderson, Cycle agent
* 97	Margaret Robertson's Pub (Anderson's Buildings)	Spirit Shop	c1905-c1920	Thomas Anderson, Cycle agent
* 97	John Marshall & Son Grocers (Anderson's buildings)	Grocers Shop	c1920-c1925	Matthew R Anderson

* 97 & 101	Hill Brothers Ltd Pawnbroker (Anderson's Buildings)	Pawn Shop	c1925-1927	Matthew R Anderson
* 97	James McTavish Butchers (Anderson's Buildings)	Butchers	c1930 - c1960's	Matthew Anderson & later James Botterill
* 97	Annie Botterils' Fishshop (Anderson's Buildings)	Fish Tearoom	c1960's-c1975	Botterill Family
* 101	Thomas Anderson Cycle Agent (Anderson's Buildings)	Bicycle shop	c1902-c1910	Thomas Anderson, Cycle Agent
* 101	John Marshalls Print Shop (Anderson's Buildings)	Printers	c1910-c1925	Thomas then Matthew Anderson
* 101	McElhone's Pawnbrokers (Anderson's Buildings)	Pawn Shop	1927-c1947	Matthew R Anderson & later James Botterill
* 101	Nancy Botterill's Shop (Anderson's Buildings)	Grocery	c1960's-c1975	Botterill Family
	Burleigh Mission Hall & Sunday School	Hall	1878-1973	Free Mission Church, EU Church, EUFC, Stonefield Par.
103	East Free Church (Burleigh Church)	Church	1892-1900	Free Mission Church
103	East United Free Church (Burleigh Church)	Church	1900-1929	Trustees of EU Church, Stonefield EU Free Church
103	Blantyre East Church of Scotland (Burleigh Church)	Church	1929-1945	Trustees of EU Church
103	Burleigh Church	Church	1945-1974	Trustees & Congregation of Stonefield Parish Church
105	Police Station	Police	1875-c1914	Commissioners of Police Supply then County Council
105	(Old) Police Station	Empty	c1914-1915	Blantyre Co-operative Society
107-125	Avon Buildings	4 houses & 4 shops (below)	1876-c1886	John Crow & James Davidson
107-125	Avon Buildings	9 houses & 7 shops (below)	c1886-1979	Blantyre Co-operative Society
*	Stonefield Medical Hall (Avon Buildings)	J&G Hogg Doctors	1876-c1880	John Crow & James Davidson
*	Walter Getty's Shop (Avon Buildings)	Saddler	1876-c1910	John Crow & James Davidson then Blantyre Co-op
*	Andrew Graham's Corner Shop (Avon Buildings)	Dairy	1876-c1885	John Crow & James Davidson
*	2 Central shops (Avon Buildings)	Co-op stores	c1886-1917	Blantyre Co-operative Society
* 105	Co-op Drapery Corner Shop	Drapery	1917-1972	Blantyre Co-operative Society
* 107	Store & Stables (rear of Avon Buildings) Later renumbered	Outbuildings, later garage	c1895-1972	Blantyre Co-operative Society
* 107	Co-op Fleshing Dept.	Butchers	1917-1972	Blantyre Co-operative Society
* 109	Coach house (rear of Avon Buildings) Later renumbered	Coach House later garage	c1905-1972	Blantyre Co-operative Society
* 109	Co-op Grocery Dept. Shop (Central Premises)	Grocery	1917-1972	Blantyre Co-operative Society
* 107 &	J.R Reid Printers (former	Printers	1976-1979	J.R Reid Printers Ltd

109	Co-op Central Premises)			
* 111	Co-op Tailors (non public at Central Premises)	Tailors Shop	1917-1972	Blantyre Co-operative Society
* 111	Glen Travel (Avon Buildings / Central Premises)	Travel Agents	1972-1979	Glen Travel c/o Davie Glen
* 113	Co-op Tailors Workshop (non public – Central Premises)	Tailors Workshop	1917-1972	Blantyre Co-operative Society
* 113	Lucky House Takeaway (Avon Buildings / Central Premises)	Chinese Takeaway	1972-1979	Lucky House
* 115	Co-op Dairy Dept. Shop (Avon Buildings / Central Premises)	Dairy	1917-1972	Blantyre Co-operative Society
* 115	Service Centre (Avon Buildings / Central Premises)	Vacuum Repairs	1972 - 1979	Blantyre Co-operative Society let to Jimmy Pollock
* 117	Co-op Fish Shop (Avon Buildings / Central Premises)	Fish Shop	1917-1972	Blantyre Co-operative Society
* 121	Hardware Dept. Shop (Avon Buildings/ Central Premises)	Hardware	1917-1972	Blantyre Co-operative Society
* 123	Co-op Boot Dept. Shop (Avon Buildings / Central Premises)	Shoe Shop	1917-1972	Blantyre Co-operative Society
* 123	Joseph Goffney's Shop (Avon Buildings / Central Premises)	Fleet Centre	c1972-c1979	Joseph Goffney, tradesman
* 125	Co-op Corner Fruit Shop (Avon Buildings / Central Premises)	Fruit Shop	1917-1972	Blantyre Co-operative Society
* 125	Electrical Corner Shop at Jackson St (Central Premises)	Electrical	c1960's-1972	Blantyre Co-operative Society
* 105-125	Co-Op Central Premises (including Avon Buildings)	Co-Op Shops, Offices & Hall	1917-1979	Blantyre Co-operative Society, possible council after 1972
127 - 137	Sprott's Buildings	2 shops & 3 houses	1879 - 1890	George Sprott, shoemaker
127 - 137	Sprott's Buildings	5 shops & 4 houses	1890-1900	William Sprott
127 - 137	Imrie's Buildings (formerly Sprott's Buildings)	5 shops & 4 houses	1900-1930	William Imrie & Son, then after 1922 Mary Ann Imrie (nee Smith)
127 - 137	Kidd's Building (formerly Imries / Sprotts Building)	5 shops & 4 houses	1930 -1979	Hughie Kidd then after 1964 others
* 127	Robert Sprott's Shoeshop (Sprott's Buildings)	Shoemakers	1879-1900	George Sprott, shoemaker then Sprott & Company Shoemakers
* 127	Co-op Bread Shop (Sprott's Building/ Imrie's Buildings)	Bread	1900-c1915	William Imrie & Son
* 127	Samuel Gilmour's Dairy Shop (Imrie's Buildings, formerly Sprotts)	Corner Dairy	c1915-1936	William Imrie & Son then from 1922 Mary Ann Imrie (nee Smith)
* 127	William Weir's Office (Imrie's/ Kidd's Building)	Commission Agent /Bookie	1936-c1964	Hugh Kidd
* 127 & 129	Mecca Bookmakers (Kidd's Building)	Bookmakers	c1964 - 1978	Mecca Bookmakers

* 129	Alexander Christies Shop (Sprotts Building)	Clothier	1890-c1910	William Sprott then from 1900 William Imrie & Son
* 129	George Valerios Shop (Imrie's Buildings)	Confectionery	c1910-c1915	William Imrie & Son
* 129	John Clark's Shop (Imrie's Buildings)	Unknown	c1915-c1922	William Imrie & Son
* 131	Neilson's Dressmakers Shop (Sprott's Buildings)	Dressmakers	1890-1900	William Sprott
* 131	Jemima Walkers Dressmakers (Imrie's Buildings)	Dressmakers	1900-c1915	William Imrie & Son
* 131	Co-op Bread Shop (Imrie's Buildings)	Bread	c1915-c1918	William Imrie & Son
* 131	James Smith's Restaurant (Imrie's Buildings)	Restaurant	c1918-1922	William Imrie & Son
* 129 & 131	Hugh Kidd's Restaurant (Kidd's Buildings)	Restaurant	1922-1930	Mary Ann Imrie (w)-nee Smith
* 131	Kidd's Fish & Chip Shop (Kidd's Buildings)	Fish & Chips Shop	1930 -c1964	Hugh Kidd
* 131	White Elephant Shop (Kidd's Building)	Second Hand Shop	c1964-1979	Unknown
* 133	George Sprott's (Jnr) Grocery (Sprotts Buildings)	Grocery Shop	1890-1900	William Sportt
* 133	John Machie's Shop (Imrie's Buildings)	Confectionery	1900-c1910	William Imrie & Son
* 133	Isa Botteril's Bootshop (Imrie's Buildings)	Bootmakers	c1910-c1940's	William Imrie & Son then from 1930 Hugh Kidd
* 135 & 137	Sprott's Public House (Sprotts Buildings)	Spirit Shop	1880-1900	George Sprott Proprietor, then William Sportt occupied by son Robert Sprott
* 135 * 137	Smiddy Inn (Imrie's Buildings, formerly Sprotts)	Public House	1900-1922	William Imrie & Son
* 135 &137	Smiddy Inn (Imrie's Buildings)	Public House	1922-1930	Mary Ann Imrie (w, nee Smith)
* 135 & 137	The Smiddy Inn (Kidd's Buildings)	Public House	1930-c1950's	Hugh Kidd managed by N Wilson
* 133, 135 & 137	The Smiddy Bar (Kidd's Buildings)	Public House	c1950's-c1979	Vincey McGuire & others
	Merry's Rows	89 tied terraced miners homes	1876-1937	Merry & Cunningham (Coalmasters)
	Former Masonic Hall	Modern Homes	1980-1988	Masonic Lodge until 1988 then private homes
	Cobbler's Bar	Public House	1988-1992	Unknown Owners
	Elm Court Flats	Residential Flats	1993-now	Unknown Owners
139	Stonefield Parish Church	Church	1880-1979	Church of Scotland
	St Andrews Church	Church	1982-now	Church of Scotland
* 141	Abbeygreen Hall & Consulting Rooms	Hall & Rooms	1892-1979	Rev John Burleigh until 1922, then Janet Burleigh until 1937 then others, possibly Masonic.
* 141	Hunter's Laundry Shop (Abbeygreen Rooms)	Laundry	c1905-c1915	Rev John Burleigh
* 141	Dr James Naismith Surgery (Abbeygreen Rooms)	Doctors	c1915-c1920	Rev John Burleigh
* 141	William Greenlie Chemists (Abbeygreen Rooms)	Chemist	C1920-1923	Rev John Burleigh then from 1922 his widow, Janet Burleigh

* 141	Dr David K Fisher's Surgery (Abbeygreen Rooms)	Doctors	1923-1930	Janet Burleigh (w)
* 141	Millinery Shop (Abbeygreen Rooms)	Women's Clothes	1930 –c1950s	Janet Burleigh (w) then unknown
* 141	Dr. Hutchison's Practice (Abbeygreen Rooms)	Doctors	c1950's-c1960's	Unknown, possibly Masonic Lodge.
141	2 homes, 1 upper 1 lower (Abbeygreen Rooms)	Houses	c1960's - 1979	Unknown, possibly Masonic Lodge or Council.
* 143	James Miller's Shoe shop (Masonic Buildings)	Shoes	1905-c1914	Livingstone Masonic Lodge 599
* 143	William Baxter & Son's Shop (Masonic Buildings)	Fruit & Veg	c1914-c1918	Livingstone Masonic Lodge 599
* 143	John Bowie's Fruit Shop (Masonic Buildings)	Fruit & Veg	c1918-c1927	Livingstone Masonic Lodge 599
* 143	Marion Young's Fruit Shop (Masonic Buildings)	Fruits, Confectionery & flowers	c1927-c1940	Livingstone Masonic Lodge 599
* 143	Bowie's Fruit & Veg & Florist (Masonic Buildings)	Fruit, Veg, Florist	c1940-c1970	Livingstone Masonic Lodge 599
* 143	Tandem Shoe Shop (Masonic Buildings)	Shoe Shop	c1970-1978	Livingstone Masonic Lodge 599
*145	Masonic Hall & Rooms (Masonic Buildings)	Hall	1905 - 1978	Livingstone Masonic Lodge 599
* 147	James Greenhorn Butchers (Masonic Buildings)	Butchers	1905-c1910	Livingstone Masonic Lodge 599
* 147	Gilbert Harper Butchers (Masonic Buildings)	Butchers	c1910-1922	Livingstone Masonic Lodge 599
* 147	Archibald Whittle Butchers (Masonic Buildings)	Butchers	1922-c1937	Livingstone Masonic Lodge 599
* 147 - 149	Aitkenhead Butchers (Masonic Buildings)	Butchers	c1937-c1958	Livingstone Masonic Lodge 599
* 147 - 149	Davidson's Butchers (Masonic Buildings)	Butchers	c1958-c1978	Livingstone Masonic Lodge 599
* 149	Gorden G Grieg Printers (Masonic Buildings)	Printers & Stationers	1905-c1910	Livingstone Masonic Lodge 599
* 149	Hugh Graham Printers (Masonic Buildings)	Printers & Stationers	c1910-c1927	Livingstone Masonic Lodge 599
* 149	Archibald Whittle Butchers (Masonic Buildings)	Butchers Machinery	c1927-c1937	Livingstone Masonic Lodge 599
* 151	James Houston's Grocery (later Masonic Buildings)	Grocers	1905-c1914	John Roberts, Wine Merchant
* 151	Commercial Bank (later Masonic Buildings)	Bank Office	c1914-c1922	John Roberts, Wine Merchant
* 151	Commercial Bank (Masonic Buildings)	Bank	c1922-c1950's	Livingstone Masonic Lodge 599
* 151	Scottish Clydesdale Bank (Masonic Buildings)	Bank	c1950's-1978	Livingstone Masonic Lodge 599
153	2 upper flats (later Masonic Buildings)	2 homes	1905-c1922	John Roberts, Wine merchant
153	2 upper flats (Masonic Buildings)	2 homes	c1922-1978	Livingstone Masonic Lodge 599
* 155	Empty Shop (later Masonic Buildings)	Empty	1905-c1906	John Roberts, Wine Merchant
* 155	James Mathieson Jewelers (later Masonic Buildings)	Jewelers	c1906-c1922	John Roberts, Wine Merchant
* 155	James Mathieson Jewelers (Masonic Buildings)	Jewelers Shop	c1922-c1927	Livingstone Masonic Lodge 599
* 155	Matthew Lennox Jewelers	Watchmakers	c1927-c1945	Livingstone Masonic

	(Masonic Buildings)			Lodge 599
* 155	Unknown Jewelers (Masonic Buildings)	Jewelers Shop	c1945-1978	Livingstone Masonic Lodge 599
* 157	Priory Bar & Cellars (Bar run by William Roberts)	Public House	c1889-c1904	James McHutchison, merchant then from 1891, his trustees
* 157	Priory Bar & Cellars (Bar run by John Roberts)	Public House	c1904-1932	John Roberts, Wine Merchant
* 157	Priory Bar, Cellars & Rooms	Public House	1932-1935	William Black, Spirit Merchant for Helen Roberts (w)
* 157	Priory Bar, Cellars & Rooms (Run by various people including Tallis, McInally & Meechan)	Public House	1935-1978	John Murray of Rutherglen then various Brewers including Scottish Newcastle.
*	Winks Inn	Public Inn	c1800-c1850	W Forest
	Winks Cottage	Cotters House	c1850-c1870's	Forrest Family
159 - 187	Turners Buildings	28 homes & 3 shops	c1877-c1885	George Turner, Architect
159 - 187	Turner's Buildings	28 houses & 3 shops	c1885-c1887	Keith Patrick Solicitors as Creditors of liquidated George Turner
159 - 187	Turner's Buildings (Central Buildings)	44 houses & 5 shops	c1885-1895	William Buchanan, spirit merchant, Motherwell
159 - 187	Turner's Buildings (Central Buildings)	44 houses & 5 shops	1895-c1915	Trustees of William Buchanan
159 - 187	Turner's Buildings (Central Buildings)	44 houses & 4 shops	c1915-1921	Mrs Marion Clifton Buchanan, (widow), Motherwell
159 - 187	Turner's Buildings (Central Buildings)	44 houses & 4 shops	1921-1925	Miss Marion Chapman Buchanan (daughter of William)
159 - 187	Turner's Buildings (Central Buildings) 159-165 demolished in 1940	44 houses & 6 shops	1925-1940	James Little, joiner Stonefield Rd then from early 1930's Jane Little (s) of Crossbasket.
* 165	Post Office Building (corner of Logan Street), Clydeview	Post Office	1954- 1997	General Post Office then Royal Mail.
167 - 187	Turner's Buildings (Central Buildings) remaining	20 houses & 3 shops	1940-1978	Jane Little and related Unknown others
* 159	Alexander McGill's Ironmongery Corner shop (Turners Buildings(	Ironmongery	1877-c1885	George Turner
* 159	Richard Livingstone's Spirit Shop (west corner Logan St at Turners Buildings)	Spirit sales	c1885-c1895	Creditors of George Turner & later William Buchanan
* 159	Torrance Grocery Corner Shop (Turner's Buildings)	Grocery	c1895-1903	William Buchanan then from 1895 later his trustees
* 159	Hugh Whyte's Shop (Turner's / Central Buildings)	Unknown	1903-c1910	Trustees of William Buchanan
* 159	James Bryce Ironmongery (Turner's / Central Buildings)	Ironmongery	c1910-1918	Mrs Marion Clifton Buchanan (w)
* 159	Samuel Brown's Ironmongers run by Samuel Brown (Turner's / Central Buildings)	Ironmongery Store	1918-1921	Mrs. Marion Clifton Buchanan (w)
* 159	Brown's Ironmongery Store (run by Elsa Meek, Turner's	Ironmongery	1921-1923	Miss Marion Chapman Buchanan

	Buildings) Liquidated 1923.			
* 159	James McGeachie Ironmongery (Turner's / Central Buildings	Ironmongery	1923-1925	Miss Marion Chapman Buchanan
* 159	William Henderson Ironmongery Shop (Turner's Buildings. Demolished 1940)	Ironmongery	1925-1940	James Little, Stonefield Rd joiner then from early 1930's Jane Little
* 161	James Hill Tailors Shop (Turner's Buildings)	Tailors & Clothiers	1877-c1885	George Turner
* 161	Marion Potter's Tailors Shop (Turner's Buildings)	Tailors	c1885-1892	Creditors of George Turner & later William Buchanan
* 161	James Gibson, Musicians Shop (Turner's Buildings)	Musician's (Pianoforte)	1892-1900	William Buchanan then from 1895 later his trustees
* 161	Marion Rae's Dairy Shop (Turner's / Central Buildings)	Dairy Shop	1900-c1910	Trustees of William Buchanan
* 161	Samuel Park's Dairy Shop (Turner's / Central Buildings)	Dairy Shop	c1910-1921	Mrs Marion Clifton Buchanan (w)
* 161	Charles & Marion McCabe 's shop (Turner's Building. Demolished 1940)	Unknown	1921-c1940	Miss Marion Chapman Buchanan then from 1925, James Little.
* 163	Empty or unknown Shop (Turner's Buildings)	Unknown	1877- c1885	George Turner
* 163	JG Birken & Co Shop (Turner's Buildings)	Lace Curtains	c1885-c1892	Creditors of George Turner & later William Buchanan
* 163	William Baxter & Son Fruit shop (Turner's Buildings)	Fruit shop	c1892-c1900	William Buchanan then from 1895, later his trustees
* 163	Marion Greenhorn's Butchers (Turner's / Central Buildings)	Butchers shop	c1900-c1910	Trustees of William Buchanan
* 163	James Powell Butchers Shop (Turner's / Central Buildings. Demolished 1940)	Butchers shop	c1910-c1940	Mrs Marion Clifton Buchanan (w) then from 1921 Miss Marion Chapman Buchanan then from 1925, James Little then from early 1930s, Jane Little.
* 167	William Baxter & Son Fruit Shop (Turner's Buildings)	Fruit shop	c1900-1914	Trustees of William Buchanan
* 167	James Maxwell & Son Sweet shop (Turner's Buildings/ Central Buildings)	Chocolate Manufacturer	1914-1925	Mrs Marion Clifton Buchanan (w) then from 1921 Miss Marion Chapman Buchanan
* 167	Mrs Little's Tailors Shop (Turner's Buildings)	Tailors shop	1925-c1940's	James Little then from early 1930's, Jane Little (s)
* 167	Scobie's Sweet Shop (Turner's Buildings)	Sweet shop	c1940's-c1960's	Unknown
* 167	Co-op Chemist Shop (Turner's Buildings)	Chemists	c1960's-1977	Unknown
* 169	John Bryson Drapery Shop (Turner's / Central Buildings)	Drapers shop	c1900-c1910	Trustees of William Buchanan
* 169	John Davidson Drapers Shop (Turner's / Central Buildings)	Drapers shop	1921-c1950's	Miss Marion Chapman Buchanan then from 1925 James Little, then from

				early 1930's Jane Little.
* 169	Janette Robertson Ladies Hairstylist Shop (Turner's Buildings)	Hairdressers	c1950's-1970s	Unknown
* 167 - 169	Charles Easton Drapers Shop (Turner's / Central Buildings)	Drapers shop	c1910-c1918	Mrs Marion Clifton Buchanan (w)
* 167 - 169	John Davidson Drapers Shop (Turner's Buildings)	Drapers shop	c1918-1921	Mrs Marion Clifton Buchanan (w)
* 183	William McManus, merchant shop (gutted by fire upon opening) Turner's Buildings	General Merchants shop	1925-1926	James Little
* 185	Dr. Adam Stewarts Surgery & Other doctors consulting room (Turner's Building)	Doctor's Surgery	1925-c1950's	James Little, then from early 1930's, Jane Little.
* 185	Dr. Gordon's Surgery & Other doctors Consulting rooms (Turner's Buildings)	Doctor's Surgery	c1950's-1970s	Unknown
*	Clydeview Shopping Centre – East with 53 businesses as listed in this book	Shopping centre	1980-present (2017)	ASDA
*	McVaneys Land	Small House, Shop & Byre	1892-1896	William McVaney, Dairyman
*	McVaney's Land (all demolished by 1915)	Small House, Shop & Byre	1896-1915	Agnes McVaney (w)
*	Marion Russell's Dressmakers shop (McVaneys Land)	Dressmakers	1892-c1900	William McVaney then from 1896, Agnes McVaney (w)
* 189-191	Repair Workshop & Petrol Pump	Workshop	c1921-c1927	Thomas Johnstone, motor hirer
* 189-191	Central Garage	Garage, Petrol Pump & Tank	c1927-1934	Blue Line Motor Spirit Co Ltd
* 189-191	Harper's Garage (formerly Central Garage)	Garage, Petrol Pump & Tank	1934 – 1960's	Barbara Harper, managed in 1934-1940 by James Ramage.
* 189-191	Central Garage (formerly Harper's)	Garage, Petrol Pumps & Tanks	1960's - 1979	Brian McLaughlin, Willie & Peggy Richardson, Isa MacMillan & Others
193-201	Nimmo's Buildings	6 houses & 2 shops	1874-1885	John Nimmo, grocer
193-201	Nimmo's Buildings	4 houses & 3 shops	1885-c1899	Hamilton Savings Investment Building Society (Bondholders)
193-201	Nimmo's Buildings (temp. Whifflet Place)	6 houses, restaurant & 2 shops	c1899-c1905	David Kerr, restaurateur
193-201	Nimmo's Buildings	5 houses, rooms & restaurant/pub	c1905-c1922	Hugh Mair, spirit merchant then from 1920, his widow Mrs Mair
193 201	Nimmo's Buildings (Hills Pawn Building)	7 houses & shop	c1922-late 1930's	Hill Brothers (Pawnbrokers) Ltd
193-201	Nimmo's Buildings	5 houses & pub	Late 1930's-c1950's	Others (Unknown)
193-201	Nimmo's Buildings	4 houses & 2 shops	c1950's-1979	Others (Unknown)
* 193/195	John Nimmo Grocers Shop (Nimmo's Buildings)	Grocers	1874-1885	John Nimmo, grocer (former miner)
* 193/195	Zachariah Nimmo Grocers Shop (Nimmo's Buildings)	Grocers	1885-c1899	Hamilton Savings Investment Building

				Society (Bondholders)
* 193/195	Restaurant with bar license (The Ale House – Nimmo's Buildings)	Public House	c1899-c1905	David Kerr, restaurateur
* 193/195	Restaurant with bar license (The Ale House – Nimmo's Buildings)	Public House	c1905-c1922	Hugh Mair, spirit merchant then from 1920, his widow Mrs Mair
* 193/195	Hills Pawnbrokers Shop (Nimmo's Buildings)	Pawn shop	c1922-late 1930s	Hill Brothers (Pawnbrokers) Ltd
* 193/195	The Ale House Pub (Nimmo's Buildings)	Public House	Late 1930s-c1950's	Others (Unknown)
* 193/195	Whyte's Plumbers Shop (Nimmo's Buildings)	Plumbers Merchants	c1950's-c1968	Unknown (Others)
* 193/195	Oreste's Chip Shop (Nimmo's Buildings)	Chip Shop	c1968 1979	Unknown (Others)
* 197	Robert Watson's Bakery (Nimmo's Buildings)	Bakery	1874-c1885	John Nimmo, grocer (former miner)
* 197	William Morrison Stationers (Nimmo's Buildings)	Stationery	c1885-1899	Hamilton Savings Investment Building Society (Bondholders)
* 197	William Wright Shoemakers Shop (Nimmo's Buildings)	Shoe Shop	c1899-c1905	David Kerr, restaurateur
* 197	Rooms (Nimmo's Buildings) House after 1920.	Rooms	c1905-c1920	Hugh Mair, spirit merchant
* 199	James Bryce Ironmongery Shop (Nimmo's Buildings)	Ironmongers	c1885-c1899	Hamilton Savings Investment Building Society (Bondholders)
* 199	Robert Sherkis Ironmongery Shop (Nimmo's Buildings). After 1905 was a house until the 1950's.	Ironmongers	c1899-c1905	David Kerr, restaurateur
* 199	Haddow's Dentist (Nimmo's Buildings) later moved to north side of Glasgow Road	Dentist Surgery	1950's-1960's	Unknown (Others)
* 199	Alex Watt's Dentist Surgery (Nimmo's Buildings)	Dentist Surgery	1960's - 1978	Unknown (Others)
203	Bloomfield Cottage	Detached House	1874-late 1880's	Hugh Dickson, enginekeeper
203	Bloomfield Cottage	Detached House	Late 1880's – early 1920's	John Watt, Shoemaker
203	Bloomfield Cottage	Detached House	Early 1920's – early 1930's	Peter Morton, miner
203	Bloomfield Cottage	Detached House	Early 1930's-late 1960's	William and Arabella B Stewart then Unknown Others
205	Stonefield Parish School	Public Junior School	1875-1957	Blantyre Parochial Board, Blantyre Parish Council, the County Council of Lanark
* 205	Blantyre employment & Labour Exchange	Labour Exchange	1957-1977	County Council
*	Clydeview Shopping Centre – west with 36 businesses as listed in this book	Shopping Centre	1980-2017 (present)	ASDA
*	Blantyre Library (Clydeview Shopping Centre)	Public Library	1999-2017 (present)	South Lanarkshire Council via lease from ASDA.
207 - 223	Annfield Terrace	25 Homes & 1 corner shop	1903-late 1920's	William Nelson, Horse dealer

207 - 223	Annfield Terrace	25 Houses & 1 corner shop	Late 1920's to early 1930s	Margaret Nelson, widow	
207 - 223	Annfield Terrace	25 houses & 1 corner shop	Early 1930's-1970	James Todd, Oil Merchant then Others (Unknown)	
* 207	Martha Rankine's Grocery Shop (Annfield Terrace)	Corner Licensed Grocery Shop	1903-late 1910's	William Nelson, Horse dealer	
* 207	Thomas Rankin's Grocery Shop (Annfield Terrace)	Corner Licensed Grocery Shop	Late 1910's-early 1930's	William Nelson, then his widow Margaret Nelson	
* 207	Gibson's Grocery & Sweet Shop (Annfield Terrace)	Grocery then Sweet Shop	Early 1930's - c1970	James Todd, Oil merchant than Unknown (Others)	
*	Blantyre Market	50 Stalls	1972-1979	Spook Erections on behalf of County Council	
223a – 223c	Council Homes	24 homes on 2 storeys	1936-now	County Council, Strathclyde Regional Council then South Lanarkshire Council	
	The Toll Brae	Part of Glasgow Road	1840's-now	Public Highway, Glasgow to Hamilton Road now A724	
	Wooden Building & Field	Stable & Paddock	1800's-c1880's	John Coats, spirit merchant	
*	Wooden office & Yard	Blantyre Miners Association	c1880's-c1900	Trustees of John Coats rented by William Rinn, Hall St.	
*	Wooden office & Yard	Cattle Storage	c1900-c1910	Trustees of John Coats rented by Archibald Borland, cattle dealer	
*	Wooden office, shed & yard	Slater's premises	c1910-c1920	Trustees of John Coats rented by William Jamieson, slater of 38 George Street, Hamilton	
	Ground (then after 1936, homes on Priory Street)	Vacant field	c1920-1936	Alexander P Smith of Hamilton then Country Council	
225	Coats Tenements (at what would become Priory St. Coat's Buildings)	8 homes	c1832-1890	Unknown originators then from 1862, John Coats farmer, Thomas Coats his son and from 1877, John Coats spirit merchant	
225	Coat's Tenements	8 homes	1890-c1914	Trustees of John Coats	
225	Coat's Tenements (top storey removed in 1930's)	8 homes then 2	c1914-c1960's	Jessie Rae then Fred Rae	
*	Coat's Tenements (single storey store now Priory Street)	Storage for pub	c1960's-2017	Multiple owners including McGuiness, Maxwells, Queen and Punch Taverns.	
*	Nicola's Salon (Coat's Tenements – now Priory St)	Hair & Beauty Salon	2017 - present	Unknown	
225	Stonefield Tavern Cellar (Coat's Buildings)	Pub Cellar	c1890-present	John Coat's Trustees, Jessie Rae from WW1, George Younger & Sons Ltd from 1932, Fred Rae after WW2, then multiple others including McGuiness, Maxwells, Queen and Punch Tavern.	
* 227-229	Changing House (Coats Buildings)	Inn or resting place	c1816-c1877	Unknown originator then from 1862 John Coats, Spirit Merchant	
* 227-229	Stonefield Tavern (Coat's	Public House	c1877-1890	John Coats Spirit merchant	

		Buildings)			
* 227-229		Stonefield Tavern (Coat's Buildings)	Public House	1890-c1914	Trustees of John Coats
* 227-229		Stonefield Tavern (Coat's Buildings)	Public House	c1914-c1960's	Jessie Rae, spirit merchant, then Fred Rae.
* 227-229		Stonefield Tavern (Coat's Buildings)	Public House	c1960's-present	Multiple owners including McGuiness, Maxwells, Queen and Punch Taverns.
		Coats' Whitewashed House (Coat's Buildings)	2 storey House	c1832-1890	Unknown originator then from 1862 John Coats, spirit merchant
		Coats' Whitewashed House (Coat's Buildings)	2 storey House	1890-late 1920's	Trustees of John Coats then from prior to WW1, Jessie Rae
*		MC Young's Grocers small shop (Coat's Buildings)	Grocers Shop	1862-c1870's	John Coats, spirit merchant
*		Bake-house (Coat's Buildings) then was partially demolished and became a ruin	Co-op Bakery	1883-c1905	John Coats, then from 1890 his trustees. Jessie Rae owned ruin.
*		Wooden Cattle Shed (rented by Archibald Boreland)	Cattle Shed	c1900-c1920	Mrs Jessie Rae, spirit merchant rented land for Boreland to build shed.
* 227		Co-op Emporium	General goods, Clothing/furniture & music store	1954-1980	Blantyre Co-operative Society, then after 1972, the rebranded Co-op.
* 227		Clydesdale Bank	Bank	1981-2016	Clydesdale Bank
* 227		Glen Travel	Travel Agents	2016 - now	Glen Travel
233-237		Stonefield Independent Co-op expansion 3 storeys	Co-Op shops & homes	1907-1932	Stonefield Independent Co-Op
233-237		Blantyre Co-Operative Society (3 storeys)	Co-Op shops & homes	1932-1972	Blantyre Co-Operative Society
233-237		Private Homes and shops (3 storeys)	Homes and shops	1972 - now	Co-op and others (unknown)
* 233		Co-Op Bread Shop & Drapery (3 storey Co-op Building)	Bread shop & Drapery	1907-1960's	Stonefield Independent Co-Op then from 1932 Blantyre Co-Op Society.
* 233		Co-Op Funeral Parlour (3 storey Co-Op Building)	Funeral Parlour	1960's-now	Blantyre Co-Op Society then Co-Op
* 235		J Estees Furniture Shop (3 storey Co-Op building)	Furniture Shop	Late 1970's - 1987	Jim & Margaret Taylor renting from Unknown landlords.
* 235		Video Vision (3 storey Co-Op Building)	Video Shop	1987 – 1990	Video Vision renting from Unknown landlords
* 235		Clyde Star (3 storey Co-Op Building)	Video Shop & Grocers, Stationers	1990-1994	Clyde Star renting from Unknown landlords
* 233-235		Londis Supermarket (3 storey Co-Op building)	Supermarket * Post Office	1994-now	Londis renting from Unknown landlords
* 237		Old Mill Barbers (3 storey Co-Op building)	Barber shop	1990's- c Millennium	Old Mill Barbers renting from Unknown landlords
* 237		Agnew's Café & Sandwich shop (3 storey Co-Op building)	Small Café	c Millennium to now	Agnews Café, renting from Unknown landlords
239-243		Stonefield Independent Co-Op (2 storey Building)	Co-Op shops & Homes	1891-1932	Stonefield Independent Co-Op
239-243		Blantyre Co-Operative Society (2 storey Building)	Co-Op shops & homes	1932-1972	Blantyre Co-Operative Society
239-243		Private Homes and Shops (2	Homes and shops	1972-now	Co-op and others

By Paul D Veverka

	storeys)			(unknown)
* 241	Co-Op Drapery & Boot Shop (2 storey Co-Op Buildings)	Drapery & Boot shop	1891-c1914	Stonefield Independent Co-Op
* 241	Co-Op Butchers Shop (2 storey Co-Op Buildings)	Butchers	c1914 – c Millennium	Stonefield Independent Co-Op
* 241	Peters Family Butchers Shop (2 storey Co-op buildings)	Butchers	c Millennium - now	Peters Family renting from unknown landlords.
*243	Co-Op Hardware & Grocery (2 storey Co-Op Buildings)	Hardware & Grocery shop	1891 – c1960's	Stonefield Independent Co-Op Blantyre Co-Op then others
*243	MacKintosh Carpets & Furniture Shop (2 storey Co-Op Buildings)	Carpets & Furniture	c Millennium - 2010	MacKintosh Carpets & Furniture renting from unknown landlords
* 243	St Andrew's Hospice (2 storey Co-Op Buildings)	Charity Shop	2010 - now	St Andrew's Hospice renting from Unknown landlords
245-251	Cameron's Buildings (3 storeys) later to become Clydeview	6 homes and 3 shops	1880-1884	Duncan Cameron, flesher and spirit merchant of Blantyre
245-251	Clydeview formerly Cameron's Buildings (3 storeys)	6 homes and 3 shops	1884-1898	Patrick Masterton, spirit merchant of Glasgow
245-251	Clydeview (3 storeys reduced to 1 storey in 1980's)	6 homes & 3 shops	1898-now	Thomas H Bennett & Co Ltd until 1935, then Alexander Thomson merchant of Perth, then unknown others.
*247	Independent Co-op Shop (Cameron's Buildings, later Clydeview)	Co-op shop	1884 & 1885	Duncan Cameron then after 1884, Patrick Masterton
* 247	Thomas Henderson Plumbers Shop (Clydeview 2 storey)	Small Plumbers shop	c1885-c1914	Patrick Masterton until 1898 then Thomas H Bennett & Co Ltd
* 247	Joseph Britton Painters Shop (Clydeview 2 storey)	Painters shop	c1914-early 1920's	Liquidators of Thomas H Bennett & Co Lrd
* 247	M Campbell Co Shop (Clydeview 2 storey)	Unknown shop	Early 1920's – late 1920's	Liquidators of Thomas H Bennett & Co Lrd
* 247	Umbeto Shivone's Ice Cream Shop (Cludeview 2 storey)	Ice cream shop	Late 1920's - 1935	Liquidators of Thomas H Bennett & Co Lrd
* 247	Charles Gray's Fish shop (Clydeview 2 storey)	Fish & Chip Shop	1935 – 1940's	Alexander Thomson, merchant of Perth
* 247	Ariel & Art Cabs (Clydeview 2 storey) then moved to Industrial Estate	Taxi company	Mid 1970's – early 1980's	Unknown landlords
* 249	Cameron's Spirit Shop (Cameron's Buildings)	Public House	1880-1884	Duncan Cameron, flesher & spirit merchant of Blantyre
* 249	Masterton's Public House (Clydeview 3 storey)	Public House	1884-1898	Patrick Masterton, Spirit merchant
* 249	Piscina Guiseppe's Ice Cream Parlour (Clydeview 3 storeys)	Ice Cream Parlour	1898-c1914	Thomas H Bennett & Co Ltd, spirit merchants of Glasgow
* 251	Joseph Lister Barbers	Barber shop	c1884-c1895	Patrick Masterton, spirit merchant
* 251	Henry Montague Shoemakers Shop (Clydeview 3 storey)	Shoe shop	c1895-1898	Patrick Masterton, spirit merchant

* 249-251	Blantyre Social Club (Clydeview 3 Storey)	Social Club	c1914-late 1920's	Liquidators of Thomas H Bennett & Co Lrd
* 249-251	Blantyre Post Office (Clydeview – 3 storey)	Post Office	Late 1920's - 1954	Liquidators of Thomas H Bennett & Co Lrd until 1935, then Alexander Thomson merchant of Perth
* 249-251	Ashley F Mack Joiners Shop	Joinery Shop	1954 – c1960's	Unknown Landlords
* 249-251	Robert Whyte Plumbers & Electricians Shop (Clydeview 3 storey)	Plumbers & Electricians	1954-c1960's	Unknown Landlords
* 249-251	Knights of St Columba (Clydeview 3 storey)	Social Club	c1960's -1975	Unknown Landlords
* 249-251	McNally's Chip Shop then Maggie Bell's Chipshop (Clydeview 3 storey)	Chip Shop	Late 1960's - 1973	Unknown Landlords
*249-251	Copper Kettle Café (Clydeview 3 storey)	Cafe	Late 1960's - 1973	Unknown Landlords
* 249-251	Shat In Chinese Takeaway (Clydeview 3 storey)	Chinese Takeaway	1973-1976	Unknown landlords
* 249-251	Sun House Chinese Takeaway (Clydeview 1 storey)	Peking, Cantonese & Thai, Chinese Takeaway and offsales	1976 - now	Mrs Lee
253-257	Gray's Buildings (2 storey)	Upper homes and lower shops	c1869-1879	Robert Gray, grocer
253-257	Gray's Buildings (2 storey)	Upper homes and lower shops	1879-1901	Mary Gray (Blantyre) widow of Robert Gray, grocer
253-257	Gray's Buildings (2 storey)	Upper homes and lower shops	1901-1928	John Gray (d1928), master grocer, son of Robert Gray
253-257	Gray's Buildings (2 storey)	Upper homes and lower halls	1928 – c1938	Blantyre Social Club & Institute Ltd then from 1935 Thomas Melville of Edinburgh
253-257	Gray's Buildings (YMCA then modern shops)	Upper homes and lower YMCA	c1938-present	Thomas Melville of Edinburgh then YMCA and Unknown others
* 253	Grays Drapers Shop (Grays Buildings)	Drapery shop	c1869-1879	Robert Gray, grocer
* 255	Grays Butchers Shop (Grays Buildings)	Butchers Shop	c1869-1879	Robert Gray, grocer
* 257	Grays Licensed Grocers (Grays Buildings)	Licensed Grocers Shop	1879-1928	Mary Gray until 1901 then John Gray, son of Mary.
*	Granary, Stable, Hayloft and Slaughterhouse (rear of Grays Buildings)	Granary, Stable, Hayloft and Slaughterhouse	c1869-1928	Robert Gray until 1879, then Mary Gray until 1901, then John Gray, their son.
* 255-257	Blantyre Social Club & Institute Ltd (Grays Buildings)	Social Club	1928-c1938	Blantyre Social Club then from 1935 Thomas Melville
*255-257	Blantyre YMCA (Grays Buildings) – used by Home Guard in WW2 years as HQ	YMCA Club	c1938-2013	Thomas Melville, YMCA and unknown others after 1990's.
* 255-257	The Roxy Youth Disco (in Blantyre YMCA Buildings)	Youth DIsco	1972 – late 1970's	YMCA
* 253	Spice of Life Indian Takeaway (Grays Buildings)	Indian Takeaway	2013 - present	Spice of Life renting from Unknown landlord
* 253	William Hill Bookmakers (Grays Buildings)	Bookmakers	2013 - present	William Hill renting from Unknown landlord

*	McSeveny's Coachworks (Grays Buildings rear yard)	Coachworks	Late 1950's and 1960's	William McSeveney renting from Blantyre YMCA
*	G Valets (Grays Buildings rear yard)	Vehicle Valet works	2009-2010	G Valets renting from Unknown landlords
*	Stoddarts Accident Repairs (Grays Buildings)	Accident repair shop	2010-present	Stoddarts renting from Unknown landlords
259	Broomknowe Cottage (formerly Milne Cottage)	Detached house	1878-1901	Robert Gray grocer until 1879, then Mary Gray his widow until 1901
259	Broomknowe Cottage	Detached house	1901-1928	John Gray, grocer and son of Robert and Mary Gray
259	Broomknowe Cottage	Detached house	1928-late 1930's	Robert Gray Junior, son of John Gray, grandson of Robert.
259	Broomknowe Cottage	Detached house	Late 1930's – 1950's	Aitkenhead Family
* 259	Felix McLaughlin car hirer then Funeral Undertaker	Car hire & Funeral Undertakers	c1950's, 1960's into 1970's	Felix McLaughlin and son Brian McLaughlin
* 259	Joseph Potts Funeral Undertakers	Funeral Undertakers	1970's - present	Joseph Potts
* 259	Kennedy Travel and Kennedy Coachworks (at rear of Broomknowe Cottage)	Bus company & Repair workshop	Millennium - present	Kennedy Family
* 261	Clydesdale Bank Office, House & Garden	Bank, House & Garden	1876-1983	Clydesdale Banking Co Ltd, then later, Clydesdale Bank
* 261	Ladbrokes	Betting shop	1985 - present	Ladbrokes
* 261	Crawford Mason Lawyers (upstairs above Ladbrokes)	Lawyers office	1985-2013	Crawford Mason (renting from Ladbrokes)
* 261	Lanarkshire Law Lawyers (upstairs above Ladbrokes)	Lawyers Office	2013 - present	Lanarkshire Law (renting from Ladbrokes)
263	Dervoch Cottage	Detached home	1882-late 1950's	William Minto a warehouseman, then from 1918, Martin Orme Minto then from WW2, Michael Devlin
265	Minto's Buildings (3 storey)	8 tenement homes	1903-early 1970's	William Minto then from 1918, Martin Orme Minto then other Minto family members.
* 267, 269 & 273	James B Dall's Drapers (lower floor of 2 storey Broompark Place)	Drapery Shop	1889-1900	Mrs. MWD Cruickshank and other bondholders in possession
* 267, 269 & 273	Henry R.S. Oliver Drapers (lower floor of 2 storey Broompark Place)	Drapery Shop	1900-1946	Mrs. MWD Cruickshank, then from 1918 John Jackson Coats then early 1930's AJ&A Graham and other bondholders.
* 267	Pat Hughes Photography (Broompark Place)	Photographers	Early 1960's – early 1980's	Unknown owners
* 269	Willie Paton's Hairdressers (Broompark Place)	Ladies & Gents Hairdressers	c1960's – early 1980's	Unknown owners
* 269	Highway One Bike Shop (Broompark Place)	Bike Shop	c 1980's	Unknown owners
* 273	Dr Terris Surgery (Broompark Place)	Doctor's Surgery	Late 1940's – early 1950's	Unknown owners
* 273	Dr. Harkins Surgery	Doctor's Surgery	Early 1950's –	Unknown owners

Blantyre Glasgow Road South – The Real Story

	(Broompark Place)		early 1960's	
* 273	Dr. Church's Surgery (Broompark Place)	Doctor's Surgery	Early 1960's – mid 1970's	Unknown owners
* 273	Batters, Malone & McKay (Broompark Place)	Lawyers Office	mid 1970's – 1993	Unknown owners
271	Broompark Place (upper floor)	2 homes	1889-c1920	Mrs. MWD Cruickshank and other bondholders in possession. John Jackson Coats from 1918
271	Broompark Place (upper floor)	1 home	c1920-1993	John Jackson Coats then AJ&A Graham Bondholders and unknown others.
275 -277	Clyde Cottages (1 storey semi detached houses)	2 homes	1865-1881	Robert Lindsay, joiner
275 - 277	Clyde Cottages (1 storey semi detached houses)	2 homes	1881 – early 1980's	Hamilton Savings, Investment & Building Society & Others
* 279	Mitchell & Forrest's Workshop & Yard	Wright & Joiners workshop	1865-1886	Robert Lindsay, joiner then from 1881, Hamilton Savings, Investment & Building Society
* 279	John Mitchell's Workshop & Yard	Joiners Workshop	1886 – c 1900	Hamilton Savings, Investment & Building Society
* 279	Smith's Workshop & Yard	Joiners & Carriage hirers	c1900-c1960's	Hamilton Savings, Investment & Building Society
* 279 - 281	David Fisher's Workshop & Yard	Blacksmiths	c1960's – early 1970's	Others Unknown
* 279 - 281	Light Fittings Shop	Electrical Shop	Early 1970's to c1975	Others Unknown
* 281	John Reid's Joinery Workshop	Joiners	c1900-c1918	Hamilton Savings, Investment & Building Society
* 281	Stewart W Allison Joinery Workshop & Yard	Joiners	c1918-c1950's	Hamilton Savings, Investment & Building Society & Unknown others
	Valerio Court	Housing estate	c 1993- present (2017)	Privately owned homes
*	Clive Place Public House	Public House & Inn	c1830's-1861	George Bruce, wright
*	Clive Place Public House	Public House & Inn	1861- 1885	Janet Craig, widowed wife of Thomas Craig, Spirit merchant
*	Clive Place Public House	Public House	1885 - 1903	Robert Craig, spirit merchant, grandson of Janet Craig
* 283 / 285	The Old Original Bar	Public House & cellar	1903 - 1917	Robert Craig, spirit merchant
* 283 / 285	The Old Original Bar	Public House & Cellar	1917 - 1925	William Francis (Frank) Benham, hardware merchant
* 283 / 285	The Old Original Bar	Public House & Cellar	1926 – c1940's	James Jones, Traveller of Rutherglen
* 283 / 285	The Old Original Bar	Public House & Cellar	c1940's - 2013	Other Private owners and Brewers (unknown)
* 283 / 285	The Old Original Bar	Public House & Cellar	2013 - present	Punch Partnership Ltd
287	Homes above Public House	2 upper flats	1903 - 1917	Robert Craig, spirit

					merchant
287		Homes above Public House	2 upper flats	1917 - 1925	William Francis (Frank) Benham, hardware merchant
287		Homes above Public House	2 upper flats	1926 – c1940's	James Jones, Traveller of Rutherglen
287		Homes above Public House	2 upper flats	c1940's - present	Other Private owners (unknown)
		Stonefield Cottage	Detached home	c1830's-c1910	Coats Family (Elizabeth, John, Margaret, William)
289		Stonefield Cottage	Detached home	c1910-early 1920's	Miss Isabella Jackson
289		Stonefield Cottage	Detached home	Early 1920's – late 1940's	Mrs Annie McGeachie, shopkeeper
289		Stonefield Cottage (then demolished & rebuilt in 1959)	Detached home	1949 - 1959	Mr. Stewart
289		Stonefield Cottage (new)	Detached home	1959-1983	Stewart family
289		Stonefield Cottage (new)	Detached house	1983 - present	Privately owned by unknown others
*		Westneuk (Stonefield House)	Concert Hall	c1840's-1859	Hugh McPherson then from early 1850's, his trustees.
		Stonefield House (formerly Westneuk Concert Hall)	2 houses	1859-c1880's	McPherson Family
291 / 293		Stonefield House (formerly Westneuk)	4 houses	c1880's-c1925	Hamilton, Brandon McDougall of Kirn
291 / 293		Stonefield House (formerly Westneuk)	4 houses	c1925-1935	Nellie McDougall
*		Vacant land	Vacant	1935-1938	County Council of Lanark
* 291		Community Centre	Community Centre	1938 - 2005	County Council of Lanark, later Strathclyde Council then South Lanarkshire Council.
		Mayberry Grange	Residential Flats	2006-present	Unknown owners.
		Stonefield Tram Terminus	Tram Terminal Point	1903 - 1930	Hamilton, Motherwell, Wishaw & Hamilton Tram Company Ltd
295		Roselea Cottage	Bungalow	1921 - 1956	John Richardson (d1956)
295		Roselea Cottage	Bungalow	1956 - 1957	Chrissie Dyer (daughter of John Richardson)
295		Roselea Cottage	Bungalow	1957 - 1977	Jock & Jean Richardson (Jock d 1977)
295		Roselea Cottage	Bungalow	1977 - 1986	Richardson Family
295		Roselea Cottage	Bungalow	1986 - now	Jimmy (janitor) and Unknown others
* 295		Roselea small Garage & sheds	Workshop, petrol pumps and sheds	1921 - 1956	John Richardson (d1956)
* 295		Roselea small Garage & sheds	Workshop, petrol pumps and sheds	1956 - 1957	Chrissie Dyer
* 295		Roselea Modern Garage with forecourt (old garage demolished)	Garage, petrol pumps & lockups	1957 - 1977	Jock & Jean Richardson (Jock d1977)
* 295		Roselea Modern Garage, MOT Centre & Forecourt	Garage, petrol pumps and lockups	1977 - now	Richardson Family, overseen by George Richardson (son of Jock) from 1983.
*		Innes Blacksmiths	Blacksmiths at rear of garage	c 1970's	Mr. Innes, blacksmith renting from Jock and Jean

				Richardson
	Rowan Place	1-23 houses	1957 - now	County Council, Starthclyde Council then South Lanarkshire Council
313	Eastern Bungalow	Bungalow	c1950's - now	Mr. French & Unknown Owners
	Arnot (number allocated in 1910's)	Detached Villa	c1906-early 1910's	William Coats, of Blantyreferme
315	Arnot	Detached Villa	Early 1910's – early 1930's	Margaret Coats & her trustees from early 1920's
315	Arnot	Detached Villa	Early 1930's – WW2 years	Helen & Margaret Weir (retired)
315	Arnot	Detached Villa	Late 1940's - now	Marion Young & Unknown owners
315a	Western Bungalow	Bungalow	c1950's - now	Eric & Margaret Averell
	Brownlea Cottages (Jeanfield)	2 storey semi detached houses	c1869 – early 1880s	Robert Lindsay, bookseller and one side from 1875 by Hugh Montgomery
297 / 299	Brownlea Cottages (was 297 and 299 Glasgow Road until 1930)	2 storey semi detached houses	Early 1880's - 1900	Penelope Galt Renfrew of Muir Street, Hamilton
297 / 299	Brownlea Cottages (was 297 and 299 Glasgow Rd until 1930)	2 storey semi detached houses	1900 – c1918	John G Johnston of Glasgow then William Johnston his trustee
297 / 299	Brownlea Cottages (was 297 and 299 Glasgow Rd until 1930)	2 storey semi detached houses	c1918 –early 1920's	Joseph Hughes
297 / 299	Brownlea Cottages (was 297 and 299 Glasgow Rd until 1930 when road widened)	2 storey semi detached houses	Early 1920's – late 1920's	Alexander & Ellen Struthers
317	Springfield Cottage	Detached cottage	c1820 - present	Unknown Owners, then latterly Reid family
319	Brownlea Cottage (was 297)	One side of 2 storey semi	Late 1920's – 1940's	Alexander Struthers (retired)
319	Brownlea Cottage (was 297)	One side of 2 storey semi	1940's - present	Unknown others
321	Brownlea Cottage (was 299)	Other side of 2 storey semi	Late 1920's – 1940's	Thomas Little, works manager
321	Brownlea Cottage (was 299)	West side of 2 storey semi	1940's - present	Unknown others
323	Korek (Brownlie House was 301)	East side of 2 storey semi	c1869-early 1880's	Robert Lindsay, bookseller
323	Korek (Brownlie House was 301)	East side of 2 storey semi	Early 1880's - 1900	Penelope Galt Renfrew of Muir Street, Hamilton
323	Korek (Brownlie House was 301)	East side of 2 storey semi	1900-c1918	John G Johnston of Glasgow then William Johnston his trustee
323	Korek (Brownlie House was 301)	East side of 2 storey semi	c1918-mid 1920's	John F Dott
323	Korek (Brownlie House was 301)	East side of 2 storey semi	mid 1920's - 1941	Mary Cumming Izett, spinster
323	Korek (Brownlie House was 301)	East side of 2 storey semi	1941-present	William Izett & family then unknown others
325	Blairhoyle (Brownlie House was 303)	West side of 2 Storey semi	c1869 – early 1880's	Robert Lindsay, bookseller
325	Blairhoyle (Brownlie House was 303)	West side of 2 Storey semi	Early 1880's - 1895	Penelope Galt Renfrew of Muir Street, Hamilton
325	Blairhoyle (Brownlie House was 303)	West side of 2 Storey semi	1895 – c1900	Mrs. Young, Cambuslang

325	Blairhoyle (Brownlie House was 303)	West side of 2 Storey semi	c1900-c1918	John G Johnston of Glasgow then William Johnston his trustee.
325	Blairhoyle (Brownlie House was 303)	West side of 2 storey semi	c1918-c1940's	Jean G Smith, wife of teacher Quintin Smith
325	Blairhoyle (Brownlie House was 303)	West side of 2 storey semi	c1940's - present	Unknown owners
327	Clifton (Moraig was 305)	Detached villa	c1902- c1910	William G Robertson, bricklayer of SA.
327	Clifton (Hilden was 305)	Detached villa	c1910-1917	Thomas Devaney, spirit merchant
327	Clifton (Hilden was 305)	Detached villa	1917-early 1920's	Robert Colquhoun
327	Clifton (Hilden was 305)	Detached villa	Early 1920's-c1936	Dugald M Norris, grocer
327	Clifton (Hilden was 305)	Detached villa	c1936- 1943	Unknown owners
327	Clifton (was 305)	Detached villa	c1943-present	Doctor Stewart and then Robert Reid & Son in the 1970's then Unknown owners
329	Laurel Cottage (was 307)	Detached villa	c1903-late 1920's	Richard McCall
329	Laurel Cottage (was 307)	Detached villa	Late 1920's-c1940's	John G Johnston, draper
329	Laurel Cottage (was 307)	Detached villa	c1940's – present	Unknown owners
331 / 333	Oakbank (was 309 and 311)	Semi Detached	c1903-1910	Thomas Crombie, builder
331 / 333	Oakbank (was 309 and 311)	Semi Detached	1910-early 1920's	Hannah Crombie, widow of Thomas Crombie, builder
331 / 333	Oakbank (was 309 and 311)	Semi Detached	Early 1920's-late 1920's	John Stirling McCallum, merchant
331	Oakbank East (was 309)	Semi detached	c1930 - present	James Pate, surface foreman then unknown others
333	Oakbank West (was 311)	Semi detached	Late 1920's – present	John McCallum then Unknown others
335 /337	Modern Homes	2 storey semi detached	1980's - present	Unknown owners
339	Modern Home	1.5 storey detached	Late 1980's - present	Unknown owners
341 / 343	Campsie View (was 313 and 315)	Semi detached	1903-1906	George Bowie, miner
341 / 343	Campsie View (was 313 and 315)	Semi detached	1906-1931	Williamson Bowie, widow, wife of George Bowie, miner
341 / 343	Campsie View (was 313 and 315)	Semi detached	1931-late 1930's	John Bowie, son of Williamson and George Bowie
341	Campsie View (was 313 and 315)	Semi detached	Late 1930's - 1968	Bowie Family
343	Campsie View (was 313 and 315)	Semi detached	1962-1983	McIntyre Family
343	Campsie View (was 313 and 315)	Semi detached	1983 - present	Unknown owners
345	Daldorch (was 317)	East side of Semi detached	1907-1931	Williamson & Jane Bowie
345	Daldroch (was 317)	East side of Semi detached	1931-late 1930's	John Bowie, son of Williamson and George

				Bowie
345	Daldorch (was 317)	East side of Semi detached	Late 1930's - present	Unknown owners
347	Dalveen (was 319)	West side of Semi detached	1907 –Late 1920's	Williamson Bowie & Jane Bowie
347	Dalveen (was 319)	West side of Semi detached	Late 1920's – late 1930's	John Bowie
347	Dalveen (was 319)	West side of Semi detached	Late 1930's - present	Unknown owners
349	Dunedin (was 321)	Semi detached	c1907-early 1930's	Gavin Semple, builder of Auchinriath
349	Dunedin (was 321)	Semi detached	Early 1930's-c1950's	William S Hamilton, newsagent
349	Dunedin (was 321)	Semi detached	c1950's - present	Unknown owners
351	Orwell (was 323)	Semi detached	c1907-c1910	Gavin Semple, builder of Auchinraith
351	Orwell (was 323)	Semi detached	c1910-c1940's	Grace McCallum, widowed spirit merchant who remarried David Livingstone Harley
351	Orwell (renamed to Larchmont, was 323)	Semi detached	c1940's - present	Unknown owners
	Dunallan Loop	Tram passing point	1903-1930	Hamilton, Motherwell, Wishaw & Hamilton Tram Company Ltd
353 - 367	Modern Flats (Loretta Housing)	8 Homes	1990 - now	Unknown owners
401 - 423	Walkers Buildings (Eastern side was 321-329 before 1930)	12 homes	c1877 -1878	J&J Walker, (Blantyre joiners)
401 - 423	Walker's Buildings (Eastern side was 321-329 before 1930)	12 homes	1878-c1895	Adam Thomson, of Castle Douglas
401 - 423	Walker's Buildings (Eastern side was 321-329 before 1930)	12 homes	c1895-early 1920's	Robert McVane (Trustee of Adam Thomson)
401 - 423	Walker's Buildings (Eastern side was 321-329 before 1930) Demolished c1952	12 homes	Early 1920's – early 1950's	John McLellan of Castle Douglas (Trustee of Adam Thomson)
425 - 441	Walker's Buildings (Western side was 337-351 before 1930)	6 houses	c1877-1878	J&J Walker, (Blantyre joiners)
425 - 441	Walker's Buildings (Western side was 337-351 before 1930)	6 houses	1878-1952	John Whelan (teacher) of Bathgate
*	Duncan MacFarlane's Grocers (Walker's Building later became 427)	Grocery Shop	c1878-c1895	John Whelan (teacher) of Bathgate
*	Janet Paterson's Grocers (Walkers Building later became 427)	Grocery Shop	c1895-c1905	John Whelan (teacher) of Bathgate
*	Elizabeth Smith's Grocers (Walker's Building later became 427)	Grocery Shop	c1905-c1915	John Whelan (teacher) of Bathgate
*	James McCartney Grocers (Walker's Building later became 427)	Grocery Shop	c1915-c1920	John Whelan (teacher) of Bathgate
* 427	Robert Craig Blacksmiths (Walker's Building)	Blacksmith's shop	c1920-c1930	John Whelan (retired teacher) of Bathgate

By Paul D Veverka

* 427	Richard B Morris's Grocery (Walker's Building)	Grocery Shop	c1930-1952	John Whelan (retired teacher) of Bathgate
*	Volunteer Arms Pub (sometimes The Cross Guns, Walkers Building was 325 / 327 Glasgow Road until 1930)	Public House	c1877-late 1920's	John Whelan (teacher) of Bathgate rented out to William Roberts, Archibald Jamieson, Charles Angus McGaughey, Charles & Annie Cook & then Annie Wilson
* 435 / 437	Hall, (formerly Volunteer Arms Public House, Walkers Building was 325/327 until 1930)	Hall	Late 1920's - 1952	John Whelan (retired teacher) of Bathgate
443 - 457	Causeway Shott Place (357-357 later Douglas Place)	6 homes in 2 storey tenement	1877 - c1878	J&J Walker (Joiners)
443 - 457	Causeway Shott Place (353-357 later Douglas Place)	2 stroey tenement of 6 homes	c1878 – early 1890's	Walter Wheeling, merchant of Hamilton
443 - 457	Douglas Place (formerly Causeway Shott Place at 353-357, changed to 443-457 after 1930)	2 storey tenement of 12 homes	Early 1890's – late 1920's	David Orr, Grocer, Hamilton
443 - 457	Douglas Place (formerly Causeway Shott Place at 353-357, changed to 443-457 after 1930)	2 storey tenement of 12 homes	Late 1920's – early 1940's	Trustees of the late David Orr, Grocer, Hamilton
	Cloudhowe Terrace	24 Double Storey Homes	1953 - present	County Council, Strathclyde Regional Council, South Lanarkshire Council and Private owners
* 487 - 501	Westend Place & Public House	Double Storey Tenement & Pub	1877 - 1895	Robert & Margaret Craig, spirit merchants, Blantyre
* 487 - 501	Westend Place & Public House	Double Storey Tenement & Pub	1895 - 1917	Robert Craig, Spirit Merchant
* 487 - 501	Westend Place & Public House	Double Storey Tenement & Pub	1917 - 1925	William Francis Benham, trustee of Robert Craig
* 487 - 501	Westend Place & Public House	Double Storey Tenement & Pub	1925 - 1929	John Anderson Gray, trustee of Robert Craig
* 487 - 501	Westend Place & The West End Bar	Double Storey Tenement & Public House	1929 - 1947	Robert Craig Junior & John Anderson Gray 50% each
* 487 - 501	Westend Place & The West End Bar	Double Storey Tenement & Public House	1947 - 1979	Elizabeth Currie MacNeil (w), spirit merchant
* 487	Jameson Newsagents (formerly McGlynn's Hairdressers in 1960's)	Shop (Westend Place)	1971 – c1970's	Ercole Di Vito
* 487	Hughes Photography (formerly Jameson Newsagents)	Shop (Westend Place)	c1970's - 1982	Di Vito Family
* 487	Di Vitos Fish & Chip Shop	Chip Shop	1982 - present	Di Vito Family
* 489 - 501	Westend Place & The West End Bar	Homes & Public House	1979 - 1991	Mary Josephine MacNeil
501	Westend Place flat above pub	Upper flat	1991 - present	Christine MacNeil, Troon & Others
* 489 - 499	Westend Place & Public House (except for 1 upper flat and shop)	Homes & Public House	1991 - 1995	Annie Winifred McGhie of 497 Glasgow Road and to Joseph MacNeil 50% share
* 489 -	Westend Place	Upper flat	1995 - present	Joseph MacNeil of Priory

	497				Bridge & others
	* 493	West End Bar	Public House	1995 - 2008	Equally Rosemary MacNeil, and Elizabeth Ann Campbell both of Priory Bridge, Catherine Clark of Calderglen, Mary Josephine McGhie of Halfway and Felix MacNeil of Jura Gardens
	* 493	West End Bar	Public House	2008 - present	Maura McLaughlin & brother Mick McCormack as licensees for brewers.
		Bardykes Grove	Private Homes built by Wimpey	1994 - present	Private Owners
		Caldergrove Estate	House, Offices and 2 lodge houses	c1830's - 1983	Various Private Owners
		Bardykes Mill (Black Mill or Priory Mill) & Millers House	Corn, then Saw Mill on River Calder	c18th Century - c1880	Jackson Family of Spittal
		Priory Bridge	Bridge	c17th Century (possibly earlier) - present	Unknown Owners but likely Jacksons of Bardykes

By Paul D Veverka

ABOUT BLANTYRE PROJECT

Independent review appearing in the October 2017 of the Lanarkshire Family History Society Journal:

Blantyre Project is one of Lanarkshire's best-kept secrets! It's a huge, free local history resource, greatly underused or known about for the former mining town of Blantyre, South Lanarkshire. Located online at www.blantyreproject.com and on Facebook at www.facebook.com/BlantyreProject it has been relentlessly added to every day without fail since February 2011 and to date has over 4,100 uniquely researched articles, many of which are illustrated. Additionally, through purchase, donation and permission the website now features over 10,200 old photographs of Blantyre from the 1860's right up until the present day, making it one of Lanarkshire's largest history collections. It's attention to detail, volume and popularity drives a superiority over any other Blantyre site.

Blantyre Project records and archives the interesting history of Blantyre from bronze age up until contemporary times, including notable timeline waypoints like the 13th Century Blantyre Priory, the 15th Century Crossbasket Castle and that famous pit explosion in October 1877 that killed over 200 men and boys, still Scotland's largest pit disaster to this day.

Followed by over 13,400 visitors on Facebook, daily posts feature a variety of Blantyre subjects, often providing a free ancestry service to those who have queries about Blantyre. What makes this all the more remarkable is that the archiving work put into this impressive endeavour, is by one local man, Mr. Paul Veverka, (* addendum by Paul Veverka: I cannot solely take credit for this. It is noted that information of interest is often provided by others).

The Blantyre Project website is easily navigable and separates aspects of Blantyre's history into interesting, searchable content. E.g. Sub sections can be found for Buildings, People Photos, Places, Poems, News and other Records. Search further and you'll find subsections including the history of 19 Churches, 44 Farms, 77 pubs (yes you read that right!) and 21 Schools. Further sub sections include expansive history about Blantyre Mills and the life of Blantyre's most famous son, the Africa Explorer, David Livingstone who was born in 1813.

A new topic for 2017 recently uploaded, charts every building, shop and home to have ever existed on Glasgow Road, the main thoroughfare of the town, an important legacy that will surely be looked upon by many future generations. Also included are many 'people' stories bringing the history of the street alive. Interesting posts document the extensive redevelopment of Glasgow Road during the late 1970's that left, for many people, an apparent lack of charm and character to the town, something community groups work so hard to this day to address.

Events and photos are sorted into chronological order and also filtered on each individual area or former hamlet within Blantyre. World War 1 and II archives have also recently been added and currently being added to. Other large sections are ongoing such as telling the stories of all individuals killed in the pit explosion, recording a timeline of when buildings were constructed and charting news like drowning's, fires, accidents and other noteworthy events that affected people more directly. The aim of Blantyre Project, no less, is simply, "to research, record and archive every noteworthy aspect of news throughout the Centuries, to explore every public building that has ever existed and make it all easily and freely accessible in one place."

In recent years, Blantyre Project has evolved into the largest collection of Blantyre history in any one place and is now both online and in 7 currently published books, offline. It has grown into a huge archive, deemed by many, including South Lanarkshire Council, Hamilton Library and the National Library of Scotland as 'Blantyre's Official History Archive' often correcting what others have previously written or assumed. All material on the site can be printed out or copied for personal use, although if intention is publication on or offline elsewhere, permissions should be sought first.

Offline, away from public sight, Blantyre Project has amassed an interesting collection of memorabilia including old quoits, banners, adverts, flags, books, newspapers, letters and we're told it's not unusual to find a Blantyre brick or two at the bottom of Paul's bed at his home in High Blantyre.

Blantyre Project often hosts public presentations in the library, church halls, for local groups, women's guilds and schools as time permits. By no means finished, and witnessing his motivation, we are assured by Paul that Blantyre Project is "only just getting started!"

www.blantyreproject.com
Blantyre's History Archives

ABOUT THE AUTHOR

Paul D. Veverka is a full time Construction Commercial Manager who has worked on several high profile major Scottish infrastructure projects such as managing financials and commercial aspects of the new Queensferry Crossing and Aberdeen Bypass. In previous years he also worked on the Millennium Canal links. It's a job he enjoys very much. Often working in claims or troubleshooting environments, he has a flair for collecting information, unraveling data, searching for facts and recording it in a way that can be understood and utilized. This skill has almost certainly assisted his hobby, in researching Blantyre's past.

Blantyre history in the form of his 'Blantyre Project' is his passionate hobby and has consumed almost all of his spare time since 2011. His passion for Blantyre and collecting memorabilia and historical data comes from his late mother, Janet Duncan Veverka (d2009) who was interested in the history of Blantyre. Paul has collected stories, news, postcards and photos about Blantyre since 1985, when he was just 14 years old!

Paul who was born in 1971 and lives in High Blantyre, writes, "Having a young child and often working away from home has afforded me the time to write each evening either when my daughter goes to bed, or if I'm working away, in hotels and B&Bs. I'm not a fan of watching TV to any extent, so relaxation for me is putting on my computer and immersing myself in yet another Blantyre story. I have a very patient and understanding wife who is proud in what I've accomplished. I never let this hobby interfere with my full time job, but I do look forward to coming home and writing in evenings. Indeed, sometimes, I just can't wait to open my computer and find out the next chapter of a building or person's history!

There are literally only a handful of evenings when I have not written about Blantyre since I started properly writing and recording, back in 2011. Making this archive free for people is particularly important to me. Getting information out freely to everybody in as accessible a fashion as possible is my driver and hopefully my legacy.

I would like to personally thank Gordon Cook, chairperson of the Heritage Group, who in recent years has unwittingly become my history mentor. He has guided me well and I hope I've reached a position now in being able to often pass him new information!"

Paul was co-founder and Chairperson of Blantyre Community Committee for 5 years from April 2012 – March 2017 volunteering to organize the town's festive event, annual music festival and gala days. However, he stepped down in March 2017 due to working away from Blantyre midweek.

He is well known in Blantyre and has a fairly high profile in community life being a member of various local community organizations including Friends of the Calder. He also runs a 'sister website' Blantyre Telegraph, a Blantyre news website, which publishes a monthly newspaper, which has so far raised a five figure sum in recent years for 75 charitable Blantyre good causes. He is sole organizer of the annual Blantyre Oscars event, personally rewarding and recognizing others of all ages in Blantyre each year that have themselves, helped others. In 2017, he also had the honour of naming the new streets in Greenhall Village, High Blantyre.

Paul is now an accomplished local history author with 7 successful Blantyre history books already published to 13 different countries, in his spare time, representing the largest volume of Blantyre history ever published globally. He has amassed an abundance of local history knowledge, his writing becoming more detailed with each book. This is his largest book by far to date.

Other hobbies include DIY and holidays are often in Tiree, an island childhood holiday destination and where his parents are now laid to rest. He looks forward to several other books in the pipeline coming out in future including a definitive immense reference volume of books in encyclopedic format called 'Blantyre Explained' covering all he has ever researched, including the content of this book. Proceeds from all his books directly benefit the community and are non-profit making.

Paul, never one to be idle, is currently progressing plans to make this large archive more official, accessible and permanent for future generations, including those offline.

AND FINALLY,

"Having enjoyed this focused, year long endeavour so thoroughly, I'll be writing a sequel exploring the North side of Glasgow Road and also plan a separate book to explore the side roads branching off Glasgow Road. I'm also quite certain further Blantyre Project books of similar detail will follow for other major streets in Blantyre. I'd love to do that soon, but the intensive research in this book has left me in need of a little break. Until then, time for a well earned rest. Thank you for your attention.

Blantyre Glasgow Road – The Real Story……will return"

Paul Veverka, 1st January 2018

Printed in Great Britain
by Amazon